Second Edition

AMERICAN EDUCATION IN A GLOBAL SOCIETY

International and Comparative Perspectives

Gerald L. Gutek
Loyola University, Chicago

Long Grove, Illinois

I dedicate this book to my grandchildren:
Claire, Abigail, Luke, and Drew Swiatek
and
Mills and Anna Hope Jordan.
May they inherit a peaceful world
where human rights and diversity are respected
and where the air is fresh, the trees are green, and the oceans blue.

For information about this book, contact:
Waveland Press, Inc.
4180 IL Route 83, Suite 101
Long Grove, IL 60047-9580
(847) 634-0081
info@waveland.com
www.waveland.com

Cover: Mike Agliolo/SuperStock

CONTENTS

PREFACE

American Education in a Global Society: International and Comparative Perspectives, Second Edition, examines the international and comparative foundations of education in the context of an increasingly interrelated world society. It is intended for use in courses in international education, comparative education, history of education, and the social and cultural foundations of education. It is a thorough revision of the first edition which appeared as *American Education in a Global Society: Internationalizing Teacher Education*. The second edition emphasizes a foundations-of-education orientation that builds a more theoretical rationale for international education by including new chapters on nationalism and ethnonationalism and globalization. The chapters that deal with American security issues as a part of international education have been updated to reflect the changing world reality brought about by the war on terrorism. The chapters on comparative education have been revised to include a more detailed discussion of the history and rationale for studying comparative education and more extended discussions of nation-state contexts. While retaining and revising the chapters from the first edition on education in the United Kingdom, Russia, Mexico, Japan, China, and Nigeria, new chapters have been added on education in the United States, France, and India.

How This Book Is Organized

The book is organized into two parts: (I) The International Foundations of Education, and (II) A Comparative Analysis of Education in Selected Nation-States.

Part I provides a general introduction to international education, the historical events and processes that have had a major impact on international education, and the ways in which the U.S. and its citizens have perceived their role in a changing world. It also includes discussions of changing perspectives on national security, development and development education, globalism, and nationalism and ethnonationalism.

Chapter 1, "Education in a Changing World," provides a point of entry into international education by identifying and examining those trends that

ix

have had an impact on the world, as well as the need to incorporate international education in teacher education programs. The chapter examines the impact of a variety of political and economic events and processes, including the cold war and the rise of a bipolar global society; the movement away from imperialism and the decolonization of the world; the advent of the nuclear era; the rise of new centers of economic power; the development of rapid systems of communication and transportation; the global ecology crisis; the end of the cold war era; conflicts in the Middle East; and the war on terrorism.

Chapter 2, "Defining International Education," discusses how international education has been conceptualized, defined, and interpreted in different ways during its long history and states the book's organizing thesis: a historically derived tension exists between education for citizenship in the nation-state and education for participation in a global society. The central ideas of educators from the past and present and their search for ways to teach about international education are identified and explored, and various dimensions and academic subdivisions of international education are examined. Although the various fields described under the heading "The Many Definitions of International Education" are often organized and taught as separate subjects, they are treated here as subfields of a general interdisciplinary area called foundations of international education. Among the fields discussed are comparative education, foreign policy studies, regional or area studies, development education, peace education, global education, and international business education. Chapter 2 concludes with the author's stipulated definition of international education as education that examines (1) the informal, nonformal, and formal educational relationships between governments and peoples of various nation-states; (2) the global educational issues that transcend national boundaries; and (3) the emergent trends that are creating greater interdependency and interrelationships among people as members of a global society.

Chapter 3 provides a historical perspective of the role the United States has played in international education. It examine the American predilection for cultural insularity and diplomatic isolation through the admonitions of early leaders such as Washington, Jefferson, and Webster, and discusses the influence of the expansionist frontier and the doctrine of Manifest Destiny in shaping America's worldview. Two conflicting approaches to American foreign and international policy are introduced: idealism based on the Wilsonian legacy and realism based on the national interest. The chapter pursues the question of America's role in international education through the impact of the cold war and its demise, the Vietnam War, and the 1991 Persian Gulf War, and concludes with an examination of recent developments in international education.

Chapter 4 is built on the idealist/realist dichotomy defined in chapter 3 and examines the issue of international security and peace education. The importance of nation-states as major actors on the world scene and the degree to which international peace is determined by their security arrangements are explored in this chapter. Difficulties in defining the U.S. national interest are illustrated by the intense debates over U.S. involvement in Vietnam and the Persian Gulf. A structural analysis of national security examines such key concepts as the nation-state, power potentialities, vital interests, and commitments, and comments on the impact of the threat of nuclear war and the limited wars of recent history.

Chapter 5 discusses international development and development education. Due to pockets of rural and urban underdevelopment, development has implications both for the world and for U.S. education in particular. Many American educators first became involved in international education through participation in development programs put in place after World War II as part of the American security effort during the cold war era. As the gap between industrial or technologically developed and less-technologically developed nations widens, development becomes an increasingly global issue. Chapter 5 analyzes "top-down" and "bottom-up" approaches to development and examines the concepts of Westernization, modernization, deinstitutionalization, and liberation pedagogy.

Chapter 6, new to the second edition, examines the process of globalization, including roles played by international global actors and agencies—especially the multinational business corporation—and looks at globalization's implications for education. It then examines how globalization has impacted national school systems and discusses the kind of education required for a global future.

Chapter 7, another new chapter, analyzes the ideologies of nationalism and ethnonationalism and their impact on education. While the older ideology of nationalism was a driving force in creating nation-state school systems, ethnonationalism was a resurrected ideology used to redefine political and educational arrangements in multinational and multiethnic nation-states. The chapter examines the possibilities of using multiculturalism as a means of reducing national and ethnonational tensions.

Part II: A Comparative Analysis of Education in Selected Nation-States is designed to put readers into the world of school systems as they function in different countries. The chapters examine how nine national school systems educate for their own particular versions of national identity and citizenship and create their own approaches to organization, curriculum, and instruction. Readers will learn how schools in other countries reflect their specific sociopolitical contexts and be made aware of the similarities and differences between systems of education in the United States and other countries. In looking outward and making these comparisons, we begin to clarify some features of American education.

Chapter 8 examines the history and development of comparative education and analyzes the concept of a national context in which educational systems function. New chapters 9 and 10 explore educational contexts, history, organization, curriculum, and instruction in the United States. These provide U.S. students with a review of education in their own country and serve as a point of departure for studying education in other countries. In those programs that include courses on the history and organization of American education, instructors may want to do a quick review of these two chapters. In teacher education and professional education programs where this content is not studied in a separate course, instructors may wish to give them a more definite emphasis. Chapter 11 examines education in the United Kingdom, a Western European nation-state that shares the same language and basic commitment to parliamentary or representative government with the United States, but also exhibits considerable traditional, cultural, and socioeconomic differences. Chapter 12, a new chapter, examines education in France to give an illustration of education in another country that is a major Western European leader. France is a model of high culture and political-educational centralization. Chapter 13 looks at education in the Russian Federation, the former Soviet Union, a region that is undergoing profound political, social, economic, and educational change. Chapter 14 examines education in Mexico, a U.S. neighbor in transition from a less- to a more-developed economy. Chapter 15 considers the Japanese educational system, the object of frequent comparisons and contrasts to that of the United States. Japan is a country that has preserved its unique cultural core while at the same time adopting modernization and technology. Chapter 16 focuses on the role of ideology in shaping educational policies in the People's Republic of China, the nation with the world's largest population and whose economic and political importance in increasing. Chapter 17, a new chapter, considers education in India, one of the world's oldest civilizations. India is examined as a religiously and culturally complex civilization that is also the world's largest democracy. Chapter 18 considers the problems of building an educational system in Nigeria, a less-developed sub-Saharan African nation.

Acknowledgments

I want to thank the following reviewers, whose suggestions and criticisms were invaluable in the development of the first edition of this book: Glenn Smith, Lawrence J. Dennis, James Van Patten, Don Adams, Pao Lindsay, George Padavil, William Paringer, Lynn W. Paine, and David R. Conrad. I also want to thank Jeni Ogilvie, my editor at Waveland Press, for her gentle encouragement to complete the second edition. Her patience, guidance, and careful editing turned a large and cumbersome manuscript into a readable book.

Gerald L. Gutek

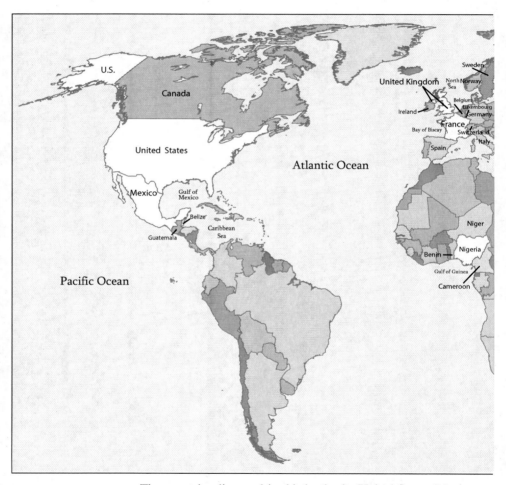

The countries discussed in this book, the United States, Mexico, the United Kingdom, France, Nigeria, the Russian Federation, the

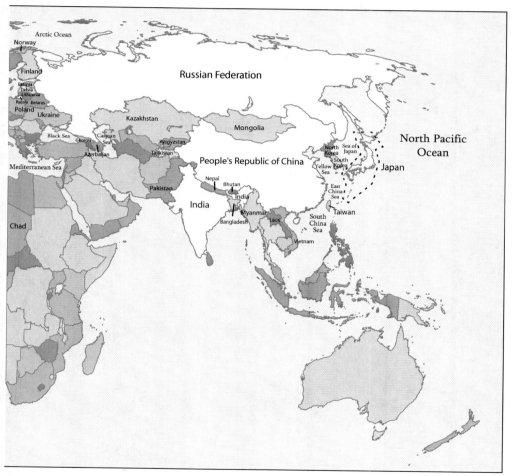

People's Republic of China, India, and Japan, are identified and
appear in white. The countries that border them are also labeled.

Part
I

Foundations of International Education

1

EDUCATION IN A CHANGING WORLD

In today's interdependent global society, it is dramatically evident that no person can be an island, and no nation can exist in isolation. Events that take place in one part of the earth ripple throughout the entire world to become global realities that impact different peoples and nations. To provide a point of departure for studying international education, this chapter provides a condensed overview of some major world events and trends that have shaped our global situation, including World War II, the cold war, and a bipolar world; decolonization; the advent of the nuclear era; the end of the cold war; the rise of new economic centers of power; rapid communication and transportation; the global effects of pollution; the long-standing tensions in the Middle East; and the war on terror. The chapter then considers the intertwined demographic, economic, political, and ecological issues impacting the need for international education.

The Legacy of World War II: The Cold War

The end of World War II saw the total defeat of Nazi Germany, imperial Japan, and the Axis powers and the victory of the United Kingdom (UK), the Soviet Union, the United States (U.S.), France, China, and the other Allied powers. The war's consequences radically reshaped the political, military, and economic relationships of the nations of the world, especially those in Europe. Germany was totally devastated, and Italy was in a weakened condition. The UK and France, though victorious, were exhausted by their war efforts. Of the world's nations, two major powers dominated the international scene—the United States and the Union of Soviet Socialists Republics (USSR), the Soviet Union. A series of events ushered in what Winston Churchill called the "iron curtain," the cold war, and the concept of bipolarity.

Because of geography and the course of the war, Soviet armies liberated the nations of Central and Eastern Europe—Poland, Czechoslovakia, Hungary, Romania, Yugoslavia, Bulgaria, and Albania—from German occupation. The eastern part of Germany was also occupied by Soviet forces, while

3

the U.S., Great Britain, and France occupied the western territory of Germany and the western sections of its capital, Berlin. From 1945 through 1948, pro-Soviet, Communist regimes were installed under Soviet auspices in these Central and Eastern European nations.

For over 40 years, from 1946 until 1989, many of the world's nations, especially those in Europe and North America, were divided into two hostile camps—those allied with the Soviet Union and those loyal to the U.S. Many of the concepts that informed the American worldview in the second half of the twentieth century were based on the politics, diplomacy, military strategy, and economics of the cold war years. Certain of these ideas from the cold war continue to influence some American policy makers. This chapter surveys how the cold war shaped America's world outlook, beginning with a discussion of the Marshall Plan.

The Marshall Plan

The Marshall Plan, named after Secretary of State George C. Marshall, provided U.S. economic aid to reconstruct war-devastated economies and to rebuild industrial and economic infrastructures in the nations of Western Europe—the UK, France, Italy, the Federal Republic of Germany (West Germany), Norway, Denmark, the Netherlands, Belgium, and Luxembourg. While there was a humanitarian dimension to the Marshall Plan, an important policy goal assumed that economic prosperity would lead to political stability in Western Europe. U.S. policy makers believed that nations that were economically viable, preferably in the free enterprise, capitalist mode, and politically stable would create the material foundations for democratic, parliamentary governments in the American or British styles. Nations with such democratic governments would be anti-Communist in their domestic and foreign policies. Along with economic aid, the Marshall Plan also encouraged cultural and educational exchanges between the participating nations. These exchanges, which involved American educators, contributed to shaping America's outlook on the world. During the postwar period, many American scientists, educators, and technicians served in overseas posts to implement the containment strategy through economic development and military assistance programs. The U.S., buoyed by its successes in Western Europe, sought to apply similar development strategies in Asia with results that were less successful.

The Marshall Plan, which was very successful in rebuilding the economies of the Western European nations, became a major concept in U.S. foreign policy throughout the twentieth century. From the Marshall Plan evolved the concept of international development and development education. This concept assumed that economically developed nations, such as the U.S., could successfully assist the economic progress of other less technologically developed countries (LTDCs). Technical, agricultural, scientific, and engineering assistance was initially given to less-developed nations, followed by teacher training and other forms of educational assistance. The thrust of the Marshall Plan mentality has continued into the twenty-first century.

Part of the war on terror as conducted by the George W. Bush administration, especially the U.S. occupation and reconstruction of Iraq, assumes that a viable economy will lead to a democratic political order in that country. Further, some U.S. policy makers assume that an economically viable and democratic Iraq will not be a base for terrorist organizations. Proponents of the Bush administration's Iraqi policy point to the rebuilding of the ruined economies and the establishment of democratic governments in Germany and Japan after World War II as a historical argument for their case. Critics of the Bush administration's policy argue that it ignores the historical and political realities of the Middle East. They contend that historical experience and the material infrastructure in Iraq is not comparable to that of Germany and Japan. Whether or not the assumptions that worked in Western Europe will be successful in the Middle East remains an open and hotly debated policy issue. It points to an important question in international education, however: To what extent should contemporary policies be based on the cultural, social, political, historical, and educational contexts of the countries that they involve?

Regional Security

The next phase in the U.S. policy in the cold war involved the development of regional mutual defense treaties aimed at containing the Soviet Union from expansion into Western Europe. A highly significant result of these treaties was the North Atlantic Treaty Organization, or NATO, which joined the signatory nations in a mutual military defense pact directed toward checking potential Soviet expansion in Europe. The Soviets countered by forming the Warsaw Pact, a military pact that linked the satellite nations of Central and Eastern Europe against an alleged threat from the capitalist nations of the West. The perception shared by each group of nations that it must be prepared to defend itself against the other became the backbone of the cold war.

The idea of the regional security pact, as epitomized in NATO, produced policy ramifications in the twentieth century that continue into the twenty-first century. An important working assumption was that U.S. policy should be multilateral, based on a coalition or concert of nations, rather than unilaterally determined and initiated solely by the U.S. This assumption was used in the first Gulf War and the NATO peacekeeping efforts in Bosnia and Kosovo in the former Yugoslavia. In the U.S. invasion of Iraq in 2003, the Bush administration, though attempting to use a multinational approach, has been accused of taking a unilateral action that ignored long-time European allies. The Bush administration, departing from the multilateral concept, also announced that it would use a "preemptive strike" against those who plan to attack the U.S. The concepts of a unilateral foreign and military policy and a preemptive attack pose new and fiercely debated policy issues.

The Cold War and Education

The ideological phase of the cold war had a significant impact on how international education was defined in the 1950s and 1960s. Domestically, the anti-Communist, anti-Soviet orientation was introduced into American schools. Many states developed mandated curriculum units that emphasized the threat that Soviet Communism posed to the democratic American way of life. Internationally, the interactions of American educators with their foreign counterparts were also framed in terms of cold war ideology. During the McCarthy period of anti-Communist investigations in the U.S. during the 1950s, some educators were accused of harboring pro-Communist sentiments or of being members of the Communist Party. The McCarthy investigations, often resembling a "witch hunt," produced a climate of fear that put tremendous strains on academic freedom and stilled dissent. Similarly, after the terrorist attacks of 9/11, the U.S. government's attempts to guard against future attacks by implementing strict security measures caused concern among many who saw these measures as a threat to freedoms protected by the Constitution.

The End of Imperialism and Decolonization

The world political map in the decades after World War II was far different than in 1939, the year the war began in Europe. World maps that hung on classroom walls before the war depicted the empires of the great world powers that extended from Europe, through Africa, to Asia. The colonies of the large British Empire, "upon which the sun never set," were usually shaded in red and included India, Pakistan, Burma, Malaya, Ghana, Rhodesia, Nigeria, and many other smaller countries as well. The French Empire, indicated in green, included Algeria, Morocco, Tunisia, French Equatorial Africa, and Indochina. The Netherlands held as a colony the Dutch East Indies in Asia, and Portugal held Angola and Mozambique in Africa.

When World War II ended, the people under European rule in Africa and Asia sought independence from colonial domination, through either negotiation or armed struggle. Often, the process of achieving independence involved a combination of both. In some cases, the European nation granted independence through protracted negotiations and without an armed struggle, as the British did in India. In other instances, the European nation sought to suppress freedom movements and maintain its control over the subject people, as was the case of the futile French efforts in Algeria and Indochina. The inevitable result was the end of European colonial rule and the rise of new independent nations. The world trend toward decolonization and the end of Western European imperialism held many important implications for international education.[1]

While the decolonized nations in Asia and Africa exhibit many unique political and cultural differences, it is possible to identify some generalizations that have significant implications for international education. First, these nations exhibit a complex cultural overlay. Although most of them are relatively young nations, having gained their political independence in the 1950s, 1960s, and 1970s, their cultural heritage dates back to antiquity. A second feature is often the presence of strong tribal, regional, and linguistic loyalties rather than a sense of national identification. Third, despite the ending of colonial rule by the European imperial powers, strong residues of the colonial influence remain. For example, because the sociopolitical elites who emerged in the newly independent countries often had been educated in European universities, the European nation's language remained as an important official and educational language; the formal educational systems that were patterned after those of the former colonial rulers have remained as well. A fourth characteristic of many of the newly independent nations is the existence of pronounced socioeconomic disparities within the country as well as longstanding problems of unemployment, overpopulation, and illiteracy. Many of the newly independent nations who share the four characteristics have been categorized as "underdeveloped," "developing," or "third-world" nations; their problems and policies are decidedly different from the first-world industrially developed nations of the West and the second-world nations of the former Soviet bloc.

In the 1960s and 1970s, the U.S. and other industrially developed nations saw these newly independent nations as countries in need of development. As mentioned previously, the U.S. implemented assistance programs. At the same time, the Soviet Union, eager to win support in Africa and Asia, also provided development assistance. Both the U.S. and the Soviet Union conducted their development policies on ideological lines, as well as by providing economic and educational assistance. Many American universities engaged in overseas development projects designed to create new economic, political, and educational infrastructures in host countries. In turn, the developing nations sent students to study in the colleges and universities in the U.S.

The decolonization of the world and the rise of new independent nations made it necessary to redraw our cognitive maps of the world. The old wall maps with the great empires shaded in red and green were no longer valid. The American school curriculum, especially in history and the social studies, needed to be revised to reflect changing international realities. No longer could courses concentrate on the history of the Western powers and regard events in Asia and Africa as merely the lengthened shadow of Spain, Great Britain, or France on the world stage. Along with the redrawing of our mental configurations, an enlightened awareness of global issues posed by the third world, with the majority of the world's population, needed to be part of our international understanding. Among these issues were overpopulation, human exploitation, undereducation, and epidemic diseases. Included with these issues is the phenomenon of globalization as multinational business corporations engage in profit-making ventures in many of the LTDCs.

The Advent of the Nuclear Age

World War II ended when the U.S. dropped atomic bombs on the Japanese cities of Hiroshima and Nagasaki. These bombs obliterated the two cities and inflicted a nuclear holocaust on their residents. While the immediate devastation of property and annihilation of life was immense, the effects of these atomic bombs were long lasting in the residual consequences of human illness and environmental contamination.

Nuclear fission, the building of the atomic and the hydrogen bombs, and the stockpiling of nuclear weapons and missiles were all part of the cold war's life-threatening legacy. The U.S. monopoly over nuclear weapons quickly ended as the Soviet Union also developed a nuclear capacity. A large part of the national budgets of both the Soviet Union and the U.S. was diverted from providing social, health, and educational services to creating and maintaining a strong military force. The massive stockpiling of nuclear weapons by the USSR and the U.S. and the capacity to use nuclear weapons against other nations posed great risks to the continued existence of human life on the planet.

The nuclear threat stimulated the organization of antiwar and peace organizations that, on a people-to-people basis, sought to end the threat of nuclear annihilation and planetary devastation. This threat further stimulated the development of peace studies as a part of international education. Today, nuclear power has been harnessed for peaceful pursuits such as the production of energy. The great threat, however, continues to be the proliferation of nuclear weapons as more nations develop and add these weapons to their military arsenals. Nowhere is the tension between the nation-state and the interests of a global society more evident than in the need to bring about disarmament and the reduction and control of nuclear weapons.[2]

The End of the Cold War

In 1989 and 1990 a series of unexpected and important events took place in Central and Eastern Europe. Beginning with the Solidarity movement in Poland, the people in the Soviet satellite countries showed restiveness and a will to independence that culminated in bringing momentous political and economic changes to the region. While attempts at independence occurred earlier, they had been ruthlessly suppressed militarily by the Soviet Union in Hungary in 1956 and in Czechoslovakia in 1968. In 1988, however, the political situation in the Soviet Union itself had changed when the new leader of the Soviet Union, Mikhail Gorbachev, embarked on a policy of *perestroika* (economic restructuring) and *glasnost* (openness). Facing a stagnating Soviet economy, Gorbachev encouraged structural changes in the Communist party, the Soviet government, and the economy.[3]

As the people of Eastern Europe challenged their Communist governments in 1989–1990, the Soviet Union under Gorbachev chose not to intervene. One by one, the Communist regimes of Central and Eastern Europe toppled. Non-Communist governments were elected first in Poland, and then in Hungary, Czechoslovakia, and East Germany, as one-party regimes were replaced by multiparty representative governments. In the Soviet Union itself, the monolithic structure created by Lenin and Stalin also showed signs of crumbling. Long-standing and unresolved nationalist and ethnic feelings for autonomy and independence surfaced in the Baltic republics of Latvia, Lithuania, and Estonia, and in Georgia, the Ukraine, and Uzbekistan.

With the tearing down of the Berlin Wall, the fortified barrier erected to keep the populations of East and West Berlin apart, the cold war's rhetoric, military systems, and ideologies grew increasingly obsolete and irrelevant as new political, social, and economic configurations emerged in Central and Eastern Europe. The end of Soviet dominance in Eastern and Central Europe and the demise and restructuring of the Soviet Union into an independent Russia, Ukraine, and other nations created a new set of political and economic realities. The ideas developed during the cold war all needed to be reconstructed or discarded.

New Economic Centers of Power

Still another important contemporary international trend has been the change and restructuring of centers of economic power. In particular, there has been the economic rise of Japan and West Germany, now reunited with East Germany. In addition, China, the Republic of Korea (South Korea), Singapore, and other Asian nations have become important centers of industry, commerce, and trade. A great deal of attention has been devoted to the high level of economic development and potential of the nations of the Pacific Rim[4] and of the European Union.[5]

Simultaneously with the rise of new economic powers has been the structural change in the economies of older industrial nations such as the UK and the U.S. In the U.S., the older, heavy, basic industries such as iron and steel production, shipbuilding, and automobile production have declined and been replaced by service occupations and high-tech industries that are so numerous in the information age. In the U.S., there is concern over the loss of jobs to other countries, where wages and salaries are much lower. Debates over free trade versus protectionism have had a long history and are currently taking place over what is called "outsourcing," that is, U.S. companies procuring goods and/or services from suppliers in other countries.

These international economic trends have had a powerful effect on national economies. In newly developing industrial economies, such as that of South Korea, there has been a shift from basic agriculture to heavy industry. In Japan, the number of people engaged in agriculture has declined markedly, and the most important area of employment has shifted to industry and technology. In the U.S., structural unemployment has occurred in the heavy manufacturing industries of the northeastern states where major employers were at one time located. Service, information, and technological sectors employ increasing numbers of people, and educational institutions have developed training and retraining programs for job requirements in these new fields. Certain educational initiatives such as those generated by *A Nation at Risk: The Imperative for Educational Reform* (1983) and No Child Left Behind (2002) were stimulated, in part, by arguments that the American workforce needed to be better trained, especially in basic skills, to compete successfully against foreign competitors.

Closely related to the changing sectors of economic power has been the rise of the international or multinational business corporation. The multinational business corporation, as its name indicates, is owned by nationals of a number of nations and conducts business throughout the world. For the multinational business corporation, production and consumption are global rather than national in scope.

An effect of the new international economy is the phenomenon of economic interdependence. Economic activities in one country or region affect those in other nations. For example, the dependence of the oil-importing nations, such as those of Western Europe and Japan, on the petroleum-producing nations is a highly important consideration for the world economy. Less dramatic but probably more significant is the fact that large numbers of Americans are employees of multinational corporations and consumers of their products.

The rapid rise of the interdependent world economy and the dominance of the multinational business corporation have produced the phenomenon of globalization. A general term that encompasses the complexity of the economic changes taking place worldwide, globalization's highly important implications are discussed later in the book.

Rapid Communication and Transportation

Innovations in the technologies of communication and transportation have eroded the sense of distance and isolation of the past. While social, political, and cultural contexts cause differences between people, technology has made it possible to transcend national boundaries in the movement of people, the flow of information, and the exposure to and influence of art, sports, and entertainment. Since the travels of Herodotus and Marco Polo, people have been educated by travel and exchange visits. Contemporary international travel, once restricted to members of elite classes, is now a common feature of education. International student and faculty exchange programs, undergraduate study abroad programs, traveling seminars, and other international field experiences give a global meaning to schooling that bridges the distance between peoples.

Global satellite television transmission and the Internet's World Wide Web and e-mail capabilities have virtually eliminated barriers to communication between people. The terrorist attacks on the World Trade Center in New York City and the Pentagon in Washington, D.C., were broadcast on television worldwide. Correspondents embedded with troops in Iraq instantaneously told the story of military combat there. Cultural isolation of the past has been reduced or eliminated by the international media. At the same time that the rapid and vivid flow of information and images occurs electronically, this phenomenon raises important educational issues. When the flow of information is so rapid, how can people integrate and gain perspective on the many pieces of information, the factoids, that they receive, indeed, with which they are bombarded? How can they sort out and judge the accuracy and validity of the many reports that they receive? International education has a mission in providing a kind of cognitive map, a worldwide mental grid, upon which to locate these bits and pieces of information. Importantly, it has a role in aiding students to make assessments and to construct a global perspective that moves them out of their own localities onto a wider world scene.

Music, art, and athletics have always had an international dimension. Today, because of wide-ranging and fast air travel, TV broadcasts via satellites, and information and pictures transmitted on the Internet, the exchange and interchange of entertainment is happening more than ever. Perhaps the Beatles and those who followed in the field of popular entertainment have done even more than formal educational programs to weaken national barriers and expose us to the creativity and abilities of others.

The developments in rapid communication and transportation are realities of modern life that advance international understanding. However, they need the balance that the more reflective modes of education can provide. The television program and the fast-breaking news event have immediacy and a dramatic effect that few classroom settings can rival. Yet, by themselves, they are highly impressionistic, unreflective, and short-lived. In their own way, they contribute to momentary and often shallow ways of viewing reality. They occur so quickly that there is not the needed intellectual pause to think deeply about their long-range effects and to create larger and broader perspectives. International education, especially in school settings, can provide the kind of reflective, critical analysis that establishes the relationships of events in time and space.

Global Environmental Issues

After decades of neglect of a deteriorating natural environment, nations and peoples are finally becoming conscious that the natural health of the earth, as a biosphere, is in a delicate and hazardous condition. Among the causes of a deteriorating natural environment are the effects of acid rain in the Northern Hemisphere as windborne industrial pollutants degrade woodlands and lakes. The deforestation of the world's rain forests further weakens the planet's ecological balance. The expansion of the deserts, caused by prolonged drought, produces famine conditions in sub-Saharan Africa. Further, a number of oil spills, such as that of the *Exxon Valdez*, seriously damaged plant and animal life in offshore Alaska. The explosion and meltdown of the Soviet nuclear reactor at Chernobyl in Ukraine resulted in loss of life and harmful consequences to human and environmental health. Contamination from the Chernobyl disaster was not limited to the Soviet Union, but was carried across frontiers to other countries—extending as far north as Norway and Sweden.

Like the wind and the rain, the earth's ecological health as a biosphere is a concern that cannot be limited to a single country or region. Environmental issues are global in scope, and their solution needs to be global as well. In defining and seeking to resolve the problems of a deteriorating environment, education can play a crucial role. Conservation in all of its aspects plays an important part in informal and nonformal education as well as in the schools' formal curriculum.

Conflict in the Middle East

The Middle East remains a region of unresolved tensions and conflict between nations and between suppressed peoples within nations. A highly volatile situation exists in the tensions between Israel and the Palestinian Authority and people. Israel seeks to preserve its integrity as a nation and to protect the security of its people against terrorist attacks that originate from Palestinian and other Arab organizations. The Palestinians recoil against frequent Israeli raids, occupations, and strikes against Palestinian towns and sites. The result has been a cycle of violence that temporarily subsides and then rekindles and escalates. The unresolved tensions between Israel and its Arab neighbors have aggravated the plight of the displaced Palestinians, some of whom remain in their former homeland; others are dispersed throughout the region in refugee camps or as migrant workers. Efforts to negotiate and resolve the issues have failed repeatedly.

In 1990 and 1991, the tensions, intrigues, and rivalries of the Middle East exploded when Iraq invaded and occupied the small, oil-rich neighboring nation of Kuwait. An overwhelming majority of the world's nations, acting through the United Nations, condemned Iraqi aggression and imposed economic sanctions to force its withdrawal from Kuwait. A key factor in the United Nations' resolution and action against Iraqi aggression was that the member nations were acting in a unified but multilateral way. In 1991, a broad based coalition of nations, of which the U.S. was a principal force, militarily intervened, defeated Iraq, and liberated Kuwait.

In 2003, the U.S., the United Kingdom, and a number of other countries formed an international coalition to invade Iraq and overthrow the regime of the country's dictator, Saddam Hussein, who was charged with creating an arsenal of weapons of mass destruction. Hussein's armies were defeated, and Iraq was occupied by the U.S. military and other coalition forces. Since the occupation of Iraq, there have been recurrent acts of violence against the coalition forces, members of the interim government, which was established with the support of the U.S., and Iraqi security forces. The Iraqi government faces the difficult challenge of restoring order in the country and establishing representative political institutions. (The Iraq war and occupation is examined in more detail in chapter 4.)

The War on Terror

The unresolved tensions in the Middle East and elsewhere in the world have produced international or global terrorism. Just as the economy and communications are now worldwide so are terrorist organizations. On September 11, 2001, operatives of the al Qaeda terrorist group hijacked four U.S. commercial airliners, and deliberately crashed them into the two towers of the World Trade Center in New York City and the Pentagon in Washington, D.C. (The fourth airliner crashed in Pennsylvania.) The number of deaths in New York alone reached 3,000. This wanton attack on civilians in the U.S. brought the country into what is called the "war on terror." The war has involved efforts to improve security at airports, nuclear installations, and other possible targets of terrorist attacks. An Office of Homeland Security was created as a federal agency to oversee antiterrorist efforts.

The war on terror brought dramatic changes to U.S. foreign and military policy. The U.S. military, particularly its special forces, was deployed to Afghanistan, where Osama bin Laden, the head of al Qaeda, established training camps for terrorists. The Islamic fundamentalist Taliban regime, which harbored bin Laden, was toppled by U.S. air strikes and anti-Taliban forces. Afghanistan is now in the process of establishing a parliamentary government. (The war on terror is examined in more detail in chapter 4).

It is dramatically clear that the U.S. and other nations of the world face the long-term threat of international terrorists who may use not only bombs but also biological, chemical, and perhaps nuclear weapons in the future. In September 2004, terrorists seized a school in Russia and held the students, teachers, and parents hostage. An explosion in the school and exchange of fire between the terrorists in the school and Russian soldiers outside led to over 300 deaths, half of whom were children. Although the events of 9/11, the fall of the Taliban, the war in Iraq, and other actions involving international terrorism are well-known and evoke a sense of national unity, the strategies to wage the war on terror are highly controversial, especially as they relate to issues about the restriction and protection of civil liberties. The war on terror carries with it some emerging and highly significant implications for education.[6] On one level, educators are responsible for teaching students why terrorism exists and strategies for dealing with it. On another, broader level, through education people can understand others and find ways to reach common ground.

Why There Is a Need for International Education

While we now live in what has been called a global village, the particular places and spaces in which people dwell are often quite different from each other. Some of us take spacious living for granted. Others live in places where space is severely limited, and they are engulfed by teeming crowds. Like the places in which we live, our lives also differ dramatically. Some of us enjoy comfortable homes, abundant food, and the amenities of life. Others have few material possessions, are ill-housed or even homeless, survive on subsistence diets, endure the ever-present threat of starvation, and face oppression and violence. While some of us enjoy extensive educational opportunities that lead from preschool and primary grades through higher education, others have never attended school and are illiterate.

The disparities between the places and conditions of peoples' lives bring us to the important international reality of changing demographics, or what has been called the population explosion. The world's population grew slowly during much of its history. It was not until 1800 that the earth's human population reached one billion. Since 1800, however, population has increased rapidly. In 1987, the world's population was estimated at five billion. In the early twenty-first century, the earth's population exceeds six billion.

While the planet's total population is growing at an accelerated rate, different places in the global village have had markedly different rates of growth. About 2.3 billion people live in Europe, North America, Australia, New Zealand, and East Asia, where population growth is slow, economies are developed, and living standards are relatively high. In the rest of the world, the population is growing at three times the rate of those more affluent countries. For example, the population of the U.S. is expected to increase by 20 percent in the twenty-first century. Nigeria's population, by comparison, is estimated to increase by more than 100 percent in the same period. In the technologically underdeveloped nations, rapidly growing populations, weak economic infrastructures, ethnic and tribal strife, and endemic diseases such as AIDS have reduced or diminished the quality of life. Consequently, the majority of the world's population is undernourished, underhoused, undereducated, and underemployed. The great disparities between the "have" and "have-not" countries of the earth are increasing and leading to such tensions and imbalances that they are becoming social dynamite that could explode at any moment.[7] One means to address these disparities and establish communities free from hunger, strife, and violence is through education.

The authors of *Education for Development* provide examples of situations that illustrate the need for change. The need for international education comes from the chronic ethnic and tribal tensions and violence that cause genocide. Campaigns of "ethnic cleansing" have forced people to flee from their homes and generated a worldwide diaspora of displaced persons. While military conflict between armed combatants causes many casualties, civilians, especially women and children, comprise the largest number of victims.[8] The use of poison gas against thousands of Kurdish refugees fleeing Saddam Hussein's oppressive regime in Iraq in 1991 was brutal testimony to the extent of the world's refugee problem. In the Sudan, in 2004, militias, backed by the government, have driven thousands of people from their homes in the Darfur region. The plight of refugees is an urgent humanitarian, social, and educational problem. It is estimated that the number of refugees exceeds 14 million, of whom 75 percent are women and children. Of these, 2.5 million are children of primary school age.[9]

In addition to the tragic plight of refugees, the movement of peoples has still another dimension. Rather than the overt violence of war, economic desperation is driving people from their homes. In developing countries demographic movement has been from rural farms and villages to sprawling cities such as Calcutta, India, Bangkok, Thailand, and Mexico City, Mexico. The migration to the large cities, especially in LTDCs, has caused economic dislocation and a largely unsatisfied need for living space, jobs, and education. At the beginning of the twenty-first century, nearly half of the world's population lives in urban areas, and the economic and social stability of rural areas, deserted by their young and often most productive persons, has declined.

The migration of peoples has produced new economic and educational phenomena. In some situations, referred to as "brain drain," highly educated and skilled persons such as physicians, scientists, and educators have left their own LTDCs to find employment in better-paying professional positions in developed countries. This worldwide migration of talent is caused by limited opportunities in LTDCs whose economic infrastructures are inadequate to absorb these highly trained persons. A larger dimension of the worldwide movement of people is that of migrant workers who leave their own countries in search of jobs to support their families. For example, migrant workers from Mexico seek employment in the U.S. In Western Europe, migrant workers usually come from Eastern Europe and Africa. Migrant workers occupy second-class status and are often economically, socially, and educationally marginalized in their host countries.

People's efforts to better their living conditions have another important ramification—the ecological health of our common planet. People living in both technologically developed and underdeveloped nations have endangered the quality of the earth's environment, but the industrialized nations are the most flagrant violators. The depletion of the earth's natural resources and damage to its ecostructure are so serious that we face an environmental crisis whose solution is critical to sustaining life on the planet. According to *Education for Development:*

> The environment knows no political boundaries: pollution and destruc-
> tion of the air, the waters, and the soil threaten all people equally. Toxic
> waste, acid rain, global warming, ground water contamination, defores-
> tation, fuel shortages, depletion of the biomass and desertification
> threaten all life on earth.[10]

We have framed the need for international education in terms of improving the quality of life for all people on the planet. The protection of the earth's
ecological health can only be done through international efforts. The plight of
the world's poor and homeless is a worldwide humanitarian issue of basic
human rights and dignity. However, international education deals not only
with these large global issues but also includes an immediate and intensely
practical concern for citizens, teachers, and students in the U.S. The economic
prosperity and progress of the U.S. is tied to our ability to understand and deal
with the new realities of an interdependent global economy. The chapters that
follow examine the educational implications of this new world order.

Conclusion

It is imperative that Americans be informed and reflective about the global society in which they now live. Events taking place in remote countries
such as Afghanistan and Iraq have an impact on our daily lives at home. We
are affected by political, religious, and ethnic conflicts in other parts of the
world and by global problems of poverty, racial and ethnic discrimination,
and environmental pollution. The rise of new sectors of economic integration
and power in the Pacific Rim and in the European Union affects the American economy and has an impact on how we educate and train people for
work in the interdependent global economy. The chapters that follow argue
that it is in our self-interest, both as citizens of the U.S. and as members of a
global society, to develop a consciousness of our relationships with people
not only in terms of other nations but also in terms of the whole planet. This
awareness involves developing political, economic, environmental, and educational interrelationships and connections between us and other peoples.

DISCUSSION QUESTIONS

1. Identify and analyze the concepts that governed U.S. foreign policy during
   the cold war. How might these concepts inhibit developing new policies in
   the post–cold war era?
2. Define colonialism and examine its impact on education in nations that
   once were part of colonial empires.
3. What are the major transnational issues that face a global society?
4. Identify the unresolved issues in the Middle East that threaten international peace and security.

5. How are homelessness and poverty both domestic and international issues?

6. Identify and examine the need for international education in elementary, secondary, and higher education and as a component of teacher education programs.

FIELD AND RESEARCH TOPICS

1. Examine the curriculum of an elementary or secondary school. Identify and describe its international aspects or components.

2. Organize a clippings file of newspaper and magazine articles that deal with international problems.

3. Invite a representative of the Peace Corps, the Red Cross, or a voluntary organization that is involved in dealing with international issues to speak to your class about such issues.

4. Using role playing in which students assume the role of diplomats, act out a conference designed to resolve the issues in the Middle East.

5. Interview international students at your college or university who are from former colonial nations. Attempt to ascertain their views on the impact of colonial rule on their education.

6. Design and use a survey to be administered to the class to determine a ranking of international issues.

SUGGESTIONS FOR FURTHER READING

Altbach, Philip G., and Gail P. Kelly. *Education and Colonialism.* New York: Longman, 1978.

Carnoy, Martin. *Education and Cultural Imperialism.* New York: David McKay, 1974.

Coombs, Philip H. *The World Crisis in Education: The View from the Eighties.* New York: Oxford University Press, 1985.

Graebner, Norman A. *America as a World Power: A Realist Appraisal from Wilson to Reagan.* Wilmington, DE: Scholarly Resources, 1984.

Griffith, William E., ed. *Central and Eastern Europe: The Opening Curtain?* Boulder, CO: Westview Press, 1989.

Kerblay, Basile. *Gorbachev's Russia.* New York: Pantheon Books, 1989.

NOTES

[1] Analyses of the impact of colonialism on education are Philip G. Altbach and Gail P. Kelly, *Education and Colonialism* (New York: Longman, 1978) and Martin Carnoy, *Education as Cultural Imperialism* (New York: David McKay, 1974).

[2] Lester R. Kurtz, *The Nuclear Cage: Sociology of the Arms Race* (Englewood Cliffs, NJ: Prentice-Hall, 1988).

[3] Basile Kerblay, *Gorbachev's Russia* (New York: Pantheon Books, 1989).

[4] Among the nations included in the Pacific Rim are: Far Eastern countries and markets bordering the Pacific Ocean, consisting of Australia, Cambodia, China, Hong Kong, Indonesia, Japan, Korea, Laos, Malaysia, New Zealand, Papua New Guinea, Philippines, Singapore, Taiwan, Thailand, and Vietnam, as well as Canada, Mexico, and the U.S.

[5] There are currently 25 member states in the European Union: Austria, Belgium, Cyprus, Czech Republic, Denmark, Estonia, Finland, France, Germany, Greece, Hungary, Ireland, Italy, Latvia, Lithuania, Luxembourg, Malta, the Netherlands, Poland, Portugal, Slovakia, Slovenia, Spain, Sweden, and the United Kingdom.

[6] One of the first books to discuss the educational implications of the War on Terror is Allan C. Ornstein, *Teaching and Schooling in America: Pre- and Post-September 11* (Boston: Allyn and Bacon, 2003).

[7] Interfaith Hunger Appeal, *Education for Development* (New York: Interfaith Hunger Appeal, 1990), 37.

[8] Ibid.

[9] Ibid., 39.

[10] Ibid., 24.

2

DEFINING INTERNATIONAL EDUCATION

Since the beginning of recorded history, humankind has engaged in a long but elusive search for peaceful forms of social organization. Ironically, however, since the time of the ancient Mesopotamian Empire in the Tigris and Euphrates river valleys and the Egyptian Empire on the Nile, the search has entailed war, conquest, insurrection, and the violence of human to human. Indeed, much human history, including that studied in schools, comprises shifting alliances, treaties made and broken, and wars between nations. This book examines the historical reality of conflict between peoples, with the equally important reality of the human desire for a peaceful and secure world. Is it possible for people, through such processes as international education, to live in ordered and peaceful environments?

In this chapter, we shall (1) examine the desire for international understanding through education as expressed by leading educational theorists from the past, (2) consider various definitions of international education that explain this important but elusive concept, and (3) stipulate the definition of international education used in this book.

The history of international education is more than the record of attempts to resolve conflicts between peoples and nations. It seeks to develop a global outlook or perspective that envisions the world in which we live as a sociopolitical, planetary biosphere.

National Citizenship and a Global Society

The tensions that exist between one's commitment and loyalty to the nation-state, to one's own country, and the imperative for a larger and broader sense of global realities are evident in schools, curriculum, and instruction. Schools in the U.S., like school systems throughout the world, reflect the commitment to shape citizens who are loyal and participating members of the country. In the U.S., public schools, through the formal curriculum and educational milieu, seek to cultivate in students a knowledge of the American past through the study of history, facility in using the English language as the national medium of communication, an awareness of the structures of American government, and a desire to participate as citizens in the affairs of the republic. In addition to teaching students the basic skills (reading, writing, and computation) and the basic academic curriculum (science, mathematics, language, the social sciences, and humanities), public schools seek to develop a sense of citizenship that is particular to the U.S. Just as schools in the U.S. undertake to cultivate a sense of American identity and citizenship, schools in other countries or nation-states, such as the United Kingdom, France, Russia, Japan, India, China, and Nigeria, are also engaged in creating civic loyalties to their own national forms of social, political, and economic organization. The structured education system provided by a nation-state is known as *formal education*.

At the same time that children are taught to become citizens in particular nation-states, they also need to understand that the world in which they live extends beyond their own nation and their specific national identity. Many of the great problems humankind faces in the twenty-first century are international or global in scope. Environmental pollution, epidemic disease, poverty, the threat of nuclear holocaust, and terrorism affect people everywhere, regardless of their geographical location and national identification. An awareness of the realities in which we live means that we need to cross not only national borders and frontiers but conceptual ones as well. International education, as developed in this book, examines the realities and tensions that exist as a result of our dual membership as citizens of both a national and world society. From this examination, a larger, broader, and more reflective concept of national and world citizenship hopefully will be constructed.

While schools cultivate particular kinds of citizenship, they can also provide the means for enlarging our sense of time and space by creating international and global perspectives. Our world can be viewed in many dimensions, each of which can be presented and interpreted though the subject matter of organized knowledge. A school's curriculum, as it reflects such disciplines, can be infused with international and global meanings. The study of geography, with its examination of landforms, topography, soils, climate, and the cultures that arise in these different places, adds to our physical and spatial understanding of the world. Political science helps us to understand the political structures and organizations that compose the governments of nation-states and the interactions between these nation-states. Throughout the world, people strive to earn a livelihood and secure the necessities of material life. Here, economics comes to bear on the world dimension, particularly on the rapidly developing interrelated global economy and the phenomenon of globalization. The humanities, literature, art, music, drama, and film, too, reflect both particular but also more universal aspects of culture.

The sense that we are part of an interdependent and interconnected global system is becoming increasingly apparent. Global interconnectedness and interrelatedness are especially salient as we consider our planet's environmental health. Damage to the biosphere caused by pollution is a problem that crosses national boundaries and affects us all. Conditions of economic growth or recession and of employment and unemployment today are linked to the interdependent global economy. Electronic means of communication, through the World Wide Web, cross national boundaries instantaneously, linking people around the world. Certainly, then, to be educated means to have knowledge from and about places that are beyond our immediate locality; we must know our relationships to a global reality and to an international society.

International education is not a new pursuit. It is as old as the human quest for peace and order. To provide a perspective on efforts to educate about the world at large, the following section examines how certain prominent educators of the distant as well as the recent past addressed issues related to international education.

Educators' Search for International Understanding

The history of education provides many examples of those who believed that the international dimension of human existence should become a conscious part of a person's education. Often, the efforts of internationally oriented educators were opposed by those who were strongly committed to and identified with local or national interests. Before discussing these internationally minded educators, we shall consider certain tendencies that motivated them to wage a difficult and often seemingly losing struggle.

Since the time of the Protestant Reformation in the sixteenth century, the major thrust of organized education, or schooling, has been to develop commitments in the young that focus more particularly on loyalty to a religious denomination, a dynasty, or a nation, as opposed to those that are global or directed to humanity in general. During the Protestant Reformation and Catholic Counter-Reformation of the sixteenth century, schools, especially at the primary or elementary level, were used to construct and reinforce denominational doctrinal commitments. Usually, the catechistic instruction, an invariable part of such denominational education, was intolerant and antagonistic toward believers of other religious faiths. The religious wars of the sixteenth century that devastated Central Europe, especially the German states, were partially stimulated by this intense denominational antagonism between Protestants and Catholics.

With the emergence of dynastic and then national states in the seventeenth, eighteenth, and nineteenth centuries, schooling was also used to build loyalties to the nation and its rulers. During the early nineteenth century, when most national school systems were created in Western Europe and North America, indoctrination of nationalism in the young was a paramount educational goal. Thus, the origin of national, or state, school systems coincided with the high tide of nationalism. This kind of education, carrying with it strong nationalistic feelings, contributed to the series of wars—the Napoleonic wars, the Crimean War, the Franco-Prussian War, World War I, and World War II—that constitute such a large part of our history.

While many educators, including classroom teachers, willingly used indoctrination to reinforce religious intolerance or chauvinistic nationalism in their students, others—probably a minority—believed that education needed to extend human horizons rather than limit them to a particular creed, dynasty, or nation. Among these more ecumenically minded educators was the Renaissance humanist Erasmus.

Erasmus and Cosmopolitan Humanism

Desiderius Erasmus (1466–1536), a Roman Catholic priest, had been educated by the Brethren of the Common Life in the Netherlands. He attended the University of Paris, one of Europe's premier institutions of higher education.[1] A widely traveled person who communicated with the leading humanists of the late Renaissance, Erasmus saw education as a liberating universal process that extended rather than limited human horizons. He believed that educators were colleagues in an international and cosmopolitan collegium rather than servants of particular denominational or nationalistic masters. Erasmus's philosophy of cosmopolitan humanism, which emphasized education as a transnational process, sharply contrasted with that which called for education to construct identification with a deliberately restricted place and state.

Consistently emphasizing education's universalizing role, Erasmus saw it as a force for establishing and maintaining peace. In his *Education of the Christian Prince*, Erasmus described the education of a prince in the humanities and prescribed the policies that such a humane ruler should follow in governing his realm.[2] Erasmus's motivation in writing this treatise was his anxiety that growing enmity between Catholics and Protestants would unleash a religious war in Europe. To turn rulers into peacemakers, Erasmus hoped to instill his cosmopolitan educational philosophy into international policy making.

In contrast to Machiavelli's portrayal of the prince as one who used manipulation, scheming, and subterfuge to maintain his power, Erasmus depicted an enlightened and cosmopolitan ruler who was prudent and humane. He encouraged a form international education that would lead to prudent diplomacy based not only on the needs of the prince's realm but also on the wishes of people who lived beyond its borders. Erasmus, an astute observer of world affairs, clearly recognized the need to balance nation-state interests with those of a larger humanity. The Christian prince that Erasmus envisioned as the ideal ruler would study history and geography. History would provide a sense of time and create a perspective on historical and contemporary events. Such a historically based perspective would inform the policy maker about the need to maintain cultural continuity and avoid reckless actions that endangered humane culture. Geography would provide a clear sense of place and location that, while it began with the ruler's own country, would also extend outward to other peoples and places.

A true humanist, Erasmus recommended that the Christian prince study the liberal arts, especially philosophy, theology, and literature, particularly the classics. These humane and liberal studies, a repository of human wisdom, would cultivate the prince's ethical sensibilities and give him a grasp of human affairs. This broad and liberal outlook would help him to appoint honest and humane individuals to public office, and provide an ethical perspective in devising and implementing the policies governing his kingdom and its relationships with other countries.

Erasmus urged the Christian prince to provide schools and teachers to educate his subjects. In well-supported and carefully supervised schools, taught by the "best and most trustworthy instructors," students would "learn the teachings of Christ and that good literature which is beneficial to the state."[3] Such a school system would provide a humane education, would develop knowledge and morality in the general population, and contribute to the realm's economic prosperity. In a kingdom, where the people were properly educated, the ruler would not have to rely on coercion and fear to maintain public order. Further, an educated and prosperous nation would be disinclined to embark on foreign adventures that might lead to war.

In *The Education of the Christian Prince*, Erasmus presents an early commentary on international education. He wrote that the Christian prince should study and practice conflict resolution, the arts of peaceful diplomacy and negotiation, to avoid war. How sad it was, Erasmus wrote, that priests and ministers should bless contending armies as they went into battle to kill their fellow Christians in the name of religion. The costs of war were high and often exceeded the expectations of those who embarked on them. They were high in the cost of human life, in material destruction, and in the psychic damage they caused. How much better it would be if the resources wasted on war were used for human betterment. Erasmus compared war to a contagious plague that spread infection across borders. While the initial conflict might be local and limited, war tended to escalate and spread, like a conflagration, from country to country.

Erasmus's fears about religiously charged "holy wars" are still very much with us. The longstanding tensions in the Middle East, such as those that provoke hostility between Israelis and Arabs, contain elements of religiously based hostility. Terrorists who take innocent lives distort Islam's teaching to inflame passions for a jihad, or holy war. The violence and tensions in Northern Ireland between Protestants and Catholics are yet another example where religion is misused to fuel antagonism. In Bosnia and Kosovo, violence and ethnic cleansing were spurred by the religious hostility of Serbian Orthodox Christians and Slavic Muslims. In urging his al Qaeda followers to engage in terrorism, Osama bin Laden invokes fundamentalist Muslims to carry out a holy war against the U.S.

When disputes between nations threatened to erupt into war, Erasmus urged policy makers to avoid fanning the flames and recommended that such disputes be referred to international tribunals composed of wise and impartial arbitrators. Erasmus's call for international adjudication of disputes is much like the peacekeeping efforts of today's United Nations and the World

Court. Ahead of his time, Erasmus's pleas for international education, however, went largely unheeded. Conflict that began in Bohemia between the
Catholic Hapsburg rulers and their Protestant subjects escalated and spread
throughout Europe. Before the Thirty Years War ended, the German states
were ravaged, as French, Spanish, Austrian, and Swedish armies fought
against each other.

Comenius and Pansophism

In the early seventeenth century, Johann Amos Comenius (1592–1670), a
Czech educator, like Erasmus before him, urged international education.
Comenius, a bishop in the Church of the Brethren, a small pietist Protestant
denomination, spent most of his life in exile as a refugee. The pietists, many of
whom were pacifists, practiced the "religion of the heart," which emphasized
a right attitude and good works rather than doctrinaire theology. The Brethren were persecuted in their native Bohemia and Moravia by the Hapsburg
authorities, who sought to restore Catholicism and suppress any challenges to
their rule. Comenius, a religious refugee, traveled throughout Europe, spending time doing religious and educational writing and teaching in Poland, Sweden, England, and Holland. Among his books are *The Labyrinth of the World*,
The Paradise of the Heart, *The Great Didactic*, and *The Orbis Pictus*.[4]

Comenius's philosophy of education, called *pansophism*, made a strong
case for international education. He believed that all knowledge comes from
God and that human beings can come to know each other, and ultimately
God, through universal knowledge. He held that the religious and national
hostilities that caused such violence to his own people, the Brethren, and to
other people of Europe were caused by ignorance. Caused by either not
knowing or of being falsely indoctrinated, ignorance led to bigotry, discrimination, and intolerance—the root causes of war and bloodshed. Complete
knowledge, which Comenius believed possible, would enlighten people, dispel ignorance, bring people closer to each other, cause them to respect human
life, and ultimately bring them to know God.

An educator with a broad ecumenical vision, Comenius lived during a
time rent by sectarian and nationalist antagonisms. Many schools in the seventeenth century were controlled by religious denominations that used them
to instill their doctrines to the exclusion of other beliefs. In contrast, Comenius believed it possible to have a value-oriented religious education that
emphasized the beliefs and practices unique to a particular church and also
embodied the common needs and hopes shared by all people throughout the
world. Much in advance of the time in which he lived, Comenius called for a
world assembly of churches to engage in common ecumenical dialogue.[5] As
an international or peace educator, Comenius believed in creating a worldwide social order that relied on peacemaking and peacekeeping institutions.[6]

To create the cultural climate for this new social order, the leaders of
church and state needed to transform schools into agencies of human enlight-

enment that would open minds and hearts to each other rather than close them through indoctrination. Comenius argued that teachers should respect children's human dignity rather than coerce them physically or psychologically. He urged teachers to develop instructional methods that encouraged children to actively use their senses in learning. Schools that were transformed into places of enlightened and humane learning would cultivate an ecumenical vision of the "peaceable kingdom" where all could live in mutual respect. Although Comenius gained wide respect for his educational ideas in both Europe and the Americas, his vision that schools should serve ecumenical purposes was not realized during his lifetime or in the centuries after his death.

Rabindranath Tagore

The Indian poet, novelist, and educator Rabindranath Tagore (1861–1941) developed both a philosophy and an institutional setting for international education. Educated in India and England, Tagore originally prepared for a career in law, but then decided to devote himself to literature. His first collection of poetry, *Songs of the Morning*, appeared in 1881. His highly acclaimed *Gitanijli* (1909) earned the Nobel Prize for literature in 1913. Interested in advancing international understanding, especially between East and West, he embarked on international travel, visiting the U.S., the Soviet Union, and China. His travels convinced him to work for cross-cultural communication and understanding, especially between East and West and between India and China.

Tagore's educational philosophy, originating in the Hinduism of his native India, encompassed both the person as an individual and all humanity as part of a divinely created and spiritually endowed universe. The unity of all human beings came, Tagore reasoned, as the potentiality of each person was developed to its fullest possibility. Giving a central place to nature in his poetry and in his philosophy, Tagore believed that it was the path to ultimate truth and unity. Nature provided the means of stimulating and unlocking the human being's creative impulses.[7]

Tagore, determined to implement his philosophy, founded a small school for boys called Shantiniketan in 1901. By 1921, under Tagore's leadership, this school had grown into Vishwabharati, an International University. At Vishwabharati, Tagore created an educational environment in which learning would originate from traditional Indian thought but would also be broadened to include an international dimension. Tagore believed that education should begin with the student's own country and then move outward to take on a global perspective. Students should learn about their country's geography, history, culture, and economy. They should study its languages and literature.[8] From this base, education would then proceed to the international dimension and create a world-minded outlook. As a philosophical idealist, Tagore saw humankind moving toward greater unity. For him, international education was the means by which different cultures, arising in varied geographical locations, would meet and speak to each other. At his International University, the cultures of East and West, while recognizing their differences, would meet on the basis of their commonalities.

Reflecting Tagore's own cosmopolitan worldview, Vishwabharati's curriculum included Asian languages and cultures; world religions such as Hinduism, Buddhism, Islam, and Christianity; Western science and technology; and fine arts, dancing, and music from an international perspective. All of these human achievements, developed across a kaleidoscopic cultural spectrum, mirrored the unity of a world spiritual force. No one culture should be regarded as superior to another, nor should any be used for exploitative purposes.[9]

Maria Montessori

Today, the Italian educator Maria Montessori (1870–1952) enjoys global acclaim as one of the world's great educational pioneers, particularly for her work in early childhood education. Her biography tells the story of a dedicated woman who used her scientific training as a medical doctor, her experience in working with children with mental handicaps, and insights gained from her Casa dei Bambini in Rome to construct an innovative method that challenged conventional schooling.[10] Although not usually thought of as an international educator, Montessori's writing and work contain a significant international dimension. She sought to disseminate her method of education to an international audience, establishing Montessori schools and training centers worldwide. Her work, which began in her native Italy, took her to the U.S., Spain, the Netherlands, the United Kingdom, India, and other countries.

In founding her first school, the Casa dei Bambini, "Children's House," in Rome in 1907, Montessori was guided by sociological and educational insights developed during her career. She located her school in a remodeled tenement apartment building where the children's families lived and designed it to make a vital organic connection between education and society. Educationally, the Children's House was to be a school-home, an educational agency in close proximity to the children's family residences. Montessori stated, "We have placed the school within the house . . . as the property of the collectivity."[11] Socializing the family as well as the child, the school would connect the individual household to the larger community. Her method was not only a means to educate children more humanely and effectively but was intended to aid in the social regeneration of the impoverished residents of Rome's San Lorenzo district.

The proximity of the children's home to their school related to Montessori's concept of "new woman." The Casa dei Bambini was located in an area where most of the mothers worked in Italy's developing industries. Montessori reasoned that not only would working-class women be employed outside of the home but that women of all socioeconomic classes would join the workforce in the future. Schools, as educational institutions, needed to recognize this technologically generated change and provide for the children of working mothers. Schools like the Casa dei Bambini would make it possible for mothers to safely leave their children and "proceed with a feeling of great relief and freedom to their own work."

Montessori then had several motives in mind when establishing the Casa dei Bambini, the prototype of all later Montessori schools, including social reform, especially the improvement of the condition of the working class. There was the motive that the school as a means of aiding working mothers would contribute to the general movement for women's equality and rights. However, the Casa was primarily a place for children's education based on the principles of scientific pedagogy.

Believing that she had developed a truly global method of education, Montessori was an international presence who traveled the world to promote her method of education. She conducted training classes and addressed conferences in Italy, the U.S., the Netherlands, Spain, France, the UK, Ireland, India, and other countries. Living through two world wars, she argued that the true way to peace would come as children were educated in the ways of peace.

For Montessori, children have a nature that is as universal as the periods of human development. Although cultural contexts have some conditioning significance, Montessori claimed the nature of childhood and her method of early childhood education are universal and not culturally relative, nor culturally determined. Individuals everywhere experience the same process of development, regardless of place or clime. Because of this universality, the Montessori method is transnational and transcultural. Its application may be conditioned by the cultural context but is not determined by it. Although different cultural settings may require some slight adaptation, Montessori believed her method could function in any culture because of the universality of human and child nature. She stated:

> There is no sense in talking about differences of procedure for Indian babies, Chinese babies, or European babies; nor for those belonging to different social classes. We can speak of one method; that which follows the natural unfolding of man. All babies have the same psychological needs, and follow the same sequence of events, in attaining to human stature. Every one of us has to pass through the same phases of growth.[12]

More Contemporary Theories of International Education

Like Erasmus, Comenius, Tagore, and Montessori, contemporary educators continue to reassert the need for international education and its importance in school curricula. Although the literature on international education is vast, we examine the work of three such educators: Harold Taylor, Kenneth Melvin, and Elise Boulding.

Harold Taylor

In *The World as Teacher,* Harold Taylor argues that international education should be the integrating focus of study and activity in departments and colleges of teacher education. Knowledge of world cultures should be integrally diffused throughout the teacher education program. History, he says, has reached the stage where human loyalties and commitments need to be extended from identification with a particular national context to the entire human race. Without a world perspective, the rapidly expanding and accelerating rate of specialized information will result in a fragmented understanding of reality. In an emerging world culture, the teacher and the school must be conscious agencies of crossing the boundaries of subject matter, integrating knowledge, and creating human unity in a world culture.[13] Defining education as "the way in which each person becomes aware of himself and his place in the world at large, and learns how best to conduct himself in it and to contribute to it," Taylor urges educators to create a larger, broader, and more interpenetrating awareness in their students.[14] Taylor gives a special role to schools and departments of teacher education in developing effective programs of international education. Teacher education programs should become genuine laboratories that facilitate international dialogues for educators around the world.

Taylor calls for a "seriously concerned teachers college" that makes the world its classroom and moves the world into its curriculum. Using the Peace Corps as a model, Taylor's proposed teachers college would immerse prospective teachers in world culture by providing a range of multicultural educational experiences in both domestic and international contexts; arranging student teaching and other clinical experiences in diverse multicultural settings both in the U.S. and in other countries; and including in the curriculum of teacher education the study of the cultures and languages of other peoples.

Some of Taylor's recommendations are found in contemporary teacher education programs. Many institutions include study abroad as part of the general teacher education program; a number of institutions also provide student teaching opportunities in schools in other countries. However, the general interpenetration of international education into teacher education programs has not yet occurred.

Kenneth Melvin

In *Education in World Affairs,* Kenneth Melvin, like Taylor, examines the international dimension of teacher education. Using an approach somewhat similar to this book's, he identifies the strains and tensions that exist between education for the national interest and education for a global society. Commenting on how nations engage in *realpolitik,* Melvin finds they pursue their own interests and try to achieve them if they have sufficient power to do so. In contrast to realpolitik, Melvin stipulates the term *idealpolitik* as an alternative position based on "principled conviction rather than expediency." To create a synthesis between policies based on the interests of nations and the broad humane goals of a world community, Melvin turns to education. He argues, somewhat like Erasmus and Comenius, that education should advance international understanding and create a *weltpolitik*, a principled worldview.

Like Taylor, Melvin views teacher education programs as vital centers for developing a global perspective. He states that international education

> has much to learn from the social sciences; as a study of the mastery of the human environment it must incorporate a number of the applied sciences; as a search for Weltanschauung it must draw heavily upon international literature, prose, [and] poetry, both verbal and iconic.[15]

Broadening their scope, teacher education programs should include the international and comparative studies of politics, sociology, psychology, and economics. Melvin emphasizes, like Taylor, international practicum experiences and third-year abroad programs. He, too, would make teacher education a scene of international dialogue by encouraging the worldwide exchange of students, artists, scholars, and performers. Both Taylor's and Melvin's proposals harken back to Erasmus's cosmopolitan humanism, which relished the free, open, and international exchange of ideas and educators.

Elise Boulding

Elise Boulding's *Building a Global Civic Culture: Education for an Interdependent World* presents a philosophy for international education that has programmatic goals for shaping a new world society. For Boulding, the peoples of the world are becoming increasingly interdependent. From this sense of international commonality, international education becomes the vehicle for creating a common civic culture. Boulding asserts, "Civic culture represents the patterning of how we share a common space, common resources, and common opportunities and manage interdependence in that company of strangers."[16]

In working toward a new definition of the international order, Boulding points out the new importance of voluntary, international, nongovernmental organizations that pursue policies and development on a grassroots, people-to-people basis that does not depend on the foreign policies and interests of nation-states. Among such voluntary international nongovernmental organizations are the International Coalition for Development Action, Health Action International, the World Health Assemblies, the World Wildlife Fund, and churches, service organizations, and youth groups. There are more than 18,000 organizations that transcend national boundaries and continents, representing a new global force that could become the basis for creating the needed world civic culture.

Urging us to create new futures, Boulding emphasizes social imagination as a tool for conjecturing alternatives to current international threats to human and planetary survival. Using their social imagination and encouraged by international education, people throughout the world are to develop a feeling of relatedness to others and a sense of how that relatedness functions. Boulding's book is rich in suggestions of new visionary and utopian vistas for creating a world civic culture.

Despite the richness and variety of the literature on international education, progress in incorporating the international dimension into teacher education and elementary and secondary education programs in the U.S. has been slow and uneven. At times, there is a great but often unrealized enthusiasm for incorporating a strong international presence in American education. In the past, such enthusiasm has often been dissipated by the need to deal with what appears to be more urgent local and national issues. Part of the difficulty has been the vagueness and polemical tone of many proposals for international education. The next section examines the various definitions of international education in order to focus more directly on the topic.

Definitions of International Education

International education has had a long and varied history. At times, American educators have been enthusiastic about incorporating international education into the school curriculum and programs of teacher education. But at other times, they have neglected international education. Over time, international education has had varying definitions that reflect different points of emphasis. This section examines some of the major approaches to and fields related to international education.

Comparative Education

Comparative education's long history begins in the classical Greek and Roman period, when historians, such as Herodotus, and travelers commented on the various peoples and cultures of the Aegean and Mediterranean worlds. More directly, comparative studies in education can be traced to the nineteenth century, when educators visited other countries to examine educational systems and to ascertain what elements might be used in the schools of their own countries. Examples of such comparative studies and educational borrowing are the visit of the French educator Victor Cousin to inspect the Prussian schools and the travels of American educators such as William Maclure, Calvin Stowe, Horace Mann, and Henry Barnard to visit European schools and import European educational ideas to the U.S. In the late-nineteenth and twentieth centuries, comparative studies became increasingly sophisticated and well developed through the efforts of educators such as Paul Monroe, Isaac Kandel, George S. Counts, William Brickman, and others.[17]

Essentially, comparative education can be defined as studies or examinations of education, including and often emphasizing school systems and structures, and analyzing their similarities and differences. For example, it is possible to compare and contrast education in the U.S. and Russia, or the UK and France, or China and India. Comparative studies, though broad in scope and often using cultural contexts, generally focus on formal educational structures and institutions such as primary, secondary, and higher schools. Often related to international education, the scope of comparative education focuses more on structures and systems of organized or formal education.

Certain contemporary trends in comparative education focus on comparative analyses of specifically defined characteristics or issues in education. For example, among this type of comparative study are topics such as how students are socialized politically, retention rates in higher education, or the relationship of vocational education to economic change in selected countries. There are also the frequently cited comparisons of academic achievement and rankings in specific subjects such as mathematics and science that have been used to support educational policy initiatives in the U.S. such as *A Nation at Risk* and No Child Left Behind.

Foreign Policy Studies

Foreign policy studies include international relations, usually part of political science and diplomatic history. From the American viewpoint, foreign policy studies analyze the policies of the various nations of the world in terms of their relationship to U.S. interests. The emphasis is on the vital interests, commitments, alliances, and treaty obligations of the U.S. as they promote the national interest. Educationally, foreign policy studies have at least two important implications: first, the education of Americans about the world role of their country vis-à-vis other nations; second, an examination of how educational programs of the U.S., both informal and formal, are part of foreign policy considerations.

As they study government, civics, and history, American students in elementary, secondary, and higher education acquire a perspective on their own country in relationship to other countries. The emphasis, however, is often focused on political, military, and economic considerations rather than on cultural and educational relationships. It is also often charged by ideological considerations. When examined in the broader context of international education, foreign policy studies illustrate the role and impact of nation-states and their relationships on the world scene. A weakness of many of the arguments made by advocates of international education is that they neglect or minimize the reality of the foreign policy considerations of nation-states. Unless these important relationships are included, international education tends to become highly utopian and based on what the proponents regard as an emergent rather than actual reality.

Regional or Area Studies

Regional or area studies form still another subset of international education. While more often found in higher education, such programs—as units in social studies courses—can also be found in elementary and secondary school curricula. Regional studies, for example, concentrate in an interdisciplinary way on a particular region or area of the world such as the Middle East, Latin America, the Caribbean, Western Europe, Eastern Europe, or Southeast Asia. Because of the war on terror and the U.S. involvement in Iraq, there has been an emphasis on the Middle East and the Arab world. Also, the Pacific Rim nations and the European Union, regions of growing economic and political power, are attracting serious attention. Rather than using a single discipline to examine a region, area studies are typically interdisciplinary. For example, the history, politics, economy, society, religion, art and music, and language or languages of a particular area are studied. Regional studies are particularly useful in developing insights into world cultures and affairs through a wide range of academic disciplines, subjects, and methods.

International Development and Development Education

After World War II, international development and development education appeared as still another dimension of international education when the U.S., through the Marshall Plan, sought to reconstruct the war-ravaged economies of Western Europe. According to the strategy developed by U.S. Secretary of State George C. Marshall, the U.S. would provide monetary loans and technological assistance to recovering nations. American strategists believed that once a nation's economic infrastructure was restored to health, political and social stability would follow.

After the success of the Marshall Plan, international development became more generalized as "developed nations" provided assistance, including educational assistance, to the "underdeveloped" or "developing" nations. The developed nations were characterized as those that had attained some degree of modernization, were urban, and had extensive industry and technology. These nations were also characterized by high rates of literacy and well-developed educational, health, and social service systems.

The underdeveloped nations, later called third-world nations and now referred to as less technologically developed countries (LTDCs), were generally characterized as having pervasive residues of traditional institutions and customs. They were predominantly rural, with economies at the subsistence level. These nations also faced serious and chronic problems of illiteracy, poverty, and endemic diseases. The operating assumption was that the developed nations could help the less-developed nations to modernize their institutional infrastructure, including education. It was further assumed that the developing nations could borrow institutions, procedures, and techniques from the developed nations. Experts, often scientists, technicians, and educators from the developed country, would work with their counterparts in the underdeveloped host country. International development programs and development education reached a high point in the mid- to late-1960s.[18] By the mid-1970s, in the aftermath of the Vietnam conflict and soaring rates of inflation in developed nations, development and development education declined. In the 1980s, a revival of development programs and development education occurred, but its operating principles were grassroots and linked to international nongovernmental organizations rather than being derived from the "top-down" government-negotiated and government-implemented policies of the 1960s.[19]

Peace Education

Peace education or world-order education represents an old form of international education that has its origins in the ideas of Erasmus and Comenius. It identifies the major goal of international education as world peace or the reduction of international tensions. Today, it is also referred to as conflict resolution education. It assumes that international tensions and wars that result from unresolved tensions are caused by nationalism, chauvinism, and ethnic stereotyping. It further proposes that the dissemination and analysis of knowledge about the peoples of the world and their problems can foster international understanding. Such understanding will reduce tensions that cause violence and war. At times, it also recommends that psychological and sociological techniques that reduce tensions between people and small groups be applied to the major actors on the international scene.[20]

Betty Reardon, an expert on peace studies, has identified three significant approaches to peace education: the reformist, the reconstructionist, and the transformational. The reformist approach seeks to reform rather than alter or radically abolish the current international system. Its goals are to prevent war and reduce the threats to peace presented by the arms race. Operating largely in a realist frame of reference, it sees the greatest possibilities for peace arising from changes in the behaviors of nation-states. It seeks to educate both leaders and citizens to the peace-maintaining possibilities that can be found in diplomacy, international organizations, and negotiations. The knowledge base for reformist approaches to peace education emphasizes the study of international institutions, international law, foreign policy, and national security systems. It identifies the causes of war as uninformed foreign policies, aggression, and highly nationalistic behavior on the part of the leaders of nation-states.[21]

The reconstructionist approach is similar to the educational philosophy of the same name that originated with certain socially oriented progressives such as Theodore Brameld, who proposed that education should create a new social order. The general approach used by reconstructionist philosophers is to identify viable elements in the cultural heritage and to integrate these elements with emergent trends. The integration of the inherited, viable cultural elements with the emergent ones is guided by human purposes and planning designed to create a new, more humanistic and egalitarian society. According to Brameld, "American civilization cannot survive, much less reorganize itself, unless its reconstruction is geared throughout to that of other countries. On our planet, the lands of which are technologically and economically interdependent, isolation is now completely impractical even if it were morally defensible."[22]

Reardon sees reconstructionist peace educators working toward the basic reconstruction of the international system, especially national security structures and processes, so as to achieve a "just and lasting peace." This reconstruction is likely to require limitations on the sovereignty of nation-states. The reconstructionist knowledge base is oriented toward international problem solving and relies on critical and futures research. Related to the basic theme of war and conflict resolution is addressing the problems that lead to international violence, such as poverty, repression of human rights, and environmental pollution.[23]

The transformational approach is most comprehensive in that it seeks profound changes in institutional structures, human behavior, and consciousness. It asserts that these changes are necessary because violence and war are caused by how we think. Examining relevant literature in a critical fashion, it uses such recently developed areas of scholarship as "macro-history, feminist scholarship, human ecology, process theology, and action research" for its knowledge base. Its goals are to stimulate and raise consciousness about global realities and to develop the human capacity to transform the conditions that diminish or threaten life on the planet.[24]

International Exchange Programs

International exchange programs and study-abroad programs, such as the "junior year abroad" programs in which education majors do their student teaching in another country, represent still other approaches to international education. These types of programs promote the exchange of professors, scholars, researchers, teachers, and students between countries. One of the best known of these programs is the Fulbright exchange program. Today, many school districts, colleges, and universities offer study abroad programs.[25]

Global Education

Global education represents one of the most recent approaches to international education. Indeed, the proponents of global education see it as distinct from international education in that its perspective is global rather than between nations. Global education portrays humankind as inhabiting a global village, a biosphere that is "spaceship Earth." Global educators tend to look for commonalities rather than differences among the earth's peoples and nations and are concerned with "emergent trends" that come from futuristic studies. They see a world of growing interdependency and emerging forces. They have identified world or global problems and issues that need to be studied and resolved. Among such problems are population explosion, environmental pollution, inequitable distribution of resources, famine, drug abuse, and disease. They see the role of the nation-state diminishing and that of a transnational global society emerging. The Study Commission on Global Education has recommended emphasis on the following curricular areas:

- developing a "better understanding of the world as a series of interrelated systems: physical, biological, economic, political, and informational-evaluative";
- devoting "more attention to the development of world civilizations as they relate to the history of the U.S.";
- devoting "greater attention to the diversity of cultural patterns both around the world and within the U.S."; and
- providing more "training in policy analysis both of domestic and international issues."[26]

International Business Education

Education for the multinational or transnational business corporation is yet another form of international education. This rapidly growing area of economic activity involves economics, management, advertising, and marketing. It represents the involvement of worldwide corporate financial interests and conglomerates in the global economy. (See chapter 6 on globalization for a more extended discussion of the global economy.) Educators associated with international education have often overlooked the importance of this new form of international business or tend to see its profit-making objectives as contrary to the more altruistic motives associated with peace education or global education. However, the multinational corporation has been a force for creating greater economic interdependency. It should be considered a contributor to the dynamics of a new kind of world economy because it will involve many students of U.S. schools as employees, and it will certainly involve them as consumers of its products.

As we see in the various forms of international education, it is difficult to define the area of study specifically. Each of the categories identified has valid claims as an intrinsically important area of study. Each also has educational inadequacies that result from being either too limited or two sweeping in scope. For example, foreign affairs education is too closely tied to the interests of the nation-state to provide the more general kind of perspective that relates to global or planetary issues and concerns. Global education, in contrast, is so sweeping in its orientation that it neglects the realities of the nation-state. In later chapters of the book, we shall examine certain categories, such as comparative education, development education, and globalization in greater depth. We shall see them as dimensions or subspecies of a more general and broader field that we identify and define as international education. We now come to a stipulated definition of international education that presents my orientation to the subject.

Creating a Stipulated Definition of International Education

Although each of the preceding definitions related to international education describes education in a world context, each also brings with it a sense of ambiguity and occasional ideological polemics. In this section I provide my own definition of international education, which also states the thesis or unifying theme of the book.

Approaching a stipulated definition is a challenging task. It is made more complicated by the convergence of the historical past, in which major power struggles and wars have occurred between nation-states, and by the long-standing human desire—expressed in religion, philosophy, and literature—for a peaceful and nonviolent world. The definition I stipulate recognizes the twin realities of human history—a record of conflict and the desire for peace. The definition recognizes that the present moment in human history is one that carries a tension of what was and what might be.

While international education examines informal as well as formal education, a large and important part of the subject deals with schooling, or organized education, and its philosophies, policies, organization, curricula, and modes of instruction. It is in this area—organized education—that the tensions between the nation-state and its school systems and a global society become even more evident. In reaching our stipulated definition of international education, a brief review of the history of schooling in relationship to the nation-state is instructive.

Nation-States and Their Schools

Today, there are almost 200 countries or nation-states in the world. A nation-state is a polity, a country that is independent and sovereign with its own government. It enacts its own laws and controls the territory within its borders. Among nation-states are such large ones as the U.S., Canada, the Russian Federation, the People's Republic of China, and India. Next in area of land mass are France, Spain, Germany, Nigeria, Mexico, and many other countries. There are the highly significant island-nations of the UK and Japan. There are many small nation-states such as Latvia, Estonia, Jamaica, Belize, Monaco, Belgium, and Luxembourg. We have named only a few of the nation-states that appear on the political map of the world. These nation-states share the following common characteristics: (1) they are sovereign with their own governments; (2) they are independent in that they are not officially controlled by another country; and (3) they have their own political, legal, military, and educational institutions. It is important to reiterate that they have their own school systems that socialize children as national citizens.

Each nation-state has its own vital interests that relate to preserving, maintaining, or extending its power. Primary goals of nation-states are to provide security for their independence, protect their interests, and protect their citizens' way of life and freedom of action. The interests and the policies of nation-states have come into conflict in the past and will continue to do so in the future. While wars have occurred throughout history when the interests of nation-states conflicted, the situation today is even more perilous for the future of the planet and human life on it. While war has always been a dangerous threat to humanity, the total destructiveness of nuclear and other weapons of mass destruction make war in the future especially perilous.

Any viable theory of international education needs to recognize the reality of the nation-states as primary actors on the world scene. To the degree that international education involves developing programs of change and designs for shaping the future, these plans need to emerge from existing realities. One of these important realities is that all the people of the world are citizens of independent and sovereign nation-states.

In Europe, North America, and South America, the modern nation-state developed in the eighteenth and nineteenth centuries. On these continents, governmental or state and public school systems were established in the nineteenth century. The emergence of government school systems is closely related to the nation-state system. Thus, there was convergence between the nation-state and its policy objectives and the school systems established to educate the citizens of the nation-state.

Today, each nation-state maintains a national, state, or government school structure. An important part of the formal curriculum, and the hidden curriculum as well, is citizenship education, also called political socialization, which educates the young person to identify with and become a loyal citizen of the nation. Schools, institutions either maintained by nation-states or private ones that function with their approval, use organized and formal education, as distinct from informal education (learning through experience, reading, and social contact) and nonformal education (noncompulsory education that takes place outside of the formally structured school, such as continuing education classes for adults), to construct a concept of cultural and political socialization that includes learning the roles and duties of citizenship. Nation-states use their school systems to mold individuals into citizens and productive workers.[27] In most countries, schools tend to reproduce the existing social and economic structure. However, there are philosophies of education, such as critical theory, that seek to use schooling for social and economic change.

Since most of the readers of this book will be students in professional education programs in the U.S., we comment on the U.S. as an important but nonetheless typical nation-state. In the U.S., authority and responsibility for education are constitutionally reserved for each of the fifty states. Nevertheless, a variety of forces—teacher education, certification requirements, textbooks, the media, and the mobility of the American population—have worked to shape a system of schools that exhibits certain unifying or homogeneous characteristics. Public schools in the U.S., regardless of the state in which they are located, emphasize the English language as the medium of instruction and require the study of U.S. history, literature, and government. This common curricular core builds a shared sense of national identity in which children learn that they are citizens of the U.S. and are part of the same political culture.

The philosophy of public education in the U.S. is especially influenced by the ideology of American democracy. Students are encouraged to be law-abiding, to respect freedom of speech and assembly, and to be involved in the political processes of representative government. A significant component of this ideological ethos emphasizes the economic values of private ownership of property and individual competition.

Schools throughout the world, especially those that are government or publicly controlled, use strategies of political socialization to construct identification with the nation-state. Schools in China educate Chinese children in that nation's history, language, and the Marxist political ideology. French schools perform a similar citizenship role. In other words, formal education, or schooling, is always contextual in that it occurs in a particular place and in a given historical period and reflects a particular economic, political, and social orientation. (The chapters in part II on comparative education emphasize how contexts shape education and schooling.)

Reflecting the reality of the nation-state, international education can be defined as *the study and examination of the educational relationships among and between nation-states*. Such a definition includes those aspects of education that are informal, or cultural, and those that are school-situated in terms of being part of organized education.

Transnational Problems of a Global Society

The reality of the nation-state discussed above, however, is only part of the definition of international education. When one views the peoples of the earth as inhabiting a common planet with common resources, limitations, and problems, it is clear that many of humankind's most pressing issues, including planetary and human survival, transcend the boundaries of particular nation-states. A brief survey of the pressing problems facing humankind reveals the transnational or international dimension of what needs to be included in international education.

First, the control and proliferation of nuclear, biological, and chemical weapons and their disarmament is a problem not only to be addressed by great world powers but also by smaller nations as well. Nuclear weapons arsenals have been proliferating, and several of the world's smaller nations now possess nuclear capability. Nuclear war carries the real possibility of annihilating life on this planet and turning it into a lifeless desert. The resolution of the problem of nuclear weapons lies beyond the power of any single nation-state to solve. It requires international security agreements between nation-states.

Second, ecological damage to the environment in a variety of forms such as the effects of acid rain, the deforestation of rain forests, the depletion of the earth's ozone layer, and global warming has reached acute proportions that threaten the earth as a biosphere. Again, the restoration of the health of the natural environment transcends national boundaries and involves everyone.

Third, the health of the peoples of the earth, while dependent on national health-care services, has a dimension that extends beyond these national services. Epidemic diseases do not respect national frontiers. For example, the AIDS epidemic is wreaking havoc around the world. The SARS epidemic and Mad Cow disease are not confined by national boundaries but are truly global problems that can be solved only by international measures.

Fourth, international terrorism is a wanton force that threatens the entire world. It takes the form of large-scale attacks on civilian populations such as those that occurred in Spain, Indonesia, Russia, and the U.S. Its perpetrators, not identified with particular nation-states, move across national boundaries to murder and maim civilian populations. The suppression of terrorism requires an international plan and cooperation among nation-states and their security agencies.

Emerging Trends

Today, powerful new economic configurations shape our lives. International or multinational corporations, owned and controlled by people who are citizens of a variety of nation-states, affect the economic destinies of workers and consumers around the world. The forces of supply and demand, production and consumption, are not limited to national markets. For example, many Americans work for and use products made by international or multinational corporations. The importation of goods to the United States and the outsourcing of jobs from the United States are major political issues that need to be part of the entire structure of international education.

Satellites and microchips have changed the world of communication, allowing for instantaneous global communication. News is broadcast throughout the world as rapidly as it occurs. Dramatic events, such as the war in Iraq and Israeli-Palestinian conflicts, are viewed by a worldwide audience. The media have a drama and quickness that schooling and textbooks lack, but the vivid images and the accompanying reports often are not conducive to reflection and critical evaluation. A worldview provided by international education can assist us to process the changes and events occurring around the globe in a reflective and critical way. Just as satellites make it possible for us to be exposed to world events in our own homes, computers have changed the way we disseminate, access, and store information for our own personal use. The World Wide Web and e-mail enable people to access information and share ideas instantaneously. E-mail, especially, makes it possible for individuals who live in all parts of the world to communicate and learn from each other rapidly and easily. The ease of information exchange can heighten our awareness of others and the forces that shape their lives.

Art, music, athletics, travel, and recreation are broad and powerful cultural forces that traditionally have transcended national boundaries and been a means of informal education. With improved communication and transportation systems, global cultural linkages between peoples are facilitated easily and quickly, making them an even more viable component of international education.

A Stipulated Definition

Now we can state our stipulated definition of international education. It is education that examines:

- informal, nonformal, and formal educational relationships among peoples of various nation-states;
- issues that are global in nature and that transcend national boundaries;
- emergent trends that are creating greater interdependency and interrelationships among people as members of a global society.

Such a definition avoids the egocentrism of the older, nationalist view of education. It also avoids the "wishful thinking" of those who take a view of international education that neglects the reality of the nation-state. It is both content and problem centered. While considering the impact of historical forces, it also anticipates the emergence of new economic, political, social, and educational configurations. It recognizes the reality that we are all both citizens of nation-states and participants in a global society. It further recognizes that there are and will be inevitable tensions between these two ideational foci of our lives, but also that there are many creative possibilities that grow out of this tension.

Conclusion

International education's subcategories of development education, peace education, and global education provide insights into the worldwide dimensions of our lives and expand our knowledge beyond the more limited realm of citizenship in a nation-state. While international education involves relationships between nation-states, it includes global issues that transcend national boundaries. It must include emergent trends, such as globalization, that make us increasingly economically interdependent as producers and consumers of goods. The stipulated definition of international education stated above takes into account the issues, problems, and trends that shape education today. However, we must be aware that the world is not static; needs change, power shifts, new ways replace old ones. As change occurs, the definition of international education will be recast with new stipulations so that it continually serves as an important guide for all educators.

DISCUSSION QUESTIONS

1. Identify and analyze the tensions that exist between education for the nation-state and education for a global society. Assess the possibilities for resolving these tensions.

2. In your opinion, do the governance and organization of American public schools contribute to or limit the development of an international perspective?

3. Assess the effectiveness of past and contemporary educators in defining and encouraging the internationalizing of education.
4. Define the following and indicate their uses in developing an international perspective: comparative education, foreign policy studies, regional studies, development education, peace education, and global education.
5. Describe the various approaches to peace education.
6. What are the major transnational issues that face a global society?
7. Assess the adequacy of the author's stipulated definition of international education.

FIELD AND RESEARCH TOPICS

1. Examine the curriculum of an elementary or secondary school. Identify and describe its international aspects or components.
2. Examine the teacher education program in your college or university. Identify and describe its international components.
3. Review two or three books on the history of American education or textbooks used in the foundations of education. In a review essay, assess how these books deal with international education.
4. Review several recent critiques or proposals for reforming American education. Determine the extent to which these proposals use a comparative rationale.
5. Examine your college or university catalogue. Determine if your institution offers regional or area study programs. Identify and analyze the philosophy, requirements, and courses that are part of the program.
6. Examine your college or university catalogue. Determine if your institution offers foreign study abroad programs.
7. If you have participated in a foreign study abroad program or have been involved in education in another country, reflect on your experiences in a paper.

SUGGESTIONS FOR FURTHER READING

Altbach, Philip G., and Gail P. Kelly. *Education and Colonialism*. New York: Longman, 1978.
Barbet, Elinor G., Philip G. Altbach, and Robert G. Myers. *Bridges to Knowledge: Foreign Students in Comparative Perspective*. Chicago: University of Chicago Press, 1984.
Boulding, Elise. *Building a Global Civic Culture: Education for an Interdependent World*. New York: Columbia University, Teachers College Press, 1988.
Carnoy, Martin. *Education and Cultural Imperialism*. New York: David McKay, 1974.
Coombs, Philip H. *The World Crisis in Education: The View from the Eighties*. New York: Oxford University Press, 1985.
DeBenedetti, Charles. *Peace Heroes in Twentieth-Century America*. Bloomington: Indiana University Press, 1988.

Erasmus, Desiderius. *The Education of the Christian Prince*, Lester K. Born, trans. New York: Columbia University Press, 1936.

Fraser, Stewart E., and William W. Brickman. *A History of International and Comparative Education: Nineteenth-Century Documents*. Glenview, IL: Scott Foresman, 1968.

Johnson, David, ed. *Education for Justice and Peace*. Maryknoll, NY: Orbis Books, 1985.

Kerblay, Basile. *Gorbachev's Russia*. New York: Pantheon Books, 1989.

Lebow, Richard Ned. *Between Peace and War: The Nature of International Crisis*. Baltimore: Johns Hopkins University Press, 1981.

Melvin, Kenneth. *Education in World Affairs: A Realistic Approach to International Education*. Lexington, MA: D. C. Heath, 1970.

Salomon, Gavriel, and Baruch Nevo, eds. *Peace Education: The Concept, Principles, and Practices Around the World*. Mahwah, NJ: Erlbaum, 2002.

Study Commission on Global Education. *The United States Prepares for the Future: Global Prospects in Education*. New York: Global Perspectives in Education, n.d.

Taylor, Harold. *The World as Teacher*. New York: Doubleday, 1970.

Thomas, David C., and Michael T. Klare, eds. *Peace and World Order Studies: A Curriculum Guide*. Boulder, CO: Westview Press, 1989.

NOTES

[1] Biographies of Erasmus are Albert Hyma, *The Youth of Erasmus* (New York: Russell and Russell, 1968); Johann Huizinga, *Erasmus of Rotterdam* (London: Phaidon Press, 1952); Christopher Hollis, *Erasmus* (Milwaukee, WI: Bruce Publishing, 1933). Also, see Hans J. Hillebrand, ed., *Erasmus and His Age* (New York: Harper and Row, 1970).

[2] Desiderius Erasmus, *The Education of the Christian Prince*, trans. Lester K. Born (New York: Columbia University Press, 1936). Also, see Frank E. Schact, "The Classical Humanist: Erasmus," in *The Educated Man*, eds. Paul Nash, Andreas Kazamias, and Henry Perkinson (New York: John Wiley, 1965), 140–162.

[3] William Woodward, *Vittorino da Feltre and Other Humanist Educators* (Cambridge, Eng.: Cambridge University Press, 1921).

[4] Biographies of Comenius are John E. Sadler, *J. A. Comenius and the Concept of Universal Education* (New York: Barnes and Noble, 1966) and Mathew Spinka, *John Amos Comenius, That Incomparable Moravian* (Chicago: University of Chicago Press, 1943).

[5] Eva Chybova Bock, "Seeing a Better World," *Christian History* 6(1) (1987): 7–8.

[6] Gerald L. Gutek, "Knowledge the Road to Peace," *Christian History* 6(1) (1987): 29–30.

[7] V. R. Taneja, *Educational Thought and Practice* (New Delhi: Delhi University Publishers, 1965), 154–155.

[8] Ibid., 159.

[9] K. G. Saiyidain, *The Humanist Tradition in Modern Indian Educational Thought* (Madison, WI: Dembar Educational Research Services, 1967), 37–57.

[10] Gerald L. Gutek, ed., *The Montessori Method: The Origins of an Educational Innovation: Including an Abridged and Annotated Edition of Maria Montessori's The Montessori Method* (Lanham, MD: Rowman & Littlefield Publishers, 2004), 1–42.

[11] Ibid, 100.

[12] Maria Montessori, *The Absorbent Mind* (New York: Henry Holt and Co., 1945), 75.

[13] Harold Taylor, *The World as Teacher* (New York: Doubleday, 1970), 3–5.

[14] Ibid., 8.

[15] Kenneth Melvin, *Education in World Affairs: A Realistic Approach to International Education* (Lexington, MA: D. C. Heath, 1970), 171. See pp. 1–15 and 145–176 for Melvin's rationale for international education.

[16] Elise Boulding, *Building a Global Civic Culture: Education for an Interdependent World* (New York: Columbia University, Teachers College Press, 1988), xviii.

[17] For the nineteenth-century origins and development of comparative education, see Stewart E. Fraser and William W. Brickman, *A History of International and Comparative Education: Nineteenth-Century Documents* (Glenview, IL: Scott Foresman, 1968).

[18] For representative works on development and development education, see Paul E. Sigmund, ed., *The Ideologies of the Developing Nations* (New York: Praeger, 1972); John W. Hanson and Cole S. Brembeck, *Education and the Development of Nations* (New York: Holt, Rinehart, and Winston, 1966); and Don Adams and Robert M. Bjork, *Education in Developing Areas* (New York: David McKay, 1969).

[19] For the changing directions in development and development education, see Philip H. Coombs, *The World Crisis in Education: The View from the Eighties* (New York: Oxford University Press, 1985).

[20] Curricular approaches to peace education are outlined in Daniel C. Thomas and Michael T. Klare, *Peace and World Order Studies: A Curriculum Guide* (Boulder, CO: Westview Press, 1989).

[21] Betty Reardon, "Pedagogical Approaches to Peace Studies," in Thomas and Klare, 20–22.

[22] Theodore Brameld, *Toward a Reconstructed Philosophy of Education* (New York: Holt, Rinehart, and Winston, 1956), 170–171. Also, see Theodore Brameld, *Education for the Emerging Age* (New York: Harper and Row, 1950).

[23] Reardon, 22–23.

[24] Ibid., 24–25.

[25] Elinor G. Barber, Philip G. Albach, and Robert G. Myers, eds., *Bridges to Knowledge: Foreign Students in Comparative Perspective* (Chicago: University of Chicago Press, 1984).

[26] Study Commission on Global Education, *The United States Prepares for Its Future: Global Perspectives in Education* (New York: Global Perspectives in Education, n.d.), 3.

[27] Richard Rubinson and Irene Browne, "Education and the Economy," in *Handbook of Economic Sociology*, ed. Neil J. Smelser and Richard Swedborg (Princeton: Princeton University Press, 1994), 592.

3

THE AMERICAN ROLE IN INTERNATIONAL EDUCATION
A HISTORICAL PERSPECTIVE

What events and trends influenced American thinking about international issues and education? To answer this question, first the chapter examines the historical perspectives that worked to isolate the U.S. from other countries, especially those in Europe. Leaders of the early republic, such as Washington and Jefferson, inaugurated a policy of isolation, which continued until the end of the nineteenth century. Further, the American worldview was shaped by the ideological belief that the U.S. was endowed with a providential mission and with a Manifest Destiny that gave U.S. policy a moral righteousness. The American common school ideology, grounded in localism and assimilation, also isolated American education from world affairs. Second, the chapter examines the emergence of the U.S. as a world power after the Spanish-American War and President Woodrow Wilson's efforts to make the U.S. an active international participant in the League of Nations after World War I. It assesses the legacy of Wilsonian idealism on international education and its critique by those claiming to be realists. Third, the chapter examines the development of American international attitudes as part of a larger worldview.

The Insularity of American Education

With some exceptions, American educators have tended to be preoccupied with domestic issues and with internal school affairs rather than with international issues. This type of insularity of American educators can be examined in the context of the history of American education in which school administrators and teachers saw themselves functioning within the immediate locality rather than within the wider world community. Furthermore, historians of American education generally have emphasized the

American public schools' differences from rather than their similarities to school systems in other countries. The accentuation of the uniqueness of American public education is derived from the long-standing perspective of the new frontier—brave and determined settlers carving a path to new territories and taming the land to make new lives form themselves—as a shaping influence on the American character. The common school was portrayed as a civilizing institution that brought enlightenment to the communities established along the westward-moving frontier. Added to this emphasis is the persistent theme of public elementary and secondary schooling as having local and state rather than national responsibilities.

Isolationism

In the early history of the U.S., isolationism emerged as the policy that guided American relations with other countries. Americans believed themselves to be a separate and exceptional people, set apart from Europe's traditions, prejudices, and aristocratic social-class distinctions. In his farewell address on September 17, 1796, George Washington advised the new republic's citizens to avoid "entangling alliances" with European nations.[1]

Washington's admonition that the U.S. should avoid foreign entanglements had a significant impact on American attitudes toward the world. Even Thomas Jefferson, one of the new republic's most cosmopolitan political leaders, warned against imitating Europe's aristocratic vices. Advising Americans to educate their children in their own country rather than in Europe, Jefferson warned that a European education induced a fondness for "luxury and dissipation, and contempt for the simplicity of his own country."[2]

The prolific textbook writer, compiler of dictionaries, and educator Noah Webster promoted American cultural nationalism through his efforts to standardize a new American form of the English language. President James Monroe, in 1823, warned the European nations in his Monroe Doctrine to keep out of the Western Hemisphere, which was an American sphere of interest.

What emerged from the isolationist origins of the U.S. was a belief that God had a special interest in the new republic and that the two great oceans—the Atlantic and Pacific—provided natural moats to keep foreign invaders out and to permit the American people to shape the North American continent according to their own democratic character and temperament. Isolationism generated two important attitudes that influenced American policies toward other countries: a sense of a special providential mission and Manifest Destiny.

Sense of Providential Mission

From the first days of independence onward, America's relationships with other countries have been shaped by the belief that it has a special, almost providential, mission to perform in the world. Although originating in the concept of isolationism, this sense of a special providential mission often ran at cross-purposes with the desire to stay uninvolved with foreign countries. Because American foreign policy was always on the side of righteousness, morality, and divine purposes, it saw itself as the republican and democratic beacon, the "city on the hill," whose light would inspire democracy throughout the world. At the same time that this sense of mission shaped policy and rhetoric, American diplomats pursued their nation's special political, economic, and military interests. Thus, when leaders and diplomats of other countries dealt with American policy makers, they encountered a self-proclaimed moral righteousness but also demands based on special interests. The history of international education, especially in its world affairs components, was not immune to this dichotomy. The U.S. was portrayed to students as a nation that was exceptional and unique—a moral exemplar of how other people should govern themselves. A key element in the American version of international education is that Americans have something special, something unique, to teach people of other countries.

Derived from the special sense of mission was the concept that the U.S. had a "Manifest Destiny" to occupy and to establish its unique political and educational institutions across the North American continent. Motives of political and military security and economic development and profit were easily subsumed under the cultural expansionism that accompanied the Manifest Destiny. The Native Americans could be forcibly resettled west of the Mississippi River, wars of annihilation could be waged against them, and then policies that veered from confinement on reservations to assimilation could be imposed upon them in the name of Manifest Destiny. An equally expansionist war against Mexico could be justified in the name of bringing a superior culture to the southwestern territories. While the causes and results of the wars against the Native Americans and Mexico fill the pages of history books, the most important concept for education was that the U.S. and its people had a destiny that gave them a special purpose among the earth's nations and peoples.

The American belief that the U.S. has a special moral mission to play in the world carries with it the following assumptions: (1) the goals of U.S. foreign policy, unlike those of other countries, are always noble and altruistic; (2) the U.S., since its goals are morally right, has the right and obligation to be the moral teacher of other countries; and (3) when other countries disagree with or seek to impede U.S. policy goals, the U.S. has the right to act unilaterally. An example from the twenty-first century illustrates this sense of moral righteousness. In the invasion to remove Saddam Hussein from power in Iraq and in the reconstruction of that country, U.S. policy makers tended to assume their ideological beliefs applied to the geopolitical realities of the Middle East and would be embraced by the citizens of Iraq. Policy makers found out that their assumptions were questionable.

Although Manifest Destiny was the rationale that justified American expansionism in the nineteenth century, it is more than an ideological artifact of history. In the twenty-first century, Manifest Destiny is still at work. It takes the guise of a cultural, economic, and sometimes educational attitude—that Americans have a mission to bring their ideas of politics (being democratic), economics (being productive and efficient), and education (being pragmatic and comprehensive) to the rest of the world. It is further assumed that other peoples need to have these ideas and if they reject them that they need to be reeducated to want them.

Interpretations of American Character

Of importance in developing this ideological belief in America's special mission and Manifest Destiny was the equally compelling belief that the American character differed from that of other peoples. Although contemporary historians have challenged Frederick Jackson Turner's thesis that the westward-moving frontier profoundly shaped American character, Turner's interpretation has influenced many textbook writers and commentators on the American experience.[3] According to Turner, the American character, with its propensity for change, innovation, and mobility, was formed by the ever-moving frontier. The frontier that originated on the Atlantic Coast with the thirteen original colonies moved westward through the Ohio Valley, the Mississippi Valley, and the plains states of the trans-Mississippi West, to the shores of the Pacific Ocean. A unique character was forged as successive waves of westward-moving migrants adapted to and transformed the land and created a new and different American culture.

Although the frontier account is overly generalized, it has shaped the historical myth that is at the base of the pervasive ideology about American uniqueness. For example, this generalized account neglects the Spanish and French frontiers, which were not westward moving but were historically present in the Southwest and the Mississippi Valley. It also neglects the way in which Native Americans perceived the westward movement of whites into their native lands as an invasion that threatened their lives and culture. Nevertheless, myths such as that of the frontier are the stuff from which the past is often perceived and upon which policies are based. Ideological legacies that remain lodged in the American psyche from the frontier experience include the belief that: (1) the frontier experience transformed Americans into a unique and exceptional people who have a special ability in surmounting the obstacles that impede their progress; (2) Americans are an especially inventive and innovative people who possess a commonsense, practical intelligence that is often lacking in other people; (3) the best, most efficient, and effective way of accomplishing goals is by individual initiative like that of the settlers in dealing with a new and often inhospitable environment; and (4) American's "know how" will shape a progressive and better future. With their emphasis on the uniqueness and special quality of the American character, the American people's attitudes and their leaders' policies developed a sense of meaning and destiny that often had little to do with people in other countries.

The Common School Legacy

While the frontier theme fascinated earlier generations of historians, the common school movement had an equally powerful hold on historians of education. Despite the interpretations of contemporary revisionist historians of education, the ideology of the common school movement has persisted and attained the status of a myth that has influenced popular and professional concepts about the public school and the policies that govern education in the U.S.

Basic Ideology

According to the long-standing interpretation of the common school movement, the creation of common, or public, schools was a result of something unique to the American character. It was a legacy of the Puritan ethic that saw the health, well-being, and prosperity of the political commonwealth linked to education. It expressed the Jeffersonian-Jacksonian ideal of equality of educational opportunity for all people. It also reflected the Whig ideology, expressed by Horace Mann, that public education could serve as an agency for national economic development and for political order and stability. As a unique institutional creation of the American people, the common school moved with the westward settlement to the territories that became part of the U.S. The common school legacy passed down from generations of American educational historians and policy makers held that: (1) the common school was a unique creation of the American people; (2) it originated in New England, particularly Massachusetts, where it was supported by public taxation and open to all children; (3) the local community, through elected school boards, knew the best way to set educational policies and determine educational practices; and (4) a public school education opened the way for individual advancement and mobility and social and economic progress for the entire nation.

Although some American educators borrowed ideas from European educators such as Lancaster, Pestalozzi, Froebel, Herbart, and Montessori, their importation of these ideas was for methodological purposes rather than to bring about structural changes in school organization. That is, they might be used to make classroom teaching more effective and efficient but were not to affect how schools were organized and governed. On institutional or structural matters of school organization and governance, American educators acted in deliberately chosen cultural isolation. As a result, little attention was paid to the theme that American schools should have a connection to schools in other countries. Thus, the international dimension of education was largely undeveloped. In those instances when American educators looked abroad, it was often in the belief that education in other countries would do well to imitate the American model of public schooling.

Americanization

Another highly important cause for the neglect or even denial of international education in the common school legacy came from the Americanization ideology and policy that public schools followed in the nineteenth and through much of the twentieth centuries. Americanization meant that the public schools should socialize non-English-speaking peoples, especially immigrants, into American society through a deliberate program of imposing the dominant cultural group's model, or definition, of what it meant to be an American. Although the desirability of Americanization, the melting pot, and cultural pluralist theories were debated, Americanization prevailed as a major component of public school ideology. Americanization formed educational policies and practices that, in turn, shaped the schools' formal curriculum and the educational milieu of the hidden curriculum.

The Americanization ideology had been used with the Mexican Americans.[4] As a result of the Treaty of Guadeloupe Hidalgo in 1848, which ended the Mexican War, Mexico had been forced to cede the vast territories that now comprise Arizona, California, Colorado, Nevada, New Mexico, and Utah to the U.S. This territory, along with Texas, was home to a large Mexican population.[5] Mexican American children attending public schools were taught in the English language and were required to use English while in school. The curriculum reinforced an Anglo-American culture that ignored the students' own Mexican heritage.

Although there were many proponents of Americanization, the most respected and articulate was the veteran administrator and educational historian Ellwood P. Cubberley. Cubberley postulated a version of Americanization that was imposed on the massive numbers of immigrants who came to the U.S. from eastern and southern Europe in the period from 1880 through 1920. According to Cubberley, American institutions and character were finished products, closed to reconstruction from the changing linguistic, ethnic, and religious pluralisms of the new immigrants. The new immigrants, according to Cubberley, had little to offer from their own cultures, traditions, and customs. Instead, their characters were to be remade along lines that were English in language and Protestant in values. The public school was deliberately used to remake the children of immigrants into what Cubberley and other members of the dominant culture regarded as true Americans. An important part of the process of Americanization was to separate immigrant children from their ethnic heritage.

In the public schools, Americanization encouraged a movement away from ethnicity and from seeing direct relationships between the ethnic culture and homeland and the new world. Immigrants, of course, had their own ways of offsetting the public schools' efforts at Americanization. They often created their own ethnic parochial schools such as those that became important parts of the Catholic school system, as well as social and fraternal organizations and foreign-language newspapers. However, the public school's Americanization ideology and the policies that stemmed from it worked to eradicate direct relationships between formal schooling and ethnicity and between the United States and other countries, including Mexico, the countries in southern and eastern Europe, China, and Japan. Opportunities for intercultural exchange and the expanding views that came from multicultur-alism were deliberately lost. Today, when the importance of multiculturalism is being realized, many opportunities for multicultural education that once existed have been lost for the offspring of older immigrants. The opportuni-ties to enjoy the riches of two cultures remain, however, for the new immi-grants. An important educational possibility is to create linkages between multicultural education and international education.

The U.S. on the World Scene

By the end of the nineteenth century, the U.S. was playing a more signifi-cant military and economic role in the world. Although it had achieved status as a world power, the U.S. continued to harbor concepts from its isolationist past, especially the belief in its special destiny. Its victory in the Spanish-American War of 1898 had made the U.S. a world power. Not long after the Spanish-American War, the United States became involved in World War I and reevaluated its isolationist policies.

Spanish-American War

The rationale for going to war against Spain combined several inconsis-tent motivations, but it expressed how U.S. foreign policy was often formu-lated, articulated, and implemented. In some respects, it is instructive to consider the war against Spain in 1898 with current issues, particularly the war in Iraq in 2003.

1. Spain's control of Cuba and the presence of the Spanish fleet were regarded as a security threat to the U.S.; the Bush administration's allega-tion that Saddam Hussein's regime in Iraq possessed weapons of mass destruction was presented as threat to national security.

2. The American press, especially the Hearst newspapers, gave extensive cov-erage to accounts of atrocities against the Cuban people. An often-stated justification for hostilities against Spain was the American altruistic desire to liberate the Cubans from the repressive yoke of Spanish colonialism and to establish a democratic republic in Cuba, modeled on the American example. In the war on Iraq, part of the U.S. rationale was that military action would liberate the Iraqi people from a ruthless dictator and that a democracy would be established in Iraq that would be a model for the Middle East.

3. The immediate cause of the war with Spain was an explosion that sunk the U.S. naval vessel, the *Maine*, with the loss of life of American sailors; in the case of the Iraq War, it was alleged that Hussein's regime had ties with ter-rorist organizations that had perpetrated the attacks on New York City and the Pentagon in Washington, D.C., on September 11, 2001.

4. There were real but officially unarticulated American economic interests in Latin America; in the case of Iraq, there was the matter of that country's vast oil resources.

The Spanish-American War of 1898 combined the messianic view of America's special mission and morality with the economic and military interests of power politics. As a consequence of the war, the U.S. joined the ranks of the European colonial powers with its own overseas empire that included Puerto Rico and the Philippines, which Spain was forced to cede.

American models of government, civil service, and schooling were transported to the Philippines and to Puerto Rico. The patterns of school administration, organization, and curriculum that were then current in the U.S. were established in these dependencies. Puerto Rico became a U.S. possession. Its people were made U.S. citizens in 1917 and it was granted Commonwealth status in 1952.[6] Believing that Puerto Rico needed American-style social and economic development, U.S. officials overhauled the old Spanish school system.[7] They made school attendance compulsory, established American-style public schools, and employed English-speaking teachers to promote the English language and Americanization.

World War I and Wilson's Legacy

Not long after the aftermath of the Spanish-American War, World War I erupted. Its aftermath established many of the contours of international education that remain today. After the armistice that ended World War I in 1918, the victorious allies met at Versailles, in an international conference, to negotiate the treaty for formally ending the war and creating the peace. The major Allied powers that were to shape the Versailles Treaty were the United Kingdom, France, Italy, and the U.S. President Woodrow Wilson, a former professor of political science and former president of Princeton University, represented the U.S. Wilson's vision of the peace rested on an association of nations, a League of Nations, that would establish a world order and eliminate recourse to war in the future.[8]

Wilson, an idealist in foreign policy, believed that once the central powers—Germany, Austria-Hungary, and Turkey—had been defeated, peace should be established on open covenants and international law rather than on secret agreements and the great power politics that satisfied the victors' special interests. Wilson's Fourteen Points, announced during the war, eloquently expressed his vision of the peace and a world governed by international law.[9]

At the Versailles conference, however, Wilson quickly discovered that his lofty goals were not shared and viewed as utopian ideas by Lloyd George, the English prime minister; Clemenceau, the French premier; and Orlando, the Italian premier. These European leaders wanted the defeated Germany to pay reparations for the war and to arrange a new set of mutual security agreements that would protect them from a resurgent Germany in the future. Although he had to negotiate and compromise with the European leaders,

Wilson secured the acceptance of the League of Nations, which he considered his major achievement and a guarantee of world peace in the future.

Based on the principles of one nation, one vote, the members of the league were to use parliamentary processes of discussion, debate, and majority rule to settle their disputes rather than recourse to war. A key element in the Wilsonian perspective was that foreign policy decisions were essentially moral ones. Using the idealism that came from the American concept that the U.S. was a providentially blessed and inspired nation, Wilson believed that moral principles, albeit a morality conceived in the Anglo-American experience, should and could be imposed internationally.

When Wilson returned, he found that the Senate, which had to ratify the Versailles Treaty, was deeply divided over U.S. membership in the League of Nations. The inherited legacy of isolationism resurfaced, and several senators who were quite progressive on domestic matters were adamantly opposed to U.S. membership in the league. Following George Washington's admonition of "entangling alliances with none," they vehemently objected to Wilson's view that the U.S. should play a leading role in world affairs. The result was that the Senate did not ratify the Versailles treaty, and the U.S. did not become a member of the League of Nations. The ensuing decade of the 1920s and early 1930s saw the U.S. return to a policy of isolationism that was not broken until the nation's entry into World War II after Japan's attack on the American naval base at Pearl Harbor.

Idealism and Realism: Two Views of International Relations

Wilsonianism in international affairs and international education has remained a strong legacy. Textbook writers told the story of President Wilson's failed dream of a League of Nations as a lost opportunity for world peace. Many advocates of international education were infused with the spirit of the Wilsonian approach to world affairs; for them, education could persuade people that an international order could be created on the basis of the rule of law and the application of moral principles. The conceptions of international educators have rested on the Wilsonian-inspired assumption that Anglo-American concepts of parliamentary processes and common law can be extended to other countries, including those with far different cultural and political traditions. Those who took a Wilsonian orientation were often designated idealists. That is, they held it possible to achieve an ideal, nonviolent world order. In such a world order, nations would be willing to submerge their interests to a greater international good that would be arrived at by majority rule or a kind of international consensus. The effort to create a Western-style democracy in Iraq by the Bush administration represents a current application of this part of the Wilsonian legacy.

Wilsonianism has also had its severe critics, especially among political scientists and diplomatic historians who consider themselves to be realists.

These critics allege that Wilsonian idealism ignores basic international realities. Among the principles of realism are:

- The world order is based on the interactions of nation-states, each with their own interests. Foreign policy, trade relationships, educational exchange, and other areas of international relations are between nations.
- Each nation seeks to protect its way of life and the vital interests that preserve its integrity and sovereignty.
- In order to do so, nations enter into agreements, form alliances, maintain armies, and seek to maintain the political, economic, and military power that preserves their vital interests.
- Power relationships between nations are dynamic and changing. These changes will result in conflicts of interest between nations.
- Nations will not abandon their particular vital interests to adjudication by world governments such as the League of Nations or the later United Nations.[10]

According to the realist critique, approaches to world affairs and international education that deny these realities are miseducative in that they ignore the very structure of relationships between nations.

The dichotomy between the idealist and realist orientation brings us to the tension that exists in international education between two divergent positions: the idealist who sees the international order in a state of an emergent world without war and violence and the realist who sees it as the interplay of the power relationships of nation states. My position is that international education needs to recognize and be based on two sets of realities that may appear to be in conflict: the historical reality of the nation-state and the equally present reality of an emerging global society and economy. The realist position is instructive for an orientation that stresses the nation-state and policies arising from national interests and security. The idealist position, such as that advocated by Wilson, points to the recognition of the planetary needs of people that extend beyond national borders.

Conclusion

Washington, Jefferson, Madison, and other leaders of the early American republic feared involvement in different nations' problems and urged a policy of isolationism. American westward expansion and a belief in the nation's Manifest Destiny instilled in Americans a belief in the moral righteousness of their nation's foreign policy that continues today. In addition, the common school movement with its emphasis on local control and assimilation of immigrants into a homogeneous citizenry insulated Americans from a broader world perspective.

Despite a predilection for isolationism, the U.S. became involved in world affairs in the Spanish-American War, World War I, World War II, and in the creation of and participation in the UN. The tension experienced by Americans regarding involvement in world affairs was dramatically illustrated by President Wilson's inability to persuade the Senate to agree to U.S. participation in the League of Nations. Since World War II, the U.S. has been actively participating in world affairs.

Knowledge of historical events and outcomes provides helpful insights that guide us in our current and future decisions. These insights should not cloud our understanding but instead crystallize it so that we can be effective participants in an ever-changing global environment.

DISCUSSION QUESTIONS

1. How have general interpretations about the origin of American public schooling contributed to an emphasis on domestic rather than national issues?

2. How did the founding fathers of the early American republic encourage a policy of isolationism?

3. Examine the impact of the frontier and Manifest Destiny in shaping American attitudes to other countries and peoples.

4. How did the public school ideology and policy of Americanization weaken international education?

5. Describe Wilsonian idealism and assess its impact on proponents of international education.

6. Describe the realist approach to foreign policy and world affairs.

7. Examine current American foreign policy. Do you find evidence of an idealist or realist orientation?

FIELD AND RESEARCH TOPICS

1. Review two or three books on the history of American education. In a review essay, analyze their accounts of the common school movement. Did the authors tend to interpret the common school as a uniquely American phenomenon?

2. Review two or three books on international education. In a review essay, determine if the authors have used an idealist or realist frame of reference?

3. Review several secondary school textbooks on American history. Analyze their treatment of international relations.

4. Interview several students in your college or university. Attempt to determine their perceptions of the U.S. role in world affairs. Do they appear to have a realist or idealist orientation?

5. Interview several veterans of the war from the Vietnam and Gulf wars. Attempt to determine their perceptions of the U.S. role in world affairs.

6. Interview several students who have participated in study programs in other countries. Attempt to determine their perceptions of the U.S. role in world affairs.

7. Interview several professors who have participated in international exchange programs. Attempt to determine their perceptions of the U.S. role in world affairs.

8. Read an autobiography, memoir, or biography of a U.S. secretary of state, for example Henry Kissinger or Madeline Albright. In a review essay, determine his or her orientation to world affairs.

SUGGESTIONS FOR FURTHER READING

Dockrill, Michael. *The Cold War 1945–1963.* Atlantic Highlands, NJ: Humanities Press International, 1988.

Carroll, John M., and George C. Herring. *Modern American Diplomacy.* Wilmington, DE: Scholarly Resources, 1986.

Gaddis, John L. *Russia, the Soviet Union, and the U.S.: An Interpretive History.* New York: Alfred A Knopf, 1978.

Garcia, Luis Garcia. "I Am the Other: Puerto Rico in the Eyes of North Americans, 1898," *The Journal of American History* 89 (June 2000).

Graebner, Norman A. *America As a World Power: A Realist Appraisal from Wilson to Reagan.* Wilmington, DE: Scholarly Resources, 1984.

Lynn-Jones, Sean M. *The Cold War and After: Prospects for Peace.* Cambridge, MA: MIT Press, 1991.

Monge, Jose Trias. *Puerto Rico: The Trails of the Oldest Colony in the World.* New Haven: Yale University Press, 1997.

Nordholt, Jan W. S. *Woodrow Wilson: A Life for World Peace.* Herbert H. Rowen, trans. Berkeley: University of California Press, 1991.

Nye, Joseph S., Jr. *The Paradox of American Power: Why the World's Only Superpower Can't Go It Alone.* New York: Oxford University Press, 2002.

Perlmutter, Amos. *Making the World Safe for Democracy: A Century of Wilsonianism & Its Totalitarian Challengers.* Chapel Hill, NC: University of North Carolina Press, 1997.

Wittner, Lawrence S. *Cold War America: From Hiroshima to Watergate.* New York: Praeger, 1974.

NOTES

[1] Washington's Farewell Address (September 17, 1796) in *Documents of American History,* ed. Henry Steele Commager (New York: Appleton-Century-Crofts, 1949), 174.

[2] Letter from Thomas Jefferson in Paris to J. Bannister, Jr., October 15, 1785, in Steward E. Fraser and William W. Brickman, *A History of International and Comparative Education: Nineteenth-Century Documents* (New York: Scott Foresman, 1968), 26–27.

[3] Richard Hofstadter, *The Progressive Historians: Turner, Beard, Parrington* (New York: Alfred A. Knopf, 1968), 47–164.

[4] Victoria-Marie MacDonald, "Hispanic, Latino, Chicano, or "Other"?: Deconstructing the Relationship between Historians and Hispanic-American Educational History," *History of Education Quarterly* 41 (Fall 2001): 368–369.

[5] Histories of Mexican Americans are Manuel G. Gonzales, *Mexicanos: A History of Mexicans in the U.S.* (Bloomington: Indiana University Press, 1999) and Richard Griswold del Castillo and Arnoldo De Leon, *North to Axtlan: A History of Mexican Americans in the U.S.* (New York: Twayne Publishers, 1996).

[6] For the history of Puerto Rico as U.S. possession, see Jose Trias Monge, *Puerto Rico: The Trails of the Oldest Colony in the World* (New Haven, CT: Yale University Press, 1997).

7 Gervasio Luis Garcia, "I Am the Other: Puerto Rico in the Eyes of North Americans, 1898," *The Journal of American History* 89 (June 2000): 41.

8 For the legacy of Wilsonianism, see Amos Perlmutter, *Making the World Safe for Democracy: A Century of Wilsonianism & Its Totalitarian Challengers* (Chapel Hill: University of North Carolina Press, 1997).

9 An interesting account of Wilson's attempt to interject moralism into foreign policy can be found in Robert M. Crunden, *Ministers of Reform: The Progressives' Achievement in American Civilization 1889–1920* (Urbana: University of Illinois Press, 1984), 225–273.

10 For a realist's analysis of America's role in world affairs, see Norman A. Graebner, *America as a World Power: A Realist Appraisal from Wilson to Reagan* (Wilmington, DE: Scholarly Resources, 1984).

4

NATIONAL AND INTERNATIONAL SECURITY AND EDUCATION

Philosophically, the approach used in our discussion of national and international security is that of moderate realism. It is realist in the assumption that international relations can be analyzed as interactions between nation-states, the major entities on the world scene. It further assumes that nation-states have their own structure and functions. The processes of international interaction involve how these nation-states relate to each other—sometimes in cooperation and other times in conflict. Cooperation and conflict between nation-states is largely determined by how the individual nation-state seeks to maintain its security—its vital national interests. This essential realist position is modified, however, by the recognition that in the contemporary world there are other important players on the international scene, including international organizations such as the United Nations, regional security pacts such as NATO, nongovernment agencies (NGOs), and multinational business corporations. There are also global terrorist organizations, such as al Qaeda, whose activities take place without being limited by nation-state borders. Despite these modifications or changes in the international situation, the guiding assumption in the chapter is that the nation-state remains the basic entity in world affairs.

This chapter introduces national security systems by establishing a contemporary context that considers such recent events as the wars in Vietnam, the Persian Gulf, and Iraq, and the war on terror. It then identifies and examines such key concepts in international relations as nation-states, power potentialities, commitments, and vital interests. This is followed by a discussion of diplomacy as a means of resolving tensions without violence and the impact of weapons of mass destruction on the nation-state system. The chapter concludes by returning to the theme of tension between the nation-state system and the issues of a global society. Recent changes in world affairs such as those in Central and Eastern Europe and the former Soviet Union, terrorist organizations, conflict in the Middle East, and the rise of new economic regions such as the Pacific Rim and the European

Union are discussed to illustrate the need for developing new ways to conceptualize international reality.

Recent Events and National Security

Since the demise of the Soviet Union in 1989, the U.S. is the world's sole superpower. This distinction makes the U.S., with its preponderant military and economic power, the paramount global actor. This distinction carries with it immense opportunities and definite perils, especially in a time of international terrorism, in which anti-American conspiratorial groups rather than definably hostile nations pose a threat to national security. The preeminence of the U.S. does not mean that there are not other centers of power on the international scene. Russia, France, the United Kingdom, and Germany remain major nation-states. Japan is a significant economic power. China, with the world's largest population, possesses great economic as well as military potential. While the nation-state was the most significant actor on the world scene throughout the modern period of history, from the eighteenth through the twentieth century, new constellations of economic and military power have appeared in the twenty-first century. Among them is the European Union (EU), composed of the majority of Western European countries.

Among other contemporary trends is the rise of ethnonationalist groups that seek either greater autonomy within or freedom from the larger nation-states that have jurisdiction over them. (For an extended discussion of such groups, see chapter 7.) The strife and violence in Chechnya in Russia, in the Basque regions of Spain, and in the western region of the Sudan in Africa are symptomatic of the efforts of multiethnic nation-states to suppress separatist movements and of the efforts of ethnic groups to free themselves from that control. The rise of ethnonationalist tendencies has produced instability in several areas of the world. Still another player on the world scene are terrorist organizations such as al Qaeda. The terrorist group aims to destabilize the traditional nation-state though wanton acts of violence.

Today, the world is divided into many nations, each seeking to promote its own national interests. Some nations are united in regional security pacts such as NATO. The spread of nuclear, chemical, and biological weapons makes international security delicate and fragile. To explore these national security issues, we now examine some events that involved the U.S. in recent history.

The Vietnam War

The recent history of the U.S. reveals the degree to which it has been involved in alliances, pacts, and actions designed to promote its security and vital interests. For many Americans, especially the men and women in the armed services, what has been called "peacekeeping" is actual combat and has brought home the realities of the U.S. role in international affairs with respect to the defense of national interests. America's longest war, the Vietnam conflict, vividly demonstrated the difficulties that a democracy has in defining and defending its interests. During that conflict, President Lyndon Johnson and his advisers based their policy in Southeast Asia on the domino theory. Johnson, who inherited the American role in Vietnam from his predecessors, Presidents Eisenhower and Kennedy, believed that the North Vietnamese forces were Communist aggressors who intended to subdue South Vietnam in order to gain control of Southeast Asia. To prevent the spread of Communism, these aggressors needed to be stopped.

The leaders who formulated the domino theory and American military policy in Vietnam received their education about world affairs during World War II. One lesson that they learned from World War II was that appeasement of a dictator such as Hitler merely whets the dictator's appetite and leads to further demands and aggression. From a historical perspective, the lessons of World War II were misapplied in Southeast Asia.

At the same time that President Johnson and his diplomatic and military advisers argued that the defense of South Vietnam was important to the national interests of the U.S., others disagreed and opposed military involvement in the region. The social, political, and educational ferment generated by the war in Vietnam in the 1960s was so powerful that it continues to shape America's outlook on the world. Those who opposed American military involvement in Vietnam did so for a variety of reasons. Some opponents believed that U.S. vital interests were not threatened by the Viet Cong and North Vietnamese. Others interpreted the conflict in Vietnam as a civil war rather than an invasion by Communist forces. Still other opponents of U.S. policy in Vietnam rejected using U.S. military forces to settle international disputes. Still others did not want to serve in the armed forces. Some based their opposition on their belief that it was more important to fight racism and poverty at home than the Viet Cong in Vietnam. Among the opponents were young people, especially some college students, who demonstrated against the war and conducted "teach-ins" and "sit-ins." The intensity of emotions and the degree of commitment on both sides of the Vietnam issue illustrated the difficulty that a democratic nation has in formulating foreign policy and in defining and sustaining its own vital national interests.

Still another important dimension of the Vietnam War experience was the power of informal educational agencies and agents in conveying messages to the public. While World War II and the Korean War had been covered by the news media, especially the press, the coverage of the Vietnam War by television dramatically brought the conduct of the war, the casualties, and the terrible violence into American homes each night on television news programs. The media also covered the protest demonstrations against the war.

The power of the television media in presenting images and shaping meanings, particularly about the nation's role in world affairs, brought with it important implications for formal education, especially classroom instruction. Television coverage was vivid, dramatic, and quick, but rarely systematic or reflective. Although the school curriculum—history, government, social studies, and geography—provided the foundations of a civic and international education, it was not focused on the pressing issues facing the nation during the war in Vietnam. Moreover, while the perspective provided by formal education was indispensable to reflective and critical thinking about America's foreign policy interests, the mode of delivery in these areas paled in comparison with the vividness of television programming.

The Gulf War of 1991

In August 1990 the Iraqi army, under the orders of Saddam Hussein, occupied the small neighboring country of Kuwait. Both Iraq and Kuwait, located in the volatile Middle East, are important petroleum producers and exporters. President George H. Bush, who condemned the Iraqi occupation, dispatched a large U.S. military force to protect Saudi Arabia against a possible Iraqi attack. Bush and Secretary of State James Baker also commenced a concerted diplomatic effort to persuade the UN Security Council to condemn the Iraqi occupation of Kuwait. Bush succeeded in building a large coalition of nations, backed by a UN Security Council resolution, which organized to disengage Iraq from its occupation of Kuwait.

In the U.S. Congress, a dramatic debate occurred in the Senate and the House of Representatives over the president's constitutional authority to commit U.S. forces to the proposed action against Iraq. The debate is instructive for national security issues and for international education in that it relates to defining the national interest and to how to best defend it. Although most commentators would agree that nation-states have the right to defend their national interests in general terms, it is not always easy to define what the national interests are in specific cases. Definition of the national interest is especially difficult in democracies such as the U.S. and the UK where different political parties and groups hold diverse opinions on what constitutes the national interest. In addition, it is difficult to relate the national interest of a particular nation-state to those of international bodies, such as members of the UN.

Supporters of President Bush's call for the use of force against Iraq argued that it was in the U.S. national interest. Among their reasons were that (1) Iraq's dictator, Saddam Hussein, in Hitler-like fashion, was violating international peace and security by his invasion and occupation of Kuwait; (2) Saddam Hussein's seizure of Kuwait, unless reversed, would give him strategic power over the Persian Gulf area and its important oil-producing nations, Saudi Arabia and the United Arab Emirates; and (3) Iraq possessed and was adding to an arsenal of biological and chemical weapons, and was also developing a nuclear capability that threatened the peace and security of the Middle East.

Congressional opponents of using military force against Iraq argued that military action was premature and that economic sanctions imposed by the

UN should be given more time to have an effect on Iraq. They also argued that Iraq's occupation of Kuwait, while violating the United Nations charter, did not threaten vital U.S. interests. After debate, Congress voted to support President Bush's request for authorization to use force in liberating Kuwait.

On January 16, 1991, one day after the UN deadline for the evacuation of Kuwait by Iraq had expired, the U.S. and other coalition nations attacked Iraqi military units and forced them from Kuwait. The coalition forces had limited objectives and did not attempt a major invasion of Iraq. Saddam Hussein, the Iraqi dictator, remained in control of Iraq and commenced to attack the Kurds and Shiite Muslims in his own country. Part of the agreement to end hostilities required Iraq to allow UN weapons inspectors access to the country to make sure that Iraq was carrying out its agreement to eliminate weapons that could be used to attack other countries. UN inspectors conducted inspections in Iraq until 1998 when they were suspended because of Iraq's obstructive noncompliance in the process. Inspections by UN inspectors resumed in November 2002 when Iraq agreed to permit inspections once again. The U.S. and the UK were pressing the UN Security Council to take stronger action against the Iraqi regime, which was alleged to possess weapons of mass destruction. The inspection process was suspended in March 2003 when the U.S., the UK, and a coalition of other countries began military action against Saddam Hussein's regime.

9/11 and the War on Terror

On September 11, 2001, terrorist operatives of al Qaeda hijacked four commercial American passenger planes. The flight crews of the planes were overwhelmed and killed by the attackers who used two of the planes to crash into the twin towers of the World Trade Center in New York City and the other to attack the Pentagon in Washington, D.C. The crew and passengers of the fourth plane struggled with the al Qaeda operatives, forcing the plane to crash in rural Pennsylvania, diverting it from the attack on Washington.

The unexpected wanton attack on American soil that claimed over 2,500 lives at first stunned Americans and then unified them against their unseen enemy. President George W. Bush, in the first year of his term of office, rallied the country in what was proclaimed as the "war on terror." The war was carried to Afghanistan, a country ruled by a fundamentalist Islamic regime, the Taliban, which was harboring Osama bin Laden and was used as a training ground for al Qaeda terrorists. The Taliban regime was overthrown by internal forces, aided by the U.S. military. However, bin Laden eluded arrest.

The war on terror dramatically brought changes to American life and society. A Department of Homeland Security was established to monitor terrorist threats, coordinate antiterrorist actions, and keep the American people informed about the level of threats to their security. Airport security was heightened. Suspected terrorists were placed on surveillance and arrested by the Justice Department. A debate began between those who wanted even greater security measures taken and those who feared that some of the anti-terrorist methods were eroding civil liberties. An important and continuing issue is the degree and extent to which antiterrorist and security measures can and should be debated.

For national discourse in general, and education in particular, there is the continuing issue in the American experience over the need to unite to oppose terrorism and the right to dissent and the appropriate ways to either support or question the national policy. American history provides a series of times when international threats resulted in the limitation of civil liberties. In 1920–21, there was a "red scare," a strong domestic reaction against the Bolshevik Revolution in Russia, during which the U.S. attorney general ordered the deportation of anarchists, radicals, and other dissenters. During World War II, thousands of Japanese Americans were interned for fear that they might commit sabotage against the U.S. Again, in the 1950s, in a time of fear of Soviet espionage and Communist subversion, the U.S. experienced what is known as McCarthyism, named after Senator Joseph McCarthy, who conducted a number of security investigations against citizens alleged to be subversive. For freedom of thought and expression, key elements in a democratic education, there is the need—often implemented with great difficulty—to educate citizens to protect the nation's security while maintaining civil liberties.

The perpetrators of the 9/11 terrorist attack were Arabs, mainly Saudi Arabians, who were members of the Islamic religion. There was the possibility that the U.S. would have a strong anti-Arab reaction because of the attack. In analyzing this possibility, the internment of Japanese Americans by the U.S. government during World War II is highly instructive. The U.S. government's reaction against Japanese Americans was based on unfounded fears that they might commit acts of sabotage. No such attacks occurred. The internment of Japanese Americans was also based on racial discrimination. Many years later, the U.S. government formally apologized and compensated those who had been interned and denied their civil liberties. As a case study in national security and civil liberties, the lessons learned from the internment of Japanese Americans can be applied to protect the civil liberties of Arab Americans: It is unconstitutional and inhumane to withhold civil liberties from innocent people who have no involvement with acts of war committed by others who share their ethnic, racial, or religious orientation. So that Americans might be better informed, educational institutions, especially those of higher education, developed more courses and programs on Arab culture and on Islam; knowledge and understanding function to eliminate fear and discrimination.

Still, another important implication of the war on terror relates to the security of educational institutions and schools; it is highly difficult and emotionally trying to prepare children to take precautionary action in the event of an attack. School administrators in cities and areas placed on high security alert are advised to take security precautions, but the guidelines for what plan of action to implement tend to be underdeveloped. It is possible that security measures might be derived from guidelines to protect students during hurricanes, tornadoes, and other natural disasters. During the cold war, especially during the 1950s and 1960s, school districts developed elaborate plans and exercises to protect students during an atomic attack. In retrospect, the atomic bomb drills and hiding under the desk activities of the cold war era appear now to be over reactive and highly ineffective. Nevertheless, practical security issues relating to schools and students are serious matters during a time of terrorism, and plans and strategies need to be developed.

Another important implication of terrorism is to examine and address the effects of the war on terror in the lives of children. The images of planes toppling and destroying the World Trade Center towers were carried throughout the world by television. The images created a sense of fear, anger, and depression throughout the U.S. population. How children react to and interpret this and other events into their psyches and understanding of the world are crucial educational concerns. Educational strategies need to be developed that teach students about the presence and possibility of violence and terrorism in the world but that alleviate the sense of anxiety that comes from something that is both incomprehensible and real. In other words, in an age of international terrorism when national security is a paramount concern, building a sense of personal security becomes a key dimension in education.

The Iraq War of 2003

During 2002, President George W. Bush and members of his administration focused their attention on the regime of the Iraqi dictator Saddam Hussein, who was accused of possessing weapons of mass destruction in violation of the agreement that had ended the first Gulf War. After the first Gulf war, Hussein's regime agreed to the return of UN weapons inspectors who began their search for the hidden weapons. In the meantime, the Bush administration, growing impatient with the search process, continued to warn that Hussein's regime posed a threat to world security and sought to prove Hussein's complicity in international terrorism. Some Bush administration spokespersons put forth the doctrine of a "preemptive strike" in which the U.S. would be justified in attacking a nation planning an attack against the U.S. Secretary of State Colin Powell went before the UN Security Council to make the American case against Saddam Hussein but failed to win council action.

As the debate over what course of action to take against Hussein's regime continued, former U.S. allies such as France and Germany opposed a military invasion of Iraq. Bush was supported by Prime Minister Tony Blair of the United Kingdom as well as by the governments of Italy, Spain, and Portugal. Domestically, there was a debate in Congress over the proposed action against Saddam Hussein, with the result that President Bush was authorized to take necessary force against the Iraqi regime. In March 2003, the U.S., the UK, and other members of what President George W. Bush called a "coalition of the willing" invaded Iraq to defeat Hussein's armies. After the defeat of Saddam Hussein's Baathist regime, the U.S. undertook to establish a Western-style democracy in Iraq, hoping to unite various ethnic and religious groups into a federal system. Whether or not the transitional Iraqi government, established under coalition auspices, can succeed in moving to a viable democratic nation-state is an open question. As of 2004, the Iraqi government and security forces and the occupying coalition forces faced serious unrest and sporadic attacks from insurgents. In January 2005, democratic forces in Iraq were encouraged when an election for a national assembly to draft a new constitution for Iraq was successfully carried out despite insurgent threats.

While the events leading up to and subsequent to the war in Iraq are well known, the following major foreign policy issues have emerged and are significant considerations for international education. Is the U.S. reverting to a doctrine of unilateral action on the world scene? If so, does unilateral action reflect the concepts of Manifest Destiny in world affairs and an attitude of American moral righteousness or is it a manifestation of the U.S. military superiority as the world's sole superpower? Does the division over Iraqi policy between the U.S. and former allies such as France and Germany signal a major change in world affairs? Will leading European nations take a separate course of action from the U.S. on other issues? Is the concept of a "preemptive strike" a justifiable concept in foreign relations? Is it a defensive act or an act of aggression? As the Iraqi situation persists, there has been more debate over and questioning of the Bush administration's policy. During a time of international terrorism are there limits on foreign policy debate or is such debate a characteristic right of those living in a democratic nation?

Nation-States and National Security

The following sections examine key concepts that relate to the national security and vital interests of nation-states. The discussion provides a structural framework for considering the components of a national security system.

Nation-States

As argued in this book, the basic units in the international system consist primarily of independent and sovereign states or nations, referred to as nation-states.[1] These political-historical-geographical entities are the basic but not the sole entities in foreign affairs. Diplomacy, the conduct of international relations, involves the art of negotiating between nation-states, whose interests may coincide or be in conflict. Each nation-state is sovereign to the degree that it possesses the necessary power, or material and human resources, to determine and implement its domestic and foreign policies. Should the policies of nations conflict, the nation-state with the strongest aggregate of power can limit the self-determination of the weaker nation.

Decisions of war and peace, in the last analysis, are made by the leaders of nation-states, some of whom are democratically elected and others are not.

In the twentieth and twenty-first centuries, nation-states, still the primary players on the international scene, tend to pursue their interests in association with other nations that share or have similar interests. For example, the Triple Alliance of Germany, Austria-Hungary, and Italy and the Triple Entente of the UK, France, and Russia were formed before World War I. During the cold war, NATO was formed as an alliance of North Atlantic nations that aimed to contain the expansion of the Soviet Union. In the Gulf War of 1991, nations joined a coalition to dispel the Iraqi army from Kuwait. In the Iraq war of 2003, the U.S. sought to build a coalition of nations to quash Saddam Hussein's regime and bring democracy to Iraq.

The decision of the Bush administration to invade Iraq reveals the difficulties in defining the national interest and determining what policies, strategies, and actions are needed to defend the national interest. A review of the debates concerning the Bush decision to invade Iraq are highly instructive about how a democratic nation such as the U.S. defines and safeguards the national interest.

Working with International Agencies

In 2002, UN inspectors were once again in Iraq conducting on-site inspections to determine if the regime of Saddam Hussein was hiding weapons of mass destruction (WMD). The U.S. claimed that the Iraqi regime, which had obstructed weapons inspections in the past, was following a similar pattern of deceit. In turn, Saddam Hussein's government denied the existence of WMD. Although unable to find the alleged weapons caches, the UN inspectors claimed they needed more time to complete the inspection process. At this juncture, heated debates took place in the UN Security Council. The U.S. and the UK argued that there was a clear threat that Iraq possessed and would use weapons of mass destruction against its neighbors and posed a threat to world peace and security. France and Germany argued that the inspectors should be given more time to complete the inspection process. At this point the following policy options were available to the U.S.: (1) the U.S. could take unilateral action against Iraq; (2) the U.S. could try to create a coalition similar to that in the first Gulf War to oppose Iraq; (3) the U.S. could agree to let the UN inspectors continue their search for weapons of mass destruction. The U.S. took the second option and attempted to create a coalition of nations. However, the coalition was not as broad and as large as in the first Gulf War. Opponents of the U.S. policy accused the Bush administration of unilateralism—pursuing a policy without the agreement and consent of other nations.

In terms of international education, the concept of the nation-state needs to be examined to understand how one's own country acts in international relations. When the concept of the nation-state is abstracted and extended to other nation-states, one can understand the extent of a nation-state's sovereignty and the limitations of national power in relationship to other nation-states. In formal education, the concept of the nation-state can be developed historically. It is also developed through courses in political science, government, geography, and related social science and social studies subjects.

Some international educators disagree with emphasizing the nation-state as the primary entity in international relationships. They often argue that the nation-state system is either obsolete or is becoming obsolete and will be replaced in the future by a world government such as the UN or some other world body. Others contend that economic forces such as globalization will drive world events and that nation-states as primary actors will be displaced by these new forces. Others believe that world public opinion or the actions of key individuals or private voluntary organizations can mute the power of the nation-state in conducting foreign affairs. For these educators, it is more important to envision a world governed by peaceful, nonviolent means of conflict resolution than to accentuate nation-states, which have caused so many wars in human history.

As previously mentioned, the impact of nation-states in world affairs is being modified by the appearance of new global players such as international organizations, multinational corporations, and unfortunately global terrorist organizations. It has also been pointed out that pressing world issues such as pollution of the biosphere, epidemic diseases such as AIDS, global terrorism, and the threat of nuclear war transcend the boundaries of nation-states. Although these contemporary modifications of the world international system have occurred, the nation-state remains the basic unit of international relations and international education needs to recognize that reality. Easing world tensions, solving world problems, and even the threat of war can be realistically addressed and hopefully alleviated by multilateral agreements between nation-states. In the UN itself, membership is based on the reality of nation-states in which each country has one vote in the General Assembly. However, the inequality of power among nations is also recognized by the veto power that certain nations—the U.S., France, the UK, Russia, and China—can exercise in the Security Council.

Changing Potentialities of Nation-States

Although nation-states are structurally definable, like the populations that inhabit them, they are socially, politically, and economically dynamic and changing, as are the relationships among nations. Clear evidence of the dynamism of nation-states is provided by the momentous changes that occurred in Central and Eastern Europe and in the former Soviet Union since 1988. The Soviet-backed and -controlled governments of Poland, Czechoslovakia, and Hungary have been replaced by non-Communist governments. Germany, divided in 1945 into East Germany and West Germany, has been reunited as one country. The former monolithic Soviet Union has dissolved and been replaced by a number of independent nation-states such as Russia, Ukraine, Uzbekistan, and Georgia. At the very moment when a changing international situation promised relaxation from the decades of tensions between the U.S. and the Soviet Union during the cold war, tensions were exacerbated in the Middle East, especially in the continuing struggle between Israel and the Palestinians and by the actions of international terrorist organizations. The world of nation-states is one of constant change, of development and decline, of the resolution of conflicts and the emergence of new conflicts.

International relationships are dominated by the shifting power potentialities of nation-states. Power refers to the total economic, military, population, scientific, technological, and natural resources that a nation can draw upon to maintain its sovereignty, protect its vital interests, achieve its policies, and prevent other nations from imposing their policies on it. A nation that pursues policies unrelated to its interests or pursues goals that exceed its power potentiality acts both unrealistically and imprudently in that these goals may weaken the nation's power potential, its economic wealth, and its security.

History, as a subject in the school curriculum, clearly demonstrates the rise and decline of the power potentialities of nations. In the sixteenth century, Spain was a world power of first magnitude. By pursuing ends that exceeded its means or that were not in its vital interests, Spain dissipated its power. Throughout the nineteenth century, France and Great Britain were great powers. Through the attrition of World Wars I and II and the rise of even greater world powers such as the U.S. and the Soviet Union, French and British power to influence world affairs diminished. Although the rise and fall of nations are presented in many history courses and books, the concepts of interactive change and interrelationships are not as clearly developed. The concept that the power potentialities of nations and regions are dynamic and shifting is a necessary element in understanding world affairs and needs to be developed in international education.

Vital Interests

The national interest, also referred to as vital interests, of a particular nation in world affairs refers to whatever a nation-state needs to continue as a nation, to maintain its particular way of life and cultural heritage, and to exercise domestic self-determination. The national or vital interests are what a nation undertakes to defend for its own survival. The goal of a nation's foreign policy—with its economic, diplomatic, security, and cultural dimensions—is to protect and preserve its vital interests. The total aggregate of material and human resources, the nation's power potentiality, is the means to this end. Since vital interests are intimately related to national self-preservation and security, it is crucial that the nation's leaders and people determine what is genuinely in the national interest. Using power for unattainable or unnecessary goals ultimately undermines vital interests and the nation itself.

In a democratic society with representative institutions, such as Congress in the U.S. and the Parliament in the UK, the identification of the national interest and particular vital interests is subject to intense political debate. Before the Japanese attack on Pearl Harbor in 1941, Americans debated the issue of aid to Great Britain, which was under severe attack by Nazi Germany. The America First Committee took an isolationist stand and argued that assistance to Great Britain would involve the U.S. in a foreign war that was not necessary to its survival. Equally determined individuals united in the Committee to Defend the Allies, contending that the fall of Great Britain to Nazi Germany would change international power relationships to the degree that Hitler would dominate the world. War came for the U.S. with the Japanese attack on Pearl Harbor, and the debate ended.

A dramatic instance of defending vital interests occurred in 1962, when the Soviet Union positioned offensive missiles in Cuba. President Kennedy regarded the Soviet action as a threat to the vital interests and security of the U.S. The U.S. undertook a naval embargo to halt the delivery of military equipment and other supplies to Castro's Cuba. The U.S. and the Soviet Union came perilously close to war. Conflict was averted only when the Soviet leader Khrushchev agreed to remove the missile systems from Cuba.

In the late 1960s, the American presence in Vietnam was hotly debated. While President Johnson and many Americans believed the defense of South Vietnam was necessary to American security interests in Southeast Asia, many other Americans disagreed. Johnson pursued his foreign and military policy in Vietnam against a backdrop of antiwar protests and demonstrations. Most recently, in 2002, the debate over what constituted the vital interests of the U.S. shifted to the Middle East, to the Persian Gulf. Here, the question was whether Iraq threatened America's vital interests. After intense debate, a majority in Congress agreed that it did. However, large numbers of Americans disagreed and organized demonstrations protesting the U.S. military action against Iraq.

What is clear is that nations have vital interests and seek to defend them to the best of their abilities. Power, or the resources available, constitutes the means of defending the national interest. International education, in the past, however, has generally not addressed the issue of vital interests, national security, and power potentialities. This is probably because many writers in this field prefer a world governed by the peaceful settlement of disputes between nations through international organizations and tribunals. However, even international organizations, such as the UN, depend on the resources that nations make available to them for the implementation of their decisions.

The angst that has motivated many who write, teach, and work in international education is the fear of a nuclear holocaust, which has the capacity to extinguish life on earth. This is a painful reality of modern life and international affairs because not only do the great world powers have nuclear capacities, so do many smaller nations. In the interplay of nations, it is sometimes assumed that the major actors will calculate, reflect, and use power prudently. This formula for estimating the interplay of interests assumes that world leaders will exercise diplomatic rationality. However, the twentieth century has taught us that some individuals, such as Adolf Hitler, will abandon rationality to achieve their goals or will define these goals in grandiose, utopian visions in which the end justified the means.

Clearly, then, a realistic approach to international education will include a discussion of national interests and power. It also needs to point out that great tension exists between national interests and a global society. It is important for teachers and students to realize, however, that a global society involves the people of the earth within the contexts of their respective nations. Often, this is more easily done in the abstract because there are complex issues and there is disagreement on what specifically constitutes the nation's vital interests. It is crucial, however, that international education include examinations of nations and their interests and how these relate to dynamic and changing world relationships.

Commitments

To preserve their vital interests, nations enter into commitments with each other. Commitments in international affairs generally take the form of treaties or pacts in which nations agree to economic cooperation, mutual security arrangements, nonaggression, economic and military assistance, cultural and educational exchange, environmental and species protection, and disarmament, for example. These agreements express a commitment between the signatory nations. Although there are humanitarian reasons for these agreements as well as economic and security reasons, they affect the preservation of the vital interests of the signatory nations.

If a nation undertakes a commitment necessary to the national interest, it must possess the necessary power, the resources, to fulfill the commitment and thus contribute to its national self-preservation and interests. A realistic commitment is one that is necessary to the preservation of the guarantor nation, but it needs sufficient resources to honor claims made upon it by the agreement. Walter Lippman once wrote that a foreign policy is created only when a nation balances its commitments and its power:

> Without the controlling principle that the nation must maintain its objectives and its power in equilibrium, its purposes within its means and its means equal to its purposes, its commitments related to its resources and its resources adequate to its commitments, it is impossible to think at all about foreign policy.[2]

Peace and War

Diplomacy between nations involves interactions and negotiations designed to maintain the various nations' national security and interests. Nations that enjoy dominant positions in the world—economically and militarily—will pursue diplomatic relations, allies, and commitments that preserve their position. They will tend to see maintenance of the status quo as the best means of promoting world peace and security. Indeed, they would like to see world events frozen in time at the moment of their dominance. For example, the reunification of Germany in 1990 raised some fears, based on memories of World War II, in Europe and particularly in Poland. German reunification means that the European nation-state system will not be frozen in time, but will see an economically powerful Germany exercising increasing influence in Europe, particularly in the EU.

In 1989 and 1990, the Soviet satellite nations in Central and Eastern Europe regained full political sovereignty. Poland, the Czech Republic, Slovakia, Hungary, Romania, and Bulgaria have gone from being dependent on the Soviet Union to acting as independent and sovereign nation-states, defining and pursuing their own national interests. These changes in Europe alone attest to the dynamic relationships that exist internationally. Such changes inevitably cause readjustment in trade and security relationships. For example, NATO is redefining its purpose as a mutual security organization as it accepts more members from Central and Eastern Europe.

Just as dominant nations seek to minimize threats to their preeminent positions, other nations pursue readjustment in international relations. Those that seek readjustment are rising powers, economically and militarily. They may seek new and expanded spheres of influence and economic markets and may also be courted by lesser-developed nations that need their economic assistance and sometimes their military protection. For these nations, the status quo needs to be altered to reflect new realities. An example of a rising great power is the People's Republic of China (PRC) with the world's largest population. As the PRC grows in economic strength, it is likely to seek readjustments in the relationships between nations in Asia.

The conduct of diplomacy in all of its forms is a way in which nations act in their interests through peaceful means and by negotiations. Diplomacy is a way of bringing about readjustments without war and military conflict. However, nations that conduct successful diplomacy need to accurately self-appraise their own national interests and make the commitments needed to maintain them. They also need to accurately appraise the interests and resources of other nations. In democracies, where diplomacy often reflects popular attitudes and domestic politics, successful diplomacy requires internationally literate citizens who have a general knowledge of the world and its peoples. Cultural arrogance, stereotyping of other nations and peoples, and ignorance about world affairs put great constraints on a nation's ability to conduct a diplomacy that maintains peace and avoids war. International education so conceived becomes a national diplomatic tool.

Nuclear War

World War II ended in 1945 when the U.S. dropped atomic bombs on the Japanese cities of Nagasaki and Hiroshima with great loss of life. President Truman, who made the decision to use these nuclear weapons to end the war, announced that the world had entered a new stage in its history—a nuclear era. Like any technological instrument, nuclear power can be used either negatively or positively, for either good or evil. When used as an instrument of war, however, nuclear energy has the potential of extinguishing life on this planet. Since the onset of the nuclear age, human beings have lived with the threat of nuclear war and global devastation.

While the nation-state system of international interaction developed in the early nineteenth century long before the nuclear era, it remains in place. The existence of nuclear weapons and their delivery by guided missiles has introduced a new factor in the traditional diplomatic and military interplay between nations. Nuclear weaponry little resembles the kind of military operations described in the standard history textbook. The application of science and technology to modern warfare has created the possibility of total war in that the theater of operations can be extended to virtually the whole earth by any nation equipped with nuclear weapons systems. Nuclear weaponry becomes an instrument of universal destruction capable of annihilating both aggressor and defending nations. If the objective of a conflict is preservation of the national interest, the use of nuclear weapons can destroy that which a nation seeks to preserve.[3]

Limited Use of Military Power

Since the end of World War II, the U.S. has been directly involved in four significant military actions where the conflict was deliberately limited to a specific geographical area—Korea, Vietnam, Persian Gulf, and Iraq. The U.S. military has also been a participant in peacekeeping efforts, primarily keeping contentious ethnic groups from engaging in genocide, in Bosnia and Kosovo. Engaging in limited military actions, especially peacekeeping missions, represents a new role for the armed forces.

For individuals who conceive of military conflict with a past-centered orientation, especially those who think about war in terms of the unconditional surrenders in World War II, limited war is frustrating because it implies a limited peace. According to the ideology of total war, the world will be remade according to the victor's view of what it should be. When put into sloganeered formulas, the idea of war based on unconditional surrender was expressed as making the world safe for democracy after World War I, which was the goal of the League of Nations, and making the world safe for freedom after World War II, through the framework of the United Nations and its Security Council.

Neither dream of world order was realized, however. Instead, there emerged a world that was far different and often even more frustrating than the world that existed before either war. Clearly, a world free of tensions and frustrations has never existed. In a dynamic international reality, change produces tension. The degree of the tension and the urgency of resolving it depend upon how close the point of potential conflict is to the particular vital interests of the nation.

In reviewing the American experience with limited war, we should note that the conduct of such conflicts has produced severe domestic strains. For example, the Korean conflict was conducted by the Truman administration as a war with limited objectives that were to be confined deliberately to a limited operational sphere. General Douglas MacArthur, the U.S. general commanding the United Nation's forces, claimed that a war without a total victory over the enemy was futile, even if the combat had to be extended to China. The differences in MacArthur's and Truman's objectives resulted in the dramatic dismissal of MacArthur by President Truman and illustrate the American dilemma over limited war.

By the mid-1960s, the U.S. found itself embroiled in another limited war, the conflict in Vietnam. Here the U.S. was bogged down in the jungle, fighting against an adversary who used guerrilla tactics in which conventional battle lines and strategies were meaningless. As the war dragged on, the debate over American presence in Vietnam and its conduct was waged throughout the U.S. Lyndon Johnson, who wanted to be recorded in history as the builder of the Great Society, instead is linked to America's tragic involvement in the war in Vietnam.

In the 1991 Persian Gulf War, the goals once again were limited because the danger of spreading the war threatened not only the nations of the Middle East but the entire world. The rapidity of the coalition nations' victory over Iraq stilled the recurrence of domestic debates on the war.

In 2003 the Iraqi army was quickly defeated by coalition forces, but the reconstruction of Iraq by the coalition nations proved to be exceedingly difficult and costly. The role of U.S. military forces in the occupation and rebuilding of Iraq is controversial. The Bush administration's initially stated cause for the war—finding and destroying Saddam Hussein's weapons of mass destruction—proved to be unfounded. Then, the administration revised the cause of the war to be the establishment of a democratic government and society in Iraq. Opponents of the U.S. invasion and occupation of Iraq countered that the military intervention was not related to American vital interests, had been waged on false pretenses, and had placed the U.S. in the role of being an unwelcome occupying power.

While the ideal state of affairs is that nations avoid conflict through diplomacy, the persistent danger of war is a reality. Because of the threat of the total destructiveness that a nuclear war will bring to humanity, future conflicts are likely to be limited and conditional. While it can be a diplomatic instrument for peace, realistic international education needs to educate Americans about the nature of limited military action and about the changing role of armed forces. It needs to alert them to Erasmus's observation that war, once begun, tends to spread like a conflagration. As a conflict consumes more and more countries and larger areas of the world, the immediate causes of the conflict are often lost. Such conflicts then become framed in ideological rhetoric that bears little resemblance to international reality.

Conclusion

In presenting the preceding structure on foreign relations in the nation-state system, the objective was to describe key concepts about how nations conduct their relationships. It was not intended to imply that the conduct of international relations is based on some indelible natural law that construes the behavior of nation-states to be like that of natural organisms. It rather assumes that the international behavior of nation-states is the result of patterns derived from historic forces. The purpose of the discussion is to suggest that a realistic view of international education needs to begin with current conditions. Any efforts to reconstruct the international order will be based on the actions and interactions of the principal actors on the world scene—the nation-states. Indeed, a major theme in this book is that international education needs to reflect realistically the tension experienced by people because of their particular nation-state's vital interests and their membership in a global society.[4]

DISCUSSION QUESTIONS

1. Examine the impact of the "war on terror" on your life.
2. Why is the definition of vital interests often so controversial in democratic countries?
3. Identify and define the key elements in a nation's security system.
4. What are the vital interests of the U.S.?
5. Is the nation-state system still viable in the modern world?
6. What are the current major foreign policy objectives of the U.S.? By whom and how are these objectives determined?
7. How is the international system changing and dynamic?
8. What problems does the U.S. face in maintaining its national interests?
9. How does international education relate to the nation-state system?

FIELD AND RESEARCH TOPICS

1. Invite a political science professor from your college or university whose specialty is national security to speak to your class on the topic.
2. Do a survey of students in your college on how they define the national interest.
3. Invite a professor from your college's or university's department of military science to discuss the military's role in national security.
4. Invite a representative from an organization whose major concern is world peace and disarmament to speak to your class on that subject.
5. Organize a clippings file of newspaper and magazine articles that deal with national security and disarmament.
6. Debate the following: "Resolved, the nation-state system is an obsolete mechanism for providing national security in the international order."
7. Invite veterans who have served in the armed forces to speak to your class about their impressions of the military in providing national security.

8. Invite activists, pro or con, who were involved in demonstrations for or against U.S. military action in Iraq to share their views with your class.

SUGGESTIONS FOR FURTHER READING

Bogart, Sandra C., and Allan E. Goodman, eds. *Making Peace: The U.S. and Conflict Resolution.* Boulder, CO: Westview Press, 1992.

Bremer, Stuart A., and Barry B. Hughes. *Disarmament and Development: A Design for the Future?* Englewood Cliffs, NJ: Prentice-Hall, 1990.

Clarke, Richard, et al. *Defeating the Jihadists: A Blue Print for Action.* New York: Century Foundation Task Force, 2004.

Florini, Ann. *The Coming Democracy: New Rules For Running the World.* Washington, DC: Brookings Institution Press, 2005.

Haley, P. Edward, and Jack Merritt. *Nuclear Strategy, Arms Control, and the Future.* Boulder, CO: Westview Press, 1988.

Hollins, Harry B., Averill L. Powers, and Mark Sommer. *The Conquest of War.* Boulder, CO: Westview Press, 1989.

Kurtz, Lester R. *The Nuclear Cage: A Sociology of the Arms Race.* Englewood Cliffs, NJ: Prentice-Hall, 1988.

Lamb, Christopher J. *How to Think about Arms Control, Disarmament, and Defense.* Englewood Cliffs, NJ: Prentice-Hall, 1988.

Levering, Ralph B. *The Cold War, 1945–1972.* Arlington Heights, IL: Harlan Davidson, 1982.

Mead, Walter R. *Special Providence: American Foreign Policy and How It Changed the World.* New York: Alfred A. Knopf, 2001.

Miller, Lynn H. *Global Order: Values and Power in International Politics.* Boulder, CO: Westview Press, 1990.

National Commission on Terrorist Attacks on the U.S. *9/11 Commission Report.* Washington, DC: U.S. Government Printing Office, 2004.

North, Robert C. *War, Peace, Survival: Global Politics and Conceptual Synthesis.* Boulder, CO: Westview Press, 1990.

Pillar, Paul R. *Terrorism and U.S. Foreign Policy.* Washington, DC: Brookings Institution, 2001.

Thomas, Daniel C., and Michael T. Klare, eds. *Peace and World Order Studies: A Curriculum Guide.* Boulder, CO: Westview Press, 1989.

NOTES

[1] The discussion of the nation-state system and national security interests is based on Gerald L. Gutek, "Education for a Realistic Conception of Foreign Affairs," *Educational Forum* 29 (May 1965): 493–501. Also, see Gutek, "Examining Idealistic Attitudes in Foreign Affairs Instruction," *International Education* 2 (Spring 1973): 75–83.

[2] Walter Lippman, *U.S. Foreign Policy: Shield of the Republic* (Boston: Little, Brown, 1943), 7.

[3] Useful discussions of nuclear weapons, the arms race, and disarmament are Lester R. Kurtz, *The Nuclear Cage: A Sociology of the Arms Race* (Englewood Cliffs, NJ: Prentice-Hall, 1988) and Christopher J. Lamb, *How to Think about Arms Control, Disarmament, and Defense* (Englewood Cliffs, NJ: Prentice-Hall, 1988).

[4] Recommended discussions of the nation-state system and global order are Robert C. North, *War, Peace, Survival: Global Politics and Conceptual Synthesis* (Boulder, CO: Westview Press, 1990) and Lynn H. Miller, *Global Order: Values and Power in International Politics* (Boulder, CO: Westview Press, 1990).

5

CHANGING PERSPECTIVES ON INTERNATIONAL DEVELOPMENT AND DEVELOPMENT EDUCATION

The concepts of development and development education are important in international education. Throughout the history of cross-cultural and cross-national exchange, the interaction between technologically developed and less-technologically developed peoples, cultures, nations, and civilizations has been a recurrent theme. *Developed, developing, and undeveloped* are not judgmental terms; rather these terms were coined originally by economists, sociologists, and educators in Western, industrial, and technological societies to designate or explain the degree of development of a nation's infrastructure, especially its economy. Currently, the term *less technologically developed* is preferred in the professional literature. Although the earlier designations of "underdeveloped" or "developing" were usually applied to the economies of countries, they sometimes were used as general descriptors without the necessary economic quantification. In the use of terminology, it is important to consider how the particular country defines itself.[1]

This chapter begins with a historical overview of development. It moves to a discussion of the top-down model of development and development education, followed by a discussion of modernization and education that includes some dimensional comparisons of education in developing and developed societies. The chapter then presents the perspectives of some respected critics of top-down development and explores the bottom-up approach to development.

A Historical Perspective on Development and Development Education

Long before the concepts of development and development education gained currency, cultural interaction and the borrowing of ideas, processes, and institutions occurred throughout history. In the ancient world, there was the interchange of ideas—often in religion and art—between such great civilizations as the Indian, the Chinese, the Egyptian, the Mesopotamian, and the Greek. Cultural elements from one civilization were borrowed by another, reconfigured to fit the borrower's culture, and then incorporated into the cultural fabric of the recipient group.

Sometimes cultural borrowing resulted from the peaceful interaction of peoples through trade and economic exchange, and other times it came from war and conquest. In the history of education, Rome's conquest of the Greek city-states eventually led to the introduction of Greek philosophy, rhetoric, arts, and sciences into Roman culture and then into what became Western civilization. The crusades of the twelfth and thirteenth centuries stimulated cultural interchange between Europeans and Arabs. Arabic mathematics, medicine, and architecture were carried into Western culture. In such borrowing, there was often a sense that one group was taking a more complex cultural form and grafting it onto a simpler one. The process of cultural engrafting involved both informal education and deliberate instruction.

Westernization

The Renaissance marked the onset of the period of exploration and colonization by Western nations that bordered on oceans and developed a high degree of political consolidation. Portugal, Spain, England, and France subsidized voyages of exploration such as that of Christopher Columbus. The explorations that began in the fifteenth century and continued until the end of the nineteenth century led to conquest and colonization of North America, South America, Africa, and parts of Asia by the European powers. While chapter 1 described colonization, imperialism, and decolonization and their educational consequences, this chapter considers how European colonization shaped the contemporary concept of development.

Throughout South America, Africa, and to some extent Asia, a similar pattern of European imperialism occurred. In their first encounters with Europeans, native peoples met soldiers, missionaries, and traders. The well-documented history of the Spanish conquest of Central and South America recounts the conquistadores' search for gold and silver, the often forced conversion of Indians—the Mayas, Incas, Aztecs, and others—to Catholicism, the exploitation of subject peoples, and the attempts to eradicate their cultures and replace them with an Iberian-Hispanic version of culture (see chapter 14 on Mexico).

The story of the British in India presents an example of interaction between Europeans and indigenous people. India was the location of one of the world's enduring civilizations. Two of the world's great religions, Hinduism and Buddhism, originated in India. While some British officials appreciated Indian culture, the majority did not. The British people who settled in India lived apart from Indian society in self-preferred isolation. The British also decided that the means of education and language of instruction in India would be English (see chapter 17 on India).

Despite the achievements of Asians, Africans, and Native Americans in literature, art, and architecture, Europeans regarded indigenous peoples as culturally inferior. In the colonizers' minds, for indigenous peoples to be developed culturally they had to be Westernized. Thus, the Europeans imposed their culture, language, religion, and educational practices on the indigenous peoples. Mission schools conducted by various Christian churches or specialized secondary schools that trained natives to be of service to the European colonialists were established in the colonies (see chapters 17 and 18). Primary schools and basic literacy programs, based on the Western model, served most of the indigenous population but were separate from those of the Europeans. Indigenous educational programs instituted by the Europeans often did not adequately serve the vast majority of the native population.

The process of colonization was repeated in all the empires of the European nations, and from this can be generalized that the ruling colonial class determined that the most developed cultural model was the European one.

Industrialization

The next major impact on the history of development came with the Industrial Revolution of the early nineteenth century. The Industrial Revolution, which integrated science, machinery, and energy to produce goods abundantly and inexpensively, occurred initially in Western Europe and North America. Industrialization generated new economic, social, and political configurations, including: (1) large-scale, machine-driven assembly lines that replaced handicraft production; (2) industrial factories as centers of mass production; (3) industrial workers who were concentrated in large, urban population centers; (4) the large-scale marketing of goods, which stimulated economic exchange and consumption; and (5) owners and managers of industries joining the ranks of the middle classes. The concept of development became increasingly driven by economic factors, such as the demand for raw materials and the marketing and consumption of manufactured products.

The definition of what constituted a developed society was framed by industrial owners and managers in Western Europe and North America. A "developed" society was industrialized and urban while an "underdeveloped" one was agricultural and rural. Accordingly, the role of development education was to introduce scientific and technical knowledge and processes that were compatible with and facilitated industrial efficiency. The industrialized nations of Western Europe and North America were called first-world nations. Conversely, because the nations of Africa, Asia, and South America had the majority of their populations engaged in agricultural production in rural settings, they were identified as third-world countries. The then-existing Communist bloc nations of the Soviet Union and Eastern and Central Europe were identified as second-world countries. The demise of the Communist regimes in Central and Eastern Europe and the movement of their new governments to market economies signaled the end of the second-world designation. From this historical context our discussion of development can now move to the more contemporary views of development and development education, beginning with the top-down model.

The Top-Down Model of Development and Development Education

The top-down model originated from the success of such large-scale foreign aid projects as the Marshall Plan. Recall that the Marshall Plan provided aid from the U.S. to the war-torn nations of Western Europe for reconstructing their economic infrastructures. According to the premises of the Marshall Plan, a stable economy would result in a stable, parliamentary political structure. The implementation of the Marshall Plan was intergovernmental and international. It resulted from negotiations between the U.S. government and the governments of the nations receiving the assistance. The nature, amount, and implementation of the aid were negotiated by government officials and their expert scientific and technological consultants. It is generally agreed that the Marshall Plan had positive consequences in restoring the economic health of the recipient Western European nations. As of 1953, the U.S. had channeled more than $12 billion into the reconstruction of the European industrial and agricultural infrastructure. At the same time, Western Europe's gross national product had increased by 32 percent.[2] It should be remembered, however, that prior to World War II these nations had been industrialized and had large educational systems and well-trained managers and workforces. Here, the aid program was directed at restoring war-torn industrial economies to health, rather than creating the basic economic infrastructures from scratch.

In 1950, Congress passed the Act for International Development, and throughout the 1950s and 1960s the U.S. government, through the Agency for International Development (AID), encouraged and supported a wide variety of foreign assistance programs to nations that were identified as having underdeveloped economies. Among AID's premises were:

- Underdeveloped economies were primarily backward, inefficient, labor intensive, and overly dependent on subsistence agriculture, with effort concentrated at the local village market level.

- Political and social instability was a consequence of underdeveloped economies characterized by massive unemployment or underemployment.

- Formal educational systems were underdeveloped, with poorly attended primary schools and a few selective academic secondary schools and universities.

- A large part of the population, often the majority, was illiterate and unprepared for either popular civic participation or economic modernization.

- Health-care services were few and underdeveloped, and epidemic diseases were present because of unsanitary water supplies and waste disposal and the lack of medical services.

- Transportation networks were primitive, unreliable, and underdeveloped and failed to link the sections of the country in an efficient way.
- Conditions of political, economic, and educational underdevelopment resulted in extremes of social and political behavior that ranged from non-participatory passivity to revolutionary insurgency.

The proponents of development believed that economically underdeveloped nations' inefficient traditional institutions and behavioral patterns inhibited efficient productivity.[3] Conditions of underdevelopment were so large and pervasive, only concentrated and centralized efforts could change them. From this constellation of conditions, the model of top-down development emerged.

Conceptually, in top-down development, success is economically based on increases in the gross national product (GNP). To successfully develop, a nation-state needs to concentrate on promoting the production of goods and their consumption both domestically and for export to other countries. This requires new technologies to increase productivity and a good transportation system so that products can be moved quickly and efficiently to markets in various locations. For the effective implementation of new technology, educational and training programs in science, technology, and engineering need to be established or expanded.

From 1960 through 1980 many of the less technologically developed countries (LTDCs) opted to implement the top-down development model and established national planning departments to devise development strategies and promote their implementation. Following is a simplified version of how the top-down model worked: First, representatives of the developed nations' government met with their counterparts in the recipient nation to identify the recipient nation's development needs and devise a general strategy to fulfill them in a master plan. These governmental agents were generally experts in education, health care, transportation, agriculture, and so forth. Next, lower-level agents and agencies from both countries became involved to implement the plan. For example, if the project were designed to improve agricultural education, agricultural experts and educators from the developed country would be sent to work with educators in the recipient country to establish an agricultural college, improve instruction in existing schools, or introduce new agricultural techniques, such as the use of hybrid seeds, fertilizers, irrigation, and perhaps even mechanization. It was believed that the visiting representatives would act as change agents in the recipient country; that is, the improvement programs they devised would catch on and radiate throughout the country. The same strategy was also used in health-care education, secondary education, vocational education, and so on.

While it was anticipated that the majority of the population of the recipient country would benefit from the top-down development process, the results were often mixed and did not always turn out as expected. One example occurred with the "Green Revolution" that took place in countries such as India and the Philippines in the 1960s. The Green Revolution development plan included: replacing native grains with hybrid rice and wheat to produce more abundant yields; developing irrigation systems to lessen dependence on seasonal monsoon rains; encouraging the use of chemical fertilizers to enrich overused soils; and improving transportation systems so that grains and other foodstuffs could be moved from region to region, rather than be restricted to local markets.

The Green Revolution's focus on introducing technical innovations often neglected the cultural context within which the innovation was to operate—local villages where daily life was governed by long-standing customs and traditions. These village societies had always supported themselves by growing their own food. An increase in total agricultural production did not necessarily benefit the majority of the people because it upset the hitherto balanced subsistence economy. For example, a few large landowners or corporations owned by native elites or foreign investors purchased small plots of land and consolidated them to grow a single cash crop dependent on the world market. This shift from a subsistence to a market economy had a negative effect on local farmers who were dispossessed of their smaller plots. Without subsistence farming to support their livelihood, small farmers relocated to large cities where there was large-scale unemployment. They ended up losing on both rural and urban fronts. From this simplified example, we can understand why the process of centralized innovation, with little regard for the cultural context and local needs, often caused cultural and psychological dysfunction. Many who were meant to benefit from development viewed it as intrusive and threatening. In some instances, top-down development was not only resented, it was also resisted.

The proponents of top-down development viewed the modernization of traditional societies as a process that required several stages and components. A valuable component of this process was development education. In other words, American educators working in foreign recipient nations were change agents bringing about the modernization of backward societies. While local people might be dislocated, progress would result, and its fruits would eventually reach and benefit the entire population.

Modernization and Education

To focus on our discussion of modernization, we shall rely on the clear and succinct definition established by C. E. Black in his book *The Dynamics of Modernization: A Study in Comparative History*.[4] Black defines modernization as "the process by which historically evolved institutions are adapted to the rapidly changing functions that reflect the unprecedented increase in man's knowledge, permitting control over environment, that accompanied the scientific revolution." According to Black's definition, modernization occurs when institutions such as the family, the community, the church, the state, and the school are functionally altered and redefined or reconstructed because of social and technological change. Accompanied by efficiency, modernization is seen as making life less dependent on the vicissitudes of nature by giving individuals greater control over the environment. During the 1960s and 1970s, many scholars conceived of modernization as a global process that functioned independently of contextual variables such as ethnicity, culture, and history.

Seeing modernization as a universal phenomenon, modernizing theorists subscribed to the sociological theory of structural-functionalism, which linked the structures of society to the functions that they performed. Based on structural-functionalism, political, social, economic, and educational structures were seen as interrelated and an alteration in one of these structures would produce changes in the other structures.[5] Based on their performance, structures could be compared. Nation-states accordingly could be ranked on how well their structures functioned on a scale from the least modern to the most modern.

Michael Latham, who discusses modernization theory as an ideology, identifies the following key assumptions at the theory's core: (1) "traditional" societies and "modern" societies are sharply different; (2) economic, social, and political changes are interrelated and interdependent; (3) the movement from traditional to modern is linear—moving in a unilateral direction; and (4) the modernization of traditional societies can be accelerated by their contact with developed ones.[6] These assumptions can also be applied to education in that educational changes are related to and dependent on socioeconomic and political change.

As an educational agency, the school can be used either to perpetuate the status quo of traditional knowledge and values or to implement social reconstruction. That is, the school's curriculum and milieu can reflect what already exists or act as an agency of social change. Educational modernizers see the school as an agency that induces change and themselves as building nations out of developing societies. For these educational nation builders, the process of development involves an inevitable and necessary tension between the poles of modernity and tradition. While the tension brings with it cultural dislocation and discomfort (as in our Green Revolution example above), the intended goal is to move custom-bound traditional societies toward modernity.

To illustrate the process of change, we shall view four basic human dimensions through the framework of hypothetical traditional and modern societies.[7] The dimensions are: (1) intellectual, (2) political, (3) economic, and (4) social. Our discussion first illustrates the particular dimension in a traditional society; next, it contrasts it with a modern society; and then it highlights the way in which education acts to alter the traditional society and move it toward modernity.

The Intellectual Dimension

In a traditional society, the interactions between human beings and the environment are governed by customs, mores, and folkways that evolved over time. Such a society reveres the past as the source of wisdom and the guide that governs behavior. The decisions that govern life are often made by the elders. Intellectual education in such traditional societies tends to take two forms: informal and formal. At the local, often village, level where family and kinship groups are most important, there is a natural reliance on direct kinds of informal education, a kind of on-the-job vocational training in which the young learn household, agricultural, or handicraft occupations directly from their parents or other village elders. In LTDCs, the emphasis on informal education is often accompanied by sporadic attendance at primary schools. Irregularity in attendance and early school leaving or dropping out results in high rates of illiteracy (see chapters 17 and 18).

The elite groups in traditional societies, a small percentage of the population, tend to have a highly traditional education that is academic and formal. Formal schooling is primarily literary and based on religious and philosophical classics. In India, traditional education was based on the Vedic classics. In China, it was based on the works of Confucius. Such classical study often continues to be stressed. If the LTDC was once a colony of a European nation, it also incorporates the literary education associated with the upper classes in that country into its own secondary and higher education patterns. This kind of education stresses literary, philosophical, and historical knowledge rather than technological, managerial, and engineering knowledge and skills.[8]

The impact of traditional intellectual education is antagonistic to development designed to bring about modernization. The masses of population, located in rural villages or sprawling cities, are undereducated and, consequently, often illiterate. The impact of custom and tradition creates a suspicion of change and innovation. Although the very different education experienced by the elite creates a wide gulf between the upper and lower classes, the upper classes also tend to be oriented to the status quo, which protects their privileged position.

In contrast, a modern society views knowledge more pragmatically. Knowledge is regarded as something obtained by discovery and research rather than from the wisdom of the past found in religious or philosophical texts, or in the sanctity of custom. Modern knowledge is tentative, dynamic, and evolving rather than certain or static. One looks not to the past but to the future by manipulating and controlling the environment. Rather than feared, change is welcomed as an opportunity for a better life. A better life, however, is generally defined in quantitative, material, economic terms rather than qualitatively. The modern intellectual outlook sees the system as creating more things, more goods, and more commodities. In contrast, the traditional outlook sees the quantity of goods as inevitably and invariably limited.

In a modern society, the educational objective, both in terms of institutions and processes, is a command of processes, particularly problem-solving methods, rather than familiarity with religious and philosophical literature. In terms of schooling, modernizing educators have debated which educational level should receive priority. Some development educators see primary education as a necessary base for modernization; others stress secondary and higher education. However, in the top-down development strategy, secondary and higher education generally receive the emphasis and allocation of resources from experts in ministries of education. Secondary education is highly selective and competitive. Science, agriculture, and engineering are introduced as studies in technical schools. (This represents the course to modernization taken by government and Communist party planners in China, as described in chapter 16).

With top-down development, educational results in LTDCs have been uneven. Although more primary schools have been established, they are often underfinanced because they are not a priority among government planners. Among the elites, the holding power of the older literary curriculum is so strong that young people still seek it over newer, applied educational programs. There is often an aversion to technical studies based on the idea that educated people do not work with their hands, which causes them to avoid education that could lead to managerial and technical positions.

The Political Dimension

In the modern world, educational systems—primary schools, secondary schools, and colleges and universities—generally are part of the total institutional structure of the nation-state. Top-down, modernizing development educators have often called their educational task "nation building." Nation building implies that a nation may not exist in the Western sense and needs to be created. (This aspect of nation building is illustrated by the case of Nigeria, in chapter 18.) By comparing and contrasting the political orientations of traditional and modern societies, it is possible to examine education as nation building.

In a traditional society, local authority figures have the greatest contact and exert the greatest power over villages and rural populations. Political identification and loyalty are based on kinship, clan, tribe, or caste membership, rather than on the nation. In the case of India, for example, significant political divisions are based on language identifications; those who speak Hindi are often in contention with those who speak Dravidian-rooted languages. In addition, there are sectarian conflicts between Hindus, Muslims, Sikhs, and others, and caste identification further complicates political loyalty. In sub-Saharan African nations such as Nigeria, tribal and language loyalties are often primary bases of identification and sources of political divisiveness. For those who see the nation-state as a focal center of political activities, ethnic and language loyalties in traditional societies weaken central authority.

Development educators who stress modernization as a goal direct their primary efforts toward creating a central and unifying sense of identity in nations. In modern societies, especially those of Western Europe and North America, national governments rather than the locality often command the greatest attention. Policy making, planning, and administration are done centrally. The national or central government extends its authority and power outward, from the center, throughout the country on a functional basis that extends to such areas as education, transportation, communication, health care, defense, and social security. The nation-state becomes the focus of identification and commitment and is capable of mobilizing popular support.

In traditional societies citizenship responsibility and political socialization are generally focused on the locality rather than on the nation. Societies in the throes of the movement from traditionalism to modernity are beset by a range of political tensions and conflicts among various language, tribal, and religious groups (see chapter 7). Modernizing development educators who pursue an agenda of nation building seek to extend identification and loyalty from the locality to the nation. At the primary level, they infuse the curriculum with a sense of nationhood by using national history, national heroic personages, and common national symbols to build loyalties. If the country was once ruled by a colonial power, a national freedom ideology may also be stressed. National systems, like those of many developed Western countries, emphasize homogeneity rather than individual local customs, traditions, and sensibilities. In contrast, people in LTDCs often ignore or deliberately resist political centralization.

Nation-building tendencies and localism and regionalism, especially when reinforced by language and ethnicity, are points of serious political and often educational conflict. For example, Nigeria has had difficulties in achieving peaceful national integration. Beginning with the Gorbachev reforms of the 1980s, the nationalities issue in the former Soviet Union also spurred controversy and often violent confrontations, which have continued in Russia and in some of the other new nations that emerged from the demise of the USSR. It is in the area of nation building, language and ethnic diversity, and autonomy that an internationalized concept of multicultural education is badly needed.

The Economic Dimension

Along with nation building, modernizing development educators have emphasized that LTDCs need to create a modern economic infrastructure. Indeed, in many top-down development strategies, economic growth is the chief goal. As mentioned previously, proponents of top-down development believe that if the economy is improved, the benefits will be diffused to the larger population.

In traditional societies, production and consumption are locally based; the chief occupation for most of the population is labor-intensive agriculture. Farming at the subsistence level generates little or no surplus for sale elsewhere. Most of the products are consumed where they are grown. Industry, too, is local and often of the handicraft or small-scale variety. The traditional rural economy of the market type is geared to locally based production and consumption with little or no surplus for investment. In striving for self-sufficiency in producing their own food, goods, services, clothing, and tools, people in LTDCs are limited in their range of production and specialization. The young often follow in their parents' occupations, and the chief form of education is a kind of apprenticeship, with sons and daughters learning directly from fathers and mothers. Because of the intensity of labor, children also form an important part of the local labor force, performing chores related to farming or caring for younger siblings. Traditional societies regard child labor as a family economic resource that augments the family's income and do not place a high value on school attendance.

Top-down development educators seek to reshape traditional economies into modern ones where economic surplus can be generated and used for investment in further development. The modern economy, frequently defined as industrial, is one of mass production, specialization, and integration. In contrast to the handicrafts of the local artisan, factories mass produce goods. Mass production rests on efficiency that is based on the mechanization of labor. In developing countries, where there is a large force of unskilled laborers and high unemployment, mechanization may exacerbate these problems. However, this structural unemployment is regarded as a necessary but temporary condition that will lead to a higher standard of living in the future. In modern societies agriculture also assumes a large corporate pattern, in contrast to traditional societies' small farms consisting of a few strips or plots of land. Specialization in production and services is part of the industrial-corporate pattern. Local markets are replaced by mass markets linked by mass transportation systems. The process of economic modernization affects educational institutions in that it generates a demand for larger numbers of trained engineers, managers, technicians, and clerical workers. This demand causes tensions between those who want a new-style, scientific, and technological education and those who resist it in favor of older educational patterns.

The creation of a modern economy, as envisioned by top-down development educators, requires a particular kind of education system. First, a basic change is required of secondary and higher education from an orientation toward the classics and literature to technical, engineering, and managerial specializations. Second, secondary schools need to be more diversified and offer a range of options such as those provided by the American comprehensive high school. Third, attitudes and behaviors need to be changed from less efficient but stable to efficient and dynamic use of time and resources.

The Social Dimension

The intellectual, political, and economic transformation envisioned by top-down modernizers requires such momentous and pervasive social change and adaptation that it can produce social disruption and alienation. Top-down modernizers recognize these consequences as unfortunate but necessary for improving the quality of life for the whole population.

In a traditional society, social patterns are highly stable, with little geographic or socioeconomic mobility. People may spend their lives in their place of birth. Moving upward to a higher socioeconomic class is also unlikely. The familial and kinship network provides security for its members by caring for the very young, for the ill, and for the elderly. The young are impressed with their responsibility for caring for all of the family members. Social concern for those who are not members of the family or kinship group may be absent. It is also unlikely that traditional governments provide the kind of social and health-care services found in a modern society.

Because mobility is limited, the behavioral patterns learned by the young arise from norms developed by a group that has lived in a place for generations. There is likely to be a strong sense of appropriate behavior, especially toward elders and parents. The social stability of such situations impedes change; indeed, change may be feared. Traditional social stability may also become a kind of social stagnation in which individuals passively accept their situation. Here, the forces of informal education, the ways of the ancestors and the family, set the standards of individual behavior and role expectations. Further, the roles of men and women are also carefully defined based on gender specifications. Most traditional societies are patriarchal with males playing the dominant roles at home and in public life. Men's roles are also defined by the agricultural or handicraft work they do. Appropriate women's roles often are defined as being a wife and mother and are specific to the conventional tasks of childrearing, cooking, and housekeeping that cluster about such roles. To maintain these traditional female roles, women may be denied entry or have very limited access to schools. When they attend school, it likely to be at the primary rather than the secondary and higher levels.

In contrast to the traditional society's social stability, the modern society is one of continuing, dynamic, and pervasive change with multiple roles and occupation alternatives. In developing countries, as the pace of industrialization quickens, a significant migration of people from rural to urban settings occurs. Indeed, a phenomenon in many developing countries has been the rapid growth of sprawling urban centers such as Bangkok, Calcutta, and Mexico City. Frequently, the central business core, with its modern office buildings, is surrounded by slums that duplicate but also multiply and intensify the conditions of rural poverty. Because of restrictions on space and a different kind of occupational structure in urban settings, the extended family tends to erode and be replaced by the nuclear family.

The changing social relationships of a modern society also shape educational arrangements. Modern societies are characterized by much higher rates of literacy, indeed almost universal literacy, in comparison with traditional ones. Primary schooling also tends to be universal, and more individuals participate in secondary and higher education, which exhibit differentiation from strictly academic to vocational and technical programs. Further, educational opportunities in modern society are more open to both genders. Greater numbers of women have increased educational opportunities and enter the workforce. Modern societies base their education on people's physical, psychological, and social stages of development. There is a longer period of adolescence in the more modern and the more affluent societies; young people are permitted to make a gradual transition from being cared for by parents to taking total responsibility for themselves. In contrast, people in traditional societies are likely to go abruptly from childhood to adulthood without an extended transitional period of social adolescence. In modern societies, marriage is more likely to take place at an older age than in traditional societies where it is often arranged and can take place at a very early age.

Finally, modern societies possess an extensive communications network that includes radio, newspapers, popular periodicals, television, and the Internet. Everyone—not just a select group—has access to information. The explosion of information decreases the authority of traditional high-ranking figures such as family elders and religious figures. Furthermore, modern communication methods replace the oral tradition in which certain members of the society were responsible for communicating news or passing on information for posterity.

In modern societies and in societies moving toward modernization, powerful communication forces and the widespread availability of information and entertainment facilitates the construction of a national culture and is likely to erode the distinctive cultures found in isolated rural villages and provincial settings. As local and regional differences diminish, the national culture becomes more homogeneous and standardized. Critics of modernization theory contend that modernizers have exaggerated the unifying tendencies of the process. They argue that the rapid transmission of information, especially electronically, creates autonomous subgroups, often ethnic and religious ones, that seek independence from the centralized state.

The educational system that serves a modern society simultaneously exhibits signs of specialization and standardization. Schools offer more career education options, provide more technical programs, and give students greater educational choices. At the same time, a standardized curriculum emerges in which teacher training follows a national pattern as mass-produced textbooks are graded and standardized, and standardized learning responses become the norm for successful academic completion. Mass communication and mass education in the modern society tend to produce a mass culture.

Thus far, we have examined development based upon a strategy that originates with experts at the top, is designed to bring about a modern society, and is patterned after the historical experience of the industrial societies of Western Europe and North America. Such a development pattern was prevalent in the 1960s and continues to have its advocates, especially in the corporate sectors of both developed and less-developed nations. In the 1970s, critics appeared on the educational scene to challenge the top-down version of modernization through development and began arguing for alternatives.

Critics of Top-Down Development

While participating in a seminar on "Modernization in India" in 1969, I heard presentations by Indian economic and educational planners. Although some Indian educators supported the top-down model described above, others argued it was in reality a strategy of neocolonial Westernization. They wanted to find a way to eliminate the economic and social stagnation and illiteracy that beset much of rural-village India without the problems that besieged modern Western industrial societies, such as environmental pollution, violent crime, disintegration of family life, and alcoholism and drug abuse. They wanted, they said, an India in which modernity arose from and within the values of the indigenous cultural context. They often pointed to Japan as a modern but not Western society.

Neo-Marxist dependency theorists argued that the societies labeled as LTDCs were underdeveloped because of economic relationships that deliberately kept them dependent on technologically developed countries (TDCs).[9] They identified the new forms of capitalism, such as multinational corporations, as key agencies in developing and maintaining the exploitative economic relationships that keep LTDCs, primarily located in the Southern Hemisphere, locked in a state of dependency and poverty.

Rather than sequentially improving urban and rural areas, top-down modernization strategies often widened urban-rural differentials. Rural economic, social, and educational problems were often accelerated and aggravated. Although formal education was a key element in top-down development strategies, rural school systems remained weak or had deteriorated. Primary schooling, often incomplete, was characterized by sporadic attendance and high dropout rates. In many less-developed countries, less than 10 percent of the rural school-age population completed primary schooling. Only 10 to 15 percent of those who completed primary schooling continued to secondary school. In the cities, primary schools were more numerous and better equipped. While educational opportunities for city children improved, the disparity of educational services between urban and rural areas increased. Further, secondary schools, which provided the institutional route to higher education, were also concentrated in the cities. The secondary curriculum was often an amalgamation of the language, literature, and values of the former colonial rulers, with a thin overlay of modern technological skills. It was more suited to the needs of an urban elite than to those of the more general population.[10]

In the 1970s, a group of social and educational critics challenged the long-accepted version of the benefits of modern industrial society and the educational systems that served it. In Western Europe there arose a critical philosophy based on the works of Antonio Gramsci and Juergen Habermas. In the U.S., revisionist historians of education challenged the celebrationist historiography associated with Ellwood P. Cubberley that extolled the virtues of schooling as an instrument of the modern industrial state. Revisionist critics also challenged the moderate liberal, middle-of-the-road version of educational history associated with Lawrence Cremin, Bernard Bailyn, and others who had broadened their interpretation of education to include agencies other than the school. Critics contended that the liberal educational historians continued to interpret formal educational processes, especially schooling, in generally positive terms. Revisionists such as Joel Spring, Clarence Karier, Michael Katz, and others constructed an interpretation of schooling that emphasized the concept of social control in which the upper and middle classes use formal education to empower themselves in the dominant political and economic position and to disempower lower socioeconomic classes and minority groups.[11] Neo-Marxist writers on curriculum, such as Michael Apple, analyzed the power of the hidden curriculum as a covert agency used to indoctrinate suppressed groups to accept the values imposed by the dominant groups.[12] In addition to the revisionist historians, two significant critiques of top-down development originated in the works of Ivan Illich and Paulo Freire.

Illich's Deschooling

Illich, cofounder of the Center for Intercultural Documentation, developed a strategy for social and educational change based upon the deinstitutionalization of society's coercive institutions, including schools. In *Deschooling Society*, Illich argues for the abolition of the formal school and the deschooling of society as a first step in eliminating coercive social institutions.[13] In many respects, Illich's arguments for deschooling are directly contrary to educators' advocacy for top-down modernization and development. Modernizing development educators, it should be remembered, often see their role as transforming traditional societies into modern ones by creating learning institutions that fit with the scheme of nation building. Much of the modernizing process relates to economic development or growth and to the centralized planning for such economic development.

Illich contends that the values of a modern society have become embedded in institutionalized structures.[14] Further, institutionalized values are measured largely as the outputs or products of particular institutions such as corporations, hospitals, or schools. According to Illich, "When values have been institutionalized in planned and engineered processes, members of modern society believe that the good life consists in having institutions which define the values that both they and their society believe they need."[15] Illich argues that schools play a particularly pernicious role in that they indoctrinate the young to relinquish their own value-creating potentialities to institutions and to become consumers who want institutionally produced goods and services.

Schooling and Development

Illich's attacks on schools and other coercive institutions foreshadowed the theory of bottom-up development or sustainable development described later in this chapter. He attacked the concept that all important learning is organized and controlled by institutions of formal education such as schools, colleges, and universities. Primitive human beings, he contended, learned by direct involvement and interaction with the environment. Illich sought to restore learning that is informal and direct rather than formal and indirect.

Illich's arguments for informal and nonformal education rest on his rejection of modernizers' attempts to construct a totally planned and manipulated environment. He abhorred the modern ideal of a totally planned world in which the value of all human interactions is determined by a calculus of social engineering. In the developed economies and societies of the Western nations, highly trained specialists perform specific functions. Around the specialists, specialized institutions produce the goods and services determined by the economic planners, marketing experts, and profit makers. These institutions and their specialists are rationalized by the false ideology of the "myth of unending consumption," which holds that valuable products are being produced and should be desired, purchased, and consumed.

Schools in modern societies indoctrinate the young to accept the theory of unending consumption by training and certificating them to become specialists and to fit into institutionally defined roles. Furthermore, in an institutionalized society, promotion within institutions and within the economic structure depends upon holding the appropriate certification. The institutionalized system is sustained by schools through their use of graded promotions; their focus on certification confuses learning with specialization. School, the initial exposure to institutions, conditions people to depend on institutionalized life. This dependency is then transferred to other institutions.

Whether located in a developed or a developing country, schooling's educational monopoly is the same throughout the world. Having the same structure, curriculum, and consequences, schooling is a universally coercive "age-specific, teacher-related process requiring full-time attendance at an obligatory curriculum."[16] It shapes a consumer mentality that values institutional commodities and services over the friendly assistance of concerned but uncertificated neighbors. Schooling brainwashes students into believing that the bureaucracies of coercive institutions are truly scientific, efficient, and benevolent.

Liberating Learning

Illich's arguments for deschooling society are directed toward liberating learning from schooling's domination. Free from institutionalized constraints, education could become a form of skill or drill learning in which a person learns a particular skill—from reading, writing, swimming, and sewing to computer programming. Much of skill learning would occur informally or nonformally in specific or on-the-job training. Specific learning would be appropriate, for example, for villagers in a less-developed country who want to learn to dig a community well, improve sanitation, irrigate a field, or use a sewing machine or a loom. What Illich calls "liberal education" is general, open-ended learning about ideas, literature, history, art, and any subject about which people have an interest. Here, interested individuals meet in mutual association and participation to share ideas and opinions for as long as they are interested in the topic.[17] The general, open-ended, liberal education might be used by people concerned with political and economic exploitation for meeting and discussing political alternatives and actions. The kind of learning Illich recommends as an alternative to schooling is very similar to that which bottom-up development educators emphasize.

Illich's Critique of Top-Down Development

In assessing development and development education, Illich proposes a strategy for "outwitting developed countries."[18] He argues that in developed Western societies the quality of life is based on the quantitative dimension of life—more products, more schooling, and more consumer goods. Industries, the media, and governmental and educational agencies are defined as producers of commodities that are packaged to reflect the Western modernization and domination. Progress is defined as a continuing expansion of these agencies, and development is merely the exportation of these agencies to the LTDCs.[19] In top-down development, Illich contends, "rich nations benevolently impose a straight jacket of traffic jams, hospital confinements, and classrooms on the poor nations and by international agreement call this development." In reality, the poor, not the wealthy, bear the cost of modernizing top-down development. According to Illich:

> Every dollar spent in Latin America on doctors and hospitals costs a hundred lives. . . . Had each dollar been spent on providing safe drinking water, a hundred lives could have been saved. Each dollar spent on schooling means more privileges for the few at the cost of the many; at best it increases the number of those who, before dropping out, have been taught that those who stay longer have earned the right to more power, wealth, and prestige. What such schooling does is to teach the schooled, the superiority of the better schooled.[20]

The top-down development programs of the advanced nations that are exported to the less-developed nations are designed, says Illich, to create a mass demand and market for consumer goods produced by developed nations. The consumerization of the population of the less-developed nation creates a demand for packaged solutions that are not only beyond the reach of the masses but are also undesirable for them. Illich argues that underdevelopment results from rising aspirations caused by intensive marketing. What has been called development, he contends, is contrary to a genuine education. A genuine education awakens "awareness of new levels of human potential and the use of one's creative powers to foster human life."[21]

Freire and Liberation Pedagogy

Paulo Freire, like Illich, argues that oppressed peoples in LTDCs are not only repressed by the traditional structures controlled by the dominant classes but also by certain modernizing projects that create sophisticated patterns of social control. Oppressors, according to Freire, use their monopoly of science and technology for economic exploitation and political repression of the poor.

In *Pedagogy of the Oppressed,* Freire advocates liberation pedagogy, an education that raises the consciousness of oppressed people in less-developed nations and encourages them to develop their own political and educational alternatives to end exploitation.[22] It involves people within the local community, rather than experts from outside, who participate in a critical dialogue to identify, define, discuss, and determine ways to solve their mutual problems. A critical dialogue develops trust and mutual understanding that leads to agreed-upon action for solving the problem and to the creation of grassroots political, social, and educational organizations that will empower their creators.[23] Liberation pedagogy enlightens oppressed people to become conscious that they are in an indeterminate historical situation, which they can define for themselves and then end by transforming it in directions that eliminate oppression and contribute to greater humanization.[24]

Important elements of Freire's theory that contributed to the strategy of grassroots sustainable development are: (1) genuine development should originate locally; (2) locally initiated development should focus on problems or projects significant to those who initiated them, rather than being imposed by outside experts; (3) the initial stage in development projects involves a raising of consciousness so that people know they can change their living conditions; (4) development should encourage a broader humanization or empowerment of people; and (5) grassroots development leads to new political and educational configurations that will challenge and alter the oppressive conditions of the status quo. Freire's site-based local development stands in sharp contrast to the centralized, nationwide, programs of modernization associated with top-down development.

Postmodern Critique

The most philosophical critique of top-down development, particularly modernization, comes from postmodernist philosophers. Indeed, postmodernism is antithetical to modernism and the theory of modernization discussed earlier in the chapter. Postmodernists assert that we are now living in the postmodern era, a time after modernity. The period in which we now live is also a postindustrial era. While the proponents of modernization argue that it is a universally applicable and scientifically objective theory, postmodernists challenge the very possibilities of universalism and objectivity. For them, theories such as modernism are not descriptions of universal phenomena but are the constructions, often transmitted through social discourse, of particular groups who seek dominance over others, at specific times in history. Postmodernists contend "modernization" is a construction of those who want to impose their version of Western for-profit capitalism on others, especially those living in what are labeled less-developed societies and countries.[25]

As its name suggests, postmodernism is a reaction against and a rejection of modernism, especially its emphasis that development, as progress, can be measured quantitatively by economic indicators. It also rejects the concept that societies can be ranked according to economic development. According to postmodernists, what is needed is a liberating or opposing discourse, such as that suggested by Freire, to raise the consciousness of exploited groups so that they can begin to empower themselves. Possessing a real consciousness about the agents and agencies of oppression, such as exploitative capitalism, marks the beginning of true self-development. A liberating kind of education can deconstruct the rationales of oppression, one of them being the ideology of modernization.

Emergence of a New Development Strategy: Bottom-Up Development

As a consequence of the interpretations of revisionist historians, neo-Marxist curriculum theorists, advocates of deschooling, proponents of liberation pedagogy, and postmodernist critics, a new development strategy—the bottom-up strategy—emerged in the 1980s. Along with these more theoretical perspectives, two other factors contributed to the newer strategy: (1) NGOs such as churches, philanthropic organizations, foundations, and organizations of private individuals entered the scene and added a new dimension to development and development education; and (2) changing economic conditions in the developed countries caused them to focus on domestic issues and question top-down development strategy.[26]

The bottom-up strategy of development relies less on projects initiated by governments and experts and more on local grassroots community efforts. These local efforts are sometimes aided by private, voluntary international organizations. The contours of the new strategy emphasize local participant sovereignty to ensure equal access to goods and services, and grassroots decision making in which local participants determine the kind of community in which they wish to live.[27] This bottom-up, more humanistic pattern, according to Coombs, is broader in scope and suited to a greater diversity of needs than is the top-down linear pattern.[28] The bottom-up pattern rests on the following assumptions:

- Development planning and projects should originate in the local community in which they are to occur.

- Development should be multidimensional and improve the social, political, and educational as well as the economic quality of life.

- Development should serve the needs of the greatest number of people and not only the elite.

- The trickle-down economic theory in which economic benefits are supposed to work their way down from upper to lower economic groups has actually increased rather than reduced disparities; it should be reversed to encourage a more equitable distribution of resources.

- Since the great majority of people in LTDCs live in rural areas, development strategies should be directed toward improving the quality of rural life.
- Although external assistance may be needed for development projects, the control and direction of these projects should be in local hands.

The bottom-up strategy has led to an emphasis on rural development that involves the social, economic, political, and educational transformation of rural societies. Rural development goals tend to feature food production and distribution, family planning, sanitation, education, and employment. The bottom-up strategy uses an integrated grassroots approach to development in which members of rural communities work together in the kind of consciousness-raising and dialogue suggested by Freire for making plans and mobilizing their own resources and energies to implement their own goals.[29]

While top-down modernization relies heavily on formal, or institutionalized, education through primary and secondary schools and colleges and universities, the bottom-up strategy uses nonformal education. In many respects, nonformal education resembles the skill and liberal education recommended by Illich and the liberation pedagogy suggested by Freire. Nonformal education is not a separate and distinct educational system, but may parallel the formal or institutionalized school system. Coombs defines nonformal education as "any organized, systematic, educational activity, carried on outside the framework of the formal system, to provide selected types of learning to particular subgroups in the population, adults as well as children."[30] Nonformal education may include agricultural extension and farm training programs, adult literacy programs, youth clubs, or meetings of community groups to discuss family planning, health, nutrition, or sanitation. It may relate to organizing rural cooperatives to improve agricultural production and distribution. In some respects, nonformal education is compatible with the older, oral education found in traditional societies as it creates fewer cultural conflicts than does formal schooling.

While formal school systems and nonformal school arrangements may coexist in parallel fashion, their differences are significant. Formal schooling is age specific to children and adolescents, involves a fixed curriculum, and requires cumulative and sequential organization and instruction. The institutionalization of formal education in sequentially arranged primary, secondary, and higher education institutions is geared to centralized planning, management, and financing. It also includes control of instruction by certificated personnel arranged in a hierarchical staffing pattern. Nonformal education is part-time, involves learning by both children and adults, is limited in scope, and is directed toward solving particular problems or meeting specific needs. The consequences of nonformal education are not deferred to the distant future as in formal education. Rather than rely on certificated and hierarchically arranged personnel, nonformal education draws from a variety of support sources—government and nongovernmental private, voluntary organizations such as foundations and churches.[31]

Conclusion

Simultaneously, throughout the world small-scale grassroots, decentralized, bottom-up development is taking place. While many differences exist between the conceptualization and motivation of development strategies, both the top-down and the bottom-up approaches may be fruitfully employed. The top-down strategy has the weakness that it may conflict with local interests and have consequences other than those intended. Further, it may serve special rather than popular interests. Top-down development, however, has an asset in that it possesses the potential to mobilize needed resources that local communities do not possess. Additionally, it has a staying power, a duration that is unlikely to exist in voluntary small-scale projects.

In contrast to the top-down strategy, the bottom-up strategy has much to commend it. It is popularly initiated and locally controlled and may have limited but tangible results for the local population. However, it too has built-in weaknesses. It may be so localized that its impact is isolated. Local communities may be unable to mobilize needed resources to accomplish their goals. Further, the activities of voluntary agencies may be short lived, depending on often temporary funding and the enthusiasm of volunteers.

I recommend a synthesis of the positive and constructive features of both approaches. Centralized, long-range, coordinated planning and mobilization associated with top-down development may provide the resources and the invited expertise needed to sustain development. However, the centralized efforts of governments should not lead to an imposition of the views of experts or special interests that violate local prerogatives. It is possible in a genuinely integrated pattern of development that the provided resources and expertise be governed by local wishes as expressed through the community. Such a synthesis would avoid doctrinaire either-or approaches and would unite the positive features of the top-down and bottom-up models. In such a synthesis, the formal school and nonformal education can coexist.

DISCUSSION QUESTIONS

1. Define the concepts of development and development education.
2. Identify and examine key events in the history of international development and development education.
3. Describe the strategy used in top-down programs of international development.
4. What are the benefits and the limitations of top-down development programs?
5. Analyze Ivan Illich's critique of the imposition of Western patterns of development on third-world nations. Do you agree or disagree with Illich's argument?
6. Describe the strategy used in bottom-up programs of international development.

7. What are the benefits and the limitations of bottom-up development programs?
8. Analyze the uses of formal education, or schooling, and nonformal education in both the top-down and the bottom-up strategies of international development.

FIELD AND RESEARCH TOPICS

1. Interview several international students from developing nations about the process of international development as they have observed it in their own countries. Based upon your interviews, prepare a report for the class.
2. Invite a professor who has participated in an overseas development project to speak to the class about his or her experiences.
3. Identify and describe areas of underdevelopment in the U.S. If such an area is located near your college or university, arrange a field trip to the site.
4. Identify an LTDC. Prepare a statistical profile of that country. If several students in the course wish to participate in a project of creating such demographic profiles, arrange to share the information in a cooperative learning experience.
5. Contact the Peace Corps and request information that describes the work of volunteers in LTDCs.
6. Contact area churches and private organizations. Inquire if they are involved in development projects in third-world nations. If so, arrange interviews and collect information about the work of such private voluntary organizations.
7. Arrange a classroom debate on this issue: "Resolved, the most effective programs of international development take place through the activities of governments that rely on expert advice."
8. In a role-playing situation, act out the roles of villagers in an LTDC who are engaged in a dialogue on local problems and their resolution.

SUGGESTIONS FOR FURTHER READING

Adams, Don, and Robert M. Bjork. *Education in Developing Areas.* New York: David McKay, 1969.
Appadurai, Arjun. *Modernity at Large: Cultural Dimensions of Globalization.* Minneapolis: University of Minnesota Press, 1996.
Apter, David E. *Rethinking Development: Modernization, Dependency, and Postmodern Politics.* Newbury Park, CA: Sage, 1987.
Black, Jan Knippers. *Development in Theory and Practice: Bridging the Gap.* Boulder, CO: Westview Press, 1991.
Blumberg, Rae Lesser. *Women, Development, and the Wealth of Nations: Making the Case for the Gender Variable.* Boulder, CO: Westview Press, 1991.
Boulding, Elise. *Building a Global Civic Culture: Education for an Interdependent World.* New York: Columbia University, Teachers College Press, 1988.

Brandt Commission. *Common Crisis North-South: Cooperation for World Recovery, 1983.* Cambridge, MA: MIT Press, 1983.

Brown, Janet Welsh, ed. *In the U.S. Interest: Resources, Growth, and Security in the Developing World.* Boulder, CO: Westview Press, 1990.

Coombs, Philip H. *The World Crisis in Education: The View from the Eighties.* New York: Oxford University Press, 1985.

Escobar, Arturo. *Encountering Development: The Making and Unmaking of the Third World.* Princeton: Princeton University Press, 1995.

Freire, Paulo. *Pedagogy of the Oppressed.* New York: Continuum, 1984.

Hamilton, John Maxwell. *Entangling Alliances: How the Third World Shapes Our Lives.* Cabin John, MD: Seven Locks Press, 1990.

Hanson, John W., and Cole S. Brembeck, eds. *Education and the Development of Nations.* New York: Holt, Rinehart, and Winston, 1966.

Illich, Ivan D. *Celebration of Awareness: A Call for Institutional Revolution.* New York: Doubleday, 1970.

Illich, Ivan D. *Deschooling Society.* New York: Harper and Row, 1970.

Joy, Carol, and Willard Kniep, eds. *The International Development Crisis and American Education: Challenges, Opportunities, and Instructional Strategies.* New York: Global Perspectives, 1987.

Kidron, Michael, and Ronald Segal. *The New State of the World Atlas.* New York: Simon and Schuster, 1986.

Lai, Deepak. *The Poverty of Development Economics.* Cambridge, MA: Harvard University Press, 1985.

Latham, Michael E. *Modernization as Ideology: American Social Science and "Nation Building" in the Kennedy Era.* Chapel Hill, NC: University of North Carolina Press, 2000.

Sigmund, Paul E., ed. *The Ideologies of the Developing Nations.* New York: Praeger, 1967.

Todaro, Michael. *Economic Development of the Third World.* New York: Longman, 1989.

Weaver, James H., and Kenneth P. Jameson. *Economic Development: Competing Paradigms.* Lanham, MD: University Press of America, 1981.

Weisband, Edward, ed. *Poverty amidst Plenty: World Political Economy and Distributive Justice.* Boulder, CO: Westview Press, 1989.

Wilber, Charles F., ed. *The Political Economy of Development and Underdevelopment.* New York: Random House, 1987.

NOTES

[1] Wikipedia the free encyclopedia, http://en.wikipedia.org/wikiDeveloping_country (accessed February 2, 2005).

[2] Michael E. Latham, *Modernization as Ideology: American Social Science and "Nation Building" in The Kennedy Era* (Chapel Hill: University of North Carolina Press, 2000), 25.

[3] James H. Weaver, Steven H. Arnold, Paula Cruz, and Kenneth Kusterer, "Competing Paradigms of Development," *Social Education* 53 (April/May 1989): 209.

[4] C. E. Black, *The Dynamics of Modernization: A Study in Comparative History* (New York: Harper and Row, 1966), 1–34.

[5] Latham, 34.

[6] Ibid., 4.

[7] These activities have been identified by Black in *The Dynamics of Modernization*, 1–34. The educational implications are developed further by the author of this book.

[8] For a well-written analysis of the modernization process in a traditional society, see Milton Singer, *When a Great Tradition Modernizes: An Anthropological Approach to Indian Civilization* (New York: Praeger, 1972).

[9] Latham, 5.

[10] Philip H. Coombs, *The World Crisis in Education: The View from the Eighties* (New York: Oxford University Press, 1985), 15–18.

[11] For example, see Joel Spring, *The Sorting Machine: National Educational Policy Since 1945* (New York: Longman, 1976); Samuel Bowles and Herbert Gintis, *Schooling in Capitalist America: Educational Reform and the Contradictions of Economic Life* (New York: Basic Books, 1976); Michael B. Katz, *Class, Bureaucracy, and Schools: The Illusion of Educational Change in America* (New York: Praeger, 1971).

[12] Michael W. Apple, *Ideology and Curriculum* (London: Routledge and Kegan Paul, 1979), 82–104.

[13] Ivan Illich, *Deschooling Society* (New York: Harper and Row, 1971).

[14] For themes related to deschooling, see Ivan D. Illich, *Celebration of Awareness: A Call for Institutional Revolution* (New York: Doubleday, 1971); Alan Gartner, Colin Greer, and Frank Riessman, *After Deschooling, What?* (New York: Harper and Row, 1973); Everett Reimer, *School Is Dead: Alternatives in Education* (New York: Doubleday, 1970).

[15] Illich, *Deschooling Society*, 113–114.

[16] Ibid., 25–26.

[17] Ibid., 76.

[18] Ivan Illich, "Outwitting Developed Countries," *New York Review of Books*, Nov. 6, 1969, 20–24.

[19] Ibid.

[20] Ibid., 20.

[21] Ibid., 22.

[22] Paulo Freire, *Pedagogy of the Oppressed*, trans. Myra Bergman Ramos (New York: Continuum), 1984.

[23] Ibid., 102–103.

[24] Ibid., 72–73.

[25] For postmodernism see: Joe L. Kincheloe, *Toward a Critical Politics of Teacher Thinking: Mapping the Postmodern* (Westport, CT: Bergin and Garvey, 1993); William E. Doll, Jr., *A Post-Modern Perspective on Curriculum* (New York: Teachers College Press, 1993); Stanley Aronowitz and Henry Giroux, *Postmodern Education: Politics, Culture, and Social Criticism* (Minneapolis: University of Minnesota Press, 1991).

[26] For a discussion of nongovernmental international actors, see Elise Boulding, *Building a Global Civic Culture: Education for an Interdependent World* (New York: Columbia University, Teachers College Press, 1988), 35–55.

[27] Weaver et al., 211.

[28] Coombs, 18.

[29] Ibid., 18–19.

[30] Ibid., 23.

[31] Ibid., 24–25.

6

GLOBALIZATION AND EDUCATION

This chapter examines the contemporary phenomenon of globalization, a term widely used in economics, sociology, policy studies, and comparative education. Because it has multifaceted and interconnected economic, political, social, and educational consequences, globalization is a highly complex but significant worldwide process.[1] A generic term, it has implications for a wide range of international areas such as international trade and finance, information technology, environmental policy, and the transnational business corporation.[2] Since these areas all involve an educational component, globalization is an important area of study for international and comparative educators.

First we shall define globalization and situate it in a historical context. While aspects of globalization resemble modernization, in reality the two phenomena are different. We explore what makes them different and then look at how individual nation-states are impacted by globalization. As an important institution within the nation-state, education is affected by globalization, but it also plays a role in shaping the nation-state to become a viable global producer and consumer. The last section of the chapter discusses globalization's impact on curriculum, instruction, education systems, and possibilities for the future.

Defining and Situating Globalization

Because it is a wide-ranging, multifaceted, and dynamic world force, it is difficult to establish a specific definition for globalization. Sociologists, political scientists, and comparative educators have had long and complicated discussions over its meaning and its impact. In his insightful commentary on globalization, Erwin Epstein, referring to Roland Robertson, an expert on globalization theory, describes globalization as an "accelerated compression of the contemporary world and the intensification of . . . the world as a singular entity."[3] Tending to homogenize rather than diversify, this compression is reducing social and ethnic differences around the world. Because of the complexity of the term and disagreements over its meaning, it is necessary to stipulate a definition of globalization as used in this book.

We can begin to stipulate a definition for globalization by examining its root, the term "global." Global refers to a system or a process that relates to, involves, includes, or is adapted to the entire world. Climatic, environmental, and health conditions are examples of natural processes. Globalization also refers to human engineered and developed processes such as economics, communication, travel, and transportation that encompass the entire world. Globalization, then, can be defined as the systems or processes that promote worldwide involvement, relationships, adaptations, and connections between peoples of different countries, cultures, and languages. Globalization needs to be considered in terms of characteristics that are transnational and worldwide together with those that are within nation-states and are, in turn, affected by national contexts. Globalization operates worldwide as a process but this process functions within particular contexts such as individual nation-states or regions comprised of nation-states such as the European Union or the Pacific Rim.

While I contend that globalization as a general process needs to be considered in terms of contextual settings, such as the nation-states in which it functions, other commentators see it as a transnational and supranational process that reduces the power of local contexts, that is, reducing the power of local circumstances on people's lives.[4]

Throughout history, global or worldwide interactions have taken place between different peoples, often because of trade or war. There have been interactions caused by the diffusion of religions from their place of origin to more distant regions. Although early trade, military, and religious interactions had broad implications, when compared to contemporary globalization they tended to function regionally rather than globally.

The age of exploration in the fifteenth and sixteenth centuries witnessed the transoceanic explorations of Western Europeans in North and South America, Asia, and Africa. These explorations brought cultural and economic interactions between the Europeans and the indigenous peoples they encountered and led to the establishment of European colonies, especially in North and South America. While Western exploration and settlement were certainly global occurrences, they lacked the rapidity, intensity, and interrelatedness of contemporary globalization and were deeply rooted in the politics, commerce, and diplomacy of particular European imperial nations, such as Spain, Portugal, England, and France. Specifically, European exploration was oriented to the agenda of the particular nation-state to become an empire.

European imperialism and colonization reached its high tide in the nineteenth century with colonies established in Africa and Asia. The U.S., too, participated in the worldwide race for overseas areas of control in Puerto Rico and the Philippines. Nineteenth-century imperialism, though a worldwide process, again differed from contemporary globalization, as it was oriented to the policies of specific nation-states.

World War I and World War II were conflicts whose battles were waged throughout the world. The League of Nations was established after World

War I. The United Nations, which today has a membership of 191 sovereign states, was established after World War II to maintain international peace and security, develop friendly relations among nations, and promote social progress, better living standards, and human rights. The goals of the United Nations are truly global in scope and have led the way in looking at nation-states from a global perspective.

During the cold war from 1948 to 1990, there were two conflicting paramount economic-political-military paradigms operating in the world: the American and Western European model of essentially free market capitalism and the Soviet model of centralized state control. Other models operating in the period were the Western European social welfare state, a hybrid of socialism and capitalism, with extensive social welfare and health-care provisions as in the Scandinavian nations and the UK. Another model, found in some nonaligned nations such as India, was a hybrid whereby certain sectors of the economy were controlled by the state, especially major industries such as steel and energy production, and others by market demands. Several concurrent trends in the 1980s and 1990s moved globalization to assume its contemporary economic features and policy positions. In 1990, the Soviet Union dissolved and Soviet control of the satellite nations in Eastern and Central Europe ended. The demise of the Soviet bloc ended Communist party rule and its economic policy of centralized state economic planning, ownership, and control in this region. With the collapse of the Communist system in the USSR and its satellites, the Marxist model of state centralized control was generally discredited in those regions. Important causes of the collapse of the Soviet system were military spending that exceeded resources and the stagnation and gross inefficiency of state-run industries. At the same time that the Soviet Union was in its death throes, there was a decided political shift in the UK from social welfare state economic policies to the free enterprise capitalist system, and in the U.S. with the passage of legislation that further promoted a market-driven economy.

With the ascendancy of neoconservative politics and market-driven capitalism in the U.S. and the UK and the disappearance of their major global rival, the Soviet Union, the following occurred: (1) the dramatic triumph of the capitalist over the Marxist model left capitalism without a significant economic counterforce; and (2) under neoconservative governments, social welfare policies were dismantled by policies of privatization and deregulation in the U.S., the UK, and other countries. The globalization process that moved with great acceleration and momentum since the early 1990s took on the following characteristics: (1) state economic planning and centralization no longer provided a viable alternative policy to the now-triumphant free market capitalist model; and (2) market-driven capitalism, identified with the U.S. and other technologically developed Western nations and Japan, was closely associated with political democracy. World economic organizations such as the World Bank and the International Monetary Fund developed criteria for loans to the former Soviet bloc nations and to the less technologically developed countries (LTDCs) in Asia, Africa, and South America that were based on the free market capitalist model. These criteria required borrowing countries to reduce the central government's economic role and to privatize some of its social, health, and educational services. The rationale supporting these criteria was that such reforms would reduce government expenditures and bring about the competition that would engender greater efficiency and productivity.

Certain aspects of globalization were not an entirely a new process but had been operative throughout history. One may ask—why the great contemporary focus on globalization? The next sections seek to answer that question.

The Intensity of Contemporary Globalization

In some ways, globalization can be considered as an extension of the twentieth-century processes of internationalization and modernization. Internationalization refers to interactions such as trade between nation-states. The international relationships between nation-states have been augmented by global contacts between individuals, resulting from high-tech communication systems. Modernization is the process by which traditional, rural societies become technologically advanced and industrialized (as discussed in chapter 5). Recall that modernization relied on nation-states, often ignoring local contexts, and relied on the industrial model that originated in the U.S. and Western Europe. Epstein criticizes modernization for its "focus on changes within societies or nations and comparisons between them—with Western societies as their main reference." He also argues that modernization neglects the themes of interconnectedness and interdependence between nations and societies.[5]

Both modernization and globalization are forces that move economic, social, and educational interactions and relationships out of local contexts and place them in world settings, interactions, and relationships.[6] Both modernization and globalization: (1) are worldwide processes that affect nation-states, especially their economies and societies; (2) are highly attuned to the role of economic forces in shaping the world's social and political order; (3) tend to subordinate the contextual features of given countries, societies, and cultures to what is regarded as a worldwide process; and (4) have generated wide interest among academic historians, economists, sociologists, and comparative educators.

In the twenty-first century, globalization, while containing some aspects of internationalization and modernization, is considered a transformative process that transcends nation-states and involves global communications systems and multinational economic interests and relationships. For example, Roger Dale argues that "globalization is distinct from" earlier processes in that it refers to a "global economy that includes all nations of the world."[7] Although globalization goes beyond nation-states, it is the nation-state that molds itself to be an effective global operator. The nation-state, especially its institutions, is responsible for reshaping or redirecting the effects of the globalization process. Globalization affects educational systems; issues of gender, ethnicity, language, and social class; the labor market; migration and immigration patterns; international finance and banking; and mass media and international communications systems.[8]

One of the twenty-first century's major transformative innovations is the development of worldwide communications systems in reporting news, providing international entertainment, diffusing information, and making it possible for people to interact with each other via the Internet. As very powerful agencies of informal and nonformal education, these systems have had a pronounced influence on how people view themselves, other peoples, and the world. Worldwide news agencies, ranging from CNN, based in the U.S., and Aljazeera, serving the Arab world, provide almost immediate coverage and commentary on events occurring around the world. As a result, people are instantaneously and dynamically informed about what is happening in other countries. With this instantaneous reportage, television programming has outdistanced the printed page, newspapers, magazines, and books as a source of information. Today the World Wide Web and e-mail make it possible for people within and across countries to share ideas with an ease and rapidity unknown in the past. While in most cases this type of communication has positive benefits, it also has a negative side because it makes it possible for global terrorist groups such as al Qaeda to plan and coordinate their attacks.

Globalization and the World Economy

Economic globalization refers to the international integration of economies worldwide. It involves global capital, investments, production, marketing, and distribution of goods and services worldwide. These economic aspects of globalization have highly significant educational implications, especially those that relate to the nature of the curriculum and the degree to which education is geared to the arts and humanities or to technological and vocational training. They relate to a nation-state's investment in education, especially to the funding of particular sectors in the school system. Finally, economic aspects of globalization relate to the role of education in creating understanding of and competency in functioning in a global society and economy. In the next sections we will discuss some of the forces that have contributed to the creation of a global economy.

Multinational Business Corporations

One of the most powerful of the twenty-first century's agencies of globalization is the multinational or transnational business corporation. These transnational corporations (TNCs) may have headquarters and ownership in several countries and have factories and production centers located throughout the world. TNCs operate across national borders, and their capital comes from investors from all over the world; components of their products are manufactured in different countries and assembled in others; their marketing departments may be located at headquarters in still another country; and the final products are sold in still other countries.[9] TNCs range from agribusinesses, to automobile manufacturing companies, to media corporations. The extent to which and the rapidity by which the TNCs can transfer financial and personnel resources from nation to nation or region to region exerts a new unprecedented force on the world economy.

Globalization and Regionalization

Globalization has stimulated the growth of regional trade organizations. These organizations of nation-states, affiliated on a regional basis, represent new configurations that raise important social, political, economic, and educational implications. The most of significant of these regional organizations are the European Union (EU), the North American Free Trade Agreement (NAFTA), and Asia Pacific Economic Cooperation (APEC).[10] The establishment of these organizations is a sign of the economic interdependence of the member nations on each other. Regional trade organizations seek to reduce trade barriers, encourage economic interactions between their members, and secure international trade agreements favorable to the region.[11] While they compete against each other to obtain the trade arrangements that benefit them, these regional organizations share a mutual recognition that they need a world that is safe for international commerce.[12]

The European Union: EU

After World War II ended with its massive loss of life and property, the nation-states of Western Europe attempted to reduce national antagonisms and to develop some semblance of European unity that would reduce future conflicts and aid in Europe's economic recovery. The slow but sustained process that began with the Treaty of Rome in 1957 and culminated in the Treaty of European Union in 1992 led to today's European Union.

The EU seeks to reduce nation-state nationalism and conflict in Europe, maintain peace and security, and promote a more integrated European economy. The EU has standardized market access to its members, increased the movement of workers, and regulated working conditions, wages, and social insurance in its member nations. Its social and educational policies seek to develop a sense of European social cohesion among the citizens of the member nation-states.

In the EU, as in other regional agreements, education, particularly schooling, tends to remain a direct prerogative of the nation-states. Although elementary and secondary schooling remain primarily in the jurisdiction of the member nations, the EU is concerned with the broad policies of encouraging a sense of European-ness through the curriculum. It is most concerned with training programs to increase technological skills and with supporting research and development in higher education.[13] Research, development, and technological and information-age training are especially relevant to making the EU into an effective and competitive trading bloc. The EU has a Directorate General for Education and Culture. Among its goals are improving teacher preparation standards, improving technological training programs, preparing skilled workers, and encouraging cultural programs and educational exchanges.

The North American Free Trade Agreement: NAFTA

The North American Free Trade Agreement between Canada, Mexico, and the U.S. took effect on January 1, 1994. Involving 363 million people and a $6.3 trillion economy in the three countries, it seeks to promote market liberalization, stimulate trade, and encourage the flow of capital across borders by eliminating or reducing tariffs and border taxes. One of the motivations behind the agreement is to stem the tide of illegal Mexican immigrants into the U.S. by encouraging American businesses to shift part of their production costs to Mexico, which has lower labor costs (see chapter 14 on Mexico). NAFTA allows freer access of Mexican products to U.S. and Canadian markets.[14] While the direct effects of NAFTA on education in the three countries are limited, NAFTA's related implications for education are more significant, especially regarding the promotion of technological training programs and the generation of technology research, for higher education.

Asia Pacific Economic Cooperation: APEC

A highly important economic development has been the rise of certain Asian nation-states as significant economic actors on the world scene. In the 1980s, South Korea and Singapore joined Japan, which was already an economic leader, as significant economic forces in the Pacific region. Further, Thailand, Taiwan, and Malaysia enjoyed gains in economic development. In addition, the Peoples Republic of China (PRC) is undergoing a major economic shift as it supplies resources for industrial and technological development in its coastal provinces, privatizes its economy, and reduces central planning. By the 1990s, the Pacific Rim, which includes the U.S., Canada, Mexico, Russia, and Australia as well as the Asian nations, was recognized as an area of tremendous economic importance. Though the economic downturn of the late 1990s in Asia dampened some of the more enthusiastic predictions, Asia and the Pacific Rim remain highly significant economic players on the world scene.

APEC is an arena of economic cooperation whose diverse members are nation-states that border the Pacific Ocean, including the U.S., PRC, Japan, Russia, Australia, Brunei Darussalam, Canada, Indonesia, South Korea, Malaysia, New Zealand, the Philippines, Singapore, Thailand, and Mexico. Its members account for half of the world's trade and range from those that are among the world's most technologically developed countries (TDCs) to those at the lower end of technological development. Despite these differences in economic development, APEC's member nations are working to liberalize and facilitate trade and establish economic and technical cooperation.[15]

As with the other regional economic organizations, the governance and control of education, particularly school systems, remains within the domain of each nation-state. APEC members have issued policy statements that recognize the importance of human development and technological skill training in the global economy. APEC encourages its members to share information and strategies to improve literacy, skills, and distance and teacher education programs. There has been a particular emphasis on development programs and education in the LTDC member nation-states.[16]

Economic Change and Controversy

Globalization has generated considerable controversy between those who see it as a possibility for improving economic conditions and raising living standards for people throughout the world and those who see it as a deteriorating force, one that includes the exploitation of the world's poor. Proponents of privatization and a worldwide free market economy argue that globalization's long-term benefits will reduce production costs and make goods available to more buyers in an expanding global marketplace. Similar to the arguments of *laissez-faire* economic theorists in the nineteenth and early twentieth centuries, the proponents of free trade globalization contend that the elimination of tariffs and other trade barriers erected by individual nation-states will make production more efficient and bring jobs to more people, especially those who live in LTDCs. Specifically, the proponents of globalization contend that it has (1) improved Asian economies; (2) reduced the isolation of the LTDCs, giving them greater access to the world economy; and (3) generated programs that have improved rural education and health care.

Opponents of globalization include members of trade unions in TDCs who see it as causing the movement of jobs to other countries where pay and benefits are low; environmentalists who see the spread of huge agribusinesses as producing environmental damage; and social activists who see it as a another means of exploiting the poor in LTDCs. The opponents contend that globalization benefits the few at the expense of the many. They claim that poverty has actually increased in some countries, particularly those in sub-Saharan Africa. The opponents see globalization as creating a more stratified world society, with greater economic disparities between the haves and have-nots. Some critics fear that globalization is eliminating the uniqueness of local cultures and creating consumer-generated conformity, uniformity, and sameness—a kind of worldwide strip mall.[17]

Market-driven globalization has caused significant economic changes in both TDCs and LTDCs. In the older, industrial nations, such as the U.S. and the UK, heavy industries such as iron, steel, and coal have downsized dramatically, resulting in unemployment in these older industrial sectors. Steel production, for example, has shifted to other countries, such as South Korea, where it is produced at a lower cost. The defenders of market-driven globalization argue that this kind of unemployment is temporary; workers in the older industries can be retrained for different kinds of jobs in the postindustrial high-tech information age. Many opponents to globalization, especially in the U.S., argue that high-paying jobs, with health-care and pension benefits, are being outsourced by corporations to other countries that do not meet safety standards for working conditions, nor do they enforce environmental protection requirements.

In some LTDCs, especially in South America and Africa, agribusinesses, in which multinational corporations own most of the land, engage in the large-scale production of a single crop, such as sugar, pineapples, palm oil, or bananas. This has caused a change in land occupancy as the large agribusinesses gain control of vast acreages. Often, local farmers, with small tracts of land, are displaced to make way for the large agricultural units. Advocates of market-driven globalization argue that such single-crop, large-scale agriculture is more efficient, produces more food at less cost, and employs local people. Critics argue that the dispossessed farmers become an impoverished, landless, lower class, who struggle as rural poor or migrants in urban slums.

Globalization's Impact on the Nation-State

Participation in a global community means that nation-states must shift their political, economic, and social focus from within to the multidimensional, dynamic, and often unknown regions of the world. Globalization requires nation-states to be open to greater international understanding and cooperation. Globalization offers nation-states new opportunities, such as the economic benefits of foreign investments. These opportunities, however, require nation-states to make changes and experience the strains and tensions that accompany changes. In the next sections, we first will look at establishing an environment that attracts global opportunities and the controversial impact of globalization on nation-states. We then explore democracy as a model that fosters success in the global arena and how schools can participate in achieving that success.

Nation-states range from technologically developed to less-technologically developed nations and from democracies with representative institutions and political processes to repressive authoritarian regimes. How a nation-state is organized will have an effect on its success and presence in the global community. Increasing global economic competition requires nation-states to focus on policies that attract investment, create new industries, and develop markets for their products. A well-organized, efficient institutional structure that is capable of regulating and implementing coherent economic and social policies is much more likely to attract capital investment and skilled managers and workers than those that are inefficient or mired in bureaucracy and political instability.[18] For example, nation-states that: maintain civil order; have few incidents of violence; offer tax breaks and other investment incentives; charge reasonable tariffs and duties; and have laws that protect foreign investment from seizure, expropriation, labor conflicts, or nationalization have created a climate that attracts foreign investors. This climate also makes it easier for nation-states to negotiate for their own investments abroad.[19]

The formula for creating an environment conducive to attracting foreign investors and industries is not always easy to implement, especially in nation-states whose political processes historically have been operating in isolation from the world or are unstable. In many nation-states, contesting political forces are likely to disagree about the types of social and educational policies and the economic concessions needed to attract investment. Some political parties, often with mass support, may oppose economic concessions and/or reductions in social services to attract foreign investors. In LTDCs indigenous elites may oppose globalization, seeing it as bringing in new foreign elites that threaten their favored position.

Globalization introduces new variables into the political context, often creating new economic class divisions or exacerbating existing ones. It may increase economic disparities between groups and generate new social divisions, movements, and conflicts in the nation-state. There is likely to be class-based political realignments or conflicts. For example, the control of the economy may generate conflicts between old and new elites for political power. If there is a market dominant ethnic group, such as the Chinese minority in Southeast Asia, it may cause ethnic tensions that spill over into the political arena.

Structural Adjustment Policies

Many of globalization's economic consequences, especially as they impact the LTDCs, are closely related to the structural adjustment policies of the World Bank and other international lending organizations. Structural adjustment refers to changes that international financial organizations require in the governmental institutions and agencies of debtor nation-states as a condition for loans. The structural adjustment rationale rests largely on the free market capitalist model's basic assumptions that economic competition produces greater efficiency and productivity and that government interference that impedes the operations of the free market results in a costly bureaucracies and inefficiency that saps productivity. Nation-states seeking to borrow funds from the World Bank and other international lending agencies generally must meet the following requirements: (1) streamline government bureaucracies and civil service components; (2) reduce government expenditures for subsidized housing, food, and social services; (3) liberalize trade policies by reducing or eliminating protective tariffs; (4) devalue currency when necessary; (5) reduce or eliminate government price controls and subsidies for products produced in the country; (6) shift production toward export goods for sale on the world market; (7) privatize health, social welfare, and some education programs; and (8) place state-owned industries in private ownership.[20]

Although the nation-state remains the paramount agency in governing and providing education, structural adjustment policies have caused reductions in funding social services related to education. As governments reduce educational subsidies, certain expenses, such as those for textbooks, supplemental materials, and activities, are passed on to students and their families. These user fees, which fall heaviest on the poor in urban slum and rural areas, may cause lower-income students to leave school for financial reasons.

In many countries, school administrators and teachers are part of the national administrative structure and may be civil servants. Although structural adjustment may not have a direct effect on the number of teachers and the essential conditions of teaching, it alters the role and function of national educational bureaucracies. Structural adjustment advocates view large government bureaucracies as having vested interest in maintaining the status quo and perceive them as fostering "red tape," resistance to change, and inefficiency. Rather than maintaining centralized national agencies to control education, structural adjustment policies encourage greater devolution of authority to local levels.

Globalization and Democracy

The dominant model of globalization combines free market capitalism with democratization, the establishment of representative institutions of government, and a media free of official censorship and control. After the disintegration of the Soviet system with its one-party rule by the Communist Party, democratization became an important theme in Russia, in the other newly independent former Soviet states, and in the satellite countries in Central and Eastern Europe. The extent to which democratic institutions have been established in the former Soviet region differs from country to country. Poland, Hungary, the Czech Republic, Lithuania, Latvia, and Estonia have had success in reestablishing democratic institutions. Russia's movement to establish democratic institutions has tended to move forward but with significant retrograde lapses. In 2004, President Putin announced plans to recentralize provincial governments under Kremlin control, a move that may limit democratization processes in Russia. Establishment of democratic institutions in the former Yugoslavia has suffered reverses due to ethnic conflicts in some of its former constituent republics, especially Bosnia and Kosovo (see chapter 7).

An important corollary growing out of the democratization assumption is that education can be an agency that furthers the establishment of democratic institutions and processes. The validity of the assumption, however, rests to a large extent on the national context in which educational institutions function. If the political climate and institutional structure of the nation-state is favorable to representative institutions as in the Czech Republic and Poland, globalization is likely to aid democratization. In such situations, the school governance, curricula, and instruction will be organized to promote knowledge, skills, and values that support and encourage representative institutions.

In contrast if the political climate and institutional structure is hostile to representative institutions as in Saudi Arabia, North Korea, or Iran, globalization is unlikely to enhance the development of democratic institutions. Current U.S. policy assumes that democratic institutions can be created in Afghanistan and Iraq, both of which are countries with a long history of authoritarianism.

An important question is—will globalization processes contribute to representative institutions in nation-states that have an increasingly mixed economy such as in the PRC, where there is both state ownership and a growing private sector? Despite globalization, the PRC remains a single-party nation ruled by the Chinese Communist Party. Then, there are nation-states where there is serious political instability as in Nigeria. Will globalization promote democracy in countries with marked political instability as in Nigeria and other African nations? It is necessary to contextualize globalization as a transnational process within the nation-state to determine its political and its educational ramifications. The political context—the existing political structures and climate—acts as a filter through which the process of globalization must flow.

The role that schools play in the democratization process depends on how the particular nation-state functions. If the country's political structures and climate, especially its history, are favorable to democratic institutions and processes, the schools, as part of the institutional structure, are likely to feature democratic governance; if, on, the contrary, such structures are absent or underdeveloped in the country's political and governance structure, they will be absent or underdeveloped in the school system.

Educational Implications of Globalization

Globalization, especially via high-tech communication systems, has affected the origin and flow of information between peoples that takes place outside of schools and agencies of organized education. News coverage, entertainment such as motion pictures and music, and athletic events such as the Olympic Games are carried to a worldwide audience through television. The growing use of personal computers makes it possible for people to communicate with each other via e-mail, and the World Wide Web is a source of instantaneous information. This flow of information affects how people construct their images and concepts of reality and of each other. It is a highly important kind of informal education. Globalization has important implications for formal education as well; we explore these implications in the following sections.

Globalization's Impact on Educational Content and Processes

In terms of curriculum and instruction, there is a need to provide knowledge about globalization as a process and analysis of how it affects people in a multidimensional way. As indicated earlier in the chapter, globalization has an obvious impact on the economy but also on society, politics, and culture.

As Epstein observes in his analysis of globalization, schools should: (1) prepare people to participate in their economy and politics; (2) provide the knowledge needed to make responsible judgments; (3) motivate them to contribute to their society's well-being; and (4) develop a consciousness about their behavior.[21] Education for globalization is both conceptual and applied. It involves infusing knowledge about the meaning, processes, and implications of globalization for society and the economy into the curriculum. It involves training in the technological skills needed for competency in a global society. Curriculum needs to impart conceptual knowledge about globalization, its meaning, and its impact as a worldwide phenomenon. It also needs to provide interdisciplinary and transdisciplinary analyses in the social sciences and humanities about globalization's impact.

In addition to constructing a conceptual understanding of globalization, students need to develop competency in using globalization's tools, particularly in the rapid acquisition of information via computers, the Internet, and World Wide Web. They also need to learn how to authenticate and interpret this generally unreferenced and unrefereed information.

Globalization's Impact on Educational Systems

As indicated in earlier sections of the chapter, globalization has had an impact on the administration, organization, and funding of educational systems throughout the world. For example, structural adjustment policies in LTDCs alter educational priorities and reduce the social service aspects of educational funding. International financial agencies put pressure on government in LTDCs to reduce the growth of public spending on education and to find other sources to fund the expansion of their educational system. It is important to note that globalization has generated conflicting demands in LTDCs—to reduce expenditures but also to expand the system to meet rising educational expectations, especially in the new middle-class sectors. (For example, see the chapters on Mexico and India.)

Globalization is a force that causes the setting of new educational priorities and the restructuring of the curriculum. It calls for training an industrially skilled labor force in countries that were hitherto primarily agricultural and in developing managerial and technological skills in the middle occupational rungs. This means that priorities shift to training programs and to a restructuring of secondary and higher education to technology programs. In many LTDCs, secondary and higher education historically emphasized the arts and humanities as the appropriate education for the governing elite. As globalization proceeds, this emphasis will be shifted to science, technology, and more applied professional and vocational programs.

Some advocates of globalization, especially those who identify with its private market-driven orientation, contend that administrators and teachers need to be made accountable for students' academic performance. They argue that students' performance can be measured by using standardized achievement tests. This assumption has accentuated the use of standardized testing to measure students' academic progress and the use of statistical analysis to interpret that progress in effectiveness studies that compare and rank results in different countries.

Alternative Educational Directions of Globalization

In a highly instructive article on globalization, Roger Dale analyzes two approaches for examining globalization and its implications for education: the Common World Educational Culture (CWEC) and the Globally Structured Agenda for Education (GSAF).[22] CWEC assumes that the international community consists of nation-state systems, composed of individual sovereign countries. It argues that the nation-state system, based on its European origins and thrust to modernization, is a universal structure in which the individual actors, the nation-states, conform to general world patterns. GSAF, in contrast, argues that social and economic forces are "operating supranationally and transnationally, rather than internationally," and are working to break down nation-state boundaries and are reconstructing "relations between nations."[23]

Dale's discussion of globalization reiterates the point made in earlier chapters in this book about two realities in tension when considering international education: the nation-state and an emerging global society. An important point in this consideration is that the nation-state is an existent and historically defined entity. The emergent global society and economy is fluid and ill defined and subject to various ramifications. Though noting the differences between the CWEC and GSAF models, Dale finds that both approaches agree: (1) on the importance of supranational forces; (2) that nation-state educational policies can be externally influenced; and (3) that policy-making in nation-states is shaped by both national and supranational forces.[24]

Dale then turns to fundamental differences between the CWEC and GSAF models. The most fundamental difference, he says, is how the two approaches interpret the nature of the supranational level. For CWEC, the interpretation of globalization is based on the Western cultural experience. For GSAF, globalization is driven by the need to maintain the capitalism.[25] Dale claims that while the CWEC model considers education to be a resource that is mandated by a nation-state in a prescribed curriculum, the GSAF model construes it as a topic. When seen as a topic, the crucial question becomes "Who gets taught what, how, by whom, and under what conditions and circumstances?"[26] The answer to this question will reveal how educational institutions and structures are organized, governed, and used.

Conclusion

Today, some interpreters of globalization seem to be repeating the same mistake made by the earlier advocates of modernization. They seem to be minimizing the reality that a process always occurs in a context—somewhere, at some time, and in some place. Processes, such as modernization and globalization, are conditioned and often reshaped by the context in which they are placed. In turn, the processes work to restructure the context. It is important to recognize that there is an interaction between the context, the nation-state's culture and society, and the process of globalization. Educators, sensitive to this interaction, can design curricula that prepare students to be aware of and to reflect on the global dynamics occurring in their local communities as well as in the broader nation-state and world societies.

DISCUSSION QUESTIONS

1. Examine the various definitions of globalization; then construct your own definition.
2. Compare and contrast modernization and globalization.
3. Do you believe that globalization's effects have improved or reduced the quality of life for most people? Defend your answer.
4. Why has globalization generated controversy?
5. Do you agree or disagree with the statement: Globalization is necessarily related to free market capitalism and democratic political institutions.
6. How has globalization affected your local community in terms of employment opportunities?
7. How has globalization affected the products that are sold in your community?
8. Discuss globalization's impact on nation-states and their educational systems.

FIELD AND RESEARCH TOPICS

1. Consider the impact of e-mail and the Internet on how you communicate and acquire information. How often have your contacts been international or global?
2. Do a survey of businesses in your community. Identify which of them are international corporations.
3. Examine some of the items in your possession such as clothing and other items. Determine which of them have been produced in another country.
4. Research the most highly enrolled programs at your college or university. Try to analyze these programs in terms of their relationships to globalization.
5. Examine your college or university catalogue. Identify the courses that are related to globalization.
6. Identify specific ways in which globalization has had an impact on your family, friends, and yourself.
7. Conduct a survey in class that examines the students' opinions on free trade and the outsourcing of jobs to other countries.

SUGGESTIONS FOR FURTHER READING

Bhagwati, Jagdish. *In Defense of Globalization.* New York: Oxford University Press, 2004.

Burbules, Nicholas C., and Torres, Carlos A., eds. *Globalization and Education: Critical Perspectives.* New York: Routledge, 2000.

Clarke, Ian. *Globalization and Fragmentation: International Relations in the Twentieth Century.* Oxford: Oxford University Press, 1997.

Cox, Robert W. *Approaches to World Order.* Cambridge: Cambridge University Press, 1996.

Daun, Holger. *Educational Restructuring in the Context of Globalization and National Policy.* New York: Garland, 2001.

Epstein, Erwin, "Globalization of Education," in James W. Guthrie, ed., *Encyclopedia of Education III*, 2nd ed. New York: Thomson Gale, Macmillan, 2003.

Hall, I. Stuart, David Held, and Tony McGrew. *Modernity and Its Futures.* Cambridge: Polity Press/The Open University, 1992.

Hoogvelt, Ankie. *Globalization and the Post-colonial World: The New Political Economy of Development.* Basingstoke, UK: Macmillan, 1997.

Irwin, Douglas A. *Free Trade Under Fire.* Princeton, NJ: Princeton University Press, 2002.

Lingard, Bob, and Fazal Rizvi, eds. "A Symposium on Globalization and Education," *Educational Theory,* Vol. 50, No. 4 (Fall 2000) Urbana: University of Illinois, 2000.

Mansfield, Edward O., and Helen V. Milner, *The Political Economy of Regionalism.* New York: Columbia University Press, 1997.

Popkewitz, Thomas S., ed. *Educational Knowledge: Changing Relationships between the State, Civil Society and the Educational Community.* Albany: State University of New York Press, 2000.

Samoff, Joel. *Coping with Crisis: Austerity, Adjustment, and Human Resources.* London: Cassell, 1994.

Sen, Amartya. *Development as Freedom.* New York: Knopf, 1999.

Shiller, Robert. *The New Financial Order.* Princeton, NJ: Princeton University Press, 2003.

Schriewer, Juergen, ed. *Discourse and Comparative Education.* Bern: Peter Lang, 1999.

Stiglitz, Joseph. *Globalization and Its Discontents.* New York: W.W. Norton, 2002.

Wolf, Martin. *Why Globalization Works.* New Haven, CT: Yale University Press, 2004.

NOTES

[1] John Hinkson, "Globalization: Political Economy and Beyond," *Arena Journal* 12 (1998): 67–81.

[2] Peter J. Dougherty, "The Wealth of Nations: A Publisher Considers the Literature of Globalization," *The Chronicle of Higher Education* (July 16, 2004), B6.

[3] Erwin Epstein, "Globalization of Education," in *Encyclopedia of Education*, 2nd ed., vol. 3, ed. James W. Guthrie (New York: Macmillan Thomson Gale, 2003), 936. Epstein's reference is to Roland Robertson's article, "Globalization Theory and Civilizational Analysis" in the *Comparative Civilizations Review* in 1987.

[4] Stuart Hall, David Held, and Tony McGrew, *Modernity and its Futures* (Cambridge: Polity Press/The Open University, 1992), 66–67.

[5] Epstein, 937.

[6] Hall, Held, McGrew, 66–67.

[7] Roger Dale, "Globalization and Education: Demonstrating a Common World Educational Culture or Locating a 'Globally Structured Educational Agenda'?" *Educational Theory* 50(4) (2000): 436.

[8] Nelly P. Stromquist, "Preface," *Comparative Education Review* 46(1) (2002): iii.

[9] Paige Porter and Lesley Vidovich, "Globalization and Higher Education Policy," *Educational Theory* 50(4) (2000): 460.

[10] Joseph Grieco, "Sources of Variation in Regional Institutionalization in Western Europe, East Asia, and the Americas," in *The Political Economy of Regionalism*, ed. Edward O. Mansfield and Helen V. Milner (New York: Columbia University Press, 1997), 167–187.

[11] Roger Dale and Susan L. Robertson, "The Varying Effects of Regional Organizations as Subjects of Globalization of Education," *Comparative Education Review* 46(1) (2002): 15.

[12] Dale, 435.

[13] Dale and Robertson, 436.

[14] Ibid., 20–23.

[15] Ibid., 29.

[16] Ibid., 29–32.

[17] Fazal Rizi and Bob Lingard, "Globalization and Education: Complexities and Contingencies," *Educational Theory* 50(4) (2000): 419–420.

[18] Martin Carnoy and Diana Rhoten, "What Does Globalization Mean for Educational Change? A Comparative Approach," *Comparative Education Review* 46(1) (2002): 5.

[19] Ibid., 3.

[20] Epstein, 937.

[21] Ibid., 938.

[22] Dale, 427–448.

[23] Ibid., 428.

[24] Ibid., 435.

[25] Ibid., 436.

[26] Ibid., 438.

7

NATIONALISM, AMERICAN EXCEPTIONALISM, AND ETHNONATIONALISM
IMPLICATIONS FOR EDUCATION

Throughout modern history, nationalism has been a highly significant ideology in constructing the primary identification and the mobilization of the members of nation-states. Significant in engendering national identity and "we-feeling" in the young are nation-states' school systems. In the U.S., nationalism takes the form of American exceptionalism, the belief that Americans are an exceptional, special people who live in an exceptional land. Since the beginning of history, ethnicity and race have had a profound effect in shaping cultural identity, character, and behavior. Ethnicity and race can either enhance a nation-state's identity or weaken and fragment it. In the late twentieth and the twenty-first centuries, ethnonationalism, based on ethnicity or race, resurfaced as a strong and often untamed force on the world scene. This chapter discusses the implications of nationalism, American exceptionalism, and ethnonationalism for international education.

Nationalism

Although there are several definitions of the term *nation*, the most often used meaning designates a nation as a group of people, citizens, who live within its political boundaries and participate in its cultural, political, religious, and educational institutions. Derived from the core word "nation," *nationalism* is the sense of belonging to and sharing common membership in a particular nation-state. *Nationality* further identifies persons legally with a nation-state and designates them as being born in the country or naturalized in it as citizens.

Nationalism and the Nation-State

The modern relationship between nation-states and nationalism began in the late eighteenth and early nineteenth centuries. Key events that stimulated nationalism's rise were the American Revolution in 1776 and the French Revolution in 1789. An important ideological premise of the American rebels against British colonial rule was their emerging sense that they were no longer English men and women living apart from the mother country but had become a unique and distinct people.

In the nineteenth century, the idea of the country as a nation-state rather than a realm of a dynastic monarch took hold in Europe. A popular revolution against the monarchy and aristocracy, the French Revolution stimulated nationalism as it proclaimed that the French people rather than the Bourbon monarchy constituted France. Later, Napoleon's efforts to conquer Europe and remake it into a system of French satellite states generated a counternationalist tide among the British, the Russians, the Spanish, the Germans, and other groups.

Throughout the nineteenth century, nationalist rivalries drove the major European powers to colonize Africa and parts of Asia. European imperialists exported the idea of the nation-state model of political organization to South America, Asia, and Africa. When Spain's Central and South American colonies revolted and became independent sovereign states, they adopted the nation-state model of organization. When British, French, Dutch, and Portuguese colonies gained independence in the twentieth century, they, too, adopted the nation-state model.

Nation-States and Schools

Nation-states create institutional structures—governments, parliaments, and other legislative bodies, law courts, police and armed forces, and school systems—to maintain national security and interests. Important institutions in the nation-state's infrastructure are the schools that comprise the educational systems used to educate children and young people. Schools are used to socialize the young in the political ideology and processes that maintain the nation-state and reproduce it for future generations.

In the nineteenth century, nation-states began to establish national school systems. In the United Kingdom, Parliament gave financial grants to voluntary school societies in the 1830s to promote primary education. France, under the leadership of François Guizot, established national primary schools. Although not establishing a national or federal system of education, the individual states of the U.S. established locally controlled common, or public, school systems. In some countries, the national schools either cooperated with or replaced the existing religious schools. In nation-states such as France and Mexico, there were strong and prolonged conflicts between state and religious authorities for control of the schools. In the twentieth century, as new nation-states emerged after winning independence from colonial powers they, too, established national school systems. National, state-operated schools became key agencies in constructing a sense of national identity and in bringing about political socialization that instills patriotic and civic values in the young.

The close relationship between nation-states and a national system of education raises some serious implications for international education. For comparative educators, the national school system of each nation-state provides a large but definable unit of education for purposes of comparison and contrast. For example, it is possible to describe, compare, and contrast schools in the UK, Russia, Mexico, the U.S., and other nation-states (as is done in part II of this book). It is also possible to focus on a particular element or characteristic within these national systems, such as primary schools, vocational education, expenditures, or the role and compensation of teachers, for comparative purposes. In the broad view of international education, there is the question of the degree to which national systems of education tend to create an inward-looking perspective, often based on a narrowly defined identity, or a more globally centered perspective. For much of the nineteenth and twentieth centuries, national school systems tended to foster patriotism in the young that glorified their own country over all others.

Constructing a National Identity

As an ideological force, nationalism is typically identified with the nation-state, where it is used to construct a sense of primary identification with the nation. It means learning how to be and feel French, English, Italian, Chinese, or American, for example. This political-cultural identity is generated by the experience of living in a national political space, marked by boundaries and frontiers that separate it from other spaces, and by participation as a citizen in the nation's affairs. The chords of national identity are constructed in the young by the common experience of shared origins, language, beliefs, and values. An issue that the emphasis on a common primary national identification raises for international education is: Is this identification so basic that it limits other kinds of identification, or can it be broadened to include multiple identifications?

A person's national identity is often shaped by hearing and speaking the same language; by learning to respect the same national symbols; by celebrating commemorative events that generate a feeling of patriotism; by being members of the same religion; and by being acculturated in the same culture. A reflection on one's own school experiences easily demonstrates how these elements—being taught language arts, pledging allegiance to the flag, and studying literature, art, music, architecture, and dance—can construct a feeling of nationalism. The role of religion, especially in the American experience, needs a special interpretation. Before exploring this important topic, we will first address language and patriotic symbols and events.

Language

The words that a child first hears and learns to speak and read mark the beginning of forming group identity. Hearing and speaking a language means not only acquiring the ability to interpret the group's symbols and expressions, it is also the way in which the group's values are conveyed to and internalized by a child. A common language unites people by providing a way to construct shared meanings and understandings—ideas, beliefs, and values—about themselves as group and about their relationships to others who, not speaking the same language, are different from them. Language helps individuals create a sense of identity—of who I am, where I am, and how I relate to others.

For these reasons, the language issue in education is a vital and highly contested one. If one language is spoken in a nation-state, such as in Japan, then the construction of national identity proceeds more directly and more easily than it does in a nation-state that has multiple languages, such as in Nigeria, Canada, Belgium, or India. In these countries, there are intense debates and often political party divisions based on the question of which language will be the official or dominant one. Consider how carefully the French government and its ministry of education seek to preserve the integrity of the French language by blocking foreign words and phrases from entering it. As the countries of the world become more multicultural and multilingual, language issues also become more complex. Should the schools conduct instruction is one language or in two or more languages? For example, consider the controversies related to bilingual and bicultural education in the U.S. to accommodate the influx of Spanish-speaking students. Should classes be conducted in English or Spanish? Should textbooks be rewritten to consider a Hispanic perspective?

School curricula throughout the world give priority in time and resources to teaching language. In the primary or elementary schools, reading instruction as a central activity commands much time and resources. A child's academic access to and success in the secondary and higher levels of education are often determined by how well she or he masters the language. If there is an official or dominant national language, as there is in most countries, mastery of this language is the key to passing school examinations, especially university entry examinations, which are set by national educational authorities. Furthermore, language is not only related to education, it is a determinant of future work, employment, and economic success.

Patriotic Symbols and Events

A sense of primary national identity is constructed in the young by teaching them to respect national symbols, such as a nation's flag and anthem, and by their participation in patriotic celebrations and times of remembrance through songs, stories, and observances. In the U.S., such common celebratory occasions of remembrance are Thanksgiving and Independence Day commemorated by parades, speeches, and fireworks. In France, citizens fly the tricolor flag, sing the "Marseillaise," and participate in parades on Bastille Day, July 14th, to invoke memories of the past. In schools, these days of national celebration or remembrance are part of the process of political socialization and constructing personal identification with the nation-state. While patriotic symbols and events can be positive sources of identity, they can also engender animosity and rivalry between groups. For example, commemoration of the Battle of the Boyne, in which the Protestant army defeated the Catholic forces in Ireland, still generates sectarian divisions in Northern Ireland.

Religion

Still another element that has been historically powerful in constructing national identity in many countries is a common religion, often an "official church." In Greece, Russia, Serbia, Bulgaria, and Romania, the Orthodox Church provides not only religious cohesion but also a sense of cultural homogeneity. In Italy, Poland, Ireland, Portugal, and Spain, Roman Catholicism provides a religious and cultural sense of belonging. In Israel, Judaism is the religious and cultural link. In Egypt, Pakistan, Malaysia, Afghanistan, Iraq, and Iran, Islam is deeply embedded in the culture. In Thailand, Buddhism is embedded in the culture. From a historical perspective, the origin of schooling can be traced to temples, churches, mosques, and synagogue. In all countries, churches and religious institutions still are powerful informal educational forces. In many countries, the teaching of religion, especially that of the dominant church, takes place in state-operated schools. While it is still is a powerful force in constructing national identity in many countries, the role of religion, like language, needs careful interpretation.

In the Western countries, especially those in Europe, the influence of religion has diminished and has been separated from government. For example, in 2004, the French government reasserted its secular orientation by banning the wearing of religious symbols by students in state schools. Like other countries in Western Europe, France is growing increasingly multicultural and has a growing Islamic population. The French government's ban on the wearing of religious symbols generated a protest from Muslim girls and women who traditionally wear head scarves as a religious practice.

In the U.S., where church and state are separated constitutionally, the government does not sponsor or sanction religion; neither does it interfere with the free exercise of religion. Religiously as well as culturally pluralistic, the U.S. is home to a variety of Protestant denominations as well as to Roman Catholics, Orthodox Christians, Jews, Muslims, and other religious denominations. However, there is a sharp division in the U.S. between those who argue that the U.S. is a Christian country and those who see it as a secular nation. The issue manifests itself over such matters as prayer in the public schools, teaching creationism or evolution in the science curriculum, and the presence of denominational clubs as extra curricular organizations.

Cultural Artifacts

Nationalism is portrayed though the artifacts of the culture; it is expressed in the art, history, literature, poetry, drama, music, and architecture that exemplify a national ethos. As far back as the ancient Greeks, cultural symbols and artifacts were used to instruct the young Greeks about their history and culture. Powerfully blending history with myth, Homer's epic poems, the *Iliad* and the *Odyssey*, gave young Greeks a profound sense of what it meant to be a hero struggling against the Trojan adversary. The Parthenon, the temple on the Acropolis in Athens, was an ever-present monument that identified Athenians with their religion and culture.

In the U.S., the novels of James Fennimore Cooper, Henry James, Edith Wharton, Ernest Hemingway, and F. Scott Fitzgerald and the essays of Ralph Waldo Emerson, Henry David Thoreau, Herman Melville, and Mark Twain crafted a distinctive American literary style. The poetry of Emily Dickinson and Robert Frost captures the American mood in verse. The architecture of Louis Sullivan and Frank Lloyd Wright expresses American architectural design. The White House, the Washington Monument, the Statue of Liberty, Mount Rushmore, the Lincoln Memorial, and the Sears Tower evoke an American consciousness. "Yankee Doodle," "Dixie," the "Battle Hymn of the Republic," "This Land is My Land," and "God Bless America" stir American pride through song.

For Germans, the literary masterpieces of Johann Wolfgang von Goethe and Friedrich Schiller and the music of Beethoven and Wagner evoke the sense of being a German. Wagner, a renowned composer who wrote some of the world's greatest operas, was also a strident nationalist. In France, nationalist themes were conveyed by Alexander Dumas and Victor Hugo, especially the latter's literary masterpiece, *Les Misérables*. The epic murals in the Louvre and the Chamber of Deputies portray events in French history. The stirring strains of the "Marseillaise" and vistas of the Eiffel Tower and the Arc de Triomphe call to mind France. For Italians, Giuseppe Verdi's dramatic operas portray Italia. Frederic Chopin's stirring *Polonaise* inspired Polish patriots to rally for their country's freedom. In China, the Great Wall, the Forbidden City, Tiananmen Square, and Mao's tomb tell the story of the country's cultural heritage. In India, the Red Fort, the statue of Gandhi in Bombay, and the Taj Mahal are physical symbols of the Indian past.

Works of artistic, literary, musical, and architectural referents illuminate a common national culture. In the school curriculum, these cultural artifacts are used as points of contact between the young and their nation's heritage. Courses in literature, music, art, and drama as well as field trips to museums and historic sites are used to introduce the young to their national monuments.

Nationalism and International Education

So far, nationalism has been discussed as a feeling of primary identification. Scholars have attempted to analyze the more intellectual meanings of that sense of we-feeling. The pioneering studies of nationalism were done by Hans Kohn in political science and J. H. Carlton Hayes in history. Using a broad comparativist approach in analyzing nationalism, Kohn wrote:

> A study of nationalism must follow a comparative method; it cannot remain confined to one of its manifestations; only the comparison of the different nationalisms all over the earth will enable the student to see

what they have in common and what is peculiar to each, and thus allow a
just evaluation.[1]

Kohn's admonition is useful in studying comparative educational systems.

In international education, the early studies of the impact of nationalism
on education were done by Isaac Kandel and Edward Reisner who focused
their analyses on the contexts of particular nation-states such as France, Germany, Italy, and Russia. Kandel and Reisner examined nationalism as a force
used to construct an individual's identity with the nation-state and in mobilizing the people of these nation-states for politically based agendas such as
defense, war, imperialism, and modernization. Nationalism, often identified
with modernization, was seen as an ideological force that eroded residues of
feudalism, localism, and provincialism. Kandel, Reisner, and other scholars
concluded that: (1) nationalism was a powerful emotional force for constructing individual primary identification with and social cohesion for the nation-
state; (2) modern national school systems were used as agencies for deliberately cultivating national identity and consensus; and (3) the modern curriculum, dating from the early nineteenth century, too, was a medium for
instilling national sentiments, loyalties, and values. Kandel and Reisner's pioneering studies were useful in establishing definitions of nationalism, in
assessing its power in mobilizing nation-state energies, in examining its educational uses, and in identifying nonrational elements embedded in the concept.

A theoretical tension, also reflected in this book, developed in educational theory about nationalism's nature and impact. While nationalism was
seen as necessary to the modern nation-state and in schooling for the nation-
state, extreme nationalism, especially when chauvinistic, was condemned as
generating conflicts between nations that led to war and as a menace to world
peace and security. The educational problem then became how to use nationalism as a constructive force in building nations while circumscribing those
conflict-generating elements that threatened world peace and security. This
tension between nationalism's constructive and destructive potentialities
remains an important unresolved issue in international education.

Exceptionalism as an Expression of American Nationalism

In the American experience, the idea that the U.S. is a "shining city on a
hill," "a beacon to the world," a special country blessed by Providence, and a
country with a Manifest Destiny all express nationalism. Underlying American nationalism is the pervading ideology of American exceptionalism, the
belief that the U.S. is an extraordinary, unique land and that its uniqueness
makes it better than other countries.

The young French intellectual, Alexis de Tocqueville, who in 1831 and
1832 conducted what might be called ethnographic research, traveled
throughout what was then the U.S. In many ways, he was an early comparativist who was skilled in developing insights about countries and peoples other

than his own. De Tocqueville was a sensitive and penetrating observer of American society, institutions, and behavior. When he returned to France, he wrote about his insights into the American character in a comparative way that analyzed the similarities and differences between Americans and Europeans. He caught a glimpse of American exceptionalism when he noted Americans "have an immensely high opinion of themselves and are not far from believing that they form a species apart from the rest of the human race."[2]

As the U.S. frontier moved westward and Americans settled the vast expanse of land between the Atlantic and the Pacific in the nineteenth century, many Americans believed it was their Manifest Destiny to occupy the entire North American continent. Manifest Destiny proclaimed that divine providence, in bestowing a vast continent with immense expanses of land and abundant natural resources on Americans, had favored them above all other peoples. Protected from hostile and less-deserving nations by the great Atlantic and Pacific ocean barriers, God had given Americans a secure environment in which to establish their unique form of government—a democratic republic. As a special people, a people set apart, the U.S. was to be a beacon light of freedom to people living in the darkness of subjugation. It had the great moral mission of being the democratic exemplar for other less-fortunate people. Although the words "Manifest Destiny" are not spoken today, they still have a subconscious influence on many Americans, even U.S. policy makers. They influence the assumption that the American system of government can be exported to and implemented in other countries. They influence the belief that other countries have much to learn from Americans, who after all are an exceptional people, living in an exceptional land.

American exceptionalism influenced beliefs and attitudes about education. American public schools were to be agencies for constructing a sense of identification with and loyalty to the U.S. While this function was not exclusive to American schools, the assumption was that public schools, like the country they served, were unique institutions established to educate the sons and daughters of an exceptional people. The public schools, originally called common schools, differed from European schools established for the different socioeconomic classes. Unlike Europe's schools, American public schools, open to all the children of all the people, were the country's great social equalizers. While Europe's schools reproduced and perpetuated the class-based socioeconomic status quo, American public schools generated upward social and economic mobility.

American exceptionalism has influenced how Americans view international education. It contributed to a general self-assurance and confidence that American schools were superior to those in other countries. This self-assurance caused American educators to be inward looking and disinterested in educational ideas and schools in other nations. It assumed that Americans have much to teach people in other countries but little to learn from them. Educators in other countries could improve their schools by borrowing American ideas about curriculum and instruction. Many of the strategies of development education and of modernization rested on the premise that American know-how could be transported abroad and lead other countries on the path to becoming more productive and efficient—just like America.

Ethnonationalism

We now turn to ethnonationalism, an important contemporary ideology that is producing unrest and change in the relationships between people, especially in multiethnic nation-states. While nationalism emphasizes identification with the nation-state, *ethnonationalism* focuses on constructing primary identification with the racial, ethnic, or tribal group. In nation-states where the national population belongs to the same racial or ethnic group, as in Japan, nationalism and ethnonationalism coincide and reinforce each other. In situations where the nation-state's population is multiethnic or multiracial, as in Nigeria, ethnonationalism tends to weaken identification with the nation-state by focusing it on a particular group.

Ethnonationalism rests on the belief, often embodied in a powerful myth, that an individual is a member of a unique group because of descent from a common ancestor and a blood relationship shared with others descended from this common ancestor as is the case of Serbs, Croats, Québécois, Ibos, or Basques.[3] The belief in common ancestry is not based on genetic verification but is mythic and emotional. Myth, as used here, refers to a highly powerful sense of meaning that may be partially historical or pseudohistorical but nonetheless is the reference point for belief in a common ancestral identity. Highly emotional, the mythic element in ethnonationalism creates self-identification in the ethnic group. For ethnonationalist identity, the anthropologically or sociologically correct description of ethnic group membership is not important; most important are the group's beliefs about itself. Various ethnonational groups often merge myth and history creating powerful stories about their origins, history, triumphs, and adversities. The transmission of the group's language and heritage from the older generation to the younger one takes place through informal as well as formal education. In situations where the particular ethnic group is suppressed by another dominant group, its ethnic heritage may be passed on informally or even secretly.

Ethnonationalism and the Nation-State

There are examples of ethnonationalism all over the world. The closing decade of the twentieth century witnessed the revival of ethnonationalism with the resulting disintegration of some multiethnic nation-states. Since the end of the cold war, the unifying ideology that shaped political and educational structures and goals in the Soviet Union and its satellite Communist regimes in Eastern and Central Europe has weakened. After the disintegration of the USSR independent nation-states, such as Russia, Ukraine, Byelorussia,

Uzbekistan, Armenia, and so forth, established their own political structures. Czechoslovakia peacefully divided into two independent nation-states: the Czech Republic and Slovakia. The disintegration of Yugoslavia was marked by ethnic cleansing and violence as Croatia, Slovenia, Macedonia, and Bosnia overcame Serbian opposition to become independent nation-states. In Africa, ethnonationalism takes the form of tribalism. In countries such as Nigeria, Burundi, Rwanda, and others, the primary identification is with the tribe rather than the nation-state. In Nigeria, for example, the political and educational situation has been tortured by attempts of Yorubas, Hausas, and Ibos to gain hegemony over each other. In the Western world, ethnonationalism has asserted itself in political and educational conflicts in Canada where the French-speaking population energetically seeks to guard its language and culture against Anglicization; in Belgium, where the Flemish resist Walloons; and in Spain, where the Basques seek greater autonomy.

Nationalism, resting in the nation-state or country, and ethnonationalism, resting in the ethnic group, pose a contemporary world dilemma. Multiethnic nations, such as the UK, France, China, and the U.S., have the right to maintain their integrity and security. Ethnic groups have the right to maintain their ethnic cultures, languages, and traditions. In some instances, these two rights have erupted in violent confrontation and conflict. Some subordinated ethnic groups, such as the Kurds who live in Iraq, Iran, and Turkey; the Chechens in Russia; and the Albanians in Kosovo have resorted to armed conflict to win independence. Some of the Basques in Spain have used terrorist tactics to win greater autonomy or independence. As an emergent or reemerging international tendency, ethnonationalism is a highly consequential force in multiethnic nation-states that range from technologically-developed countries, such as Canada and Belgium, to former Soviet-bloc countries in Eastern Europe, such as the constituent republics of the former USSR and the former Yugoslavia, to less technologically developed countries (LTDCs) such as Somalia, Nigeria, Rwanda, and Sri Lanka. Ethnonationalism is a worldwide trend since the preponderant number of nation-states is multiethnic, and ethnic consciousness has been rising rather than diminishing.

Today, scholars are starting to examine ethnonationalism, but there is little consensus about how it can be accommodated in a nonviolent or noncoercive way. For international educators understanding ethnonationalism and its dynamics is highly important and includes: (1) an examination of ethnonationalism as a significant international dynamic; (2) advancing international and intercultural understanding by being aware of ethnonationalism's power to cause conflict between ethnonationalist groups, particularly in multiethnic or multinational nations; and (3) the identification of and emphasis on ethnonationalism's constructive possibilities.

Throughout the world, there are signs of ethnonationalist conflicts and a recognition that political and ethnic boundaries rarely coincide—for example: Russia's differences with the other republics of the former Soviet Union; religious conflict in Northern Ireland; ethnic and religious tension in the successor states of the former Yugoslavia; tribal conflict in Nigeria, Burundi, Uganda, Somalia, and the Sudan; ethnic and racial conflict in Tibet and other border regions of the Peoples Republic of China; communal strife in India, especially between Muslims, Hindus, and Sikhs; language conflict in Belgium between Flemings and Walloons; ethnic and language conflict in Canada between English and French-speaking groups, particularly in Quebec; conflict in Mexico between mestizos and Indians; religious and ethnic conflict in Iraq between Kurds, Sunnis, and Shiites. For international education, especially peace and conflict resolution education and multicultural education, the contemporary rise of ethnonationalism poses immense challenges.

Ethnonationalism and Education

As indicated above, education, especially schooling, is a process that creates group identity and the sense of we-feeling. Informal education, which comes from living in a particular ethnocultural milieu of family, church, and community, socializes children into that particular ethnic group. In instances where the particular ethnic group is dominant, schools, too, continue the process of ethnic socialization. However, in instances where the particular ethnic group is subordinate, its children may attend schools where the language of instruction and the curriculum reflect the dominant group's culture rather than its own. Historically, the process of Americanization in the U.S. primarily involved the use of schooling to impose the dominant white, English-speaking, Protestant culture on subordinate groups. The process, if successful, erodes the subordinate culture and assimilates its members into the dominant culture. Some of the controversies over bilingual, bicultural, and multicultural education in the U.S. reflect ethnonational issues.

In some countries, ethnonational issues are interwoven with language issues. Is there to be an official language, or are there to be several languages used in government and education? When ethnonational issues come to the surface in education, they involve: (1) using the ethnic group's language rather than the dominant group's official language; (2) including the ethnic group's traditions, literature, and history in the curriculum; and (3) constructing a school milieu that celebrates and reinforces ethnic group membership and identity. Defenders of the nation-state as the central focus of identity contend that using several languages and literatures rather than the dominant national one is divisive and weakens the nation-state. In contrast, those who seek ethnonational recognition, autonomy, or independence argue that each group has the right to ensure its ongoing existence.

In the context of education, conflicts about multiethnic nation-state identity versus subgroup ethnonational identity can involve control of schools, curriculum, and language of instruction. Cases of such conflict occurred in Canada when Québécois resisted Anglicization, in Belgium when the Flemish resisted the imposition of French, and in India when non-Hindi speakers opposed the imposition of Hindi. While ethnonationalism creates resistance to cultural and educational imposition by other groups, it also positively uses education to preserve and extend the particular ethnic group's identifying characteristics, such as: (1) the use the ethnic mother tongue rather than the official national language as the medium of instruction; (2) the inclusion of the ethnic group's literature, history, and traditions in the curriculum to create a sense of group identity; and (3) the use of the hidden curriculum to reinforce a sense of we-feeling by cultivating a group response to ethnonational symbols.

Ethnonationalism's worldwide resurgence poses a dilemma for American international educators. Embedded in the American experience is the principle of self-determination of people, enunciated by Woodrow Wilson during World War I and at the Versailles Peace Conference. While American international educators have generally endorsed a people's right to self-determination, they have also argued that nations, in the modern world, are suitably the focus for social, political, and economic integration. The dilemma becomes acute when ethnonationalism is the driving force for the disintegration of multiethnic nation-states.

Another dilemma that the revival of ethnonationalism poses for international education comes from the emphasis that American educators gave to nation building. Recall from chapter 5 that the concept of nation building was allied with modernization theory during the 1960s and early 1970s. International education, as a part of professional and teacher education, received impetus when comparativists, development educators, international educators, and others developed an extensive literature that portrayed education, particularly schooling and training, as instruments to transform less technologically developed "third world" nations into modern nation-states.

Through nation building, organized education, or schooling, would foster national loyalties, commitments, and identities that focus on the nation rather than on particular local or regional areas. International development educators believed it desirable to transform LTDCs into more highly technologically developed nations by creating the necessary infrastructures for modernity. These educators believed that nation building, while advancing modernity by reducing localism and tribalism, would not necessarily spark the older nationalist antagonisms of the pre-World War II genre. They argued that nation building would develop a constructive nationalism, and that while conducive to modernization, it would not threaten international stability. This constructive nationalism would be unlike the chauvinistic nationalism that developed in Nazi Germany, Fascist Italy, and Imperial Japan in the 1930s that led to World War II. According to Walker Connor, scholars associated with nation building generally underestimated the significance of ethnic diversity or regarded it as a "minor impediment to effective state-integration."[4]

The leading theorist who developed key concepts linking modernization and nation building was Karl Deutsch, author of *Nationalism and Social Communication.*[5] Deutsch argued that as modernization transformed traditional societies, especially those of the newly independent nations, the development

of industrial, urban, communication, transportation, and educational infrastructures would lead to greater assimilation in the nation-state. Using a func-
tionalist argument, Deutsch reasoned modernization would reduce
ethnonationalism, which would be replaced by enlightened self-interest
rather than by ethnic group loyalties. Political and economic processes, supported by an educational infrastructure, would move societies from collections of tribes and separatist ethnic and language groups into politically and
economically assimilated nation-states with a common language, culture,
and institutions. Likewise, some advocates of globalization see it as reducing
ethnic differences.

Leading American international educators affirmed that organized education could effectively promote modernization via the concept of nation
building. The theme of nation building permeated *The U.S. and International
Education*, the 1969 yearbook of the National Society for the Study of Education (NSSE).[6] The distinguished historian of education, R. Freeman
Butts, wrote:

> International Education in the late twentieth century should provide a
> two-way process by which the self-determining peoples of the world seek
> to modernize themselves through education, just as Westerners did for
> themselves when they borrowed from each other during their period of
> rapid modernization.[7]

Convinced that the "building of nationhood and of modern civilization"
rested on education, Butts argued that "the great aspirations of our times are
a unified and sturdy nationhood based upon dignity and self-identity of the
nationals concerned" united with a "satisfying modernity that will extend
widely its welfare benefits with justice and equality." Like other American
international educators who advanced nation building, Butts saw ethnonationalism in contrast with the larger nation-state nationalism to be an unfortunate residue. For him, "tensions and conflicts among groups loyal to race,
tribe, religion, or language often make achievement of a unified nation difficult or block progress toward the adoption of a modern style of life."[8] Butts
commented that educational systems in tune with modernization would be
marked by

> increased reliance upon a scientific-rational outlook, by the rational-legal
> order of public behavior, by increased participation of ever larger num-
> bers of people in public affairs, by secular validation of the knowledge
> upon which decisions in human affairs are based, and by commitment to
> the primacy of humane values.[9]

Donald Adams, another contributor to the NSSE yearbook, wrote:
"Developing a meaningful awareness of the existence of nationhood is an
important—if not the most pressing—task of many of the less developed
nations." Further, national integration meant that psychologically citizenship
education would include "identification with the nation-state and with
national symbols."[10]

The concept of nation building obscured the reality of ethnonationalism that was submerged in the former Soviet Union and Eastern Europe by the overarching monolithic ideology of Communism. Further, international educators underestimated ethnonationalism's force in the newly independent nations of Asia and Africa where it appears as tribalism and communalism. These educators overestimated economic development's impact on arresting and limiting the ethnonationalist impulse. Indeed, infrastructure developments in transportation, communication, and schooling may make ethnic groups more aware rather than less aware of cultural differences. It appears that a high degree of technological, economic, and educational integration does not guarantee that ethnonationalism will not surface in a particular nation-state. Contrary to the nation building school, Connor argues developments in communications and transportation may increase the "cultural awareness of the minorities" by making them conscious of group differences.[11]

In educational policy studies, the concept and force of ethnonationalism is one that needs analysis. Education, in its organized form as schooling, has traditionally: (1) transmitted the cultural heritage from the adult members of the particular society to the children; and (2) has been a force for creating national identity through the teaching of a national language, literature, and history in the school curriculum. While involving some degree of imposition, these two large goals have shaped educational programs in modern nation-states. American educators have debated the degree to which the school and the curriculum should transmit and cultivate both a common cultural identity and also encourage recognition and cultivation of more particular racial, ethnic, and language identities. Multiculturalism has been an American and British educational response to cultural, racial, ethnic, and language diversities.

However, there are many features of the American situation that differ from the ethnonational resurgence taking place throughout the world. One particular area of difference is the large degree of communication and assimilation between people of different ethnic backgrounds in the U.S. compared to other countries throughout the world. Further, the American educational experience, with its manifestations of assimilation and multiculturalism, does not correspond to the international phenomenon. Unlike the immigrant and racial groups that are scattered throughout the U.S., the ethnonational groups throughout the world tend to live in particular regions within nation-states that they consider to be their traditional ancestral preserve and homeland.

Nationalism, Ethnonationalism, and Multicultural Education

Throughout history, nationalism has posed serious challenges to education for international understanding. Today, the resurgence of ethnonationalism has made these challenges even more pressing. That nationalism and ethnonationalism can lead to positive personal identification and group solidarity but also to destructive rivalries presents a dilemma for educators.

Today, education in the U.S. and several other countries is infused with multi-cultural programs that seek to cultivate the positive aspects of ethnicity without accentuating the negative aspects of rivalry, antagonism, and conflict. Multicultural education emphasizes that although human beings belong to diverse racial, ethnic, and language groups, they all share a common humanity with the same needs, hopes, and fears. Multicultural education seeks to expose and examine racial and ethnic stereotyping and bigotry.

Since the end of World War II, multiculturalism and its inclusion in the school curriculum has become a worldwide educational movement. Internationally, it is possible to identify several cases where multicultural education is either being implemented or needs to be implemented. Although some nations may appear to be homogeneous at first glance, upon closer examination they are likely to have multicultural populations. Nations that have been settled by large numbers of immigrants invariably exhibit multicultural situations. Among such nations are the U.S., Australia, Canada, New Zealand, South Africa, Chile, Argentina, and other Latin American nations. In addition to the immigrant population in these nations, there is also the indigenous population that was present at the time of immigration. In the U.S., the indigenous people are the Native American population. In New Zealand, the Maoris are the indigenous population. In these nations, multicultural education examines immigrant–indigenous cultures and relationships.

A second kind of multicultural issue arises in nations, often former colonial countries, which have a large number of ethnic, language, and perhaps racial groups. In Asia, India presents an example of a nation with several large ethnic divisions, particularly those of Aryan and Dravidian stock; 17 major languages and several major religions, including Hinduism, Islam, and Sikhism. Nigeria in sub-Saharan Africa, with its more than 400 languages and dialects, is another example of a nation in this category. (For a discussion of language and ethnic diversity in these countries, see the chapters 17 and 18 on India and Nigeria).

A third type of multicultural issue can be found in Eastern and Central Europe, including the former Soviet Union, where different ethnic and language groups are included in the same nation-state. In these nations, ethnic and language tensions have a long history. Since the end of Soviet control, many supposedly dormant ethnic tensions have been rekindled. For example, the former Yugoslavia, especially Bosnia and Kosovo, composed of Serbians, Croatians, and Slavic Muslims, is a region of ethnic, language, and religious hostilities. Ethnic and language tensions are also present in Slovakia between Slovaks and Roma (gypsies), in Bulgaria between the Bulgar majority and the Turkish minority, and in Romania between the Romanian majority and the Hungarian minority. In addition to ethnic rivalries in Central and Eastern Europe, the region has a long history of anti-Semitism, especially in the former Soviet Union and Poland.

In Western Europe, the former homogeneity that characterized nations such as the Netherlands, France, Germany, and the UK has been eclipsed by immigration to these countries. People from Britain's former colonies in Asia, such as Pakistan and India, in Africa, and in the Caribbean have immigrated to the UK. In France, immigrants have come from Indochina and North Africa. In the Netherlands, there has been immigration from Indonesia. Still another kind of immigration in Western Europe has been that of workers and their families from countries such as Greece, Italy, and Turkey, who have settled in technologically developed nations such as Germany, Switzerland, and Sweden. With the European Union, Europe is becoming increasingly multinational and cross-cultural as persons from the participatory nations freely move across borders for economic, professional, and cultural reasons.

School administrators and teachers throughout the world are now experiencing and recognizing the need to develop multicultural sensitivity and pedagogical skills to educate diverse groups. The awareness of the need for multicultural education has become so significant that James A. Banks, a leading authority on the subject, has called it "an international reform movement."[12] The UK, for example, has made concerted efforts at multicultural education, especially in its larger cities, where there is significant cultural, ethnic, racial, and religious diversity. In the U.S., more attention is being given by business corporations engaged in international trade to developing international cross-cultural sensitivity in their employees.

Conclusion

The world is organized into nation-states, independent, sovereign countries, each of which uses nationalism to create and maintain a sense of national identity. National school systems socialize that nation's children into its citizens. How this socialization takes place is highly important for our future. It can involve both identity with one's own country and respect for the people of other countries. Or, it can take the form of chauvinism that exalts one's country over all others. Extreme nationalism has led to world wars and conflicts.

Ethnic identification, too, can be a force of group pride and self-esteem. It can be a positive celebration of one's ethnic heritage that also respects the racial and ethnic heritages of other people. If, however, ethnic identification becomes a strident assertion of one group's superiority over others, it can lead to suspicion of and violence toward other groups. Strident ethnonationalism can degenerate into ethnocentrism, the belief in the inherent superiority of one's group and seeing members of other groups as inferiors.

Among the questions that international educators need to examine are: (1) Can self-differentiating and self-determining ethnonational cultural groups coexist peacefully and educationally within a single nation-state's political and educational structure and system? (2) Is it possible that the transmission of the cultural heritage can be rendered into plural forms as cultural heritages within the nation-state framework? (3) Will the larger nation-state concept reassert itself and absorb smaller conflicting ethnonational groups? (4) Are we witnessing the emergence of a new global reality in which ministates based on ethnicity will replace larger nation-states? The answers to these four large questions can be used to address questions that are more specific to educational theory, such as: (1) How can ethnonationalism become part of the curriculum for international education in the U.S.? (2) How can educational theory be reconnected with the earlier theories of nationalism so that it more adequately examines ethnonationalism? (3) What are the implications of ethnonationalism for educational purposes and curriculum throughout the world? (4) How well does the concept of multiculturalism relate to the phenomenon of ethnonationalism?

DISCUSSION QUESTIONS

1. How does nationalism bring about the construction of group identity and mobilization in the nation-state?

2. How do nation-state school systems use nationalism to construct a sense of primary identity and citizenship?

3. How is American exceptionalism a variant of nationalism? Have you encountered American exceptionalism?

4. Why has there been a revival of ethnonationalism?

5. Compare and contrast nationalism and ethnonationalism.

6. Examine the educational implications of nationalism, American exceptionalism, and ethnonationalism.

7. Examine the role multicultural education can play in reducing ethnonationalist tensions and conflicts.

8. Is it possible that the transmission of the cultural heritage can be rendered into plural form as cultural heritages within the nation-state framework?

9. Is it likely that the larger nation-state concept will reassert itself and absorb smaller conflicting ethnonational groups?

10. Are we witnessing the emergence of a new global reality in which ministates based on ethnicity will replace the larger nation-state?

FIELD AND RESEARCH TOPICS

1. In an autobiographical essay, trace your ethnic and cultural roots.

2. Compile a file of newspaper and magazine articles that deal with ethnonationalist conflicts. After you have amassed a number of articles, analyze them for their educational implications.

3. Review an autobiography or biography of a person who is presented as a hero, heroine, or exemplar for persons of a particular ethnic racial group.

4. Debate the topic: "Resolved, the U.S. should have one official language."

5. Research and write a comparative paper that analyzes multicultural education in the U.S. and another country of your choice.

6. Visit a cultural center or heritage museum of a racial or ethnic group. Determine if the exhibits at the center or museum have ethnonationalist elements.

7. Interview international students from various countries who are studying at your college or university. Invite them to discuss education, schooling, and the forming of national character from their own perspectives. Then, prepare a comparative analysis based on your findings.

8. If you are engaged in fieldwork in a school setting, identity how that school, both informally and formally, builds an American sense of identity.

9. If you are engaged in fieldwork in a school setting, identity how that school, both informally and formally, shapes a multicultural sense of identity.

SUGGESTIONS FOR FURTHER READING

Alter, Peter. *Nationalism.* New York: Edward Arnold, 1994.

Banks, James A. *Multiethnic Education: Theory and Practice,* 2nd ed. Boston: Allyn and Bacon, 1988.

Banks, James A., and Cherry A. McGee Banks, eds. *Multicultural Education: Issues and Perspectives.* Boston: Allyn and Bacon, 1989.

Banks, James A., and William Joyce, eds. *Teaching Social Studies to Culturally Different Children.* Boston: Addison-Wesley, 1971.

Banks, James A., and James Lynch, eds. *Multicultural Education in Western Societies.* New York: Praeger 1986.

Branson, Margaret Stimmann, and Judith Torney-Purta. *International Human Rights, Society and the Schools.* Washington, DC: National Council for the Social Studies, 1982.

Brass, Paul R. *Ethnicity and Nationalism: Theory and Comparison.* Newbury Park, CA: Sage, 1991.

Charny, Israel W. *Genocide: The Human Cancer.* Boulder, CO: Westview Press, 1982.

Connor, Walker. *Ethnonationalism: The Quest for Understanding.* Princeton: NJ: Princeton University Press, 1994.

Diamond, Larry, and Plattner, Marc F. *Nationalism, Ethnic Conflict, and Democracy.* Baltimore: Johns Hopkins University Press, 1994.

Edwards, John R. *Language, Society, and Identity.* New York: B. Blackwell, 1985.

Eriksen, Thomas H. *Ethnicity and Nationalism: Anthropological Perspectives.* London and Boulder, CO: Pluto Press, 1993.

Farnen, Russell F., ed. *Nationalism, Ethnicity, and Identity: Cross National and Comparative Perspectives.* New Brunswick, NJ: Transaction, 1994.

Gellner, Ernest. *Encounters with Nationalism.* Oxford, UK and Cambridge, MA: Blackwell, 1994.

Gillis, John R., ed. *Commemorations: The Politics of National Identity.* Princeton, NJ: Princeton University Press, 1993.

Hunter, James D. *Culture Wars: The Struggle to Define America.* New York: Basic Books–HarperCollins, 1991.

Hutchinson, John, and Anthony D. Smith, eds. *Nationalism.* New York: Oxford University Press, 1994.

Ignatieff, Michael. *Blood and Belonging: Journeys into the New Nationalism.* New York: Farrar, Straus, and Giroux, 1994.

Kammen, Michael. *Contested Values: Democracy and Diversity in American Culture.* New York: St. Martin's Press, 1995.

Kellas, James G. *The Politics of Nationalism and Ethnicity.* New York: St. Martin's Press, 1991.

Mazurek, Kas, Margaret Winzer, and Czeslaw Majorek, eds. *Education in a Global Society: A Comparative Perspective.* Boston: Allyn and Bacon, 2000.

Nieto, Sonia. *Affirming Diversity: The Sociopolitical Context of Multicultural Education.* New York: Longman, 1992.

Reimers, Fernando, and Noel McGinn. *Informed Dialogue: Using Research to Shape Education Policy around the World.* Westport, CT: Praeger, 1997.

Shawcross, William. *The Quality of Mercy: Cambodia, Holocaust, and Modern Conscience.* New York: Simon and Schuster, 1984.

Smith, Anthony D. *National Identity.* Reno: University of Nevada Press, 1991.

Synder, Louis L. *Global Mini-Nationalisms: Autonomy or Independence.* Westport, CT: Greenwood Press, 1982.

Takaki, Ronald. *A Different Mirror: A History of Multicultural America.* Boston: Little, Brown, 1993.

Thomas, R. M. (ed.) *International Comparative Education, Practices, Issues, and Prospects.* Oxford: Pergamon Press, 1990.

Watson, Keith, ed. *Doing Comparative Research: Issues and Problems.* Oxford: Symposium Books, 2001.

Watson, Michael, ed. *Contemporary Minority Nationalism.* New York: Routledge, 1990.

Williams, Colin H., and Kofman, Eleonore, eds. *Community Conflict, Partition and Nationalism.* New York: Routledge, 1989.

NOTES

[1] Hans Kohn, *The Idea of Nationalism: A Study in its Origin and Background* (New York, 1944), ix–x.

[2] Alexis de Tocqueville, *Democracy in America*, ed. J. P. Lawrence (New York: Perennial Classics/HarperCollins, Publishers, 2000), 280.

[3] Although I have stipulated definitions for nationalism and ethnonationalism, my stipulated definition for the latter term relies heavily on Walker Connor, *Ethnonationalism: The Quest for Understanding* (Princeton, NJ: Princeton University Press, 1994), xi.

[4] Connor, 29.

[5] Karl Deutsch, *Nationalism and Social Communication: An Inquiry into the Foundations of Nationality* (Cambridge, MA: Harvard University Press, 1966); also, see Karl W. Deutsch and William Foltz, eds., *Nation Building* (New York, 1966).

[6] Harold G. Shane, ed., *The U.S. and International Education: The Sixty-eighth Yearbook of the National Society for the Study of Education*, Part I (Chicago: University of Chicago Press, 1969).

[7] R. Freeman Butts, "America's Role in International Education: A Perspective on Thirty Years," in Shane, 39.

[8] Ibid., 41.

[9] Ibid., 44.

[10] Donald Adams, "Development Education and Social Progress," in Shane, 55.

[11] Connor, 37.

[12] James A. Banks, *Multiethnic Education: Theory and Practice*, 2nd ed. (Boston: Allyn and Bacon, 1988), 3–4.

A Comparative Analysis of Education in Selected Nation-States

8

Educational Systems in National Contexts

Part II of this book's focus and development plan is designed to examine selected educational systems in their national contexts. The larger national society's politics, culture, and economy, which may seem to be external to schools, shape to a large extent educational institutions, their curricula, and processes of teaching and learning. This chapter examines comparative education as an academic discipline and describes its uses in analyzing educational systems in nation-state contexts. It provides a rationale for studying comparative education, discusses its history, and considers problems related to comparability. The chapter's major objective is to examine how comparative education can be used to gain insights into the functioning of school systems in these contexts.

We begin our study with Stewart Fraser's and William W. Brickman's very direct and straight forward definition that "comparative education is the analysis of educational systems and problems in two or more national environments in terms of socio-political, economic, cultural, ideological, and other contexts." Fraser and Brickman state further that the purpose of comparative education is "not to determine" which system is best but rather to understand the "similarities and differences in education in the various nations."[1] Though written more than thirty-five years ago, their definitions stand up well.

Why Study Comparative Education?

When we first encounter the idea of making comparisons of educational practices in different nation-states, we might think it seems irrelevant or unproductive. The rationale for studying comparative education addresses these concerns: American educators, beset by their own issues, have often tended to be isolated or insular in their educational outlook. While Americans once believed that their country was protected by the two great oceans from invasion, the involvement of the U.S. in two great world wars lessened that sense of protection. The attack on the World Trade Center in New York City on September 11, 2001, and fighting the "war on terrorism" has involved the U.S. in a struggle of global proportions. The sense of isolation and an attitude that does not care about what is happening elsewhere on the planet is no longer rationally, nor educationally, defensible, if, indeed, it ever was. While educational situations, especially in schools, vary considerably with their contexts, a comparative perspective helps one to see both similarities and differences in the role and function of educational institutions and processes that builds a professional perspective. In other words, looking out aids one to both understand a broader perspective as well as look inward and get a clearer picture of what is taking place in American education.

Comparative education, like the foundational studies of history, philosophy, and sociology of education, contributes to interpreting international comparisons of student achievement. Comparative data, especially relating to the academic achievement of U.S. students, has often been used to generate domestic educational policies in the U.S. For example, in 1958, the atmosphere of educational crisis, sparked by the Soviet Union's launching of Sputnik, resulted in the National Defense Education Act, which allocated federal funds for improving the math and science curricula in U.S. schools.

One of the highly influential reports of the reform era of the 1980s was *A Nation at Risk* (1983), compiled by the Commission on Excellence in Education appointed by U.S. Secretary of Education Terrel Bell.[2] A highly ideological document that urged restoration of American education's academic vitality, *A Nation at Risk* compared education in the U.S. with other countries to support its arguments for educational change. The report begins: "Our Nation is at risk. Our once unchallenged preeminence in commerce, industry, science, and technological innovation is being overtaken by competitors throughout the world."[3] Arguing that if Americans can restore academic rigor and quality to their schools, the U.S. can recapture the leading position it once held in the world economy. Using wartime rhetoric, the report stated:

> We have even squandered the gains in student achievement made in the wake of the *Sputnik* challenge. Moreover, we have dismantled essential support systems which helped make those gains possible. We have, in effect, been committing an act of unthinking, unilateral educational disarmament.[4]

Throughout *A Nation at Risk*, comparisons are made between American schools and those of other countries. In identifying the "indicators of risks," the report states that "international comparisons of student achievement, completed a decade ago, reveal that on 19 academic tests American students were never first or second and, in comparison with other industrialized nations, were last seven times."[5] Among the commission's findings were the following:

> In many other industrialized nations, courses in mathematics (other than arithmetic or general mathematics), biology, chemistry, physics, and geography start in grade 6 and are required of all students. The time spent on these subjects, based on class hours, is about three times that spent by even the most science-oriented U.S. students, i.e., those who select 4 years of science and mathematics in secondary school.[6]

In England and other industrialized countries, it is not unusual for academic high school students to spend 8 hours a day at school, 220 days per year. In the United States, by contrast, the typical school day lasts 6 hours and the school year is 180 days.[7]

Among the commission's recommendations that relate both to academic subject matter and to time spent on academic studies at the secondary level is that all students study what it called the Five New Basics: (a) 4 years of English; (b) 3 years of mathematics; (c) 3 years of science; (d) 3 years of social studies; and (e) one-half year of computer science. Further, for college preparatory students, two years of foreign language are recommended.[8] According to the report, foreign languages, an important area in the world's interdependent economy, need to be reemphasized.[9]

In its conclusion, "America Can Do It," the commission emphasizes America's uniqueness in providing greater opportunities to attend college and universities than do other nations. It states:

Our institutions of higher education have provided the scientists and skilled technicians who helped us transcend the boundaries of our planet. In the last 30 years, the schools have been a major vehicle for expanded social opportunity, and now graduate 75 percent of our young people from high school. Indeed, the proportion of Americans of college age enrolled in higher education is nearly twice that of Japan and far exceeds other nations such as France, West Germany, and the Soviet Union. Moreover, when international comparisons were made a decade ago, the top 9 percent of American students compared favorably in achievement with their peers in other countries.[10]

The reaction to *A Nation at Risk* produced a series of reforms in many states that increased the time spent on English, mathematics, and science and mandated academic standardized competency testing in some states. In some respects, the current movement toward using standardized tests to establish academic benchmarks of student achievement at specific grade levels partially stems from concerns about the deficiencies of American students. The No Child Left Behind Act (2002) requires states, to qualify for federal funding, to develop and administer standardized tests in reading and mathematics from grades three through eight.

While educational comparisons have been used to promote specific agendas for change, the evidence used to support such agendas needs to be carefully examined. Often the arguments are based on information taken out of context and have limited applicability to the U.S. situation. Comparative study can help to create a contextual perspective that differentiates between fair and unfair comparisons.

The study of comparative education can also contribute to selective educational borrowing and implementation from one country to another. Educational borrowing and exchange with other countries has been practiced throughout history. For example, American educators borrowed certain methods such as the Pestalozzian object lessons, the Froebelian kindergarten, the Herbartian phases of instruction, the Montessori method, and the open structures of the British Primary School. In turn, other countries have borrowed from the U.S. The structure of Japanese schools was largely borrowed from the U.S. after World War II. The movement to comprehensive secondary schooling in certain Western European nations, such as Sweden, has been influenced by the U.S. comprehensive high school.

While educational theories and practices can be transported and imported, it is crucial that the context in which they originated is understood and that their potential for adaptability in another country is carefully assessed. As a useful analogy, consider transplanting a plant from one location to another. For transplanting to be successful, the environment is a key factor. Some plants can be transplanted successfully if the soil, climate, and other growing conditions are suited to the plant's needs. Some plants may thrive in the new location and become environmental invaders, like the kudzu vine in the southeastern states. Still others may wither and die because they have been placed in inhospitable environments.

Comparative study can contribute to global, or international, understanding and cooperation. As stated in *A Nation at Risk*, we live in an increasingly interdependent global society and economy. Events in one region or part of the world affect other regions. What happens in one country is likely to affect other nations. Just as no person is an island, no nation, not even the U.S., is isolated from persons and events elsewhere. Consider, for example, prior to the events of 9/11, many Americans paid little or no attention to the people and institutions in the Middle East. But the terrorist attack on the U.S. led to military action against the Taliban regime in Afghanistan, which was harboring Osama bin Laden's terrorist cadres and training camps. Americans' eyes have been opened to issues and practices in regions of the world they formerly ignored. The more we understand people and events elsewhere in the world, the more we are prepared to function effectively in the global society and economy of the twenty-first century.

A Glimpse at the History of Comparative Education

Perceptive travelers, visiting lands other than their own, often recorded their insights about other peoples and institutions and compared them to life in their own countries. This informed travel literature reveals that these travelers gained reflective insights about themselves and their own countries as well as about the places they visited.

William Maclure, the American geologist and natural scientist, recorded his observations of other countries, their people, and their institutions in his travel journals and his book, *Opinions on Various Subjects*. After visiting Johann Heinrich Pestalozzi's educational institutions in Switzerland, Maclure, engaging in educational borrowing, the transfer of educational institutions and methods from one country to another, then proceeded to introduce Pestalozzian pedagogy to the U.S. The early advocate of women's rights, Mary Wollstonecraft, too, made such observations when she went to France to observe the revolution firsthand.

A number of important transatlantic comparisons of American and European education were done by leading American educators in the nineteenth century. For example, William Channing Woodbridge (1794–1845), in "View of the Comparative State of Instruction in the U.S. and in Europe," praised American common schools (elementary public schools) as surpassing primary schools in Europe and of educating more children than schools in any country in Europe. However, he found that instruction in the European secondary schools, especially the French *lycées* and German *gymnasium*, often surpassed that provided by U.S. colleges.[11]

Horace Mann (1796–1859), known as the father of American public education, devoted his *Seventh Annual Report* (1844), as secretary of the Massachusetts Board of Education, to his observations on education in Europe. Mann, who had visited schools in Great Britain, France, the Netherlands, Belgium, Prussia, and several of the German states, was generally critical of European education. He admired Prussia's uniformity and efficiency in governing its schools but opposed its monarchical government and militarism. He was particularly impressed by schools where the Pestalozzian method had been implemented.[12]

Marc-Antoine Jullien (1775–1848), a French educator who wrote about comparative study in education in *Esquisse d'un Ouvrage sur l'éducation comparée (Preliminary View of a Work on Comparative Education)* in 1817, is often identified as the field's founding figure.[13] Jullien developed a method, anticipating modern quantitative and qualitative research, in which the comparative educator was to: (1) use careful observations to acquire facts and insights about education in other countries; (2) arrange them in comparative tables; (3) analyze them; and (4) formulate explanatory comparative generalizations.[14]

Paul Monroe (1869–1947), a professor of education at Columbia University's Teachers College, was a leader in developing both the history of education and comparative education as fields of study. He was the founder and director of Teachers College's International Institute of Education from 1923–1938. Highly involved in comparative and international studies, Monroe conducted a survey of Philippine schools for the U.S. government in 1913 and advised the Chinese government on modernizing its system of education during that country's republican period. From his study of the history of American education, Monroe believed that the American model of democratic education had much to offer to other countries. He also stressed the importance of educational contacts on an international basis for bringing about greater communication and understanding between educators of different nations.[15]

The development of modern comparative education in the U.S. owes much to the research and writing of Isaac L. Kandel (1881–1965), a professor of education at Columbia University's Teachers College. Kandel believed that to understand the educational system of a country it was necessary to also understand its historical and cultural contexts.

George Bereday, a leading comparative scholar, divided the field into area studies and comparative studies. In area studies, the comparativist focused on one country or region and described the landscape of educational institutions. In the comparative studies focus, description was followed by multidisciplinary analysis, which, applying social science methods, sought to explain the meaning and significance of these institutions as they operated in their national or regional contexts. The approach used in this book closely resembles Bereday's strategy in that educational institutions are related and examined in terms of their supportive national context. For Bereday, comparative studies involved juxtaposing similar elements or characteristics of different educational systems in order to compare them.[16]

Also instructive is the work of comparativist W. D. Halls, who developed a model for comparative study that includes: (1) cultural analysis of the forces that influence educational systems; (2) the investigation of educational systems "abroad," in countries other than one's own; and (3) comparative pedagogy, the study of teaching and learning in other countries.[17] Halls's model is also useful in terms of this book's approach.

The Problem of Comparability

An important problem related to comparative education is comparability. What makes something comparable to something else? The more similar and focused the objects being compared, the identification of similarities and differences will be more reliable. Conversely, the greater the difference between the objects being compared, the information gained through comparative study will be more unreliable. In developing a strategy for comparability, we need to consider the following questions:

1. Are the same or similar institutions, players, and processes being compared?

2. Are the terms used to designate institutions, curricula, and processes similar from one national context to another or does their meaning weaken in translation and transition?

3. Are the purposes and goals of education similar? What must we understand about the cultural-ideological-political-economic context in order to compare educational goals and purposes?

Related to the problem of comparability are efforts to make comparative international assessments of student academic achievement in various countries. The International Association for the Evaluation of Educational Achievement (IAEEA) has been conducting cross-national academic achievement studies since the 1960s.[18] The IAEEA's early studies collected and analyzed data on the academic achievement of 258,000 students from nineteen countries in civic education, foreign languages, literature, reading comprehension, and science. The study revealed considerable differences between countries. Subsequent studies found that students in the U.S. rank near the average for technologically developed countries (TDCs) but are in the lower ranking for mathematics and science.[19]

Some commentators point out the difficulties in comparing assessments of achievement in the value-laden subjects of civic education and literature, which are deeply embedded in a country's cultural context. However, mathematics lends itself to international comparisons because it is relatively value-free and tends to be similar in content and operations across cultures.[20] In comparisons of mathematics competency, Japanese students were at the top. U.S. students were average in arithmetic but deficient in geometry and measurement.[21]

The IAEEA and the U.S. National Assessment of Educational Progress (NAEP) joined forces and conducted several studies that assessed international educational progress. In 1992, they published a survey of mathematics and science achievement in twenty countries. Again, both mathematics and science were regarded as more measurable and comparable than history and literature, which are more specific to particular cultural contexts. In the 1992 study, American students scored well below students in other TDCs such as Japan, France, and Germany in mathematics and science.[22]

The deficiencies of American students in mathematics and science have been used by domestic critics who argue that schools in the U.S. need to improve the quality of instruction in mathematics and science and devote more time to these subjects in the curriculum. These deficiencies were highlighted in *A Nation at Risk* and used to stimulate the movement in many states to increase the units in English, mathematics, and science required for high school graduation. The apparent deficiencies also contributed to the current standards movement to use standardized tests to assess and compare student achievement.

While international comparisons have been effectively used in generating domestic change in the U.S., some educators have challenged the comparability of international assessments. A major criticism is that they pay too little attention to the social, political, and cultural context. For example, in the U.S. secondary schools have high enrollments that include an academically diverse student body; in many other countries, the secondary schools are more academically selective and their students are more academically inclined. Comparability is also limited by the methods of instruction in schools. American schools tend to group students according to their ability level: some students study algebra and geometry while others are still working with basic arithmetic. In other countries, like Japan, all students study the same content in mathematics and score better on the tests.

Characteristics of Education

The meaning of education is obviously very general and has long been debated by philosophers of education. Some define education as the development of potentialities that are already present, but latent, in learners; others see it as transmission, putting ideas and information into learners' minds. Some see education as a universal human process that transcends the differences of culture and history; others identify education with formal or organized instruction, or schooling, in which learners are deliberately taught by teachers in institutional settings. While these various definitions of education are all correct to some degree, they illustrate the complexity of defining and discussing an educational system. We begin with some stipulated definitions.

In the most general sense, education can be defined as an *informal* process by which a person learns to become a participant in the social life of a group by acquiring the language, skills, knowledge, and values that the group uses and prizes. In this sense, education is an informal process of socialization and acculturation through living in and participating with a social group. Much of our early learning, our acquisition of language and our early behaviors are informally learned from our parents, family members, and peers. Education can also be a *nonformal*, noninstitutionalized process in which a person acquires skills and knowledge through learning in settings other than formal institutions of education, or schools. Nonformal education can be training that one learns on the job or by taking part in a voluntary association such as a stamp collecting, investment, or photography club. In the third sense, education in a *formal* or institutionalized setting is called schooling. Schools are institutions, either private or public, established and supported for the purpose of providing specific kinds of learning, organized in a curriculum, to learners. As institutions, they are organizations that are in part run by a staff that includes administrators, principals or headmasters, and teachers. Schooling may take place in a range of institutions that covers the human life span—preschools, elementary or primary schools, secondary schools, and various tertiary schools (such as vocational schools) and those of higher education such as colleges and universities.

In addition to the distinctions made above, we need to consider some areas of education that overlap the designations of informal, nonformal, and formal. There is also the rather new concept of distance education, which involves instruction that may be delivered by a formal educational institution but does not actually take place in a school setting. Computer-aided instruction, electronic data retrieval technology, and the Internet may be used in informal, nonformal, and formal education.

These three meanings and settings of education—informal, nonformal, and formal—point to a conclusion that education is interrelated as to purpose and setting. A person's informal education will influence learning that occurs in schools. If informal learning is conducive and supportive of schooling, then the school's program is more likely to enjoy success. In turn, learning in schools will influence the person's out-of-school life in society. To work our way to a more complete meaning of education, we shall need to examine it in its informal, nonformal, and formal aspects.

Although informal education and nonformal education need consideration, the term "an educational system" is most relevant to formal education, or schooling. Most discussions in comparative education deal with comparative schooling in which the school system of two or more nation-states, or countries, are compared and contrasted. Although variations in schooling are caused by their location in different nation-state contexts, they exhibit some stable, transnational elements that can be compared and contrasted. For example, schools are generally age-specific institutions typically attended by children, adolescents, and young adults. They are housed in certain kinds of buildings. Their curriculum is organized and structured. They are staffed by educators—administrators and teachers.

Schools are age-specific institutions in that individuals of a particular age attend them. The types of schools—elementary or primary, secondary, and tertiary or higher—are specific to particular age groups. Although there are variations as to specific ages, children attend primary schools, adolescents secondary schools, and young adults colleges and universities. Although age-specific divisions have never been precise because of how different cultures define the stages of human growth and development, they are even less so today. What are important are the changing attitudes of how to define childhood and adolescence. When does childhood end and when does adolescence begin? A modern trend is a focus on the downward extension of adolescence into childhood and its upward extension into young adulthood. Contextual attitudes regarding childhood and adolescence tend to have their greatest impact on middle and secondary schooling. In comparative terms, the issue of adolescence is most clearly apparent in how various countries define the purposes of secondary education. Along with these important contextual issues, the age-specific nature of educational institutions also has been altered by the development of lifelong learning and the entry of nontraditional learners in tertiary institutions.

Schools are organized institutions in that they have an internal structure. They are often hierarchically organized or vertically organized into grade levels, classes, or forms in which instruction is articulated according to the grade level and cumulative to the grade range. A school will have a chief or primary teacher or administrator, known variously as a principal or headmaster or headmistress. A school will have teachers—adults regarded as skilled or expert in a particular area of knowledge or in some skill or combination of these. The teachers are generally prepared in programs of teacher education or some other kind of higher study. They are likely to have some type of license, certificate, or credential. A school will have students who are either in attendance by compulsion or are there voluntarily. The students, by learning the prescribed skills or subjects, progress upward through the hierarchy of grades, forms, or classes. Upon successful completion of the prescribed program, they will be awarded a diploma or certificate.

A school will have a curriculum. The term "curriculum" historically referred to the skills or subjects that constituted the school's program of studies, which the teacher taught and the students learned. Many contemporary curriculum theorists, who consider the "program of studies" concept to be too narrow, refer to curriculum as all the experiences a student has in a school setting. Nevertheless, the curriculum has identifiable and prescribed learning experiences and these experiences are arranged in sequential and cumulative episodes.

To be in an educational system means that schools are in some kind of articulation or relationship to each other. Primary schools lead upward to middle schools which in turn lead to secondary schools which lead still upward to tertiary institutions of higher learning. School systems are found within geographical political units—in nation-states or in regions or localities of nations. The political system of the nation-state in which they are found generally determines their governance, particularly the relationship of local schools to those of larger political units such as constituent states, provinces, or regions, and finally to the nation itself.

The construction and maintenance of school buildings; the employment of teachers, administrators, and staff; and the provision of books and learning materials require funding—the allocation of financial resources for education. Although all schools require financing, the specifics of funding— sources of and distribution of revenue—will vary according to the fiscal policies, indeed, the general economy of the nation, state, or locality.

This brief and perhaps too-direct list of the characteristics of schools provides some definable elements of schooling that can be compared and contrasted:

1. Schools as institutions

2. Schools as physical facilities

3. Age cohorts at various levels of schooling: preschool, primary or elementary, secondary, tertiary, higher, or professional

4. Curriculum and instruction: scope, sequence, and methodology

5. Governance and administration of schools

6. Teachers, teacher preparation, and teaching

7. Students, their family and socioeconomic backgrounds, relationships, behavior, and expectations

8. School attendance and completion—access, participation, and rates of completion

9. Financing of schools

While schools around the world in various countries display the almost universal characteristics identified above, educational systems, or schools, also exhibit differences. Many of the differences found in schools arise from the context in which they are located and in which they function.

A National Context

A context refers to the setting, milieu, or environment in which one lives and in which human activities occur. Educational leader George S. Counts made the important point about contexts in *The Social Foundations of Education:*

> The historical record shows that education is always a function of time, place, and circumstance. In its basic philosophy, its social objectives, and its program of instruction, it inevitably reflects in varying proportion the experiences, the condition, and the hopes, fears, and aspirations of a particular people or cultural group at a particular point in history.[23]

We will not enter into the long-standing and almost perennial philosophical debate between those who argue, like Robert Hutchins and Mortimer Adler, that education is a universal process that relates to a universal conception of human nature, and those, like Counts, who see education as culturally relevant to a particular society. However, Counts's statement illuminates the need for context in educational discussions. Some preliminary comments will indicate my perspective.

I see education, in its most general terms, as a universal process, in which people everywhere, at different times and places, develop their human potentiality. Human beings, endowed with intellectual and abstractive powers, have sought to use their minds to construct meaning in the experiences of life. The desire for education and the process of learning are the same for people regardless of race, ethnicity, gender, location, and so forth. Education and educability are givens of human nature and are not subject to climate, culture, and time.

Having stated my belief that people everywhere have the potential to be educated in the general sense, I now state the degree to which I find Counts's oft-quoted statement applicable to our discussion of and the need for contexts in comparative education. Formal or organized education is, as Counts stated, highly situational or contextual. It takes the institutional form of schools, but schools are located in particular places, organized and governed in particular ways, and supported and financed in different ways. They serve purposes that depend on those who control them, and their curricula reflect different conceptions of which knowledge and values are of most worth. Their teachers and students come from and reflect the populations that they serve. Comparisons made between different schools, their students, their teachers, their curricula, how they are financed, and how they are organized need to be examined within the context in which they exist.

While it is possible to talk about civilizational contexts, as in Western, African, or Asian civilization, these designations are so broad that comparability can be done only in a very general sense. Another way of dealing with context is to focus on the nation-state (see chapter 7). Nation-states can be defined as independent, sovereign political entities that possess their own system of government, law, education, and security. The modern nation-state has historically been the central focus of its citizens' social, political, and economic life. Nation-states range in size from large countries such as the U.S., the PRC, and Russia to much smaller but still equally sovereign nation-states such as Luxembourg, Singapore, Costa Rica, and Nepal.

Historically, modern nation-states developed in the eighteenth century in Europe, North America, and South America. Of interest to educators is that state or public schools were established, often as national education systems, in the nineteenth century. This development saw a convergence between the nation-state and its school systems, especially as they educated the young to become citizens of nation-states with a patriotic identification, dedication, and loyalty to the country. An important part of the school curriculum, especially language, literature, and history, was used to build identification in the young with the nation-state in which they lived.

Education, in the informal sense, and schooling, as organized institutionalized learning, can and often is used to promote deliberate identification of persons with nation-states. Public or government-sponsored school systems are identified with nation-states. It is possible to talk about the Mexican, Russian, Chinese, and French educational systems, for example. Since the school systems of nation-states such as Japan and France are centralized and governed by the national government, it is accurate to speak about the Japanese or the French system of education. While one can argue that there is no U.S. system of education since each of the fifty states is the constitutional authority for education in its own state, it is nonetheless possible to talk about the American system of education.

In the U.S., each state's school system contributes to national homogeneity or the American system of education. For example, the use of the English language, the selection of a particular version of American history and literature, and the cultivation of democratic processes of citizenship are part of the curriculum of all schools in the U.S. and contribute to forming a common American identity and character. Certain characteristics or tendencies between the states in the U.S. contribute to national uniformity despite the fact that the fifty states are the formal, or legal, units for governing and funding schools. Among these homogenizing tendencies are such informal educational agents as the media, especially television and the Internet, and the economic and transportation infrastructures. Further, the preparation, organization, and professionalization of teachers create some professional standardization within schools in the various states (see chapters 9 and 10).

The nation-state provides not only a convenient but also a realistically useful context in which education, especially schooling, can be examined. However, context, as used in this book, means more than the geographical territoriality of a particular nation-state that is enclosed by its borders or frontiers. Context needs to be examined multidimensionally in its historical, political, social, ideological, and economic parts. Perhaps even the use of the plural term "contexts" might be a more accurate designation. The context of the nation-state is multidimensional and each of the contextual dimensions has an impact on education.

The Political Context

The political context of the nation-state refers to how the nation-state is governed. Several questions are relevant to political context: Is the political system unitary and centralized or is it a federal system in which governance is a combination of federal and state powers and responsibilities? What is the nature of local political units and how do local units relate to central and state authorities?

The organization of government in the nation-state has an important impact on educational systems. Some educational systems are closely controlled, financially supported, and monitored by central authorities in the national government, as in Japan and France. In other nation-states, such as India and Mexico, which have federal systems of government, educational authority, responsibility, and prerogatives are shared between the central and the state governments. The U.S. represents a federally organized nation-state in which the federal government exercises limited educational powers and the educational authority resides in each of the states. Still another pattern of governance can be found in the UK where the central and local governments share educational responsibilities and prerequisites.

Another aspect of the political context is that of political party organization and ideology. In the PRC, the Communist Party has been the chief determinant of educational policy. Alternating between a commitment to "redness"—loyalty to the Communist ideology, whereby students are barred from exposure to outside ideas—and pursuing expertise in science and technology that can be gained from other non-Communist countries, has resulted in dramatic policy shifts. In nation-states with representative institutions, such as the parliamentary bodies in France, the UK, Japan, India, and the U.S., political parties are driven by both ideological and pragmatic forces. For example, both the Conservative Party in the UK and the Republican Party in the U.S. emphasize greater school choice for parents, alternative schools, and increased ties between schools and business.

The Historical Context

Schools are historically evolved institutions whose structure and functions are reshaped by contemporary currents. The general history of the nation-state, especially its history of education, is important in locating and interpreting the major historically derived generalizations that impact education. Significant persons and events have shaped educational institutions and policies in these nation-states. For example, Horace Mann in the U.S., Napoleon in France, Chairman Mao in China, and Gandhi in India exerted influence on educational policy. Often, schools have a very slow response to social and technological change due to their historically generated purposes. The impact of schools' historical evolution often continues to have an effect on how they face contemporary issues and challenges.

The history of education can inform us about how school systems originate, develop, and change over time. In his analysis of comparative education, Edmund King discusses the educational idioms or styles of the educated person that are based on particular historical situations.[24] These historical

idioms or styles of the educated person tend to persist long after their significance or meaning for the particular historical period has ended. King has
identified several educational idioms, but we shall examine two that pertain
to our discussion: the priestly, monastic, literary, and classical style of the
educated person and the technical and managerial style appropriate to a
modern industrial society.[25]

The Earliest Educational Idiom
The earliest educational idiom appeared and dominated the centuries
from the era of the great Oriental empires of Egypt, Mesopotamia, and India,
through the classical Greek and Roman periods, to the medieval European
period. While many differences existed in the educational contexts of this
vast sweep of history, certain generalizations can be made. In ancient India,
the priestly Brahmin caste was educated by studying the Hindu classics, the
Vedas. In China, Mandarin civil servants devoted themselves to studying the
works of Confucius. (The earliest educational idiom is illustrated in the chapters on India and China). For the Christian monastics, the Bible and the writings of the church fathers represented the core of scholastic study. The corpus
of study for these religious and philosophical elites was literary, based on the
study of authoritative sacred texts. In the Western educational tradition, the
liberal arts (the studies for free people as contrasted to slaves) originated in
ancient Greece, entered Roman culture, and were conveyed into the medieval, Renaissance, and Reformation styles of education.

Although they originated in the preindustrial and premodern era, the
educational patterns connected to this first educational idiom have survived
and remain in place today in many countries. Schools in nations where the
first idiom survives tend to be structured into tracks—one for the masses and
the other for the elite. The schools for the masses emphasize basic literacy
and computation and lead to unskilled and semiskilled work. The schools for
the elite—often exclusive preparatory schools and highly selective universities—emphasize the liberal arts, the classics, history, philosophy, and theology. These schools tend to be attended by the children of the upper classes,
who are prepared for positions of status, power, and influence. An obvious
example of this sort of education is represented by the famous public schools
of England, which lead to the prestigious universities of Oxford and Cambridge. Attendance at these schools brings the successful graduate into a network of power and prestige. The actual subjects studied in the school are to
provide the marks of the generally educated person rather than knowledge
directly applicable to future professional activity.

The educational content and style described for the first idiom have had
a powerful hold. They formed the educational style associated with the
world's great civilizations and were preferred by Europe's upper classes, especially its aristocracy. When the Europeans colonized Asia, Africa, and South
America, this version of the educated elite was transported to these continents. (See the chapters on India and Nigeria for the transporting of the first

educational idiom). In an unusual way, it was compatible with the older literary and classical education patterns found in the cultural heritage of these regions. Its holding power is attractive in that as new socioeconomic classes seek mobility, they often imitate this older pattern of prestigious education. The newly arrived socioeconomic class wants the educational style of the older upper and privileged class, even if it is technologically and economically inappropriate for them.

The Industrial-Technological Idiom

The second stage or idiom of education reflects the industrial, technological, commercial way of life associated with capitalism and the industrial revolution. Historically, it represents a middle-class orientation rather than an upper-class version of education. The second idiom emphasizes science, technology, engineering, marketing, communications, and related subjects. It stresses the social and economic utility of knowledge or, as Herbert Spencer asked, "What knowledge is of most worth?" The knowledge most prized is that which can be applied, especially to economic production and consumption. Along with the emphasis on science and technology in the curriculum, the "hidden curriculum" or school milieu emphasizes utilitarian or functional values such as diligence, punctuality, frugality, and competitiveness.

In the second idiom, schools function to produce the planners, executives, managers, scientists, administrators, and technicians who will play functioning parts in a highly integrated functional system. Merit, rather than the gentility of birth and breeding associated with the first idiom, is prized and rewarded. In a functional system, people advance by being both competitors and team or corporate players simultaneously. Advancement in the system depends upon understanding, learning, and conforming to the system's standardized norms. This second style or idiom is found in schools in modernized, industrialized, and corporative nations such as those of North America, Western Europe, and Japan. In these countries, the model of the industrial or business corporation affects the school, which imitates the corporate style.

These two historically evolved educational styles are not the only ones that can be identified through historical analysis. In addition, there are other models. For example, in the former Communist nations of Eastern Europe a version of the industrial model was altered to fit Marxist ideological patterns. An important question arises—what is the contemporary idiom in education? Is it a reinvigorated industrial-technological-capitalist idiom found in the contemporary movement of globalization? Or, are we in the early stages of a new idiom related to the rise of the postmodern, postindustrial society?

The Socioeconomic Context

The socioeconomic foundations or context of education refers very broadly to the societal and economic factors that influence and condition schooling in a given nation-state. Here, the perspective is broadly conceived to encompass language, race, ethnicity, and gender as well as socioeconomic class and other kinds of status or social strata. Is the nation's population homogeneous or heterogeneous—linguistically, racially, ethnically, and socially? Are there dominant and subordinate groups? If so, how do these divisions impact education and schooling? Do schools tend to perpetuate and reproduce socioeconomic differences or do they work to create equality? Further, are there urban–rural differentials? Do students in urban areas have more extended educational opportunities than those in rural areas?

Economically, is the nation more or less technologically developed? What are its principal economic resources and products? Is the economy state-planned and directed or a free market situation? How do schools prepare people for occupations and professions? How are economic resources used to fund educational institutions? How are these resources distributed?

A few brief examples will illustrate the power of the socioeconomic context on education and schooling. In the PRC, there are sharp differentials in the resources and opportunities between schools in urban and rural areas. As is true in most less technologically developed nations, children living in urban areas have more educational resources available to them than those in rural areas. Further, using the program of the Four Modernizations, the national government has deliberately prioritized its objectives to develop urban areas, especially in the coastal region, at a more rapid rate than rural ones.

In the U.S., the formal school system may appear to be somewhat uniform structurally despite state and local district control and patterns. However, major distinctions arise in terms of the economic resources available to schools. The local district's property tax generates about 60 percent of school revenues. Schools located in affluent districts with high property taxes can afford to spend more on teachers' salaries, equipment, supplies, and enrichment programs than schools in less-affluent or poor districts. Where one lives is a key determinant of educational opportunity. While rhetoric in the U.S. emphasizes "equality," the fiscal reality in which schools are funded promotes inequality.

In India, certain higher castes enjoy more educational opportunities than lower castes and scheduled tribes because of the historically generated caste system. Seeking to ameliorate these inequalities, India's central government uses affirmative action procedures to reserve a certain number of places for disadvantaged castes and tribes in secondary schools and universities.

Religious and Ideological Contexts

Very important in a national context, particularly for education and schooling, are religious and ideological contexts. Again these particular contexts, while very broad and general, generate highly consequential effects on society and schooling.

Historically, education and schooling were originally connected to religion. The first schools that appear in antiquity were priestly institutions, located near or in temples. In ancient India, Egypt, Israel, China, and Mesopotamia the earliest schools were temple schools where prospective priests learned sacred literatures, scripts, and rituals. In Western Europe, from medieval times to the beginning of the modern era, schools were related to and often conducted by the Christian churches. Religious instruction generally took the form of a book-based undertaking in which the words of the sacred scripture formed the central curricular focus.

In the contemporary world, religion continues to exert a powerful force on education and schooling. Some nations continue to have official state churches such as the Church of England in the UK and the Lutheran churches in the Scandinavian nations. Islam is the powerful religious force in many Middle Eastern, North African, and some Asian countries such as Indonesia and Malaysia. Buddhism is the dominant religiocultural force in Thailand. Shintoism is a key religiocultural force in Japan. Even in nation-states without an official church, religion remains a powerful force that influences education.

Much nineteenth- and twentieth-century history of education, especially in Western nations, deals with the issues of church–state relations and controls over schools. For example, the educational history of the U.S. reveals the gradual secularization of public schools. The American movement to secularization was challenged periodically; today, it continues to be challenged by religious groups, primarily fundamentalist Christians, who argue for prayer in the public schools. Roman Catholics and others want government-funded vouchers and choice between public and private schools. A reading of France's educational history since the French Revolution reveals persistent conflicts between clericalists, supporting the Roman Catholic Church, and anticlericalists seeking to disestablish it and remove its influence from education. A contemporary manifestation of France's secular orientation in education relates to the government's banning of the wearing of religious symbols in its state schools. Especially affected by the ban are Muslim girls who are not permitted to wear the traditional head scarf in schools. Mexico's history also shows similar church–state tensions. An understanding of the nation-state context then necessarily includes its religious dimension.

Along with religion and sometimes its rival is ideology. Ideology is a highly complex concept that, while often located in nationality, ethnicity, and politics, is not limited to these areas. Ideology can be defined as the core or bonding ideas and sentiments that provide a particular group with its sense of identity. What is it that members of a particular group believe they share with each other but not with other people? The powerful resurgence of ethnonationalism throughout the world demonstrates that members of particular ethnic groups believe they share common blood and ancestry. This kind of identification has contributed to ethnonationalism and tribalism as political and educational forces (see chapter 7). Groups, especially ethnic, racial, and tribal ones, also seek to create a common past through their own group autobiography or common history, expressed in oral and written traditions. Such vistas of the past may be historical or mythic or a combination of both elements. Often, ideology is a mobilizing force for a program of action, such as nation building in Nigeria, fundamentalism in Iran and Pakistan, ethnic cleansing in the former Yugoslavia, or separatism in Canada among the French-speaking Quebecois. It is used to raise a particular group's consciousness and mobilization to action.

Regionalism

While ethnonationalism is creating more and smaller nation-states as in the former Soviet Union and in Eastern Europe, another current trend is regionalism—economic groupings or alliances of nation-states. For example, the European Union (EU) is a group of European nations that comprise an economic region with a virtually common economy and a common currency. There are also the Pacific Rim nations, which, while not as organized or formal as the EU, established favorable trade relationships between countries bordering the Pacific Ocean. Then, there is the North American Free Trade Association (NAFTA), which includes the U.S., Mexico, and Canada.

While it is true that educators need to be aware of regional economic pacts, agreements, and organizations, it is still important to note that the members of such regional groups still remain the constituent nation-states that comprise them. Although the European Union is the most rapidly evolving region as an economic force, even in this area the nation-state remains as a powerful political and cultural unit. Formal schooling in Europe will reflect greater economic integration, even to the point of having certificates and degrees that are recognized across national boundaries. In the other regional groupings, the nation-state remains the primary unit of organization and identification for school systems.

Conclusion

Education in the U.S., as throughout the world, is rooted in complex political, social, economic, and ideological relationships between schools and society. The study of comparative education, like history, sociology, and philosophy of education, can create a knowledge base, a professional perspective that examines and interprets these relationships. Comparative education helps in creating a "comparatively informed strategic vision" that is useful in understanding and assessing school organization, structures, and curricula in other countries.[26] Comparative education performs a function in which educational institutions and processes can be compared and contrasted much like political scientists do when they undertake comparative studies of governments and society in other countries.

By examining the historical, political, economic, social, religio-ideological and other forces, an effort is made to construct the context in which educational systems operate. Comparisons, which identify similarities and differences with education and schooling between one's own and other countries, are intended to develop a comparative global perspective about education. Finally, teaching and learning, curriculum and instruction, and classroom settings provide a pedagogical basis of analysis.

DISCUSSION QUESTIONS

1. What are the various meanings of the concept, "education?"
2. Distinguish between informal, nonformal, and formal education.
3. Define and provide examples of an educational context.
4. If you were asked to describe the context of your life, what aspects or elements would you include?
5. How have political and educational policy makers used comparative education to support their arguments for reform or change?
6. Identify the common assumptions that the members of your class have about equality of educational opportunity and socioeconomic mobility in the U.S. Use these assumptions to examine education in other nations.
7. Do you think that comparisons of academic achievement between students of different local or state school systems in the U.S. are fair?
8. Do you think that academic achievement comparisons between students of different countries are fair?
9. Identify the countries whose contexts seem most unlike that of the U.S. Support your choices with evidence.
10. What is a nation-state context?
11. Explain how historical, economic, political, social, and ideological contexts relate to education and schooling.
12. What are the strengths and weaknesses in using nation-state contexts in comparative education?

FIELD AND RESEARCH TOPICS

1. Through field study, research, and observation, identify and examine the context in which your college or university is located.
2. Through field study, research, and observation, identify and examine the context of an elementary or secondary school in your area.
3. Develop a panel discussion in which each presenter reviews a book that is used as an introduction to American education. Compare and contrast how the authors of these books have dealt with issues of context.
4. Prepare a content analysis of recent national or state reports on education. Determine whether and the extent to which these reports used comparative evidence.

5. As a class project, begin a clippings file on articles from newspapers and magazines that report on education in other countries. Pay particular attention to those that use such reporting to make comparisons.

6. Invite several international students to speak to your class on their impressions and experiences in the U.S. that relate to the cultural context. What problems have contextual differences created for them, and what adjustments did they have to make to relate to the American context?

7. Survey members of your class to identify individuals who have spent some time as travelers, tourists, or students in other countries. Determine if they experienced problems of cultural adjustment. How were these problems related to being in a different cultural context?

8. Through class discussion, identify those elements or characteristics of education in another country that you believe would enhance your understanding of education in the U.S.

9. Interview international students from various countries who are studying at your college or university. Invite them to discuss education, schooling, and the forming of national character from their own perspectives. Then, prepare a comparative analysis based on your findings.

10. If you are engaged in fieldwork in a school setting, identity how that school, both informally and formally, builds an American sense of identity.

SUGGESTIONS FOR FURTHER READING

Hans, N. *Comparative Education.* London: Routledge and Kegan Paul, 1958.

Halls, W. D. (ed.) *Comparative Education: Contemporary Issues and Trends.* London: Jessica Kingsley/UNESCO, 1990.

Holmes, Brian, ed. *Equality and Freedom in Education: A Comparative Study.* London: Allen and Unwin, 1985.

Ignas, Edward, and Raymond J. Corsini. *Comparative Educational Systems.* Itasca, IL: F. E. Peacock, 1981.

Jaworski, Barbara and Phillips, David. *Comparing Standards Internationally: Research and Practice in Mathematics and Beyond.* Oxford: Symposium Books, 1999.

King, Edmund J. *World Perspectives in Education.* London: Methuen, 1962.

King, Edmund J. *Comparative Studies and Educational Decision.* London: Methuen, 1968.

King, Edmund J. *Other Schools and Ours: Comparative Studies for Today.* New York: Holt, Rinehart, and Winston, 1979.

Mazurek, Kas, Winzer, Margaret, and Majorek, Czeslaw, eds. *Education in a Global Society: A Comparative Perspective.* Boston: Allyn and Bacon, 2000.

Reimers, Fernando and McGinn, Noel. *Informed Dialogue: Using Research to Shape Education Policy around the World.* Westport, CT: Praeger, 1997.

Theisen, Gary. "The New ABCs of Comparative and International Education," *Comparative Education Review,* 41 (November 1997), pp. 397–412.

Thomas, R. M. (ed.) *International Comparative Education. Practices, Issues, and Prospects.* Oxford: Pergamon Press, 1990.

Watson, Keith, ed. *Doing Comparative Research: Issues and Problems.* Oxford: Symposium Books, 2001.

NOTES

[1] Steward E. Fraser and William W. Brickman, *A History of International and Comparative Education: Nineteenth Century Documents* (Glenview, IL: Scott Foresman, 1968), 1.

[2] The National Commission on Excellence in Education, *A Nation at Risk: The Imperative for Educational Reform* (Washington, DC: U.S. Government Printing Office, 1983).

[3] Ibid., 5.

[4] Ibid.

[5] Ibid., 8.

[6] Ibid., 20.

[7] Ibid., 21.

[8] Ibid., 24.

[9] Ibid., 26.

[10] Ibid., 34.

[11] William Chandler Woodbridge, "View of the Comparative State of Instruction in the United States and in Europe," *The American Annals of Education and Instruction,* II (July 1832), 329–336.

[12] Lawrence A. Cremin, ed., *The Republic and the School: Horace Mann on the Education of Free Men* (New York: Bureau of Publications, Teachers College, Columbia University, 1957), 54–56.

[13] Stewart E. Fraser, *Jullien's Plan for Comparative Education, 1816–1817* (New York: Teacher College Press, Columbia University, 1964).

[14] Nicholas Hans, *Comparative Education* (London: Routledge and Kegan Paul, 1958), 1.

[15] Liping Bu, "International Activism and Comparative Education: Pioneering Efforts of the International Institute of Teachers College, Columbia University," *Comparative Education Review* 41 (November 1997): 414–415.

[16] George F. Z. Bereday, *Comparative Method in Education* (New York: Holt, Rinehart, and Winston, 1964), 9–10.

[17] W. D. Halls, ed., *Comparative Education: Contemporary Issues and Trends* (London: Jessica Kingsley/UNESCO, 1990), 23–24.

[18] Alan C. Purves and Daniel U. Levine, eds., *Educational Policy and International Assessment* (Berkeley, CA: McCutchan, 1975).

[19] Allan C. Ornstein and Daniel U. Levine, *Foundations of Education* (Boston: Houghton Mifflin Co., 1997), 491.

[20] For an analysis of the issues related to interpreting cross-national studies of achievement, see Barbara Jaworski and David Phillips, *Comparing Standards Internationally: Research and Practice in Mathematics and Beyond* (Oxford: Symposium Books, 1999).

[21] Thorsten Husen, *International Study of Achievement in Mathematics* (New York: Wiley, 1967).

[22] Ornstein and Levine, p. 493.

[23] George S. Counts, *The Social Foundations of Education* (New York: Charles Scribner's Sons, 1934), 1.

[24] For an extended discussion of the contextual analysis of educational systems, see Edmund J. King, *Other Schools and Ours: Comparative Studies for Today* (New York: Holt, Rinehart, and Winston, 1979).

[25] Ibid., pp. 3–62.

[26] Gary Theisen, "The New ABCs of Comparative and International Education," *Comparative Education Review* 41 (November 1997), pp. 402–403.

9

EDUCATION IN THE UNITED STATES
CONTEXT AND HISTORY

This chapter examines education in the U.S. Its purpose is to give readers a point of origin, a beginning for the study of comparative education that starts in their own country. Without a knowledge base in the context and history of education in our country, it is difficult to make comparisons and contrasts about educational systems in other countries. We first need to know ourselves to understand others. Chapter 9 begins with a general examination of the demographic, social, political, and economic contexts of the U.S. and then turns to the history of American education. The historical section examines the significant events from an international and comparative perspective. We also explore the multicultural context of the U.S. and the historical forces that have shaped educational practices involving dominant and subordinate groups in U.S. society.

Geographic, Demographic, and Sociocultural Contexts

The U.S., a large and varied nation, is approximately half the size of Russia, slightly larger than China, and is two-and-a-half times the size of Western Europe. It is bordered by the North Atlantic and Pacific Oceans and has land boundaries with Canada and Mexico.

The population of the U.S. is estimated at 290,342,554.[1] The U.S. population fits the pattern of the age cohorts found in most technologically developed countries (TDCs). Like such countries it has a relatively low rate of population growth and an increasing number of individuals over 65. The literacy rate, determined by the number of people over the age of 15 who can read and write, is a high 97 percent.[2]

While Americans have a cultural identity that is particular to the U.S. in general, they are also members of a racially, linguistically, religiously, and culturally diverse society, with origins from various ethnic groups populating different regions of the world, including Asia, Latin America, and Western and Eastern Europe. In terms of race, the population of the U.S. is 77.1 percent Caucasian, 12.9 percent African American, 4.2 percent Asian American; and 1.5 percent Native American; other groups constitute 4.3 percent of the population.[3] Although Hispanic Americans are the second largest group in the U.S., the Census Bureau does not maintain a separate listing for Hispanics. It considers Hispanic to mean a person of Latin American descent, including persons of Cuban, Mexican, or Puerto Rican ethnicity living in the U.S., who may be of any race or ethnic group. English is the dominant language in the U.S., with Spanish being used by a sizable and growing minority.

The U.S. is a religiously pluralistic country. Fifty-six percent of Americans are affiliated with Protestant denominations, 28 percent are Roman Catholics, 2 percent are Jewish, and 10 percent indicate they are not religiously affiliated.[4] The doctrine of separation of church and state is based on the U.S. Constitution, which prohibits the government from supporting the establishment of religion. The Constitution also guarantees U.S. citizens the right to exercise religious beliefs without government interference. Church–state issues have frequently arisen in education. Several of these issues have been heard by the U.S. Supreme Court, which generally has applied the "no establishment" clause to public schools. In its policy of separation of church and state, the U.S. is similar to France and Mexico.

Political Context

Unlike other countries where the positions of chief of state and the head of government are separate, the U.S. presidency unites both roles in a single office. In the UK, the monarch, as chief of state, personifies the nation in a ceremonial way, and the prime minister, as head of the government, leads the majority party or coalition in the House of Commons and makes and implements policy. Furthermore, in the U.S. the president adds the role of leader of a political party to the other presidential roles. In the U.S., the federal government is structured by three main branches.

Executive Branch

The president and the vice president are elected on the same political party ticket by the Electoral College, an assembly of representatives of the states who are elected directly by the voters in each state. The president and vice president serve four-year terms. The cabinet, which includes the secretary of education, is appointed by the president with the approval of the U.S. Senate. Since 1980, there has been a federal Department of Education with a secretary who is a member of the president's cabinet. The secretary of education is responsible for the administration of federal programs related to education, primarily supervising the distribution of federal funds to the states.

Although the constitutionally defined educational role of the president is very limited, certain presidents have taken initiatives to bring about educational reform and change in the U.S. For example, President Lyndon Johnson made education a key element in his "War on Poverty" and "Great Society" programs in the 1960s. Johnson supported the establishment of the Head Start Programs for early childhood education and sponsored the Elementary and Secondary Education Act that provided federal aid to schools. President Ronald Reagan, through the efforts of his secretary of education, Terrel Bell, popularized the recommendations of the Commission on Excellence in Education in *A Nation at Risk* in the mid-1980s. President George W. Bush secured the enactment of the No Child Left Behind law in 2002.

Legislative Branch

The U.S. has a bicameral Congress that consists of the Senate and the House of Representatives. The Senate is composed of two senators elected from each state by popular vote to serve six-year terms. The House of Representatives consists of 437 members, who are directly elected by popular vote for two-year terms from congressional districts in each state. The Congress is the law-making body of the federal government. Bills must pass both houses and be signed by the president to become laws. Both houses have committees that study education and recommend legislation, such as federal assistance programs.

Judicial Branch

The highest court of law in the U.S. is the Supreme Court, consisting of nine justices appointed for life by the president with confirmation by the Senate. The Supreme Court is the final arbiter on many constitutional issues, including those related to education, particularly those that relate to racial integration, religion and education, and discrimination and due process. For example, the Supreme Court, in *Brown v. the Board of Education of Topeka, Kansas* (1954), ruled that state-sanctioned racial segregation was unconstitutional. This decision led to subsequent cases that required school districts to develop and implement plans for the racial integration of schools. Many of the cases heard by the Supreme Court have related to the separation of church and state, such as the constitutionality of aid to religious and private schools, prayer in public schools, and other such matters. In addition to the Supreme Court, there are federal courts of appeal, district courts, and state and county courts.

Political Parties

The major national political parties are the Democratic and Republican parties. The Democrats traditionally draw their support in the northern industrial states and in urban areas. The Republicans have their greatest support in the southern and western states. The Democrats tend to support a larger federal role in education, especially in federal funding for public schools. They tend to oppose federally supported voucher programs that could be used in nonpublic, particularly church-related schools. Traditionally, the Republicans favor a more limited federal role with the major role in education being exercised by the states. In recent years, both major parties have given greater attention to educational issues. The No Child Left Behind legislation of 2002 that required standardized testing in grades three through eight in order for districts to qualify for federal aid received support from members of both parties. However, Democrat support for No Child Left Behind has weakened.

Economic Context

The U.S., a highly industrial and technologically developed nation, is rich in natural resources. Its diverse agricultural, industrial, and technological economy gives it a ranking of first among the world's nation-states. As is the case with other TDCs, the use of labor-saving technologies has replaced the need for people to be engaged in agriculture, resulting in a decrease in the population and a decline in the school-age cohort in rural areas.

The U.S. economy is essentially a capitalist, market-oriented economy in which private individuals and business corporations make the major decisions about producing and marketing products. Unlike other countries such as Japan and France where the national governments are more involved in the economic sector, the U.S. government plays a lesser role in research and planning. While "high-tech" service and communications areas have expanded, the older heavy industries such as steel and textiles have declined as these industries relocate their factories and production centers in other countries, where labor costs are lower. The result has been a "two-tier" labor market. Since 1975, increases in income have gone to the upper 20 percent of the workforce. Those in the lower tier, especially displaced industrial workers, generally lack the technical skills and training of those in the upper tier. The decline in the number of industrial jobs has brought about transitional unemployment and the need for training programs to aid in preparing individuals for the more high-tech managerial and service sectors.

Historical Context

This section of the chapter presents a historical overview of American education with emphasis on those aspects that relate to international and comparative education. It discusses (1) the colonial period, when European educational ideas and institutions were transplanted to North America; (2) the creation of educational patterns during the revolutionary and early national eras; (3) the establishment of common, or public, elementary schools; (4) the evolution of secondary schools; and (5) the development of colleges and universities.

The Colonial Period

An important comparative feature of U.S. educational history is that it, like India, Nigeria, and Mexico, shares a colonial past. Sections of what is now the U.S. were colonized by England, France, Spain, and the Netherlands, and schools, like other institutions, were transplanted versions of those in the imperial nations. After the U.S. gained independence, it reconstructed its educational institutions and processes to reflect its new political independence (as did other newly independent nations). The European colonization of North America caused complex and often violent encounters between Europeans and Native American tribes. Native American education, prior to the European entry, was largely direct and informal as children learned skills, social roles, religious beliefs, and cultural patterns from growing up as participants in tribal life.

Efforts by the European colonists in North America to "civilize" the indigenous Americans rested on the Europeans' beliefs in their own cultural superiority and the "savagery" of the American Indians. In the Mississippi Valley, French missionaries, especially Jesuits, accompanied the explorers, fur traders, and soldiers who sought to create New France on the North American continent.[5] Seeking to convert the Native Americans to Catholicism, these priests introduced the French language and culture. They established schools to educate children of French colonists and to Christianize the Indians. In the Southwest, under Spain's control, Franciscan priests established missions to convert Native Americans to Catholicism. In these mission schools, Native American children were taught religion, crafts, and reading. The missionary activities of Jesuits and Franciscans also took place at the same time in Mexico and in other Central and South American countries.

In the English colonies, Church of England missionaries established schools under the auspices of the Society for the Propagation of the Gospel in Foreign Parts. English missionary and educational activities among the Native Americans were sporadic, however, and were conducted on a small scale. The English generally saw Native Americans as culturally inferior savages to be dispossessed of their lands and forcibly resettled in western territories.[6] Noteworthy educational efforts were also made by Moravians, a primarily German pietistic denomination, associated with the Bohemian bishop and educational reformer Johann Amos Comenius. The Moravians, who saw education as a means to bring peace to the world, translated the Bible and religious tracts into the Indian languages spoken in Pennsylvania, North Carolina, and Ohio.

The white Euro-American sense of cultural superiority, which continued after the U.S. won independence from Great Britain, culminated in a forced exodus of Native Americans from their ancestral lands, in violent genocidal wars, and in cruel resettlement of the tribes to reservations. While the Spanish treatment of the Indians in Mexico was severe and exploitative, more intermarriage between members of the two groups occurred than in the U.S. Today, Mexico has a majority of *mestizos* who share both ethnicities.

Although slavery was practiced throughout the colonies, the southern colonies had the largest population of enslaved Africans. Seized by force and brutally transported in slave ships to North America, Africans were forced laborers on southern plantations. Over time, the African heritage became the genesis of African American culture. The long persistence of African enslavement in the U.S., ended by the Civil War and the ratification of the Thirteenth Amendment, produced a racial history that is quite different from that of the other countries discussed in the book. Racial tensions between African Americans and whites remain an unresolved dilemma in American society and education. Other nations discussed in the book also have sociocultural, racial, and ethnic tensions that have an impact on education. For example, the Indians in Mexico still remain disadvantaged economically; the outcastes in India, despite constitutional protections, still encounter discrimination; there are strains and conflicts among the different tribes in Nigeria such as Hausas and Ibos. While bearing some similarities to discrimination in other countries, U.S. race relations require a unique interpretation.

After militarily defeating the Dutch and the French for control of North America, the English had the greatest influence on the development of colonial educational institutions. However, the various colonies approached education and schooling somewhat differently.

New England Colonies

Massachusetts, settled primarily by Puritans, Calvinist dissenters from the officially established Church of England, enacted some of the earliest laws governing education. Stressing Bible reading and congregational church governance, the Puritans recognized the need for a literate clergy and laity. They saw schools as necessary agencies of social control; along with home and church, schools would keep a sinful humanity in conformity to Biblical law.

In addition to its religious orientation, Puritanism also emphasized the relationship between a proper education and economic productivity and prosperity. Schools were to prepare diligent, thrifty, and industrious men and women who would be self-supporting economically and law abiding politically. This utilitarian bent often overshadowed intellectual aims and decreased the tendency to separate school and work, unlike other societies, particularly in Asia and Africa where schooling and work tend to be separated. The theme that tied schooling to economic productivity would be recurrent in U.S. educational history.

As early as 1642, the Massachusetts General Court made parents and guardians responsible for ensuring that their children could read and know the principles of their religion and the Commonwealth's laws. In 1647, the General Court enacted the "Old Deluder Satan" Act requiring every town of fifty or more families to appoint a reading and writing teacher. Towns of one hundred or more families were to engage a Latin teacher to prepare young male students for admission to Harvard College.[7]

Massachusetts, followed by the other New England colonies, developed the town school, a locally controlled, usually coeducational school, attended by pupils ranging in age from six to thirteen or fourteen. The school's curriculum included reading, writing, arithmetic, catechism, and religious hymns. An important characteristic of the town school that shaped later U.S. schooling was that it was locally controlled and financed. The American concept of local school control and funding would persist in the U.S., in contrast to centralized national educational systems like those of France or Japan.

Imitating Europe's educational models, America's colonists initially fashioned a class-based dual school system in the New World. Children of the lower socioeconomic classes attended vernacular primary schools that offered a basic curriculum of reading, writing, arithmetic, and religion. Girls could attend primary schools but not secondary schools or schools of higher education. Upper-class males went to the Latin grammar school, a classical preparatory school that stressed classical Greek and Latin languages and literature needed for college admission. The Latin grammar school was modeled on similar institutions in England, which, in turn, resembled the classical humanist schools that originated in the Renaissance-Reformation periods.[8] In terms of comparative educational history, the North American Latin grammar schools were the trans-Atlantic equivalents of European counterparts.

Entering the Latin grammar school at age eight, the upper-class male students might complete their preparatory studies by age fifteen or sixteen and then enter such colonial colleges as Harvard, Yale, or William and Mary.[9] If from a very wealthy family, a young man might be sent to university study in England or Scotland. Originally, the colonial colleges were to prepare ministers for the church that sponsored the institutions. Structured on the traditional arts and sciences, the college curriculum consisted of grammar, logic, rhetoric, arithmetic, geometry, astronomy, ethics, metaphysics, and natural sciences. In addition, Hebrew, Greek, and ancient history were taught for their usefulness in scriptural study.

Middle Atlantic Colonies

One of the important characteristics of education in the U.S. is cultural, religious, racial, and ethnic diversity. The degree to which the public schools should encourage a common or a pluralist culture had been debated historically and continues to generate heated disputes. Some of the origins of U.S. cultural diversity can be traced to the religious, linguistic, and ethnic diversity of the colonial period, particularly in such Middle Atlantic colonies as New York, New Jersey, Delaware, and Pennsylvania. The diversity of the Middle Atlantic colonies contrasted with Puritan New England's religious and cultural conformity and orthodoxy. In addition to the English-speaking English, Scots, and Scotch-Irish, there were Dutch in New York, Swedes in Delaware, and Germans in Pennsylvania. Religiously, the Dutch were members of the Dutch Reformed Church; the Society of Friends, or Quakers, was present in Pennsylvania, and Germans might be Lutherans or members of small pietistic denominations such as the Moravians, Ephratans, or others. There were also Baptists, Roman Catholics, and a small Jewish population.

The Middle Atlantic colonies' religious and language diversity had important educational implications. During the colonial era, schools were generally founded by and supported by churches, which used them to educate children in their religious creeds and practices. Because of the Middle Atlantic colonies' diversity, parochial schools, established by the different churches, reflected these religious and language differences.

Southern Colonies

The southern colonies—Maryland, Virginia, the Carolinas, and Georgia—presented yet another educational pattern. In the South, where enslaved Africans were forced to labor on the plantations, the origins of North American racial diversity and inequality were most evident. Over time, southern culture, economics, politics, and education reflected the slavery system's impact on the region.[10] The plantations, often producing a single, staple crop such as tobacco, cotton, or rice, were part of an export agricultural economy sustained by the large slave labor force. Unlike New England and the Middle Atlantic colonies, which had some population concentrations in cities and towns, the southern population was for the most part dispersed over a large land area.

Wealthy southern families employed tutors, an educational practice used by the upper-class gentry in England and other countries, or sent their children to private schools conducted by the Church of England.[11] By the late colonial period, boarding schools were established, usually in towns such as Williamsburg or Charleston. Enslaved Africans were trained to be agricultural workers, field hands, craftspeople, or domestic servants, but legally they were forbidden to learn reading or writing. There were notable exceptions who learned to read secretly.

Early National Period

The victory of the rebellious American colonists against British rule led them to create a new republican form of government. Although the existing vernacular and denominational primary and Latin grammar schools inherited from the colonial period continued for a time, the new republic's leaders sought to eliminate neocolonialism by devising new educational patterns suited to a republican concept of citizenship and civic education.

The new republic's earliest national educational legislation was included in the Northwest Ordinance of 1785, which divided the Northwest Territory into townships of thirty-six square miles. Each township was further divided into thirty-six sections, each of 640 acres. Each township's sixteenth section was to be used for education. The provisions of the Northwest Ordinance established the pattern of financing education through land grants—a pattern often followed in the early nineteenth century.

Unlike constitutions or basic laws in other nations, the U.S. Constitution did not refer specifically to education, but the Tenth Amendment's (ratified in 1791) "reserved powers" clause (which reserved to the states all powers not specifically delegated to the federal government or prohibited to the states by the Constitution) left education as the prerogative and responsibility of each state. In the American educational experience, the New England tradition of local school control and the general Jeffersonian-Jacksonian reservations against centralized political power contributed to a state rather than a national system of education in the U.S.

In the early national period, opinions expressed about education were that it should: (1) prepare people for republican citizenship; (2) emphasize the utilitarian skills and scientific knowledge needed in developing a nation with vast expanses of frontier land and abundant natural resources; and (3) be purged of European attitudes and values to create a uniquely American culture. Prominent American leaders such as Benjamin Franklin, Thomas Jefferson, and Noah Webster generated educational proposals.

Franklin: The Academy

The ideas of Benjamin Franklin (1706–1790) reflected Americans' propensity for science and utility which became ingrained in U.S. education. A self-educated scientist and self-made entrepreneur, Franklin helped establish important scientific and educational organizations in Philadelphia.[12]

Franklin rejected the Latin grammar school as an obsolete residue of the old European colonial order. His "Proposals Relating to the Education of Youth in Pennsylvania" argued that an alternative institution, the English grammar school, replace it. Franklin's English school would offer vocational and scientific subjects and would accentuate English language and literature studies, composition, and rhetoric rather than Latin and Greek. Introducing the elective concept, students would choose a second language based on their vocational interests. Mathematics would be taught for its practical application to bookkeeping, surveying, and engineering rather than as an abstract subject. Franklin's curriculum was especially noteworthy because it brought into the school utilitarian skills that hitherto had been ignored. These included carpentry, shipbuilding, engraving, printing, painting, cabinetmaking, farming, and carving. With prophetic insight, Franklin recommended special attention to science, invention, and technology.[13]

Jefferson: Education for Citizenship

Thomas Jefferson (1743–1826), primary author of the Declaration of Independence, a governor of Virginia, third U.S. president, and founder of the University of Virginia, was committed to advancing civic education in the new republic. Jefferson was especially determined that, unlike in Europe, there should be no state establishment of religion in the U.S. He also argued that education should be directed to citizenship. His "Bill for the More General Diffusion of Knowledge," introduced in the Virginia legislature, sought to shift education from religious to civil control. The state of Virginia would establish, maintain, control, and finance schools. Jefferson's bill stipulated that free children, both girls and boys, could attend elementary schools, financed by public taxes, where they would study reading, writing, arithmetic, and history. Jefferson further proposed that twenty grammar schools be established throughout Virginia to provide secondary education for males. In the grammar schools, students would study Latin, Greek, English, geography, and higher mathematics. Select academically talented students would receive merit scholarships to attend the College of William and Mary. Jefferson's educational proposal pointed to the future direction of American education.

Although at the end of the eighteenth century and even through the early decades of the nineteenth century churches remained involved in education, Jefferson's arguments for separation of church and state would shape future policy and legislation and become an important characteristic of American education. Jefferson also saw scientific exploration, research, and education as a key element of nation building, or national development. His commission of the Lewis and Clark Expedition to explore and map the trans-Mississippi American West was a forerunner to the settlement and development of the West.

Webster and American Exceptionalism

Noah Webster (1758–1843), a native of Connecticut and a Yale graduate, was a lawyer, schoolmaster, politician, and writer.[14] Webster's widely used *American Spelling Book* and *American Dictionary* emphasized American cultural identity. He was one of the early republic's leading cultural nationalists who sought to create a distinctive sense of American identity.

After the Constitution's ratification in 1789, Webster argued that the U.S. should achieve cultural independence by having its own "language as well as government." British English "should no longer be our standard; for the taste of her writers is already completed, and her language on the decline."[15] Believing strongly that national identity is constructed by a distinctive national language and literature, Webster worked to construct an American version of the English language.

Webster closely related language learning to schooling, especially to reading, writing, and literature in the primary curriculum. He reasoned that as children learned a distinctively Americanized English, they would be acculturated into a unique American cultural identity. Webster's *Grammatical Institute of the English Language* was published in 1783. The *Institute's* first part, titled the *American Spelling Book*, was a widely used school text that had sold fifteen million copies by 1837. Based on twenty-five years of careful research, Webster's definitive *American Dictionary* appeared in 1825. Webster's emphasis on the unique character of the American language buttressed the predilection found in U.S. schools for a monolithic American cultural identity. As a nation of immigrants, the public schools were used to Americanize immigrants.

The Movement to Public Schooling

In the 1830s and 1840s, educational reformers were lobbying for the creation of a public school system in the U.S. At that time, the U.S. was experiencing the first stages of industrialization in its northeastern states and was undergoing westward expansion across the Mississippi River. Industrialization was also occurring in the UK and to a lesser degree in Western Europe. In terms of the comparative history of education, several parallel developments occurred in the U.S. and the UK. Among them were voluntary approaches to education such as Sunday schools and monitorialism. The Sunday school, developed by Robert Raikes, an English religious leader and publicist, reflects the trans-Atlantic movement of educational ideas and institutions. Raikes designed Sunday schools to provide child laborers with basic literacy and religious instruction on the one day of the week factories were closed. Borrowing the concept from the UK, American voluntary groups, often under church auspices, established Sunday schools in the larger eastern cities.

Monitorialism was a method of instruction in the early nineteenth century. It was an international educational movement that some claimed had originated in India and was used in the UK, the U.S., Argentina, and other countries. Monitorialism was promoted by two rival English educators, Andrew Bell, an Anglican churchman, and Joseph Lancaster, a Quaker teacher. Similar to the Sunday school, monitorialism was a voluntary rather than government response to education. Its basic goal was to provide literacy and exercise social control by using advanced pupils (monitors) trained by a master teacher in a particular skill, such as basic math and reading, to teach that skill to subgroups of students, to take attendance, and to maintain order.[16] The method promised to instruct large numbers of students and was supported by those who wanted an inexpensive but large-scale approach to education.

Monitorial schools were popular in the larger American cities, such as New York and Philadelphia, where they were typically supported by private philanthropists. In the early 1840s, monitorial schooling lost popularity and quickly disappeared. However, there was an educational legacy from monitorialism in the use of large blackboards and wall charts, in the grouping of children for instruction, in the use of lesson plans, and in creating a role for supervisors of instruction.[17]

The Common School

Among the significant educational developments in the U.S. was the common school movement, which began in the early nineteenth century in Massachusetts and Connecticut. American proponents of common schools proclaimed them to be egalitarian institutions that would "educate the children of all the people." Although schooling was "common" or available to children of all socioeconomic classes, many children, particularly enslaved African Americans, did not attend. Not oriented to academic selectivity, its curriculum stressed the basic skills of reading, writing, and arithmetic, some history and geography, occasionally singing, and the civic values of patriotism and respect for law and order. The common school curriculum sought to develop the practical literacy and numeracy needed in everyday work. Eschewing the traditional classical language curriculum, the common school developed the utilitarian outlook that facilitated occupational efficiency and upward socioeconomic mobility.

Unlike republican and Napoleonic France, which developed a highly centralized national educational system, the authorities for public schooling in the U.S. were the states and their local districts. The states, in turn, delegated considerable responsibility for establishing, maintaining, governing, and financing schools to local districts. For example, Massachusetts, in 1826, required every town to elect a school committee to provide and set policy for the town schools. Again, the Massachusetts legislature established the first state board of education in 1837.[18] As the frontier moved westward and new territories and states were created, they followed the New England educational model. The southern states, with a few exceptions, were much slower in establishing common schools. It was not until the Reconstruction period (1865–1877) after the Civil War that public school systems were established in several of the southern states.

Within a particular state, especially on the frontier where many small school districts were created, resources available for schooling varied considerably from district to district. This historically generated feature of U.S. schooling created a paradox: while the common school concept emphasized equality of educational opportunity, the disparities in funding between states and local districts produced unequal educational opportunities. In contrast, the French system, based on centralized control, created greater equality between schools but at the price of autonomy.

Normal Schools and Teacher Education

The establishment of common schools created a demand for trained teachers. By the mid-nineteenth century, normal schools, modeled after the French *école normale*, from which its name was derived, were established to prepare common-school teachers. First established in New England in 1823, normal schools were two-year institutions that provided courses in history and philosophy of education, methods of teaching, and practice or demonstration teaching for prospective teachers. By the end of the nineteenth century, many normal schools were reorganized as four-year teacher-education colleges.[19]

The demand for trained teachers attracted many women to teaching careers in the expanding elementary school system. Normal schools provided women with opportunities for higher education that hitherto had been denied them. Despite low salaries, demanding conditions, and restrictions on personal freedom, teaching careers allowed women to enter the workforce when they had few other options. For example, until the Civil War, the majority of rural school teachers had been men. By 1900, 71 percent of the rural teachers were women.[20]

Public schooling's expansion and women's entry into teaching coincided with the origins of the women's rights movement. Feminist leaders such as

Elizabeth Cady Stanton, Emma Willard, Susan B. Anthony, and Catharine Beecher spoke out for women's educational and political equality. In particular, Catharine Beecher (1800–1878), who founded the Hartford Female Seminary in 1828, designed a program to prepare women for teaching careers. Similar to Webster, Beecher promoted a version of American exceptionalism that envisioned the U.S. as a developing nation with a Providential moral mission. Further, she believed that women were to fulfill a key educational role in creating a dynamic and progressive nation. Educated women, Beecher reasoned, were eminently suited to teaching careers and could contribute to national development by bringing literacy, civility, and morality to America's western frontier.[21] To prepare these young women as teachers, Beecher urged the establishment of special teacher education institutions, women's seminaries.[22]

In the nineteenth and early twentieth centuries, there were some similarities and differences between teacher education in the U.S. and in other countries. Primary and elementary teachers in the U.S. and in other countries, especially those in Europe, typically did not have college degrees. They generally completed an elementary education and then had some continuing education. In the U.S., they might go to a secondary school such as the academy or a normal school. In Europe, they might go on to advanced primary schools or to teacher training institutes. In the U.S., teacher entry qualifications were determined by each of the states, which in turn delegated them to local districts. France and Prussia in Europe were moving to more centralized national entry-level requirements. In contrast to elementary and primary school teachers, secondary school teachers typically had college or university degrees.

American Secondary Education

In discussing American secondary education, it is useful to consider the general role of secondary schooling and how American secondary schools are similar to or different from those in other countries where the structure and function of secondary schools rests upon related socioeconomic factors such as class membership and mobility, urban–rural differentials, and gender equality or bias. Traditionally throughout the world, secondary schools were selective institutions that prepared a male elite for entry to higher education. Membership in this elite was class-referenced, either as a hereditary aristocracy or an upper-socioeconomic class. In countries such as the UK and Germany, secondary institutions were often segmented, with students being streamed into them according to class and career destinations. In the U.S., by contrast, public secondary schools, particularly high schools, were comprehensive institutions, open to all students, and provided upward educational as well as socioeconomic mobility.

The Academy: The High School's Institutional Predecessor

Historically, the academy, America's dominant secondary school during the first half of the nineteenth century, replaced the colonial Latin grammar school, a European import. As of 1855, the 6,000 academies enrolled 263,000 students.[23] Unlike the Latin grammar school's limited classical language curriculum, the academy, serving the educational needs of a growing middle class, offered a variety of curricula and subjects. Furthermore, while the Latin grammar schools exclusively prepared upper-class young men for college entry, some academies were coeducational or women's institutions. For example, Emma Willard, a leader in the women's rights movement, established the Troy Female Seminary, established in 1821 in New York. Mary Lyon founded Mount Holyoke Female Seminary in Massachusetts in 1837.

Academies enrolled both college preparatory students as well as those planning to end their formal education upon graduation. Despite considerable variations, academies generally offered three curricula: (1) the traditional Greek and Latin college preparatory program; (2) the English language program, usually for students planning to end their formal education upon graduation—completing secondary school; and (3) the normal, teacher preparation program. Most academies were controlled by private boards of trustees. A few semipublic academies received some funding from cities or states. The era of the academies extended to the 1870s, when they were replaced by public high schools. Private academies still exist in the U.S. and continue to provide secondary education for a small percentage of the school-age cohort.

The High School

Although a few high schools, such as the English Classical School of Boston, operated in the early nineteenth century, it was not until after the Civil War that the high school gradually replaced academies and became the prevalent secondary school. In the 1870s, the courts upheld public taxation for the support of high schools. With such legal sanctions, public high schools were established throughout the country. By 1890 the 2,526 public high schools in the U.S. were enrolling more than 200,000 students. In contrast, the 1,600 private secondary schools and academies at that time enrolled fewer than 95,000 students.[24]

In the mid-nineteenth century, the U.S. was undergoing a profound transformation from an agricultural and rural to an industrial and urban nation, generating a need for more advanced education to which high schools responded.[25] In the late nineteenth and early twentieth centuries, high school curricula expanded to include career or vocational courses such as home economics, manual training, industrial and shop training, and clerical–commercial preparation. The high school thus provided a more advanced education for the increasing number of students who were continuing their formal education beyond the eight years of elementary schooling. Some students terminated their formal schooling at the end of high school; others enrolled in college.

The American high school became a comprehensive institution that aimed at social integration while providing some curricular differentiation. As a school for adolescents, the American high school reflected a society benefiting from an expanding economy. Free of many of the educational and cultural traditions that shaped Europe's secondary education, American society could finance educating large numbers of fourteen- to eighteen-year-olds. For example, in the UK, a strong tendency in the nineteenth century was to extend more years of primary schooling to the working classes rather than refashion secondary schooling, which remained a bastion of upper-class privilege. It was not until the twentieth century that a variety of secondary schools were established in the UK. However, these secondary schools streamed students according to academic achievement and career destinations that often reflected the students' socioeconomic class. Secondary education in France was organized into a variety of schools rather than a comprehensive one as in the U.S.

While historically the development of the comprehensive high school in the U.S. occurred rather quickly, European traditions continued to inspire some American educators. In its early decades, the high school also inherited some curricular confusion and ambiguity from the academy, its institutional predecessor. While traditionalist educators defined the high school's purpose as college preparation, progressives sought to reshape it into a "people's school," offering a range of programs to a diverse student population. Between traditionalist and progressive, the key issue was whether the high school was to be a single-purpose institution educating the college bound or a multipurpose agency.

The National Education Association's Committee of Ten, established in 1892, reinforced a single-purpose high school curriculum—the uniform teaching of subjects for both college-bound and terminal students.[26] The committee recommended four separate curricula for the high school: classical, Latin-scientific, modern language, and English. Each curriculum included foreign languages, mathematics, sciences, English, and history—the academic courses typically present in college preparatory programs. Although the committee suggested alternatives to the dominant Latin and Greek classical curriculum, its recommendations were heavily oriented to college preparatory rather than terminal students. The rationale for the committee's decisions argued that the recommended subjects provided mental discipline and trained the mind.

While the Committee of Ten brought some standardization to the potentially chaotic high school curriculum, some progressive educators challenged its recommendations. Progressives argued that the high school, as a truly comprehensive secondary institution, should provide diverse curricula with more program alternatives. Social efficiency educators, influential in curriculum design, contended socioeconomic efficiency or functionality should guide secondary education.[27] They argued that high schools should prepare students to be efficient producers, consumers, citizens, and parents. The debate between the traditionalists and the progressives provides the historical context to interpret ongoing controversies about the purpose and curriculum of the contemporary American high school.

Educators in the U.S. who believed that the high school had a single academic purpose—preparing students for college entry—argued that it was democratic to provide a single college preparatory program for all students. They believed that to segment students into different curricular tracks not only diluted the purpose of secondary schooling but was also undemocratic. In contrast, those who saw the high school as a multipurpose institution, serving an increasingly diverse student population, believed that ensuring educational opportunity for all students meant providing different programs that met the varied needs of a diverse student population.

The persistent controversy between college preparatory and multipurpose secondary educators continued into the twentieth century. Events, however, moved high schools increasingly on the multipurpose path. By 1918, thirty states required full-time school attendance until age sixteen.[28] Increasing enrollments meant that the high school population was no longer dominated by students from professional and business families but was more representative of the national population. These changes in the demographics of the high school student population were reflected in NEA's Commission on the Reorganization of Secondary Education's report, *The Cardinal Principles of Secondary Education*, in 1918. Recognizing the U.S. process of urbanization and industrialization, the commission argued that high schools should be truly comprehensive institutions that served the whole population's varied social, cultural, and economic groups.[29] The curriculum should be differentiated to meet agricultural, business-commercial, industrial, and domestic as well as college preparatory needs while maintaining the institution's socially integrative comprehensive character. Further, all public schools should be articulated, in the much-praised ladder sequence, rather than segmented or isolated.[30]

By mid-twentieth century, four curricular programs were found in the larger U.S. high schools: (1) a college preparatory program, based on college-entry requirements, which included such subjects as English language and literature, foreign languages, mathematics, natural and physical sciences, and history and social sciences; (2) the commercial-business program, with courses in bookkeeping, shorthand, and typing; (3) a program offering a choice of industrial, vocational, home economics, or agricultural classes; and (4) a general education program for students whose formal education would end with high school graduation. While these four curricula were distinct, a core of common subjects—typically English, U.S. history and civics, health, and physical education—were required by all students to maintain the high school's comprehensiveness.

Very important in U.S. secondary education were the co- and extracurricular activities—orchestra, band, dramatics, and athletics, particularly the team sports of basketball, baseball, and football—that created student solidarity in the school and community pride outside of the school. Importantly, the athletic program and activities directed to adolescent socialization gave the U.S. comprehensive high school characteristics not found in the more academic milieu of European secondary schools. However, critics, both domestic and foreign, would contend that the U.S. schools' stress on nonacademic matters weakened its academic and intellectual character.

Despite regional variations, the usual high school pattern followed a four-year sequence encompassing grades nine, ten, eleven, and twelve and generally including the age group from fourteen to eighteen.[31] There were exceptions, however, to this general pattern. There were six-year institutions in which students attended a combined junior-senior high school after completing a six-year elementary school. There were also three-year junior high schools, which comprised seventh, eighth, and ninth grades, and three-year senior high schools, which encompassed tenth, eleventh, and twelfth grades.

The junior high school concept grew out of the Committee of Ten's suggestion that secondary education begin two years earlier and reduce the years of elementary school from eight to six.[32] In many instances, the junior high school was initially the first three years of a six-year high school. In the course of its development, the junior high school often became a separate facility housing grades seven, eight, and nine. Today, the junior high school has become part of the pattern of school organization for many districts. During the 1960s, the middle school appeared. Middle schools generally include grades six, seven, and eight. The middle school was designed to meet the needs of preadolescents, usually ages eleven through thirteen years, in a transitional institution between elementary and high school.[33]

The American College and University

The colonial colleges emulated the British pattern of Oxford and Cambridge, which sought to prepare scholars and theologians to educate the well-rounded, upper-class gentleman. The early colonial colleges were established by religious denominations. For example, believing an educated ministry was needed to establish Christianity in the New World, the Massachusetts General Court created Harvard College in 1636. Although there were institutional variations, the general colonial college curriculum included: (1) Latin, Greek, Hebrew, rhetoric, and logic during the first year; (2) Greek, Hebrew, logic, and natural philosophy during the second year; (3) natural philosophy, metaphysics, and ethics during the third year; and (4) mathematics and a review in Greek, Latin, logic, and natural philosophy during the fourth year.[34]

By the early 1850s, critics of traditional liberal arts colleges were arguing for federal land grants to establish agricultural and mechanical colleges.[35] Justin Morrill, a U.S. representative from Vermont, sponsored a bill to use federal land grants to support agricultural and industrial education. The Morrill Act of 1862 granted each state 30,000 acres of public land for each senator and representative in Congress, based on the apportionment of 1860. The income from this grant was to support at least one state college for agricultural and mechanical instruction.[36] The general impact of land-grant colleges was to encourage agricultural education, engineering, and other applied sciences, as well as the more traditional liberal arts and professional education. Many leading state universities originated as land-grant colleges, including the University of Illinois and The Pennsylvania State University.

An interesting episode in educational borrowing from one country to another country occurred in the late nineteenth century when U.S. higher education was influenced by the importation of the German research model. Many American professors went to Germany to complete their doctoral studies. While in residence, they engaged in research seminars with learned professors who investigated specific topics in the sciences and the humanities. Returning to U.S., they introduced the German university's seminar method of instruction and the idea that professors should engage in research as well as teaching.

After World War II, American higher education experienced its greatest growth. This trend began with enactment of the Servicemen's Readjustment Act, the G.I. Bill, in 1944. The G.I. Bill provided federal funds to veterans to continue their education by subsidizing tuition, fees, books, and living expenses. Between 1944 and 1951, 7,800,000 veterans used the bill's assistance to attend technical schools, colleges, and universities. Doubling the nation's population of college students, the G.I. Bill ushered in the era of rapid growth in higher education that would continue until the early 1970s.[37]

The magnitude and availability of American higher education in two-year community colleges, four-year colleges, and universities can be contrasted with most other countries. In the U.S., the Scholastic Aptitude Test (SAT) and ACT tests provide information to colleges and universities about students' academic aptitudes, but there are no national entrance examinations as in the Peoples Republic of China or Japan. The wide network of institutions available to students in the U.S. facilitates a high attendance at institutions of higher education in the U.S. compared to other countries. While Americans laud the availability of higher education, critics, both at home and abroad, contend that American colleges and universities are nonselective institutions that lack the academic rigor found elsewhere.

Cultural Diversity and American Education

This section examines cultural diversity in historical perspective, concentrating on the histories of important groups such as African Americans, Native Americans, Hispanic Americans, and Asian Americans. The discussion tends to be topical as well as chronological, spanning the nineteenth and twentieth centuries.

African American Education

In the Reconstruction period after the Civil War, from 1865 to 1877, the U.S. looked to education as one means to aid the transition from slavery to citizenship. In 1865, Congress established the Freedmen's Bureau to provide aid and education to the freed African Americans. As of 1869, more than 114,000 African American students were enrolled in bureau schools. Bureau schools functioned until 1872 when the bureau ceased operations.

While the Freedmen's Bureau prepared a small number of African American teachers, most teachers who taught African American children in the South were white northerners. Although many of these teachers were abolitionists who detested slavery, they nevertheless held strong stereotypes about the education appropriate for black children. The leading expert on African American education, Samuel C. Armstrong, founder of the Hampton Institute, stressed industrial training rather than the general liberal education for blacks.[38] Armstrong believed that industrial education was most suited to black students' level of academic readiness and future career destinations.[39]

Booker T. Washington (1856–1915) became the recognized national leader for African Americans in the half-century after emancipation.[40] Educated at Hampton Institute, Washington endorsed Armstrong's industrial training ideology that emphasized vocational training as the primary means of socioeconomic uplift for blacks. In 1881, Washington was appointed principal of the Tuskegee Institute, a state-supported all-black institution in Alabama. Washington shaped Tuskegee's curriculum according to his perception that African Americans in the South formed a basically landless agricultural class. Though free from slavery, African Americans still lived in a dependent economic and oppressive political situation. To improve their economic condition, Washington believed African Americans needed to establish themselves in farming and the trades. Tuskegee's curriculum, which stressed basic literacy and agricultural and occupational skills, emphasized the values of hard work and the dignity of labor. To avoid conflict with whites in the South, Washington discouraged his students from entering higher education, law, and politics.

Washington chose not to challenge the white power structure but to conform to it. His racial ideology asserted that blacks and whites were mutually dependent economically but separate socially. Addressing the Cotton Exposition in Atlanta, Georgia, in 1885, Washington said, "In all things that are purely social, we can be as separate as the fingers, yet one as the hand in all things essential to mutual progress."[41] Today, Washington is a controversial historical figure. His defenders claim he made the best of a desperate situation and that, despite his compromises on racial issues, he gradually advanced African Americans' educational opportunities. His critics see him as the controlling head of a large educational network that promoted his own power rather than the interests of his people.

Near the end of his career, Washington met a forceful challenger in the African American scholar and activist W.E.B. DuBois (1868–1963). A sociologist and historian, DuBois challenged the segregation system that had disenfranchised black voters and limited their children's educational opportunities.[42] His important sociological study, *The Philadelphia Negro: A Social Study*, examined the situation of an urban African American population.[43]

Active in the civil rights movement, DuBois was a founder of the National Association for the Advancement of Colored People (NAACP), established in 1909. DuBois and the NAACP were determined opponents of political disenfranchisement of African Americans and their segregation in the public schools. Their efforts led to the momentous 1954 decision of the U.S. Supreme Court in *Brown et al. v. Board of Education of Topeka* (1954) that overturned the "separate but equal" doctrine and ruled racial segregation in public schools unconstitutional.

In terms of the international dimension of their ideas, Washington and DuBois were quite different. Although he was a national African American leader, Washington, in many respects, was a regional figure. He saw African Americans as a group that was located in and should remain in the South. His work sought their gradual economic improvement in the South by introducing scientific agriculture that would lessen the impact of the sharecrop system. Washington, using the phrase "put down your buckets where you are," discouraged African American migration from the South's rural areas to the large northern cities. Although Tuskegee Institute did some fieldwork in Africa, Washington did not take a broad international view of the black experience.

DuBois developed a national and international perspective on the African American experience. While the South had the largest African American population, DuBois saw the issues related to race in national and international terms. Further, he related the experience of blacks in the U.S. with those in Africa. He was a pioneer of Pan Africanism, the forerunner of the Afrocentric curriculum.

In the mid-1950s, the movement for civil and educational equality accelerated. Martin Luther King, Jr., emerged as the leader of a national nonviolent civil rights movement, which worked to increase educational opportunities for African Americans and other minority groups. At the same time that civil rights advocates were mobilizing throughout the nation, recalcitrant segregationists sought to evade compliance with the *Brown* decision. In 1957, President Eisenhower ordered federal troops to Little Rock, Arkansas, to enforce desegregation at Central High School.

The Civil Rights Act of 1964 authorized federally initiated lawsuits to compel compliance with school desegregation. It authorized withholding federal funds from school districts that failed to desegregate. To end *de facto* segregation policies based on residential patterns, some school districts initiated busing programs in which students were transported from one attendance area to another to achieve racial integration.

Native American Education

Many countries, including the U.S., have populations of indigenous peoples who were these countries' first inhabitants. The Western Hemisphere was peopled by a variety of Amerindians or Native American peoples, many of whom lived in tribal societies. The issue that developed and remains involves the relationship between the larger and more dominant groups that have populated the lands once solely inhabited by the indigenous peoples and these indigenous minorities. The educational issues often center around respect for and maintenance of the traditional indigenous cultures or the assimilation of indigenous peoples into the larger society.

During the nineteenth century in the U.S., most of the Native American tribes were expelled from the area east of the Mississippi River and, after a series of often bloody "Indian Wars," were forcibly resettled on reservations in remote areas of the Great Plains and the Southwest.[44] In the late nineteenth century, the federal government embarked on a program to "civilize" Native Americans by assimilating them into the dominant white society. Educational "reformers" were determined to purge two characteristics of tribal culture that they perceived as impediments to assimilation: communal tribal land ownership and aversion to the Protestant work ethic. Determined to inculcate dominant white values into Native Americans, the reformers relied on industrial training, which was used in African American education.[45]

From 1890 to the 1930s, the Bureau of Indian Affairs (BIA) maintained a network of boarding schools to assimilate Native American children into the dominant society.[46] Native American children were taken from their families and placed in semimilitary schools. Isolated from their indigenous tribal cultures, the students, forbidden to use their native languages, were forced to speak only English. The boarding schools stressed a basic curriculum of reading, writing, arithmetic, and vocational training.[47] Some of the children repeatedly ran away from the schools or secretly tried to maintain their connections to their parents and tribal cultures. After the boarding-school concept was discontinued in the 1930s, Native American society and education changed significantly.

The Native American population grew from 248,000 in 1890 to 357,000 in 1950, reached 1,959,000 in 1990, and exceeded two million in the early twenty-first century.[48] Leaving reservations and former tribal areas, many Native Americans migrated to large urban centers, particularly inner cities. Children living on reservations now attend a variety of schools: those maintained by the BIA, tribal schools, and other kinds of public and private institutions.[49] Native American children living in cities usually attend public schools. Despite changes in government policy, many Native Americans, especially youth, are alienated from the educational system. Although 44 percent of Native Americans are under twenty years of age—compared to 32 percent of the national population—their participation in schooling is far lower than average. Because of a very high dropout rate, the level of Native American high school completion is 67 percent below that of the U.S. population at large.[50]

Hispanic American Education

The terms "Hispanic" or "Latino" refer collectively to Spanish-speaking persons whose ethnic origins can be traced to Mexico, Puerto Rico, Cuba, or other Latin American countries. While they have speaking Spanish in common, each ethnic group has its own distinctive history and culture.

Mexican Americans constitute the largest Hispanic group. Many Mexican Americans are descendants of people who were forcibly incorporated into the U.S. after the Mexican-American War of 1848 (see the chapter on Mexico). The defeated Mexico was forced to cede large areas that are now the states of California, Arizona, Texas, Colorado, and New Mexico.[51] In these states, public schools followed the same assimilationist policy, called Americanization, that was used with immigrant and Native American children. Non-English-speaking children followed a curriculum in which English was the sole language of instruction and generally their own Hispanic culture was ignored. As in the case of Native Americans and African Americans, as well as many immigrants, schooling reinforced a negative self-image and a sense of cultural inferiority.[52]

In the late nineteenth and early twentieth centuries, the Mexican American population increased as migrant workers crossed Mexico's common border with the U.S. to provide cheap labor on ranches, railroads, and farms. Children of migrant workers, even those not working as child laborers, had no or very limited access to schooling. Although many migrants were seasonal workers in the U.S. and returned to Mexico, others remained, either legally or illegally. After World War II, there was movement of Mexican Americans from the Southwest to other states, often to northern industrial cities.[53] In the 1960s a Chicano movement, similar to the civil rights movement, was organized to improve the social, economic, and educational conditions of Mexican Americans.

The history of Puerto Rican Americans, another large Latino group, goes back to the Spanish-American War of 1898, when the defeated Spain ceded the island of Puerto Rico to the U.S. In 1917 Puerto Ricans were granted American citizenship. U.S. officials replaced the Spanish colonial education with American public schools. Although some school classes continued to use Spanish, English, as part of the Americanization policy, was made compulsory. American educators were brought to Puerto Rico to train Puerto Rican teachers in U.S. methods.

Since the early twentieth century, there has been Puerto Rican immigration to the U.S. mainland. Today, over two million Puerto Rican Americans live in large U.S. cities, such as New York, Chicago, and Philadelphia.[54] Historically, Puerto Rican high school dropout rates are high and college attendance rates are low. Since the 1960s, Puerto Rican Americans have become more politically organized and active and have improved their economic and educational situation.

The Bilingual Education Act in 1968, with the 1974 Supreme Court decision in *Lau v. Nichols*, led to the establishment of bilingual education programs. Public schools abandoned the old policies of assimilation and Americanization. Today, bilingual education is politically controversial. Opponents of bilingual education have sought to have laws enacted to make English the official language. Bilingualism, like multiculturalism, is an area of controversy.

Asian Americans

Whereas European immigrants entered the U.S. by way of the East Coast, principally New York City, Asian Americans came by way of the West Coast, especially the cities of Los Angeles and San Francisco. For these geographical reasons, the Asian American population was concentrated historically in the western states bordering the Pacific Ocean. From there Asian Americans moved eastward. The first Asian people to settle in the U.S. were Chinese and Japanese. More recent Asian immigrant groups include Filipinos, Indians, Thais, Koreans, Vietnamese, Laotians, and Cambodians.

The early Chinese immigrants arrived in California during the gold rush of 1848–1849. During the peak period of Chinese immigration from 1848 to 1882, over 225,000 Chinese immigrated to the U.S.[55] The early Chinese immigrants were miners, farm workers, and railroad construction workers. Enterprising Chinese immigrants established small businesses, such as grocery stores and laundries, in the cities of the West Coast. In larger cities such as San Francisco and Los Angeles, Chinese enclaves formed and established social, religious, cultural, and educational societies.[56]

Japanese immigration began later than that of the Chinese, occurring primarily between 1885 and 1924. Japanese immigrants came primarily from the agricultural area of southwestern Japan where labor contractors recruited a workforce for the sugar and pineapple plantations in Hawaii and for farms in California.[57] From 1881 to 1890, there were 2,270 Japanese immigrants; from 1881 to 1890, 25,942; and from 1901 to 1910, 129,797.[58] After 1910, the number of Japanese immigrants declined because of economic and political issues between Japan and the U.S.

From 1882 to 1924, the U.S. Congress enacted laws to reduce or ban further immigration of Chinese and Japanese and prevent them from becoming U.S. citizens. The Chinese Exclusion Act (1882) made the Chinese the first immigrant group to be excluded from entering the U.S. For immigrants who had arrived before these laws took effect, educational and economic opportunities were often limited by racial hostility and discrimination. In 1906, for example, the San Francisco Board of Education implemented a policy of segregating students of Asian ethnicity from other students. After strong diplomatic protests from the Japanese government, the board rescinded its policy.[59] Before World War II, few Chinese Americans or Japanese Americans attained sufficient levels of education to enter the professions.

For Japanese Americans, World War II—in particular the Japanese attack on Pearl Harbor on December 7, 1941—generated strong anti-Japanese feelings. Yielding to fears that the Japanese living in the U.S. would aid the enemy, the U.S. federal government interned 110,000 people of Japanese heritage, many of whom were American citizens, in relocation camps. Located in remote areas, the camps lacked basic services and amenities. Although camp schools were eventually established for the young people, the internment experience produced both physical hardship and psychological alienation. The government's repressive action was based on unfounded fears, since not a single act of sabotage was committed by a Japanese American. Not until the 1980s did the federal government admit its wartime violation of civil liberties and provide compensation to those it had interned.[60]

A substantial number of Filipinos had also immigrated to the mainland U.S. by the start of World War II. Because the Philippines was a U.S. commonwealth, Filipinos did not experience the immigration restrictions that applied to other Asians. Many Filipino men served in the U.S. Navy as stewards and afterwards settled with their families on the West Coast. Others, especially in the 1930s, came to the mainland as farm workers.

After World War II the economic and educational status of Chinese, Japanese, and Filipino Americans improved substantially. The McCarran-Walter Act of 1952 repealed the ban on Asian immigration and citizenship. Asian immigration then increased dramatically, and many of the newcomers were professionals with advanced education. Their arrival sparked a rise in higher education among Asian Americans generally. The change has been particularly notable for Japanese Americans, who now enjoy more participation in higher education than either the white majority of Americans or any other minority group. Nearly 90 percent of college-age Japanese Americans attend colleges or universities.

The post–World War II era also brought an increase in immigration by other Asian groups, especially Koreans, who usually located in large cities and often established small businesses. Following the collapse of American-supported governments in Southeast Asia in the 1970s, Vietnamese, Cambodians, Laotians, and Hmongs immigrated to the U.S. These recent Asian immigrants have differing educational backgrounds. For example, among the South Vietnamese are former military officers, government officials, businessmen, and professionals. The Hmongs, by contrast, do not have a written language.

Recent Trends

Several important events of the 1970s had an impact on schooling. Title IX of the 1972 Education Amendments to the Civil Rights Act prohibited discrimination against women in education programs receiving federal assistance. This legislation, and later acts such as the Women's Educational Equity Act of 1974, extended the civil rights movement to incorporate women's rights and concerns. In 1975 Congress passed the Education for All Handicapped Children Act (PL 94–142). Like Head Start and bilingual education, PL 94–142 improved opportunities for a group of children who had previously lacked full access to a quality education. In this case, the law established a national policy that children with handicaps would receive an "appropriate public education." An important provision of PL 94–142 was that, whenever possible, students with handicaps were to be "mainstreamed" into regular classrooms.

Throughout the 1980s, American education became, once again, a hotly debated topic. A series of national reports, especially *A Nation at Risk*, spotlighted failures in American schooling.[61] The decline of U.S. dominance in the world economy was attributed to academic deficiencies, particularly in mathematics and science. Stimulated by *A Nation at Risk* and similar reports, many states initiated reforms to improve academic achievement in mathematics, science, and English. The reforms of the 1980s stressed academic standards, subject-matter courses, improved school discipline, effective schooling, and teacher competency.

During the 1990s, curriculum was shaped by emphasis on subject-matter competencies in English, mathematics, and basic sciences. Computer literacy, computer-assisted instruction, and other technologies in school programs reflect the nation's transition to a high-tech information society. There was a strong concern about the impact of foreign competition on the U.S. economy and a recognition that the competencies of the American workforce needed to be improved.

Conclusion

In the U.S., historical events shaped the country's political, economic, cultural, religious, and educational milieu. While early on, Native Americans participated in an informal education process, the English colonists imported their own conventional educational institutions from Europe, based on socioeconomic class patterns. After the U.S. won its independence, the forces of democracy, social mobility, and frontier egalitarianism eroded the traditional educational structures inherited from Europe. The common or public school movement led to the establishment of elementary schools throughout the country. The emergence of the public high school in the nineteenth century contributed to the growing inclusiveness of public schooling in the United States. The rise of state colleges and universities and the enactment of the Morrill Act in 1862 created an articulated system of education. By mid-twentieth century, concerted efforts were made to bring equality of educational opportunity to the children of minority groups, especially African Americans, Native Americans, Hispanic Americans, and Asian Americans.

American educational historians typically lauded the "American educational ladder" as the means by which students could proceed in public institutions from elementary, through secondary, to higher institutions. Reflecting American exceptionalism, the U.S. educational ladder was designed to eliminate the class-based biases in European systems. The ladder concept, however, needs further examination. Although varying from state to state, the American educational ladder is a structural reality. Schools are vertically organized in an articulated pattern from kindergartens, through primary and intermediate levels, to middle and secondary school levels, to higher education. Formally, the structure allows students to climb the ladder's institutional rungs. Rather than the actual school structure posing problems of access and mobility, especially for minorities and other disadvantaged groups, the school's geographical location is usually the crucial factor. Schools in affluent suburbs provide a much higher possibility for access, retention, and mobility than schools in economically depressed areas, such as inner cities or declining rural areas. Thus, the ladder concept needs to be examined in terms of where the ladder is placed rather than its actual number of rungs.

DISCUSSION QUESTIONS

1. Reflect on American colonial history. Compare and contrast the American colonial experience with that of other countries.
2. What has been the influence of the Puritan ethic on American culture and education?
3. How did American cultural nationalism develop during the early national period? What is the continuing effect of cultural nationalism on U.S. education?
4. Compare and contrast the development of American secondary education with that of other countries.
5. Examine how the immigrant experience shaped American culture and education.
6. Explore the commonalities and differences in the educational history of African Americans, Hispanic Americans, Native Americans, and Asian Americans.

FIELD AND RESEARCH TOPICS

1. Design a project in which the members of the class conduct oral history interviews about the school experience of senior members of their family or relatives. When interviews have been completed and analyzed, prepare an interpretive history of education based on your family's experience.
2. Visit a museum that stressed American culture and history in its collections. Identify those exhibits that deal in some way with education and schooling. Interpret how the exhibit conveyed or failed to convey a sense of the American educational past.
3. Organize a group research project in which the students will examine representative books and materials that have been used to teach reading in elementary school. Identify key periods such as the 1840s, 1850s, 1860s, and so on. You might begin with the McGuffey readers. Using historical research and interpretation, try to determine how the nature of the stories, the characters, and the values in the books have changed over time.
4. Arrange a debate on the issue: "Resolved, American public schools should emphasize multiculturalism in their curriculum."
5. Organize a panel discussion in which each presenter analyzes a particular person's educational experiences based on that person's autobiography.

For example, autobiographies might be those that include themes such as a Native American's experience at a boarding school, an African American's experience in segregated schools, a woman's experience in entering a male-dominated profession, a Christian fundamentalist's rejection of cultural relativism, and so forth.

SUGGESTIONS FOR FURTHER READING

Anderson, James D. *The Education of Blacks in the South, 1860–1935.* Chapel Hill: University of North Carolina Press, 1988.

Cohen, Ronald D. *Children of the Mill: Schooling and Society in Gary, Indiana, 1906–1960.* Bloomington: Indiana University Press, 1990.

Gutek, Gerald L. *An Historical Introduction to American Education,* 2nd ed. Prospect Heights, IL: Waveland Press, 1991.

Herbst, Jurgen. *And Sadly Teach: Teacher Education and Professionalization in American Culture.* Madison: University of Wisconsin Press, 1989.

Kaestle, Carl, et al. *Literacy in the United States: Readers and Reading since 1880.* New Haven, CT: Yale University Press, 1991.

Mondale, Sarah, and Sarah B. Patton. *School: The Story of American Public Education.* Boston: Beacon Press, 2001.

Patterson, James T. Brown v. Board of Education: *A Civil Rights Milestone and Its Troubled Legacy.* New York: Oxford University Press, 2001.

Ravitch, Diane. *Left Back: A Century of Failed School Reforms.* New York: Simon and Schuster, 2000.

Rippa, S. Alexander. *Education in a Free Society: An American History.* New York: Longman, 1992.

Schlesinger, Arthur M. *The Disuniting of America.* New York: W.W. Norton, 1992.

Spack, Ruth. *America's Second Tongue: American Indian Education and the Ownership of English, 1860–1900.* Lincoln: University of Nebraska Press, 2002.

Staff of Education Week. *Lessons of a Century: A Nation's Schools Come of Age.* Bethesda, MD: Editorial Projects in Education, 2000.

Takaki, Ronald. *A Different Mirror: A History of Multicultural America.* Boston: Little, Brown, 1993.

Tyack, David, and Elisabeth Hansot. *Learning Together: A History of Coeducation in American Public Schools.* New Haven, CT: Yale University Press, 1990.

NOTES

[1] CIA (Central Intelligence Agency), "The World Factbook," January 22, 2004, http://www.odci.gov/cia/publications/factbook/geos/us.html

[2] Ibid.

[3] Ibid.

[4] Ibid.

[5] For example, see Roger Magnuson, *Education in New France* (Montreal: McGill-Queens University Press, 1992).

[6] Ronald Takaki, *A Different Mirror: A History of Multicultural America* (Boston: Little, Brown, 1993), 21–44.

[7] Nathaniel Schurtleff, ed., *Records of the Governor and Company of the Massachusetts Bay in New England,* vol. 2 (Boston: Order of the Legislature, 1853).

[8] Samuel E. Morrison, *The Intellectual Life of Colonial New England* (New York: New York University Press, 1956).

[9] Robert Middlekauff, *Ancients and Axioms: Secondary Education in Eighteenth-Century New England* (New Haven: Yale University Press, 1963).

[10] For the origins and impact of slavery in the South, see Takaki, 31–76.

[11] Jane Turner Censer, *North Carolina Planters and Their Children, 1800–1860* (Baton Rouge: Louisiana State University Press, 1984).

[12] Esmond Wright, ed., *Benjamin Franklin: His Life As He Wrote It* (Cambridge, MA: Harvard University Press, 1990).

[13] Bernard Cohen, *Benjamin Franklin's Science* (Cambridge, MA: Harvard University Press, 1990).

[14] Harry R. Warfel, *Noah Webster: Schoolmaster to America* (New York: Octagon, 1936); Ervin C. Shoemaker, *Noah Webster: Pioneer of Learning* (New York: Columbia University Press, 1936).

[15] Noah Webster, *Dissertations on the English Language* (Boston: Isaiah Thomas, 1789).

[16] William R. Johnson, "Chanting Choristers: Simultaneous Recitation in Baltimore's Nineteenth-Century Primary Schools," *History of Education Quarterly* 34(1) (1994): 1–23.

[17] John Reigart, *The Lancasterian System of Instruction in the Schools of New York City* (New York: Teachers College Press, Columbia University, 1916).

[18] Lawrence A. Cremin, *The American Common School, A Historical Conception* (New York: Teachers College Press, Columbia University, 1951).

[19] For the history of American teacher education, see Jurgen Herbst, *And Sadly Teach: Teacher Education and Professionalization in American Culture* (Madison: University of Wisconsin Press, 1989).

[20] Wayne E. Fuller, *One-Room Schools of the Middle West: An Illustrated History* (Lawrence: University Press of Kansas, 1994), 61.

[21] Polly Welts Kaufman, *Women Teachers on the Frontier* (New Haven: Yale University Press, 1984).

[22] Barbara M. Cross, ed., *The Educated Woman in America: Selected Writings of Catharine Beecher, Margaret Fuller, and M. Carey Thomas* (New York: Teachers College Press, Columbia University, 1965), 73–75.

[23] Theodore R. Sizer, *The Age of Academies* (New York: Teachers College Press, Columbia University, 1964).

[24] Edward A. Krug, *The Shaping of the American High School, 1880–1920* (New York: Harper & Row, 1964).

[25] Edward A. Krug, *The Shaping of the American High School, 1920–1941* (Madison: University of Wisconsin Press, 1972.

[26] National Education Association, *Report of the Committee on Secondary School Studies* (Washington, DC: U.S. Government Printing Office, 1893).

[27] Walter H. Drost, *David Snedden and Education for Social Efficiency* (Madison: University of Wisconsin, 1967).

[28] Krug, *The Shaping of the American High School, 1920–1941*, 7.

[29] A historical analysis of the impact of the Cardinal Principles can be found in William G. Wraga, *Democracy's High School: The Comprehensive High School and Educational Reform in the United States* (Lanham, MD: University Press of America, 1994).

[30] Commission on the Reorganization of Secondary Education, *Cardinal Principles of American Secondary Education,* Bulletin no. 35 (Washington, DC: U.S. Government Printing Office, 1918).

[31] Robert L. Hampel, *The Last Little Citadel: American High Schools Since 1940* (Boston: Houghton Mifflin, 1986).

[32] Nelson Bossing and Roscoe Cramer, *The Junior High School* (Boston: Houghton Mifflin, 1965).

[33] Judith L. Irvin, ed., *Transforming Middle Level Education: Perspectives and Possibilities* (Needham Heights, MA: Allyn and Bacon, 1992).

[34] Frederick Rudolph, *The American College and University: A History* (Athens: University of Georgia Press, 1990).

[35] Allan Nevins, *The State Universities and Democracy* (Urbana: University of Illinois Press, 1962).

[36] Benjamin F. Andrews, *The Land Grant of 1862 and the Land-Grant College* (Washington, DC: U.S. Government Printing Office, 1918).

[37] Diane Ravitch, *The Troubled Crusade: American Education, 1945–1980* (New York: Basic Books, 1983), 3–14.

[38] James D. Anderson, *The Education of Blacks in the South, 1860–1935* (Chapel Hill: University of North Carolina Press, 1988).

[39] Raymond W. Smock, ed., *Booker T. Washington in Perspective: Essays of Louis R. Harlan* (Jackson: University Press of Mississippi, 1988).

[40] Booker T. Washington, *Up from Slavery* (New York: Doubleday, 1938).

[41] Booker T. Washington, *Selected Speeches of Booker T. Washington* (New York: Doubleday, 1932).

[42] Virginia Hamilton, *W.E.B. DuBois: A Biography* (New York: Crowell, 1972).

[43] W.E.B. DuBois, *The Philadelphia Negro: A Social Study* (Philadelphia: University of Pennsylvania Press, 1899).

[44] Robert M. Utley, *The Indian Frontier of the American West, 1846–1890* (Albuquerque: University of New Mexico Press, 1984).

[45] David W. Adams, "Fundamental Considerations: The Deep Meaning of Native American Schooling, 1880–1900," *Harvard Educational Review* 58(1) (1988): 1–28.

[46] For an example of the Native American boarding school experience, see K. Tsianina Lomawaima, *They Called It Prairie Light: The Story of Chilocco Indian School* (Lincoln: University of Nebraska Press, 1994).

[47] Robert A. Trennert, Jr., *The Phoenix Indian School: Forced Assimilation in Arizona, 1891–1975* (Norman: University of Oklahoma Press, 1988). Also see Trennert, "Corporal Punishment and the Politics of Indian Reform," *History of Education Quarterly* (Winter 1989): 595–617.

[48] U.S. Department of Commerce, Bureau of the Census, *We the First Americans* (Washington, DC: U.S. Government Printing Office, n.d.), 3; U.S. Bureau of the Census, *Statistical Abstract of the United States, 1991* (Washington, DC: U.S. Government Printing Office, 1991), 22.

[49] *We, the First Americans*, 9–10.

[50] Ibid., 4–5.

[51] Leonard Dinnerstein and David M. Reimers, *Ethnic Americans: A History of Immigration and Assimilation* (New York: Harper & Row, 1982), 88–89.

[52] Julian Nava, *Mexican Americans: A Brief Look at Their History* (New York: Anti-Defamation League of B'nai B'rith, 1970), 31. Also see Richard Griswold del Castillo, *The Treaty of Guadeloupe Hidalgo* (Norman: University of Oklahoma Press, 1990).

[53] For an example of the Mexican American urban experience, see George J. Sanchez, *Becoming Mexican American: Ethnicity, Culture, and Identity in Chicano Los Angeles, 1900–1945* (New York: Oxford University Press, 1993).

[54] Dinnerstein and Reimers, 102.

[55] David J. O'Brien and Stephen S. Fugita, *The Japanese American Experience* (Bloomington: Indiana University Press, 1991), 17.

[56] Shih-Shan Henry Tsai, *The Chinese Experience in America* (Bloomington: Indiana University Press, 1986), 1–20.

[57] O'Brien and Fugita, 14–16. For the Japanese American experience in Hawaii, see Eileen H. Tamura, *Americanization, Acculturation, and Ethnic Identity: The Nisei Generation in Hawaii* (Urbana: University of Illinois Press, 1994).

[58] O'Brien and Fugita, 17.

[59] Dinnerstein and Reimers, 52.

[60] Roger Daniels, Sandra C. Taylor, and Harry H. L. Kitano, *Japanese Americans: From Relocation to Redress* (Seattle: University of Washington Press, 1991).

[61] National Commission on Excellence in Education, *A Nation at Risk: The Imperative for Educational Reform* (Washington, DC: U.S. Department of Education, 1983), 14.

EDUCATION IN THE UNITED STATES
ADMINISTRATION, ORGANIZATION, AND STRUCTURE

Unlike the centralized French and Japanese educational systems, the U.S. has neither a national nor a centralized system. Even among those countries that have a federal, or a modified federal, system of government, such as India, Mexico, and Nigeria, the U.S. federal government's educational role is much more limited. Most other countries with written constitutions make a national provision or state a national responsibility for education. Unlike the constitutions of these countries, the U.S. Constitution does not contain a specific provision that addresses education; the U.S. Constitution does not guarantee education as a fundamental constitutional right. However, some state constitutions guarantee that right. Under the reserved powers clause of the Tenth Amendment of the U.S. Constitution, responsibility for education resides with each state. With educational authority vested in the fifty states, it is more accurate legally to refer to fifty state systems rather than a national American system of education. Additionally, the states delegate considerable policy making, governance, and financing to local school districts and their boards of education.

This chapter provides an overview of how schools in the U.S. are governed, organized, and financed. To provide a framework for comparing the organization and structure of schools in the U.S. with those of other countries, an overview of elementary, secondary, and higher education is presented. At key places in the chapter, the U.S. structure is compared with that of other countries as a preview to comparisons made in later chapters on education in other nations.

The Federal Role in Education

Although the U.S. does not have a national, or federal system of schools, the federal government does exercise a role in education. The federal agency with the greatest responsibility for education is the U.S. Department of Education.

Department of Education

Although a federal Department of Education was established in 1867, it was for most of its history a subordinate unit within another federal department such as the Department of the Interior or the Department of Health, Education, and Welfare. Furthermore, throughout most of its history, the Department of Education was a center for collecting and disseminating information and statistics about American education. Rarely did it initiate general policies or reforms.

During the Eisenhower administration in the 1950s the Office of Education, as the department was then called, became part of a new Department of Health, Education, and Welfare. After the U.S. Supreme Court ruling in *Brown v. the Board of Education of Topeka* in 1954, the department was responsible for monitoring local school racial desegregation and integration plans. In 1958, after Congress passed the National Defense Education Act (NDEA), the Office of Education encouraged and distributed federal grants for new programs in mathematics, science, and guidance. It gained an even larger role during President Lyndon Johnson's Great Society and War on Poverty programs from 1964–1968.[1]

In 1979, after long and often heated debate, Congress approved President Jimmy Carter's initiative to create a separate Department of Education, whose secretary would be a member of the president's cabinet. The Department of Education was officially established in 1980. Under President Ronald Reagan and Secretary of Education Terrel Bell, the Department of Education was used to publicize a new conservative educational agenda, *A Nation at Risk*, in 1983. The rationale of the agenda emphasized that: (1) the academic achievement of U.S. students, especially in mathematics and science, was deficient in comparison to other countries such as Japan and Germany; (2) U.S. educational deficits, contributing to a declining economic productivity, had limited the country's ability to compete in the global economy; and (3) a reemphasis on academic basics and higher academic standards was needed to correct these deficits. Comparatively, the Reagan–Bell educational agenda paralleled very closely that of Margaret Thatcher's conservative government in the United Kingdom.

In more recent years, the secretary of education has become a more important national political actor, developing and articulating the administration's educational policy and using the office to promote that agenda. For example, Rodney Paige, George W. Bush's secretary of education, encouraged national testing at specific grade levels as a measure of student academic achievement and teacher accountability.

Despite this effort to effect a national policy, the agency still mainly dispenses information, sponsors publications on promising educational programs, and conducts research. Its secretary often tends to use his or her office as a sounding board to encourage educational initiatives rather than to attempt to force them. Indeed, its powers of enforcement are limited. Because of these limitations on its role, it is difficult for the federal government to implement sweeping national changes in education or to exert direct power over teachers, curricula, and standards.

Federal Funding and Support of Education

Unlike many other countries where the national or central government contributes a preponderant share of funds to operate schools, the federal contribution in the U.S. is much more limited, with the preponderant fiscal contribution coming from state and local district taxes and revenues. Indeed, the federal share of school funding rarely exceeds 6 percent of total expenditures for education.

There has been a general increase in federal support since the 1930s, especially with the Johnson administration's Great Society and War on Poverty programs from 1965 to 1968. The administrations of Nixon and Ford took the approach of revenue sharing, with the federal government distributing funds to the states. The later Republican administrations of Ronald Reagan and George H. Bush reverted to the policy that funding was primarily a state and local district responsibility. During the Reagan and Bush administrations, the working premise was that the president should stimulate educational reform through the states and local districts rather than using federal funds to encourage educational change.[2]

In most other countries, the national or central government pays a larger share of school support than in the U.S. Funding of schools throughout the world depends on the internal revenue procedures used in that country—its ability to collect taxes and to fairly and adequately provide support for schools. Less technologically developed countries (LTDCs), such as Nigeria and to some extent Mexico, have been forced to reduce expenditures on education due to declining revenues and because of economic restructuring, primarily debt reduction, imposed by the World Bank. Former Communist nations such as Russia have encountered momentous economic problems as they moved from state ownership to privatization of industry. Further, these former Communist nations have had difficulty in establishing means of collecting taxes. As a result, funds for education have declined.[3] In Europe, especially in the EU countries, changes in educational funding that transcend national borders are taking place.

The States' Role in Education

As noted earlier, each of the fifty states that comprise the U.S. has primary responsibility for and authority over education in that state, usually directed by its constitution or the state legislature. Thus, each state has the legal and statutory responsibility to establish, maintain, and support its public schools. Furthermore, the states have created local school districts that have been granted considerable latitude in governance over and in funding local schools. However, these local districts are creatures of the state rather than autonomous entities. Among the important state educational responsibilities are: (1) establishing and funding public schools; (2) establishing state-mandated curricular requirements; (3) establishing the years of compulsory education—the age at which students may legally leave school; (4) setting requirements for certification of school administrators, teachers, and other educational personnel; (5) establishing minimum academic standards and competencies required of students; and (6) establishing the health, safety, and transportation requirements that school districts must follow. The document that specifies the state's responsibilities and requirements, including those delegated to local districts, is the state school code.

Because of the preponderant authority of the states in education, the U.S. is rather unique in its educational governance. Although other nations have devolved certain educational prerogatives on regional, provincial, municipal, or other local units, the central or national government in these countries tends to be paramount. Often the local units are designated as subordinate, lower entities whose major responsibility is implementing national policies. Educational governance in the U.S. is somewhat similar to other federal systems such as India or Germany. However, in the other federal systems, the national government has more authority, as in India where its powers are concurrent with the states.

State governments in the U.S., like the federal government, rest on a threefold system of checks and balances between the executive, legislative, and judicial branches. The governor of the state, the state's elected chief executive officer, has considerable, but also limited, authority for education. The governor has the power to make the educational funding recommendations to the legislature. This then becomes the basis for the state's foundation formula that determines the amount of financial support public schools will receive. The formula should guarantee that both local and state funding provide a relatively equal and adequate amount of money for every child's essential education. Since *A Nation at Risk* launched a concerted reform effort, the nation's governors have taken a much more visible leadership role in school improvement initiatives.

The state legislature has authority and responsibility for drafting and enacting that state's laws on education. State legislatures have myriad educational powers, such as: (1) approving and amending the state foundation formula for funding public schools; (2) specifying the role and duties of state boards and departments of education; (3) determining the types of local school districts, the process for electing or appointing local district boards of education, and specifying their revenue-generating powers; (4) establishing the length of compulsory education, the minimum number of days of the school calendar, and statewide school holidays; (5) setting requirements for curriculum, school building codes, life safety, transportation, and other related items; and (6) determining student and teacher competency tests and other requirements. Recent trends in state legislatures have been to increase academic requirements and to emphasize standards as more tangible evidence of academic competency, especially through standardized testing. Comparatively, the state legislatures in the U.S. perform many of the functions that occur at the central or national level in other countries.

Governors and members of the state legislatures are elected on a partisan basis and are typically Democrats or Republicans. While both major parties have a commitment to public education, ideological differences exist between them that sometimes bears on educational policies. Another important distinction is the geographical basis of strength of each party. Traditionally, the Democratic Party has been preponderant in large metropolitan areas while the Republican Party has tended to be stronger in suburbs, small towns, and rural areas. These differences often affect educational legislation. For example, Democrats may be more supportive of the needs of urban school districts and more responsive to teachers' unions. Republicans tend to favor greater local control and, paradoxically, state-mandated competency testing and statewide standards.

Another important feature of the state legislatures in the U.S. is that their members are elected for fixed terms that range from two to four years for members of the lower house and usually six years for those in the upper house, the state senate. This differs from countries having a parliamentary system in which a party, to form and maintain a government, needs to command the majority of seats in the legislative body. Due to defections from the ruling party or its losses in elections, a government may fall and new elections be required before the expiration of terms of office in countries such as the UK and India.

Some comparisons can be made about the role of partisan politics in education in the U.S. and in other countries. In the U.S., education is paradoxically considered to be both nonpolitical in the sense of partisan political parties but also political in the sense of citizenship formation. Often, local school boards are elected in a nonpartisan way, without political party designations. Realistically, however, partisan politics enters into decisions affecting education made by governors and state legislatures. Simultaneously, the public schools are to educate for citizenship but not in a partisan political way. In other countries, there is often a more evident relationship between educational policy making and partisan politics. In countries such as France and the UK, the different political parties are likely to be more overtly political in their educational policies than in the U.S.

With the exception of Wisconsin, all states have either appointed or elected state boards of education that coordinate the states' educational activities and advise the governor and legislature on educational affairs. These boards establish the policies that guide the state departments of education and state school commissioner or superintendent. Additionally, most states have a separate board for higher education to coordinate the funding and programs for state colleges and universities.[4]

The department of education is the state agency that oversees the implementation of the laws enacted by the legislature and the policies of the board of education. Among its functions are: (1) collecting and disseminating information and statistics about education and schools in the state; (2) approving programs for preparation of and certification of school administrators, teachers, and other educational personnel; (3) overseeing school life safety and pupil transportation, health, and safety matters; (4) monitoring local district compliance with federal and state requirements on desegregation, special education, and gender; (5) developing programs to meet the needs of special student populations such as students with handicaps and bilingual students; (6) developing curriculum guides and materials for state-mandated subjects; and (7) evaluating school programs and either providing guidelines for or preparing standardized tests for student and teacher competency examination. In many ways, the state boards and departments of education exercise the functions performed by national ministries of education in other countries.

The Local Role in Education

The significant role played by local school districts is one of the unique characteristics of American education. Following historic precedents that exalted local citizen control of education, state legislatures established local school districts and their boards of education as agencies that have direct and immediate control over schools, including establishing, governing, maintaining, and financing schools. The local district is somewhat analogous to a state-established quasi-corporation, whose powers are both granted but limited by state law. Since they are state creations, the state exercises final jurisdiction over local districts but delegates important policy-making prerogatives to them. Local district policies must conform to the state's laws, guidelines, and mandates as specified in the state school code.

In contrast with countries with centralized educational systems such as France and Japan, the American local school district's geographical location, size of population, and financial resources produce important variations from district to district, even within a state. Large urban districts, such as Chicago and New York City, have many schools and attendance areas in contrast to very small districts, such as those located in rural areas, with only one school serving a single attendance area. While local school districts are immediate units that operate close to the populations they serve, the money available and per-pupil spending are affected by the district's location, size, and wealth, resulting in inequity among schools.

Local school districts in the U.S. are governed by boards, which in 95 percent of the districts are elected by citizens residing in that district. The remaining 5 percent, usually large municipal boards, are appointed, often by a higher authority such as the city council. Varying with the particular state, the number of board members generally ranges from seven to nine. Local school boards have considerable powers and responsibilities, especially in generating operating revenues by levying a local property tax. Among their other important powers are constructing and maintaining schools, establishing attendance areas, hiring the professional education staff, approving the curriculum, and establishing the school calendar. Within some latitude in these areas, the local district must follow state requirements regarding the minimum length of the school year, the presence of required subjects in the curriculum, and compliance with life-safety, transportation, and other standards. While some other countries have local boards or school councils, their functions are generally more limited than in the U.S.

A distinct feature of the boards of education in the U.S. is that their members are lay persons rather than professional educators. The premise underlying the American principle of citizen control is that as representatives of the community, board members should establish the general policies that professional educators are to follow. This feature contrasts with other countries such as Japan and France where local boards or councils primarily enforce policies made by higher national authorities, usually the Ministry of Education. In other countries, board or council membership generally includes professional educators as well as other citizens.

Local boards of education employ a professional staff, headed by a superintendent of schools, who implement board policies. Thus, boards of education are policy making while the professional education staff is policy implementing. Among the board's responsibilities are: (1) making general policies that govern the district's schools; (2) approving or reconfiguring the staffing pattern of administrators and teachers recommended by the superintendent; (3) hiring and dismissing professional staff based on the superintendent's recommendation; (4) levying the property taxes that provide revenue for the schools and approving the district's budget; (5) approving the curriculum within the state's mandates; and (6) approving policies on student attendance, discipline, and assessment.

The School Superintendent

Another important distinguishing feature of U.S. public education is the role of the district's general superintendent, who is hired by the board of education. A professional educator, the superintendent is typically an experienced former teacher and school administrator, who usually holds advanced graduate degrees, often a Doctorate of Education, Ed.D., or a Ph.D. Importantly, he or she must have the appropriate state certificate or endorsement for the superintendency.

Today, the superintendent acts more like a corporate chief executive officer than a professional educator. Paradoxically, the superintendent is hired by the board of education, which reflects the more populist view that educational policies should be set by nonprofessional educators—the community's representatives. Thus, the American system at the local level is an odd mix of local citizen control and professional educational expertise. Typically, many policies enacted by the board are made upon the superintendent's recommendation.

The superintendent's functions include: (1) providing the board with information, statistics, and data about education, generally, and the school district's, specifically; (2) supervising the district's employees—the professional educators such as other administrators, principals, and teachers, as well as the clerical and maintenance staff; (3) making recommendations to the board on hiring, promoting, remediating, and dismissing personnel; (4) preparing and administering the district's budget; (5) developing and recommending the district's staffing pattern; (6) developing and evaluating curriculum and instruction; (7) maintaining and repairing existing facilities and recommending new construction projects; and (8) ensuring district compliance with state mandates and requirements. Additionally, the superintendent is often the spokesperson for the board of education and school district, cooperating with other government units and with community organizations and the media.

The list of functions performed by superintendents illustrates that many of them focus on noneducational matters rather than on curriculum and instruction. Many deal with allocation of resources, management of personnel and facilities, and public relations. Educators from other countries are often surprised and dismayed that the chief educator in an American school district has so many duties and that only a few of them directly relate to education.

While the professional literature on school governance clearly distinguishes between the board's policy-making role and the superintendent's policy-implementation role, the line between the two areas of responsibility often is more ambiguous in practice. When the line is crossed too many times, it often leads to board–superintendent conflicts. To maintain his or her position, the superintendent needs to enjoy the confidence of a majority of board members. In the past, some superintendents were longtime fixtures who personified education in a given district. Today, however, the average term of a superintendent is typically only three or four years.[5]

Political Partisanship

The local political situation as it relates to education in the U.S. differs from that of other countries, such as France, Japan, and the UK, where educational policy is debated and implemented at the national level. In these countries, the various political parties, often from an ideological frame of reference, indicate in their party platforms the educational policies they plan to implement if elected to power. The political party with a majority of seats in the parliament and forming the government can enact educational legislation that will be implemented by a national ministry or department of education throughout the country. Although education often is an issue in U.S. national and state elections and the Democratic and Republican parties, as well as third parties, include statements about educational needs, priorities, and reforms in their national platforms, once elected, the majority party's role is basically that of stimulator or facilitator, not implementer, of educational policy. The complicated American arrangement of state and local governance of public education makes it difficult for educational reform or innovation to be implemented nationally. Furthermore, in the U.S., while virtually everyone recognizes the political nature of education, there is also a generalized principle that schools should be protected from partisan politics.

School board elections in the U.S. are often nonpartisan in that their members are not directly the nominees of the political parties. The intent is to separate partisan politics from the running of schools. However, school board elections and positions can become intensely political and often mired in special causes and issues that range from setting attendance areas, to school busing, to sex education, to values education, to teaching Creationism, and other highly charged issues. Often local pressure groups organize to advance specific causes. At times, these may be part of national coalitions such as those supporting basic education, school prayer, or the teaching of Creationism. School boards can be drastically split on these issues. Much of the superintendent's educational and administrative effectiveness depends on his or her tact, diplomacy, and political astuteness in dealing with board and district politics.[6]

Community and Parent Participation

Closely related to the American concept of local public school control is the belief that not only parents but the wider community should be committed to and involved in education. Support for parental and community involvement and support varies from district to district but is generally encouraged by boards of education and professional educators.[7] Examples of community involvement include: (1) serving on advisory committees appointed by the board of education; (2) membership in organizations such as the Parent Teachers Organization; and (3) volunteer service as aides in the school. In addition to these general supportive activities, there are also special interest groups that support particular school programs such as team sports, band and orchestra, and drama and art. Additionally, there are strong special interest and advocacy groups for other programs, including special education, bilingual education, and prayer in schools.

Local control and community involvement encourage a more personal closeness to the schools in the U.S. that may not exist in other countries. Also, Americans often do not accord teachers with the respect they enjoy in other countries. For example, parents in Mexico, France, and India are likely to regard the teachers as experts who do not need their advice and approval.

Central Office Staff and Educational Bureaucracies

A tendency in American public education, especially in the larger school districts, has been to create layers of administrative, managerial, and curricular bureaucracies. This bureaucratization replicates a civil service kind of departmentalization as well as a corporate style of managerial specialization. This merging of civil service and corporate styles has not always contributed to efficiency and innovation, however.

The central office staff, a key part of school bureaucracies, especially in large districts, consists of administrative and support personnel who occupy the administrative and managerial layer between the board of education and the superintendent, and the district's schools, principals, and teachers. Historically, the central office emerged in parallel fashion along with the superintendency. Over time, the administrative and managerial style in many school districts became hierarchical in that decision making, resource allocation, and other matters flowed downward from the board, through the superintendent, then through the central staff, to the individual schools and their principals and teachers. Though corporate in appearance, the central office staff came to resemble the traditional "civil service" model of administration, with change and innovation being slow and often guarded.

Today, the central office staff typically is charged with assisting the superintendent in operating the schools. Very large districts, typically in large cities, have an extensive central office that is bureaucratic and hierarchically layered and may consist of several deputy or associate superintendents, finance and business managers, directors and department heads, area and subject coordinators, and supervisors. In smaller districts, the very limited central office staff may include only the superintendent, an assistant superintendent, a business manager, and clerical support personnel. In some ways, the U.S. concept of the central office, which is found throughout the nation, is consolidated in other countries by the officialdom in central ministries of education.

In recent years, there has been criticism of central office bureaucracy by both the educational right and left. Finding it too costly and bureaucratic, critics on the right want to reduce its size and direct the funds saved either to lowering taxes or to basic education. The recent trend in educational policy making is to decrease the power of the central office by implementing site-based management in which more decision making resides with each school—its principal and its teachers. The trend to devolve more decision making on local units is operating almost worldwide. More autonomy is being developed in local schools in the UK, Mexico, and even France, with its long history of centralized bureaucracy.

Educational bureaucracies exist almost universally in countries around the world. In countries where educational decision making is centralized in a Ministry of Education as in France and Japan, the bureaucracy takes the civil service model. Civil servants, many of whom are professional educators, tend to be placed in the government system for their entire careers. They tend to be protective of the status quo and resistant to changes that may alter their role and functions. In countries such as India, Mexico, and Nigeria, where the government is federal, there are levels of bureaucracy at both the national level, in the Ministry of Education, and at state levels. In these countries, educational decision making occurs in a hierarchical fashion and is passed downward to local schools.

The Building Principal and the School

Typically, each school in the local district has its own building administrator, the principal, who is responsible for overall delivery of instruction and other educational services in the particular building.[8] How principals perform their roles and fulfill their responsibilities varies somewhat in elementary, middle, and secondary schools. In very small elementary schools, the principal may also teach. In large elementary and middle schools, the principal is likely to have an administrative support staff that includes an assistant principal and other school personnel. In secondary schools, administration is even more complex, including assistant principals for various functions, department chairpersons for various subject areas of instruction, and guidance and discipline directors.

In the UK, France, India, and many other countries, the head of the school is regarded as its master or most experienced teacher, a role that has either disappeared or has been greatly diminished in the U.S. Today, principals receive many "mixed messages" about their role. The principal can be considered as the individual school's overall middle manager for the school district. He or she, in hierarchical fashion, is expected to implement the districtwide policies in the particular building and attendance area. Practically, on a day-to-day basis, the principal is responsible for operating the school and ensuring that instruction takes place. "Urgent" matters, such as making sure that the buses are running on time, that the roof isn't leaking, and keeping the staff functioning consume much of the principal's time and energy. However, recent trends in the professional preparation of principals, especially as a result of the "effective school" movement, are reinstating the idea of the principal as the school's chief instructional leader.

Teachers

American teachers are the key educational professionals who provide direct classroom instruction in the school system. Most elementary teachers possess an undergraduate degree in education; those teaching at the secondary level hold a degree in education, in liberal arts and sciences, or some other area. Their counterparts in other countries such as France, Japan, and the UK are likely to hold undergraduate degrees. However, in some countries such as India and Nigeria, many elementary teachers lack higher-education degrees but have attended a teacher education program in a secondary school or at a special institute.

In the U.S., teachers are certificated (licensed) in each state. They complete a state-approved program in that state. These programs are not uniform nationally, but vary from state to state. There is, however, some uniformity in teacher education programs because of national standards of accrediting organizations such as the National Council on the Accreditation of Teacher Education (NCATE). In other countries, teachers' credentials are likely to be set by the Ministry of Education and to be uniform throughout the country.

In the U.S., teachers are employed by local districts. After a certain number of years of successful teaching in the district, teachers are granted tenure. The period of probationary standing before tenure ranges from three to five years, depending upon the state. Teachers' salaries are based on salary schedules in which compensation is determined by the degree obtained and graduate hours earned and the length of service in the district. Considerable variations in teachers' salaries exist from state to state and from district to district within a state. In contrast, teachers' salaries in other countries are typically set at national scales and are uniform throughout the country, especially in those nations where education is centralized and under the jurisdiction of a national ministry of education. Although they are part of a hierarchical system, American teachers enjoy a great deal of autonomy in their classrooms. There are no inspection visits from emissaries of a national ministry of education, but there may be several visits each year, especially with teachers in probationary status, by principals or curriculum specialists.

Trends and Alterations in Educational Governance and Organization

The organization of American educational institutions has experienced trends both to more centralization, or consolidation, and also to decentralization or the devolution of authority. The trend to consolidation, accompanied by increased centralization, began in the early twentieth century, as small rural school districts were reorganized and combined into larger ones. The pronounced trend to consolidation is evidenced by the decline in the number of local school districts from 130,000 in 1930 to the current figure of 15,000.[9] The argument for consolidation came from educational administrators who asserted that the larger district, with larger student populations, could operate more efficiently and more economically when duplication was reduced. Further, larger schools could offer a more enriched and varied curriculum than small schools with limited resources.

Since the 1980s, there has been a trend, particularly in larger urban school districts, to decentralize control of schools by creating local school councils as in Chicago in 1990. Further, there has been a trend to site-based management in which the building principal and staff have more decision-making powers in their particular school. Proponents of decentralization argue that it reduces bureaucracy and provides for more direct local control.

Although the governance and system of education in the U.S. is primarily carried out by state and local bodies, contemporary reform movements are producing some slight variations in this basic pattern. Some school boards are sharing more governance responsibilities with teachers, parents, and community members. In the UK and in France, as well, local units are being granted more governance authority over schools.

Organization and Structure of Schools

Preschools

Preschool, or early childhood education, may or may not be part of the public or state-sponsored system. In some instances, the kindergarten may be part of the system. However, most preschool and early childhood arrangements tend to be voluntary and offered by philanthropic, religious, or for-profit agencies. A trend, however, has been to extend preschool as a social service and make it part of the public or government schools.

Elementary Schools

U.S. elementary schools socialize children into American society and provide the foundations for further education. Throughout the world, elementary, or primary schools, as they are often called in other countries, perform this civic, or political, and economic function. While this function may appear to be rather direct and easily defined, socialization into a nation's civic culture and economic system is highly complex. Serious issues relate to questions of how civic culture should be defined and which groups in a given society should have the power to construct the curriculum. Furthermore, the "hidden curriculum," the cultural milieu, both in the school and in the society that surrounds it, shapes behavior on such important matters as group membership; gender roles and related behavior; a proclivity to cooperation or to competition; a positive attitude toward work, teachers, and other peoples; and other distinguishing features. For example, American schools differ greatly from Chinese and Japanese schools in issues of individual differences and group solidarity. While American schools often give conflicting messages about the values of competition and cooperation, schools in China and Japan emphasize solidarity with the group and not standing apart from it.

In the U.S., as in other literate societies, elementary schools prepare children to use language by teaching reading, writing, and comprehension. In literate societies, the ability to acquire, process, and understand information and to communicate effectively is considered indispensable for personal growth, social interaction, civic participation, continuing education, and future employment. Elementary schools worldwide devote considerable time and resources to teaching reading—the decoding and comprehension of the written word. Importantly, the stories and narratives that children learn to read are key elements in political and cultural socialization, the forming of civic character, and the shaping of behavior. Throughout the history of American education, the materials used to teach reading exemplified the nation's dominant values. For example, the "Dick and Jane" readers of the 1930s, 1940s, and 1950s, depicted the lifestyle and behaviors of the dominant group—the white, nuclear, middle-class family. Contemporary reading books and materials portray a much more multicultural orientation to family life, ranging from single-parent to extended ones. The U.S. is not alone in integrating the teaching of reading with dominant cultural patterns and national identity. In other countries, the heroic stories are about national leaders such as Gandhi in India or Mao in China. During the Soviet period in the USSR, Lenin and Stalin were portrayed in reading materials as great leaders who never made a mistake and loved children.

The language of instruction in elementary or primary schools is often highly controversial in many countries, especially in multilingual ones such as India, Nigeria, Belgium, and Canada. Mastery of an "official" language is a source of power in that it provides access to secondary and higher education and entry to professions. Multilanguage nation-states such as India, Canada, and Belgium have had protracted controversies over which language should be the official national one. India's three-language formula illustrates a compromise used to quiet language conflicts that often exacerbate political divisions (see the chapter on education in India). In the U.S., the dominant language is English and instruction in public schools is in English. The children of non-English-speaking immigrants were assimilated into American culture by the imposition of English through the elementary school curriculum. The entry of bilingual education in the U.S. is a recent and often controversial educational development. A source of controversy is whether a language other than English, such as Spanish, should be taught only until the non-English-speaking child transitions to English, or if it should be taught in a dual-language approach for the maintenance of the other language.

Along with developing language competencies, elementary education prepares children in the fundamental mathematical skills—in counting, using number systems, and performing the basic operations of adding, subtracting, multiplying, dividing, and measuring. Further, the foundations of science, social science, health, art, music, and physical education are also established.

The age range of pupils who attend U.S. elementary schools is from six to twelve, thirteen, or fourteen years, depending on the particular state or school district's organizational pattern. While a few, namely small, rural districts, retain the traditional pattern of grades one through eight, a more common pattern is grades one through six. In most school districts and in many teacher preparation programs, elementary education is organized into the following levels: primary—kindergarten and grades one, two, and three; intermediate—grades four, five, and six; and upper—grades seven and eight. A commonly found organizational pattern includes grades seven and eight, and sometimes grade six, in middle or junior high schools. When the middle school and junior high school pattern is followed, these institutions are often linked with secondary education, encompassing grades six through twelve.

The generally agreed-upon goals of elementary schooling in the U.S. are: (1) gradually leading children from their family and neighborhood to the larger society and environment; (2) providing an environment conducive to good health and physical development; (3) developing the sense of space and time through life, earth, and social studies; (4) developing democratic values of collaborative sharing and decision making; (5) encouraging creativity by storytelling, creative writing, art, and music; and (6) developing skills such as reading, writing, and mathematical computation that support further education. The goals of elementary or primary schooling in other countries are usually very similar. However, the particular country's level of economic development determines which of these goals receive the greatest priority. In countries with limited resources and facilities, the goals specific to learning reading, writing, arithmetic, and other basic skills take priority. Also, the degree to which these goals are emphasized depends on how the country's dominant cultural group defines childhood and education for childhood.

At the primary level, kindergarten through grade three, the curriculum is initially highly generalized into broad areas such as language arts, social studies, life sciences, and mathematics and then gradually becomes more specialized at the intermediate and upper grade levels into more specific subjects. The essential strategy in the broad fields approach is to integrate and correlate rather than to departmentalize areas of knowledge. Curricular departmentalization begins earlier in other countries such as Japan, China, and India than in the U.S.

The language arts, a crucial curricular area, include reading, handwriting, and spelling, listening, speaking, and visually representing. It includes reading and discussing stories, biographies, and other forms of children's literature. The U.S. emphasis on reading and writing is replicated in schools in other countries. However, the methods of teaching language arts vary. In the U.S., there are debates over the efficacy of a particular method in teaching reading. Both phonics and the whole language approach are used in school districts and in teacher preparation programs.

The social studies fuses and integrates selected elements of history, geography, economics, sociology, and anthropology. It uses a gradual, step-by-step method of leading children from their immediate home, family, and neighborhood to the larger social and political world. Social education, or social studies, has been frequently redefined and reformulated. Social studies' defenders argue that integrating elements of the various social sciences into a unified course is a more appropriate psychological way to introduce children to society than a strictly disciplinary, departmentalized approach. Critics, some of them educators from other countries, argue that American students lack the structured knowledge of place that comes from the systematic study of geography as a separate discipline or the sense of time that comes from chronologically organized history.

Like the social studies, science in the elementary curriculum integrates selected concepts and materials from the various natural and physical sciences rather than focusing on the specific sciences themselves. Frequently, science teaching emphasizes the life and earth sciences by way of field trips, demonstrations, and hands-on experiments. Critics contend that the U.S. elementary science curriculum is too unstructured and fails to develop a systematic scientific knowledge base. Defenders contend, however, that it is more important for students to develop a sense of science as a process and mode of inquiry than to amass myriad scientific facts.

The elementary curriculum is completed by mathematics, which emphasizes basic computational skills—addition, subtraction, multiplication, division, measuring, and graphing. The curriculum also includes health concepts and practices; physical education and fitness, which involves development of motor skills, games, and safety; and music and art.

As children in the U.S. progress from the primary to the intermediate grades, the emphasis on reading continues but changes from stories to more informational narratives. The goal is to develop the students' interpretive skills as well as to continue to polish basic decoding ones related to mechanics and comprehension stressed in the primary grades. The broad fields—social studies, mathematics, and science—are pursued but now become more disciplinary.

Depending on the particular organization pattern in place, the upper grades—six, seven, and eight—offer a more specialized curriculum. Subjects such as English, literature, social studies, history, natural and physical sciences, and mathematics are taught in a more differentiated way. In addition to the more conventional academic subjects, other subjects, such as industrial arts, home arts, sex education, and drug abuse prevention education are offered, especially in the upper grades and in junior high and middle schools.

Because of the generality of the elementary curriculum, especially at the primary and intermediate levels, there is often more emphasis on methods and styles of teaching in the U.S. than in primary schools in other countries. For example, U.S. teachers, in their professional preparation and in their classroom practices, are more likely to stress the process of learning, the use of inquiry skills, and collaborative participation than teachers in other countries. Teachers in other countries tend to be more specific skill- and subject-oriented.

While elementary or primary classrooms in the U.S. as well as in other countries are likely to be self-contained, the American teacher generally enjoys more autonomy and is relatively unburdened with visitations by outside inspectors. However, this autonomy is being limited by the "standards" movement in the U.S. at the state and national levels and by the mandatory testing in reading and mathematics required by the No Child Left Behind Act. The act requires that in order to receive federal funds districts must administer mathematics and reading achievement tests for grades three through eight. The standards approach means that more comparisons will be made on how well students are performing academically between states and school districts. This tendency will work its way downward into particular schools with comparisons of pupil achievement in particular grades. Results on students' academic achievement tests are likely to be regarded as indicators of their teachers' competency.

Junior High and Middle Schools

How a particular culture defines the transition from childhood to early adolescence as part of the human life cycle has a pronounced impact on schooling. Some cultures, especially the American one, have elongated the period of transition and have established schools that reflect the amplification of adolescence. In the U.S., junior high and middle schools are key transitional educational institutions that help children bridge the transition from the childhood-centered elementary school to the high school's adolescence-focused climate. The orientation of the junior high and middle school reflects the general opinion of American educators that gradual transitions in a person's educational cycle based on the periods of human growth and development are beneficial. In other countries, particularly where education is traditional, and in less technologically developed ones, the transition from childhood to adulthood is much more abrupt. In some Western countries, such as the UK and France, the traditional use of sorting or streaming children into schools based on anticipated occupational status and socioeconomic class has been softened by creating transitional or orientation cycles that give early adolescents and parents more time and a greater role in making significant educational decisions.

The American junior high and middle school concept grew out of discontent with the traditional pattern of eight grades of elementary and four years of high school. Educational change agents, particularly social efficiency administrators and educational psychologists, devised the junior high and middle schools as transitional rungs in the American educational ladder. As they developed in the 1920s and 1930s, junior high schools were either two-year institutions that encompassed grades seven and eight, or three-year institutions that also included the ninth grade. The junior high school curriculum was more differentiated than that of elementary schools in that it included some vocational and commercial courses. By 1920, there were 883 junior high schools in the U.S. By the 1940s, the junior high school was so well established that over 50 percent of young adolescents were attending junior high schools.

In the 1960s, middle schools were developed as another type of transitional institution between elementary and high school.[10] Generally including grades six, seven, and eight (ages eleven through thirteen), they facilitate a gradual transition from childhood to adolescence by emphasizing programs oriented to preadolescent development and needs. When new middle schools were designed, they often featured innovative architectural designs with learning centers, language laboratories, and arts centers. The number of middle schools grew rapidly from 1,434 in 1971 to 9,750 in 2000.[11] While most school districts today use the middle school model, a few districts retain the junior high school pattern.[12]

In the U.S., the goals of junior high and middle schools generally are to: (1) provide a comfortable transition from elementary to secondary schooling;

(2) provide a transition from the broad fields of the elementary curriculum to more differentiated subjects; (3) guide the physiological, psychological, emotional, social, and intellectual growth that occurs in adolescence; (4) introduce the range of human choices in careers and occupations; and (5) provide articulation between elementary and high schools.

The curricula of junior high and middle schools continues some of the subjects found in the earlier years of schooling and introduces subjects found in the later years in the high school. Among them are: English, language arts, and literature; mathematics, which includes practical mathematical problem solving and introduction to algebra and geometry; social studies and American history; sciences, which may include biology and botany and introductory physical sciences; health, with units on sex education and alcohol, tobacco, and drug abuse prevention; industrial arts and home economics; foreign languages; and music, art, and drama. Career and vocational education classes are also offered in American junior high or middle school, but they provide students with an introduction to a field rather than specific training for it as in other countries.

High Schools

In the U.S., secondary schools are known as high schools. As with junior high and middle schools, the U.S. high school is unique when compared with secondary schools in other countries. Its most distinguishing feature is its comprehensiveness in terms of the socioeconomic classes of its students and the nature of the curriculum they pursue. Although U.S. high schools have academic tracks, they tend not to place students into different secondary schools according to academic ability and future career destinations. The concept of comprehensiveness found in U.S. high schools means that students of various socioeconomic classes, ethnic and racial groups, and academic abilities attend the same type of institution. Although American students may enroll in differing programs within a school, all students take a general required curricular core in English, mathematics, history, social studies, and physical education. Further, co- and extra-curricular activities such as band, orchestra, and team sports involve students in different programs on a school-wide basis. In many other countries, students are streamed into specialized types of secondary schools, often according to their level of academic achievement and career destination. These factors are influenced by socioeconomic class differences. In some countries, such as Sweden and the UK, there has been a movement toward making secondary education more comprehensive.

In the U.S., the number of students in secondary schools is much higher than in some other countries, especially the less technologically developed ones. In the U.S. more than 95 percent of the age cohort between fourteen and seventeen attend high schools and other secondary institutions. Although the dropout rate is higher for Native American, Hispanic American, and African American students than for Euro-American students, about 80 percent of secondary students will graduate and more than 60 percent will go on to college.[13] In Japan, however, the rate of secondary school completion exceeds that of the U.S. In contrast to the high levels of participation in secondary schooling in the U.S. and Japan, the attendance rates in LTDCs are much lower.

The U.S. comprehensive high school, as the name suggests, is a multi-functional institution that: (1) provides a general secondary education; (2) prepares some students for college entry and others for entry into the work world upon graduation; and (3) provides for the social, civic, and personal development of adolescents. The high school curriculum reflects its comprehensive orientation in that it: (1) enrolls all students in a common core of general education courses; (2) provides parallel programs such as the college preparatory, industrial-vocational, commercial, and general programs for particular groups of students in the same institution; and (3) provides elective courses to meet students' individual interests.

The public high school curriculum is usually departmentalized into the following areas: English, mathematics, science, social science, foreign languages, computer skills, health, art and music, physical education, business or commercial education, driver education, and vocational education. While all of these high school subjects are found in the larger institutions, smaller ones typically provide a more limited curriculum. Also, the curricula of private secondary schools affiliated with churches include religious education. The curricula of private independent schools generally feature college preparatory courses.

The traditional organizational pattern of U.S. high schools has been the four-year pattern of grades nine, ten, eleven, and twelve, which persists in many states. Some states, however, use a three-year senior high school pattern of grades ten through twelve. In other countries, secondary education is often six years and divided into two basic cycles, frequently spent in different institutions.

While the public comprehensive high school is the most frequently found secondary school in the U.S., there are also public vocational, technical, and other kinds of specialized high schools, especially in large urban areas. In addition to their general courses, these more specialized schools concentrate on occupational or vocational preparation. There are also private high schools, or academies, often conducted by religious groups. About 75 percent of private school enrollments are in Roman Catholic secondary schools. There are also independent schools that reflect differing educational philosophies and religious orientations.

A significant difference between the U.S. and certain other countries, particularly Japan and China, is the absence of nationally administered testing for entry to institutions of higher education, especially universities. Japan is notorious for what is called "examination hell," the period when secondary school graduates take the national examinations that admit them to universities. The spaces in the prestigious Japanese universities are limited and only those students scoring in the upper ranks of the examinees earn a place. The U.S., in contrast, does not place such determining importance on examinations. However, many colleges and universities take into account how applicants score on the SAT and the ACT standardized tests as part of their admissions process. The weight of these tests is mitigated by the use of secondary school grade-point averages, letters of recommendation, and interviews.

Higher Education

In the U.S., there is a large and complex array of institutions of higher education, including: (1) two-year community colleges; (2) four-year colleges and universities; and (3) professional schools and institutes. Further, there is a parallel organization of state (public) and private institutions of higher education. In contrast to other countries, American higher education is accessible to diverse student populations. Participation rates in higher education in the U.S. are much higher than in other countries.

Many two-year public community colleges, a largely American institutional contribution to higher education, originated as junior colleges—two-year upward extensions of secondary schools. Like public elementary and secondary schools, community colleges, which serve specific geographic areas, have their own elected or appointed governing boards and, often with voter approval, set their own rates of taxation. The original function of many community colleges was to provide the first two years of undergraduate education, credit for which could be transferred to four-year colleges. While still performing this traditional academic function, contemporary community colleges are multipurpose institutions that offer the liberal arts and sciences courses, as well as technical, vocational, professional, and adult education programs. The community colleges award the associate's degree.

Another type of higher education institution is the four-year college, which awards bachelors' degrees. Although a small number of four-year colleges are municipal institutions, most public colleges and universities are state supported and controlled. State colleges have a variety of origins. Some were established in the nineteenth century as two-year normal schools for teacher education. They were later reorganized into four-year state teachers colleges. Many of the former teachers colleges are now multipurpose state universities. Other state colleges were established originally as four-year liberal arts and sciences institutions.

In the U.S., a university is a collection of colleges and schools organized as a single institution, with its own president or chief executive officer. State land-grant universities were established with federal land-grant funds from the Morrill Acts of 1862 and 1890, given to the states to establish agricultural and mechanical colleges. Today, large state universities are complex institutions, dubbed "multiversities," with undergraduate, graduate, and professional schools. The contemporary U.S. university includes programs in liberal arts and sciences at the undergraduate level and professional programs such as education, business, social work, and engineering, at both the undergraduate and graduate levels. Large universities have graduate schools in professional areas such as medicine, veterinary medicine, law, and others.

Historically, state colleges and universities have been governed by autonomous boards of trustees. While this pattern continues in some states, a more typical pattern is that of the state board of higher education that serves as a statewide coordinating agency to establish policies, coordinate development, and allocate funds to colleges and universities. For example, New York, California, Wisconsin, and Illinois are examples of states with integrated and coordinated state university systems. Nevertheless, universities still enjoy a great deal of autonomy.

In addition to the extensive state institutions, the U.S. has a large parallel set of private colleges and universities. These institutions range from four-year liberal arts and sciences colleges to prestigious research and graduate universities. Many private institutions originated as religious denominational college and universities.

Comparatively, there are similarities between institutions of higher education worldwide, especially between those in Europe and the U.S. Indeed, the historical model for the university originated in the Middle Ages when such renowned institutions as the Universities of Paris, Oxford, Cambridge, Prague, and Bologna were established. One of the guiding principles relating to universities was the importance given to their freedom from outside interference.

Nineteenth-century developments in Europe and Asia made the pattern of universities on those continents somewhat different from the U.S. Ministries of education in centralized nations such as France and Japan assume a greater role in higher education affairs. In the UK, government funding of state institutions through the University Grants Commission also serves to give some national direction to higher education. The British approach has been replicated in India.

Teacher Education

In the U.S., teachers are prepared in four-year colleges and universities. Many of these institutions have departments or colleges of education whose primary mission is preparation of teachers and other professional educators. The U.S. pattern of teacher education differs from that of some other countries where there is a sharp distinction in the preparation of primary and secondary school teachers. In these countries, primary teachers are prepared in teacher training colleges and institutes and secondary teachers are prepared in universities. While U.S. teachers have a bachelor's degree as a minimum requirement for entry into the profession, this is not the case in countries such as China and Nigeria.

In the U.S., undergraduate teacher education programs generally consist of five major components: (1) general education courses in the liberal arts and sciences that typically are part of undergraduate bachelor degree programs; (2) the depth, or major area, which for elementary teachers are courses that prepare them to teach the skills and subjects in the elementary curriculum; for secondary teachers, the major is in a subject specialty such as English, mathematics, science, or history, for example; (3) professional education courses in the cultural, social, and behavioral foundations of education such as history and philosophy of education and educational psychology and courses dealing with the inclusion of pupils with special needs; (4) pre-student teaching clinical and field experiences, which involve direct experience in schools and with teaching; and (5) supervised practice or student teaching. A recent trend in the U.S. is teacher competency testing designed to measure teachers' specific knowledge and skills. Since education is a state prerogative in the U.S., each state has authority over teacher certification, issuing the teaching license. This contrasts with those countries where certification is done nationally, through the Ministry of Education.

Several global or universalizing trends have been shaping teaching preparation in recent years, such as the mainstreaming of students with disabilities. Educators in the U.S., the UK, and France have grown increasingly aware of and sensitive to the educational problems faced by students with handicaps and special needs. The trend has been away from educating students with disabilities in special schools or classes and to mainstream and include them in regular classrooms. Another highly significant trend in American education has been multiculturalism—an emphasis on the underlying racial, ethnic, linguistic, and religious diversity in the U.S. A rich literature has developed around the theme of multiculturalism, which is an important part of teacher preparation programs as well as having a place in the elementary, secondary, and higher education curriculum. Multiculturalism is a relevant issue in countries, such as the U.S. and the UK, where influxes of immigrants occur on an ongoing basis. For example, the UK has a large number of immigrants from its former colonies, especially Nigeria, India, Pakistan, and the Caribbean islands. The ethnic diversity in the UK's original stock—English, Scots, Welsh, and Irish—has gained greater recognition. For these reasons, multiculturalism also is a significant trend in the UK.

Conclusion

Despite the fact that its educational governance is situated in states and local districts, education in the U.S. exhibits many more characteristics of homogeneity than found in the states or regions of India and Nigeria, two nations also with a federal–state system. While there is no national U.S. system of education, many similarities exist between the states and local districts across the country that tend to create a shared American educational climate of trends, movements, issues, reforms, and problems, which contribute to homogeneity. For example, age cohorts, curriculum, and learning expectations are for the most part uniform across the country. The trend to similarity has been infused by the movement for national standards. For example, the kind of national testing instigated by the No Child Left Behind Act of 2002 will cause greater curricular conformity in public schools as teachers prepare students for what in effect are national tests. American parents expect that when they move from one region or state to another, they can easily transfer their children to the schools located in their new places of residence.

The professionalization of education as evidenced in the preparation of school administrators and teachers also contributes to educational uniformity and standardization. While variations exist in state certification requirements, national and regional accreditation organizations, such as the National Committee for the Accreditation of Teacher Education (NCATE), promotes common course preparation and standards. The widespread use of standardized tests such as the ACT and SAT also creates similarities in curriculum, college entrance requirements, and educational expectations. Textbook publishing and the marketing of educational materials is a highly competitive market-driven industry in the U.S. Because of the competition for national markets, textbooks and educational materials tend to reflect similarities rather than differences.

Another important contributor to homogenization is the popular mass media—television, radio, motion pictures, magazines, and newspapers—that have a national audience. As a result, Americans receive much the same information and enjoy the same kind of entertainment and recreation throughout the country. This sameness contributes to a kind of cultural homogenization that also creates similar educational expectations, attitudes, and goals throughout the country. While distinctive regional variations as well as cultural and ethnic pluralism exist, the U.S. nevertheless exhibits the similarities generated in a mass society with a mass culture and market.

Thus, education in the U.S. is paradoxical. While there is no national system of education, powerful trends have produced similarities and standardization throughout the country.

DISCUSSION QUESTIONS

1. Compare and contrast the role of the federal government in education with that of the central or national government in other countries.

2. Is it correct to refer to the system of education in the U.S. as "the American system of education"? Explain your answer.

3. How is the educational system in an individual state in the U.S. comparable or different from the educational system of another country?

4. Examine the origin and development of bureaucracies in educational administration and management.

5. How does the elementary school curriculum develop a sense of national identity and political and cultural socialization? Identify those aspects of the curriculum that create a sense of American national identity.

6. What are the purposes of junior high and middle schools in the U.S. educational system? How do these institutions reflect the definition of preadolescence and adolescence used in a particular country context?

7. Is the comprehensiveness of the U.S. high school a significant distinguishing feature of American education? Explain your answer.

FIELD AND RESEARCH TOPICS

1. Spend a day visiting classes in an elementary school. Try to determine how instruction reflects the cultural context.

2. Attend a meeting of a local district board of education. Study the agenda and listen carefully to the discussion of reports and issues. Try to determine the powers and responsibilities of local boards and school districts. Reflect on how these local prerogatives in education impact educational uniformity and centralization in the U.S.

3. Review the reading materials used in elementary schools at certain periods. Identify and analyze the values that these materials convey. Determine how reading materials reflect a country's context and influence political socialization.

4. Do you believe that American high schools should offer a general secondary education or should they become more specialized as those in other countries are? Prepare a paper that examines the issues and presents your opinions.

5. Prepare a research paper that compares and contrasts college and university entrance requirements in the U.S. and Japan.

6. Prepare a chart that lists as topics, or organizers, the key features and characteristics in the U.S. system of education. Use this chart to make comparisons as you read the following chapters in the book that examine education in other countries.

7. Arrange a panel of international students that elicits their comments on how the U.S. system of education differs from education in their countries.

SUGGESTIONS FOR FURTHER READING

Alexander, Kern and David M. Alexander. *American Public School Law,* 5th ed. Belmont, CA: Wadsworth, 2002.

Campbell, Ronald F., Luvern L. Cunningham, Raphael O. Nystrand, and Michael D. Usdan. *The Organization and Control of American Schools.* Columbus, OH: Merrill, 1990.

Clubb, John E. and Moe, Terry M. *Politics, Markets & America's Schools.* Washington, DC: The Brookings Institute, 1991.

Cohen, Michael. *Transforming the American High School.* Washington, DC: The Aspen Institute, 2001.

Gordon, David. *A Nation Reformed? American Education 20 Years after* A Nation at Risk. Cambridge, MA: Harvard Education Press, 2003.

Hoy, Wayne K. and Cecil Miskel. *Educational Administration: Theory, Research and Practice*, 6th ed. New York: McGraw-Hill, 2001.

Jackson, Anthony and Gaye Davis. *Turning Points 2000: Educating Adolescents in the Twenty-First Century*. New York: Teachers College Press, 2000.

Lane, John J. *Ferment in Education: A Look Abroad*. Chicago: University of Chicago Press, 1995.

Ornstein, Allan C. and Daniel U. Levine. *Foundations of Education*, 9th ed. Boston: Houghton Mifflin, 2006.

Sergiovanni, Thomas. *Leadership for the Schoolhouse: How Is It Different?* San Francisco: Jossey-Bass, 1996.

Spring, Joel. *Conflict of Interests: The Politics of American Education*. New York: Longman, 1993.

Swanson, Austin D. and Richard A. King. *School Finance: Its Economics and Politics*. New York: Longman, 1991.

Tyack, David B. and Hansot, Elisabeth. *Managers of Virtue: Public School Leadership in America 1820–1980*. New York: Basic Books, 1982.

Wirt, Frederick and Michael Kirst. *The Political Dynamics of American Education*. Berkeley, CA: McCuthan, 2001.

NOTES

[1] For the relationship between politics and educational policy making in the Johnson Administration, see Maris Vinovskis, *The Birth of Head Start: Preschool Education Policies in the Kennedy and Johnson Administrations* (Chicago: University of Chicago Press, 2005).

[2] David L. Clark, Terry A. Astuto, and Paula M. Rooney, "The Changing Structure of Federal Education Policy in the 1980s," *Phi Delta Kappan* (November 1983): 188–193.

[3] Dennis P. Doyle, "The Role of Private Sector Management in Public Education," *Phi Delta Kappan* (October 1994): 128–132.

[4] Dinah Wiley, *State Boards of Education* (Arlington, VA: National Association of State Boards of Education, 1983).

[5] Allan C. Ornstein, "School Superintendents and School Board Members: Who They Are," *Contemporary Education* (Winter 1992): 157–159.

[6] Patricia Howlett, "Politics Comes to School," *Executive Educator* (January 1993): 14–20.

[7] An example of the literature encouraging community support for schools is Department of Education, *Strong Families, Strong Schools: Building Community Partnerships for Learning* (Washington, DC: U.S. Government Printing Office, 1994).

[8] For a discussion of the modern principalship, see Thomas J. Sergiovanni, *The Principalship: A Reflective Practice Perspective*, 5th ed. (Needham Heights, MA: Allyn and Bacon, 2006).

[9] Allan C. Ornstein and Daniel U. Levine, *Foundations of Education* (Boston: Houghton Mifflin, 2006), 209.

[10] For a discussion of middle school education, see Thomas Dickinson, ed., *Reinventing the Middle School* (New York: Routledge Farmer, 2001).

[11] Douglass MacIver and Allen Ruby, "Middle Schools," in *Encyclopedia of Education*, 2nd ed., vol. 5, ed. James W. Guthrie (New York: Macmillan/Thomson Gale, 2003), 1630.

[12] For developments in middle school education, see Anthony W. Jackson and Gayle A. Davis, *Turning Points 2000: Educating Adolescents in the 21st Century* (New York: Teachers College Press, 2000). For trends, see Jerry W. Valentine, "United States Middle Level Grade Organization Trends," www.mllc.org/docs/USMI.

11

EDUCATION IN THE UNITED KINGDOM

The United Kingdom (UK) has been selected for comparison because of its historic significance as a once-great empire, its continued importance as a modern world power, and its long association with the U.S. At its height of power in the nineteenth and early twentieth centuries, the British Empire encompassed one-fourth of the earth's surface. Three of the countries examined in this book, the U.S., Nigeria, and India, were once British colonies. The common language of both the UK and the U.S. is English, and English serves as the link language in Nigeria and India.

The original thirteen colonies in North America that united after the War of Independence as the United States had been British colonies in the seventeenth and eighteenth centuries. The American system of government owes much to British parliamentary processes, the tradition of common law, and John Locke's principles of checks and balances. Despite these common cultural, political, and language antecedents, distinct differences exist between British and American culture, society, and education. While the UK is a constitutional monarchy, the U.S. is a republic. The UK, with its traditional institutions, is much more socioeconomically class-based than the U.S. with its frontier-generated egalitarianism and class mobility. The educational systems in the two countries reflect many of these differences.

After World War II, the British Empire was dismantled as the colonies in Asia and Africa became independent nation-states. Most of these former British colonies remain part of the British Commonwealth of Nations. In the postwar years, the UK made a major adjustment from being the seat of an empire to becoming a modern European nation. Today, it is a member of NATO, one of the five permanent members of the United Nation's Security Council, and a leading member of the European Union (EU).

Geographic, Demographic, and Sociocultural Contexts

The UK is a Western European nation that lies between the North Atlantic Ocean, the North Sea, and the northwest coast of France. Officially called the United Kingdom of Great Britain and Northern Ireland, the UK consists of England, Scotland, and Wales, which are located on one large island, Northern Ireland (consisting of one-sixth of Ireland, which is located on a separate island), the smaller islands off the coast of Scotland, and the Channel Islands. Its island location contributed to two contradictory features in British history: a tendency to be isolated from the continent of Europe and simultaneously to be a maritime power that once had the world's largest navy and claimed a great worldwide empire.

The land area of the UK is 95,480 square miles. It borders only one country—Ireland. The climate is temperate and moderate, but a characteristic of British weather is abundant rainfall and overcast days. The terrain consists of some rugged hills, low mountains (particularly in Scotland), and rolling plains in the east and southeast.

The UK's population is 60,094,648. In terms of ethnic composition, 81.5 percent are English, 9.6 percent Scottish, 2.4 percent Irish, 1.9 percent Welsh, 1.8 percent Ulster, and 2.8 percent West Indian, Pakistani, and others.[1] Like other European countries, the UK is becoming more multiethnic. Along with the older ethnic groups, there are immigrants from Great Britain's former colonies in Asia, especially India and Pakistan; Africa; and the Caribbean. Programs of multicultural education are in place to provide an education that relates to these changing demographic patterns.

In terms of age distribution, 18.3 percent of the population is between 0 and 14 years of age; 66.1 percent is between 15 and 64; and 15.6 percent is over 65. The median age is 38.4 and the birthrate is a low 0.3 percent.[2] As is the case with other technologically developed countries (TDCs), the percentage of older person is increasing while the school-age population remains stable or slightly decreasing. The UK has a very high literacy rate of 99 percent.

In the UK, the Church of England is the officially established church; the monarch is the head of the Church of England, and clerical appointments are cleared by the government. In addition to the Church of England, or Anglican Church, there are also the major Protestant denominations, especially Presbyterian and Methodist, and the Roman Catholic Church. In terms of religious affiliation, 40,000,000 people identify with the Church of England or are Roman Catholics. Membership in the larger Protestant churches include 800,000 Presbyterians and 700,000 Methodists. There are 500,000 Hindus, 500,000 Sikhs, and 1,500,000 Muslims. Additionally, there are 350,000 Jews.[3] Unlike the U.S., there are religious observances in the state schools, and church-sponsored schools receive government assistance in the UK.

English is the official and major language spoken. There have been moderately successful efforts to revive the Welsh language in Wales, where it is a required subject in the school curriculum. Welsh is spoken by about 26 percent of the population of Wales. In parts of Scotland, Gaelic is spoken by about 60,000 persons.

Political Context

The UK has one of the world's oldest parliamentary systems of govern-ment. Its constitution is primarily unwritten and, in part, includes statutes, common law precedents, and traditional practices. The common law system dates back to early precedents that came with the Anglo-Saxon tribes who migrated from northern Europe to Britain in the early Middle Ages. The House of Lords is the highest court of appeal. Other courts are the Supreme Courts of England, Wales, and Northern Ireland. There are also the high courts of justice and crown courts and Scotland's Court of Session and Court of Justiciary.

The Executive Branch

The UK is a constitutional monarchy. The king or queen, the chief of state, is the titular ruler of the UK and head of the British Commonwealth of Nations. Performing ceremonial duties as head of state, the monarch person-ifies the nation, embodies national unity, and is a symbolic connection between past and present. Since February 6, 1952, the monarch has been Queen Elizabeth II. Ascendancy to the throne is hereditary and the heir apparent is Queen Elizabeth's oldest son, Prince Charles.

The prime minister, as executive head of government, leads the political party or coalition of parties that controls a majority of seats in the House of Commons. He or she formulates the policies and secures approval of the leg-islation that governs the UK. Since May 1997, the head of the government has been Prime Minister Anthony Blair, the leader of the Labour Party. The prime minister appoints the members of the cabinet.

The Legislative Branch: Parliament

The bicameral Parliament is composed of two houses: the House of Lords and the House of Commons. The House of Lords includes hereditary aristocrats and those named to the body for distinguished service and con-sists of approximately 500 life peers, 92 hereditary peers, and 26 members of the clergy. The Lords' only real power is to delay legislation enacted by the Commons.

The House of Commons holds real legislative power in that laws origi-nate in this body. It is composed of 646 members who are elected by popular vote from constituency districts. A member's term is five years, when new elections are held, unless the House is dissolved earlier. The Labour Party won a slim victory in the elections held in May 2005, and Blair continued as prime minister. Unlike members of the U.S. Congress, members of the House of Commons usually, but not always, vote as a bloc with their party.

Political Parties

The UK is a multiparty country, with a spectrum of political parties arrayed from left to right. The three major parties are the Conservative, Labour, and Liberal Democrats. The UK, like the U.S. but unlike several continental European countries, does not have proportional representation, and the candidate of the party with largest number of votes is elected in each district. The "winner takes all" determination of elections works against third and other smaller parties. British politics features party governance and discipline in that the government is party-based and the party in power is held accountable for policy successes or failures. British political parties are highly structured, centralized, and cohesive.

The Conservative and Unionist Party, as its name suggests, is a moderate conservative party. The Conservatives have opposed the extension of the welfare state and favor greater privatization of the economy. The Labour Party is a moderate party that is slightly left of center. Its origins were in the trade union movement and in the democratic socialist tradition. It tends to uphold the state's role in providing social and health-care services. The Liberal Democratic Party, a major but third-place party, consists of an alliance between the older Liberal Party and some Social Democrats who left the Labour Party. It generally takes a middle of the road position. There are a number of minor parties, including the Party of Wales, or Plaid Cymru, and the Scottish National Party. In Northern Ireland, party politics are complicated by the religious tensions between Protestants and Catholics.

Economic Context

The UK, one of the earliest industrialized nations that was once called the factory of the world, remains a leading industrially and technologically developed nation. However, the once-strong industrial sector continues to decline in importance with 25 percent of the workforce employed in this sector. Financial services, particularly banking, insurance, and business, account for the largest proportion of the GNP, and this sector employs 74 percent of the workforce. It is one of the four European nations that has a trillion-dollar economy. The economy remains strong, with low inflation, interest, and unemployment rates. The unemployment rate is 5.2 percent.[4]

The amount of its arable land, suitable for agriculture, is 26.4 percent. Agriculture is intensive and highly mechanized and efficient by European standards, producing about 60 percent of the food needs with only 1 percent of the labor force. Among the UK's natural resources are large supplies of coal, natural gas, and petroleum. The development of oil in the North Sea has especially benefited the British economy.

Despite its general prosperity, the UK's economy shows some signs of economic strain. Among the serious economic strains that have an impact on education is transitional unemployment in the heavily industrialized sector and the need for job retraining in this area. To deal with this problem, the government, in cooperation with business, has developed vocational training programs to stimulate employment and increase productivity.

The Welfare State

After World War II, the UK became a modern social welfare state with many public services, such as health care, provided by the government. Between 1950 and 1975, the Labour government, emphasizing central government economic planning and management, introduced extensive social-welfare, health-care, pension, and unemployment benefits.[5]

Arguing that Labour's policies had weakened Britain's economic competitiveness, the rival Conservative Party, which had fought a rear-guard movement to impede the welfare state, mounted a campaign in the late 1970s to reverse it.[6] Conservatives contended that the weakening economy was caused by government intervention in the free market and that excessively high taxes had stifled technological innovation and sapped private business initiative. Further, Labour's close alliance with the trade unions had led to excessive wage demands, long strikes, and uncooperative workers. Conservatives were led by Margaret Thatcher, who came to power in 1979 and was reelected in 1983 and in 1987. She reduced public ownership and contained the growth of social welfare programs. Her Conservative successor, John Major, who came to power in 1992, continued Thatcher's economic and social program. The general Conservative impetus to privatization and deregulation also extended to education where there was an emphasis on creating alternative schools and encouraging greater parental choice of schools, similar to that which occurred in the U.S.

The UK's economy, like that of the U.S., is heavily related to the world economy. As a member of the European Union, the economy of the UK reflects growing interdependency with the economies of other Western European nations. As in other technologically developed Western nations, including the U.S. and France, the agricultural sector of population has steadily declined. A pronounced shift has occurred from heavy industry to the service sector.[7] As in the U.S., technologically generated economic change has caused the displacement and the downsizing of some industry. The UK's long-standing need for improved vocational and technical training is now acute. Labour's slogan for 2005 is "schools forward, not back," and Labour has promised to provide more specialist schools (which comprise over 60 percent of all secondary schools) and city academies. Spending on education is 5.4 percent of the GDP.[8]

Historical Context

British politics, society, and education features gradualism, continuity, and evolutionary, rather than revolutionary, change. The emphasis on tradition legitimizes institutions such as the monarchy and House of Lords. While the monarch's role has persisted from the Middle Ages to modern times, the king or queen's actual political powers have lessened considerably from dynastic absolutism to constitutional monarchy. This tendency to evolutionary change also characterizes educational institutions and processes. Britain's power holders have generally, if reluctantly, accommodated to change while retaining a degree of their own power and status.[9]

In the nineteenth century, British educational policies reflected the competing political and economic ideologies of Liberals and Conservatives who contended for political power. In the twentieth century, the Labour Party's welfare-state agenda added still another ideological and programmatic dimension to educational policy making in the UK. Among the significant trends in the UK's educational history are: (1) early voluntary philanthropic efforts to reduce working-class illiteracy; (2) liberal reformist efforts to improve education; (3) the impact of laissez-faire economic policies on educational funding; and (4) the influence of public schools in perpetuating social class differences.

Early Philanthropic Efforts to Combat Illiteracy

In the early nineteenth century, illiteracy was endemic in the UK, particularly among the lower socioeconomic working classes. A long-standing issue in British politics has been that educational opportunities were based primarily on socioeconomic class. Although the UK was the nineteenth century's premier world industrial power, educational access and opportunities were still ascribed, or based on birth rather than merit. While highly selective public schools and universities educated the males of leading upper-class families for positions of future power and status, schooling for the children of the working classes was either ignored or limited.

Grounded in laissez-faire attitudes, early nineteenth-century British schools exhibited considerable variety, with private and religious schools as the most significant educational institutions. Certain selective "public" schools, really private preparatory institutions, were renowned for their academic excellence and for the influence that their graduates wielded in British politics and society. Some of the public schools, which boasted a lineage back to the classical humanist institutions that were established during Europe's Renaissance and Reformation in the fourteenth and fifteenth centuries, prepared upper-class males for admission to the prestigious universities of Oxford and Cambridge. Although their influence was reduced in the late twentieth century, the role of these elite educational institutions has been a persistent social and political force in the UK.

Charity and church-related schools in the early nineteenth century provided limited rudimentary instruction to working-class children, many of whom lived in urban slums. Among these primary institutions were parish schools, privately endowed schools, dame schools, private venture schools, and charity schools. These schools were supported by voluntary efforts of the Church of England, which was the official church; various nonconformist Protestant churches; and private philanthropic societies, such as the Society for the Propagation of Christian Knowledge.

Dissatisfied with such limited education and fearing social upheaval, certain individuals, motivated either by altruism or by social control, worked to promote increased educational possibilities. For example, Robert Raikes promoted the Sunday school to instruct child laborers on the one day of the week that factories and mills were idle. Robert Owen, the enlightened New Lanark mill owner turned utopian socialist, argued for restrictions on child labor and for the establishment of infant schools and "Institutes for the Formation of Character." Owen, who through his own efforts established schools at his mill town, became known as the "father of infant education." Despite these few attempts to ameliorate the educational situation, schools for the lower socioeconomic classes were underfinanced, poorly organized, and staffed by untrained teachers.

In the earlier nineteenth century, monitorial education was promoted as a revolutionary innovation in instruction that would make mass schooling possible for working-class children. This method of teaching was named monitorialism because it used older children as aides, or monitors, to provide instruction (see chapter 9 for a discussion of monitorialism in the U.S.). These older, more advanced students were to instruct younger, less experienced children. Instruction focused on basic skills—reading, writing, and arithmetic—graduated into small parts or units. Following a meticulously programmed series of instruction steps, a master teacher would instruct a team of monitors, who, in turn, would teach a large number of students their recently acquired skills. There was a parallel between monitorial instruction and the emerging factory system. Instruction resembled a conveyor belt on a factory assembly line with each instructional monitor teaching a highly specific lesson to a mass of children, with each child moving along like a product in the system.

A Quaker school master, Joseph Lancaster (1778–1838), and an Anglican clergyman, Andrew Bell (1753–1832), each claimed to have originated monitorialism independently of the other. Promoting monitorialism as an inexpensive, efficient, and effective teaching method, Lancaster promised that children would learn to read, write, and compute quickly and at a very low cost. Since his plan required concentrating students in large buildings to reduce the cost per student, Lancaster specified school organization and management to the very last detail such as the amount of space needed for each student and the efficient arrangement of benches and furniture. Bell, who devised a mutual instruction system similar to Lancaster's monitorialism, developed his method as a missionary in India, where he claimed success in teaching basic skills, English, and the Christian religion to the indigenous people. Bell's method was a kind of educational imperialism in which the imperial power instructed the colonial people in the approved skills and subjects. While Bell's supporters were members of the officially established Church of England, Lancaster's supporters were primarily nonconformist Protestants who dissented from the established church. In 1833, the UK began its first halting steps toward government support of education when Parliament awarded grants to the schools maintained by these societies. After a rapid burst of educational popularity, monitorialism quickly declined in the UK as well as in the U.S. and other countries. A cause of its decline was that its results were too limited.

Both Lancaster and Bell promised that monitorialism would instill working-class children with a morality that respected the established order, law, and property.[10] These promises appealed to upper-class industrialists who believed that private funding would provide basic education for the working class without government taxation. They presumed this kind of education would instill proper values in their social inferiors and curb potential social and labor unrest.

Liberal Reformist Efforts to Improve Education

Developments in nineteenth-century British education occurred against the background of the UK's sweeping industrialization and urbanization. In many factories and mills, unskilled laborers, mostly women and children, became the industrial workforce. Working on assembly lines did not require the long training used to train craftspeople; the shift to working in factories weakened apprenticeship education. The employment of child laborers in Britain's factories, mills, and mines impeded efforts to increase primary school attendance by enacting compulsory attendance laws. The reliance on child labor, plus a rising birthrate, characteristic of industrialism, actually raised illiteracy rates.

Although it was obvious that enabling more children to attend primary school depended on reducing the use of child laborers, the political power holders resisted reform. The inherited tradition held parents rather than the state responsible for educating their children. The Liberal Party, the chief reform party in the early nineteenth century, supported a laissez-faire economic policy in which government was to refrain from regulating working conditions and providing education. Manufacturers, many of whom supported the Liberal Party, claimed government intervention in the economy constrained economic growth and violated freedom of contract.

An impetus for reform came from the Utilitarians, a group of philosophical social reformers led by Jeremy Bentham, who wanted the government to promote the welfare of the greatest number of people. Arguing that the anticipated consequences of reform could be calculated quantitatively, Utilitarians believed that government, while respecting private property and individual liberties, should act in the public interest. Utilitarians, such as Bentham and his leading disciples, James and John Stuart Mill, advocated educational reform. Under Utilitarian aegis, some Liberals abandoned strict laissez-faire policies. However, even reformers like John Stuart Mill preferred private educational initiatives over state involvement.

By the 1830s, reform-minded leaders sought to improve the living and working conditions of the industrial poor. Among these reformers were the Earl of Shaftesbury and his colleague, Michael Sadler, who introduced legislation in Parliament to regulate the conditions of child laborers in textile mills. Preparatory to drafting the legislation, Sadler documented that children often worked fourteen-hour days, suffered from unsanitary and dangerous working conditions, were beaten and exposed to immoral situations, and received little or no education.[11]

In 1833, Parliament, in the "Bill to Regulate the Labour of Children in the Mills and Factories of the United Kingdom," prohibited children under age nine from working in textile mills. Children between nine and thirteen were restricted to a forty-eight-hour work week and those between thirteen and eighteen to sixty-eight hours per week. The Act of 1833 generated other reports to Parliament on the consequences of unregulated industrial capitalism: deplorable living conditions in factory towns; lack of adequate housing, water, and sanitary facilities; and inhumane working conditions. The impact of these reports caused Parliament to enact laws to improve the working conditions of the industrial classes, establishing the precedent that government had a legitimate regulative power to ensure citizens' welfare. Child labor legislation affected educational developments in the UK as in other industrial countries, including the U.S. When children were no longer being exploited as a cheap labor force, the stage was set to extend primary schooling.

Departure from Laissez-Faire in Education

The initial breakthrough in England's laissez-faire posture came in 1833 when Parliament appropriated twenty thousand pounds, about $100,000, for annual grants to recognized voluntary schools. Although these funds were inadequate to meet an industrial nation's increasing educational needs, even this limited effort raised the anxiety of some Church of England clerics who feared it might lead to a national school system from which the official church was disestablished. Also, strictly laissez-faire liberals continued to oppose state funding of schools. Primary education remained largely private and voluntary until mid-nineteenth century. Between 1850 and 1870, several royal commissions examined primary schools, endowed grammar schools, public schools, and universities, and generated recommendations for a more systematic school system.

In 1862, the Revised Code of Regulations reconfigured the school grant system, which became known as "payment by results." The Revised Code specified that: (1) achievement in reading, writing, and arithmetic was to be assessed at the end of each year as defined in seven standards; (2) each child was to work through the specific standards and sustain an annual examination; and (3) the amount of the grant to each school was to be based on the number of children who passed the examination in each subject and by the total number of days in attendance recorded for each child.[12] The national government created an Education Department to administer the assessment process. The Education Department initiated regular inspections of primary schools by a staff of school inspectors, called His or Her Majesty's Inspectors, or H.M.I.s. Since preparation for these examinations was so important, the primary school's organization and curriculum were shaped by the examinations. Primary school classes were organized into groups for each examination standard.

Although not yet a complete national school system, the outlines of a tripartite arrangement had emerged: (1) primary schools for working-class children; (2) endowed grammar schools for the middle classes; and (3) public schools to prepare upper-class males for university entry. The power of the socioeconomic class structure was clearly apparent in this emerging system.

William Ewart Gladstone (1809–1898), the Liberal Party leader for much of the nineteenth century, sought to bring about gradual, incremental reforms. Gladstone had served in several Liberal cabinets and began his first term as prime minister in 1868. He succeeded in passing several notable reforms, among them William E. Forster's Education Act of 1870, which divided the country into local school districts, each under the jurisdiction of a locally elected board. The act authorized these local boards to levy taxes to establish and maintain primary schools. As a result, board schools were supported by local taxes and national grants, as well as by student tuition, and became an alternative to voluntary schools, usually church-affiliated independent schools. In contrast to board schools, voluntary schools received national grants but no local tax funds. For both board and voluntary schools, the receipt of grants from the national government depended upon favorable reports from inspectors of the Board of Education, the central education authority.

Although the Education Act of 1870 prohibited denominational religious instruction in board schools, it required a more generalized nondenominational religious and moral instruction. Parents who objected to religious instruction could petition to have their children excused from it. In the voluntary church schools, however, religious instruction was creedal, according to the doctrines of the particular church that maintained the school.

The Education Act of 1870 exemplified the Liberal tendency to reform through gradualism, moderation, and compromise. It still retained a laissez-faire orientation by encouraging private educational efforts and requiring individual tuition payments. It also revealed the Liberal attitude of restricting or at least providing an alternative to church-controlled schooling. With its dual primary system of board and voluntary schools, it also stimulated some rivalry between these school systems. Over time, board schools, supported by local taxes, were better able to compete with church-sponsored schools. The more adequately financed board schools typically were larger, better equipped, and employed higher paid teachers. The division of the country into local school districts with locally elected authorities also quieted anxiety about a nationally dictated education policy.

Secondary Schools

In the nineteenth and early twentieth centuries, secondary schools in the UK generally served the needs of the upper- and upper-middle classes who enrolled their sons in private schools. Unlike the system of public elementary and high schools established in the U.S. by the late nineteenth century, no comparable educational ladder linked English elementary and secondary schools. British primary and secondary schools were separate institutions that served different socioeconomic clienteles. While primary schools provided basic literacy to working-class children, secondary schools prepared upper- and upper-middle class children, primarily males, for university entry.

The most prestigious private schools, the "public schools," included the nine "great schools" of Charterhouse, Eton, Harrow, Merchant Taylor's, Rugby, St. Paul's, Shrewsbury, Winchester, and Westminster. The oldest, Winchester, was founded by William of Wykeham in 1342 to prepare students to enter Oxford University. The public schools emphasized classical and humanistic studies required for university admission. They prided themselves on developing their students' character as "English gentlemen" through the residential boarding system and the emphasis on good sportsmanship, playing the game by the rules. As miniature replicas of upper-class society, public schools taught the classics and disciplined students by hazing and flogging.[13] The nine great public schools were models for other English secondary schools, which imitated their curricula and character-building milieu.

Proud of their ancient lineage and origins as classical humanist schools during the Renaissance and Reformation, public schools were bastions of tradition. When alterations occurred, they were typically slight modifications of existing institutional and curricular structures. Between 1828 and 1848, some criticisms of the public schools stimulated some moderate reforms. Thomas Arnold, Rugby's headmaster, for example, as a friendly in-house critic, made some limited reforms to broaden the curriculum, including incorporating the modern sciences and moving beyond the traditional values to include more socially conscious attitudes.[14]

Industrial modernization enlarged the British upper classes to include the capitalist nouveaux riches as well as the older landed aristocracy and gentry. The upper class, now including industrialists and professionals as well as the landed gentry, demanded the availability for more places for their children in the secondary schools. As a result, more public and grammar schools were established. Although the Latin and Greek languages and literatures were emphasized in the curriculum, other more modern subjects such as science were slowly added. Despite these gradual reforms, some critics continued to attack the public schools as bastions of special privilege.

Responding to these criticisms, Parliament appointed the Public School, or Clarendon Commission, to investigate their sources of income, style of administration, and curricula. Recommending some limited changes, the commission, in 1864, while upholding the classics, encouraged the entry of mathematics, foreign languages, music, art, history, geography, English, and natural sciences into the curriculum. Praising the public schools for preparing Britain's leadership elite, the commission commended the schools as the "chief nurseries of our statesmen." These residential boarding schools introduced many upper-class adolescent males to their future roles as leaders in British politics, religion, diplomacy, business, and higher education. The influence of these institutions was not limited to the British isles but extended overseas to Britain's colonies in Africa and Asia, and especially to India (see chapter 15).

The Taunton Commission, or Schools Inquiry Commission, established to investigate the endowed secondary schools, reported in 1868 that British secondary education was inadequately responding to socioeconomic change. The Taunton Commission recommended: (1) dividing the nation into administrative regions for coordination of secondary schools; (2) creating a commission to examine pupils, certify teachers, and publish annual reports; and (3) establishing a variety of schools for students from diverse socioeconomic backgrounds. These recommendations were deferred until the twentieth century.

Despite a general parliamentary reluctance to intervene in secondary schooling, some limited initiatives were undertaken to increase secondary education opportunities. The Technical Instruction Act of 1869 made technical training a responsibility of county and county borough councils. Some local boards established higher primary schools for students seeking education beyond that provided by basic primary schools. The Technical Instruction Act of 1889 permitted local boards to assist able students in attending "higher" or technical schools.

In 1895, a royal commission, headed by James Bryce, recommended a national educational authority for secondary schools and permitted local authorities to provide secondary schooling. While the national Board of Education was established, the provision of greater access to secondary education was again deferred until the twentieth century. The Education Act of 1902 allowed counties and county boroughs to levy taxes for secondary schooling. The funds supported a small number of scholarships for a few selected students to proceed from primary to secondary schools, but most English youths left formal education after finishing primary school. Primary and secondary schools continued to serve two distinct socioeconomic classes: primary schools educating the lower and lower-middle classes and secondary schools educating the upper-middle and upper classes.

Near the end of World War II, the Butler Act (1944) brought about major educational changes in the UK. According to the act: (1) education was to contribute to the community's "spiritual, moral, mental, and physical development"; and (2) children were to be provided an education appropriate "to their age, ability, and aptitudes."[15] The Butler Act transformed the Board of Education into a new Ministry of Education, which would later become the Department for Education and Skills (DfES), headed by the secretary of state for education, who held cabinet rank. Most significant for the organization of education, the act established a tripartite secondary school system, consisting of grammar, technical, and modern institutions, which is discussed in the section on contemporary secondary schooling.

Governance and Administration of Education

Formal education in the UK consists of government-sponsored primary schools, which serve children from ages five to eleven, and secondary schools, which serve those from ages eleven to eighteen.[16] Some local education authorities (LEAs) have established middle schools for students from ages nine to thirteen. In addition to government-sponsored institutions, private schools enroll about 7 percent of the school-age population. Private schools, though independent, are subject to inspection by the DfES. Schooling is compulsory between ages five and sixteen. The formal system is completed by higher and adult education at universities, colleges, and polytechnic institutions.

Governance and Policy Making

Because of its history and traditional suspicion of centralized educational authority, the UK's national school system is locally administered. Authority and responsibility for education are shared by the central or national government, through its DfES, and the 105 LEAs. Each school also has it own governing body, accorded enlarged functions by the Education Act of 1986. In addition, the teaching profession also has a role in formulating educational policies.[17] Authority for education in the UK can be contrasted with the federal systems in the U.S., Mexico, India, and Nigeria. In these federal systems, the state governments play a larger role in education, often an intermediary one, between the federal and local governments. In the U.S., however, the educational system is primarily state and local while that of the UK is national and local. The system in the UK is also much less centralized than in Japan, where national authorities are paramount.

In the UK's system of jointly shared responsibility, the DfES formulates policy and monitors its implementation by the other agencies, especially the LEAs. Through its allocation of the national funds to schools, it exercises an important role in providing education. The secretary of state for education and skills, a member of the prime minister's cabinet, heads the DfES. The secretary's role is to promote the "education of the people of England and Wales" and the "progressive development of" educational institutions. The secretary is to "secure the effective execution by local authorities, under his or her control and direction, of the national policy for providing a varied and comprehensive education service in every area."[18]

The LEAs are responsible for providing education under the direction of their own education committees. The organization of local authorities in the UK is complicated. There is one system for local authorities in England and

Wales, another for Scotland and Northern Ireland, and still another for the City of London. Local authorities, whose members are elected to four-year terms, are divided into larger county and smaller district councils. The county councils (called regional councils in Scotland) provide major government services such as education, social services, police and fire protection, and highway maintenance. The smaller district councils provide local services such as recreation, housing, and garbage collection. In London, the local governments are the borough and district councils. At least half of the members of the local education committee are elected to city or county councils and the remaining members are appointed because of their educational expertise and involvement.[19]

Currently, the UK, reversing an earlier trend to centralization, has decentralized more government services. Unlike the U.S., however, the UK has few historical precedents for local control. The working premise of the current trend to decentralization is that it encourages greater public responsiveness and citizen involvement. For example, the Education Act of 1988 permits schools to opt out from local district control.

Ideology, Politics, and Educational Policy

In the UK, ideology plays a role in shaping educational policies, but a lesser one than in China. The DfES's secretary's policies reflect the ideology and program of the party that holds a majority in the House of Commons and forms the government. (Note that the term *government* in the UK refers to the party in power rather than the entire governmental institutions and bureaucracy as in the U.S.) When the Labour Party forms the government, educational policy is generally more directed to social welfare needs and egalitarian and comprehensive education. The Conservative Party, in contrast, promotes greater selectivity at the secondary level and more autonomy for private schools.

When it gained political power in 1979, the Conservative Party, as its name suggests, pursued a neoconservative educational policy. Specifically, the Conservative government's basic policy objectives were to (1) raise academic standards; (2) increase parental choice in schooling; (3) relate education more to economic needs; (4) increase efficiency and effectiveness in school management; (5) restructure the examination system; and (6) restructure teacher preparation.

In the UK, the Conservative government commenced reforms of curriculum, organization, and funding. The Conservative Thatcher and Major governments pursued policies to use education as an instrument in restoring a competitive, free enterprise economic system. Government policy was directed at establishing a national curriculum, greater privatization, and closer links between business and schools. These Conservative goals paralleled the educational policy of the Reagan and the first Bush administrations in the U.S. during the same time frame. In both the UK and the U.S., neoconservative policy makers connected education to economic productivity and competition in the global economy in that they attributed economic decline to academic deficits. In the UK, the Education Act of 1988 instituted national curriculum and testing, reduced the LEA's responsibilities for education, and increased parental choice in selecting schools.[20]

In 1997, the Labour Party, led by Tony Blair, soundly defeated the Conservatives, led by incumbent John Major. Unlike the post–World War II period, Labour is now pursuing more moderate changes in the system rather than a transformative policy course. It continues traditional Labour policies of providing social service and health-care benefits, reducing socioeconomic class distinctions, improving the participation of minority groups in schools, and supporting comprehensive secondary schools over grammar schools. While the Labour Party has pursued equalization of educational opportunity by encouraging comprehensive secondary schools, Conservatives have tended to see equalization as a welfare state residue. Policy conflict has often centered on the purpose and function of secondary schooling, especially the grammar school, the UK's traditional means of entering higher education. Labour policy succeeded in turning the great majority of secondary schools into comprehensive institutions. With only limited success, some Conservatives fought with a delaying action against comprehensive schools. Conservatives sought to create an educational marketplace in which consumers could choose among alternatives.

The Labour government has emphasized the need for a better educated and more highly trained workforce to make the UK more competitive in the global economy. Labour also makes equality and equity of educational provision a high priority. The Labour government's announced agenda for education in the UK includes: (1) improving early childhood and preschool educational programs; (2) making secondary schooling more equitable and accessible, especially to groups with low retention rates; (3) redesigning the education of the age group from fourteen to nineteen so that it is more flexible; (4) increasing participation in higher education; (5) developing technological and workforce skills.[21]

Administrative Responsibilities

The civil service plays a highly important role in British government. Although secretaries of the Department for Education and Skills come and go with political shifts, the civil service, which includes professional educators, provides continuity with the assumption that it will execute policies of the party in power and administer the day-to-day functions of the DfES. In a government department such as the DfES, usually only three or four leaders (a minister and parliamentary secretaries) are politicians who are members of Parliament. The rest of the department staff are civil servants who occupy ongoing managerial positions. There is a permanent secretary, deputy secretaries, the minister's private secretaries, and other personnel who are career civil servants. The DfES, at the national level, bases its policies on the platform of the governing party, the expertise of the civil service personnel, the reports of Her Majesty's Inspectors of Schools (H.M.I.s) who are in the field, and the national Advisory Council for Education in England and Wales. Though officially neutral, the civil service nonetheless influences policy through its selection of information and use of precedents based on prior practices.

While overall national responsibility is with the secretary of education and the DfES, the 105 LEAs retain much actual authority for operating the schools. The LEAs are directly responsible for providing maintained, or publicly financed, schooling and for determining the location, size, organization, and staffing of schools under their jurisdiction. They employ teachers and other staff, provide and maintain buildings, supply equipment and materials, and provide grants for students proceeding to further and higher education. Decision making at the local level causes some variations in the instruction received by children in the UK—but not to the extent as in the U.S., where much of it is set by local school boards. The DfES works to reduce disparities between regions.

In governance, the schools in a given district have a governing body, a school council composed of equal representation of elected parent representatives and members appointed by the LEA. The council is responsible for the general conduct of schools and is expected to ensure that the national curriculum is implemented. Since 1988 particular school councils can vote to withdraw their school from local authority and apply to be directly funded by the central government as a grant-maintained school. If the application is approved, the council receives an annual maintenance grant to pay operating costs, and the school is required to provide a free education to its pupils and to follow the prescribed national curriculum.[22] Only a few school governing councils have left the jurisdiction of the LEAs. Some of those who left sought to operate secondary schools along more traditional grammar school, emphasizing a more academic curriculum, rather than along comprehensive lines. Under the Labour government elected in 1997, funding is more directed to the LEAs than to schools that take the option of leaving their jurisdiction.

In the UK a particular school climate is most affected by its socioeconomic composition, as in the U.S. Inner-city schools in the UK exhibit similar dropout and discipline problems as urban schools in the U.S. do. Education is further complicated in inner-city areas by growing multicultural complexity. Since the 1960s, there has been significant immigration from former British colonies in Asia and Africa to the UK. British society, once generally racially and linguistically homogeneous but divided on class lines, now shows greater racial, ethnic, and language diversity. Educators in the UK, like their U.S. counterparts, are sensitive to multiculturalism and have developed strategies and materials appropriate to the nation's changing racial and ethnic composition.

Traditionally, the LEAs took the most responsibility for setting and revising the curriculum. The teaching profession, especially the unions, supported the policy that curriculum is a local educational responsibility. This traditional policy on curriculum development was changed by The Education Reform Act of 1988, which established a national curriculum (1989) and national examinations. The national curriculum consists of core subjects in English, mathematics, science, and specified foundation subjects such as history, geography, technology, music, art, physical education, and (for secondary students) a modern foreign language. In Wales, Welsh is a core subject. For each of these subjects, the act sets attainment goals, programs of study, and assessment provisions for the four key stages of compulsory education: ages five through seven, seven through eleven, eleven through fourteen, and fourteen through sixteen.[23]

The DfES is responsible for the training, registration, and regional allocation of teachers. Salaries, negotiated between the local education authorities and the teachers' unions, are formally approved by Parliament upon the recommendation of the secretary of education. The education profession, the professional staffs, and especially the headmasters and headmistresses also shape educational policy by their direct involvement in the schools' day-to-day activities. In addition to their local school involvement, teachers are also organized into several national professional organizations, the largest of which is the National Union of Teachers. The School Council for Curriculum and Examinations is financed jointly by the DfES and LEAs. Its committees, on which representatives of the teachers' organizations comprise the majority of members, sponsor research and initiate proposals for curricular and examination reforms.

The system of dual and shared responsibility between the DfES and the LEAs has historically been one in which change is slow. Although the national government, through the DfES, has a considerable impact on standards for facilities and teachers' compensation, LEAs may be slow to implement change or resist it altogether unless compelled by Parliament to do so.

Within the school itself, the day-to-day administration is done by the headmaster or headmistress. This position evolved from the concept of the head teacher, an experienced teacher who served as educational mentor for the professional staff. Traditionally, headmasters in the UK have been more involved in teaching than U.S. principals. This is changing, however, as they take on more administrative tasks.

Teachers in the UK consider themselves to be skilled instructors rather than theoreticians or change agents. While primary school teachers are very child-centered, secondary teachers emphasize subject knowledge. As in the U.S., primary methods in the UK are highly activity based.

British schools generally have less parental involvement in the educational process than those in the U.S. They do schedule the usual parent evenings when children's progress is discussed with teachers. Recent policies have encouraged more school choice and a larger parental role.[24]

Financing

Like educational practices in the other countries examined in this book, schooling in the UK is tax supported and compulsory. Funding comes from national taxes, especially the income tax, and from local property taxes. Eighty percent of funding comes from the national government, through the DfES to the LEAs. The remaining 20 percent is from the local property tax, or rates, set by the local municipal or county governments.[25] Schools administered by LEAs are "maintained schools" since they are established and supported by public funds. Pupils attending maintained schools do not pay fees, and books and equipment are provided by the LEAs. The amount of locally generated revenue varies from LEA to LEA. As in the U.S., the more affluent districts have the capacity of generating greater educational revenues. In the UK, the national government uses the rate support grant as an equalizer to ensure a minimal standard of education throughout the country, while this effort at equalization is done via each state's foundation formula in the U.S. However, fiscal distributions in the U.S. and the UK can be contrasted with practices in Japan, whose centralized funding ensures equity in the amount of money spent on each child's education.

Funds from the British central government come from several national departments such as the Treasury and the Home Office in addition to the DfES. Similar to elementary and secondary school spending in the U.S., the British expend most of their funds on school facilities and on administrators' and teachers' salaries. Again, as in the U.S., only about 2 percent of funds go for research. In the UK, the national government also funds categorical needs related to the education of immigrants and the training of unemployed youth in inner-city areas.

In the UK, decentralization, or site-based management, of schools is an important recent trend. Headmasters/headmistresses and school councils have been given more authority over budgets and planning. The LEAs allocate 85 percent of a projected school budget to the school itself. The LEAs also provide many voluntary independent schools with aid in the form of "recurrent" or operations costs for teachers' salaries and assistance for capital expenditures for facilities.

Administration and Organization of Schools

Approximately 9.5 million children attend the UK's 36,000 schools. LEAs administer approximately 31,000 of these schools—26,000 primary and nursery and 5,000 secondary schools.[26] About 7 percent of the school-age population attend independent voluntary schools. Many voluntary schools are operated by churches, especially the Church of England and the Roman Catholic Church. There are also independent or private voluntary secondary schools, including the prestigious "public schools."

Relationships between the LEAs and the voluntary schools follow several patterns. While some voluntary schools are virtually autonomous, others are heavily controlled by the LEAs. The majority of the voluntary schools receive financial assistance from the LEAs and the DfES. The trustees or governors of some voluntary schools also contribute privately to capital costs. The varied arrangements between maintained and voluntary schools represent ways of resolving church–state and religious education issues. In England and Wales, religious instruction as well as a daily act of corporate worship are required in both maintained and voluntary schools. In the maintained schools, religious education follows a locally approved nondenominational format. Upon petition, parents may have their children excused from religious exercises in maintained schools. If a school has a sufficient number of non-Christians, it may conduct a separate assembly for these students. There is a growing population of Muslims as well as Hindus in the UK. Schools, whose students are members of different religions, may participate in a multifaith assembly.[27]

Religious education and observances are typically based on the doctrines of the church that controls a particular voluntary school. The UK's compromises on religion have created a dual school system, with the voluntary sector receiving subsidies from the national government. The policy in the UK contrasts with the anticlerical tradition in Mexico, with the constitutional mandate in the U.S. that prohibits tax support for church-related schools, and with the Marxist rejection of religion in the Peoples Republic of China. Somewhat similar to the UK is the educational situation in Japan where moral, but not religious, values are taught as a unit or course in the government schools.

Early Years Education

Preschool and early childhood education is referred to as "early years education" in the UK. Early years education, directed to the three- and four-year-olds, is provided by government-maintained nursery and primary schools and by private and voluntary ones. In 2002, 96 percent of the age cohort was enrolled in either government-maintained or private early years programs. Nursery classes in government-maintained schools are required to have a qualified teacher and nursery assistant on staff. Day nurseries are supported by the county social services department or education department in the public sector and by business and industrial companies and voluntary organizations in the private sector. They provide care during the length of the working day. Each LEA is required to have an early years development and child-care plan.[28] Early years education has the same goals as those found in preschools in other countries. Among them are personal, social, emotional, physical, and language development; developing readiness for reading and mathematics; and providing physical and creative activities.

Primary Schools

Enrolling children between ages of five and eleven, British primary schools are subdivided into the early stage, traditionally called the infant stage, from five to seven and the junior or later stage from eight to eleven years. In the early stage, instruction, emphasizing language arts and numeracy, is informal and individualized. Classes are organized heterogeneously rather than homogeneously and pupils are seated at group tables rather than individual desks. Teachers move about the classroom, working with particular groups. At the junior level instruction becomes more systematic and subject-centered. The informality of the early stage diminishes with the focus on students completing assignments, following instructions, and being evaluated by external standards.

The Education Reform Act of 1988, which established a national curriculum, broke the long-standing precedent that curriculum should be set by local authorities and teachers. The national curriculum mandated for England and Wales requires all children between ages five and sixteen to study nine foundation subjects. The rationale stated for making curriculum part of the legal framework is to ensure that each school's program: (1) is broad and balanced; (2) promotes students' spiritual, moral, cultural, mental, and physical development; and (3) prepares students for the experiences, responsibilities, and opportunities of adult life. British primary schooling follows the general primary or elementary pattern found worldwide in emphasizing language, communication, socialization, and mathematical skills.[29] The practice of nationally prescribing the curriculum in the UK differs from the pattern in the U.S. where curriculum requirements are a composite of state mandates and local school board policies. However, the UK's prescription is less detailed than that of Japan where most subjects are nationally mandated.

The national curriculum is organized into two categories of foundation subjects: core and other. The core foundation subjects are mathematics, English, and science. Core instruction emphasizes language, number, and science skills, including reading, writing, listening, speaking; counting, adding, subtracting, multiplying, dividing; and an introduction to elementary life and earth sciences and to scientific processes. Other foundation subjects are history, geography, technology (including design), music, art, and physical education. Modern foreign language study begins at age eleven. In addition to the core subjects, each school must provide religious education. In Wales, the Welsh language is also a foundation subject. There is also national testing in the core subjects at determined stages in a child's education: at ages seven, eleven, fourteen, and sixteen. The requirement of a mandatory curriculum and testing, which is relatively new in British education, has caused uneasiness among teachers who believe that it will force them to abandon a less-formal learning environment in order to teach for the tests. In the U.S., the No Child Left Behind Act (2002) requires school districts to conduct tests in reading and mathematics in grades three to eight to qualify for federal funds.[30] Some American teachers, like their British colleagues, fear that the required testing may cause curriculum and instruction to be geared to teaching for the test.

As in primary schools throughout the world, in the UK the number of students per teacher is higher than in secondary schools. The student–teacher ratio in primary schools in the UK is twenty-five to one, and it is seventeen to one in secondary schools.[31] In addition to primary schools, a few LEAs operate middle schools, which enroll children from ages nine to thirteen.

Secondary Education

In analyzing the educational policies of a nation, how that country provides access to secondary education reveals its socioeconomic and political orientation. Traditionally, in Western European nations (including the UK), secondary schooling has sorted people into their future career destinations along socioeconomic class membership. Until the early twentieth century, only a small proportion of British adolescents, usually from upper- and upper-middle-class families, attended secondary schools. Working-class children either continued in postprimary arrangements or left school for work. Gene Maeroff, an American educator visiting the schools in the UK, found strong residues of the impact of social class on participation in secondary education and later career destination. He comments that socioeconomic class "has a devastating effect on the aspirations" of many lower-class youth who do not believe they have real possibilities to improve their economic condition. Class orientation also limits their aspiration for continuing and higher education. This results in many young people leaving school at age sixteen and entering a job market where unemployment is high.[32]

Debate regarding secondary education has centered around the "eleven-plus" examination administered after a student's eleventh birthday. With the Butler Act, the Education Act of 1944, three alternative types of secondary schools were put in place: grammar, technical, and secondary modern schools. Pupils sat for the "eleven- plus" examination and their scores determined which of the three secondary schools they would attend. Although educational authorities claimed that the three institutions were equal, it was widely known that academically promising students were streamed into grammar schools. Of lesser prestige, the technical schools were available only to a small number of students. The majority attended secondary modern schools, which, despite their name, were regarded as schools for those who lacked academic ability.

In the debate on secondary educational policy, the two major political parties took opposing sides. The Labour Party argued that the "eleven-plus" examination was unfairly biased toward the upper and upper-middle classes, that it came too early in a child's education and was too powerful in determining a child's future. The Labourites wanted to establish a genuinely comprehensive secondary system to replace the existing tripartite system of grammar, technical, and modern schools. The Conservatives, in opposition, defended the examination system and the grammar schools, which they argued had served the nation well by providing an able leadership group.

The movement toward comprehensive schools depended upon which party held power. During the 1960s and 1970s, the tendency was toward comprehensive schools. During the 1980s, the reverse was true. Despite the policy stances of the major political parties regarding comprehensive schools, the majority of students now attend comprehensive secondary schools. Over 90 percent of the students attending maintained schools are enrolled in comprehensive schools. Seeking to provide a broad curriculum, comprehensive schools accept students without reference to academic aptitude.

Since comprehensive education is a relatively new educational pattern in the UK, it still utilizes a variety of arrangements rather than taking a standardized approach. Although there are other age-range patterns, the majority of comprehensive secondary schools enroll students from ages eleven to eighteen. While the English education tradition has stressed "streaming" or rigid grouping, comprehensive schooling emphasizes more heterogeneity in students' socioeconomic backgrounds and academic abilities. Students enter the comprehensive secondary school at slightly different ages. Those in LEA schools begin at age twelve while those in independent schools tend to enter at age fourteen. Some secondary schools transfer students at age sixteen to sixth-form colleges (discussed below).[33] Those comprehensive schools that developed from the selective grammar school approach may retain a university preparatory orientation. Other factors affecting the comprehensive arrangement are the location of the schools and the composition of the student population.

A relatively new concept, the Specialist School Program, has taken hold in the UK. Specialist schools are privately and publicly funded and each one emphasizes a specific subject area but also must meet the National Curriculum requirements and deliver a broad and balanced education to pupils. Any maintained secondary school in England can apply for specialist status in one of ten specialisms: arts, business and enterprise, engineering, humanities, languages, mathematics and computing, music, science, sports, and technology. Schools can also combine any two specialisms. Specialist schools represent the government's goal to raise educational standards and to have all secondary schools become specialist schools.[34]

In addition to maintained secondary schools, the UK continues its private education tradition that includes the "public schools." The five hundred public schools, which enroll students from ages eleven through nineteen, charge rather high tuition and board fees. A strong educational network exists between the public schools and Oxford and Cambridge, the leading universities, which enroll a high proportion of public school graduates. Supporters of the private education sector argue that it allows parents and students to choose among secondary education alternatives. Private secondary schools also provide a means of avoiding comprehensive schooling and government regulations.

The curriculum in the early years of secondary schooling tends to be similar for all students, with courses such as English, mathematics, geography, history, science, art, and physical education. In the third year of secondary school, at age thirteen-plus, there is differentiation in the course schedules followed by students, especially in subjects such as craftwork, physical education, and modern languages. After the fourth year, the secondary school curriculum becomes increasingly specialized, especially for students seeking university admission. This is when students enter the sixth-form colleges. Now, the students' course schedules consist of subjects, which together with general studies emphasize either the arts or the sciences. For example, students taking a concentration in arts may study English, history, and French while those in a science concentration may study physics, chemistry, and mathematics. These curricular concentrations lead to the "A" or advanced-level examinations.[35]

British education, with its inherited tradition of payment by results, emphasizes the external examination of students. Study programs have been designed for each core subject to ensure cumulative progression in instruction from year to year and to provide for continuity and articulation between schools. Curriculum and instruction in secondary schools has been influenced by the need to prepare students for the examinations administered at ages sixteen-plus and eighteen-plus. Often instruction, especially from the fourth year of secondary education on, mirrors the examination syllabus. The importance of these examinations has made teaching highly subject-matter centered with the teacher serving as a transmitter or conduit of information to students.

The principal examinations taken by secondary school students, usually administered at age sixteen, lead to the General Certificate of Secondary Education (GCSE) upon completion of five years of secondary school. Students' knowledge is evaluated according to a seven-point grading scale denoted by the letters A through G. Grades A through C qualify students to enter higher education. The syllabi and assessment procedures for the examination follow national criteria. Coordinated and supervised by the Secondary Examinations Council, the examinations are prepared by agencies external to the school called examining boards that are associated with universities.[35] The examining board establishes subject-area committees of teachers from secondary schools and university professors to prepare the examinations and establish the criteria for their evaluation. These committees also appoint examiners who evaluate the examinations. Each particular school is free to select an examining board.

As does the U.S., the UK faces the problem of obsolete and deteriorating secondary schools. The Labour government launched a major policy initiative in 2003 to renovate and improve the physical facilities of secondary schools and to create "state-of-the-art school buildings." More than five billion pounds have been allocated to improve the facilities in 20,000 schools.[37]

Vocational Education

Although once called the "factory of the world," British industrial productivity did not lead, historically, to the development of extensive industrial and vocational training programs. In contrast to Germany with its highly segmented and specialized vocational secondary training tracks, the UK neglected this kind of training, preferring class-centered general education. By the 1920s, British industry was showing symptoms of stress and obsolescence. By the 1970s, as in the U.S., British industries, facing more efficient and cheaper global competition, shifted from heavy industries to other areas of production, to information technology, and to services. Large sectors of industry had obsolete equipment, outmoded systems of production, and underskilled workers. As in the large cities of the U.S., the UK's industrial cities suffered from high rates of unemployment in the 1970s. Unemployment, underemployment, and feelings of economic insecurity remain high among British youth. In 1998, for example, the British rate of youth unemployment was a little over 15 percent for youth sixteen to seventeen years old and approximately 12 percent for youth eighteen to twenty-four years old.[38]

With the organization of the European Common Market and the European Union, vocational training and technological education are now being given a high priority in Western Europe, especially in the UK. Unlike Germany, school-leavers in the UK (those who leave the formal academic system) have either entered the workforce directly or become unemployed rather than entering continuing vocational education programs or apprenticeships.

The Conservative Thatcher and Major governments, emphasizing closer links between education and business, pursued policies to make technological and industrial training more prominent in the curriculum and to encourage industry and business to become more active in education. This trend in the UK is similar to U.S. efforts to create school–business partnerships. According to the British government:

> In line with the concern to maintain British expertise in science, engineering and technology, a shift in provision is occurring in post-school education from the arts and social sciences towards these subjects and towards directly vocational courses, while higher education institutions and industry are being encouraged to collaborate more closely for their mutual benefit. The responsiveness of many courses in further education to the needs of the economy is also being increased. The role played by further education institutions in providing training and continuing education is considered to be of great importance, especially at a time of rapid technological change. The Government is considering taking measures to ensure that everyone up to the age of 19 should undergo some form of structured education or training.[39]

The Thatcher government established the Youth Training (YT) program to integrate young persons into work by establishing industrial training possibilities, subsidized by public resources. Financial incentives are used to encourage business and industry participation. Aimed to train and employ unemployed school-leavers, the YT was designed to combine training and planned work experience in a business with off-the-job training in a college. Unlike the mandatory dual system in Germany, the British program is voluntary. Eighty-two Training and Enterprise Councils (TECs) were established in 1989 to place the responsibility for vocational training on British employers. The TEC approach rests on the concept that local business firms should identify training needs in their locality. However, the practice of entering the workforce upon leaving school without continuing training is still strong. For example, the number of sixteen- to seventeen-year-olds who entered the labor market directly in 1990 was 497,000 in contrast to 281,000 who participated in YT programs.[40]

To achieve the goal of more technological and industrial training as well as to alleviate unemployment in large cities, The Education Act of 1988 sought to develop a network of secondary-level "city technology colleges" in economically disadvantaged urban areas. Sponsored by industry and business, these schools, with a strong technological- and business-oriented curriculum, are state-aided but independent of LEA jurisdiction. Also, the government, through the Manpower Services Commission, has promoted the Technical and Vocational Education Initiative to prepare students with up-to-date commercial and industrial skills. Projects have been geared to providing general, technical, and vocational education for the fourteen- to eighteen-year-old group.[41]

Higher Education

Universities, polytechnic institutes, colleges of education, and colleges of higher education provide postsecondary higher education for about 15 percent of the age group. Although participation in higher education in the UK is much smaller than in the U.S., enrollments in British higher education, like its American counterpart, increased after World War II.[42]

The highly prestigious universities Oxford and Cambridge historically have dominated British higher education. In addition to Oxford and Cambridge, forty-five other universities enroll more than 310,000 full-time students. While there has been a general increase in university enrollments, the more prestigious ones have remained the cultural preserve of the historically socially and economically advantaged classes. In the UK, more children from managerial and professional families are likely to enter universities, complete degree programs, and earn professional qualifications than those from lower-middle- and working-class families.[43] While economically favored groups enjoy greater access and completion rates in higher education in most countries, including the U.S., the effects of socioeconomic class historically have been more evident in the UK.

University enrollments in the UK are revealing greater gender equity than in the past. This trend to greater representation of women is also found in other Western industrialized nations such as Germany and the U.S. In

Germany, Poland, and the U.S., more women are currently enrolled in higher education institutions than men. In the UK, the proportions of men and women entering universities are nearly equal, but women still tend to be educated in less prestigious institutions than men.[44]

Until 1989, universities were funded by the University Grants Committee (UGC) and enjoyed a great deal of autonomy. Throughout the 1980s, the national government reduced funding to the UGC for distribution to the universities and ended the policy of subsidizing large numbers of foreign students. These measures caused retrenchment in higher education. In 1989, the national government replaced the UGC with the new Universities Funding Council (UFC). Composed of members from higher education, industry, commerce, and finance and appointed by the national government, the UFC recommended funding allocations for instruction, research, and other university matters. The UFC was replaced by Higher Education Funding Councils (HEFC). The councils, linked to the national Treasury Department, are now more responsible and accountable to the Department for Education and Skills, thus reducing university autonomy.[45]

Universities still retain a great deal of their traditional autonomy, however, and continue to control their own entry requirements and curricula. They offer the usual range of degree programs in the arts, sciences, social sciences, business studies, and medicine. Bachelor degree programs in science and technology attract about 40 percent of the enrollment, followed by 20 percent in English, modern languages, and other arts subjects, 20 percent in the various social sciences, and the remaining 20 percent in such professional studies as medicine, dentistry, and education.

The LEAs, especially in large urban areas, have established polytechnic institutions that stress scientific and technical programs and are closely affiliated with local business and industry.

A highly innovative approach to adult and higher education occurred in 1969 when the Open University, a nonresidential institution, was established. Using a variety of distance education strategies such as television, radio, the Internet (now), and summer study experiences, the Open University has made higher education accessible to many who were excluded in the past. It also provides a network of regional study centers throughout the country at which students can interact with tutors, counselors, and other students.[46] In 2005, 150,000 undergraduate and over 30,000 postgraduate students were enrolled in Open University classes.[47]

Teachers and Teacher Education

Candidates for teaching positions must complete a recognized program in teacher education offered by institutes of higher education, universities, and polytechnics. The teacher education program is a three- or four-year course that leads to the Bachelor of Education, B.Ed., degree. The Council for Accreditation of Teacher Education monitors teacher preparation programs for their conformity to approved criteria. To teach in a government-maintained school, teachers are required to have qualified teacher status (QTS). There are two main paths for achieving QTS: (1) successful completion of an undergraduate course of initial teacher preparation; or (2) successful completion of requirements for the Postgraduate Certificate in Education (PGCE). There has been some experimentation with alternative patterns that provide for the entry of individuals into teaching who have "relevant qualifications and experience" but who lack formal teacher training qualifications. This provision is similar to proposals in the U.S. that provide for alternative approaches to teacher certification.

The School Teachers' Pay and Conditions Act of 1991 created the School Teachers Review Body (STRB), which makes recommendations for the compensation and working conditions of teachers. In 1999, teachers' pay increases were linked to the achievement of performance objectives. The General Teaching Council (GTC) was established in 2000 to monitor teachers' performance, which is reviewed each year. All teachers are required to register with the GTC, which has the power to remove teachers from its register for unacceptable professional conduct or serious incompetence.

In the UK, two-thirds of teaching positions are filled by women, including seven out of ten classroom teaching posts. Nearly half of all full-time teachers are age forty-five or over. Less than 20 percent are under thirty. The Labour government, in 2001, pledged to increase the number of classroom teachers by 10,000 in the next several years.[48]

Special and Multicultural Education

Two movements in the UK that parallel those in the U.S. are special and multicultural education. As in the U.S., special education in the UK provides services to pupils with physical handicaps and learning impairments caused by emotional and behavioral disorders. Somewhat different from the civil rights and advocacy climate in which special needs issues surfaced in the U.S., the UK movement for special education services for pupils with handicaps was stimulated more by the general development of comprehensive schooling and efforts to make these schools more democratic than selective.[49] The Warnock Report (1978) estimated 18 percent of the school population in the UK would require special educational services at some time in their school experience.[50] The LEAs in the UK are responsible for ensuring that students with special needs are educated in regular schools. The guidelines for integrating children with handicaps into regular classrooms respect parental wishes as far as possible, ensure that children's special needs are met, and ensure compatibility with the efficient education of other children.

An area of discussion in the UK is the impact of the national curriculum, which requires detailed programs of study, attainment targets, and assessments of core subjects, on children with handicaps and special needs. Greater sensitivity to students with special needs and the movement to mandate curricular uniformity has required increased support personnel and services such as consultants, special education teachers, auxiliary support, and volunteers.[51] Similar to special education concerns in the U.S., the issues in the UK deal with providing adequate funding, the need to retrain teachers to deal with more inclusive classroom populations, and establishing the appropriate parental role.

The UK today, like other Western European nations, is a multicultural nation and like these other countries has experienced some multicultural tensions. Immigrants, especially from former colonies in Asia, Africa, and the Caribbean, are concentrated in economically disadvantaged sections of the large industrial cities. These minorities have a higher rate of unemployment and lower school retention rates. As with children living in U.S. cities, children living in the poorer urban areas of the UK often attend older, rundown, overcrowded schools. Educators in the UK (and in the U.S.) have made concerted efforts to make the schools and curriculum more sensitive to multicultural issues. To meet multicultural needs, the schools teach the English language as well as provide instruction in the vernaculars of non-English-speaking children. Education practices in the UK seek to infuse multiculturalism into the curriculum and to provide multicultural preservice and inservice to teachers.

In 2003, the Labour government of Prime Minister Blair launched a new initiative, "Aiming High: Raising the Achievement of Minority Ethnic Pupils," to improve the academic participation and performance of students from minority groups. It established an annual census to monitor the academic achievement of minority students throughout the country. The initiative's strategy seeks to: (1) meet the needs of bilingual students and raise the academic achievement of minority ethnic pupils; (2) maintain and publish data annually on the academic performance of minority students; (3) direct the inservice of teachers to include more attention to working with minority students; and (4) work to improve retention rates of students from minority groups.[52]

Conclusion

National politics has more influence on educational practices in the UK than in the U.S. Educational practices reflect the agenda of the political party in control of the national government and filter down from the Department for Education and Skills to the local education authorities. Although the national government and the local authorities share educational responsibilities more today than ever before, the national curriculum and national examinations, established by the central government and implemented by local school councils, are examples of parliamentary control of education.

When we look at education in the UK from a historical perspective, it is evident that establishing an educational structure that prepares students to perform roles articulated by the UK's standing as a highly technologically developed nation and that provides long-term opportunities to socially diverse groups is a continually evolving process. Traditionally, entry into higher education was available only to students from upper-middle- and upper-class families. This characteristic is slowly changing, now that secondary education is free to all students who attend maintained schools. The development of vocational training programs, another example of educational change, has occurred in response to the needs of the economy and rapid technological change.

Just as in the U.S., education in the UK is a continual process that reflects the past, attempts to meet the needs of the present, and molds the future. Educating a population is not done in a vacuum, but in varied contexts that exist within a nation-state. Comparing education in the UK with that in other countries (such as those discussed in this book) hones our understanding about how education can best serve humankind.

DISCUSSION QUESTIONS

1. How have the British generally accommodated their institutions to socio-economic change?
2. Identify the traditions in British educational history that contributed to gradual reform and change.
3. Analyze the ideologies, with special reference to education, of the UK's major political parties.
4. Historically, what distinctions existed between primary and secondary education in the UK?
5. Compare and contrast educational patterns in the UK and the U.S.
6. How is education in the UK a national system that has been administered locally?
7. Describe the features of primary school in the UK.
8. Describe the features of secondary schools in the UK.
9. Compare and contrast the educational policies of the Conservative and Labour governments.
10. Identify and analyze the major problems facing education in the UK.

RESEARCH TOPICS

1. In a paper, compare and contrast education in the UK and the U.S.
2. Read and review a book on the British public schools.
3. Prepare a "clippings file" of articles dealing with education in the UK.
4. If there are international students from the UK on your college or university campus, interview several of them on their educational experiences. Then, write a paper describing and interpreting their comments.

5. Reflect on the similarities and differences relating to religious and church–state relationships in education in the U.S. and the UK and then arrange a debate on the proposition: "Resolved: The pattern of state support for voluntary schools in the United Kingdom should be adopted for non-public schools in the United States."

6. Arrange a viewing of a motion picture about education in the UK such as *Good Bye Mr. Chips* or *The Prime of Miss Jean Brodie* and then discuss the portrayal of the teachers in the film.

7. Consult the Web site for the Department for Education and Skills for information on specific developments and issues in education in the UK.

SUGGESTIONS FOR FURTHER READING

Aldcroft, Derek H. *Education, Training, and Economic Performance, 1944–1990.* Manchester, UK: Manchester University Press, 1992.

Allsobrook, David I. *Schools for the Shires: The Reform of Middle-Class Education in Mid-Victorian England.* Manchester: Manchester University Press, 1989.

Docking, Jim. *New Labour's Policies for Schools.* London: David Fulton, 2000.

Duke, Benjamin C. *Education and Leadership for the Twenty-first Century: Japan, America, and Britain.* New York: Praeger, 1991.

Gearon, Liam, ed. *Education in the United Kingdom: Structures and Organization.* London: David Fulton, 2002.

Glenn, Allen D. *Lessons in Teacher Education: A Comparative Analysis of Teacher Education in the United Kingdom and the United States.* Washington, DC: ERIC Clearing House on Teaching and Teacher Education, 2001.

Gordon, Peter, Adrich, Richard, and Dean, Dennis. *Education and Policy in England in the Twentieth Century.* London: Frank Cass and the Woburn Press, 1991.

Green, Andy. *Education and State Formation: The Rise of Education Systems in England, France and the U.S.A.* New York: St. Martin's Press, 1990.

Green, James E. *Education in the United Kingdom and Ireland.* Bloomington, IN: Phi Delta Kappa International, 2001.

Hayes, Denis. *Planning, Teaching and Class Management in Primary Schools.* London: David Fulton, 2003.

Higher Education Funding Council for England. *Higher Education in the United Kingdom.* Bristol, UK: Higher Education Funding Council for England, 2005.

Hopkins, David. *Improvement in the Quality of Education for All.* London: David Fulton, 2002.

Knight, Christopher. *The Making of Tory Education Policy in Post-War Britain, 1950–1986.* London and New York: Falmer Press, 1990.

Marsden, W. E. *Unequal Educational Provision in England and Wales: The Nineteenth-Century Roots.* London: Frank Cass and the Woburn Press, 1987.

McCulloch, Gary. *Philosophers and Kings: Education for Leadership in Modern England.* Cambridge, UK and New York: Cambridge University Press, 1991.

Silver, Harold. *An Educational War on Poverty: American and British Policy-making, 1960–1980.* Cambridge and New York: Cambridge University Press, 1991.

Tabor, Daniel C. *Curriculum Continuity in English and the National Curriculum: Working Together at Transition.* London and New York: Falmer Press, 1991.

Thomas, Norman. *Primary Education from Plowden to the 1990s*. London and New York: Falmer Press, 1990.

Wolford, Geoffrey. *Privatization and Privilege in Education*. London: Routledge, 1990.

NOTES

1. CIA (Central Intelligence Agency), "The World Factbook," January 22, 2004, http://www.odci.gov/cia/publications/factbook/geos/uk.html.
2. Ibid.
3. Ibid.
4. Ibid.
5. Frank L. Wilson, *European Politics Today: The Democratic Experience* (Englewood Cliffs, NJ: Prentice-Hall, 1990), 92–98.
6. Christopher Knight, *The Making of Tory Education Policy in Post-War Britain, 1950–1986* (London and New York: Falmer Press, 1990).
7. Wilson, 37.
8. BBC News. "Election 2005: Blair Wins Historic Third Term—Majority of 67," http://news.bbc.co.uk/1/hi/uk_politics/vote_2005/constituencies/default.stm (accessed June 14, 2005).
9. Wilson, 21–24.
10. Monitorialism is described in Joseph Lancaster, *Improvements in Education, As It Respects the Industrious Classes of the Community* (London: Darton and Harvey, 1805) and Lancaster's *The British System of Education* (London: Royal Free School Society, 1810).
11. *Report from the Committee on the Bill to Regulate the Labour of Children in the Mills and Factories of the United Kingdom* (London: House of Commons, 1832), 94–104.
12. Brian Simon, "Classification and Streaming: A Study of Grouping in English Schools, 1860–1960," in *History and Education*, ed. Paul Nash (New York: Random House, 1970), 117–119.
13. Edward C. Mack, *Public Schools and British Opinion Since 1860* (New York: Oxford University Press, 1941), 10.
14. Ibid., 69.
15. As quoted in Crispin Jones, "Education in England and Wales: A National System Locally Administered," in *Equality and Freedom in Education: A Comparative Study*, ed. Brian Holmes (London: Allen and Unwin, 1985), 25.
16. We focus on education in England and Wales; Scotland and Northern Ireland, while constituent parts of the United Kingdom of Great Britain and Northern Ireland, have their own educational systems.
17. *Education in Britain* (London: Central Office of Information, 1989), 164.
18. Holmes, 27–28.
19. Philip H. Taylor and Roy Lowe, "English Education," in *Comparative Educational Systems*, eds. Edward Ignas and Raymond J. Corsini (Itasca, IL: F. E. Peacock, 1981), 166.
20. Brian Elliott and David Maclennan, "Education, Modernity, and Neo-conservative School Reform in Canada, Britain, and the United States," *British Journal of Sociology of Education* 15(2) (1994): 165–185.
21. Department for Education and Skills, "Creating Opportunity, Releasing Potential, Achieving Excellence," March 3, 2003, http://www.dfes.gov.uk.
22. *Education in Britain*, 166.
23. Ibid., 3.
24. Ibid., 163.
25. Taylor and Lowe, 167–169.
26. *Education in Britain*, 166.
27. Ibid.
28. Department for Education and Skills, "Early Years Education and Day Care," March 5, 2003, http://www.dfes.gov.uk.
29. Gene I. Maeroff, "Focusing on Urban Education in Britain," *Phi Delta Kappan* 73(5) (1992): 355.

30 U.S. Department of Education, Office of the Secretary, "No Child Left Behind" (Washington, DC: U.S. Department of Education, 2001).

31 Maeroff, 357.

32 Ibid.

33 Jones, 41–42.

34 Department for Education and Skills, "The Standards Site: What Are Specialist Schools?", http://www.standards.dfes.gov.uk/specialistschools/what_are/?version=1 (accessed June 14, 2005).

35 Taylor and Lowe, 157–158.

36 *Education in Britain*, 170.

37 Department for Education and Skills, "Every Secondary School to Be Transformed with Buildings Fit for the Future," March 5, 2003, http://www.dfes.uk.

38 Richard Barwell, *Age Structure and the UK Unemployment Rate*, http://www.bankofengland.co.uk/qb/qb/qb000301.pdf (accessed March 22, 2005).

39 *Education in Britain*, 169.

40 Thomas Deissinger, "The Evolution of the Modern Vocational Training Systems in England and Germany: A Comparative View," *Compare* 24(2) (1994): 19–21.

41 *Education in Britain*, 2.

42 Muriel Egerton and A. H. Halsey, "Trends by Social Class and Gender in Access to Higher Education in Britain," *Oxford Review of Education* 19(2) (1993): 183.

43 Ibid., 189.

44 Ibid., 190.

45 Edward Shils, "The British Universities in Tribulation," *Minerva* 32(2) (1994): 201.

46 *Education in Britain*, 5.

47 The Open University, http://www.open.ac.uk/ (accessed March 15, 2005).

48 Department for Education and Skills, "Teaching Population," March 5, 2003, http://www.dfes.gov.uk; and *Statistics of Education—School Workforce in England, 2002* (UK: DfES, 2002).

49 Brahm Norwich, "The Relationship between Attitudes to the Integration of Children with Special Education Needs and Wider Socio-political Views: A U.S.–English Comparison," *European Journal of Special Needs Education* 9(1) (1994): 91–106.

50 Department of Education and Science, *Special Education Needs. Report of the Committee of Enquiry into the Education of Handicapped Children and Young People* (The Warnock Report) (London: H.M.S.O., 1978).

51 Rachelle M. Bruno, Janet M. Johnson, and Jack Gilliland, "A Comparison of Reform in Special Education in England and in Kentucky, USA," *International Journal of Special Education* 9(1) (1994): 53–64.

52 Department for Education and Skills, "Aiming High: Raising the Achievement of Minority Ethnic Pupils," March 5, 2003, http://www.dfes.gov.uk.

12

EDUCATION IN FRANCE

France is selected for discussion because of the great influence it has had on world culture. France, historically, was one of the world's great powers. In the Napoleonic era, France dominated Europe. In the eighteenth and early nineteenth centuries, she was a rival of Great Britain. After German unification in 1871, her major rival was Germany, with which she fought three wars. Until the post–World War II era, France maintained an empire with colonies in Africa, Asia, and the Caribbean. With few exceptions, the colonies won independence after World War II. France still exercises a considerable influence in her former African colonies. Since World War II, France has played a significant role in the United Nations, often taking an independent course based on French and European interests. France has been an active leader in the European Union, and plays a leading role in NATO.

Geographic, Demographic, and Sociocultural Contexts

France is Europe's second largest country, exceeded in size only by Russia. Its boundaries are: on the north, the English Channel, the Straits of Dover, and the North Sea, separating it from the UK; on the northeast, Belgium, Luxembourg, and Germany; on the east, Germany, Switzerland, and Italy; on the southeast, the Mediterranean Sea; on the south, Spain; and on the west, the Bay of Biscay, an extension of the Atlantic Ocean. What remains of the once-large French empire are the four overseas *départements* of Guadeloupe, Martinique, French Guiana, and Reunion. Its other overseas territories are the Pacific islands of New Caledonia and French Polynesia and Miquelon and St. Pierre off the coast of Canada.

France is Europe's fourth most populous nation, but its population density is low for Western Europe. Over half of the population lives in cities of more than 50,000 inhabitants. Paris, the largest metropolitan area with more than 2,000,000 inhabitants, contains 19 percent of France's total population.[1] After World War II, France, like the U.S., experienced a "baby boom." Between 1951 and 1956, more than 1.2 million new pupils entered primary schools, a 40 percent increase over the preceding period. A declining birth-rate after 1965 resulted in a decreasing school-age population from 1972 to 1982 that, as in the U.S., caused the closing of some smaller schools.[2]

Approximately 18.6 percent of the French population is in the age range from 0–14 years; 65.1 percent is in the 15–64 year range; 16.3 percent is 65 and over. The current birthrate is 0.42 percent and the median age is 38.3 years. France has a very high literacy rate of 99 percent.[3] Like other techno-logically developed nations France's rate of population growth has been slow. Thirty-two percent of the population is under age 25.[4] The school-age cohort, in proportion to the rest of the population, is decreasing.

Like other technologically advanced countries, the percentage of the French population engaged in farming has declined, although agriculture is an important sector of the French economy—33 percent of France is arable and agriculture benefits from the country's generally temperate climate. As the rural population declines, France is becoming more urban. Urbanization has been accompanied by increases in technological and service areas, which in turn has stimulated expansion of technological secondary schools (*lycées techniques*) and vocational schools.

French society is paradoxically both traditional and modern, liberal and conservative, and Catholic and secular. Avant garde in the arts, it is also a society where traditional family values reign. While the majority of people are nominally cultural Catholics, only a minority are practicing Catholics. Despite paradoxes, the French perceive their country as culturally preemi-nent—a world cultural force and trendsetter.

The sense of *mission civilisatrice*, civilizing mission, has had a deep impact upon French culture and education. By the eighteenth century, the French language had reached such prominence that it replaced Latin as the interna-tional diplomatic language. Emphasizing the intimate relationship between French cultural identity and the French language (the country's national lan-guage), educators stress the schools' key role in transmitting and maintaining language purity, cultural tradition, and the maintenance of French identity.

Like the U.S., France does not define citizenship in ethnic terms as does Germany and Japan. About 85 percent of the population is of French ethnic-ity. France is experiencing a modest rekindling of ethnic regional cultures and languages in Brittany, Alsace, the Basque area, and Corsica. In addition to French, some regional dialects such as Breton are spoken in Brittany, Catalan and Basque in the Pyrenees mountain region, Provencal in Provence, Flem-ish in Flanders, and German in Alsace and Lorraine. Teacher training is pro-vided in these regional languages.

Like other postindustrial European nations, France, especially in its larger urban areas, has a multicultural, multiethnic, and multiracial character. The number of guest workers and their families is estimated at 4,000,000. There also are immigrants from France's former colonies in Africa and from the former French Indo-China, including Vietnam and Cambodia.[5] The most noticeable increase has been from Arab countries. The largest groups of foreign-born residents are Italians, Spanish, Portuguese, Poles, and West and North Africans. About 6.3 percent of the population is comprised of foreign residents. An issue in French education relates to how the schools should maintain the dominance of French culture and language.

French history reveals often contentious relationships between its republican governments and the Roman Catholic Church. Church–state issues have had reverberations in education. Since 1905, France has been an officially secular state. Nominally, however, 81.4 percent of the population is Roman Catholic, but the number of those who regularly practice their religion has declined sharply. Although difficult to ascertain, it is estimated that only 20 percent of those identified as Roman Catholics regularly attend Sunday Mass. Nevertheless, Catholicism is a persistent intellectual and cultural force. Islam with 4,000,000 adherents, or 6.9 percent of the population, is the second largest religion. In addition, there are 950,000 Protestants, or 1.6 percent of the population, and 750,000 Jews, 1.3 percent of the population. There are also Buddhist and Orthodox communities.[6] Fifteen percent of primary and 20 percent of secondary school pupils attend church-related schools, most of which are Roman Catholic.

Political Context

France's political structure consists of a central national administration in Paris, the capital, regional and departmental administrations, and local units known as *cantons* and *communes*.

The Central Government

France is a parliamentary democracy. The functions of head of state and head of government are separate. The president of the republic, the head of state, is elected by popular vote for a five-year term and has more powers than other continental European heads of state, whose positions are primarily formal and ceremonial.[7] The president promulgates the laws, has exclusive power in granting pardons, appoints the prime minister, and, upon the prime minister's recommendation, appoints the cabinet. The president can dissolve the National Assembly, which eventuates in new elections, and may invoke special measures in national emergencies. The prime minister heads the government. In charge of the national administration, the prime minister determines policies, submits government bills to the National Assembly, and is responsible for executing laws.

Cabinet ministers compose the government and are responsible for the national administration in their respective jurisdictions. For example, the minister of education frames the government's educational policies and executes and supervises laws relating to education. While both the French minister of education and the U.S. secretary of education hold cabinet ranks, the powers of the French minister are much more extensive. Cabinet ministers, such as the minister of education, are assisted by a permanent civil service staff. While governments come and go, depending on their party's political fortunes, the civil service ensures administrative continuity (as in the UK).

The French parliament, the national law-making body, consists of two houses: the Senate and the National Assembly. The Senate's 321 members are indirectly elected by an electoral college for nine-year terms. One-third of the senators are elected every three years. The National Assembly's 577 deputies are elected by direct popular vote for five-year terms. The National Assembly can force the prime minister's resignation by a majority vote of no confidence or by voting down the government's program. All finance bills originate in the National Assembly. Other national institutions include those that deal with judicial, legal, and economic matters.

Regional, Departmental, and Local Government

Metropolitan France, which includes continental France and Corsica, is divided into twenty-two regions and is subdivided into ninety-six administrative units called *départements*. Départements are divided into cantons and communes. Additionally, the four overseas départements of Guadeloupe, Martinique, French Guiana, and Réunion have the same rights and duties as those in metropolitan France.

Each region is administered by an elected regional council. An economic and social committee serves in an advisory capacity to the general regional council and (1) implements the national development plan in the region; (2) prepares and executes the regional development plan; (3) prepares the regional budget; and (4) advises on internal regional economic and social matters. Each region has a regional prefect, appointed by the national cabinet, to represent the national interests in the region.

The General Council, elected by voters in the cantons for six-year terms, administers the affairs of the département. The decentralization law of 1983 devolved such responsibilities on the département as: (1) providing public works and improvements; (2) organizing school transportation; (3) developing health, social service, and cultural programs; and (4) instituting and monitoring environmental protection. The General Council's president, chosen by its members, is the département's chief executive. The president implements council policies, manages the budget, and exercises general police powers. The département préfet, appointed by the national cabinet and representing the national government, directs national services in the département.

France's 36,934 communes, local government (township) units, are its smallest administrative units.[8] Each commune is administered by a municipal council, its legislative body, elected by direct popular vote for six-year terms, and a mayor. The mayor, elected by the municipal council from its members, is the agent of both national and communal governments. Responsible for proclaiming and implementing laws and regulations, the mayor has authority over municipal police, performs marriage ceremonies, implements council decisions, and drafts and submits the local budget.

The Trend to Decentralization

While the preponderance of authority remains with the central government, the Decentralization Acts of 1982 and 1983 increased the role of elected local authorities, especially in the regional, departmental, and communal assemblies. With the move to limited decentralization, local authorities provide 20 percent of funding for education and have limited responsibility in providing and maintaining educational facilities. Communes provide the nursery and primary school buildings, equipment, and their maintenance. They also pay the salaries of the nonprofessional staff. Note that the national central government retains authority over the professional education staff and curriculum and instruction. At the secondary level, the départements are responsible for building, equipping, and maintaining the *collèges* and providing the school transportation system. The regions provide the same services for the *lycées* and participate in planning the regional training plan.

The limited educational prerogatives accorded to local government units in France contrasts with other countries such as the UK and the U.S. where local authorities enjoy greater educational powers. In the UK, where educational responsibilities are shared by national and local governments, each unit of government has defined powers. In the U.S. where the federal government has limited authority, the states have significant educational responsibilities to local school boards.

Political Parties

France's multiparty political system has always seemed complex to Americans who are used to a two-party system. French parties, ranging from the far left to the far right, are presently organized into four major coalitions. The *Rassemblement pour la République* (RPR), a moderately conservative party, is composed of Gaullists. More centrist factions form the *Union pour la Démocratie Française*, or Union for French Democracy (RDF), associated largely with former President Valery Giscard d'Estaing. The RDF supports a free market economy and a strong French role in the European Union (EU). The largest leftist party is the Socialist Party. There is also the French Communist Party, which once had but has lost support among industrial workers. In addition to these major political groupings, there are myriad others.

Economic Context

France has a well-developed modern economy. Its diverse industries produce machinery, chemicals, automobiles, aircraft, electronics, textiles, and food items. Large manufacturing and commercial areas are located in

France's northeastern section and Paris.[9] While the economy is essentially free enterprise capitalist, there has been a large government role in public service enterprises, such as railways and telecommunications, and a role in providing subsidies in the private sector, particularly in banking, insurance, automobile and aircraft manufacturing, and armaments. The French economy is currently undergoing a transition from extensive government ownership and intervention to an increasingly greater reliance on free market forces. At the same time that forces of privatization are at work, the government has tried to maintain social equality through tax policies and social service spending.

Complementing industry, France has a stable and prosperous agricultural sector, which enjoys government subsidies. France is self-sufficient in food production and exports many of these products. The government role in subsidizing agriculture will be subject, in the future, to the policies of the European Union. When efforts are made to reduce government subsidization of agriculture, a strong backlash can be expected from farmers.

France generally has enjoyed a high rate of employment but has recently experienced a slight rise in unemployment,[10] attributed to the displacement of industrial workers in an economy that has become more service- and technology-based. The same phenomenon has occurred in Germany, the UK, and the U.S. France's labor force is divided into 71 percent who are employed in service areas, 25 percent in industry, and 4 percent in agriculture.[11] France, along with Germany and the UK, is a leading economic power in the European Union.

Historical Context

French education has a long and distinguished history that reaches back to Charlemagne's court school at Aachen, where Alcuin presided as chief educator. In the Middle Ages, it boasted the famous University of Paris, founded in 1150, which was Europe's leading theology center, home to such great educators as Abelard and Thomas Aquinas. Other universities were founded at Toulouse in 1229, Lyon in 1245, Orléans in 1306, Poitiers in 1431, Bordeaux in 1441, Nantes in 1460, Reims in 1548, and Lille in 1560.[12]

During the Renaissance, French classical humanists such as Rabelais, Bude, Montaigne, Descartes, Pascal, Ramus, and others made significant contributions to Western education. During the sixteenth and seventeenth centuries, Roman Catholic religious communities such as the Jesuits, Oratorians, and Christian Brothers established schools noted for distinctive pedagogical styles. An important cultural legacy that influenced French education was the emphasis on the humanities and literature as the corpus of knowledge.

Paris was the leading literary and cultural center of the eighteenth-century Enlightenment. Denis Diderot and the other Encyclopedists constructed a literature that presented a rationally organized body of knowledge. The

Enlightenment's emphasis on critical reason was a potent influence on French education. France also had its great romantic and naturalist theorists. Jean Jacques Rousseau's iconoclastic didactic novel, *Émile*, has been a great influence on naturalist and progressive educators.

Although France was Western Europe's premier cultural and political power, educational access, like political and economic rights, were unevenly distributed among the French people. On the eve of the French Revolution of 1789, more than 50 percent of the male population and 75 percent of the female population were illiterate. While France boasted a distinguished intellectual elite, the masses had limited access to schooling. For them, education was limited to sporadic attendance at Roman Catholic parish schools that offered a basic curriculum of reading, writing, arithmetic, and religion.

The years of the French Revolution were heady with educational theories but scarce on actual implementation. The Constitutions of 1791 and 1793, however, identified education as a universal right. The various revolutionary assemblies and legislative bodies approved educational policies that sought to replace Roman Catholic schools with new republican schools. The revolution's secular thrust against the church's prerogatives spawned the long-lasting secular versus clerical controversy in French politics and education. Since the French Revolution, church–state issues have resurfaced episodically in struggles between pro-Catholic and anticlerical factions. Comparatively, similar controversies took place in Mexico, a country with both Roman Catholic and anticlerical traditions.

The First Empire: 1804–1815

During the First Empire, Napoleon made peace with the Catholic Church so he could concentrate on his ambitious imperial designs. The concordat, restoring Church control of primary schools, allowed priests and members of religious orders to be school principals and teachers. Wanting to train military officers, engineers, and reliable administrators, Napoleon concentrated on secondary and higher education.

Napoleon's imperial decree, in 1808, placed French universities' faculties under national jurisdiction. Furthering imperial centralization, the Napoleonic educational system was administered through *l'Université Impériale*, a hierarchical government corporation headed by an advisory council and an imperial grand master, the nation's chief educational minister. Next in the educational chain of command were the rectors, national officials responsible to the central government, who presided over the *académies*, the educational regions into which France was organized. Napoleon's centralization policies generated an important tendency in French educational governance. With some temporary reversals, a guiding principle in French education has been national control, centralization, and uniformity. Teachers were made civil servants and governed by nationwide career regulations and salary schedules.

The Bourbon Restoration: 1815–1830

After Napoleon's defeat at Waterloo and exile to St. Helena in 1815, the Congress of Vienna, controlled by the victorious allies, restored the Bourbons as France's legitimate rulers. The Bourbon restoration saw an effort to reassert prerevolutionary social, political, and educational patterns. Kings Louis XVIII and Charles X returned primary and secondary schools to religious control with priests and nuns in administrative and teaching positions.

The Citizen King: 1830–1848

Recalcitrant against Bourbon exertions to set back the clock, the French people mounted a successful revolution in 1830 that swept Charles X from the throne. The new regime of Louis Philippe, dubbed the "citizen-king" and the "bourgeois monarch," was controlled by upper-middle-class liberals who proceeded with moderate but limited reforms. François Guizot, an eminent historian and proponent of cultural nationalism, was Louis Philippe's first minister of national education. In 1833, he introduced the Guizot Law. While the law did not enforce compulsory attendance, it did mandate that the local units of government (communes) establish public primary schools and pay their teachers. It required larger towns and cities to establish higher elementary schools in which students, with the exception of the very poor, were to pay tuition. Further, the law authorized each département to establish a normal school to prepare primary school teachers.[13] Civil authorities assumed responsibility for licensing and appointing teachers, including those in private schools.

While reducing the Catholic Church's educational authority, the Guizot Law did not eliminate it. The local priest remained a member of the communal councils that supervised local schools. Upon parental petition, however, children could be excused from religious instruction, which was included in the national curriculum. As in most countries where liberals controlled the government, educational reforms were incremental and gradual. During Louis Philippe's regime, the number of public and private schools increased from 30,000 to 62,000 and enrollments rose from 1.95 million to 3.53 million. Seventy-two normal schools were established. Among males, the literacy rate increased from 50 to 67 percent.[14]

The Second Republic and the Second Empire: 1848–1870

In the revolutions that swept Europe in 1848, Louis Philippe's regime was overthrown. Exploiting political uncertainty, Louis Napoleon Bonaparte, the first emperor's nephew, emerged as the strongman. He was elected president of the short-lived Second Republic in 1848, and then, following his uncle's career, was crowned emperor of the Second Empire in 1852. Louis Napoleon consolidated his position by reconciling with the Catholic Church. To appease Catholics, the Falloux Law restored much of the church's traditional influence: it appointed bishops to each academy's administrative council, permitted clergy to teach in public schools, and increased the time allotted to religious instruction. The law permitted any French citizen over twenty-five who held a *baccalauréat* (secondary school diploma) and had five years teaching experience to open a private school and receive government funding. Near the end of the Second Empire, Victor Duruy, the minister of education, convinced Louis Napoleon to pursue a more liberal education policy. The Duruy Law extended free primary education for poor children and required all communes to establish public primary schools for girls.

The Third Republic: 1870–1940

France's crushing defeat by the German armies in the Franco-Prussian War of 1870 brought the collapse of Louis Napoleon Bonaparte's Second Empire, his exile to England, and the establishment of the Third Republic. Humiliated by the German victory, the republic's government, bent on revenge, sought to rekindle nationalist pride. School curricula and textbooks emphasized patriotic love of country and the need to revenge its defeat.

The republic's educational policy again moved in an anticlerical direction as liberal ministers maneuvered to curb the Catholic Church's influence. Seeking to withstand the liberals' offensive, the church, an entrenched traditional force, firmly resisted efforts to curtail its educational role. Though on the defensive, the church, with nearly half of the schools under its control, sustained some of its educational prerogatives. The state continued to subsidize church schools and the clergy continued to be represented on the National Council, the major advisory body for public education. The Jesuits continued to operate the most prestigious secondary schools.

Winning majorities in the election of 1878, the liberal parties mounted a concerted campaign to secularize and modernize the national education system. Jules Ferry, the minister of education, designed an educational policy to limit the church's educational role and to centralize education. The government restricted the educational activities of Catholic religious orders. Religious instruction was dropped from the public school curriculum and clergy were no longer permitted to teach in, inspect, or supervise public schools. Extending its authority over private schools, Ministry of Education inspectors ensured compliance with national standards.

The liberal republican government, in the 1880s, reorganized the *école normale d'instituteurs* to prepare more primary school teachers. It abolished primary school fees and mandated compulsory attendance for children between ages six and thirteen. The Law of 1896 reconfigured higher education. It divided France into twenty-three académies, or districts, each with its own university. Given limited autonomy over their academic affairs, universities remained under central government control with instruction, examinations, and degrees conforming to national standards.

In early twentieth century, the Third Republic took its most determined anticlerical stand. In 1901, the French government prohibited members of unauthorized religious orders from teaching in any school, public or private. Priests, brothers, and nuns were forced to leave their schools, which were then closed. Crucifixes and other religious symbols were removed from public schools. The government, in 1905, ending the concordat with the Vatican, officially separated church and state and placed church property under state supervision. The Laic Laws of 1904, which banned members of authorized religious orders from teaching, resulted in the closing of over 13,000 Catholic schools that were still functioning.[15] Some reopened as private schools of Catholic persuasion. In 1909, the French bishops conceded that Catholic children could attend public schools, if they received religious instruction outside of school. France's desperate struggle against Germany and the Central Powers in World War I brought a truce between clerical and anticlerical factions. The government suspended enforcement of the law that had closed religious schools.

The period from the end of World War I in 1918 to the beginning of World War II in 1939 saw expansion of the education system. The Depression of the 1930s caused retrenchment and budget cutting in France as it did in most countries. During this era, French politics were unstable as the political parties in the governing coalitions shifted from right to left of center. Among the educational developments of this period were the Astier Laws of 1919, which made part-time technical education compulsory for young workers and authorized the establishment of institutes in higher education in 1920. In 1933, the school-leaving age was raised to fourteen.

Though religious issues remained, socioeconomic class controversies focusing on the issue of elitism and egalitarianism became preeminent in education. As in most Western European countries, France's schools reflected, reinforced, and reproduced socioeconomic class differences. Its generally conservative secondary and higher educational establishment dedicated itself to maintaining an elitist school system that emphasized the rigorously selective study of the classics and mathematics.

The educational status quo was challenged by a group of French teachers, many of whom were World War I veterans, who organized *Les Compagnons de l'Université Nouvelle*, the Companions of the New Educational System. Rebelling against the traditional examination-driven system, the companions wanted more humanistic and egalitarian schooling. They advocated creating a unified school system, *école unique*, to replace the existing dual system that tracked lower-socioeconomic-class and middle- and upper-class children into separate schools. The French government made a modest movement toward a unified school system by easing restrictions on transferring between various types of schools. Further, all children between ages six and thirteen were to attend common primary schools. After completing the common school, they were streamed into specialized schools. In 1937, Jean Zay, the minister of education, moved the system toward greater articulation between elementary and secondary schooling. Zay's plan created *classes d'orientation,* guidance or orientation classes, to identify student aptitudes and interests as a means of assigning students to appropriate tracks. World War II, the German occupation, and the authoritarian Vichy regime ended the Zay experiment.

The Vichy Government: 1940–1944

In 1940, the German army, using a highly mechanized strategy, the *blitzkreig,* crushed the French armed forces. In a humiliating treaty, the Germans occupied France's northern and coastal areas, leaving the southern part of the country to be governed by a collaborationist regime, the Vichy government of Marshall Petain. The Vichy regime established a paternalistic, authoritarian style of government. It emphasized patriotism, work, and family as the core values of the truncated nation and its schools. Semifascist youth organizations were organized. Like its Nazi overseers, the Vichy regime enacted anti-Semitic laws, banning Jews from teaching and government service. It also cooperated in transporting Jews from France to Nazi death camps. With France's liberation in 1944, the Vichy regime collapsed, and prior to the establishment of the Fourth Republic, a provisional government was in place from 1944 to 1946.

The Fourth and Fifth Republics: 1946–Present

Following World War II, the Fourth Republic sought to rebuild France's damaged economic and educational systems. The agenda for educational reconstruction included promoting: (1) equality of educational opportunity; (2) programs to train personnel for the postwar economy; and (3) greater attention to children's individual needs and development.[16] These efforts generated intense educational debate and identified issues that reverberated throughout the twentieth century.

After the war, church–state tensions resurfaced. Despite strong opposition from the Radical, Socialist, and Communist Parties in the National Assembly, the government, headed by René Pleven, enacted the Barange and Marie Laws in 1951 that provided subsidies to parochial schools. The Barange Law provided national grants to all primary schools, both public and private. The grants to private schools were paid to parents' associations. The Marie Law made national scholarships available to both public and private school pupils; however, the private schools were required to meet national standards for facilities, teacher qualifications, and instruction.

As in the Federal Republic of Germany, Czechoslovakia, and the U.S., France was swept by a wave of student protests in higher education in the 1960s. Protesting students took to the streets against the de Gaulle government's educational policies. Seeking to quiet student protests, the government, with the *Loi d'Orientation de l'Enseignement Supérieur,* reformed higher education, especially universities. As in the U.S., reforms included more student participation in university governance and created interdisciplinary academic programs. Contrary to the French tradition of centralization, the 1968 reforms granted universities more freedom in: (1) teaching, research, and examinations; (2) internal governance and administration; and (3) the development of internal budgets and greater discretionary use of funds.[17] The Higher Education Act of 1983, the Loi Savary, established a Secretariat of State for Higher Education as the national coordination agency for postsecondary education.

An important trend in French education is the marked increase in retention and completion rates that have occurred since the 1980s. The Outline Act of 1989 affirmed that 80 percent of students would complete secondary school and obtain the baccalauréat. About 70 percent of French young people now complete secondary education, reversing the earlier pattern of leaving school at age 16.[18] As in other countries, efforts are underway to improve retention and expand secondary and university enrollments

Governance and Administration of Education

While France was Europe's first modern republic and the French revolutionaries exalted liberty, equality, and fraternity, the French educational system has exhibited considerable elitism, reflecting socioeconomic class differences. The French model, characterized by universal primary schools where children learned basic skills and subjects, especially the French language and culture, also featured secondary and higher education geared to academically elite students. The paradox between equality and elitism is rooted in centralization. In order to overcome regional and class differences, the French Republic designed its highly centralized system, not only to promote cultural uniformity, but also to maintain equality of entitlement for all children by providing the same curriculum and instruction no matter where they live. Concurrently, however, the French insistence on maintaining rigorous standards throughout the republic produced elitism.

Administration

Today, the state schools, which have a strongly republican and strictly secular character, are agencies for constructing French identity and citizenship in students. Throughout France, the Ministry of Youth, National Education, and Research (hereafter referred to as the National Education Ministry), and the Ministry of Universities exercise national educational authority. The National Education Ministry is organized into the following directorates, or subdivisions: preschool and first-level schools; the first and second cycles of secondary education; lycée teaching staff; administrative staff; general administration; equipment and buildings; finance; statistics and information; and international relations.

The French system is organized hierarchically, from nursery school to postgraduate work.[19] The National Education Ministry, at the apex of the organizational pyramid, is responsible for the overall administration of primary, secondary, and technological education. It establishes and implements policies and curricula, trains teachers, and sets teachers' salaries.

Policy made in Paris is passed down the administrative line through the hierarchical bureaucracy. Communications are sent to the local schools in an official weekly bulletin specifying new regulations and guidelines. Teachers are expected to implement these regulations, and inspectors verify compliance. The Ministry of Universities is responsible for higher education, particularly universities, certain *grandes écoles* (great schools; see p. 265), national libraries, and research.

In the 1990s, France experimented with decentralization to bring diversity and flexibility to the educational system. This process was a response to critics' charges that the system is too rigid, uniform, and monolithic. More discretionary authority was given to regional and other local authorities who, nevertheless, remain under the overall jurisdiction of the National Education Ministry. Below the national authorities in the organizational flow chart of French education are three subordinate units: the académie, the département, and the commune.

The académie, a regional division, is responsible for implementing national policies. France is divided into twenty-six académies; there is also an académie for France's Caribbean colonies. The schools in each académie are administered by a *recteur*, an agent of the National Education Ministry. *Recteurs d'académie* are appropriated funds by the national ministry, which they then allocate to the schools in their jurisdiction. The recteurs also assign new teachers and promote and transfer teachers within their académie. National control is reinforced by school inspectors whose supervision ensures conformity to national standards.

The académies are divided into départements, headed by a *préfet* (prefect), who has general supervisory powers over public primary schools in his or her jurisdiction. The prefect chairs a council on elementary education. While having little power over curriculum or instruction, the council has some authority over the appointment of teachers to permanent positions, teacher promotion, approval of new private schools, and inspection of school facilities. The actual appointment of teachers is done by a joint administrative commission composed of members of the teaching profession. Each département has a head inspector of schools and a corps of inspectors working under his or her direction who are primarily concerned with elementary schools. Secondary school inspection in the collèges and lycées is conducted by *inspecteurs pedagogigues régionaux,* assigned to subject specializations such as history, French language and literature, and science.[20]

At the local level is the commune school board whose limited powers include maintaining records to verify compulsory school attendance and administering a small fund to provide extra services.

Funding

The funding for French education reflects traditional centralization as well as the trend to devolve more responsibility upon regional and local authorities. Although annual variations in educational appropriations vary, the national government, through the National Education Ministry, contributes about 66 percent; the regions, départements, and other local government authorities contribute about 18 percent; and other sources provide the remaining support. Nearly 80 percent of the total expenditures support general instruction, which includes teachers' compensation and benefits. Vocational education is partially funded by an apprenticeship tax levied on industrial and commercial businesses. In the 1990s, the national government, giving high priority to educational improvement, increased spending for education to offset rising operating costs, to fund more teachers' positions, and generally to improve instruction.[21]

Organization and Structure of Schools

Preschools

France's well-developed system of early childhood education provides almost all three- to six-year-old children with the opportunity to attend preschool. While *l'enseignement préelémentaire* (early childhood education) is optional for children between the ages of two and six, it is an important and highly used component of French education. Nearly 100 percent of four- and five-year-olds, 91 percent of three-year-olds, and 32 percent of two-year-olds attend public or private programs.[22] Preschool attendance is highest for low-income families in which the mother works outside of the home, and it is lowest in rural areas.

While French preschool programs perform socialization and child-care functions, academic preparation for later education also receives attention. The basic preschool institutions are the *écoles maternelles* (nursery schools), operated by municipalities, and *jardins d'enfants* (kindergartens), usually operated by private agencies. The école maternelle enrolls children from ages two through six. In small towns of less than 2,000 inhabitants, children are likely to attend *classes enfantines* (infant classes) in the local primary school rather than an école maternelle. Regulations require that upon a family's request, a place be available for any three-year-old child in a nursery or infant class in the primary school nearest to the child's home. Regulations also give priority in school places to two-year-olds in socially underprivileged localities. In the école maternelle, children are grouped into three levels according to age and level of development: beginners, two to four years old; middle, four to five years old; and upper, five to six years old. The upper section of nursery schooling is articulated with the "basics" stage, *cycle des apprentissages*, the first cycle of elementary school.

The typical day in the école maternelle consists of two three-hour sessions: one in the morning from 8:30 to 11:30 AM and an afternoon session from 1:30 to 4:30 PM. Schools providing child care may be in session ten to twelve hours each day, opening as early as 6:30 or 7:00 AM, to meet needs of working parents. About one-third of the children spend the entire day at school. The école maternelle is likely to provide bathing facilities, meals, clothing, and medical services.

The curriculum of an école maternelle must be approved by the National Education Ministry. Programs include games, movement exercises, songs, drawing, general knowledge, exercises in correct speaking, stories, and elements of reading, writing, and arithmetic. They also emphasize development of sensory and motor skills, socialization, and learning readiness.

Primary Schools

School attendance in France is compulsory from six to sixteen years of age. Primary schooling encompasses children from ages six to eleven who attend one of the country's 60,000 primary schools. While most children begin elementary school, l'école élémentaire, at age six, those identified as gifted may begin at age five. There are both single-sex and coeducational schools. Primary schooling is divided into five levels: (1) the preparatory course, from ages six to seven; (2) the first-year elementary course, from ages seven to eight; (3) the second-year elementary course, from ages eight to nine; (4) the first-year middle course, from ages nine to ten; and (5) the second-year middle course, from ages ten to eleven.

The primary curriculum, prescribed by the National Education Ministry, is mandatory for all schools, public as well as private; it emphasizes academic preparation for the next stage of schooling. The ministry states: "The main objective of primary school remains the learning and consolidation of the basics (reading, writing, and mathematics)," so that children can proceed smoothly to secondary school.[23] The largely skill- and subject-based primary curriculum is organized into three major clusters: (1) French language, history, geography, and civics; (2) mathematics, science, and technology; and (3) physical education and sport, art and craft work, and music. Although the local schools are allowed some flexibility, ministry regulations specify the instruction time to be devoted to each cluster.

As is true worldwide, primary schooling in France emphasizes language acquisition and skill development—reading, writing, spelling, and grammar. Giving high priority to literacy, the National Education Ministry has set the following goals for the primary schools: (1) to improve children's language skills for knowledge acquisition; (2) to establish special programs for children whose native language is not French; and (3) to encourage parents and local authorities to promote reading, particularly through public libraries.[24]

The school year, which begins in mid-September, continues to the end of June. Short vacations occur at the end of October, at Christmas, in February, and in the spring. The summer vacation is eleven weeks. The school day is from 8:30 AM to 4:30 PM. Most schools are closed on Wednesday and open Saturday mornings.[25] The twenty-seven hour, four-and-a-half day academic week in primary schools is scheduled into: (1) fifteen hours of basic studies, divided into nine hours of French and six of mathematics; (2) seven hours of history, geography, moral education projects, handwork modeling, music, and other creative activities; and (3) five hours of physical education and sports.[26]

Although not selecting textbooks directly, the National Education Ministry influences their selection through a procedure in which: (1) the teachers in each commune meet with the elementary school inspector to compile a list of possible textbooks; (2) the list is then forwarded to the académie inspector to be evaluated by a commission of inspectors, teacher educators, and representatives of classroom teachers; and (3) the revised list is then submitted for approval to the rector and the National Education Ministry. Unauthorized books or materials may not be used in public schools. Textbooks typically adhere to syllabi authorized by the ministry.[27]

French elementary school instruction has often been criticized as a lock-step mechanism that requires students to accumulate and recall detailed factual information. Defenders of the system argue that its uniformity provides equality of instruction throughout the country. The ministry's precisely delineated curriculum guides and periodic visits by the national inspectors reinforce instructional standardization and conformity. Schedules and timetables, approved by school inspectors, are posted in the classrooms. Inspectors expect teachers to follow the nationally prepared syllabi closely. Principals in French primary schools have no direct responsibility for evaluating the performance of teachers in their schools. Supervision is the responsibility of the inspectors. The French system of teacher evaluation by external inspectors contrasts with the supervision of teachers in the U.S., where it is typically performed by the school principal or another supervisor in the school district.

An inspector's visit to a primary school focuses on the particular classroom and teacher rather than on the school. Since inspections are scheduled in advance, teachers know when they will be visited and prepare for the inspections. Inspectors evaluate teachers on such items as: (1) orderly classroom materials and desks; (2) displays about the French language and mathematics; (3) clear lesson plans, discipline, and motivated pupils; (4) pupils' exercise books that demonstrate the teacher is implementing curricular standards; (5) teachers' preparation books; and (6) the presence of ministry documents, especially the curriculum schedule and timetable.[28] For teachers, the evaluations, which are maintained in teachers' permanent files, are crucial to their career advancement. Their upward promotion and salary increases depend heavily on the cumulative record of inspectors' assessments.

Because of strong external controls, the teaching style tends to be formal and uniform. A basic teaching method is a meticulous, line-by-line reading of textbooks, followed by recitations in which pupils answer the teacher's questions about the textbook assignment. Teachers may not use corporal punishment. Typical punishments for infractions of the rules are assigning extra work, deprivation of recreation periods, and detention. Despite some efforts to meet children's interests and needs, foreign observers in French classrooms note that teachers seem most concerned with pupils' academic performance. A German educator visiting French schools commented, "In France, anyone who does not achieve the highest possible school diploma is regarded, more or less, as a school failure. It is assumed that a pupil who can read, write, and do arithmetic . . . must be capable of acquiring a Baccalauréat."[29]

An attempt to reform school climate and instruction occurred in 1989 with the enactment of the Law for the Orientation of Education. The law, designed to encourage more innovative teaching, encouraged greater attention to children's needs and interests. It requires teachers to teach in a more individualized and differentiated manner as a response to the growing diversity of the school population. At the same time, however, the system of external inspections and adherence to nationally designed policies remains in effect. An English educator visiting French schools commented that paradoxically the law may generate a conflict "between inspectors promoting the new approach and teachers who are ideologically opposed to greater autonomy for themselves." He found that many teachers continue to teach in standard ways, using techniques they regard as "tried, tested, and successful."[30]

The French elementary teacher is both constrained and free at the same time. Working within a bureaucratic and highly centralized school system, curriculum content and teaching methods are predetermined at the top. The chief external intrusion into their classrooms comes from important periodic visits by inspectors, their real supervisors. Otherwise, they are virtually autonomous, if not isolated, in their classrooms since principals and head teachers lack supervisory power and customarily do not intrude into another teacher's domain. Further, parents are expected to support but not interfere with schooling.

Based on examinations, students are ranked at regular intervals throughout their schooling. Decisions about repeating a class, promotion to a higher class, and changing classes are made through a process that involves teachers, administrators, parents, and pupils. Parents also have the option of appealing a decision. Elementary education concludes with oral and written examinations that require intensive preparation by students. Administered by a committee of teachers, these comprehensive examinations include dictation, arithmetic, history, geography, science; exercises in drawing, handicraft, or sewing; and reading a passage.

Secondary Schools

The general control of secondary education is exercised by the National Education Ministry, through the rector of the académie, and more directly through the académie inspector who is in charge of education in the département in which the school is located.

Secondary education, compulsory to age sixteen, takes place in three types of schools: the *collège*, which includes forms sixth through third; the *lycée*, which includes forms second, first, and terminal; and the *lycée professionnel*. (Note that forms are arranged in descending order from sixth through terminal. Sixth form is the lowest or beginning level, which leads upward to the first form and then to termination.)

Collèges

Upon completion of primary school, almost all students proceed to four-year comprehensive secondary schools, *collèges d'enseignement secondaire* (CES). Collège schooling, encompassing ages eleven through fourteen, is subdivided into two two-year stages: observation and orientation.

In the observation stage, *cycle d'observation*, in the sixth and fifth forms, all students follow a common core curriculum of twenty-four hours a week of French; mathematics; a modern foreign language; history-geography-economics; civics; physics, chemistry, biology, and geology; technology; and art, physical education, and sport. Because of strict separation of church and state, no religious instruction occurs in the state schools. Music is elective. The average class size is 24.3 students.[31] After completing the fifth form, students proceed to the fourth form.

In the past, after completing the fifth form, about 20 percent of the students were streamed into prevocational classes, *classes preprofessionnelle de niveau* (CPPN). These classes, which often included remedial instruction, especially in French and mathematics for those repeating the fifth form, were followed by a *classe préparatoire à l'apprentissage* (CPA) for students moving into apprenticeships or two years of *classes préparatoires* within vocational secondary schools. This tracking, occurring when the student was thirteen or fourteen, often streamed students who were identified as less academically able into vocational training. From an American perspective, this streaming, which was largely determined by educational authorities, was done prematurely, before the student had matured academically and emotionally. Further, the preciseness or academic calibration of the curriculum locked students, especially those in vocational tracks, into a career path that may not be the best one for the particular person.

Streaming students into either academic or vocational tracks after fifth form is now delayed until secondary school. Students can now follow an alternative technological curriculum, paralleling the general curriculum, which offers more applied subjects and practical experiences.[32] Special education sections provide educational services for students with psychological, emotional, or behavioral disorders.

The orientation stage, *cycle d'orientation*, which includes fourth and third forms, is designed to orient students to future academic work. Students in these forms pursue the same core subjects found in sixth and fifth forms, with an additional hour of mathematics. Along with the core curriculum, students choose one or two additional subjects such as a second modern foreign language, advanced work in their first modern foreign language, a regional language, or a classical language such as Greek or Latin. A current trend is to take additional modern languages, such as English, which advances Europeanization related to the EU.

Classes in technology in the fourth and third forms provide a more practical educational experience than the traditional highly academic classes. Technology instruction occupies ten out of thirty hours of instruction per week for students pursuing this option. These students can then obtain a *certificat d'aptitude professionnel* (CAP) in either a vocational school or in apprenticeship.

Students completing the four-year general program in the collège may apply for the *brevet des collèges* (diploma). The brevet is awarded without further examination to students proceeding to more advanced academic studies at a lycée. Those not advancing to the lycée must sustain an examination to receive the brevet.[33]

Lycées

The general and technical secondary schools, *lycées d'enseignement général et technologique*, start with the second form, progress to the first form, and end at the terminal form. They prepare students, ages fifteen to eighteen, for the highly important baccalauréat examination. The lycée d'enseignement général leads to the *baccalauréat d'enseignement général*, a university entry diploma. The lycée technologique leads to a *baccalauréat technologique* or to a *brevet de technicien,* a vocational training diploma. Like other continental European school systems, the lycées stream or differentiate students institutionally into career lanes based on their academic ability. This contrasts with the American philosophy of locating secondary students in a common facility, even if tracked within the school.

The lycée's second form, *classe de second de détermination*, begins to prepare students for the type of baccalauréat examination they will take. All students in the second form follow the required core curriculum in French, mathematics, a modern foreign language, history and geography, physics and chemistry, biology and geology, and physical education and sports for twenty-three-and-one-half hours per week. They also choose compulsory subjects from one of the following two groups: Group A consists of a required introduction to economics and social sciences and an elective from among a second modern, a regional, or a classical language; management, automation technology, or art and sports. Group B consists of one or two specialized technology subjects such as industrial technologies, science and laboratory technologies, medical science, and social science. Students must choose at least one technology subject to move to the first form leading to the technology baccalauréat series.

Upon completing the second form, students advance to more specialized courses leading to the examination they will take. Unlike the American comprehensive high school, advanced secondary schooling in France is geared to students' careers.

Instruction in the lycée is driven by the crucial baccalauréat examinations. Adhering to national syllabi, French secondary teachers see their role as being responsible for preparing students for the examinations and for their ongoing education. This tendency is also found in other countries such as Japan and China where a person's future is based on success on examinations. Critics of the French system compare it with the Japanese system for its emphasis on cramming information into students' minds. Memorizing information dictated by teachers is often the focus of instruction. Defenders of the system claim that it has contributed to the academic quality of French secondary education.

The academically rigorous baccalauréat examination traditionally has been a highly selective screening device, with a failure rate often reaching 35 percent. However, the French government's announced policy is to increase the number of persons holding a baccalauréat.[34] Though the lycée remains highly selective in terms of academic specialty and streaming, there has been, in response to popular demand, an increase in the number of candidates preparing for baccalauréat examinations and earning the degree. While only 24 percent earned the baccalauréat in 1975, 60 percent earned it in 2000.[35]

Vocational Schools and Professional Schools

There are two types of vocational schools, *lycées professionnels*, with highly specialized programs that lead to various vocational certificates and diplomas such as the CAP or *brevet d'études professionnelles* (BEP), and lycées professionnels that award a baccalauréat professionnel, which entitles a student to university admission. Two-year programs in vocational lycées lead to vocational certificates. A reorientation class is provided for pupils who change tracks and wish to prepare for a technology baccalauréat. After completing the third form, students begin to prepare for the BEP and/or the CAP. Along with course work, on-the-job internships are provided. Students possessing either the BEP or CAP can proceed to earn a technology baccalauréat.

Higher Education

In France, higher education has historically included two major institutions: universities and the grandes écoles. Although either controlled directly or supervised by the Ministry for Higher Education, the 300 institutions of higher learning exhibit some diversity. In some specific cases, the Ministry of Higher Education shares administrative responsibility with the Defense, Agriculture, and Health Ministries. While universities have large enrollments, the highly selective grandes écoles admit only a small number of applicants.

The reforms of 1968 brought important changes to French universities. National government control and authority was reduced as universities gained more autonomy. The universities are generally interdisciplinary, multipurpose, and autonomous institutions that offer programs in a range of fields such as law and public service; medicine, pharmacy, dentistry, and other health-care areas; cultural programs in publishing, library science, communications, and museums; education; and commercial areas such as business, trade, and banking. Depending on the institutions, enrollments range from 5,000 to 35,000 students.[36] The universities are largely open to every baccalauréat holder who applies. Tuition and fees are very low. Nearly one million students are enrolled in universities.

Universities are administered by a president who is elected for a five-year term by a university board or council composed of teachers, students, administrative personnel, and eminent public figures. Universities are organized into departments that are chaired by elected councils. The departments offer the same types of programs as in the U.S. and most other countries. Universities also may include special professional institutes of technology, engineering, management, or foreign languages. Universities award national diplomas, degrees, and doctorates. The three *instituts nationaux polytechniques* (INP) have university status and provide advanced training in engineering and award the doctoral degree. Faculty designations are similar to those in the U.S., but the number at the upper ranks is much smaller.

Organization of University Studies

Students enroll in one of the faculties, completing most of their course work in a specific field. Courses are divided into three successive two-year cycles. A national diploma is awarded at the completion of each cycle.

The first cycle, open to students who possess the baccalauréat, offers general education and orientation curricula. Many courses are interdisciplinary and provide basic knowledge in a major and complementary knowledge in a minor. Upon completion of the cycle, students qualify for a diploma, the *diplôme d'études universitaires générales* (DEUG).

The second cycle provides higher-level general, scientific, and technical education in specific professions. Students may concentrate on one of the following: (1) fundamental professional and specialized training leading to the *licence*, after one year, and the *maîtrise*, after two years; (2) professional training that leads to the maîtrise in science, technology, management, and computer science; (3) programs leading to engineering degrees; and (4) three-year university programs that combine fundamental knowledge, research, and practical professional application, leading to the *magistère* diploma.

The third cycle of university study is very specialized and includes research. Students accepted into the third cycle must possess a maîtrise or engineering diploma or their equivalent. Among the programs are: (1) one-year programs leading to the *diplôme d'études supérieures spécialisées*, DESS diploma, that offers professional training and requires an internship; and (2) a one-year program leading to the *diplôme d'études approfondies*, DEA diploma.

The doctorate can be pursued in fields in which accreditation to supervise research, the *habilitation*, has been granted. The habilitation, the most advanced university diploma, is awarded to professors recognized as having expertise in research and the ability to supervise students who are writing their thesis. The *doctorat d'université*, obtained mainly by foreign students, requires two or three years of course work and writing and defending a thesis. The *doctorat d'état*, France's highest and most prestigious university degree, is open to holders of either the DEA or DESS and is awarded after the successful submission and defense of a thesis.

Critics of French university instruction contend that it, like the lower schools, exaggerates transmitting information so that students merely memorize it rather than understand it, interpret it, and draw meaningful conclusions about it. The examination process that drives the system contributes to a high failure and dropout rate.

The Great Schools

The grandes écoles are a distinctive feature of French education. At the summit of the institutional hierarchy, these prestigious institutions educate highly selected elites in rigorous academic programs that lead to high-level careers in politics, education, and economics.[37] The grandes écoles enjoy greater acclaim than the universities whose courses of study are regarded as insufficient for top positions in engineering, commerce, and administration. Graduates of the grandes écoles include France's most distinguished scholars, scientists, and political leaders.

To be admitted to the grandes écoles, students must pass the baccalauréat, complete classes préparatoires (CPGE, a program of preparatory studies), and pass rigorous competitive examinations. While academic preparatory classes are integral in the lycées, some are occasionally found in the grandes écoles. Admission to the CPGE is a highly selective hurdle on a complicated academic race track. While a baccalauréat is necessary, it is not sufficient for admission to the preparatory classes. The admission process also requires evidence of academic ability and teacher recommendations. Students who fail their admission examination to the grandes écoles often enroll in universities.

The grandes écoles vary in governance. Some are controlled by the National Education Ministry and others are either public or private institutions. All have highly selective admission policies that limit the number of students who can enroll in them. There are several types of grandes écoles. Among them are scientific schools, *grandes écoles scientifiques*, which offer three-year programs to prepare scientists and civil, mining, and other engineers and executives. Grandes écoles of business and management prepare higher echelon administrators and civil servants. The *écoles normales supérieures* offer a three-year program to prepare secondary teachers, university instructors, and researchers. The *École Militaire Saint-Cyr* prepares high-ranking military officers. Somewhat like the graduates of the public schools and Oxford and Cambridge in the UK, graduates of the grandes écoles in France form a closely knit network in government, private industry, and the highest ranks of cultural and intellectual life.

Other Higher Education Choices

Technological Education

There are a variety of post-secondary technological education programs. They are offered in first-cycle professional, scientific, and technical programs at universities, at university institutes of technology, and in advanced technical studies sections of public and private vocational high schools, or at schools offering specialized study in the social, paramedical, or business sectors. Candidates are admitted on a selective basis. About 30 percent of those holding a baccalauréat choose these programs.

University institutes of technology (UITs) offer two-year specific training programs leading to the diploma of technology, which is especially attractive to those seeking manufacturing and service industry careers. The post-secondary technical studies (*section de techniciens supérieures* [STS]) offer more advanced specialized programs. After two years of study, students are awarded the BTS diploma (*brevet de technicien supérieur*).

Catholic Institutes

The Roman Catholic institutes of Paris, Lille, Lyon, Angers, and Toulouse are private institutions accredited by the National Education Ministry. They include both university-level programs and specialized advanced schools. Their students must take examinations supervised by public university examining boards.

Continuing and Distance Education

Higher education in France also includes continuing and distance learning programs and courses, many in the evening, for working students. The *Conservatoire National des Arts et Métiers* (CNAM) and its regional centers admit working students to its evening classes without entrance requirements. Students who complete these courses may earn engineering degrees. A university distance learning system also is available to nontraditional students unable to attend a university on site. Several offer televised distance learning programs. The *Centre National d'Enseignement à Distance*, using televised instruction, also prepares students in specific fields or for entrance examinations to other institutions.

Teacher Education

Many factors shape teachers' professional roles in a given country, especially the national context and educational system. These factors influence teachers' professional preparation and socialization.[38]

For teachers in France, the highly standardized school experiences are likely to create a well-defined image of teaching. For many, the decision to become a teacher is a deliberate career choice rather than a result of "drifting" into the field. Teaching is perceived as a positive career with prestige, respect, and status. This contrasts with the perception of teaching in the U.S., where many elementary and secondary teachers find that their profession lacks high social status. As civil servants, teachers in France identify job stability and economic security as important career considerations.[39]

Prospective elementary teachers for grades one through five must possess the secondary school baccalauréat and have passed a competitive admission examination to enter an *école normale primaire*, a primary teachers' training school, offering a two-year preservice program. Those who have taught for a year after graduation usually are awarded full elementary certification and the title *instituteur*. Often instituteurs continue to study for the *certificat d'aptitude au professorat d'enseignement général des collèges* (CAPEGC). Those who complete a specialized two-year course may also qualify as a school psychologist or a special education teacher.[40]

Prospective teachers for the lower secondary grades, six through nine, follow a more complex three-year preparation program. Preservice programs leading to lower secondary certification are offered by *centres pédagogiques régionaux* (regional pedagogical centers) affiliated with normal schools near universities. After completing two years of university study, students are awarded the *diplôme d'études universitaires générales*. After an additional year of study at the regional center, they receive the CAPEGC, the lower secondary general education teaching certificate. Upper secondary school teachers for grades ten through twelve must hold the *licence*, a diploma requiring three years of university study. An additional year is spent preparing for a *concours*, a competitive examination, leading to the *certificat d'aptitude au professorat de l'enseignement secondaire* (certificate of aptitude for a secondary school professorship), the CAPES. Those preparing to teach secondary technical subjects must qualify for the CAPET, *certificat d'aptitude au professorat de l'enseignement technique*, (certificate of aptitude for a technical school professorship). Full CAPES-CAPET certification status is not awarded until completion of a second year of professional training and practice teaching at a regional pedagogical center. Both CAPES and CAPET lead to certification and tenure.

Some university students prepare for the CAPES and complete their maîtrise, the diploma awarded after four years of university study, during the same academic year. This option is possible because the CAPES examination tests competency in an academic specialty rather than educational theory and methodology. Students from the highly selective écoles normales supérieures as well as normally matriculated university students also may take the CAPES examination.

The elite of France's teachers are the *agréges*, a select minority of academically able students who have passed the fiercely competitive *agrégation* examination. Candidates for the agrégation must already have earned the maîtrise or the CAPES. Many agréges pursue graduate studies leading to university teaching. Those continuing as secondary teachers enjoy special assignments and higher salaries.[41]

Teacher education is marked by a basically didactic pedagogy designed to reproduce rather than transform the culture. The process of transmitting information has been standardized by imposition of national norms. Comments by comparative researchers from the UK suggest that French teachers are often not concerned with their "teaching style" but rather regard teaching to be a highly regulated and well-defined contract that is "largely unexplicated and unproblematic." For French teachers, "teaching" means transmitting the cultural heritage, usually construed as bodies of information, within the four walls of the classroom. They identify their primary responsibility as ensuring students' academic preparation and progress.[42] Their concern with larger social issues appears to be less than that of teachers in the UK or the U.S.

While the "four walls" academic specialist role is well established in French schools, some teachers want reforms that will reinvent schools to be more responsive to children's and society's needs. As in other post-industrial, technologically developed nations such as the UK and the U.S., children and youth problems are present in France. Among these problems are the remoteness of curriculum from contemporary issues and a failure to respond to changes in family life. In response, the government has initiated more educational theory and application in pre- and inservice training and more involvement of universities in teacher preparation.

Conclusion

Since the creation of modern France with the revolution and the Napoleonic periods, French education has been tied to the service of the nation. In establishing and maintaining their nation, the French, unlike the English and the Americans, veered strongly toward centralization. The centralization of French schools, under the governance of the National Education Ministry, is like that of Japan. Educational philosophy, curriculum, and instruction tend to be centrally determined. This has resulted in greater uniformity and a uniformity-induced equality not found in the U.S.

As a member of the European Union moving toward greater economic and political integration, French policy makers recognize the need to modernize education and make it more responsive to economic and technological change. A major challenge, not unique to France but pronounced because of its inherited system, is to resolve the often conflicting demands of academic excellence and educational equality. This is particularly acute in France where the system has prized elitism and selectivity. Still a second challenge relates to the inherited proclivity to national control and centralization. Will the French consider it desirable to devolve greater policy making and implementation authority to regions and local communities so that schools can better serve their students and their families?

DISCUSSION QUESTIONS

1. How did political changes such as revolutions have an impact on education in France?

2. Examine the issue of clericalism and anticlericalism in French education.

3. What social and political forces contributed to the centralization of French education?

4. What is the purpose of primary education in France?

5. Examine French secondary education in terms of access, tracking, and selection.

6. What forces have had an impact on French higher education in the post–World War II era?

7. What is the role of the grandes écoles in French society, politics, and economics?

8. Compare and contrast the supervision of teachers in France and the U.S.

9. Compare and contrast the style of teaching in France and the U.S.

RESEARCH TOPICS

1. Write a paper that compares and contrasts the effects of the American and French revolutions on educational development in the two countries.

2. Determine if there are international students from France on your college or university campus. Interview them regarding their educational experiences. Prepare a paper that describes and analyzes their experiences.

3. Develop a "clippings file" of articles on French society, politics, and education.

4. Write a paper that compares and contrasts the role of examinations in French and American secondary education.

5. Compare the role of the *grandes écoles* in France with Oxford and Cambridge in the UK.

SUGGESTIONS FOR FURTHER READING

Baumgartner, Frank R. *Conflict and Rhetoric in French Policymaking*. Pittsburgh: University of Pittsburgh Press, 1989.

Clark, Linda L. *Schooling the Daughters of Marianne: Textbooks and the Socialization of Girls in Modern French Primary Schools*. Albany: State University of New York Press, 1984.

Enders, Jurgen, ed. *Academic Staff in Europe: Changing Contexts and Conditions*. Westport, CT: Greenwood Press, 2001.

Glenn, Charles L. *Choice of Schools in Six Nations*. Washington, DC: U.S. Department of Education, 1989.

Green, Andy. *Education and State Formation: The Rise of Education Systems in England, France, and the USA*. New York: St. Martin's Press, 1990.

Gordon, David M. *Liberalism and Social Reform: Industrial Growth and Progressive Politics in France, 1880–1914*. Westport, CT: Greenwood, 1996.

Price, Roger. *A Concise History of France*. Cambridge, UK: Cambridge University Press, 1993.

Schonfeld, William R. *Youth and Authority in France: A Study of Secondary Schools.* Beverly Hills, CA: Sage, 1971.

Singer, Barnett and Langdon, John. *Cultured Force: Makers and Defenders of the French Colonial Empire.* Madison: University of Wisconsin Press, 2004.

Smith, Paul. *Feminism and the Third Republic: Women's Political and Civil Rights in France, 1918–1945.* New York: Clarendon Press of Oxford University Press, 1996.

Stone, Judith F. *Sons of the Revolution: Radical Democrats in France, 1862–1914.* Baton Rouge: Louisiana State University Press, 1996.

Tiersky, Ronald. *France in the New Europe.* Belmont, CA: Wadsworth, 1994.

NOTES

[1] *La Documentation Française* (Paris: Ministre des Affaires, 1996), 15.

[2] Torsten Husen and T. Neville Postlethwaite, eds., *The International Encyclopedia of Education: Research and Studies*, vol. 4 (Oxford and New York: Pergamon Press, 1985), 1963.

[3] CIA (Central Intelligence Agency), "The World Factbook: France," January 22, 2004, http://www.odci.gov/cia/publications/ factbook/geos/fr.html.

[4] Discover France! "Education in France," January 23, 2004, http://www.discoverfrance.net/France/Education/DF_education.shtml.

[5] Brian Fitzpatrick, "Immigrants," in *France Today*, ed. J. E. Flower (London: Metheun, 1987), 88–91.

[6] Roger Price, *A Concise History of France* (Cambridge, UK: Cambridge University Press, 1993), 203.

[7] The chapter examines the general structure of France's political system. Since the officeholders change with elections, readers are advised to consult articles in newspapers and journals, as well as the World Wide Web, for specific changes.

[8] Husen and Postlethwaite, 1963.

[9] Brian Holmes, ed., *International Handbook of Education Systems: Europe and Canada*, vol. 1 (New York: John Wiley and Sons, 1983), 311.

[10] Discover France!

[11] CIA (accessed March 23, 2005).

[12] George T. Kurian, ed., *World Education Encyclopedia* (New York: Facts On File Publications, 1988), 418.

[13] Guy Vincent, "The École Normale in the Year III of the First French Republic," *European Education* 25(2) (1993): 6.

[14] Kurian, 407.

[15] Ibid., 408.

[16] Husen and Postlethwaite, 1964.

[17] Kurian, 418.

[18] Discover France!

[19] Alison Wolf and Marie-Therese Rapiau, "The Academic Achievement of Craft Apprentices in France and England: Contrasting Systems and Common Dilemmas," *Comparative Education* 29(1) (1993): 30.

[20] Keith Sharpe, "An Inspector Calls: An Analysis of Inspection Procedures in French Primary Education," *Compare* 23(3) (1993): 263.

[21] *Primary and Secondary Education in France* (Paris: Ministry of National Education, Youth, and Sport, 1990), 3–4.

[22] Kurian, 413.

[23] *Primary and Secondary Education in France*, 6–7.

[24] Ibid., 7–8.

[25] Holmes, 312.

[26] Kurian, 414.

[27] Ibid.

[28] Sharpe, 271.

[29] Franz Noichl, "The National Education Target in France: 80 Percent Secondary School Graduates," *European Education* 24(1) (1992): 33.

[30] Sharpe, 265.

[31] Noichl, 29.

[32] Wolf and Rapiau, 31.

[33] Noichl, 31.

[34] Ibid., 26.

[35] Discover France!

[36] Alain Bienayme, "France," in *International Higher Education: An Encyclopedia*, vol. 2, ed. Philip G. Altbach (New York and London: Garland, 1991), 662.

[37] Michael G. Roskin, *Countries and Concepts: An Introduction to Comparative Politics* (Englewood Cliffs, NJ: Prentice-Hall, 1989), 105.

[38] Marilyn Osborn and Patricia Broadfoot, "Becoming and Being a Teacher: The Influence of the National Context," *European Journal of Education* 28(1) (1993): 105.

[39] Ibid., 111.

[40] Kurian, 422.

[41] Ibid.

[42] Osborn and Broadfoot, 106–107.

13

EDUCATION IN THE RUSSIAN FEDERATION

The Russian Federation (RF), the largest republic of the former Union of Soviet Socialist Republics (USSR, or Soviet Union; we will refer to the former Soviet Union as FSU), presents a rich lode of useful comparative generalizations. Because of its adversarial and competitive relationship with the U.S. during the long cold war from 1948 to 1989, the USSR's educational system was frequently compared and contrasted with the American educational system. Indeed, scientific and educational developments in the USSR, such as the successful orbiting of *Sputnik* in 1957, generated educational critique and reform in the U.S. Since 1991, the RF has experienced profound social, political, and economic transformation, which in many ways affects education in this somewhat enigmatic country.

Geographic, Demographic, and Sociocultural Contexts

The RF's large land mass, which covers an area of approximately 6,659,328 square miles (1.8 times that of the U.S.) is located in both Europe and Asia. The RF borders the Arctic Ocean to the north and the North Pacific Ocean to the far east. It is bordered on its western frontiers by Finland, Norway, Poland, and the now independent states of the FSU, Estonia, Latvia, Lithuania, Belarus, and Ukraine.[1] Lying to the south are Georgia, Azerbaijan, and Kazakhstan. The vast eastern region (Siberia) is bordered by Mongolia, China (PRC), and North Korea. Both the RF and the PRC share a Marxist past, but they also have experienced border tension.

The European part of the RF, the vast agricultural regions west of the Ural Mountains, includes large broad plains bordered by areas of low hills. Siberia, in the Asian part, east of the Ural Mountains, is covered by vast coniferous forests and tundras. The southern border regions contain upland plateaus and steep mountains. A country as large as the RF has a varied climatic range. The summers vary from warm in the steppes to cool along the Arctic coast. The permafrost that covers large areas in Siberia poses a major obstacle to the region's development.

The RF's population is 143,782,338.[2] The age cohorts in the population are 16 percent in the age group 0–14, 70.4 percent in the age group 15–64, and 13.6 percent 65 years and older. The median age is 37.6 and the rate of population growth is a low 0.3 percent. The RF's demographic profile is like that of a more technologically developed country (TDC) with a larger middle-age and senior-age population and a very high literacy rate of 99.6 percent.[3] For the school-age cohort, the major issue is to maintain and improve existing educational facilities.

The RF is a multiethnic and multilingual nation-state. Although the Soviets were well aware of ethnic and language differences and often exploited them, the Communist ideology sought to veil ethnic distinctiveness in the Marxist doctrine of proletarian classlessness. Despite the breakup of the FSU, the RF remains a giant complex of land and peoples, with Russians constituting 81.5 percent of the population. The RF is also home to a large variety of non-Russian ethnic groups and languages, including: Tatars, 3.8 percent of the population; Ukrainians, 3 percent; Chuvash, 1.2 percent; Bashkirs, 0.9 percent; Byelorussians, 0.8 percent; Moldavians, 0.7 percent; and other ethnic groups, 8.1 percent.[4] Since the breakup of the USSR, there has been unrest among some of the ethnic groups.

The Russian Orthodox Church has an important position in Russian life, society, and culture. In addition there is a large Islamic minority, especially in the border regions; a significant Jewish presence; a representation of Protestants with a growing fundamentalist membership; and a community of Roman Catholics, some of whom are Uniates, who follow eastern rite rituals but are in allegiance with the Pope.

Political and Economic Contexts

In the RF the president is the head of state. The first president after the demise of the USSR in 1991 was Boris Yeltsin. Vladimir Putin has been president since 1999.[5] The head of the government, the premier, is appointed by the president. Under Putin, the president's role has grown more powerful and the premier's position has become increasingly subordinate. The government ministries are composed of the premier and his deputies, ministers, and selected officials who are all appointed by the president. A presidential administration provides staff and policy support to the president, drafts presidential decrees, and coordinates policy among government agencies.

The RF's legislative branch consists of the bicameral Federal Assembly, *Federalnoye Sobraniye*, and the State *Duma, Gosudarstvennaya Duma*. The Federal Assembly, the upper house, consists of 178 members who are appointed by the executive and legislative officials in each of Russia's federal units for four-year terms. The State Duma, the lower house, consists of 450 members elected by direct popular vote for four-year terms. The actual relationships and powers of the president, premier, and Duma have been fluid and uneasy. Putin has consolidated greater power in the presidency.

There are many political parties in the RF, ranging from those favoring a completely market-driven economy and democratic institutions to those, like the Communist Party (CP), who desire a return to a centralized government and statist economy. The party structures, too, are fluid, centering on personality or ideology. Yeltsin's supporters favored political and educational democratization and economic privatization. Currently, Putin seeks to restore the RF among the world's great powers and develop social and economic stability. Since the demise of the USSR, nationalist and ethnonationalist feelings have risen: nationalists seek to create a solidly Russian nation with Russification policies; ethnonationalists identify more with their primary ethnic and language group.

The end of the Communist government's monolithic and centralized control has brought momentous but also uncertain political and economic change to the RF. Under the Soviet system, economic decisions were all determined by the central government. Priority was given to heavy industry and the military; little attention was directed to consumer goods. Under the Soviet system, the collective was the economic unit of production with individual initiative and competition forbidden as an unhealthy virus of capitalism. As the revolutionary ardor dissipated in the 1970s and 1980s, the economic system became sluggish and inefficient. The large state-run industries were becoming increasingly obsolete, producing goods of inferior quality.

The collapse of the USSR and its Communist Party and government caused deep anxiety about the future of the economy. There were fears of unemployment as the state-owned industries were privatized, fears that social programs and health-care services would diminish, and fears of inflation. After the demise of the Soviet Union on December 22, 1991, Boris Yeltsin, hoping to stimulate greater productivity, moved toward establishing a free enterprise economy. The RF ended the policy of state-controlled and state-subsidized food and other products to allow these items to reach market prices. During the transition to a market economy in the early 1990s, the RF suffered shortages of food supplies and other consumer goods, resulting in price increases, some at 60 percent. By 1993, the rate of inflation was contained.

From 1991 to 1996, the president, premier, and duma disagreed on the country's economic course, especially the extent to which the free market should operate. The RF managed a slight but short-lived economic recovery in 1997. Large budget deficits and an unstable business climate weakened the recovery, which collapsed in 1998. The 1998 crisis brought about a depreciation of the ruble, a debt default by the government, and declining living standards for most of the population. In 1999–2000, an economic rebound saw the economy growing by more than 6 percent, aided by higher oil prices and a 60 percent devaluation of the ruble.[6] As of 2004, the RF had a large labor force of 71,800,000. By occupation 12.3 percent work in agriculture, 22.7 percent in industry, and 65 percent in services. The unemployment rate is estimated at 7.9 percent, with significant underemployment.[7]

The transition to a market economy produced some unanticipated consequences for Russian society and politics. Under the Communist system, the social ideal ensconced in Marxist-Leninist ideology was that of a classless society. As the new market system emerged, there was a sharp division in the Russian class structure as a newly rich entrepreneurial capitalist class emerged and gained control of many of the privatized industries. At the top of the new economic structure was a group of Russian-style "robber barons," referred to as the oligarchs. However, on the opposite end of the spectrum, with the Soviet social security network in shreds and many of the state subsidized jobs eliminated, the number of Russians at or near the poverty level increased. Furthermore, organized crime, political corruption, and lawlessness increased.

The RF's economic direction remains unclear as it takes uncertain steps from its state planned and directed economy to something that resembles a Russian-style modern market economy, highly dependent on the supply and demand in the world market. Many of Russia's industries, constructed in the Soviet period, need modernization or replacement. Other economic problems are an underdeveloped banking system, an uncertain business climate that discourages investment, political corruption, and a general mistrust of all institutions. In 2003 Putin's regime exerted greater controls over the media that limited freedom of expression, especially criticism of the government.

Historical Context

For much of history, the Russian people have clung to hopes of economic and political stability and equality, only to be subsumed by the will of a series of autocratic leaders, foremost among them, the tsars. At the head of a government that did not include popular representation, the often eccentric, self-serving tsars created an agenda of regulations whereby the masses, who were permitted very limited educational opportunities, unquestioningly served the ruling class. At the same time that the tsars were oblivious to the will of the people, they struggled to keep up with Western progress. The challenges in building and perpetuating a strong nation-state were no different than those of Western European nations, yet Russia was always strides behind.

> While the Renaissance spread from Italy over northern Europe, while the West made enormous technological strides, Russia stood still and then slipped below the level it had reached earlier. If in the early sixteenth century Russia was not far behind the West, [but] from then on it rapidly lost ground while Europe moved ahead.[8]

For centuries Russian tsars were deaf to the cries for reform and blind to the lives of the masses: "For decades on end they [the Russian people] go unnoticed, serving the needs of the state anonymously, working and dying without identity. . . . Momentarily the observer's attention focuses on the Russian masses and on the leaders who arose from their midst to lead them."[9] In 1917, the Russian people had finally had enough. Tsar Nicholas II was forced to abdicate the throne, and a provisional government was established. Then, that same year, under the leadership of Vladimir Lenin, Bolshevik rebels overthrew the provisional government and established the USSR as a Communist nation.

During the tsarist period, Russian Orthodox Christianity was the officially established religion. The tsarist government, through the office of the Procurator of the Holy Synod, was heavily involved in church governance. In turn, the Orthodox Church was expected to be a reliable and steadfast support of tsarist autocracy. The Russian Orthodox Church was also invested in primary education, maintaining village schools, often run by parish priests.

The USSR

After the Bolshevik Revolution terminated the tsarist era in 1917, the Communist regime took over and Marxism-Leninism became the official ideology. Favoring dialectical materialism, the Communist Party was openly and actively antireligious and determined to eradicate religion from Russian life. Despite its proscription and persecution, the Orthodox Church was sustained by those Russians who continued to practice religion, often in secret. As well as being a religious force, Orthodoxy was also closely intertwined with Russian culture, festivals, and memorial occasions.

As with all things in the USSR, the CP Central Committee was the key agency in setting educational goals and establishing programs to achieve them. The Central Committee's pervasive goal was to eradicate old tsarist loyalties and replace them with ideological conformity to the new Soviet system. In Soviet schools, the curriculum was designed to instill conformity to Marxist-Leninist thinking and behavior.[10] An important priority of the Soviet regime was to use education to transform the backward agricultural economy that the Communists inherited from their tsarist predecessors into a modern, industrial, technological giant. Based on Marxism, the Soviet educational ideology emphasized a complete plan of general education to shape students intellectually, morally, polytechnically, aesthetically, and physically.

Academic Education

When the Bolsheviks seized power, Lenin and his commissar for education, Anatoly Lunacharsky, were determined that intellectual education should eradicate residues of tsarist attitudes, loyalty to the Russian Orthodox Church, and bourgeois middle-class values. After purging the ideological remnants of the old order, educational institutions were to instill the Marxist ideology of dialectical materialism. Experimenting with a variety of methodological approaches in the 1920s, such as collective group learning and socially useful labor projects, the Soviet regime remained steadfast in its determination to turn the younger generation into staunch Communists. When Joseph Stalin consolidated power in the 1930s, intellectual education was redesigned to inculcate academic subjects within the interpretive framework of Marxist-Leninist scientific materialism and class conflict. Instruction in Soviet schools was to be orderly, systematic, and follow dialectical logic.

Stalin, a ruthless dictator who held absolute power from 1925 to 1953, launched a series of five-year plans to build heavy industries and force agricultural collectivization. To achieve this modernizing goal, Stalin determined that the USSR needed cadres of trained scientists, engineers, and technicians. Thus, the Soviet school curriculum emphasized mathematics and physical sciences, particularly chemistry and physics, to develop industrial and military technology. Although industrial modernization and technical training were emphasized, political indoctrination in CP ideology remained thorough going. (See the chapter on education in China for another scenario in setting educational priorities between ideological indoctrination and technological development.) Instruction in literature, history, social studies, and the arts—the value-laden areas in the curriculum—closely mirrored shifts in the official ideology. For example, in the early Soviet era, the role of the proletariat as the truly revolutionary class was emphasized. This was followed in the 1930s by an emphasis on working to build socialism through industrialization. During World War II and at the height of the Stalinist period, history and literature were used to glorify Stalin's often gruesomely attained achievements in what Nikita Khrushchev, Stalin's successor, later condemned as the "cult of personality."[11]

Ideological Indoctrination

The USSR's educational institutions' paramount goal involved shaping the character of new Soviet man and woman through ideological indoctrination—moral education—an important component of what Soviet educators called the total upbringing of children and youth.[12] For the early Communist educators, moral education meant eradicating the Russian Orthodox Church's traditional religious beliefs and values and eliminating middle-class "bourgeois sentimentality." After these archaic values were eradicated and local family and village loyalties fit into an enlarged Marxist vision of collective responsibility, a new classless morality would arise. Soviet moral upbringing developed into a code in which the end—the establishment of a classless society—justified the means, no matter how ruthless.

Stalin ruled the USSR by establishing a totalitarian police state whose ideology was reinforced by show trials, purges, and imprisonment of suspected dissidents in forced labor camps, known as gulags.[13] The official Soviet morality incorporated traditional Great Russian patriotic nationalism with Marxist proletarian values. The CP, calling for constant and total mobilization, warned the Soviet people that their socialist motherland was encircled by hostile capitalist nations bent on destroying the Soviet Union. The Soviet people were constantly mobilized to make sacrifices to protect Communism in their country.

During World War II, called the "Great Patriotic War" by the Soviets, the USSR was invaded by the armies of Hitler's Nazi Germany. Stalin's regime rallied the Soviet people by rekindling patriotism, especially nationalist love and loyalty to Mother Russia. The USSR, a wartime ally of the UK and the U.S., suffered great physical devastation and massive loss of life. The epic struggle of the war remains embedded in Russian collective memory. Cities like St. Petersburg, formerly Leningrad, which was besieged for three years, were designated "hero cities" for their resistance against the German invaders. Many schools have museums that depict the nation's heroic efforts during World War II.

Polytechnic Education

Soviet educators emphasized Marx's concept of polytechnic education aimed at developing socially useful technical labor.[14] Marx condemned capitalists for exploiting the proletariat, the industrial workers, by expropriating the economic value the workers' labor had created. Workers, under capitalism, were alienated from their work. To overturn capitalist exploitation, Marx proposed polytechnic education to educate working-class children in the techniques of useful, nonexploitative labor. In the promised classless society, Marx predicted workers would enjoy the value their labor created. Lenin and especially his wife, Krupskaya, an important person in setting educational policy in the first Soviet decade, enthusiastically promoted polytechnic education. The early Soviet educators charged that tsarist schools, especially secondary and higher ones, had separated academic learning from productive labor. Under the tsars, it was assumed that educated persons would not engage in physical labor. The Soviet educators determined that the inherited attitude that separated education from work was to be replaced by exalting socially useful productive labor in polytechnic education.

In its development, the Russian empire that the Communists controlled was still an economically backward and inefficient agricultural nation that was just beginning its serious industrialization. In terms of both Marxist ideology and the USSR's modernization program, polytechnic education seemed well suited to instill the ideologically correct attitudes about work as well as develop the necessary technical skills for industrial development.

Aesthetic Education

Under the Soviets, especially Stalin, aesthetic education was to create an artistic outlook supportive of the Marxist-Leninist worldview.[15] Radio, motion pictures, and even the circus, as well as the more conventional art forms of painting, dance, and music were used as important forms of informal and nonformal education in promoting Marxist-Leninist ideology. Although artists and writers typically value their freedom of creative expression, the Soviet regime put the arts under tight party control. The official criterion for judging a work of art, poetry, fiction, a play, music, or a motion picture was its conformity to socialist realism. Artists, writers, composers, and filmmakers, for example, were to use realistic or representational forms that portrayed the struggle of the working class and the Soviet people to achieve a classless society. The canons of socialist realism imposed straight-jacket-like conformity on artists and musicians.

In conjunction with the arts, Soviet educators, using the concept of "upbringing," shaped the ideological attitudes and behavior of Soviet children and youth through CP-controlled recreational agencies. Supplementing schools, CP youth organizations such as the *Komsolmol* provided recreational and other activities to build party loyalty. Offering crafts, sports, music, dance, and recreation, these officially sponsored organizations reinforced ideological commitment to the CP through a continuous program of indoctrination through the recreational milieu. From ages nine to fourteen, most Soviet children enrolled in the Young Pioneers. Older Soviet youth, ages fourteen to twenty-six, were members of the Komsolmol, the All-Union Leninist Communist Union of Youth.

As indicated, Soviet schools, reflecting Marxist-Leninist ideology, had a deliberate political character. Nearly every classroom had a centrally and prominently displayed picture of Lenin. School bulletin boards carried CP slogans, calling upon children and youth to put forth their best efforts in building a strong and modern Soviet nation. In ceremonies and exhibitions about the "Great Patriotic War," Soviet children were imbued with patriotic love for their motherland. In and out of school, evidence of the cult of Lenin could be seen.

Reforming the Soviet System

Despite its self-laudatory rhetoric, Soviet schooling, like other aspects of the tightly state-controlled society and economy, showed symptoms of bureaucratic inertia during the 1970s. The Soviet monolithic structure, brutally erected by Lenin and Stalin, had grown increasingly fossilized. Although the Soviet leadership issued policy statements about educational reform that echoed the USSR's more dynamic revolutionary past, actual educational practices, resisting change, limped along in halting contradictory and vacillating patterns. For many Soviet educational administrators, success required conforming to rather than challenging top-down hierarchical decisions. Even at the top levels of the party and government apparatus, maintenance rather than innovation was viewed as the safest course in a fearful land once victimized by Stalinist purges and gulags. Among the contradictions in Soviet educational policies were vacillation between gender-based and non-gender-based education, between raising and relaxing academic standards, between ten and eleven years of general education, and between polytechnic and more conventional academic curricula.[16]

Gorbachev, Perestroika, and Glasnost

Efforts at reform were inaugurated in the Soviet Union and in Soviet–American relations in 1985 when Mikhail Gorbachev became the CP general secretary and brought momentous changes in Soviet internal and foreign policies that had serious, unexpected consequences for the Soviet Union.[17] Gorbachev realized that the stagnant Soviet economy and bureaucratic rigidity were slowing reform efforts to a snail's pace. He boldly announced new policy directives: *perestroika*, restructuring or transformation; *glasnost*, public openness; *demokratizatsiia*, democratization; and *novoe myshlenie*, a new foreign policy. Struggling to stimulate a stagnating economy, Gorbachev made cautious moves toward limited privatization. His policies opened the Soviet Union to change and brought about a political earthquake that would topple the Communist regime's government in Central and Eastern Europe.[18] The former Soviet satellites—Czechoslovakia, Poland, and Hungary—established non-Communist governments. In 1989, the Berlin Wall, erected during the cold war to isolate East Berlin from West Berlin, was demolished, and in 1990 the German Democratic Republic, a Soviet satellite, was reunited to the Federal Republic of Germany. The rapidity with which these pivotal events unfolded moved far beyond what Gorbachev had anticipated and brought about the end of the USSR itself.

Gorbachev's Proposed Educational Reforms

Just as he criticized the stagnant economy and fossilized bureaucracy, Gorbachev also challenged the ideological and bureaucratic conformity that dominated Soviet education and schooling. Since the Bolshevik Revolution in 1917, the schools had been used for indoctrination in the official Marxist-Leninist ideology. Now, Gorbachev urged their reformation so that they could become agencies of social, political, and economic innovation rather than conformist indoctrination. However, the ills of Soviet society—indifference, low quality standards, social passivity, and bureaucratization—were also endemic to the educational system.

In the spirit of perestroika and glasnost, the schools, once used to create the conformist "new Soviet man and woman," were now to educate the young in "nontraditional attitudes and values" and a risk-taking willingness to innovate.[19] Some educators, stimulated by glasnost's speaking openly, urged basic internal school reforms before dealing with larger socioeconomic change. These critics within the schools claimed the centralized educational bureaucracy, with its vested interests, made it virtually impossible to restructure the educational system. While official statements recommended decentralizing the system, actual policy making in the Gorbachev era was contradictory.

To reduce bureaucracy, the Ministry of Education, the Ministry of Higher and Specialized Secondary Education, and the Committee on Public Education were merged into one All-Union Committee on Public Education. Specific reform efforts focused on: (1) changing the age for entry to schools from seven to six years of age; (2) improving curriculum, instruction, and materials; and (3) modernizing technical and vocational training.[20] Although Soviet planners believed existing facilities and teaching staff could accommodate the larger enrollment resulting from lowering the school-entry age, they miscalculated. The CP Central Committee, in 1989, had already admitted that 20 percent of the schools were either too dilapidated or unsuited for the younger children and understaffed by teachers prepared in early childhood methods.[21]

Gorbachev admonished that curriculum and instruction had "suffered the most from the personality cult, from bureaucratic methods of management, from dogmatism and incompetent meddling."[22] His reform-minded associates recognized that real educational reforms depended on revitalizing curriculum and instruction that suffered from extensive ideological indoctrination in Marxism-Leninism and from the approved teaching method of recitation, in which students answered teacher-originated questions, most of which had only one correct and approved answer. Realistically, reform required extensive revision of subject-matter curriculum, state-approved textbooks, and teacher training—all of which needed funding and time. Nevertheless, Gorbachev urged "radical and immediate changes" in educational research, textbook preparation and publication, and use of creative teaching methods. After decades of following the approved methodology, teachers were told to be more flexible in their methods and to use discussion rather than memorized recitations.

Increasing political and economic instability as well as internal contradictions in the educational system weakened reform efforts. One reform sought to develop quality control of teachers' performance through assessment by supervisors and peer reviewers. Devising and implementing effective assessment is a difficult and highly charged challenge in any educational system, especially one dominated by fear of change. The effort at quality assessment ran into serious obstacles, especially the Soviet practice of inflating achievement scores to very high levels. While some educators saw potential rewards in accurate assessment, others feared it as another bureaucratically imposed "administrative nightmare."[23] The last gasp Soviet efforts to improve curriculum and instruction were seriously flawed by inertia, self-interest, and fear of change.

Gorbachev's desperate stratagems to save the ailing Soviet system were impeded by an increasingly obsolescent industrial system. For decades, the Soviet leadership had concentrated on heavy industrial production rather than consumer goods. By the end of the 1980s, the system was in serious trouble. Educationally, the Gorbachev regime sought to modernize vocational training in light of actual economic needs. However, vocational and technical education, like the general economy, had deteriorated. Equipment used to train technical and vocational students was decrepit and obsolete. Furthermore, many instructors were unqualified. Gorbachev called for a new system of labor education that would modernize workers' technical skills and unite training and economic needs.[24] However, these reforms were frustrated by lack of resources and will.

The Demise of the USSR

Gorbachev's attempts to reform Soviet political, economic, and educational structures caused consequences he had not anticipated, especially the rekindling of ethnonationalism among the various ethnic and language groups comprising the USSR. The Baltic states of Latvia, Lithuania, and Estonia demanded and gained independence in 1991. Demands for autonomy and then independence surfaced among Georgians, Ukrainians, Byelorussians, Azerbaijanis, and other groups.

By 1991, Gorbachev was very much a "man in the middle" who had to balance and appease contentious political and ethnic factions. The CP bureaucracy sought to reverse the process of change and to reassert its once dominant position. Leaders in the various republics, including the large Russian Republic, demanded more decentralization and autonomy. On August 19, 1991, hard-line leaders of the old Communist establishment attempted a coup to depose Gorbachev and restore party control. Due to dramatic popular opposition led by Boris Yeltsin, president of the RF, and the armed forces' unwillingness to support the coup, it failed, and the CP was banned from government agencies.

Though restored to the Soviet presidency, Gorbachev was in a tenuous position and his struggle to salvage the USSR failed. The USSR ceased to exist and it was replaced by a confederation, the Commonwealth of Independent States (CIS), on December 22, 1991. On December 25, 1991, Gorbachev officially resigned as the president of the now defunct USSR. As a significant shaper of world events, Gorbachev should be credited with contributing to the end of the cold war, refraining from attempts to block the Soviet satellites of Eastern and Central Europe from regaining their independence, and creating the preconditions leading to German reunification.

Restructuring in a Changing Russia

With the disappearance of the Soviet Union, the former constituent republics declared their independence as sovereign nation-states. Education in the newly independent states assumed the conventional nation-state pattern that fosters nationalism. While the various states are generally populated by a majority ethnic group, each has sizable ethnic and language minorities. At the same time that each newly independent state asserted the dominant group's culture and language, other ethnic groups have grown restive, resentful, and potentially rebellious. An important question is: Can the schools of the RF and those of the other independent states, like those in Western Europe, embrace a greater pluralism with strategies for multicultural education? Unfortunately, much in the Russian past suggests that a positive answer to the question will be very difficult to implement.

Along with the resurgence of ethnonationalism, the movement to a free enterprise market economy is an important new dynamic in the RF. After seventy years of the Marxist collective economy, the new Russian leadership initially saw a free market economy as the best hope for improving a stagnant economy. Despite considerable opposition, Yeltsin's government moved toward greater economic privatization by breaking up the large state-run industries. To facilitate the movement toward a free enterprise economy, the RF had to borrow large amounts of money from Western countries. Inflation, unemployment, and other economic factors further retarded the process, as did the emergence of a new economic class that monopolized the new industries and banks. The move to free enterprise is continuing under Putin, but with more government intervention.

If the economic reforms are to succeed, an appropriate education is needed to replace the old-style collectivism and centralized planning with the values of individualism, competition, and the profit motive. Many Russian educators emphasize the need to restructure the educational system. Elizaveta Sokolova and V. M. Likhacheva, two Russian educators, note that a new "social ideal" has not yet replaced the Soviet collectivist model. They ask, "What is the schoolteacher to do in such a situation?" Teachers can no longer repeat "ready-made" textbook formulas about the glories of Communism. While the old concepts are "a thing of the past," new ones are needed.[25]

Restructuring Inherited Ideas about Education

Academic education needs to be reconceptualized so that more creative alternative ways of thinking and of viewing the world are possible. Unlike the regimentation of the Soviet past, teachers are now encouraged to deviate from rather than adhere to textbooks, to rely on their own initiative and creativity rather than on central directives, to develop a repertoire of teaching strategies, and to search for the truth rather than follow the party line.[26]

The decades during which the younger generation was imbued with Communist values ended in a sudden but total discrediting of the old credo. The failure and rejection of the Communist orientation left a general ideological cynicism and void. Articulation of a viable and society-sustaining value core remains a significant challenge. Russian educators, while still conceptually committed to moral upbringing, recognize the need to reconceptualize moral education, a profoundly challenging and controversial task.

A key moral issue remains in dealing with the Stalinist legacy. A survey of school students between ages ten and fifteen revealed some interesting findings (published in 1993) on how the younger generation viewed Stalin and Stalinism. Forty-one percent of the students believed that while "Stalin was guilty of many things, . . . he also did many good things." Thirty-eight percent of the students polled thought that "Stalin did great harm" to the country; 9 percent answered that "Stalin was a great man who is not to be spoken ill of"; the remaining 12 percent had no opinion. Those who were most critical of Stalin were males from urban areas, especially children of artists, scientists, engineers, and technicians. Defenders of Stalin were young people in rural areas and children of workers in services and trades.[27]

Approaching the dilemma of Stalinism, Russian and other historians in the FSU are researching Stalin's reign of terror, the rigged purge trials of innocent people, the mass exiles of Soviet citizens to the forced labor camps of the gulags of Siberia, and the mass executions conducted by his regime. Historians and social studies educators face the challenge of writing textbooks that present the truth about the Stalinist past. They need to present a balanced treatment of the Soviet heritage that recounts in an unbiased way the achievements in eradicating illiteracy, in industrialization, and in resisting Hitler's Nazi hordes but that also tells of repression by the totalitarian system.[28]

Another dimension of moral upbringing lies in renewing religious values in the RF and the other successor states of the FSU. The Communist regime, regarding religion as the "opiate of the people," sought to eradicate the influence of religion, especially Russian Orthodoxy but also Judaism and Islam. A religious revival is having an impact on the concept of upbringing and character formation. Religious schools and religious education have reappeared. M. G. Taichinov, a Russian educator, writes that "a new interpretation of religion's role" is needed in the moral development of the young. Such a new interpretation requires turning away from "the dismissive rejection and prohibition" of using religion in moral education. Religion should no longer be seen as the "enemy but as the ally" in moral education.[29] The Russian Orthodox Church is actively involved in education, particularly religious education.

Polytechnic education and its correlative concept of socially useful labor carry the stigma of its Communist origins. It is associated with the centralized state-run economy that floundered and stagnated in the USSR's last decades. As the RF moves in a free market direction, polytechnic education needs to be redesigned to correspond to the new economic reality. Some reformers urge reconceptualizing polytechnic education, or vocational education, to include guidance about career options that were not available under Soviet collectivist state controls. They want to establish the technical foundations for advanced training in a variety of occupations, careers, and professions. Others, however, contend that a new concept of work education, directly related to the market economy, needs to emphasize cost accounting, profit making, and productive efficiency.[30] The market economy approach, they contend, accentuates individual initiative and enterprise over socially useful labor.

In the debate over work education, some fear the trend away from socially useful labor education to one that is market driven may reintroduce the pre-Soviet gap between academic and vocational education. For example, I. N. Nazimov argues that "productive labor—especially manual labor—has been given the label of secondary or even inferior status."[31] The debate takes the lines of argument found in the U.S. over the merits of general versus vocational education.

In the post-Soviet era, artists and musicians have greater freedom of expression than was allowed by Soviet state censors who scrutinized music, art, films, drama, and literature for its ideological correctness. With declining state control, however, there has also been a reduction in state subsidization of arts and the humanities. Music, art, and drama from Western countries are now available throughout the RF. Some Russians, however, are uneasy about these new art forms. As Russian education develops its new philosophy, there will be a need for more open aesthetic education.

Problems in Implementing Educational Reform

The first minister of education of the independent RF, Eduard Dneprov, was a critic of the rigid Communist ideology who encouraged democratization, humanization, and internationalization. Dneprov wanted the reformed educational system to reflect the movement to a market economy and privatization.[32] Although Dneprov and his successors in the Russian Ministry of Education were motivated by bold idealism, economic limitations and political uncertainties have weakened their reformist efforts.

The reform of educational institutions is a difficult task in any country. Schools, as institutions, are especially resistant to transformative change. Often what seems to be a successful reform will be blunted and reshaped so that it resembles the status quo rather than real change. Again, the word "reform" is used so commonly throughout the world that it is necessary to define it in its different contexts. We need to ask such questions as: Who are the reformers? What are their motives? What is being reformed? What are the consequences of reform? For example, a reform will be viewed quite differently by liberals and conservatives, and by the religiously minded and the secularist. Still, another important consideration is that of the "unexpected consequence," results, problems, or situations that were not planned by the reformer—as Gorbachev, himself, experienced.

Educational reform initiatives are often stated as policy directives that originate in upper administrative echelons but may be inadequately and frequently unenthusiastically implemented. In the old Soviet system, reforms generally reflected bureaucratic policy restatements rather than substantive innovation.[33] The tendency to regard an upper-level policy statement as a reform and to neglect implementation remains a problem, not only in the RF, but also in other nations accustomed to top-heavy bureaucracies such as India and Nigeria. Furthermore, reforms require the necessary funds to implement them. Again, there is a tendency in education to announce or mandate a reform but not provide the resources necessary to implement it. This has been the case with nations with weak economies or with uneven economic growth. For example, the RF, now an economically challenged nation with an underdeveloped taxation system, has difficulty in allocating the needed resources for innovations in the schools.

Financing Education

Before the demise of the USSR, Soviet education was funded by the central government, the various constituent republics, and the local districts. The local educational districts paid about half of the schools' operating expenses. Locally generated funds came from income earned by state operated industries and agricultural collectives in the local district. The remaining revenues for education came from the republics and the central government.

Educational funding in the RF and the other successor states to the FSU has suffered from the high rate of inflation and the general difficulty in raising revenue through taxation. Educators are concerned that educational funding will be inadequate to meet the demands of restructuring and reorganizing the educational system, such as incremental increases in teachers' salaries, teachers' pensions, facility construction and maintenance, and preparation and distribution of books and materials. In the RF, incremental increases in teachers' pay are based on years of teaching experience and advanced academic hours and degrees earned. In congruence with democratization and privatization, the RF will need to develop new strategies for educational financing. As the private economic sector develops, corporate and income taxes will be needed to produce revenues for education and other social services.

Organization and Structure of Schools

The structure and organization of the school system in the RF were inherited from the highly centralized system of the USSR and from educational reforms stimulated by Gorbachev's perestroika. In the RF and other successor nations of the FSU, the once centralized Soviet authority is now lodged in each independent successor nation. Each successor nation reconstructed its schools into its own national system of education.

Preschool

Under the Soviets, preschool education received considerable attention since it was believed that ideological formation should commence as early as possible. As soon as the Communists consolidated power, they began to use early childhood institutions, especially orphanages and kindergartens, to create what they envisioned would be the first generation to build the world's first totally socialist society.[34] Furthermore, early childhood institutions provided a nurturing environment for young children while their parents worked. The USSR, which constitutionally guaranteed women's equality, decreed that women were to be free to pursue socially useful labor. Practically, the USSR as a developing industrial nation relied on women, as unskilled and skilled workers as well as professionals, as part of the workforce. To bring more women into the labor force, the Soviet government expanded early childhood and kindergarten education.[35]

Encouraged by state support, Soviet educators devoted considerable research to children's early development and education. The Pre-School Education Institute of the USSR Academy of Pedagogical Sciences and the USSR Academy of Medical Science cooperated in preparing a comprehensive early childhood development program. The future of early childhood education in the post-Soviet RF and other successor states depends on availability of resources. In a climate of limited resources, priorities are likely to shift to general primary and secondary education. Further, the reorganization of the basic general education school from a ten to an eleven-year school has brought the kindergarten into the formal school system. The RF, freed from the strong Soviet tendency to act in *loco parentis*, gives more early childhood decision making to parents and local agencies.

Today, early childhood education is less constrained by ideological objectives but is less adequately supported. Many Russian educators criticize the former tendency to "confine childhood to granite channels."[36] When Russian educators identify the goals of early childhood education, they appear similar to those in other countries and include: enhancing children's physical and mental health; humanizing the principles of early childhood education; ensuring continuity between early and later education; improving the preparation of early childhood educators; developing children's learning readiness by cultivating observing, listening, and communicating skills; and instilling cooperative behavior.[37]

Among the early childhood preschool facilities that provide care and education for children under age six are nursery schools, combined nursery schools and kindergartens, and orphanages. Although the trend is to add kindergartens to the general school, some combined nursery and kindergartens still operate. Nurseries, *yasli,* accept children between six months and age three. Kindergartens, *detskie sady,* typically enroll children from ages three through six. Although early childhood education is often subsidized by government and industry, parents also pay a fee for their children to attend nursery schools and kindergartens. Depending upon their parents' working hours, children attend kindergartens from nine to twelve hours a day and are provided with appropriate meals. The educational experiences of the three- and four-year-old children are broken down into ten short fifteen-minute lessons per week. Older children, from ages four through six, have fourteen lessons per week devoted to developing reading readiness and introducing skills of language, numeracy, art, music, physical activities, and practical work.

The General Eleven-Year School

Although a trend to the more institutional and organizational diversification in the RF and the other successor states is discernable, many students still attend the unified eleven-year school, which incorporates primary and secondary education. During the Soviet era, the institution was designated officially as the general and polytechnic school with vocational training. It was a ten-year institution until 1984 when the kindergarten was added. In some regions, however, the school is still a ten-year institution. In the last year of Soviet rule, it was estimated that approximately 50,000,000 students were attending some 190,000 of these schools throughout the USSR. The major goals of the general and polytechnic schools were to: establish a foundation in basic academic skills and subjects; cultivate a receptive attitude to socially useful work; and instill proper ideological values. These goals have been reconstructed to reflect the political change to democracy and the economic change to a free market economy.

The Law on Education, approved in 1992, established the structure and organization of the RF's school system. While the combined primary and secondary school (the ten- and then eleven-year school) was retained, the 1992 law permitted differentiation of types of schools. Though most of the RF's schools remain the traditional general education school, which enrolls students from ages six to seventeen (in contrast to the various patterns of enrollment in the U.S.), other types of schools have opened. The older pattern persists in rural areas, while more institutional variation is found in cities. The new RF exhibits characteristics of both a technologically developed as well as a less technologically developed country (LTDC). As in many LTDCs, urban and rural regions exhibit educational differentials in quantity and quality.

Some schools now follow the inherited eleven-year pattern of general education but include more curricular options than in the Soviet era. Specialty schools, which also existed in the FSU, offer highly specialized program in mathematics, art, dance, or a particular foreign language, for example. A new addition to Russian schools is the *gymnasium* or lyceum, an academic secondary school resembling the German academic secondary school. Proponents of the gymnasium envision it as a selective secondary school with a curriculum that includes Latin, philosophy, logic, advanced mathematics, and science.[38] These academically selective preparatory schools concentrate on preparing students for university admission.

Since the concept of institutional and curricular alternatives is new to RF, the future of diversification is unclear. The traditional pre-Soviet tendency toward religious schools is reasserting itself. During the tsarist period, there was an extensive network of parish parochial schools, operated by the Russian Orthodox Church, which received government subsidies. Under communism, religious education and church-sponsored schools were ruthlessly proscribed. Today, Orthodox and other clergy speak out openly on education issues and there is a growing number of church-related schools. The legal status of private and other schools, outside of the official state system, remains unclear. Among government officials, there are both strong proponents and opponents of private schools. The economic situation, with growing socioeconomic class differences, further clouds the future of alternative educational institutions.

A recent development in RF is author schools, which resemble charter schools in the U.S. American charter schools are schools within public school systems that may be organized by teachers or others who hold a contract or charter from a district school board to implement an innovative pedagogical approach. In author schools, educational personnel within a school district may organize a nontraditional school based on an innovative curricular or instructional approach. Though currently small, the number of author schools is likely to increase.

The reforms of the Gorbachev era and the emergence of the new independent nations have also had an impact on the school's milieu and student behavior. Among the changes in the RF, for example, are the abolition of wearing the compulsory school uniforms and the institution of more flexible rules for classroom behavior. This more open attitude to classroom management replaces the old Soviet pattern whereby boys wore a required blue uniform and girls a black or dark blue dress with a white apron. Most children also wore the red kerchief that identified them as a member of the Young Pioneers, the official CP organization for school-age children. Children also wore medals depicting Lenin or other Soviet leaders. In the past, students followed officially sanctioned rules on the proper way to sit at one's desk, to stand at attention while reciting, and to be seated only when permitted by teacher. These behaviors associated with the ideological rigidity of the past have disappeared or are disappearing in Russian schools.

Curriculum

This section first examines the general features of the curriculum based on grade levels and then turns to revisions of key subjects.

General Curricular Features

During the Soviet period, especially from Stalin onward, the curriculum in the general and polytechnic schools was generally uniform throughout the USSR. The devolution of educational authority to each of the former republics, now independent states, has generated greater curricular differences. New programs of civic education, reflecting the revival of nationalism, emphasize the history, culture, and language of each country. Curriculum has moved to reflect democracy, nationalism, and a market economy. The major trends in curriculum change have been to remove residues of the Communist ideology, to restore some subjects and topics excluded by the Soviet regime, and to add new subjects that align with the RF's changing social, political, and economic realties.

During the Soviet regime, curriculum making was a formally complex and detailed process. Curriculum review and change involved decision making by the formal government apparatus—the Supreme Soviet, the All-Union Ministry of Education, the Soviet Academy of Pedagogical Sciences, and the ministries of education of the various constituent republics. Many important policy decisions were first made by the CP Central Committee, the chief curriculum maker in the USSR. In post-Soviet Russia, the responsibility for curriculum making is divided between the central and local authorities. Further, local schools now have some on-site discretion in curriculum matters.

At the close of the Soviet period, pupils in the primary forms, grades one through three, began language study in their own vernacular. If the pupils lived in a non-Russian-speaking region, they began with their own vernacular and then also began to study Russian in the second form. Mathematics included basic computation, weights and measures, and rudiments of algebra and geometry. Natural science included geography and elements of earth and life sciences. The curriculum for the primary grades was completed by craft work, vocational training, art, music, and physical education. The current curriculum in the RF for the primary grades remains much the same in content, plus the major change in political and economic orientation. It includes mathematics and computing; the native language, if other than Russian; the Russian language; art and music; local cultural studies; physical education; and labor training. Although statistics are somewhat unreliable, it appears that almost all children of the appropriate age cohort attend primary schools in the RF.

Grades, or forms, four through eight continue and offer more advanced mathematics. The curriculum continues the native language, if other than Russian, as well as Russian language, literature, and cultural studies. It also includes the study of physical sciences such as physics, astronomy, and chemistry; natural science, especially biology; geography, history, and social studies; foreign language; art and music; physical education; labor training; and electives. In grades nine through eleven, the following are offered: advanced mathematics; continuation of physical science such as physics, astronomy, and chemistry; continuation of natural science study, especially biology; fundamentals of market economics, history, world culture, and social studies; continuation of native language and Russian language studies; foreign language; technical drawing; physical education; labor training; and electives.

Revising Mathematics and Science

The less obvious effects of the changing situation in the FSU are in mathematics and science, areas more value free and less prone to ideological intrusions than history, literature, and social studies. During the Soviet period, these areas were emphasized for their potential in providing the foundational skills needed for technology, modernization, and the military. In the RF and other successor states, mathematics and science easily lend themselves to the transformations needed for a free enterprise, market-based economy.

Highly valued for its relationship to science and technology, mathematics is rigorously taught and includes algebra, geometry, trigonometry, and calculus. Since mathematics education is relatively free from ideology, the content change is relatively slight. However, the methods of teaching mathematics likely have changed. After laying a general science foundation in the primary and intermediate grades, the secondary level includes chemistry, physics, astronomy, biology, and geography. Physics and chemistry were given high priority during the Soviet period. The relevance of the sciences to technology, industry, and agriculture were emphasized in their relationship to polytechnic education. In the past, Soviet science education was also given priority for its role in developing military technology. As this emphasis lessens, changes may occur in the stress that science once received.

Language Policy

The RF, like most of the successor states of the FSU, is a multiethnic and multilingual country. Although Russian is the language of a great majority of people in the RF, several non-Russian languages such as Ukrainian, Chuvash, Bashkir, Moldavian, and Chechen are spoken. The revival of ethnonationalism both among Russians and non-Russians is a phenomenon occurring not only in the RF but also throughout the successor states of the FSU. To preface our discussion, several important points need to be reiterated about the centrality of language in education, schooling, and curriculum. Language learning, a generative skill, is necessary for success in learning other school subjects. Because of its generative centrality, language instruction occupies much space and time in the primary and secondary curriculum. The language arts—reading, writing, composition, and literature—are key foundational skills and subject areas.

While occupying a central focus in the curriculum, language also should be considered in its much broader sense—as an agency of cultural identity and reproduction and a means to social, political, and economic power. One's vernacular, or mother tongue, is an important source by which a person identifies with and is enabled to participate in the cultural life of the ethnic group. Language expresses ethnic conceptions of belief and value.

The RF's language policy is based on the laws, "On the Languages of the Peoples of the Russian Federation," enacted in 1991, and "The Conception of a State Program for the Preservation and Development of Languages of the Peoples of the Russian Federation," enacted in 1992. These laws recognize the languages of the RF as a "historical-cultural heritage," under state protection. Further, the RF is accountable for promoting "favorable conditions for the free development of all the languages" of Russia.[39]

Language policy and education in Russia, however, is highly complex. During the Soviet era, the government encouraged migration and settlement of Russians to non-Russian ethnic and language areas of Russia as well as to the other republics. Often, Russian speakers were Communist Party bureaucrats or technical workers charged with the economic development of areas in the Asiatic and Siberian parts of Russia. In these non-Russian-speaking regions, the Russian speakers became permanent residents but did not learn the local language. Similar language issues also exist in what is referred to as the Near Abroad, the successor states of the FSU such as Latvia, Ukraine, Kazakhstan, and Uzbekistan, that contains large Russian-speaking minorities.

To reduce ethnic and language tensions, an important educational issue is the need to develop multicultural and bilingual strategies. Bilingual education has encountered strong opposition, however, from Russian speakers who, savoring their former dominant position, resist learning a non-Russian local language. The Ministry of Education has followed a bilingual education policy in that the whole population of the RF is to learn Russian and that the populations of the national regions, regardless of their ethnic and language affiliations, are also to learn the local language most used in a particular region. The underlying assumption is that children and youth will have less cultural resistance than adults to learning a non-Russian local language.

Literature

During the Soviet regime, the teaching of literature and the arts followed the prescribed interpretive canons of socialist realism. Literature was included

or excluded from the curriculum according to its correct ideological orientation. Soviet literature—books and poetry—that described the class struggle
and the struggle to achieve socialism in the USSR were included and those
appraised as reflecting bourgeois sentimentality excluded. Today, the selection of authors in the literature curriculum is being revised. Those too closely
identified with the Soviet past are being downgraded or deleted while more
attention is being given to those excluded by the former Soviet authorities.

History and Social Studies

History and the social studies, two curriculum areas rigorously controlled
during the Soviet era, have been especially susceptible to political change. During Gorbachev's perestroika reforms, Russian educators challenged the once
officially sanctioned Marxist-Lenninst ideological portrayal of Soviet history as
"a path of solid accomplishments" and an "ascent to brilliant heights" led by
"infallible" leaders, not subject to criticism.[40] The text, *The History of the USSR*,
published in 1990, signaled the more open trend by criticizing Stalinist repression and the mistakes of Soviet leaders. However, there is now a concerted tendency, encouraged by the government, to make history textbooks and teaching
less critical of the Soviet past and to use them to instill nationalism and patriotism. When President Putin addressed Russian historians in 2003, he emphasized that history textbooks should "cultivate in young people a feeling of pride
for one's history and one's country." Igor Dolustky's once widely used history
textbook, *National History: 20th Century*, which examined such sensitive topics
as Stalin's purges and gulags, anti-Semitism, and the conflict in Chechnya, is
being replaced in Russian schools by more nationalist renditions of history. For
example, current historical interpretations highlight the industrial development
that took place in the Stalinist period as a proud fact of Russia's past.[41]

Like history, the social studies conformed to Marxist-Leninist ideological canons and require extensive revision. Since political structures changed
radically, political and civic socialization requires serious curricular redefini-
tion. The existence of multiple political parties rather than one and the presence of a relatively free media are relatively new experiences. The political
geography of the FSU has changed. Former constituent republics are now
independent nations. States and cities have been renamed. Leningrad is now
St. Petersburg, its name before the Bolshevik Revolution. These changes need
to be reflected in new geography texts and in the teaching of geography.

Still, another subject neglected in the past is environmental studies. In its
rush to industrialize, the USSR ignored environmental protection. The rivers,
lakes, and air of the FSU are dangerously polluted by industrial wastes and
by-products. The bleak environmental prospects are further complicated by
the threat of potential nuclear disasters such as that at Chernobyl in 1986. In
addition, the knowledge base and value orientation appropriate to a free
enterprise economy needs emphasis in the economic units of the social sciences. Research and teaching methods in the social sciences need revitalization now that they are freed from dogmatic Marxism.[42]

Russian history and social studies educators have departed from the Soviet canon that viewed historical causation based on Marxist dialectical materialism and class struggle.[43] Now, they are reinterpreting the tsarist heritage and the role of the church and "bourgeois" liberals in a more objective way. Russian social studies educators have developed a new curriculum that seeks to: (1) replace the old Soviet pattern with a revitalized sense of Russian national identity; (2) introduce new developments in social education, whose entry was blocked by narrow Soviet ideological strictures; and (3) replace the old pattern of Soviet collective upbringing with values of humanism, individualism, and democracy.

To implement these goals, Russian educators have developed a social studies course for grades eight through eleven called "Man and Society" that abandons the former orientation to separate disciplines and instead integrates selected knowledge from various social sciences such as history, economics, politics, sociology, social psychology, and philosophy. The new interdisciplinary approach resembles social studies education in the U.S. (It should also be noted that the course title continues to use gender-biased language unlike American trends to non-sexist terminology.) The course's general orientation locates the person as a biosocial being in the world of natural, social, political, and economic phenomena. The course further seeks to develop a political-legal orientation that is conducive to parliamentary democracy and participation and that embodies the RF's constitution, the Fundamental Law of the Russian Federation.[44] The old Soviet economic concepts that condemned individual ownership of property, the free market, and capitalism and that praised collectivism and state-operated industries have been discredited and replaced in the curriculum. Now, market economics, once thoroughly proscribed, is included.

Other Subjects

Vocational education may include courses in metallurgy, electrical work, radio electronics, and agriculture. The industries or economic activities in the locality served by the school are stressed. Cooperative educational arrangements may also be developed between the schools and collaborating industries.

Foreign languages include English, French, German, and Spanish in which instruction begins in the fifth grade and continues through grade ten. Music, art, and physical education complete the curriculum.

Instructional Innovation

While evidence of the Soviet past are disappearing from Russian schools, styles of instruction, especially among older teachers, often reflect the rigidity of the Soviet methodological style with its emphasis on the prescribed teacher-directed recitation of the approved textbooks. The Soviet method included precise phases in which the teacher: (1) reviewed previous lessons;

(2) checked students' homework and heard recitations of assigned material; and (3) then assigned new material. In the standard Soviet classroom, the teacher asked questions about the assigned textbook reading and students answered them with a correct answer that conformed to the textbook.

While reformers have persistently urged development of new strategies for instruction that encourage greater teacher and student freedom and creativity, change has been slow and difficult to implement. The early efforts at liberalizing instruction were designated as the Pedagogy of Cooperation. Eduard Dneprov and other proponents of the Pedagogy of Cooperation urged teachers to work collaboratively to free themselves from inherited ideological and bureaucratic constraints in order to develop liberating and humanistic teaching methods. The new pedagogy was hailed as an "integrated methodological" approach that offered teachers a "diversified range" of teaching tools to facilitate children's well-rounded development.[45] The new approach sought to develop both personal and cooperative skills and behaviors in children.

The Pedagogy of Cooperation attracted favorable comments from many teachers and teachers' organizations. However, endorsements of the new method did not guarantee implementation. Some critics saw the method as too Western in orientation and rejecting too much of the Russian educational heritage. While some teachers began to experiment with new methods, there was a strong resistance to altering the status quo. Not only did teachers need to be motivated to experiment with new methods but the school system, itself, had to be redesigned to encourage such innovation.

To overcome teachers' reluctance to introduce innovative practices, the Russian Federation Law on Education (1992) modified the general requirements for admission to schools, curriculum content, and program revision and implementation.[46] These changes sought to encourage local schools and teachers to engage in more independent planning for curriculum and instruction and implementation of innovative methods.

In such a large country as the RF, as in the U.S. or India, efforts at innovation take a variety of formats that have varying degrees of success. Factors that have a bearing on educational innovation are: (1) the degree to which the innovation is congruent with the general educational philosophy or ideology in place; (2) the degree to which administrators and teachers really understand the innovation and how it will affect teaching and learning; (3) the teachers' motivation to accept the innovation and their willingness to implement it their classrooms; and (4) the extent to which teachers have been in-serviced in the content and process required to implement the innovation. These conditions for successful innovation generally apply in schools worldwide. However, in the case of the RF, the difficulties relating to innovation are compounded by: (1) the attitudinal baggage of past inertia and resistance to change; (2) the unsettled political, social, and economic situation; and (3) the scarcity of adequate funding to support educational innovation.

To illustrate the process of educational innovation, certain specific instances can be identified. In some of the schools of Moscow, there has been an effort to make instruction more individualized and to pay more attention to the individual student's level of readiness and needs in the primary grades. In the past, the tendency was to emphasize collectivity rather than individualism and to deny that pupils might have learning deficits and special needs. Additionally, there has been a movement away from curricular uniformity in that classes are being offered for students with special interests, such as in the fine arts, music, and aerobics.[47] The recognition of special interests and needs by schools also brings co- and extracurricular activities into the schools and away from organizations once dominated by the Communist Party.

As is generally the case, curricular and instructional innovations are easier to introduce in the primary rather than in the upper grades. The primary curriculum is less differentiated and has greater possibilities for teachers to be more flexible in using a variety of methods. The upper grades, often dominated by entry requirements to higher and technical institutions, are more impervious to change. The Soviet educational legacy has left embedded administrator and teacher attitudes against innovation in the upper grades of general education. For all of its faults, the uniformity of the old Soviet system did provide a rough equality in access to the curriculum. Today, there are contradictory tendencies—for uniformity, which promotes equality, and for greater differentiation, which encourages inequality. The question becomes, which method best serves the student population? In some schools there may also be a tendency to emulate the German system, particularly the academically selective gymnasium, which involves a more intensive study of particular academic subjects; other schools, however, are introducing nontraditional classes in debate, discussion, and conferencing approaches.[48] In addition, some schools are introducing alternatives to textbook-dominated instruction. It is unclear what course innovation will take at this level.

Higher Education

Higher education in the Soviet Union consisted of universities, polytechnic and technical institutes, and a variety of post-secondary schools. These institutions now form the core of higher education institutions in RF and the other nations in the FSU. Specializations offered by the universities include social sciences, natural and physical sciences, humanities, and history. The polytechnic institutes offer combinations of related technical areas. Specialized institutes offer training in mining, metallurgy, petroleum, communications, transportation, railroading, agriculture, forestry, medicine, and pedagogy, for example. There are also advanced institutions for the fine arts—dance, music, theater, and film. It is estimated that 50 percent of the students in higher education study science and engineering, 10 percent study agriculture, and the remaining 40 percent concentrate on other fields. In addition to on-site attendance, some institutions also offer correspondence courses. The general curricular pattern in higher education consists of course work in the general knowledge base related to the specialization and a concentration on the specialty.

An important feature in Soviet higher education was the establishment of scientific centers for research and training. These centers continue to involve faculty and students of the universities in a given region. The prototype science center is Academy of Sciences at Akademdorodok associated with the University of Novosibirsk in Siberia.

Higher education in RF and the other nations of the FSU faces serious problems related to internal restructuring and financing and the external realities of an economy, society, and political order that are in deep transition. There is an effort, however, to make admission more dependent on academic ability rather than political reliability and class membership. In the past, applicants who were already employed were given admission preference. The age limit, which was thirty-five, has been eliminated. The practice of reserving places for applicants in special categories, often on a party or class basis, also has been eliminated.

Teacher Education

Teachers are prepared in secondary specialized pedagogical schools, in pedagogical institutes, or in universities. The secondary specialized institutes prepare teachers for the primary grades by providing a general secondary education and pedagogical training. Among the courses offered are child development and health, child and educational psychology, children's literature, and methods of teaching. Clinical and practice teaching are also emphasized.

The pedagogical institutes prepare teachers for the upper and secondary grades, four through ten. The concentration in the pedagogical institutes is to prepare subject-matter teachers who are specialists in the content of their subject and in the methods of teaching it. In the institutes the curriculum is organized into two major areas: (1) courses in pedagogical theory and practice such as the history of education, educational psychology, child development and health, educational issues, and the methods of teaching; and (2) courses in the subject-matter area such as science, mathematics, history, or some other subject found in the secondary level curriculum. As with teachers in the U.S., the prospective teacher is involved in clinical experiences and in student teaching.

In addition to the specialized pedagogical schools and the pedagogical institutes that prepare the majority of teachers, a smaller number are prepared in universities. For these students, the preparation concentrates on a particular academic subject such as mathematics or science.

Under the Soviet system, students in teacher education programs, as well as other students, were required to take courses in Marxism and the history and role of the Communist Party. The nature of the emerging foundations will depend on the course of events in RF and the nations of the FSU. It is hoped that Russian and other educators will integrate multiculturalism into the teacher education program as an antidote to the revived nationality and ethnic tensions.

Conclusion

It is an understatement to say that writing a conclusion to a chapter on education in the RF is difficult. The political and economic situation remains volatile and subject to unexpected and sudden changes. Despite these uncertainties, it should be remembered that the RF and the other nations of the FSU have long histories and well-developed cultures that equal those of Western Europe. As events unfold in the RF, they need to be carefully observed and studied by students of international and comparative education.

RF and the successor states of the FSU face momentous political, social, economic, and educational issues as they depart from the constraints of the past and enter a new and largely undefined landscape. In a system geared to issuing and taking orders from the top downward, teachers at the grassroots level will need to assert themselves in risk-taking innovations. Implementing educational reforms will be problematic; policy statements, no matter how democratic their rhetoric, do not guarantee that reforms will be implemented throughout the system unless teachers are motivated to do so. Russia's challenge is to ensure that statements of policy intentions result in actual implementation and not remain rhetorical.

While it is difficult to predict the future of the RF, several scenarios are possible: (1) Although it is very unlikely that the Soviet style will return, elements of the authoritarian past may remain or resurface. For example, freedom of information may be limited with the central government increasingly controlling expression of ideas in society and schools. (2) The processes of change may continue but move forward and backward and then forward again. (3) Some segments of society will give their primary allegiance to the ethnic and language group with whom they identify rather than to the larger nation-state. (4) The RF and some of the more developed nations of the FSU will be able to create new political structures that allow greater freedom while still maintaining social and political stability; this will make it possible to engage in cooperative interaction, especially economically, with the European community, the U.S., and other regional trading blocs. (5) The RF, as the largest successor nation, may return to its historic role and pull the other smaller states back into its orbit.

As in any country, educators in the RF need to develop new philosophies that address political and social realities. In a nation-state that is undergoing such profound change as the RF, disassembling the ideological and political influences of the educational past and discarding and revamping them to fit the present and prepare for the future is a tremendous challenge for government leaders and educators alike.

DISCUSSION QUESTIONS

1. Identify and analyze the major social, economic, and political changes that have taken place in the RF since the demise of the USSR.

2. What were the basic features of the Communist (Marxist-Leninist) ideology and how did they shape education in the USSR?

3. What is the nature of the ethnic and language issue in the RF and the other successor states? How is it like or different from that of the U.S.?

4. Examine the organizational structures of the Russian system of education and compare them with those in the U.S.

5. Describe the contours of the Russian economy and project the kind of education required to sustain it.

6. Examine ethnonationalism and multiculturalism in the Russian education context.

RESEARCH TOPICS

1. Maintain a clippings file of recent newspaper and magazine articles about education in the RF and some of the independent states of the FSU.

2. If there are international students on your campus from the RF or the FSU, invite them to speak about their educational experiences.

3. Read and review a recent book about the RF or the FSU.

4. Invite an expert on the RF who is a professor at your college or university to speak about recent developments in that country.

5. Read a novel by a Russian author. Examine the ideas and values conveyed by the narrative.

SUGGESTIONS FOR FURTHER READING

Baker, Peter, and Glasser, Susan. *Kremlin Rising: Vladimir Putin's Russia and the End of Revolution.* New York: Simon & Schuster, 2005.

Ball, Alan. *And Now My Soul Is Hardened: Abandoned Children in Soviet Russia, 1918–1930.* Berkeley: University of California Press, 1994.

Billington, James H. *Russia in Search of Itself.* Baltimore: Johns Hopkins University Press, 2004.

Eklof, Ben, and Dneprov, Edward. *Democracy in the Russian School: The Reform Movement Since 1984.* Boulder, CO: Westview Press, 1993.

Filtzer, Donald. *Soviet Workers and Late Stalinism: Labour and the Restoration of the Stalinist System after World War II.* New York: Cambridge University Press, 2002.

Gorsuch, Anne E. *Youth in Revolutionary Russia: Enthusiasts, Bohemians, Delinquents.* Bloomington: Indiana University Press, 2000.

Grant, Bruce. *In the Soviet House of Culture: A Century of Perestroikas.* Princeton: Princeton University Press, 1995.

Keller, Shoshana. *To Moscow, Not Mecca: The Soviet Campaign Against Islam in Central Asia, 1917–1941.* Westport, CT: Praeger, 2001.

Kirschenbaum, Lisa A. *Small Comrades: Revolutionizing Childhood in Soviet Russia, 1917–1932.* New York: Routledge Falmer, 2001.

Pearson, Landon. *Children of Glasnost: Growing Up Soviet.* Seattle: University of Washington Press, 1990.

Sakwa, Richard. *Russian Politics and Society.* London: Routledge, 2002.

Webber, Stephen L. *School, Reform and Society in the New Russia.* London: Palgrave Macmillan, 1999.

NOTES

[1] For a history of these nations, see Timothy Snyder, *The Reconstruction of Nations: Poland, Ukraine, Lithuania, Belarus, 1569–1999* (New Haven: Yale University Press, 2003).

[2] CIA (Central Intelligence Agency), "The World Factbook: Russia," April 5, 2005, http://odci.gov/cia/ publications/factbook/geos/rs.html.

[3] CIA (January 22, 2004).

[4] Ibid.

[5] As in other chapters, the intention is to describe the major structure of the government. Since particular officials change frequently, readers should consult appropriate newspaper, journal, and Web site articles for the current situation.

[6] CIA (January 22, 2004).

[7] Ibid.

[8] Melvin C. Wren and Taylor Stults, *The Course of Russian History,* 5th ed. (Prospect Heights, IL: Waveland Press, 1994), 123.

[9] Ibid., 120.

[10] Lisa A. Kirschenbaum, *Small Comrades: Revolutionizing Childhood in Soviet Russia, 1917–1932* (New York: Routledge Falmer, 2001), 156.

[11] George S. Counts, *Khrushchev and the Central Committee Speak on Education* (Pittsburgh: University of Pittsburgh Press, 1959).

[12] J. Tomiak, "Education in the USSR: Equality and the New Soviet Man," in *Equality and Freedom in Education: A Comparative Study,* ed. Brian Holmes (London: Allen and Unwin, 1985), 137. For this attempted transformation, see Richard Pipes, *The Russian Revolution* (New York: Alfred A. Knopf, 1991).

[13] Galina M. Ivanova, *Labor Camp Socialism: The Gulag in the Soviet Totalitarian System,* ed. Donald J. Raleigh, trans. Carol Flath (Armonk, NY: M. E. Sharpe, 2000).

[14] Tomiak, 137.

[15] Ibid., 138.

[16] Cathy C. Kaufman, "De-Sovietizing Educational Systems, Learning From Past Policy and Practice," *International Review of Education* 40(2) (1994): 151.

[17] Harley D. Balzer, ed., *Five Years That Shook the World: Gorbachev's Perestroika* (Boulder, CO: Westview Press, 1991) and William E. Griffith, ed., *Central and Eastern Europe: The Opening Curtain* (Boulder, CO: Westview Press, 1989).

[18] Ben Eklof, *Soviet Briefing: Gorbachev and the Reform Period* (Boulder, CO: Westview Press, 1989), 1.

[19] Gerald H. Read, "Education in the Soviet Union: Has *Perestroika* Met Its Match?" *Phi Delta Kappan* 70 (April 1989): 600–602.

[20] Kaufman, 152.

[21] Ibid., 152–153.

[22] "Mikhail Gorbachev's Address at the 19th All-Union Party Conference," *Moscow News* (November 27, 1988), 2, quoted in Read, 611.

[23] Kaufman, 154–155.

[24] Ibid., 156.

[25] E. S. Sokolova and V. M. Likhacheva, "The *Perestroika* Generation," *Russian Education and Society* 35(10) (1993): 7.

26 Ben Brodinsky, "The Impact of *Perestroika* on Soviet Education," *Phi Delta Kappan* 73(5) (1992): 318.

27 Sokolova and Likhacheva, 13.

28 Brodinsky, 318.

29 M. G. Taichinov, "Religious Culture and Upbringing," *Russian Education and Society* 36(7) (1994): 91.

30 For a discussion of the dilemma regarding work education, see I. N. Nazimov, "School Students' Labor Under Conditions of the Transition to the Market Economy," *Russian Education and Society* 35(1) (1993): 56–71.

31 Ibid., 59.

32 Ben Eklof and Eduard Dneprov, eds. *Democracy in the Russian School: The Reform Movement since 1984* (Boulder, CO: Westview Press, 1993), 1.

33 Kaufman, 149–158.

34 Kirschenbaum, 103–104.

35 Ibid., 146.

36 "A Conception of Preschool Upbringing," *Russian Education and Society* 34(3) (1992): 3.

37 Ibid., 7.

38 Brodinsky, 384.

39 M. V. D'Iachkov, "Language Policy in Today's Russia," *Russian Education and Society* 36(9) (1994): 42–56.

40 Sokolova and Likhacheva, 12.

41 Alex Rodriguez, "Omitting the Past's Darker Chapters," *Chicago Tribune* (May 19, 2005), p. 3.

42 "Upheaval in the USSR: Experts Foresee Benefits, Dangers for Education and Research," *The Chronicle of Higher Education* (September 4, 1991), A54.

43 For a review of the teaching of history, see L. N. Aleksashina, "Didactic Aspects of the Teaching of History," *Russian Education and Society* 36(8) (1994): 5–17.

44 L. N. Bogoliubov, L. F. Ivanova, A. T. Kinkul'kin, and A. I. Lazebnrikova, "Social Studies in Today's Schools," *Russian Education and Society* 36(8) (1994): 18–32.

45 Eklof and Dneprov, 93–94.

46 O. G. Khomeriki, "Innovations in the Practice of Instruction," *Russian Education and Society* 36(8) (1994): 33–42.

47 Ibid., 38–39.

48 Ibid., 40.

14

EDUCATION IN MEXICO

Mexico, officially the United Mexican States, is selected for comparison as a representative of Latin American nations with Hispanic cultures. The southern neighbor of the United States, Mexico affords interesting comparisons between the two countries. For U.S. educators, Mexico is of special interest since a large number of Latinos are of Mexican ethnic heritage. Mexico is examined as a nation that has steadily progressed economically but still must surmount serious obstacles to its educational development.

Geographic, Demographic, and Sociocultural Contexts

Mexico is Latin America's third largest country. Its northern boundary is the 2,000-mile-long border with the U.S.; on the south, Mexico's neighbors are Guatemala and Belize. Mexico has 6,000 miles of coastline on the Caribbean Sea, the Pacific Ocean, and the Gulf of Mexico.

Mexico's topography is that of two narrow low-laying coastal plains, each with high mountain ranges, the western and eastern Sierra Madres, on their landward side. A plateau, at an elevation between 5,000 and 8,000 feet, lies between these mountain ranges. The differences in topography, particularly altitude, create a range of climates. While its southern region, especially the Yucatán Peninsula, is tropical or semitropical with abundant rainfall, 70 percent of Mexico's land area in the north and west is semiarid or arid. The plateau on which Mexico City, one of the world's largest cities and the country's capital, is located has distinct wet and dry seasons.

Like other less technologically developed countries (LTDCs), Mexico is experiencing significant population growth. In 1960, its population was 36,046,000; currently, the population is estimated at 104,907,991. In terms of age structure, 32.3 percent of the population is from 0 to 14 years of age; 63.1 percent is between ages 15 and 64; and 4.6 percent over age 65. The median age is 23.8.[1] Similar to other LTDCs, such as India and Nigeria, a high percentage of the population is of elementary and secondary school age.[2] While such a large school-age cohort requires extensive primary and lower second-

301

ary schooling, the provision of educational services lags behind population growth. Limited access to schools occurs in remote rural areas and in urban slums. While imbalances between rural and urban education in Mexico are not as marked as in Nigeria or India, they are characteristic of other LTDCs.

A historically rural and agricultural nation, Mexico now is growing increasingly industrial and urban. Factors such as population increase, shortage of arable farmland, and the search for improved living conditions have stimulated urban migration. The urban population in Mexico's largest cities continues to grow at a rate of 10 percent annually.[3] Mexico City, the world's largest metropolis, has had rapid and largely unplanned growth. Providing social, health-care, and educational services to its large population is a challenge of great magnitude.

Fifty-five percent of Mexicans are *mestizos*—people of mixed Indian and European (primarily Spanish) ethnicity. Twenty-nine percent are of Indian ethnicity and 15 percent are of European ethnicity.

Spanish, Mexico's official language, the national language spoken by 85 percent of the population, is the medium of instruction in the schools. About 15 percent of the population, primarily Indians, lacks fluency in Spanish. Among the Indian languages spoken are Nahuatl, Otoml, Maya, Zapoteca, and Tarasca.[4] The literacy rate is 92.2 percent.

Ninety-six percent of the population is nominally Roman Catholic. Although its government and politics, since independence, have been anticlerical, Roman Catholicism is deeply ingrained in Mexico's culture and society. In many places, Catholic liturgy blends with residues of precolonial indigenous religious practices. Officially, Mexico, a secular republic, prohibits religious instruction in public schools.

Political Context

Like the U.S., Nigeria, and India, Mexico is a federal republic. It consists of thirty-one states and the federal district of Mexico City. Each state has a chief executive, a governor who is elected to a six-year term, and a chamber of deputies, which is its legislature.

The federal executive branch is headed by a president who, like the president of the U.S., is both the chief of state and the head of the federal government. Elected by popular vote for one six-year term, the president appoints the cabinet. In its recent history Mexico has had strong presidents who exercised control over the republic. The current president, Vicente Fox Quesada, was elected in 2000.[5]

The federal legislative branch, *Congreso de la Unión*, the National Congress, consists of two houses—the *Cámara de Senadores*, the Senate, and the *Cámara Federal de Diputados*, the Chamber of Deputies. The Senate is composed of 128 members. Two senators are elected for six-year terms from each of the thirty-one states and the federal district, with the remaining number allocated on the basis of each party's popular vote. The lower house, the

Chamber of Deputies, consists of 500 members who are elected for three-year terms. Three hundred deputies are directly elected and 200 deputies are allocated on the basis of each party's popular vote for three-year terms.

There is also a federal and state legal system. The *Corte Suprema de Justicia*, the Supreme Court, has the power of judicial review. Justices on the Supreme Court are appointed by the president with the consent of the Senate.

In the 1920s, Mexico became a one-party state as the *Partido Revolucionario Institucional* (the Institutional Revolutionary Party), or PRI, dominated politics and continuously controlled the government. Despite the one-party nature of its politics, Mexico has been a democratic republic. There are now several active opposition parties, ranging to the left and right of the PRI. In 1997, the PRI lost control of Mexico City. In 1998, the PRI lost its majority in the lower house of the national legislature. Also, opposition parties have increased their representation in the Chamber of Deputies. Vicente Fox, a candidate of the National Action Party (PAN), won a historic victory in 2000 that ended 71 years of rule by the PRI.

Economic Context

Mexico has a free market economy with the private dominant over the public sector. Its economic development has been uneven with a mixture of very modern and outdated modes of industry and agriculture. The economic pattern has seen spurts of development accompanied by inflation followed by recession and retrenchment. Its economic situation resembles that of other LTDCs. Income distribution is highly unequal, with an estimated 40 percent of the population living below the poverty line.

Mexico's fairly diversified economy includes the once dominant agricultural and the now growing industrial sectors. The chief industries are food and beverage, tobacco, chemicals, iron and steel, mining, textiles, motor vehicles, tourism, and petroleum. Fifty-six percent of the workforce is engaged in service, 24 percent in industry, and 20 percent in agriculture.[6] Mexico's petroleum and oil-related industries make it, like Nigeria, a leading world oil producer. Again, like Nigeria, Mexico's economy, though more stable, is subject to the booms and recessions that have affected oil-producing nations.

As in the case with other nations experiencing rapid industrialization, Mexico has problems of environmental pollution. There is scarcity of hazardous waste disposal facilities and some serious fresh water pollution. In particular, air and water quality has been impacted negatively in the Mexico City area and in the rapidly expanding urban areas along the U.S. border.[7] Deforestation also has occurred in some areas with intense agricultural cultivation. The national government recognizes the seriousness of the problem and is making plans and taking measures to improve the quality of the environment.

Still another trend affecting Mexico is economic regionalization. With the U.S. and Canada, Mexico is a member of NAFTA. Since 1994, trade with the

U.S. and Canada has tripled. New industries in Mexico's border states with the U.S. have stimulated a migration of population to these locations. As these industries develop, there are demands for training of managers and technicians.

Mexico has experienced some of the typical economic problems that impact LTDCs, especially a large foreign debt. To qualify for international loans, it has restructured its economy by reducing funding for the government sector and state-supported social services. Mexico has devalued its currency, the peso, on several occasions to stem inflation. Economic restructuring in Mexico, as well as in other LTDCs such as Nigeria, has consequences for funding public education. While funding educational expansion grows more difficult, Mexico faces demands for greater access to education, especially at postsecondary levels. Due to population growth, the secondary school and university age cohort is large in Mexico. Also, economic growth has stimulated rising educational expectations. The path to an improved socioeconomic status is seen to be through education, particularly through university degrees. Spending on education reached a high point in 1975 at 3.8 percent of its GNP. Since then, government spending on education has decreased.

While all nations have issues in setting educational priorities, Mexico faces difficult policy choices in making its priority decisions. The essential question facing Mexico as well as other countries with limited resources, such as Nigeria, India, and China, is which area or level of education should receive the most funding. Comparatively, Mexico, India, China, and Nigeria face similar decisions despite their highly different cultural contexts. Should the most money be spent on primary education to develop basic literacy and civic and economic competencies or on higher education, especially the universities, to prepare the scientific, technological, and managerial experts necessary for economic modernization? Policy makers who choose higher education believe that top-level modernization will raise the country's GNP and that the fruits of a growing economy will trickle downward throughout society.

Since the late 1920s, the Mexican government has been committed to providing basic education as a necessary social service. Since the 1970s, however, the growing middle classes have demanded more emphasis on higher education. The government, encouraging modernization, also has given higher education greater priority. For example, in 1970, the proportion of the total educational budget was 47.7 percent going to primary education and 10.4 percent going for higher education. By 1986, primary education's funding had declined to 27.4 percent while higher education's had increased to 31.8 percent.[8]

Historical Context

Before the Spanish conquest, Mexican education, from 500 BC to AD 1519, reflected the sociocultural patterns and religions of the various Mesoamerican Indians that occupied present-day Mexico. Chief among these were the Aztecs, Mayans, and Toltecs who developed sophisticated and intricate cultures. Education for the Aztecs and Mayans, people led by warrior kings, was heavily caste or class-based. Aztec society was stratified hierarchically into the warrior nobility, priests, merchants, free farmers, and serfs.[9] The highly religious education of upper-class Aztec youth emphasized astronomical calculation, calendar reading, and ritual. The priests, the guardians of Aztec traditions, plotted an astronomically based calendar and maintained the cultural records. Grounded in an oral tradition, education was highly informal and nonformal as it transmitted Aztec culture from generation to generation.

The emphasis on an oral tradition also is found in the educational history of the tribal groups in Nigeria and India. Schools attended by children of free commoners, merchants, and peasants stressed military tactics as well as religious and ritualistic training. For the village farmers and craftsmen, occupational activities were learned informally and transmitted from parent to child through the work activities of daily life.

Like the Aztecs, the Mayans, located in the Yucatán Peninsula, also developed an advanced civilization ruled by kings who governed in a close alliance with the priests. Large Mayan cities were dominated by pyramids, temples, royal palaces, astronomical observatories, and other prominent edifices. Surrounding these massive state buildings were the dwellings of the commoner class who engaged in agriculture and trade. Radiating from the central urban areas, the majority of the Mayan population were farmers who raised subsistence crops. Mayan culture also featured a written language, an elaborate chronology, and a code of ritualized religious ceremonies and behaviors. Although much of the Mayan literature was destroyed by Catholic priests who accompanied the Spanish conquistadors to Mexico, it is being recreated today by painstaking archeological research. To have sustained such an elaborate culture, the Mayans maintained schools, especially for the education of the nobility and the priests.[10]

Mexico was invaded by the Spanish who, initially in search of the quick riches of gold and silver, turned the area into a colony of Spain in 1521. Spain's long colonial rule lasted until 1821 when Mexico won its independence.

The Spanish were determined to exploit Mexico's mineral wealth, especially gold and silver. Along with the sword of the conquering Spanish conquistadors came the cross of Catholic missionaries who accompanied the soldiers. Jesuit and Franciscan Roman Catholic missionaries secured mass conversions of the indigenous peoples. Despite deliberate efforts to eradicate native religions, indigenous religious practices persisted under a veneer of Catholicism. The king of Spain granted large estates, *haciendas,* as well as the Indians who lived on the land, to the occupying military officers. Many of the indigenous people were treated like agricultural serfs. The missionaries, primarily the Jesuits until their expulsion and then the Franciscans, seeking to shelter the Indians from this ruthless exploitation, created missions with their own craft industries, agriculture, and schools. While the missions were protective they could also be exploitative of the Indians. Indian laborers were conscripted to construct the mission buildings such as the church, chapel, factories, and schools. Children attending mission schools were taught to be Catholics and to abandon their native religions, which also meant losing part of their cultural heritage. In comparison with the English settlements in North America, however, the Spanish did not attempt to eradicate the native peoples or to displace them completely from their lands. They were, however, put into the category of a dominated group.

During Spain's long colonial rule from 1521 to the early nineteenth century, distinct social groups emerged. The *peninsulares*, of pure Spanish ancestry, constituted the elite governing class. Those of Spanish ancestry born in Mexico, the *criollos*, were the originators of the upper-middle classes. Considerable intermarriage and assimilation of the Spanish and the indigenous Indian population produced a large population of mixed Spanish-Indian extraction, the mestizos. A large number of Indians were not assimilated into the Hispanic culture and Spanish language. This group constituted the agricultural workers who worked on the large landed estates.

Throughout the eighteenth and early nineteenth centuries, the Catholic Church, especially its hierarchy, increasingly allied with the Spanish colonial elite and the upper-socioeconomic class. Along with the large landowners, the church was a strong conservative pillar of the status quo. There were, however, exceptions among the clergy, especially parish priests, who sought to improve the situation of the lower classes.

During the three centuries of Spain's colonial rule, the Roman Catholic Church was Mexico's principal educator. Under church auspices, educational arrangements reflected the transfer of Spanish educational institutions to the New World. A similar transference occurred in other European colonies such as those in North America, India, and Nigeria where schools were often under church control. Ideologically, the church's educational institutions, in hierarchical fashion, emphasized what were considered to be proper human relationships, namely commitment to existing ecclesiastical and patriarchal rubrics. As in Europe, upper-class males enjoyed the greatest educational privileges. Following the general pattern in Catholic countries, upper-class girls and young women were educated by nuns in convent schools. The church maintained some primary and mission schools for the lower socioeconomic classes and Indians, who received only a rudimentary education.

The Nineteenth Century

The Mexican War for Independence, launched in 1810, did not win total victory until 1821. Independent Mexico's leaders were influenced by Enlightenment and continental European ideology, especially French liberalism, with its emphasis on private property, individualism, and rational progress.[11] Like their European counterparts, Mexico's anticlerical revolutionary leaders were antagonistic to the Catholic Church and determined to reduce its political and educational prerogatives. The long entrenched church, opposed to the policies of the various revolutionary regimes, became a recalcitrant opponent of the new order. A long period of political-religious conflict ensued, resembling that which occurred in France during its revolution and its later nineteenth-century history. Anticlerical government officials sought to restrict and often suppress traditional prerogatives of the Catholic Church. Conservatives and religious Mexicans rallied to defend the faith and the church against what they regarded as agnostics and atheists.

In 1833, the church's control of education ended when the religious foundation of the University of Mexico was abolished. In its place, the Mexican Republic established the General Directorate of Public Instruction for the Federal District and Territories, whose main function was to issue regulations for schools, oversee the appointment of teachers, and select textbooks. With a generally federal direction, state governments were empowered to organize education in their territories.

From 1821 until 1857, educational institutions served the needs of Mexico's ruling political elite. The new elite, modeling themselves on the upper-middle-class liberals of Europe, sought to bring about limited reforms that displaced the old Spanish colonial rulers. As in other former colonial nations in the twentieth century, the socioeducational situation in the early Mexican republic favored elites rather than the entire population. A Mexican elite replaced the former Spanish colonial officials, but rather than sharing power, the new ruling elite monopolized it in their own self-interest. The revolutionary tension that developed in Mexico was between the new elite of landowners and upper-class businessmen and the underrepresented and often suppressed masses.

In the 1840s, border tensions developed between Mexico and the U.S. These tensions were exacerbated when Texas won its independence from Mexico. By 1848, Mexico and the U.S. were at war, and the U.S. army invaded Mexico. Mexico was defeated and under the terms of the Treaty of Guadalupe Hidalgo was forced to cede the vast territories north of the Rio Grande River that now comprise Arizona, California, Colorado, Nevada, New Mexico, and Utah to the U.S. This territory, along with Texas, was home to a large Mexican population, which became the original Mexican American population.[12] The war generated suspicion and hostility between the two countries, which persisted into the early twentieth century.

The next significant occurrence in Mexico's history happened when the popular Mexican president, Benito Juarez, challenged the ruling landowning elite and the still powerfully entrenched Catholic Church. Juarez attempted to bring about reforms to improve the conditions of the lower socioeconomic classes. He and his like-minded political followers were determined to end church control of educational institutions. The constitution of 1857 and subsequent laws, separating church and state, established public education as secular, free, and compulsory.[13] The degree to which the constitution's provisions were enforced depended, however, on the policies of the particular regime in power.

Juarez's efforts to create popular political and educational institutions were interrupted by the French interlude in Mexican history. Seeing that the U.S., engaged in its own Civil War, was unable to block European involvement in the Western Hemisphere, French Emperor Louis Napoleon, styled Napoleon III, engineered a coup and installed a Hapsburg prince, Maximilian, as Mexico's emperor from 1860 to 1867. The attempt to install a monarchy, backed by French military forces, precipitated civil war in Mexico. Although Maximilian's French-supported puppet government was defeated and the Mexican republic sustained itself, French cultural and educational influences penetrated the ideology of the Mexican upper classes. These tendencies reinforced the continental European liberal ideology that was already popular among Mexican intellectuals.

Throughout the nineteenth century, Mexico's educational history, like that of France, was marked by conflict between anticlerical liberal governments and the Catholic Church, a bulwark of traditional conservatism. Influenced by continental European liberalism, the Mexican republic rejected official state churches and church-controlled education. Mexican liberalism's greatest supporters were the upper-middle classes who encouraged *laissez faire* economic policies. The Mexican peasantry, the agricultural poor, and the Indian population received few benefits from Mexico's economic development.

The liberal reformers defined educational goals that fostered national patriotism for the republic, encouraged economic development, and maintained upper- and middle-class hegemony over the lower socioeconomic classes. Regarding the state rather than the church as the paramount political authority, liberals gave the government responsibility for providing and controlling education. They enacted laws to create a single system of public instruction and prohibited a church role in public education.

From 1876 to 1910, Mexico was ruled by Porfirio Diaz, a virtual dictator, who developed the country by exploiting its natural resources. Diaz's regime, which had the features of both one-man rule and control by an economic oligarchy, repressed the peasant workers. Diaz and his associates styled themselves *científicos*, men of science and technology influenced by Auguste Compte's Positivism. They applied technological development selectively, however. Economic developments in mining, industry, and agriculture benefited the ruling elite who exploited the peasants, especially the Indian agricultural laborers on large, landed estates. Although knowledgeable about educational developments in Europe and the U.S., the científicos discouraged general popular education and channeled resources to benefit the upper classes. Indeed, educational opportunities were deliberately restricted. With educational resources directed to the upper classes, two-thirds of the population remained illiterate. Less than 25 percent of Mexico's school-age children attended schools.[14]

The classical, liberal social and economic doctrines, inspired by continental European Enlightenment ideology, have had a strong and continuing influence on Mexico's educational history. For the Mexican liberals, the major goals of education were to: (1) reduce the powers of the church in politics and education; (2) apply science and technology to achieve economic development; and (3) construct a selective educational system that would prepare the most able people to lead the nation.[15]

The Twentieth Century

The Revolution that began in 1910 swept Diaz from power. It marks an important watershed in Mexican history that demarcates the old from the new order. For seven years, from 1910 to 1917, civil war waged in Mexico. The revolutionary spirit of the early twentieth century engendered a strong sense of nationalism that emphasized the solidarity of the Mexican people. It helped to create a distinct sense of Mexican national identity and a collective self-interest. Education was seen as an instrument for bringing about greater sociopolitical equality and Mexican nationalism.[16] Educational arrangements, like political ones, were designed to meet both popular demands and to create a strong centralized government.

The constitution of 1917 was a key document in setting Mexico's educational future course. The constitution's educational provisions increased federal control over schools' structure, organization, and curricula. The federal government was empowered to enact educational legislation and determine the revenue contributions that federal, state, municipal, and other local governments would make to education. Compulsory attendance was mandated but not strictly enforced for children ages six through fourteen in public or officially sanctioned private schools. Instruction in public or state schools was to be completely free and secular. Agricultural, industrial, and mining enterprises were to establish and maintain schools for their employees' children.

The constitution of 1917 divested the Roman Catholic Church from its remaining educational prerogatives. Article III prohibited priests and members of religious communities from involvement in public elementary, secondary, and teacher education.[17] It prohibited religious instruction in public schools. While private schools could be established and maintained, they were subject to official government supervision. The church and its supporters resisted, and church–state tensions continued to be a persistent feature in Mexico's educational history, much as they were in France in the late nineteenth and early twentieth centuries.

In 1921, the revolution was consolidated and President Alvaro Obregón was firmly in power. The federal Secretariat of Public Education, *Secretaria de Educación Publica,* under the direction of Jose Vasconcelos, was established. Vasconcelos reorganized the educational system according to the regime's two guiding ideological goals: to educate citizens with a sense of Mexican national identity and to use education for national economic development.[18] The government embarked on a thoroughgoing nation-building program to cultivate both a sense of national identification and an impetus for economic modernization. To foster nationalism, the school curriculum accentuated

Mexican history and geography. The lives of leading heroes in Mexican history became models for emulation by the young. Schools were also used as community centers in which patriotic celebrations commemorated important events of Mexican history.[19] To advance Mexico's economic modernization, the government's educational policy emphasized more technical, vocational, and practical programs.

The secretaria faced enormous practical as well as ideological issues. Many existing schools had to be repaired from the damage caused by revolutionary battles, and new schools had to be built in places where they had never existed. In the early 1920s, there were few complete primary and virtually no secondary schools in Mexico's rural areas. The government gave a high priority to primary education in its literacy campaigns. In its program of rural development, the government introduced the concept of rural primary schools as *casas del pueblo* (houses of the people). Teachers were given a multifaceted mission to teach basic skills and subjects to eradicate illiteracy and also to serve as cultural representatives of the new Mexican nation.[20]

In the 1920s, Mexican educators directed attention to developing the secondary school system. As a former colony of Spain, Mexico had inherited the traditional classical European attitude that defined secondary education as the academic preparation for university studies. In 1923, the undersecretary of education proposed that secondary education should be both an upward cultural extension of the primary school as well as a preparatory vehicle for higher studies. The discussion over the purpose of secondary education was not unique to Mexico but mirrored similar debates in other countries where reform-minded educators sought to broaden the function of secondary schools.

During the world economic depression of the 1930s, Mexico's government moved ideologically toward the left. During the administration of President Lázaro Cárdenas, from 1934 to 1940, government policies took on a moderate socialist orientation. A major ideological goal of the Cárdenas regime was *igualización,* social equality. As a result of the government's campaign to have working-class children stay in school instead of dropping out, primary and secondary school enrollments increased. More curricular emphasis was given to socially and economically productive activities and cooperative work. A civic education course was included in the curriculum that emphasized the benefits of a socialist society.

In 1940, Avila Camacho, who succeeded Cárdenas as president, returned to a liberal rather than a socialist ideological orientation. References to socialism were replaced by liberal calls for more equality of opportunity and socioeconomic mobility. Since then, Mexico has developed industrially and technologically, moving in the direction of becoming a modern and urban society. While the country was changing from a rural to an urban society and economy, the agricultural regions remained important. However, the urban middle classes were becoming a new and significant factor in Mexico's politics, economy, and education. Changes in educational policy accompanied this more general social transformation. Educational planners began to stress secondary and higher education, especially in urban areas. Between 1950 and 1970, there was a very dramatic 1,000 percent increase in secondary enrollments.[21]

In 1964, the constitutional article that specified the goals of the educational system was revised to accentuate the relationship between advancing equality and national identity and solidarity. Special attention was to be given in curriculum and instruction to affirming a patriotic love of country, celebrating national traditions, and achieving an equitable return to all from the development of the nation's natural resources.[22]

The Federal Education Law of 1973 continued the prohibition that barred religious congregations and organizations from involvement in public elementary, secondary, and teacher education. Continuing the government's power to license, regulate, and supervise private schools, it mandated the use of state-approved curriculum materials in all schools. Private schools found in violation of the government's guidelines could have their licenses revoked without judicial review. The law's provisions, directed against private schools, intensified tensions between Catholic and other private schools and the federal government.[23] In addition to its restrictions on religiously sponsored schools, the 1973 Federal Education Law sought to increase participation of historically underrepresented groups, such as Indians and rural residents, in education.[24]

Despite the reforms of the early 1970s, the education system did not fully respond to the transformative socioeconomic changes in Mexico. During 1970s, there were demands for the extension of higher education to more people. In particular, the growing middle classes were demanding greater access to university education. University students staged demonstrations and strikes, protesting deficiencies in classrooms and instruction. By the end of the 1970s, the federal government declared its intention to decentralize certain features of the educational system. To begin work on decentralization, the National Ministry of Education established Coordinated Services of Public Education (SCEPs) in each of the thirty-one states.

In the early 1980s, President de la Madrid signed education reform agreements with the thirty-one states. By the late 1980s, Mexico, under President Carlos Salinas de Gortari, announced *El Plan de Modernización Educativa,* the Education Modernization Plan, to reform the system by: (1) improving the quality of education, especially basic education; (2) raising the general level of schooling among the population; (3) increasing community participation in education; and (4) gradually decentralizing the system.[25] Devolution of educational authority from the central to the state governments was a key element in the reform strategy. The assumption underlying decentralization was that greater state rather than federal management would be more effective in meeting local needs. Again, the trend to decentralization was not unique to Mexico but was found in other countries as well.

By 1992, the administration of President Salinas de Gortari had firmly aligned itself with economic globalization, increased productivity, privatization, and modernization that were occurring worldwide. In 1992, the Secretariat of Public Education promulgated the first National Agreement on the Modernization of Basic Education (ANMEB) that was negotiated by the federal and state governments and the national teachers' union (SNTE). The agreement formally began the movement to lodge more authority with the states. It also included such innovations as reformulation and privatization of basic textbook production, decentralization of educational administration, a merit structure for teachers' career advancement, and an obligatory secondary school cycle. In 1993, the agreement was written into a new General Education Law, *Ley General de Educación*, which replaced the existing law of 1973.[26]

Governance and Administration of Education

Although Mexico's government is a federal system like that of the U.S., Mexico's governance of education historically resembles the more centralized systems of Japan and France. Since 1993, there have been initiatives toward greater decentralization, with the federal government delegating more authority to the states. Indeed, Mexico's handling of church–state issues, resting on an anticlerical ideology, is similar to France.

The Secretaria de Educación Publica, a large bureaucracy headed by the minister of education, includes major divisions for general, technical, and higher education and cultural affairs, and some thirty directorates, councils, and committees. The secretaria is responsible for implementing the Organic Law of Public Education and administrative regulations and curricula throughout Mexico.[27] The Federal Education Law of 1981 decreed that the national system of education encompasses all educational services by the federal and state governments. The minister of education, assisted directly by subordinate underministers, is responsible for the formal institutional sector as well as for nonformal education and popular culture.

Approximately 27,000,000 students are enrolled in educational institutions, encompassing preschool to higher education. The length of compulsory education was increased from six to nine years in 1992, but the requirement is not uniformly enforced throughout the country. Federally controlled institutions enroll 65 percent of students. State-controlled institutions enroll 25 percent and private institutions enroll approximately 10 percent.[28] While public schools are supervised by the secretaria, other federal ministries such as defense, navy, health, and agriculture maintain specialized schools and institutes. The state and municipal governments exercise day-to-day responsibility for operating the schools.

The secretaria prescribes textbooks, curricula, and syllabi for all public and private primary and secondary schools. In public primary schools, it prepares and provides required textbooks at government expense to pupils. At the secondary level, it publishes lists of "approved" textbooks for each subject. State schools, as well as private ones incorporated into the federal system, follow the same prescribed curriculum. Adherence to a nationally prescribed curriculum is similar to the controls exercised by the national education ministries in France and Japan. This contrasts with the local control found in the U.S. Program evaluation is also a central government function in Mexico. A central government agency is responsible for constructing, maintaining, and equipping schools.

In recent years, Mexico, like France and other countries with historically centralized systems, has devolved limited educational responsibilities to state and local authorities. The ANMEB, supported by the federal administration, the teachers' union, and representatives of parent associations, created a framework for controlled decentralization that gives state and local officials an increased role in implementing educational decisions. The central government, nevertheless, controls the process of devolution, allowing state and regional units limited responsibilities that do not interfere with overall federal planning, financing, and implementation.[29] While the federal government establishes the national curriculum and monitors assessment through a national evaluation system, state and regional authorities determine the instructional strategies for reaching these objectives. While the federal government still largely determines funding allocations, state and other regional authorities now enjoy more discretionary powers. In the late 1990s, the Mexican federal government embarked on a policy of moderate decentralization that devolved more authority and responsibility to the states. The decentralization strategy called for: (1) developing more democratic governance models such as school councils; (2) using teachers as active agents of school improvement; and (3) implementing curricular innovation and change.[30]

A key part of the process of decentralization is the *Consejos Técnicos Escolares* (CTEs), or technical councils, in each school and in each district that includes several schools. The councils are composed of the school principal and teachers. The establishment of school councils parallels trends to site-based management in other countries. The overall purpose of the school councils is to develop and monitor change in the school climate by: (1) encouraging more site-based management; (2) developing more subject-matter curriculum; (3) promoting a more interactive and process style of instruction; and (4) developing closer relationships between the school and community. At the school level, *Sociedad de Padres de Familia*, parents' organizations, are participating more in school matters. Further, teachers are encouraged to be more actively involved in community relations.[31]

An assumption underlying decentralization is that greater local and community involvement will improve educational outcomes. However, in the Mexican situation, the actual movement to site-based management has been limited by strong remnants of traditional centralization of authority. Often the councils are instruments of implementing the national ministry's mandates and of monitoring teacher compliance rather than bodies that initiate change.[32]

Mexico's public schools receive federal and state funding. Because of limited financial resources in several states, the federal funding provides 70 percent of the total revenues. Forty-six percent of the federal contribution is allocated to primary education, 19 percent to the middle (secondary) level, and 17 percent to higher and technical education.[33] Funds for education come from general revenue rather than specific taxes. A recent exception, however, is a salary tax to support secondary and higher education expansion.

Subject to federal policies, the state governments are required to establish and staff the schools and colleges in their territories. Because of limited resources in some states, the federal government has established a parallel network of educational institutions throughout the country. In the poorest states, federal authorities provide most of the secondary schooling. They also maintain institutions located in the federal district.

In 1980, the federal government allocated 14.9 percent of its expenditures to education, or 3.1 percent of GNP. The state governments spent approximately 22 percent of what the federal government spent on schools and a smaller percentage came from the private sector. Forty-nine percent of these appropriations were allocated for primary schooling and 37 percent were for secondary schooling.[34] Students attend public schools without cost or pay only nominal fees. Private schools and universities, which do not qualify for government subsidies, generally charge high tuition fees.

Traditionally, universities and other institutions of higher education have enjoyed significant autonomy. Federal authorities are assuming more direct responsibility for education at the higher-middle level, particularly in technical and vocational training.

Organization and Structure of Schools

The Mexican educational system consists of three distinct levels: elementary (preschool and primary), secondary (basic and upper), and higher. Between 1980 and 1990, the proportion of primary-age children enrolled in schools increased from 90 percent of the age cohort to 98 percent.[35] However, the dropout rate is high. Between the ages of fifteen and nineteen the proportion of students attending school declines to 23 percent and between the ages of twenty and twenty-four it declines further to 4.3 percent.[36]

Preschool and Early Childhood Education

As in most countries, preprimary education in nursery schools and kindergartens is an available but optional, noncompulsory part of the school system. While the secretaria provides educational advice and operates some preprimary schools, the Ministry of Public Health and Welfare, the Social Security Institute, and other ministries and private or religious agencies also operate early childhood centers and schools.

Participation in preprimary arrangements is much less in Mexico than it is in the U.S. and other Western nations, but is proportionally higher than in other Latin American countries.[37] Approximately 56 percent of the kinder-garten enrollment (ages four to six) is in federal schools, 36 percent is in state schools, and 7.5 percent is in private schools.[38] Preschool arrangements are much more available and have higher participation rates in urban areas than in rural areas. The majority of kindergartens are in large urban centers, with nearly one-third in Mexico City. In Mexico, as well as in most countries, the stated goals of kindergarten education seek to develop children physically, mentally, and socially, especially in developmental skills and social behaviors that contribute to readiness for primary schooling.

In addition to kindergartens, there are also *guarderías*, or nursery schools, for children under age four. The secretaria exercises some supervision and coordination of these guarderías, which provide health, welfare, and educational services and activities. Often, government departments operate these nursery schools for their employees' children. Upper- and middle-class families are the most frequent users of kindergartens and nursery schools.

Primary Schools

The primary school, a six-year institution, enrolls children ages six to twelve. While most urban primary schools offer the complete six-year cycle, some schools in remote rural areas offer a more limited program. Approximately 20,000 rural schools offer primary schooling only through third grade. In some very remote regions, primary schools offer only one grade.[39]

In the 1990s, about 98 percent of the primary age cohort was enrolled in school. The national rate of pupils completing the school year is 93 percent and the average promotion rate is 84 percent. A high dropout rate persists, particularly in rural areas, where the completion rate for the primary cycle is one-seventh of that in urban areas. The number of students who complete the primary cycle at the final year, grade six, is about 37 percent of those who began five years earlier.[40] The high dropout rate has resulted in a large number of functional illiterates. In the lower primary grades, the enrollment of boys and girls is about equal. In the higher primary grades, however, the number of boys exceeds girls.

Women constitute 61 percent of primary teachers. The national teacher–student ratio for the primary schools is one teacher to forty-four pupils. The ratio is higher than in other Latin American countries. These higher ratios are attributable to inadequate funding rather than teacher shortages.

The school year, which begins in September and ends in July, is divided into three terms, with vacations in December and April. Primary school classes meet for five hours, five days per week. The primary school curriculum, developed at the national level, is uniform in terms of skills and subjects for all schools, both public and private, throughout Mexico. The officially stated objectives are to: (1) relate schooling to life in the home and the outside world; (2) promote the understanding of the environment and society; and (3) develop skills in practical activities. The curriculum consists of: Spanish language and literature; mathematics; an introduction to natural science; history, geography, and elements of other social studies; health; art and music; physical education; technological education, usually manual training for boys and home science for girls; and regional education (in specific areas).[41] Major subjects are subdivided into eight units, one for each month of the school year.[42]

Promotion from grade to grade is based on teacher evaluation of student performance, aptitude, and behavior rather than by scores on standardized examinations. This feature of Mexican education is somewhat different from the national assessment used in other countries with a national curriculum.

While Mexico's official language of instruction is Spanish, some groups use their local Indian language as their first language. *El Servicio Nacional de Promotores Culturales y Maestros Bilingües*, the National Service for Cultural Promoters and Bilingual Teachers, administers and provides special programs in which instruction is in the Indian vernacular language. In these programs, Spanish is taught as a second language. Like many other former colonial and immigrant societies, Mexico's population is multicultural and multilingual. It exhibits regional variations as well as those based on various ethnic backgrounds, especially among indigenous peoples.

Secondary Schools

Secondary education in Mexico reflects several divergent tendencies that arise from tradition, the needs of economic development, and greater attention to the specific needs of adolescence. The inherited tradition, as in most countries, emphasizes the role of secondary education as preparation for higher university studies and eventual entry into recognized professions. Mexico's programs of national economic development, geared to industrial modernization, emphasize applied technical studies. Along with other modernizing countries, Mexico's educators are aware of and seek to integrate the psychology of adolescent needs into school programs.

Secondary schooling in Mexico, the *secundaria*, starts with a three-year general cycle or a three-year technical cycle, which roughly corresponds to the U.S. middle school and encompasses postprimary grades seven through nine. About 60 percent of secondary students are enrolled in general secundarias. Twenty-eight percent of secondary students are enrolled in technical secundarias.

The general secondary cycle covers three years for students between the ages of twelve and fifteen, although some may attend beyond those ages. Until the 1970s, the secundaria was an optional continuation from primary school. Most students who continued from primary to secondary education intended to pursue professional studies and used the secundaria as a means to gain entry in a college-linked *preparatoria,* an introductory component of higher education.[43] The general secondary cycle requires thirty hours of classroom instruction per week. Vocational secondary schools are supplemented by training centers, which offer one academic year of technical training for those who leave primary school to prepare them for semi-skilled agricultural or industrial jobs. Some technical secondary schools and some higher technical institutions also offer these one-year programs.

During the 1970s, however, secundaria enrollments steadily increased as socioeconomic development, especially growth in an industrially dominated labor market, caused more nonuniversity-bound students to complete secondary education. Approximately 4,267,000 students, 19 percent of the total national student enrollment, attend some type of secondary school.[44] Participation in secondary education still involves only a minority of the age cohort due to the high dropout rate in the upper grades of primary school. It is estimated that only 15 percent of those who begin primary education will enter middle, or secondary, schools.[45] In addition, boys participating in secondary schooling outnumber girls by about four to three.

In 1993, the Mexican constitution was amended to mandate compulsory secondary schooling. By 1994, all secundarias had implemented a new national curriculum as part of the Program for Educational Modernization. The program for secondary education reform emphasized: (1) education's role in modernizing and increasing the productivity of the Mexican economy as part of a global world economy; (2) providing more students with access to higher education; and (3) the entry of more people into active participation in the nation's cultural and political life.[46]

The middle, or secondary, school curriculum articulates with and builds on such basic subjects studied in the upper grades of the primary schools as Spanish language and literature, mathematics, and social sciences such as history and geography, and then adds natural sciences such as biology, chemistry, physics, and foreign languages, especially English and French. The popularity of English rests on the belief that it will lead to a better job in the post-NAFTA era. In the third year, there is an orientation course that provides vocational and career counseling and a final elective course. For the elective course, students have the choice of ecological study, photography, state and local history, and the local indigenous language. In addition, the curriculum includes activities, not defined as courses, in art and physical and technical education. Spanish is the medium of instruction throughout the general secondary cycle. Similar to the U.S. pattern and unlike the European and Japanese systems, promotion in middle school is based largely on teachers' evaluation of student performance rather than external examinations.

At the middle, or secondary, school level, there are 233,000 teachers. The majority of middle-school teachers are men who constitute 65 percent of the professional staff. In middle schools, the teacher–student ratio is one to seventeen. The ratio, which has remained generally stable in middle schools, is similar to other Latin American countries.

Higher Secondary Schools

After completing the secundario cycle, students are awarded a certificate of completion and are then eligible for admission to three-year preparatory or advanced vocational cycles, similar to high school in the U.S., which take place in separate schools. Students in the vocational track, enrolled in technical institutes, may use it as terminal preparation as technicians and skilled craftsmen in the middle levels of industry. Higher secondary study leads to the bachillerato (the higher secondary school graduation certificate), or to a professional certificate.[47]

Mexico's economic development from an agricultural to an industrial nation has had important implications for vocational and technical education, where the policy has been to shift training programs from agriculture to industry. Mexico, like India, has the challenge of preparing a workforce of technicians, managers, and para-engineers who can operate and maintain industrial and other technologies, especially at midlevels.

To prepare its vocational and technical workers, Mexico has developed three types of institutions that offer programs related to industry, agriculture, and fishing: (1) vocational/technical institutions, (2) institutions of professional studies, and (3) regional technological institutes.[48] Institutions of professional studies that require completion of the basic secondary cycle for admission offer courses ranging from eight months to several years. A variety of institutions provide higher technical secondary education, with the National Polytechnic Institute of the National University in Mexico City as the model imitated throughout the country. Technical institutes offer three pre-university programs in such fields as engineering, mathematics and physical sciences, chemical and biological sciences, economics, commerce, and administration. Controlled directly by the national Ministry of Education, the federal government has established Centers of Scientific and Technical Studies, often located on the same premises as technical and agricultural secondary schools, in key industrial and agricultural areas. Technical preparatory schools are linked to regional institutes of technology in the provinces and offer technical education at the upper-secondary and higher-education levels. Also, professional and trade schools prepare students for a recognized professional qualification over a period of three or four years or for entry to appropriate first degree courses in an institution of higher education. After completing a program, students may enter a trade or occupation or proceed to more advanced technical programs.

The traditional university preparatory schools are the *preparatorias* and *colegios de ciencias y humanidades* (schools of sciences and humanities) and the *colegios de bachilleres* (upper comprehensive secondary schools). Students completing these programs are awarded the bachillerato diploma needed for entry to universities and other higher education institutions.[49] While the usual preparatory program is three years, some schools offer a shorter, two-year program, followed by a "prepedeutic" year at the university.

Following the model of the National University's Preparatory School, many public universities prepare entering students in their own preparatory schools. In addition there are private preparatory secondary schools. In Mexico, graduates of university-related higher secondary schools generally proceed automatically to first-degree programs.

Higher Education

In Mexico, a large variety of institutions, ranging from multipurpose universities to technical institutes, offer higher education leading to the bachelor's and advanced graduate and professional degrees. As in the U.S., Mexican higher education began to expand in the late 1940s and has continued to grow. In 1940, the eight existing universities enrolled about 14,000 students; by the 1980s, enrollments had climbed dramatically to more than 600,000 students in 124 institutions of higher education. Current enrollment exceeds one million students.

Mexico's universities include both public (federal and state) and private universities. Although they receive direct government subsidies, public institutions, which enroll 80 percent of college and university students, enjoy considerable autonomy from federal interference. Some autonomous institutions that are financed by the federal government are largely self-governing and others fall under state government jurisdiction. In the late 1960s and 1970s, Mexico, like the U.S., began to use strategic planning to coordinate its public institutions of higher education. Until that time, institutions of higher learning, operating under their own organic regulations, were virtually self-governing. In 1973, the Federal Education Law incorporated the universities into the national system to provide more coordinated growth and development and reduce duplication of facilities.[50]

Nominal tuition and fees, paid by students, cover only a small portion of operating costs. In contrast, private universities, like those in the U.S., depend heavily on student tuition and fees and on support from private donors and foundations. Technological institutes, primarily preparing engineers and business administrators, are centrally controlled by the federal government, which makes decisions on faculty, programs, and curriculum. Enrolling 15 percent of higher education students, technological institutes are important in regions of the country with limited higher educational options.[51]

Of the 124 institutions of higher education, 39 are in the federal district, including the two largest and most prestigious institutions, the National University and the National Polytechnic Institute. The National Autonomous University of Mexico (UNAM), established in 1910, with more than 100,000 students, is the largest and most influential institution of higher learning. It consists of ten faculties, or departments and schools, as well as thirty-four research centers and institutes. Its large central library and attached specialized libraries hold a collection of two million volumes. The National Polytechnical Institute is the largest and most prestigious institution providing technical education in Mexico. It has general responsibility for planning, establishing, and coordinating technical programs, as well as supervising higher-level regional technical institutes. The Autonomous University of Guadalajara is the largest private institution. In contrast, many provincial universities are small, some having less than 1,000 students.[52] Smaller public universities model themselves after the UNAM.

Mexican universities are highly autonomous and establish their own agendas for curriculum, instruction, and research. Their governance and structures follow traditional academic patterns. An important part of autonomy in higher education is faculty members' "academic freedom." Although universities publish syllabi for all courses, professors are free to determine their own teaching methods and materials. However, universities are subject to some government control through membership in the National Association of Universities and Institutes of Higher Education, a centralized agency for strategic planning. While the UNAM emphasizes both teaching and research, most public universities are primarily teaching institutions. A recent trend, however, has been to establish research institutes, often separate from teaching faculties. Each faculty, or department, within a university tends to prepare students for a particular discipline or profession.

In the past, institutions had a more selective admissions policy, often maintaining their own preparatory schools. Admission requirements vary among institutions. The basic requirement is the *bachillerato*. Other requirements may include entrance examinations and psychological tests. Today, admissions policies have become more flexible, and many institutions have an "open door" admission policy.

Universities in Mexico tend to follow the European model of governance that evolved during the Middle Ages. They are presided over by rectors. In the universities in the various states, rectors are appointed by the state governor. In the UNAM, however, the rector is elected by a university council composed of faculty, administrators, and student representatives. All universities have councils that serve as internal institution-wide governing bodies. University academic programs are administered by faculties, which are similar to academic departments in colleges and universities in the U.S. A feature of Mexican as well as other Latin American universities is that the number of full-time faculty is small. Many professors are professionals who hold full-time positions outside of the university. In the Latin American educational tradition, university teaching, while highly prestigious, is considered to be a part-time occupation. For example, even at the highly prestigious National Autonomous University of Mexico, only 1,100 of the 18,000 teachers are full-time faculty. The high number of part-time professors limits the out-of-class professor and student contact.

In the public autonomous or state-controlled universities, the majority of students are part-time, working their way through college. The large universities operate double shifts, mornings and afternoons, Monday to Friday. Courses of study in Mexican universities vary from three to seven years. Since many students are part-time, a longer period of time is needed to complete degree programs. The usual mode of instruction is the lecture with little discussion. The highest program enrollments are in accounting, medicine, law, engineering, and business administration. The first degree is the *licenciado*, or licentiate, similar to the bachelor's degree in the U.S. Graduate programs lead to the *maestría*, or master's degree, and the *doctorado*, or doctorate.

The National Polytechnic Institute in Mexico City, the preeminent higher technical institution, offers programs leading to first and higher degrees in engineering, pure and applied sciences (including medicine), economics, commerce, and administration. The Institute of Technology and Higher Studies of Monterrey is also a highly regarded institution. To spur technological development, the federal government has developed the National Center for Technical and Industrial Education and a network of regional institutes of technology. Several private institutes of technology are located in the larger cities. These institutes of technology emphasize engineering and applied sciences. Admission to higher technical institutes, like university entry, requires completion of the higher secondary program. Students who attended secondary institutions attached to specific technical institutes usually have direct access. Other students, however, must pass an entrance examination.

Since the 1970s, the private sector in higher education has grown rapidly to meet accelerating demands. There are basically two types of private institutions: elite universities and smaller, less prestigious ones with limited offerings. While elite institutions offer a full range of academic programs staffed by full-time faculty, most private universities are small, locally based, nonselective institutions, with limited programs typically in fields such as accounting, business, or psychology. These institutions rely heavily on part-time instructors. Other than granting initial licenses to private universities to begin operations, the state exercises only limited regulation over them.[53] Private universities, charging high tuition fees, draw more students from economically affluent classes. Their curricula parallel that of state institutions. Much of the instruction is in the lecture format.

Expansion of Higher Education

Mexico's expansion of higher education corresponds to the general international pattern found in other LTDCs such as Nigeria and India. Higher education's dramatic growth in Mexico can be illustrated statistically. In 1940, the then existing eight universities had a total enrollment of 14,000 students, 10,000 of whom attended the National University in Mexico City. By 1981, enrollment had grown to 600,000 students, 25 percent at the National University.[54] Currently, Mexico's institutions of higher education enroll one million students; 15 percent of the age cohort between twenty and twenty-four is enrolled in higher education. An important trend, also observed worldwide, is increased participation of women, who constitute about 40 percent of enrollments. The expansion of higher education has been primarily urban, expanding from Mexico City to other large cities.

The rapid and generally unplanned expansion of higher education generated an increase in numbers of faculty, changed socioeconomic expectations related to higher education, and raised quality issues. The chief issue facing colleges and universities is how to maintain quality standards while admitting larger numbers of students. This question involves the adequacy of facilities such as classrooms, libraries, and laboratories, the academic preparation of faculty, and the instructional patterns between faculty and students. On the eve of the expansion in 1970, Mexico had approximately 24,000 university professors, many of whom were professionals who taught part-time. Unlike the U.S. where the Ph.D. is typically required for university professors, this was not the case in Mexico. Also unlike the U.S., Mexican faculty were not expected to be researchers. With the great expansion of enrollments, more than 75,000 new professors were hired. To accommodate expansion in higher education, two inherent conditions have had to change: (1) the tradition of using part-time professors; and (2) the lack of appropriate graduate programs to prepare new faculty. As a result, Mexican higher education has had to work through the process of combining teaching and research.[55]

As in other LTDCs, such as India and Nigeria, Mexico's expansion of higher education in education was primarily a political response to a climate of rising educational expectations, especially by the middle class. Though costly and supported by the government, there was little overall strategic planning. Greater access tended to benefit the urban middle class and to generate more urban–rural differentials. Furthermore, with some institutions literally opening their doors to all who applied, selectivity in admissions suffered. Without entrance examinations or other selection processes, students tended to move from secondary to higher education for social, political, or economic rather than academic reasons.

Higher education's expansion also reflected important socioeconomic changes in Mexico. Economic growth, enlarging the middle class, accelerated traditional educational expectations. The emerging urban middle classes believed their children's higher education would guarantee upward mobility. The enlarged urban middle class's outlook carried important political implications. In return for generous state funding of higher education, the middle class would contribute to Mexico's stability by supporting the political establishment that had made their upward climb possible.[56]

The federal government's generous policy for funding higher education rested on what proved to be faulty economic assumptions. It assumed the high oil prices and low international interest rates of the 1970s would continue. The same assumptions also were at work in other oil producing LTDCs, like Nigeria. However, economic changes, particularly the depression in oil prices of the 1980s, forced government fiscal retrenchment and restructuring. Priorities shifted from supporting institutions of higher education to repaying foreign loans, controlling inflation, encouraging privatization, reducing government bureaucracy, and opening Mexico to the world market.

Higher education in Mexico historically has been selective with students coming from the upper and upper-middle classes.[57] For example, 95 percent of the students at the National Autonomous University of Mexico come from families whose income is in the upper 15 percent of the population. During the 1970s and 1980s, Mexico and its educational system continued to move from underdevelopment and selectivity to serving the needs of an increasingly industrialized and modern society. Education was viewed as a significant contributing force for future economic development and the creation of strong national consciousness. These two elements—national consciousness and economic development—follow the pattern of using education for modernization and nation building that is found in many LTDCs. For example, Nigeria has employed a similar but less successful strategy for its development.

Teacher Education

Teacher education programs are offered in separate institutions, called normal schools, for the various levels of schooling. After earning a secondary school certificate, prospective preprimary and primary teachers are prepared in teacher training programs in federal and state normal or higher normal schools. There are also a few private normal schools. The teacher preparation program is typically three or four years, consisting of general and professional educational studies.

The program for pre- and primary school teachers includes courses in scientific-humanistic, physical-artistic, and technical areas as well as in professional education courses, including practice teaching.

Higher normal secondary schools provide four-year training courses for secondary and normal school teachers. The entrance qualification is possession of a bachillerato or a normal school certificate. Many higher normal school students are in-service primary school teachers who attend part-time to prepare for more remunerative and prestigious secondary school positions. It often takes four or five years to complete the program and qualify for secondary school positions. Special education teachers are prepared in *escuelas normales de especialización*, normal schools for special education. Teachers for industrial, technical, and agricultural specialties are prepared in specialized upper secondary institutions.

As in the U.S., many teachers attend summer school in-service programs. These summer courses are popular with primary school teachers in rural areas where there is limited access to training colleges. Higher normal schools offer summer programs by which students can obtain their teacher certification.

The national teachers' union (SNTE), the largest trade union in Latin America, has over 250,000 members. In its early history, the SNTE was a strong force for social and educational change. Over time, however, it has become increasingly tied into the federal system and Ministry of Education. Often, union members who climb the organizational structure receive official appointments, which tends to make them supporters of the status quo rather than agents for change. Further, the recent tendency to decentralization has weakened the union's national power since it now has to negotiate with state, regional, and local authorities.

Nonformal and Open Education

Mexico, like other LTDCs, struggles in the war against illiteracy. The high primary school dropout rate contributes to illiteracy. While children may learn reading basics in the early primary grades, their leaving school at an early age reduces reinforcement of decoding skills so that they often lapse into functional illiteracy. A similar but more serious problem of educational waste exists in Nigeria and India.

As in other LTDCs, people in rural areas, where access to schools is limited, tend to be illiterate. Literacy is highest in the federal district and the northern areas; illiteracy is high in the Gulf Coast and southern areas. To combat illiteracy, the federal secretaria has inaugurated a radio and television distance education project, called *alfabetización*. There are also some boarding schools, *albergues escolares*, which offer elementary and vocational training to children between ages twelve and fifteen who have not completed elementary education. These schools provide instruction and room and board for children from rural communities without schools. *Las brigadas de desarrollo*, brigades for regional development, are mobile educational units that work among the Indians in remote areas.

Mexico has developed "open learning" alternatives to meet its serious undereducation problems. Open learning emphasizes independent self-instruction, supplemented by contact with professional educators. The 1973 Education Act allowed limited certification based on qualifications earned through open education. In higher education, UNAM operates an Open University in which students attend courses on Saturdays. The Federal Centre for Study of Advanced Methods and Processes in Education provides a higher secondary option. Its Open Preparatory School at Monterrey operates its own educational TV channel. Teachers involved in open and nonformal education use specially designed textbooks.

There is also a television program, *Telesecundaria*, which provides general secondary education according to the general secondary school syllabi for students in deprived urban and rural areas that lack regular secondary school facilities.

Conclusion

The imprint of Spanish colonialism is clearly evident in language, religion, social class, and education in Mexico. After gaining independence in the early nineteenth century, Mexico's political and educational leaders worked to create a sense of Mexican cultural and political identity, as did U.S. educators during the common school movement. Mexico's history was different from that of the U.S. in that Mexico experienced political instability due to frequent revolutions, dictatorships, and a strong role by the army. Here,

Mexico's history bears some similarity to Nigeria's history of political instability, coups, and a military government. Like the U.S., Mexico had and still has a large indigenous population; unlike the U.S., Mexico's largely mestizo population is descended from Indian as well as Spanish ethnicity.

Economically, Mexico is like India and China, a country that is rapidly moving through developmental processes from an agricultural to an industrial society. Mexico, like Nigeria and other LTDCs, is attempting to restructure and reduce its government services. The result is a decrease in available expenditures for education and other social services.

In education, Mexico exhibits the structural and organization patterns that exist worldwide: preschool, primary, secondary, and higher education. However, culture and context work to reshape this structure. Preschool arrangements, following the Latin American pattern, are less developed and less available than in other Western-influenced countries. Mexico, like India and Nigeria, still suffers from a high dropout rate from primary schooling. This contributes to problems of educational wastage, especially in the struggle against illiteracy. Although the number of students moving through secondary school is less than in the U.S., Mexico's secondary structure is not as selective as those found in Western Europe. Higher education in Mexico, too, follows trends found in LTDCs in that more people, especially the urban middle class, are developing higher educational expectations for their children and are demanding greater access to universities.

A persistent issue facing educational planners, decision makers, and practitioners in Mexico is that of quantity versus quality. Resources need to be allocated to primary and secondary schools with a goal of retaining students so they can advance to higher and vocational schools. At the same time, growth without quality controls is likely to exceed Mexico's economic capabilities and lower academic standards.

DISCUSSION QUESTIONS

1. Which characteristics of Mexican history are unique to Mexico and which ones are shared with other countries?

2. Describe the demographics in Mexico's population. How do these factors have an impact on education?

3. Compare and contrast the status and role of indigenous groups in Mexico and the U.S.

4. What features of LTDCs are present in Mexico's economy and education?

5. Is the school structure significantly different in Mexico than in other countries?

6. Are the problems in Mexican education similar to or different from those in the U.S., Western European countries, and LTDCs?

7. Why has there been an expansion of higher education in Mexico? Is this expansion similar or different from other countries?

8. Why is nonformal education so important in Mexico? Is this importance similar to or different from other countries?

9. What challenges do educational reformers face in Mexico?

RESEARCH TOPICS

1. Interview several international students from Mexico and elicit their impressions of their education. Try to make some comparisons with education in the U.S.

2. Interview several recent immigrants from Mexico and elicit their impressions of their education. Make some comparisons with the experiences of other recent immigrants to the U.S.

3. Conduct an Internet search and identify sites that provide information about education in Mexico.

4. Develop a clippings file about culture, politics, the economy, and education in Mexico.

5. In a research paper, write a comparative analysis of an aspect of education, such as primary, secondary, or higher education, in Mexico and the U.S.

6. Prepare a comparative organization chart that illustrates the organization of education in the U.S. and Mexico.

SUGGESTIONS FOR FURTHER READING

Brachet-Marquez. *The Dynamics of Domination: State, Class, and Social Reform in Mexico, 1910–1990.* Pittsburgh: University of Pittsburgh Press, 1994.

Cook, Maria Lorena. *Organizing Dissent: Union, the State, and the Democratic Teachers' Movement in Mexico.* University Park: Pennsylvania State University Press, 1996.

Foweraker, Joseph. *Popular Mobilization in Mexico: The Teachers' Movement, 1977–87.* Cambridge: Cambridge University Press, 1993.

Gonzales, Manuel G. *Mexicanos: A History of Mexicans in the United States.* Bloomington: Indiana University Press, 1999.

Griswold del Castillo, Richard, and Arnoldo De Leon. *North to Aztlan: A History of Mexican Americans in the United States.* New York: Twayne, 1996.

Hale, Charles A. *The Transformation of Liberalism in Late Nineteenth Century Mexico.* Princeton, NJ: Princeton University Press, 1989.

Levinson, Bradley A. "Una etapa siempre dificil: Concepts of Adolescence and Secondary Education in Mexico," *Comparative Education Review* 43(2) (1999): 129–161.

MacDonald, Victoria-Marie. "Hispanic, Latino, Chicano, or 'Other'?: Deconstructing the Relationship between Historians and Hispanic-American Educational History," *History of Education Quarterly* 41 (Fall 2001): 368–369.

Martin, Christopher C. *Schooling in Mexico: Staying In or Dropping Out.* Aldershot, UK: Ashgate, 1994.

Morales-Gomez, Daniel A., and Carlos A. Torres. *The State, Corporatist Politics, and Educational Policy-Making in Mexico, 1970–1988.* Westport, CT: Praeger, 1990.

Morales-Gomez, Daniel A., and Carlos A. Torres. *Education, Policy and Social Change: Experiences from Latin America.* Westport, CT: Praeger, 1992.

Tatto, Maria T. "Education Reform and State Power in Mexico: The Paradoxes of Decentralization," *Comparative Education Review* 43(2) (1999): 251–282.

Vaughan, Mary Kay. *Cultural Politics in Revolution: Teachers, Peasants, and Schools in Mexico, 1930–1940.* Tucson: University of Arizona Press, 1997.

Vaughan, Mary Kay. *The State, Education, and Social Class in Mexico, 1880–1928.* DeKalb: Northern Illinois University Press, 1982.

NOTES

[1] CIA (Central Intelligence Agency), "World Factbook: Mexico," January 22, 2004, http://www.cia.gov/cia/publications/factbook/geos'mx.html.

[2] *Book of Vital World Statistics* (London: Hutchinson Publishers, 1990), 16–28.

[3] Robert Cowen and Martin McLean, *International Handbook of Education Systems: Asia, Australasia and Latin America, III* (New York: John Wiley & Sons, 1984), 726.

[4] Ibid.

[5] Since the political situation in Mexico is subject to frequent changes, only the general outlines are presented here in terms of the specific designation of officeholders.

[6] CIA.

[7] Ibid.

[8] Ibid.

[9] Lawrence J. Estrada and Thomas J. LaBelle, "Mexican Education," in *Comparative Educational Systems*, ed. Edward Ignas and Raymond J. Corsini (Itasca, IL: F. E. Peacock, 1981), 288–289.

[10] An important work on the Mayans is Linda Schele and David Freidel, *A Forest of Kings: The Untold Story of the Ancient Maya* (New York: William Morrow, 1990); also, see Michael D. Coe, *The Maya* (London: Thames and Hudson, 1987).

[11] Bradley A. Levinson, "Una etapa siempre difícil: Concepts of Adolescence and Secondary Education in Mexico," *Comparative Education Review* 43(2) (1999): 137.

[12] Victoria-Marie MacDonald, "Hispanic, Latino, Chicano, or 'Other'?: Deconstructing the Relationship between Historians and Hispanic-American Educational History," *History of Education Quarterly* 41 (Fall 2001): 368–369. Histories of Mexican Americans are: Manuel G. Gonzales, *Mexicanos: A History of Mexicans in the United States* (Bloomington: Indiana University Press, 1999) and Richard Griswold del Castillo and Arnoldo De Leon, *North to Axtlan: A History of Mexican Americans in the United States* (New York: Twayne, 1996).

[13] George Kurian, "Mexico," in *World Education Encyclopedia*, II, ed. George T. Kurian, (New York: Facts on File, 1988), 861.

[14] Ibid.

[15] For the changes in liberal thinking in Mexico, see Charles A. Hale, *The Transformation of Liberalism in Late Nineteenth Century Mexico* (Princeton, New Jersey: Princeton University Press, 1989).

[16] Mary Kay Vaughan, *Cultural Politics in Revolution: Teachers, Peasants, and Schools in Mexico, 1930–1940* (Tucson: University of Arizona Press, 1997).

[17] Kurian, 862.

[18] Carlos Ornelas, *El sistema educativo mexicano* (Mexico City: SEP/Centro de Investigación y Docencia Económica, 1995), 49.

[19] Kurian, 861–862.

[20] Levinson, 141–142.

[21] Ibid., 150.

[22] Ibid., 143–44.

[23] Kurian, 862–863.

[24] Estrada and LaBelle, 295.

[25] Maria T. Tatto, "Education Reform and State Power in Mexico: The Paradoxes of Decentralization," *Comparative Education Review* 43(3) (1999): 257.

[26] Levinson, 152.

[27] Educational policy making and implementation is treated in Daniel A. Morales-Gomez and Carlos Alberto Torres, *The State, Corporatist Politics, and Educational Policy Making in Mexico* (New York: Praeger, 1990).

[28] Library of Congress, "Country Studies," http://lcweb2.loc.gov/cgi-bin/query/ (accessed June 1, 2005); Secretaria de Educación Publica, *Sistema Nacional de Educación Tecnológica* (Mexico City, Mexico: Secretaria de Educación Publica, 1991), 21–22.

[29] Tatto, 259–261.

[30] Ibid., 251–252.

[31] Ibid., 261–263.

[32] Ibid., 261.

[33] Kurian, 870.

[34] Cowen and McLean, 746–747.

[35] Christopher J. Martin, *Schooling in Mexico: Staying In or Dropping Out* (Aldershot, UK: Ashgate, 1994), 24.

[36] Kurian, 863.

[37] Estrada and LaBelle, 302.

[38] Kurian, 864–865.

[39] Ibid.

[40] Ibid.

[41] Cowen and McLean, 734.

[42] Estrada and LaBelle, 302.

[43] Levinson, 131

[44] Secretaria de Educación Pública, 21–32.

[45] Kurian, 865–866.

[46] Levinson, 153.

[47] Cowen and McLean, 736.

[48] Kurian, 866.

[49] Ibid.

[50] Secretaria de Educación Publica, 21–32.

[51] Rollin Kent, "Higher Education in Mexico: From unregulated expansion to evaluation," *Higher Education* 25 (1993): 74.

[52] Cowen and McLean, 738.

[53] Ibid., 74.

[54] Kurian, 867.

[55] Kent, 75.

[56] Ibid., 76.

[57] For higher education development, see Daniel C. Levy, *University and Government in Mexico: Autonomy in an Authoritarian System* (New York: Praeger, 1980).

15

EDUCATION IN JAPAN

Intrigued by Japanese education, American commentators, scholars, and professional educators have frequently compared Japanese and American schools and students, highlighting Japanese students' higher academic achievement. For example, a *Chicago Tribune* editorialist asked, "Are Japanese children smarter than American youngsters? Have the Japanese found a way to produce not only high quality cars and stereos but brighter people?"[1] The *Tribune*'s editorialist advised Americans to learn from the following lessons from Japan: (1) Americans "should raise their assumptions of what children are capable of learning, especially in math and science"; (2) American students "should spend more time," in and out of school, on academic study; (3) American schools and teachers should instill productive work habits such as "concentration, attention to detail, order, diligence"; and (4) students should be responsible for their school and their academic progress.[2]

The *Tribune*'s editorialist recommended that U.S. educators might borrow selected features from Japan and transplant them to U.S. schools. However, the effectiveness of importing an educational structure or method from one country to another depends on how well it fits with the cultural context into which it is transplanted. When the Japanese devised their educational system in the late nineteenth and early twentieth centuries, they borrowed selectively from the UK, France, Germany, and the United States, taking care that the transplanted elements did not alter Japan's core values.

Japan is selected for discussion in the book because it is a major economic power in the global economy and because it presents a fascinating problem of comparability for educators.

Geographic, Demographic, and Sociocultural Contexts

The island-nation of Japan, located east of the Korean peninsula, occupies an island chain between the North Pacific Ocean and the Sea of Japan. The country is slightly smaller than the state of California, with a land area of 147,356 square miles.[3] The climate ranges from tropical in the south to cool and temperate in the north. The terrain is mostly rugged and mountainous. Despite its economic successes, Japan has few natural resources and is heavily dependent on imported minerals and fuels, especially petroleum.

Japan's population of 127,214,499, half that of the U.S., occupies a very small and thus crowded living space. The population's age structure is that of a technologically developed country (TDC) with 14.4 percent of the population between 0 and 14 years; 67 percent between 15 and 64 years; and 18.6 are 65 years or older. The median age is 42 years. Life expectancy is 80.93 years. The rate of population growth is small at 0.11 percent.[4] The literacy rate is a very high 99 percent. The cohort group of preschool and elementary school age is 14.4 percent, while the group over age 65 is 18.6 percent. As is true for other TDCs, such as the UK and France, the statistics reveal a stable school-age population and an increasing senior-age population. The literacy rate of 99 percent shows a country with a well-schooled population. The Japanese demographic profile is significantly different from that of the other Asian countries, China and India, examined in the book. Although they are in the process of technological and economic development, these two larger Asian nations still show considerable underdevelopment.

Japan is very homogeneous in terms of ethnicity, language, and religion. Ninety-nine percent of the population is ethnically Japanese, and Japanese is the universally used language. All other ethnic groups equal less than 1 percent of the population. The largest non-Japanese ethnic groups are the Koreans, estimated at 511,262, and the Chinese at 244,241.[5] Migration of non-Japanese people into Japan is negligible.

When recommendations are made that the U.S. transplant educational arrangements from Japanese schools, it is important to compare and contrast Japan's high degree of ethnic and cultural homogeneity with American racial, ethnic, language, and cultural diversity. While 99 percent of Japanese are of the same ethnic stock, the U.S., with the exception of the Native Americans, is a country of people who came there from other nations—Europe, Asia, and Africa. Japan is a monolingual country; in the U.S., many languages are spoken in addition to English. The differences between a monocultural Japan and a multicultural U.S. have important implications for education.

Shinto and Buddhism, Japan's major religions, are observed by 84 percent of the population. Shinto, which originated as an indigenous religion unique to Japan, is a kind of national religion. Historically, it combined worship of the emperor, as one who is semidivine, with elements of nature worship. Although no longer considered a deity, the emperor remains a highly revered person who, as constitutional monarch, is the head of state. Shinto contributes to the Japanese sense of identity in which individuals feel that they are part of a national family, which, in turn, is responsive to the natural order.[6] Originating as a reform movement in India, Buddhism was introduced into China and than transported to Japan. These two religions have a long history in Japan where traditions and rituals from Buddhism have become intertwined with Shinto. Many Japanese observe both religions and simultaneously follow their traditions and rites. There are also Christians and other smaller religious groups. Christianity was introduced by Europeans and Americans in the nineteenth century. However, less than 1 percent of Japanese are Christians. Unlike Mexico, France, and the U.S., where religion has affected church–state relationships, the role of religion is not a point of conflict in Japanese politics and education.

Rather than religion, the philosophy of Confucius exerts a powerful influence on Japanese culture and education. Confucianism, like Buddhism, was introduced from China (see chapter 16) and is more of a philosophical or an ethical system than a religion. Of significance in Japanese culture and religion are the following ethical principles of Confucius: (1) the importance of maintaining harmony in family, personal, and work relationships by minimizing conflicts; and (2) the need to maintain and respect rankings in social and work relationships. These principles infuse Japanese values, which are learned first at home in the family, are reinforced by the schools, and are observed in the work place. Respect for one's parents is transferred into respect for one's teachers, which, in turn, becomes respect for one's supervisor on the job.

Confucianism's importance in the Japanese collective psyche and consciousness lies in the emphasis that it gives to the group over the individual. The authority of the group takes priority over the desires of the individual. Indeed, the individual is expected to behave in a way that does not jeopardize other people's needs.[7] The pervasive values and preferred behaviors generated by Confucianism have a strong influence on the milieu of Japanese schools.

Political Context

Japan's government is based on the constitution adopted in 1946 during the post–World War II Allied occupation. Article 1 of the constitution transformed the emperor's position from the living embodiment of the Japanese nation to a constitutional monarch.[8] Inheritance to Japan's throne is hereditary. Rejecting Japan's militaristic past, the constitution renounces war as an instrument in settling international disputes.

Like the government structure in the U.S., Japan's government consists of three branches—executive, legislative, and judicial. However, Japan's parliamentary government resembles European political systems, such as the British, rather than the American Congress. The Diet, a bicameral legislature, is Japan's supreme parliamentary body.

Legislative Branch

The Diet is composed of two houses: the House of Representatives with 511 members and the House of Councilors with 252 members.[9] Members of the House of Representatives are elected for four-year terms or less if the Diet is dissolved. Members of the House of Councilors serve six-year terms, with one-third elected every three years. Enactment of a law requires passing both houses. However, the House of Representatives holds the most important prerogatives. In approving the budget and treaties, the vote of the House of Representatives carries in situations where the two houses differ or when the House of Councilors fails to act within thirty days of receiving a bill from the House of Representatives. The prime minister, who holds executive power, is also a member of the Diet. Like the prime minister in the House of Commons in the UK, the Japanese prime minister, who is selected by the members of the Diet, leads the party or coalition of parties holding the majority of seats in the House of Representatives.

Executive Branch

As the leader of the majority party or coalition of parties, the prime minister is effectively the government's chief executive. Like the British prime minister, he reports to the Diet on the government's program, submits bills, conducts foreign relations, and supervises the government's administrative branches. Unlike the U.S. president who is elected to fixed four-year terms, the prime minister's tenure in office depends on his ability to command a majority of votes in the Diet. Should he lose his majority on a confidence vote, he may either resign or call new elections. When the prime minister is forced to resign because of a no confidence vote, the Diet selects a new prime minister who can muster a majority vote. If the prime minister chooses, he can dissolve the Diet and call for new elections. However, as soon a new house is elected, he and his cabinet must resign. If his party has won a majority, he is likely to become prime minister again.

The cabinet, the executive branch, consists of the prime minister as its head, and twenty ministers of state, appointed by the prime minister. At least half of the cabinet members must be members of the Diet. Of importance to education is the minister of education, culture, sports, science, and technology who is a cabinet member.[10]

Judicial Branch

Japan's legal system is modeled after the European civil law system, with strong influences from the Anglo-American legal tradition. The 1946 Constitution established an independent judicial system consisting of the Supreme Court, eight high courts, a district court in each prefecture, with the exception of Hokkaido which has four, and a number of summary courts. Additionally, family courts adjudicate domestic complaints. The Supreme Court, composed of fifteen members, as Japan's highest court, exercises the power of judicial review. Like the U.S. Supreme Court, it has the power of determining the constitutionality of any law, order, regulation, or official act. Its chief justice is appointed by the prime minister upon designation by the cabinet. The other fourteen justices are appointed by the cabinet. Lower court judges are appointed for ten-year renewable terms by the cabinet from a list nominated by the Supreme Court.

Political Parties

Japan has a multiparty system. The major party that has generally controlled the government since World War II is the Liberal Democratic Party. Although in the 1990s it lost several elections to a coalition of opposition parties, it has regained control. The Liberal Democratic Party, a pro-business and free enterprise party, tends to promote conservative social and economic policies. Other parties are the Democratic Party of Japan, Japan New Komeito Party, Social Democratic Party, Japanese Communist Party, and New Conservative Party. The Komeito Party was originally related to a religious faction associated with Buddhism. It advocates humanitarian socialism and neutrality in foreign affairs. The Social Democratic Party was organized by right-wing defectors from the Socialist Party, which sought to create a planned social welfare state and a more equitable economy.

In the 1990s, Japanese politics changed as other parties were able to mount successful challenges against the Liberal Democratic Party. Mounting economic pressures, generated by the uncertainty of the Asian economy, has challenged the political parties to devise new economic policies to regulate Japanese banks and to spur economic growth.

Economic Context

What captured American attention was Japan's dramatic economic revival from being a war-devastated country after its defeat in World War II to becoming a leading world economic power. In 1950, five years after World War II ended, Japan's GNP was only 6 percent of that of the U.S. Forty years later, in 1990, it rose to 75 percent of the U.S. GNP.

Japan's impressive economic growth from devastation to prosperity was facilitated by the following factors: (1) a close working relationship between the national government and business and industrial corporations; (2) a strong cooperative work ethic; and (3) a tendency to quickly adapt technological innovations. In terms of technology, Japan's economy ranks second in the world, being surpassed only by the U.S. The Japanese government takes an active role in the corporate business sector, encouraging and coordinating investment and industrial growth. The Ministry of International Trade and Industry takes a strong role in determining areas of industrial and technological research and development.[11] The working relationship between government and business leaders rests on their shared background and education in that many of them are graduates of Japan's most prestigious university, Tokyo University.

A unique feature in the Japanese economy are the *keiretsu*, alliances of manufacturers, suppliers, and distributors who work together in a particular sector of the economy. The strong cooperative work ethic is constantly reinforced in the home, the school, and the work place. Still another unique feature of the Japanese economy is job security, the guarantee of lifetime employment that most of the workforce enjoys. Whether or not this kind of job security will be maintained in the future, however, is not certain. Despite these strengths, Japan has a major problem of needing to import most of its raw materials, especially minerals and fuels.

Asia's economic crisis in the 1990s caused a serious downturn in Japan's economy that revealed the island-nation's economic fragility and need for restructuring. Despite its economic downturn, Japan remains a major economic global actor. It is one of the world's largest and most technologically advanced producers of motor vehicles, electronic equipment, machine tools, steel, ships, chemicals, and textiles. Japan's "high tech" capability makes it a leading provider of robotics, computers, and optical electronics.[12] By occupation, 70 percent of the workforce is employed in service-related jobs, 25 percent in industry, and 5 percent in agriculture.[13] The agricultural sector is heavily subsidized and protected by the government.

Many foreign observers attribute much of Japan's economic successes to its people's strong work ethic, especially to the high value given to teamwork and cooperation. Japanese society tends to define a person's role according to the degree that he or she is a respected participant in group-centered collaborative efforts. Of particular importance in Japanese culture is *wa*, the value of harmony, which permeates the society and has important implications for the economy, especially for work and occupations.[14] Seeking to minimize conflict and confrontations, wa requires that in work relationships personal conflicts be submerged and resolved for the good of the business corporation. Further, it requires employees to give their loyalty to the corporation, as they did to their families and schools. Of importance to the corporate group—the executives, managers, and workers—is that the product that the company produces be of high quality so that it can be marketed with a good profit. Shoddy products reflect on all those involved in their production; thus, it is crucial that the group work toward efficiency and quality.

Japan's group-based value orientation is constantly rewarded and reinforced by its occupational system that closely calibrates employment with educational attainment. The Japanese emphasize education and school achievement, believing that successful students will merit secure, life-long employment in major corporations. Since individual employees are not expected to leave the company for other jobs, the corporation will spend time and resources on in-house training programs to develop the employees' technical skills.[15] In return, the employee is expected to become a devoted member of the corporate family, giving loyalty to the corporation. Although the traditional value and economic rewards anticipated from education continue to motivate Japanese students, recent downward economic trends, pointing to restructuring and perhaps downsizing, threatens to erode the optimism of the past.

Historical Context

Although historians frequently identify the Meiji restoration of 1868 as the key event in Japan's modernization, an examination of education in the earlier Tokugawa period contributes to understanding the dynamics that transformed an isolated and feudal Japan into a modern nation.[16]

In the tenth century, political power in Japan gravitated to the *samurai*, or *bushi*, a military class, somewhat analogous to medieval Europe's knights. Similar to the knights in European feudalism, the samurai's monopoly over military power gave them control of land ownership and local government. By the twelfth century, the samurai were clearly the dominant class and their military code provided core values for the rest of Japanese society.[17] The social role of the samurai and their chivalric code of *bushido*, which called for such qualities as loyalty, self-sacrifice, justice, honor, and refined manners, left a strong imprint on Japanese culture, especially on its central values.

The Tokugawa Period: 1600–1867

The Tokugawa era was named after Sekigahara Tokugawa, the paramount feudal lord, or *shogun*. The shogun was the strong military overlord who ruled in the name of the emperor, who was a figurehead. During the Tokugawa shogunate, considerable power was delegated by the shogun to local feudal warlords.

While political power was decentralized under the Tokugawa shogunate, the Japanese were an ethnically homogeneous people with a common culture and language. They believed they were a unique and distinctive people. This ethnic "we-feeling" nurtured a strong sense of national identity that would be important in creating a modern nation-state during the Meiji restoration. The concept of a well-run polity, governed by an elite, composed of people of the same ethnicity, culture, and language, facilitated the Meiji program of modernization.[18]

Confucianism, the regnant Chinese philosophy that stressed harmonious social and political relationships and responsibility to higher authority, was engrafted onto the samurai military code of bushido during the Tokugawa period. In China, government officials were recruited from the scholarly elite, but in Japan they came from military warriors. Confucianism's emphasis on the need for social and political hierarchy and harmony and cooperation in society became a core value in Japan.

Based on the amalgamation of Confucianism with bushido, the Tokugawa shoguns developed an educational philosophy that embraced both learning the Confucian classics as well as training in military skills. The sho-

guns institutionalized their educational philosophy by establishing academies—domain schools—to educate young and aspiring samurai. Between
1781 and 1871, an estimated two hundred domain schools were training the
sons of the samurai class. While only 2 percent of Japan's population were
samurai, these feudal warriors, administrators, and officials had an influence
that greatly exceeded their small numbers.

While the shoguns gave priority to domain schools that educated the
samurai, they also established and supported schools for commoners. By the
1870s, more than one million Japanese were attending some kind of school.
The schools of the Tokugawa era accustomed the Japanese to accept the idea
that schools were important and needed in a well-regulated society. The
Tokugawa school infrastructure would be used as the foundation for the
Meiji modernizers' educational program.

By the 1840s, the shogunate's power weakened as it faced increasing internal political and social unrest aggravated by economic problems and growing
pressure from Western nations. The newly emergent Japanese business class,
resisting the Tokugawa regime's cumbersome feudal barriers to trade, wanted a
more modern political structure. Western nations, eager for Japanese markets,
were pressing the shogunate to open the country to Western trade. The
Tokugawa era ended when the last shogun, the Lord of Mito, voluntarily surrendered his power to the Meiji emperor in 1867. With the emperor now fully
restored to paramount power, the key role in shaping Japan's future was exercised by a group of young samurai, mainly from western Japan, who supported
the Meiji restoration. Japan embarked on its path to rapid modernization.

The Meiji Period: 1868–1912

By 1868, the young emperor, Meiji, and his modernizing elite were
firmly in control of Japan. Inheriting the Tokugawa shogunate's governmental and educational institutions, they proceeded to modernize these institutions to make them function more efficiently. Recognizing that a modern
Japan required a literate and orderly population, a technically skilled workforce, and a Western-trained army and navy, they gave education a high priority in their strategy for national modernization. Imperial Japanese officials,
astutely orchestrating the modernizing efforts, carefully integrated core values of Japan's Shinto-Confucianist tradition with models borrowed selectively from Western Europe and the U.S. Several critical factors advanced
Japan's successful efforts to construct a modern national system of education.
With the exception of a few very small minorities, Japan's highly homogeneous population, unlike the geographically vast Chinese empire with its different languages and dialects, spoke a common language. Unlike the Chinese,
the Japanese tended to welcome rather than resist technological change.

The Meiji modernizers inherited an educational infrastructure of primary schools, or *terakoya*, and elite training schools, the shogunal clan
schools, from the Tokugawa shogunate. Although these separate schools edu-

cated distinct classes, they provided an institutional base upon which the modernizers could build. The terakoya, originally founded by Buddhists, were already providing basic education to commoner children in reading, writing, arithmetic, and moral training.[19] It is estimated that 14,000 terakoya, enrolling approximately 900,000 Japanese students, were functioning when the Meiji emperor was restored to power in 1868.[20]

The Meiji modernizers faced a daunting challenge to their vision of a modern Japan. Their task was to reconstruct 280 feudal domains into a new nation-state. They determined to achieve this by eliminating feudalism's divisive encumbrances and to revivify the inherited Shinto-Confucianist core of values as an ideology that would stimulate national patriotism. In 1871, the Meiji government officially abolished feudalism. It then ended the reliance on the feudal armies by creating a new national army that would be staffed by military service conscription. They used Shinto as a moral religious force that could be used to transfer loyalties from feudal lords to the emperor, proclaimed as divine living embodiment of the nation. The samurai, unlike China's mandarin scholar-officials, accommodated themselves to these changes. While they retained their ethical code, they moved into other areas of Japanese life and came to play a role in modernizing Japan.[21]

Like the French revolutionaries, the Meiji modernizers believed that they needed a national centralized school system to build their new vision of Japan.[22] However, linking modernization and education required an initial reconstruction of the inherited Japanese educational philosophy that, as indicated earlier, blended Confucianism with bushido, the indigenous warrior code. Confucianism, more of an ethical than metaphysical philosophy, on its face resisted change. It accentuated respect for the past, for traditional values, and for the established system; obedience to authority; and loyalty to hierarchical superiors. Confucianist-inspired schooling featured learning the Confucian classics and inculcating traditional values.

Upon analysis Meiji modernizers realized that certain Confucian subtleties could be enlisted to support the Meiji nation-building program. The value of filial piety, essential to Confucianism, could be reconstructed into a dynamic loyalty to the emperor.[23] Traditional hierarchies could be recast into a structured efficient administrative chain of command that could move the nation forward with rapidity. Unlike imperial China's Mandarin scholars who generally resisted Western knowledge, Japan's emerging educational leadership was open to it. They were willing to put the Confucian classics temporarily on the shelf while they imported Western science. Then, they would return to the traditional Confucianist wisdom and the military code of bushido as a moral code that would implement technological change within the Japanese cultural context.

Selective Educational Borrowing

Like imperial China, Japan was threatened by imperialist European powers seeking to establish colonies or economic enclaves and spheres of influence in Asia. Determined to preserve their country's sovereign integrity, the Meiji leaders followed a policy of defensive modernization but with greater success than the Chinese. The Japanese defensive modernization strategy encompassed three related emphases: (1) preserving the nucleus of Japanese ethical values, derived from Confucianism and bushido, as the essential cultural core of national identity; (2) selectively borrowing Western scientific and technical knowledge and processes to modernize the nation; and (3) grafting the new knowledge on the trunk of inherited Japanese core values.[24] Thus, Japan embarked on a strategy of selective borrowing and adaptation of Western science and technology that would be confined within a purely Japanese value core.

The Meiji emperor's Charter Oath, in April 1868, affirmed that knowledge would be "sought all over the world in order to establish firmly the foundations of the Empire."[25] The highly adaptable but equally selective Meiji modernizers sought to identify foreign models to import and graft on to Japan's traditional culture and values. Teams of Japanese educators visited Europe and the U.S. searching for acceptable educational models to import to their own country. In addition, foreign educational advisers were invited to Japan from Germany, France, the UK, and the U.S. to advise the government on educational policy.

One of these missions, led by Prince Tomomi Iwakura, came to the U.S. in 1872. The U.S. Commissioner of Education briefed the Japanese team on the American system of education, presented them with a collection of educational reports and documents, and arranged a program of school visits. Concurrent with the Iwakura Mission, Arinori Mori, the Japanese Charge d'Affaires in Washington, approached leading American educators for advice on Japan's projected educational development. Pragmatically, the American educators encouraged Japan to end its isolation and participate in the world economy. Following the land grant approach, they counseled the Japanese educational planners to develop institutions for applied scientific and technological education to improve Japan's agriculture and industry.[26]

In 1873, Fujimaro Tanaka, once part of Iwakura's delegation to the U.S., became Japan's vice minister of education. He engaged David Murray, a Rutgers University professor of mathematics, as his chief advisor. Murray, while supporting modernization, cautioned the Japanese to fit educational imports from the West into their own cultural context.[27] Murray recommended that Japan: (1) establish normal schools to prepare Japanese teachers in what were then the new Pestalozzian and Herbartian methods; and (2) import, translate, and print in Japanese, books on Western science, technology, and education. Based on Tanaka's and Murray's efforts, Japanese education began its process of what Murray called "naturalization." Classrooms were outfitted with Western-style desks, blackboards, and wall maps. Students read translations of Western textbooks instead of memorizing Confucius's *Analects*. The Japanese language, too, was standardized according to the Tokyo dialect. Despite these achievements, Tanaka's and Murray's attempt to create local school boards, on the U.S. model, failed. Local control of education was at cross-purposes to the Meiji modernizers' design for a nationally centralized system.

Constructing Japan's Modern Educational System

The construction of Japan's educational system and institutions began with the Meiji Fundamental Code of Education in 1872, which projected a highly centralized national system. Designed by Shimpei Eto, the code announced a very ambitious plan modeled on the educational systems of the Western nations, especially France and the U.S. The implementation of the code followed the modernizers' strategy of borrowing elements from several foreign countries rather than from just one. To eradicate remnants of feudal localism and to focus authority directly with the central national government, the Japanese took the idea of a highly centralized national authority from France and used it to construct their own centralized educational administration. Top-level administrative decision makers in the national Ministry of Education were given top-down authority over educational and cultural affairs. This kind of authority also resonated nicely with the Confucianist emphasis on order and rank.

Eto's plan called for universal education based on a pyramid-like school system. The country was divided into eight collegiate divisions, similar to the French *académies*, each of which was to have a university. Each collegiate division was subdivided into thirty-two middle school districts, and at the local level, each middle school district was to be further subdivided into 210 primary school districts. Overall, there would be eight universities, 256 middle schools, and 53,760 primary schools.[28] The primary schools, modeled after the American common school, formed the pyramid's base and were to provide compulsory elementary education for children from ages six to fourteen. The middle schools, at the pyramid's center, were to prepare selected students for university admission. At the educational pyramid's summit were the universities, modeled on the German research institution. In this instance, the plan revealed carefully selected educational borrowing from the French, German, and American models.

Like the French pattern of school and teacher inspection, the Japanese plan set up regional school inspection bureaus under the national ministry's direct jurisdiction. Under the regional bureaus' control were local school district supervisors. With the exception of the primary schools, the proposed system of school inspection gave control to the central Ministry of Education much like the situation in France. This contrasted with the U.S. model where the federal government, at the time, exercised no supervisory authority over elementary and secondary schools.

When it began to implement the Fundamental Code, the Japanese government found that the funds needed for building construction and professional staffing exceeded available financial resources. The Japanese educational officials still lacked the administrative experience as well as the financial resources to create and maintain the complete system of educational institutions envisioned by the modernizers. Although the plan could not be fully implemented, it provided the blueprint for the coming modern school system. Moving incrementally, Japanese school enrollments increased, and by 1878, 41.3 percent of the school-age population was attending school.[29]

In the 1880's, Japan's educational officials, consolidating their gains, moved in a more nationalist direction. In 1885, Arinori Mori was named Minister of Education in Count Herobumi Ito's cabinet. Militaristically inclined policy makers such as Ito and Mori believed the Japanese state and education should embody its own samurai and Shinto nationalistic and military heritage.[30] Mori was guided by his own principle that, "In the administration of all schools, it must be kept in mind, what is done is not for the sake of the pupils, but for the sake of the country." According to the "three pillars" of Mori's philosophy, education was to: (1) develop national power; (2) enlighten the general population; and (3) keep Japan free of foreign domination.[31]

Ito and Mori wanted to recast Japan's modernization along imperial Germany's Prussian lines rather than in the style of Western liberal democracy. The Japanese believed their situation was like that of imperial Germany, which had gained great-power status rather late in the game. Germany's example appealed to the Japanese policy makers who believed that Japan, like Germany, had to "catch up" to the other great powers, especially France, the UK, and the U.S.

Adapting Germany's policy of national centralization was one step that Japan took on its road to great-power status. The School Ordinances of 1886, promulgated by Mori, continued the process of educational system building. These ordinances provided for a uniform, standardized school system under the centralized authority of the national Ministry of Education and for four years of compulsory primary schooling. The authority of the Ministry of Education was continuously expanded as it developed a complete series of standardized textbooks in all school subjects and reviewed and approved all syllabi. Books were scrutinized to remove "material dangerous to the national peace or injurious to public morals."[32] Mori's policies continued the modernizing strategy that sought to make Japan a modern nation without succumbing to Western cultural values. Certain aspects of Confucianism and bushido resurfaced to fortify Japanese core values without jeopardizing modernization. Moral education stressing Confucian duties and responsibilities and military drill, conducted by army officers, was introduced into the schools.

At the same time that German statist concepts were influencing Japan's political and educational policy makers, German educational methods also had a pronounced impact on instruction in schools. Japanese scholars were sent to study at German universities and German educators, in turn, were called upon to advise Japanese educators. It should be noted that many American scholars, too, earned advanced degrees in German universities.

Japanese educators were attracted to the educational philosophy and method developed by the German realist educator, Johann Friedrich Herbart. Herbartianism was also very popular in the U.S. where it dominated instruction until the early twentieth century. The Japanese were very attracted to Herbart's emphasis on a carefully structured sequence of steps by which teachers instructed their pupils. Further, Herbart's emphasis on moral education nicely conformed to Mori's educational goals. The traditional Confucian moral virtues of filial piety, obedience to paternalistic authority, the practice of social civility, and fidelity to tradition could be reconstructed to accommodate Herbart's accentuation of the values of sincerity, integrity, will, justice, and reward.[33]

In 1890, an Imperial Rescript on Education announced an educational ideology that integrated the Shinto emphasis on the emperor's divinity with the Confucian ethical concepts of loyalty, filial piety, and obedience to superiors. Reinforcing the impetus of nationalism, educational goals affirmed loyalty to the emperor and nation. Importantly, Japanese nationalism did not resist Western technology but used it to fortify Japanese values.

Kowashi Inouye, who succeeded Mori as the Minister of Education in 1893, emphasized the role of vocational education and industrial training to prepare a highly trained workforce. Again, Japan's development of vocational training schools paralleled similar efforts in Germany and the U.S. The Japanese established vocational training institutes, agricultural schools, industrial schools, and commercial schools as well as supplementary vocational and apprenticeship schools.[34] Following French and American patterns, Japan established normal schools to prepare primary school teachers. Their curriculum was prescribed by the Ministry of Education. Those seeking admission to normal schools needed to be recommended by the head of the regional administrative unit. Normal school students received state financial support and upon graduation were required to take specific teaching assignments. Imperial universities provided specialization in law, medicine, literature, engineering, and agriculture. They emphasized research and professional training, especially in science and technology, for the needs of the modernizing nation. Samurai nobility no longer dominated higher education as more children of landowners and businessmen attended universities.

By 1903, 90 percent of the primary school-age group were in attendance. In 1907, the government required six (instead of four) years of compulsory primary school attendance.[35] A crucial element in the success of plans to use schooling for national development depends upon the extent to which education is available and attendance enforced. Frequently, developing nations have made rhetorical commitments to universal education but have not enforced attendance. Japan's pattern, however, unlike China and India, not only made primary schooling accessible but enforced compulsory attendance. While primary schooling in Japan was becoming a mass system, middle schools and higher education remained selective. Unlike the American "ladder" concept, the Japanese adhered to European dual track system.

The Imperialist Period: 1912–1945

Changes were taking place within Japan and with its place in the world. By the 1920s, Japan, an emerging industrial and military power, had developed both light industries such as textiles and heavy industries such as machine and chemical manufacturing. However, the island-empire still lacked the raw materials needed for mass industrial production. Modeling European colonialism, government officials, military leaders, and some industrialists urged an expansionist policy in Asia, especially against China.

As Japan experienced an economic cycle of industrialization, it faced the issue of redefining the goals of secondary education.[36] How a nation defines its secondary education purposes relates to its ideology and plans of economic development. For example, the United States, by the 1920s, already had established and consolidated comprehensive high schools that encouraged upward educational mobility from elementary schools to colleges and universities. In contrast, European nations, such as Germany and France, established a range of specialized secondary options and institutions; some secondary schools prepared students for higher education and other secondary schools offered terminal programs leading to semiprofessional occupations, the trades, and other fields directly connected to the economy. The Japanese developed their newer secondary options in vocational education while their middle schools continued to perform the university-preparatory academic function.

From 1930 to 1945, Japanese education, like Japan itself, was extremely nationalistic and militaristic. For Japan to achieve a much-deserved great-power status, military leaders argued Japan would need to begin a campaign of territorial expansion, even if it meant war. The Japanese military and their industrial allies saw Asia as the sphere of Japan's projected empire. In 1931, Japan conquered China's large province of Manchuria, where they established a puppet regime under China's last emperor Pu Yi. When the League of Nations condemned and imposed economic sanctions on Japan, it withdrew from the league. In 1937, Japan joined Nazi Germany and Fascist Italy in the Anti-Comintern Pact, directed against the Soviet Union. In 1941, the Japanese attacked Pearl Harbor, bringing the U.S. into World War II. Japanese military forces defeated American and Philippine armies in the Philippines, the British in Malaya, and the Dutch in the East Indies. By late 1943, the fortunes of war began to turn against the Japanese who were decisively defeated and surrendered in 1945 after two devastating atomic bombings, with great loss of life, on the cities of Nagasaki and Hiroshima.

When Japan was ruled by the promilitary faction from 1930 through 1945, educational policy stressed maximum central control. In 1937, the Ministry of Education, designating primary schools as national schools, dedicated them to basic skills and training in conformity to the principles of the Japanese empire.[37] Schools also experienced some structural changes. Two more years were added to compulsory primary schooling for a total of eight years.

Five years of compulsory part-time postprimary education was required for those who had completed primary schooling. A national Science and Technology Council, advising the government on policy in areas vital to the war effort, emphasized science, technology, and engineering in the universities.

Postwar Reconstruction

On August 15, 1945, Japan surrendered unconditionally to the Allies. Unlike Germany, which was occupied by the British, French, Soviets, and Americans, Japan's occupation, while theoretically an Allied undertaking, essentially was controlled by the U.S. armed forces. The principal figure in Japan's post–World War II reconstruction was General Douglas MacArthur, supreme commander of Allied forces in the Pacific. MacArthur inaugurated a policy of pervasive democratization in Japan that included the right of workers to organize and full civil rights for women. The emperor, Hirohito, was retained as head of state but was relegated to the position of a constitutional monarch rather than a divine figure.

During the U.S. occupation, MacArthur began significant educational reforms. As in defeated Germany, the occupation authorities sought to eliminate militarism and extreme nationalism from the schools, the curriculum, and the textbooks. Administrators and teachers suspected of harboring military and nationalist ideological views were dismissed. Textbooks were reviewed and revised to eliminate their nationalist orientation. Instruction in Japanese history, geography, and ethics was suspended until more democratically oriented curricular materials were prepared. The emphasis on Shinto, the state religion featuring worship of the emperor, was removed from the schools.[38]

In 1946, MacArthur invited a U.S. education mission to Japan to advise occupation authorities on how to proceed with the democratic reconstruction of education. The mission, headed by Dr. George Stoddard, included the respected educators George S. Counts and Isaac Kandel. The commission's recommendations included: curriculum revision, underscoring democratic principles and values; administrative and organizational decentralization to provide for local control of schools; establishing an institutional educational ladder, like the American pattern, to encourage socioeconomic mobility; provision of more individualized instruction and counseling services to students; and simplifying the Japanese language by using roman letters rather than Japanese script.

The mission's recommendations for democratization, decentralization, and establishment of articulated educational institutions were embodied in the Fundamental Law of Education in 1947. The recommendation for changing the Japanese language was disregarded, however. The Fundamental Law created a twelve-year elementary and secondary school system modeled on the American pattern. At the base of the system were six-year primary schools, followed by three-year lower secondary schools and three-year upper secondary schools. Education was compulsory for the first nine years of primary and lower secondary schooling. As in the U.S., Japanese higher education was reorganized into two-year junior colleges and four-year universities.

Further resembling the U.S. pattern, the Education Law of 1948 decentralized school administration and limited the powers of the Ministry of Education to issuing very general guidelines rather than the specific requirements and mandated syllabi of the past.[39] A radical innovation for Japan was that elected local commissions, like American school boards, were to operate schools, hire teachers and administrators, and select textbooks. The American pattern of local control, however, was incongruous with Japan's historical and political pattern of centralized national educational control. After the American military occupation ended, Japan abandoned decentralization and reasserted its traditional centralized pattern of education.

Since 1950, Japanese education has experienced significant change, development, and growth. Among the significant changes were the establishment of new colleges and universities, the appearance and growth of *jukus* (schools that prepare students for examinations or provide enrichment classes), greater upward social mobility via education, and the general expansion of schools at all levels.[40]

Schooling and Society

Modern Japan is often cited as a nation that makes education a national priority. The terms *gakureki shakai*, or "educational path society," and *kogakureki shakai*, "a society of long educational routes," portrays Japan's respect for and commitment to education.[41]

Conditioned by its historical and social foundations, Japanese education calibrated with the national values of social cohesiveness and harmony. These values generate clearly defined predispositions and beliefs that govern personal behavior and socioeconomic expectations. Along with social cohesiveness, the school system, controlled by the Ministry of Education, reinforces national uniformity and standardization in administration, organization, curriculum, and standards.

Unlike continuing debates about the purposes of education in the U.S., the Japanese have a clear understanding about the expectations they have for schools and of the role of schools in their society. For them, the school is an academic, rather than a multifunctional, institution that prepares students in basic skills and transmits the basic subjects considered necessary for the country's economic and social well-being. Japanese schools reinforce conformity to approved collaborative group behavior. Because of this comprehensive societal consensus, schools and teachers can be clear about what conforms to and what violates acceptable behavior. Further, these behaviors build upon and reinforce the values of the home and family, which, in turn, mirror the larger society and economy.

When a child is born, Japanese parents plan and save for her or his education. The family, especially the mother, is devoted to encouraging, supporting, and sustaining their children's educational efforts and feels responsible for their children's preparation and success in school. Mothers instill the basic values of harmony and cooperation in group life and in society. Mothers are careful to avoid confrontations with children who, in turn, are conditioned to refrain from creating embarrassing situations that cause discomfort for others. Mothers emphasize readiness for school, especially completing one activity or task at a time.[42] The role of the Japanese mother can be contrasted with recent American trends. The Japanese woman's role as wife and mother is rather rigidly ascribed with little ambiguity regarding her life choices. In the U.S., women have achieved greater independence and freedom of choice in their social and career roles. Approximately 50 percent of American women with children under age seventeen work full-time. Japanese children begin schooling with a more predictable predisposition to schooling than American children, whose early childhood experiences are more varied due to American cultural pluralism.

Governance and Administration of Education

The contemporary Japanese educational system is again highly centralized. The Ministry of Education, the *Mombusho*, is the national agency responsible for education at all levels, overseeing the administration of government services for education, science, culture, sports, technology, and religious affairs. The minister of education, who heads the Mombusho, is a member of the prime minister's cabinet. Among the Mombusho's administrative subagencies are the Department of Facilities, the Elementary and Secondary Education Bureau, the Higher Education Bureau, the Private School Department, the Science and International Affairs Bureau, the Social Education Bureau, the Physical Education Bureau, and the Agency for Cultural Affairs.

Like Japanese society, Japan's educational system is a hierarchical structure in which the Mombusho develops and enforces national policies, including countrywide curriculum, to be implemented locally at the prefectural (Japan is divided into forty-seven prefectures) and municipal levels.[43] Each local government unit has a board of education whose function is to ensure that national policies are implemented. The Mombusho's inauguration of policies moves slowly, as most of the officials of the Mombusho are civil servants who tend to resist sweeping changes. The Japan Teachers' Union (JTU) is a large and highly proactive organization. Its reaction to government initiatives and policy represents an important check on major changes.

Another important feature of Japan's centralization of education relates to school financing. The Mombusho, like the French Nation Education Ministry, provides relatively equal funding for Japanese schools, regardless of their location. As a result, there is uniformity in facilities, supplies, and the quality and experience of the teaching staff throughout the country. In contrast, in the U.S., school facilities, supplies, and the quality and experience of the teaching staff differs significantly from state to state and from local district to local district. This means that the school experiences of Japanese students are nationally uniform but equitable. In the U.S., the school experiences are uneven and inequitable because of differences in funding and in other matters at the state and local levels.

Japan's Mombusho works collaboratively with business and industry in economic planning. Many of the leaders in the government and the major corporations are graduates of the prestigious Tokyo University and form a network of policy makers with similar backgrounds and economic orientations. As a result of this business–school alliance, the Mombusho has emphasized scientific and technological education. The partnership between business, industry, and education is a cornerstone of Japanese educational policy. Recent educational policies in the U.S. and the UK have encouraged similar educational and business cooperation.

The Mombusho, in consultation with a Curriculum Council of Professional Educators, prepares the national Course of Study used at each level of the school system: elementary, lower secondary, and upper secondary.[44] This highly prescribed curriculum details the scope and sequence for each subject and level of schooling. Unlike the local curricular variations in the U.S., the Japanese system sets the stage for uniform national educational outcomes.

Another feature of centralization relates to textbooks. The Mombusho reviews and approves the textbooks that will be used in the schools, ensuring uniformity in curriculum and educational standards. In the U.S., the process is much more diffuse and decentralized in that the states and local school districts rather than the national government approve textbooks.[45] Although commercial publishers in both countries produce and sell textbooks, the Japanese publishers follow a specific set of national standards. In contrast, U.S. textbook publishers need to accommodate their products to variations in school organization and curriculum from state to state and from district to district within a particular state.

Brief by American standards, Japanese textbooks provide a specific and succinct format that facilitates the memorization and retention of information that is useful in passing examinations.[46] In contrast, a typical American textbook is much larger than a Japanese text, often containing three or four times the number of pages. While the Japanese prefer a structured presentation of essential information about a subject, American publishers are concerned with expanding the content to meet what they call the "knowledge explosion." Market-driven American textbooks compete with each other in rushing to include the latest developments and methods of teaching and strive to make interdisciplinary connections between subjects.

While some American teachers follow textbooks closely in instruction, many do not. Teachers may use chapters selectively or supplement the textbooks with their own self-prepared materials. American teacher education programs frequently encourage critical thinking in which students use constructivist, discovery, or inquiry methods and problem solving to create their own knowledge base rather than rely on predetermined textbook conclusions. However, the more important that national tests become in the U.S., the less likely it will be that teachers will be free to be so experimental in using classroom materials.

A controversy over Japanese history textbooks erupted in 2005 in Asia as demonstrators in China and South Korea protested a new series of books that downplayed Japanese aggression and atrocities during World War II. The new texts were prepared by the Society for History Textbook Reform, a group of nationalistic academics, who want to instill national pride in Japanese secondary students. The protests in China were provoked when Japan's Ministry of Education authorized new textbooks that the Chinese claimed whitewashed Japan's invasion of China (1931–1945). The most contentious text removes references to the Japanese army's forced use of "comfort women" and to the Nanking massacre in which 300,000 Chinese casualties occurred, and suggests that Korea invited the Japanese occupation.[47]

Organization and Structure of Schools

School attendance is compulsory from ages six through fifteen, the years of elementary and lower secondary schooling. Over 99 percent of the respective age group attends school. The lower secondary school is organizationally similar to the U.S. junior high school.[48] Students generally attend the schools nearest their home.

Preschools

Approximately, 2,500,000 children, about 75 percent of the preschool age cohort (ages three to five), attend the 15,000 preschools, either nursery schools, *yochien*, or day schools, *hoikuen*. As is in other countries, most preschool teachers (96 percent in Japan) are women. Although the Japanese are heavily preoccupied with long-term academic success, the generally play-oriented preschool program reinforces the mother's efforts in developing cooperative attitudes and readiness skills such as listening, speaking, concentrating on tasks, and being a worthy group member.[49]

Elementary Schools

Japanese children begin elementary school at age six and complete it by age twelve, after which they attend the three-year lower secondary school. The elementary school curriculum consists of Japanese language arts and literature, which receive heavy emphasis, social studies, arithmetic, science, music, drawing and handicrafts, homemaking, physical education, moral education, and special activities. There are many field trips and excursions of an enrichment nature during the school year.[50]

Because of the complexity of the Japanese script, language instruction dominates the elementary school curriculum. Each year, children learn by rote a prescribed number of *kanji*, the Chinese characters upon which written Japanese is based. By the end of the six years of elementary school, children are expected to know one thousand characters.[51] Japanese schools place emphasis on mathematics and science, which, according to the national curriculum, are to receive 25 percent of in-class instructional time. In these areas, Japanese children learn complicated skills and concepts at an earlier age than do children in the U.S. For example, Japanese elementary students are taught such mathematical concepts as correspondence of geometrical figures, statistics, and probability that for American students are reserved for high school and college.[52]

The school year in Japan consists of three terms: from April first through July first, from September first through December first, and from January first through March first. The school year is 240 days compared with 180 in the U.S. The school week is five seven-hour days and a half-day on Saturday.[53] Japanese students also spend much more time on homework and out-of-school educational activities than American students.

The typical Japanese school building has been described as a pleasant but plain two- or three-storied concrete, L- or U-shaped structure. In elementary schools the furniture is not fixed and can be moved to accommodate varied classroom activities. In secondary schools, the rows of desks are arranged in conventional fashion, side by side.[54]

Average class size in Japanese schools, forty-two students per teacher, is higher than in the U.S. Because of the large class size and the emphasis on group behavior, individual differences between children are not accentuated as much as in U.S. schools. Children, considered as having equal potential, are not classified or grouped in elementary school according to their academic ability. All students are expected to keep up with their class as a whole and are generally promoted with their age group.[55] Assignments are directed to the group, and children learn that completing them on time and following directions reflect on the group as a whole.

The importance of functioning as a harmonious team member is reinforced in school milieu as necessary to being an effective and worthy member of adult and business communities. Teachers accentuate the importance of the individual being a committed and loyal member of the class. They reiterate the Confucianist ethical value of fulfilling one's responsibility to the other members of the class and the to school. They impress upon students that their in- and out-of-school behavior reflects on the school and on their families as well. Since students have a stake in maintaining the reputation of their class and school, they are given a role that makes them stakeholders in some well-defined areas of school life, such as planning field trips and excursions. They also are responsible for keeping their school clean, maintaining equipment, and taking care of books and supplies.[56]

Certain features identified as contributing to Japan's educational success are also perceived as possible deficits for the future. The pervasive tendency to emphasize the same level and type of instruction for all children rather than to consider individual needs and differences inhibits divergent and creative thinking. Japanese teaching methods, which become examination-driven in the upper grades, emphasize memorization of facts rather than critical thinking and problem solving. Whether the group-centered, other-directed behavior that Japan's schools prize will be adequate for future challenges is an open question, particularly in a nation that shows increasing need of political and economic restructuring.

Secondary Schools

Secondary education in Japan is divided into the three-year lower secondary school, equivalent organizationally to the American junior high school, and the three-year upper secondary school, similar to the American senior high school. While attendance at the lower secondary school is compulsory, attendance at the upper secondary school is not. At the present time, attendance at and completion of secondary school is virtually universal for both males and females. The dropout, or noncompletion, rate among secondary students in Japan is very low. Ninety-seven percent of students between the ages of fifteen and eighteen enroll in upper secondary schools and 94 percent complete it. Nearly 40 percent of the graduates continue to junior colleges or universities.[57] To accommodate the growing secondary school enrollments, the number of private as well as public institutions has increased.[58] Although the increase in secondary schools has promoted upward socioeconomic mobility, it has also spawned differentiation, with certain institutions serving specific groups of students.

The lower secondary school curriculum consists of Japanese language studies, social studies, mathematics, science, music, the arts, health and physical education, industrial arts and homemaking, moral education, elective subjects, and special activities.[59] Japanese secondary schools begin foreign language instruction in seventh grade and continue it through the six years of secondary education. About 10 percent of instructional time is devoted to foreign language learning. Students can choose the foreign language they wish to study, and English is a very popular choice. The Japanese emphasis on continuous study in one foreign language is similar to that of European schools. In contrast, foreign language study in the U.S. continues to be a neglected subject, despite frequent recommendations that it receive greater emphasis.[60] Japanese secondary students, like elementary students, spend much more time on homework, attending juku classes, and participating in out-of-school educational activities than American students do. The more academically able Japanese students select the schools that will give them a better chance at success on the national Joint Achievement Test required for entry to colleges and universities.

The political, social, and economic principles and expectations of a nation are generally revealed by the way that the particular country organizes its secondary schools. In a country that is committed to an egalitarian social philosophy, such as the U.S., secondary schools offer all adolescent members of the population the chance to participate in the educational experience with an equal opportunity for socioeconomic mobility. In nations that seek to arrange their population into some kind of hierarchical pattern, secondary schools are ranked, and only a select group of students can attend the higher ranked upper secondary schools. Rankings are based on the schools' ability to get their graduates into prestigious universities that are also hierarchically ranked. In Japan, generally the public schools have a higher status than the private ones, which are considered to be a second choice for students. Teachers, students, parents, and the general public are well aware of how the schools in their district are ranked.

Although some Japanese upper secondary schools consider students' academic performance and teacher evaluations, the crucial element in student selection is the entrance examination that is given in the last year of lower secondary school. The highest scoring students win entry into the highly ranked secondary schools and universities. If students fail to score high enough on the examination to secure admission to the upper secondary school of their choice, they cannot then take the examination for another public upper secondary school. Instead, they are limited to applying to a public vocational school or to a less-prestigious private secondary school, deflating their chances of admission to a highly ranked university and ultimately their chances for status, prestige, and power in their adult life.[61] The idea that these kinds of rankings create an elitist society is not given much credence in Japan. According to Japanese opinion, every student has the same opportunity to study and to take the examinations, and a high score on the examination boils down to the individual's resourcefulness and determination.

In contrast to the Japanese-style transition from lower secondary school, or middle school, to upper secondary school, or high school, based on ranking students academically, the transition from middle school to high school in the U.S. is automatic. Indeed, middle school is often seen as a time of personal development and exploration rather than as an intense academic experience that significantly impacts their adult life.

At the upper secondary level, Japanese students once again face intense pressure as they prepare for the Joint Achievement Test that determines entry to state colleges and universities. The Joint Achievement Test, administered annually each January, is a nine-hour battery of examinations consisting of multiple-choice questions. Those who score high enough on these texts win the right to take the two-day entrance examinations developed and administered by the university to which they seek admission. Each department in a university sets the standards and determines the acceptable score for study in the department. Those who fail the Joint Achievement Test will have to study for another year to try to pass it. Some may even have to try for a third time.

Those who have attempted but failed the examination several times are cast into a large group, called *ronin*, or wandering masterless samurai, who are consigned to an educational limbo.[62] With such examination-based demands, the upper secondary school curriculum is heavily oriented to the examinations. Critics, such as American educator Thomas Rohlen, contend that the Japanese examination system deadens students' "curiosity" and imposes "dated knowledge on students." He states that "with so much riding on examinations" there is a reluctance to make major changes in curricular content. For example, there is often as much as a ten-year delay in introducing new theories and trends since a great deal of time, resources, and energy have been invested in preparing for the examinations that are already set in place.[63] Although these criticisms could spark reform, the examination hurdle appears impervious to change.

Juku

In addition to public and private elementary and secondary schools, private schools, called juku, which students attend after their regular school day, are a huge industry in Japan. Juku refers to for-profit, independently operated tutorial schools that provide intensive drill and "cram" sessions that prepare students for upper secondary and university entrance examinations.[64] These private schools are supplementary to the state schools rather than substitutes for them. Juku is a vital connection in the educational system between instruction at state schools and the powerful demands of the examination system. It is estimated that more than 60 percent of the students enrolled in public schools attend a juku after the regular school day. Juku classes meet from 4:30 to 10:00 PM. Juku may range in size from a small school taught by one teacher to a large business chain that employs thousands of teachers. The average Japanese family may spend 5 percent of its income on tuition for their children's instruction in juku.

Higher Education

In Japan, the prestige of the university from which a person graduates carries a great deal of social, political, and economic status and directly affects one's career possibilities. Most of the key officials in the national government are graduates of Tokyo University, the most prestigious institution of higher education in Japan. It is a public institution that is theoretically open to all Japanese students. However, in reality, it is a highly selective institution in that those who are admitted must score very high on the entrance examinations. This selective aspect makes the institution one that serves an elite group of high testers.

While a great deal of power lies with Tokyo University, Kyoto University, and a few other prestigious institutions, there has been an expansion of higher education that has accompanied the growth of secondary education. There are also a number of newly created national universities and community colleges. At the bottom of the higher education ranking are the private universities, which have rather open admissions policies and standards. Tuition and fees at national universities are relatively low but the examination structure remains the key to admission to higher education.

Since many occupations in Japan remain male-dominated, there are noticeable differentials in the education of women. While women are represented in elementary, lower secondary, and upper secondary schools in proportion to their numbers in the general population, they are underrepresented in colleges and universities. According to a recent survey, only 23.8 percent of students in undergraduate university courses were women, only 13.2 percent of students in graduate courses were women, and less than 4 percent of students enrolled in technical schools were women.[65] The underrepresentation of women in universities, among the highest of industrialized countries, can be attributed to the staying power of traditionally ascribed gender roles in Japanese society and to limited employment prospects in fields, agencies, and business firms that normally employ university graduates.

Conclusion

Despite its very real successes, Japanese education, like Japan's economy and society, faces the difficult problem of transforming its intellectual and social foundations. This problem has two important dimensions, one that relates to core values and one that relates to functional behaviors.

Throughout its history of interacting with and selectively borrowing from Western nations, Japan's policy makers were adamant that a core of indigenous values remains as the stable heart of Japanese education. Some Japanese educators believe that the core of traditional values is eroding because of the introduction of non-Japanese cultural variables. Those who fear value change have called for reforms to increase the amount of moral education received by students in Japanese schools.

The second transformational issue deals with functional behaviors. Japan has succeeded in its policy of reaching and surpassing the economic development of most of the Western nations. Much of this economic success has rested on Japan's ability to develop and improve upon innovations developed elsewhere. It now needs to make an intellectual transformation from being a follower and imitator of Western technology to becoming a leader. Can Japan now create, develop, and apply original innovative ideas?

According to Sheppard Ranbom, a commentator on Japanese education, such an intellectual transformation requires the development of "a strong national capacity for research and innovation" and behaviors such as "originality, diversity, creativity, risk-taking, and inventiveness" that are presently not valued and rewarded in Japanese society and education.[66] These behaviors conflict dramatically with the traditionally prized other-directed behaviors of cooperation, loyalty, obedience, and group conformity.

DISCUSSION QUESTIONS

1. Consider the proposition that it is possible for one nation to borrow educational elements from another. Are their limitations in such educational borrowing?

2. Why has Japanese education attracted the attention of the American public and educators?

3. How did the major periods in Japan's educational history contribute to forming the modern system of schools?

4. Compare and contrast Japanese and Chinese culture and education on the degree to which they have been successful in selectively borrowing and adapting technological and educational models from other countries.

5. Both Japan and the United Kingdom are "island empires." What similarities and differences exist in their cultural contexts and educational patterns?

6. Compare and contrast Japanese and American cultures and education.

7. Is it valid to assert that educational attitudes and school structures have contributed to Japanese economic success?

8. How does Japanese society support and reinforce schooling?

9. How are Japanese society, institutions, and families both a support and a source of pressure on Japanese students?

10. Describe the organizational structures of Japanese education.

11. Analyze the power of university entrance examinations and the "doctrine of preparation" in Japanese society and education.

12. How do the schools and occupations in Japan reinforce each other?

RESEARCH TOPICS

1. Develop a "clippings file" of articles from newspapers and magazines that examine economics and education in Japan.

2. If there are international students from Japan on your campus, invite them to speak about their educational experiences to your class.

3. Prepare a research paper on a selected aspect of education in Japan.

4. If there is a Japanese business firm operating in your community, invite a member of the firm to discuss the Japanese economy.

5. Attend a Japanese motion picture and identify and analyze the attitudes and values depicted in the film.

6. Read a novel by a Japanese author; identify and analyze the attitudes and values conveyed in the narrative.

SUGGESTIONS FOR FURTHER READING

Aso, Makoto and Amano, Ikuo. *Education and Japan's Modernization.* Tokyo: The Japan Times, Ltd., 1983.

Beasley, W. G. *The Japanese Experience: A Short History of Japan.* Berkeley: University of California Press, 1999.

DeCoker, Gary, ed. *National Standards and School Reform in Japan and the United States.* New York: Teachers College Press, 2002.

Dore, Ronald P. and Sako, Mari. *How the Japanese Learn to Work.* London: Routledge, 1989.

Ellington, Lucien. *Education in the Japanese Life-Cycle: Implications for the United States.* Lewiston, NY: E. Mellen Press, 1992.

Feiler, Bruce A. *Learning to Bow: An American Teacher in a Japanese School.* New York: Ticknor & Fields, 1991.

Feinberg, Walter. *Japan and the Pursuit of a New American Identity: Work and Education in a Multicultural Age.* New York and London: Routledge, 1993.

Hanley, Susan B. *Everyday Things in Premodern Japan: The Hidden Legacy of Material Culture.* Berkeley: University of California Press, 1997.

LeTendre, Gerald. ed. *Competitor or Ally: Japan's Role in American National Debates.* New York: Falmer Press, 1999.

Mungazi, Dickson A. *Educational Policy and National Character: Africa, Japan, the United States, and the Soviet Union.* New York: Praeger, 1993.

Ministry of Education, Science, and Culture. *Education in Japan: A Brief Outline.* Tokyo: Ministry of Education, Science, and Culture, 1984.

Peak, Lois. *Learning to Go to School in Japan: The Transition from Home to Preschool Life.* Berkeley: University of California Press, 1991.

Richardson, B. *Japanese Democracy: Power, Coordination and Performance.* New Haven, CT: Yale University Press, 1997.

Rohlen, Thomas P. *Japan's High Schools.* Berkeley: University of California Press, 1983.

Rose, Barbara. *Tsuda Umeko and Women's Education in Japan.* New Haven: Yale University Press, 1992.

Smith, Robert J. *Japanese Society: Tradition, Self and the Social Order.* Cambridge: Cambridge University Press, 1983.

Stephens, Michael D. *Japan and Education.* New York: St. Martin's Press, 1991.

Stevenson, Harold W. *The Learning Gap: Why Our Schools Are Failing and What We Can Learn from Japanese and Chinese Education.* New York: Summit Books, 1992.

White, Merry. *The Japanese Educational Challenge: A Commitment to Children.* New York: The Free Press, Macmillan, 1987.

NOTES

1 "How Japan Builds Brains," *Chicago Tribune,* sec. 2, November 24, 1985.
2 "Japanese Lessons for the U.S.," *Chicago Tribune,* sec. 1, September 21, 1985.
3 CIA (Central Intelligence Agency), "The World Factbook: Japan," January 22, 2004, http://www.cia.gov/cia/publications/factbook/geos/ja.html.
4 Ibid.
5 Ibid.
6 Walter Feinberg, *Japan and the Pursuit of a New American identity: Work and Education in a Multicultural Age* (New York and London: Routledge, 1993), 35.
7 Ibid., 24.
8 "Government," *Facts about Japan* (Tokyo: Ministry of Foreign Affairs, n.d.), 1.

[9] Since the party membership of the Diet and the prime minister and cabinet change with elections, the discussion is about the structure and functions of the Japanese government rather than its current membership.

[10] Prior to January 2001, the ministry was called the Ministry of Education, Science, and Culture; its role has been expanded to include sports and technology. Hereafter, the ministry will be referred to as the Ministry of Education or Mombusho for simplicity of expression.

[11] Feinberg, 110–11.

[12] Sheppard Ranbom, "Harnessing Education for Growth," *Education Week* (February 20, 1985): 13.

[13] CIA.

[14] Thomas Rohlen, *For Harmony and Strength* (Berkeley: University of California Press, 1974), 47.

[15] Feinberg, 48.

[16] For a highly readable history of Japan, see W. G. Beasley, *The Japanese Experience: A Short History of Japan* (Berkeley: University of California Press, 1999).

[17] Edwin O. Reischauer, *Japan: Past and Present* (New York: Alfred A. Knopf, 1967), 21.

[18] John W. Hall and Richard K. Beardsley, *Twelve Doors to Japan* (New York: McGraw-Hill, 1965), 146.

[19] Makoto Aso and Ikuo Amano, *Education and Japan's Modernization* (Tokyo: Japan Times, 1983), 4.

[20] Sheppard Ranbom, "A History of Learning," *Education Week* (February 20, 1985): 16.

[21] Aso and Amano, 4.

[22] Ronald S. Anderson, *Japan: Three Epochs of Modern Education* (Washington, DC: U.S. Office of Education, 1959), 3–6.

[23] Herbert Passin, *Society and Education in Japan* (New York: Teachers College Press, Columbia University, 1965), 62.

[24] Aso and Amano, 7–8.

[25] Anderson, 4; also, see Passin, 62–63.

[26] Arinori Mori, *Education in Japan: A Series of Letters* (New York: D. Appleton-Century, 1873).

[27] Hall and Beardsley, 398.

[28] Anderson, 6.

[29] Aso and Amano, 1–2.

[30] G. B. Sansom, *The Western World and Japan* (New York: Alfred A. Knopf, 1950), 459.

[31] Aso and Amano, 17–18.

[32] Hall and Beardsley, 400.

[33] Ibid., 401; also, see Anderson, 12.

[34] Aso and Amano, 21, 26.

[35] Ibid., 33.

[36] For the industrialization of Japan and its impact on Japanese culture, see Susan B. Hanley, *Everyday Things in Modern Japan: The Hidden Legacy of Material Culture* (Berkeley: University of California Press, 1997).

[37] Aso and Amano, 57.

[38] Ibid., 61.

[39] Ibid., 57–66.

[40] Gerald K. LeTendre, "Setting National Standards: Educational Reform, Social Change, and Political Conflict," in *National Standards and School Reform in Japan and the United States*, ed. Gary DeCoker (New York: Teachers College Press, 2002), 27.

[41] Ulrich Teichler, "Equality of Opportunity in Education and Career: Japan Seen in an International Perspective," *Oxford Review of Education* 18(3) (1992): 283.

[42] Merry White, *The Japanese Educational Challenge: A Commitment to Children* (New York: Free Press, 1987), 95–100.

[43] Ministry of Education, Science, and Culture, *Education in Japan: A Brief Outline* (Tokyo: Ministry of Education, Science, and Culture, 1984), 12–13.

[44] Sheppard Ranbom, "The Total System," *Education Week* (February 20, 1985), 22.

[45] Catherine C. Lewis, Ineko Tsuchida, and Samuel Coleman, "The Creation of Japanese and U.S. Elementary Science Textbooks: Different Processes, Different Outcomes," in *National*

Standards and School Reform in Japan and the United States, ed. Gary DeCoker (New York: Teachers College Press, 2002), 46–47.

[46] Ranbom, "The Total System," 23–24.

[47] David McNeill and Mark Selden, "Why Is Japan Indulging in Rosy Reinterpretations of the Past?", Center for History, George Mason University, http://hnn.us./articles;11354.html (accessed April 26, 2005).

[48] Ministry of Education, Science, and Culture, 1.

[49] White, 101–107.

[50] Ibid., 7.

[51] Ranbom, "The Total System," 23.

[52] Ibid., 22.

[53] OERI Japan Study Team, *Japanese Education Today* (Washington, DC: U.S. Government Printing Office, 1987), 10.

[54] White, 67.

[55] Delwyn L. Harnisch, "Supplemental Education in Japan: Juku Schooling and Its Implication," *Journal of Curriculum Studies* 26(3) (1994): 323.

[56] Feinberg, 115.

[57] Ministry of Education, Science, and Culture, 1.

[58] LeTendre, 8.

[59] Ministry of Education, Science, and Culture, 7.

[60] Ranbom, "The Total System," 22–23.

[61] Feinberg, 112–114; 196–197.

[62] Ranbom, "Harnessing Education for Growth," 15.

[63] Thomas P. Rohlen, *Japan's High Schools* (Berkeley: University of California Press, 1983), 95–110.

[64] Harnisch, 324.

[65] Teichler, 292.

[66] Ranbom, "Harnessing Education for Growth," 14.

16

EDUCATION IN THE PEOPLE'S REPUBLIC OF CHINA

The People's Republic of China (PRC), the world's most populous nation with more than 2,286,975,468 inhabitants, is selected for comparative treatment because it represents one of the world's oldest ongoing civilizations, because its history has reflected the tensions of continuity and change, and because of its role as a world power. The Chinese culture has influenced other Asian cultures such as Korea and Japan, especially in its transmission of the Confucian tradition.

Geographic, Demographic, and Sociocultural Contexts

The PRC is the world's fourth largest country, after Russia, Canada, and the U.S. Slightly smaller than the U.S., it occupies 3,742,814 square miles of land.[1] Located in eastern Asia, the PRC is bordered by the East China Sea, the Yellow Sea, and the South China Sea. It has borders with Russia, Mongolia, Kazakhstan, Kyrgyzstan, Tajikistan, Afghanistan, Pakistan, India, Nepal, Bhutan, Myanmar, Laos, Vietnam, and North Korea. Bordering the Pacific Ocean, China is a key player in the Pacific Rim economy.

The PRC's large population is unevenly distributed. The highest concentration of population is along the Pacific coast and exceeds one thousand inhabitants per square mile. In contrast, fewer than twenty-five persons per square mile live in China's vast arid western expanses. Despite the government's one child per family policy, its population, with an average family size of 3.9 persons is growing at a rate of 17.40 per 1,000.[2] Though 22 percent of the world's people live in China, it possesses only 7 percent of the earth's arable soil. The pressure of the growing population on limited resources is similar to the problems faced in other less technologically developed countries (LTDCs) such as India, Nigeria, and Mexico. Also fitting the demographic profile of other LTDCs, the PRC's population is preponderantly rural, with 73 percent engaged in agriculture. Most of the remaining population lives in coastal China's large cities, which receive preferential treatment as economic development zones, or in the sparsely inhabited remote border regions.

Because of these factors, China has a very large school-age cohort of nearly half a billion students. Chinese educational planners give priority to the urban population in the economically developing coastal areas.

The dominant ethnic group in China is the Han, which constitutes 91.8 percent of the population. Other ethnic groups constituting the remaining 8.2 percent are the Zhuang, Uygur, Hui, Yi, Tibetan, Miao, Manchu, Mongol, Buyi, Korean, and other small groups. Official policy simultaneously recognizes the legitimacy of ethnic cultures and languages while stressing loyalty to the PRC and the Communist Party. The officially promoted language is standard Chinese or Mandarin (Putonghua, based on Beijing dialect), but other dialects and languages are spoken throughout the country. Language learning and literacy efforts are complicated by the need to master the many characters of Chinese script. Literacy is defined as the mastery of 2,500 characters. Approximately 86 percent of the population is literate.[3]

China's major historic religions are Buddhism and Taoism. There are also Christian and Islamic minorities. Today, it is estimated that more than 60 percent of the population does not identify with any particular religion. This lack of religious identification contrasts with India, another great Asian civilization, where Hinduism is practiced by the majority of people. Rather than religion, Confucianism, an ethical rather than religious system, exercises a powerful impact on Chinese culture, despite the Communist regime's periodical efforts to suppress it.

In modern China itself, Confucianism has had an interesting and contradictory history. During the Cultural Revolution (1966–1976) Confucianism was condemned for its reliance on tradition rather than revolution. Mao Zedong encouraged children and students to denounce the traditional authority of elders and teachers as being counter-revolutionary. Despite attacks by Mao and other Communist leaders, Confucianism has survived and remains a cultural force in the PRC. In many respects, it is seen in the Communist leaders' political style that emphasizes working for the good of the state, party, or collective and submitting to its authority.

Political Context

The PRC's political system rests on a parallel interlocking network of government units and Communist Party organizations. Policy making involves both the government structure and the Communist Party hierarchy with paramount authority in the party's Central Committee. In reality, however, Chinese Communist Party (CCP) leaders dictate policy making.

The PRC's government is highly centralized. Policy originates with the Communist Party's Central Committee and is then implemented by the central government (the State Council) throughout the country's twenty-three provinces. The State Council is composed of a premier; several vice premiers; several state councilors; a secretary general; and many ministries (including the Ministry of Education), administrations (including the State Commission of Education), offices, and bureaus. China's formal government structure appears democratic, with hundreds of lower units electing representatives to units at the next higher level. For example, the local units elect delegates to the Local People's Congresses, which then elect delegates to the County People's Congresses. The process continues upward from the County People's Congresses, to the Provincial People's Congresses, culminating in the National People's Congress. The National People's Congress is a single-house body composed of 2,985 members who are elected by municipal, regional, and provincial people's congresses to serve a five-year term. Its chairman is the head of state.[4] Real decision-making power, however, is in the central government's forty-member State Council, the chief executive branch, which includes the premier and vice premiers. The regional level of government consists of autonomous regions, provinces, and centrally administered cities, such as Beijing and Shanghai. Below these larger regional divisions are local subdivisions such as non-centrally administered cities, prefectures, counties, townships, and urban districts.

The CCP, with its forty-six million members, is the nation's major political force. Several small parties exist, but they are really controlled by the CCP. Although there is some political dissent, there is no substantial political opposition. Party structures parallel the state, or government, units. At its lowest level of party organization are the local units, or cadres. Through an ascending network of party congresses, moving upward from local, county, and provincial to national levels, party committees are elected. The National Party Congress of 1,900 delegates elects a Central Committee of 175 members, which then chooses a Politburo of eighteen members. The general party secretary heads the Communist Party.[5]

Economic Context

Since the establishment of the PRC in 1949, the country has had difficulty in striking a balance between sociopolitical and economic goals. This imbalance is not unique to the PRC but is also found in other LTDCs such as Mexico, Nigeria, and India. In the PRC there is tension between economic development and modernization and the Marxist social orientation to reduce class inequalities. Since 1949, educational policy has zigzagged between promoting economic development and encouraging an egalitarian society.[6] In the 1980s, government leader Deng Xiaoping, seeking to modernize the country, opened it to Western science, technology, and education.[7] Communist ideology was reconfigured to rationalize the new economic policy. While still voicing ideals of public ownership, the government began to lease some state land, factories, and other enterprises to private owners.[8] Because of the government's modernization policy, the PRC's economy has moved from the old Soviet-style centrally planned model to a more market-oriented system.

By the 1990s, the PRC had a growing market economy with private businesses coexisting with state-owned enterprises. Agriculture, too, became more privatized as state control lessened. Individuals were allowed to lease land, giving an amount of their produce to the state as lease payment, and sell the surplus on the open market. Agricultural production increased, as did farmers' incomes. Importantly, the PRC, potentially a major Pacific Rim economic power, openly courted foreign investment and business.

Although the economic system operates within a political framework of CP control, the economic influence of nongovernment organizations and individual entrepreneurs has steadily increased. The economy has grown as foreign trade and investment has increased. Today, the PRC, after the U.S., has the world's largest economy. Among its industrial products are iron and steel, coal, machinery, armaments, textiles and wearing apparel, petroleum, cement, chemical fertilizers, footwear, toys, consumer electronics, and telecommunication equipment. It is an agricultural producer of rice, wheat, potatoes, sorghum, peanuts, tea, millet, barley, cotton, oil seed, pork, and fish. Industry and technology have made major gains, especially in coastal development zones. With its vast labor force of 744,000,000 workers, China has attracted foreign investment. By occupation, 50 percent of the workforce is engaged in agriculture, 22 percent in industry, and 28 percent in services.[9] The urban unemployment rate is estimated at 10 percent. There is a much higher rate of unemployment in rural areas.

The modern PRC is an unusual mixture but not yet a blend of capitalism and socialism. While the free market sector is growing, there are strongly embedded residues of the state-run Communist economic system. The position of the ruling CP elites has not always been clear. At times, the government and party have encouraged the free market approach and then have periodically backtracked, reasserting central controls at intervals. The regime has continued to subsidize inefficient state-run industries.

Although voicing the Marxist rhetoric that the PRC is a classless society, its rapid economic development has generated significant socioeconomic class differences. The class differentials between the urban and rural populations are becoming increasingly evident. A major problem is the large number of unemployed rural workers, estimated at 80–120 million, who have attempted to relocate to urban areas. Many of these individuals are at the poverty level, and subsist on low-paying, part-time jobs.

The developing market economy is producing an enlarging middle class, which is enjoying greater social freedoms and economic opportunities. Some observers believe the middle-class revival will eventually lead to greater political freedom. Other commentators, however, interpret it as an outgrowth of state capitalism and see it having only limited political influence. They contend the middle class will support the regime, which created the economic base that supports it.[10]

A major change has been the departure from the Marxist economic orientation to state-owned collective agriculture and heavy industry to market-driven, consumer-oriented production and retailing. Remaining state-owned enterprises are constantly being pressured to adapt more efficient management techniques based on open rather than controlled market mechanisms.[11] In the "new China," of the "Four Modernizations," economic change has challenged and weakened old-style Marxist controls. There has been an accelerating demand for consumer goods. Stores feature consumer-demanded stylish clothes, jewelry, televisions, and other items.

The PRC is a nation where economic change is bringing about other kinds of social, cultural, and educational transformation. While some enterprising Chinese are becoming wealthy, others have lost their once lifetime employment in state industries. The education system, too, is changing as economically driven careers replace those that were more politically based. A similar process of economically generated sociocultural, political, and educational change is taking place in the RF and other former Communist nations. However, in the PRC, paradoxically, Marxism remains the official ideology in what is becoming an increasingly capitalist nation.

A potential serious problem facing the PRC is degradation of the environment, especially air pollution, soil erosion, and the steady fall of the water table, especially in the north. China continues to lose arable land because of soil erosion. The government has embarked on a gigantic program of managing its water resources, building dams and reservoirs to prevent flooding and to harness hydroelectric power.

Historical Context

Chinese civilization's long history highlights the processes of continuity and change in education. The examination of Chinese educational history generates some leading questions that are useful in studying education in any country: What is the relationship between cultural continuity and change? Why and how do such societies as the Chinese attempt to bring about profound political, social, economic, and educational change? Why do some attempts at change and innovation succeed while others fail? What kinds of conflicts, particularly ideological ones, result from change? What are the planned and unplanned, or unanticipated, consequences that result from change?

Imperialist Rule

For over two thousand years, China was a vast empire.[12] In imperial China, Confucian philosophy, especially its ethics, regulated political, social, economic, and education relationships.

Confucianism

Promoting stability and order as positive ethical goals, Confucius (551–448 BC) sought to curb change. Confucius esteemed ethics, tradition, order, and stability as characteristics of a harmoniously functioning society. Constructing a relational ethical system, Confucius saw the world balanced between chaos and order, a world in which change needs to be small and limited. When change occurs, it must be harmonized with tradition. The goal of transgenerational continuity therefore has been a powerful cultural force with educational implications in China.

The Confucian ethical code ordered society into a hierarchical pattern of subordination. For example, politically, the subject should be compliantly subordinate to the paternalistic ruler, the emperor. The family, which is where one learns piety, benevolence, and following the right path,[13] should be headed by the father and the chain of subordination is: wives to husbands, sons to fathers, and younger to older siblings. The most direct and binding relationships are familial and kinship, and it is within the family that the basic ethical principles of ordered relationships are transmitted from generation to generation.

Confucianism instilled and revered honor. Those who developed their talents and behaved appropriately according to their station brought honor to self and family. This honor-based code also conveyed a shame-based side in that inappropriate behavior dishonored self, family, and ancestors. The Confucian emphasis on familial relationships and the paramount need to maintain the family's honor contributed to the veneration of ancestors. Through fame, a person achieved symbolic immortality. To be famous meant the person had earned public esteem because of his or her virtue; in turn, virtue meant the person had observed appropriate behaviors. Next to the emperor, those of the greatest fame were the scholar-officials, the *shih,* who earned their rank by passing highly competitive examinations. Becoming a shih added fame to the family.[14]

Confucius's philosophy influenced the traditional Chinese worldview. Like the ancient Greeks, the Chinese saw their country as the center of the civilized world. For them, the Chinese language and culture were superior to that of the barbarians who surrounded them and to that of the Western Europeans who sought entry to China. This sense of cultural superiority caused the Chinese to be an inward- rather than an outward-looking people. Instead of being a change agent, education in imperial China emphasized cultural preservation and social control. Traditional informal education in family and kinship groups accentuated the elders' wisdom. The attribution of higher rankings to males versus females was seen not only in families, where females as wives were subordinate to husbands, but also in education; women were denied or had limited access to schooling.

Confucianism had powerful educational implications. According to imperial ideology, knowledge of the Confucian classics would cultivate meritorious and virtuous ethical persons who were capable of governing a politically and socially harmonious state.[15] The classics would illustrate the advantage of maintaining the Confucian status quo and the dangers of diverting from it.

Scholarship and Hierarchies

Imperial China's schools, reproducing the hierarchical social class structure, rested on the assumption that humans were inherently unequal in talent. At society's summit were the shih, civil servant administrators, who were believed to be best suited by temperament and talent to maintain cultural continuity and universal harmony. The shih commanded the highest social status and authority after the emperor and governed in the emperor's name. In descending rank, the shih were followed by the wealthy landowners, or the gentry, with whom they were closely affiliated. In the lower ranks were smaller landowning farmers, artisans, and merchants. At the bottom were the masses of landless workers.

Since intellectual activity was prized over applied and manual work, the formal educational system sought to reproduce scholar-official class. The shih studied the gentleman's arts—art, philosophy, poetry, and history. Thus, there was an absence from the shih's intellectual repertoire of science and technology, so important to Western modernization. Though the Chinese invented gunpowder, paper, and other items useful to modernization, they saw them as curiosities, novelties, and toys rather than instruments of technological change.

The education of the scholar-officials emphasized the all-important state administrators' examinations that had to be passed before a candidate could be assigned a position in the imperial civil service. The examinations required an exacting recall of memorized texts. Students prepared for the examinations by studying ancient Chinese literature and Confucian texts with learned master teachers at imperial or temple schools. Ineligible for government positions, women were not admitted to schools or to examinations. Stressing recall of highly literary information rather than a candidate's potential for solving actual administrative problems, the examinations required candidates to write highly stylized essays and poems based on Confucius's texts and Chinese classical literature. Mistakes in word choice and grammar, improper use of rhyme, and poor calligraphy as well as factual errors automatically disqualified a candidate.[16] Today, university entrance examinations in China and Japan still emphasize recall of masses of information.

The examinations were arranged like a ladder; passing each rung gave a candidate a higher rank and potentially a higher position in the imperial bureaucracy. The first step in the process took place in the counties; then, those who passed the county examinations climbed upward to the more demanding provincial examinations; those who succeed at the provincial rung were eligible to take the national imperial examinations in Beijing, the capital. Only a predetermined number of highly selected candidates successfully reached the top of the examination ladder. Successful candidates who reached the top were ranked, and those with the highest scores received the highest positions.

Though highly competitive and theoretically open, the examination system reproduced the ruling elite. The shih came from the wealthy gentry class, who supported the preparatory schools. The process favored the male relatives of those already invested in the system. It sustained an immense social gulf between those with extensive formal education and those who had only a primary schooling or were illiterate.

The shih were inextricably linked to the imperial system in which the emperor was regarded as the head of great family. Thus, family relationships and values by extension became imperial relationships and values. China's intellectuals, during the long imperial rule, were the governing elite. Unlike other countries such as prerevolutionary France and imperial Russia where intellectuals were alienated from the regime, China's shih were tied to the state that gave them honor, prestige, status, and rank. As policy makers, the shih guarded against change emanating from both internal dissent and from external forces.

Administratively, imperial China was divided into 1,500 local districts, each about 300 square miles with a population of 250,000. A shih presided as the emperor's agent, or magistrate, in each district where he implemented imperial judicial, fiscal, and military policies. Land and produce were heavily taxed, and among the magistrate's important duties was tax collection. Through a highly bureaucratic chain of command, local district magistrates reported to provincial magistrates, who, in turn, reported to the imperial court in Beijing. Although magistrates were frequently reassigned and could not serve in their own home districts, the system was sullied by corruption, bribery, and favoritism.

The long endurance of the shih gave China the appearance of a permanent bureaucracy. A combination of internal dissent and pressures from the European nations and Japan would eventually bring down the shih and the imperial system. The last imperial dynasty, the Qing, (Ch'ing), which ruled from 1644 to 1912, had difficulty in reacting to threats to its survival. Resisting modernization and relying on tradition, the regime demonstrated a customary inertia in mobilizing resources to meet its challenges. Confucianism was impotent in facing the escalating crisis. The regime's stagnating bureaucracy locked out potential change agents and its army and navy, with antiquated weapons and strategy, were no match for the European nations' modern military might.

Threats to Imperial Rule

At the nineteenth century's beginning, imperial China faced serious dangers: internal rebellion and external pressures from Western European nations and Japan. From 1830 to 1860, the European powers, especially Great Britain, had breached China's traditional isolation, forcing trading concessions from the empire. Violating imperial ordinances, British merchants introduced Indian-grown opium to China and profited from the illegal drug trade. The Chinese imperial government's efforts to end the opium trade led to the Anglo-Chinese War of 1839–1842. The Chinese forces, especially the antiquated imperial navy, were defeated decisively by the more powerful modern British fleet. The victorious British, in the Treaty of Nanking, on August 29, 1842, forced China to accede to British economic exploitation.

Others followed the British in forcing concessions. In 1897, Germany secured a ninety-nine-year lease on Kiachow and the right to develop mines and railroads in Shantung. In 1898, Russia procured a twenty-five-year lease on the Liaotung Peninsula and the right to build a railroad in South Manchuria. In 1898, the British secured a ninety-nine-year lease of Hong Kong and its adjacent territories, which did not end until 1997 when Hong Kong returned to Chinese rule.

With treaties that opened China to foreign trade, Christian missionary activity (which had started with the Roman Catholics in 1582) that included both Roman Catholic and Protestant missionaries increased dramatically in the nineteenth century. Initially, Protestant missionaries worked in east coast port cities where the influence of the European powers and the U.S. was strongest. Then, venturing into China's interior, they established churches, medical clinics, and schools. Roman Catholic missionary activity was renewed by the Jesuits, Franciscans, Lazarists, and Dominicans. The presence of educated women, Protestant missionaries and Roman Catholic nuns, was a new phenomenon for many Chinese.[17] The missionaries established day and boarding schools for girls. Though offering some Chinese women new educational opportunities, the girls' schools, reflecting traditional gender bias found in Western education, stressed home economics, sewing, and child care.

Resenting Christian missionaries who were protected by the Western nations, the imperial government covertly encouraged periodic antimissionary demonstrations. In 1870, French Sisters of Charity, who had established an orphanage in Tientsin, were massacred. The anti-foreign Boxer Rebellion, put down by Western and Japanese armies, was covertly supported by the imperial government.

Imperial China's last decade, from 1901 to 1911, witnessed belated futile reform efforts to stave off collapse. China attempted to transform its absolutist court into a more functional government like that of Meiji Japan by planning for a new school system that would replace traditional Confucian scholarship with a more functional program of training officials.[18] Still hierarchical, the proposed school system projected schools at local, provincial, and imperial levels. Each level was to feed candidates into the examination system. When the schools were fully operational, the examination process was to be phased out with graduates directly entering the imperial administration.[19]

The new system consisted of a four-year higher elementary school, a five-year middle school, a three-year higher school, and a three-year imperial university. In 1906, an imperial Ministry of Education was established to create and supervise these government schools. Government planners, following a top-down strategy, gave priority to the upper institutions—the higher schools and the imperial university. The system was to follow a minutely prescribed syllabus developed by the Ministry of Education. In developing the new school system, Ministry of Education officials selectively borrowed ideas from the Japanese. Several thousand Chinese students were sent to study in Japanese schools.

China's last emperor, a young child, Pu Yi, reigned briefly from 1909 to 1912. Rather than being suddenly overthrown by revolutionary forces, imperial China, which had endured for centuries, lost the mandate of heaven and disintegrated. Although years in the making, imperial China's death knell began when an army unit defected on October 10, 1911. The rebellion spread throughout the country. The remaining imperial forces were commanded by General Yuan Shih-k'ai, a politically ambitious intriguer.

The Republic

Among the revolutionary groups were China's republican forces, led by Dr. Sun Yat-sen, (1866–1925), a Western-educated physician. Organizing a "Revive China Society," Sun's ideology rested on three principles: (1) "nationalism," asserting China's destiny to be a modern nation; (2) "democracy," the right of China's people to self-government; and (3) "socialism," the Chinese people's right to economic livelihood.[20] As the situation destabilized for the imperial government, Sun Yat-sen, on January 1, 1912, was inaugurated as the new Chinese republic's provisional president. To avert civil war, Sun Yat-sen reached a compromise with Yuan Shih-k'ai. For Yuan's support of the republic, Sun offered to resign as president. Accepting Sun's compromise, Yuan was installed as president, ruling as virtual dictator from 1912 until his death in 1916.

During the "Warlord Era," 1916–1928, China's central government controlled only a small part of the country while real power was held in the provinces by petty military tyrants. Using their local armies, generals seized control of a region, exploiting it for personal profit. Despite its political instability, China saw economic growth and development, often with foreign investment and control. Industries developed in the coastal cities where urban classes of industrialists, merchants, and factory workers emerged. The era also was significant for its intellectual ferment. Chinese students studied abroad, especially in Japan, the U.S., the UK, and France. Returning to China, many students sought to apply their learning to the Chinese situation. When Japan pressed demands for special commercial and territorial concessions in China's Shantung peninsula in 1919, students organized a national patriotic protest strike. The strike led to the "New Culture Movement," organized to reassert Chinese nationalism. Many students joined the Kuomintang, or Nationalist Party, led by Chiang Kai-shek, who claimed to be Sun Yat-sen's ideological successor.

Along with the Nationalists, a rival political party, the Chinese Communist Party, was organized by a professor at the University of Peking. In July 1921, the CCP Congress met at Shanghai with Mao Zedong in attendance.

The CCP attracted disaffected intellectuals who, following Marxism, endeavored to create a Chinese proletariat by organizing industrial workers.

By 1928, the Kuomintang, led by General Chiang Kai-shek, had defeated the warlords and was moving to reconstitute central political control. Nationalist support came primarily from upper- and middle-class professionals such as government officials, industrialists, and businessmen. A fragile truce between Nationalists and Communists erupted into civil war. To escape annihilation by the militarily superior Nationalists, Mao Zedong's Communists embarked a desperate long march northward to Shensi province where they proclaimed the Chinese Soviet Republic in 1931. From his remote base in rural China, Mao, revising Marx's doctrine, proclaimed the poor agricultural peasants as China's revolutionary class.[21]

Successfully holding off Nationalist attacks, Mao's Communists secured their position in Yenan where they forged a highly disciplined fighting force for the coming struggle against their Kuomintang foes. They won grassroots peasant support by expropriating and redistributing the wealthy landlords' estates to the impoverished farm workers. They organized literacy campaigns and CP schools to indoctrinate the rural masses and to win their allegiance with promises of economic improvement.

The Japanese invasion of China in 1931 began the long and devastating conflict that did not end until 1945 when the Allies defeated Japan in World War II. Nationalists and Communists temporarily put aside their differences to combat the Japanese invaders. Upon Japan's defeat, however, Nationalists and Communists resumed civil war. From 1946 through 1949, the Nationalists, with U.S. support, and the Communists, with Soviet backing, were locked in combat. Chiang's Nationalists lost popular support, and Mao's rural-based strategy proved effective as isolated Nationalist armies were confined to the cities, while the surrounding countryside fell to the Communists. In 1949, Chiang's vanquished Nationalists fled to Taiwan, claiming to be the Republic of China's legitimate government. Chiang remained as president of the republic until his death in 1975.

Mao Zedong proclaimed a new government, the People's Republic of China, on October 1, 1949. For more than twenty years, the U.S. recognized the Nationalist government on Taiwan as China's legitimate government and refused to recognize the PRC. Though the U.S. recognizes the PRC as the legitimate government today, it also continues to support Taiwan. Despite improved relations between the U.S. and the PRC, the issue of Taiwan remains unresolved.

Chairman Mao's Rule

No account of China's history would be complete without frequent references to Chairman Mao Zedong. In Chinese Communist ideology, Mao was the doer of heroic transformative deeds. Today, Chinese politicians and historians still praise him as the PRC's founding father but criticize certain of his policies such as the Great Leap Forward and the Cultural Revolution, which deterred China's technological development. A consistent revolutionary, Mao believed it more important to create zealously revolutionary new Communist men and women than to prepare scientific and technological experts necessary for creating a modern nation. Urging unrelenting struggle against counterrevolutionary forces, he believed a new Communist China could be created out of chaos.

After establishing the PRC in 1949, the Communists consolidated power. Staging mass public show trials, Mao's government ruthlessly purged capitalists, landlords, and those suspected of bourgeois leanings. Land, initially expropriated from landlords and distributed to poor landless farm workers, was collectivized into large state-owned agricultural communes. Private and foreign-owned businesses were expropriated and, on the Soviet model, operated as state enterprises. The new Communist regime mounted a massive campaign to eradicate illiteracy and indoctrinate the people in Marxist ideology.

In 1949, the PRC faced severe educational problems. The illiteracy rate was a staggeringly high 80 percent; less than 40 percent of the school-aged children were enrolled in inadequate and deteriorating facilities.[22] The government's educational policies, emphasizing needed facilities' expansion at both the primary and secondary levels, sought to overcome these serious deficits. As is true in LTDCs, the PRC's new leaders grappled with whether to concentrate on urban areas and build onto the school infrastructure already in place or to focus on the rural areas, which were plagued by the highest rates of illiteracy and general undereducation. In the 1950s, China's policy makers decided on a two-pronged educational strategy: they would improve access to education by expanding rural schooling and would use the existing urban educational infrastructure, especially in secondary and higher education, for development purposes. While all schools were to build ideological loyalty to the new Marxist social order, rural schools, in particular, were to reduce illiteracy by educating more pupils.

By 1951, ten million rural students were attending regular school and a larger number were attending *minban* (people-run) local schools. For rural adults, winter and spare-time literacy programs were an important part of the literacy campaign.[23] Between 1949 and 1957, the number of primary schools increased from 346,800 to 547,300, and the number of secondary schools increased from 4,000 to 11,100. Primary enrollments increased from 24.4 million to 64.3 million and secondary enrollments from 1 million to 6.3 million.[24]

From 1953 to 1957, the Chinese government, emulating the Soviet model, launched an ambitious five-year plan to reconstruct society, the economy, and education to conform to Communism. Imitating Soviet agricultural collectivization, the government organized agricultural cooperatives and communes. Industrial development, too, copied the Soviet's emphasis on heavy industry rather than consumer goods. Chinese schools, emulating Soviet education, used a transplanted Soviet curriculum and translations of Soviet textbooks.

Like primary and secondary education, higher education in the PRC was ideologically driven. In its reorganization of higher education, from 1949 to 1965, the government relied on the Soviet Union for advice and support. Like their Soviet counterparts, Chinese planners decided that higher education should train needed scientists and engineers. The higher education system included general universities as well as polytechnic and technical institutes. Student admission was selectively determined by passing rigorous entrance examinations, with emphasis on science, engineering, and technology.

By the late 1950s when tensions between the Soviet Union and the PRC, two Communist giants, were present, Mao determined China would follow its own path of socialist development. He argued China's vast population should be mobilized as a human resource to quickly build the Communist state. In 1958–1959, Mao Zedong boldly initiated "the Great Leap Forward," a new ideologically driven economic policy. China's population was mobilized into a frenzied effort to overtake the Western industrialized nations.

The Great Leap Forward

In educational policy, the Great Leap followed the politically correct dogma of "redness"—a proletarian orientation rather than an orientation to expertise. Mao's educational strategy, called "walking on two legs," called for more alternative education while maintaining traditional schools. Rural primary and secondary schools were combined, with the years required for graduation shortened. Vocational, work-study, and spare-time educational programs were expanded and accelerated. In the late 1950s, primary enrollments dramatically increased from 64.3 million in 1957 to 93.8 million in 1960, with secondary enrollments climbing less dramatically from 6.3 million to 10.3 million in the same period.[25] The increased enrollments, like the efforts to double agricultural and industrial productivity, masked a serious failure in quality. More students were attending but for shorter periods of time; academic courses gave way to sessions devoted to political exhortation; and more unqualified teachers were used in the hastily opened schools.

Mao also wanted to move higher education into the Great Leap Forward. He wanted to lessen emphasis on highly selective entrance examinations, which he regarded as a relic of Confucianism and a serious deviation from Marxist "classlessness." He also wanted to create a more proletarian-minded university faculty that emphasized Marxism and classlessness rather than scholarship.

Contrary to Mao's predictions, the Great Leap Forward was a disaster. Instead of moving forward, China fell backward.[26] In education, the "walking on two legs" policy was reversed. Educational policies returned to the premise that the PRC needed more trained experts in mathematics, science, and technology. Many of the hastily established rural schools with unqualified teachers were closed. Enrollments in elementary and secondary schools declined. The emphasis on scholarship reappeared in universities. Thus, another policy change had taken place in China's education. After the Great

Leap Forward's failure, Mao Zedong was still revered as the father of the Communist revolution, but his actual role in policy making diminished. From 1960 to 1965, the government and the party sought to restore agricultural and industrial productivity and academic quality.

The Cultural Revolution

Though enshrined as the revolution's venerable father, Mao was relegated to the political background until he launched his next major ideological effort, the Cultural Revolution, in 1966. Promoting revolutionary cleansing, Mao dramatically took center stage from 1966 to 1976.

Believing a renewed revolutionary Communist China could be created out of chaos, Mao challenged the very bureaucratic and educational structures he had created. Guided by his own standards of ideological purity, Mao's dramatic and often violent Cultural Revolution sought to reshape cultural and educational thought and structures. From 1949 to 1966, the Ministry of Education had made and implemented policy. Like other state agencies, the Ministry of Education conformed to guidelines dictated by the Communist Party Central Committee. During the Cultural Revolution, Mao and his followers vilified administrators in the Ministry of Education, which became virtually nonfunctional. Rather than having policy made by educational bureaucrats, Mao wanted it made by the masses.

Bent on rooting out inherited Confucianist cultural residues that emphasized merit based on scholarship and veneration of scholars, Mao called for the revolutionary virtue of "redness," pervasive political loyalty and activism.[27] Mao's ideological purification campaign generated an intense emotional commitment from the young, especially students, who mobilized as Red Guards and scoured the country harassing administrators, professors, and teachers.[28] Replacing academic selectivity and expertise with proletarian political correctness, the following educational goals were foremost during the Cultural Revolution: (1) education was to promote Maoist political ideology; (2) education should eliminate rather than perpetuate class divisions; (3) students were to be treated as equals, regardless of their academic abilities and achievement; (4) practical, socially useful labor should take precedence over academic subjects; and (5) secondary school graduates were to devote two years to productive work before entering a university. The different types of secondary schools were reorganized into ordinary secondary schools, and entrance examinations were abolished. There was a dramatic increase in the number of secondary schools. The 8,102 regular secondary schools existing in 1965 had increased to 193,152 by 1976. Secondary enrollments, reflecting the Cultural Revolution's egalitarianism, expanded prodigiously from 14.4 million secondary students in 1965 to 68.5 million in 1977.[29]

From 1966 through the early 1970s, universities and other institutions of higher education were either closed or radically reconstructed; like secondary schools, universities were thoroughly politicized with Maoist proletarian ideology; higher learning, too, was to be penetrated by the ideal of socially useful productive work. Technicians were trained from among the workers in part-time universities. University administrators and professors suspected of bourgeois intellectual sentiments were tried and purged by gangs of Red Guards. Suspect professors were assigned as factory or farm workers.

By 1970, the Cultural Revolution's higher education system was in place when ninety culturally purified universities reopened. University revolutionary committees ran the universities, replacing the abolished Ministry of Higher Education and disgraced administrators. These committees abolished entrance examinations, condemned as perpetuating bourgeois dominance.[30] The new proletarian admission requirements were: graduation from a secondary school; two years of work experience in industry, agriculture, or the army; being between age twenty and twenty-five, unmarried, and possessing correct political recommendations.[31]

University classes emphasized Maoist ideology, discussion of correct politics, and revolutionary activities. Students made up their own examinations and shared answers in the spirit of proletarian egalitarianism. Using the method of Maoist self-criticism, study groups discussed party documents or sayings from Chairman Mao. Participants engaged in mutual self-criticism of any negative thoughts they might be harboring. Group pressure enforced social control and political correctness.[32]

The Cultural Revolution grew increasingly chaotic as factions in the loosely organized Red Guards fought pitched battles, often on school grounds. When the disorders threatened to get completely out of control, the Communist Party and the army suppressed the Red Guards and resettled sixteen million young people in rural areas as agricultural laborers. The aging Mao, father of the Communist revolution, was again isolated from real power as the government and party reasserted control over China.

When the Cultural Revolution ended, higher education was demoralized with disgraced professors working at menial jobs as part of their "proletarian reeducation." Students had sacked libraries searching for objectionable books and few acquisitions had taken place for nearly a decade. Laboratories had been misused and wrecked by revolutionary committees. Many students, admitted under proletarian admission policies, were totally unprepared for higher education. After the Cultural Revolution, some professional educators returned to their positions in the Ministry of Education and in schools and universities, but their efforts to restore academic quality were often thwarted by political appointees.

The Four Modernizations

In 1977, the Chinese government and the Communist Party launched the concerted campaign of the Four Modernizations in four key sectors—agriculture, industry, national defense, and science and technology. Emphasizing science, technology, management, and planning, the modernization campaign sought to remedy the Cultural Revolution's deleterious effects. Government and party leaders now asserted that "the loss of a generation of technicians and scholars during the deemphasis on academic quality and technical expertise had produced a deep crisis in which the PRC was essentially endangering its future as a modern socialist country."[33] "Redness" as a paramount goal was suddenly replaced by scientific and technological expertise. Linking economic productivity to education, government and party leaders, reversing their prior ideological stance, emphasized competition, efficiency, and productivity. Government and party leaders called for renewed academic discipline.

To achieve modernization, the PRC's policy makers determined that elite cadres of scientific and technological experts, trained according to Western standards, were needed. The Chinese government believed modernization could be selectively introduced and centrally controlled without jeopardizing the political status quo. However, change could not be confined to science and technology but penetrated into Chinese society, culture, and education.[34]

Deng's modernization policy endeavored to double and then quadruple the PRC's GNP within twenty years. Though not rejecting Marxism, capitalist-like efforts were initiated to attract foreign investors and open foreign markets to Chinese exports. Priority was given to key regions—five special economic zones consisting of fourteen coastal cities and the Pudong District in Shanghai—rather than the entire nation. This decision produced economic and educational differentials between urban and rural areas, with the favored coastal economic zones moving beyond the rest of the country.

The PRC's educational policy paralleled the modernization program with emphasis on renewing academic discipline and quality to prepare needed scientific and technological experts. Secondary schools returned to their pre–Cultural Revolution curricula, offering academic curriculum for university entrance or specialized training. An ambitious program, launched to improve science and technology curriculum and instruction in higher education, included international exchange; Chinese professors of science, technology, and engineering were sent to developed nations, including the U.S., to learn about recent innovations in their fields. Professors from developed countries came to the PRC to advise and teach.

To restore academic credibility to universities, the Ministry of Education reinstituted selective entrance requirements, especially examinations, to ensure that entering students were academically qualified. These highly selective examinations admitted only a small percentage of applicants to universities. The reemphasis on university admission examinations hearkens back to the PRC's imperial legacy and is also similar to the power that examinations have in Japan and Korea, nations with a Confucianist legacy. Such selectivity contrasts with the more open admissions policies in U.S. colleges and universities.

In the summer of 1989, university students motivated by a desire for political and intellectual freedom organized to liberalize Chinese society and politics. Loosely organized as the prodemocracy movement, students staged a sit-in in Peking's Tiananmen Square to press their demands for political and cultural liberalization. (It should be remembered that the other Communist giant, the USSR, was undergoing unprecedented change at the same time under Gorbachev.) The students' prodemocracy movement was a dramatic illustration that the forces of change, once unleashed, could not be confined to designated sectors of life. The government's response, after some hesitation, used the army to ruthlessly suppress the movement and to massacre students in Tiananmen Square in 1989.

Modernization's social and economic changes that generated such unanticipated consequences as individualism, consumerism, and class consciousness produced a "crisis in values" among Chinese youth. Thus, in the PRC two value models compete—Mao's old order Marxism and Deng's Four Modernizations. Maoist core values epitomize national collectivity in which individuals sacrificed themselves for an officially proclaimed common good. In contrast, modernization's values are material rewards, efficiency, entrepreneurship, and individualism.[35] The material changes brought about by the Four Modernizations are eroding Maoist values that are still enshrined in party ideology and entrenched in Chinese collective memory.

The CCP and government have attempted to synthesize certain selected Maoist values with modernization. Official pronouncements and approved textbooks tell young people to serve the PRC by contributing to its modernization, which improves the economy and gives it a high ranking among the world powers. Unlike Mao's bungled Great Leap Forward, the new modernization's leap forward is to be systematic, scientific, and technological. One can now be both an expert and a loyal Communist. Government-sponsored media messages feature such key words conducive to modernization as *efficiency, knowledgeable, expert, creative,* and *industrious* along with the more collectivist terms of *altruism, generosity, helpfulness,* and *eagerness* to work for the common good.[36]

With the Four Modernizations, the Ministry of Education again functions as the national educational authority and was given centralized control over education. Educational policy follows a top-down, linear model, in which decisions at the central level filter downward through a three-tiered central, provincial, and local set of structures.

Organization and Structure of Schools

In countries like the PRC, where policy is driven by ideology, schooling reinforces clearly prescribed, ideologically grounded, acceptable social and moral behaviors.[37] Ideology refers to the ideational mortar that unifies individuals into a collective group. Featuring an interpretation about a people's past, ideologies blend history and myth, often with inspirational tales enshrining heroic events and heroic figures in the nation's cultural memory.[38] For example, in Chinese Communist ideology, Chairman Mao, the PRC founder who led his followers on a long march of five thousand miles to escape annihilation by his Nationalist foes, is a heroic figure. While all countries have such ideologies, such as the U.S. with George Washington and Abraham Lincoln as heroic figures, the PRC relies very heavily on ideology to mount and drive policy.

The organization and presentation of knowledge in the school curriculum serves ideological purposes; the values embedded in the school milieu reflect the nation's official ideological prescriptions and proscriptions. Along with schools, the media and entertainment are mobilized as informal educational forces to shape public opinion to fit the preferred ideological molds. Ideological shifts in the PRC drive educational policy. For example, when official policy in the PRC emphasized Marxist ideological correctness, educational positions were filled according to party loyalty, credentials, and service. In contrast, modernization emphasizes technological and scientific expertise rather ideological conformity.[39] While Chinese schools seek to instill socially and politically approved values in their young, there is uncertainty as to what these approved values will be. This is not due to moral ambiguity or relativism found in many postmodern societies, such as the U.S., the UK, or France, but instead to the regime's ideological rigidity at particular periods in time. While schools have responded obediently to party dictates, party leaders have shifted between reproducing the Communist culture and educating scientific experts.

Preschool and Early Childhood Education

Since the establishment of the PRC, policy makers have encouraged early childhood education and agencies because: (1) they are useful in forming politically correct Marxist ideological values early in a child's life; and (2) they facilitate the entry of more mothers in the labor force—an important consideration in economic development. As the PRC continues to modernize, early childhood care will become more attractive for economic as well as ideological reasons.

Chinese day-care, nursery, and kindergarten facilities include boarding, full-day, part-day, and rural seasonal schools. While some early childhood schools are state agencies, others are locally sponsored by urban neighborhood committees or rural work units. Since the 1980s, private kindergartens have also opened. Chinese early childhood education emphasizes group activities and movements in which children often act in unison. The passive learning climate contrasts with more active Japanese and American arrangements.

Primary Schools

The PRC is officially committed to universalizing primary schooling throughout the country. Priorities, however, have shifted from earlier efforts at rapid universalization to more cautious decisions to allocate resources according to demographic and economic realities. As a result, government efforts to provide universal primary schooling have been inconsistent. A major obstacle in making primary schooling uniformly accessible is the PRC's geographical vastness, its immense school-age population, its limited financial and educational resources, and its uneven pace of national development. Since the onset of the modernization initiative, government policy realizes the need to base decisions on existing realities and move steadily but gradually to achieve future goals.[40]

Until the 1980s, Chinese primary schools, depending on their location, offered either five- or six-year programs, with children beginning school at either age six or seven. In 1982, the government mandated six-year primary schools throughout the PRC. The PRC's approximately 629,000 primary schools enroll 139,950,000 pupils. The proportion of girls enrolled is 45 percent. Approximately 10,513,000 pupils are members of minority groups. The total primary school staff is 6,084,700, of whom 5,433,800 are full-time teachers. The average class ratio of pupils to teacher is 24 to 1. While these statistics are impressive, the number of pupils enrolled is much higher than the number in regular daily attendance or the number completing primary schooling.[41]

Urban–Rural Differentials: A Two-Track System

Primary schooling, like secondary and higher education, has been shaped by shifts in political ideology and availability of economic and educational resources.[42] Although the PRC is officially committed to establishing universal primary education, government resource allocation has caused differences in the expansion of schools in urban and rural areas. The greatest growth is in areas where educational infrastructure already exists. In less-developed rural areas, primary school improvement has proceeded more slowly, relying more on local rather than central government resources.[43] Currently, the central government makes general policies and contributes 50 percent of funding and the remaining funds are raised by local authorities. Thus, Chinese primary schooling has become a two-track system with considerable quantitative and qualitative differences between urban and rural schools. The full-time, mainly urban schools constitute one track and rural and part-time primary schools another. Urban children, with access to more extensively developed school systems, are much more likely to complete the full cycle of primary schooling than are rural children. Additionally, Chinese primary schooling is still burdened by such historical residues as disadvantaging women and ethnic minorities, especially in rural areas.

Three types of primary schools exist in this two-track system: (1) five-year schools; (2) part-time schools; and (3) full-time six-year schools. Five-year schools, which are being phased out, still exist in rural areas, offering a limited basic curriculum. The part-time, or every-other-day primary school, offers only Chinese language and arithmetic.[44]

The full-time six-year school, with a complete curriculum, is usually found in urban areas. In line with the Four Modernizations, urban primary schools, serving 25 percent of the school-age population, prepare students academically for secondary and higher education. The Ministry of Education's "Teaching Plan for Full-Time Primary Schools" standardizes the complete six-year primary school curriculum throughout the country. The curriculum includes Chinese language and literature, moral education, mathematics, geography, history, natural science, physical education, music, drawing and fine arts, physical labor, and foreign language, with English being the most popular. As is generally true of primary schooling, language arts occupies 40 percent of instructional time. Language learning is complicated in that pupils are expected to master both the Chinese phonetic alphabet and a minimum of 2,500 characters in Mandarin script, defined as necessary for functional literacy. Moral education, retaining aspects of ideological indoctrination, reinforces the "five loves" of motherland, people, work, science, and socialism.

Some full-time schools are also key schools, or *Zhongdion,* which offer experimental or model programs, featuring innovative curricula and attended by highly select students. The Ministry of Education operates the highest ranked key schools, but key schools are also operated at provincial, municipal, and prefect levels. The vast majority of key schools are urban. Their greater funding enables them to have better physical plants, libraries, equipment, and more academically qualified teachers than other full-time schools.

Rural primary schools, serving about 75 percent of the PRC's primary students, are financed largely by local communities. Their dependence on the local economy causes them to be generally underfinanced. Consequently, they vary in organization and quality. Among the types of rural primary schools are full-day, half-day, spare-time, double-session, and winter schools. In these schools, the standard curriculum is abbreviated to Chinese language study, arithmetic, general knowledge, and moral lessons. The central government no longer subsidizes teachers' salaries in rural areas.[45]

Rural primary schools face many problems. In farm areas, some parents have removed children, especially girls, from school to help with farm chores. In addition, the curriculum, even in its abbreviated format, is oriented to urban rather than rural situations. Some rural schools also charge tuition, which keeps poorer children from attending full-time. These problems cause high dropout rates, especially for girls. While 90 percent of rural children enroll in primary schools, regular attendance is at 60 percent, with a 30 percent completion rate.[46] For ethnic minorities, in remote or mountainous areas, educational opportunities are limited. For nomadic peoples in pastoral areas in the Mongolian autonomous region, boarding and headmen's primary schools provide basic education.[47]

The two-track primary system, called "multiple ways of running schools" or "standing on two legs," reflects both the pressures of setting funding priorities as well the ambivalent policy gravitation between modernizing and instilling politically correct socialist attitudes, producing the usual consequences of dual systems: advantaging urban children (especially in the coastal development zones) over rural children, thereby perpetuating the gulf between urban and rural classes[48] in what is officially claimed to be a "class-less society."

Attempting to justify a two-track primary school system in Marxist society, PRC officials argue the policy rests on a necessary relationship between the economy and education. For example, one such interpretation is:

> But given the actual economic base and level of productivity, all people cannot be provided with an education that is absolutely the same. China, a populous nation with a backward economy and educational system, cannot set up large numbers of schools or universalize full-time secondary and tertiary education all at once. [49]

The decision to proceed at uneven levels of educational development is one that developing countries with limited resources frequently make.[50] Policy in the PRC, like that in India and Nigeria, generally favors urban over rural areas and secondary and higher education over primary schooling. These priorities are established by policy makers who believe such decisions will facilitate development most effectively. However, in LTDCs, rural children are often at an educational disadvantage, which affects later socioeconomic opportunities. In reality, the policy makers, influenced by their own socioeconomic and educational backgrounds, are for the most part reproducing their strata or class. These practices contrast with the trend in more technologically developed countries (TDCs) such as the U.S. to make educational access available to all groups.

Objectives of Primary Schooling

Children begin primary schooling at age six and continue their studies for six years. The official objectives of primary schooling are:

> (1) to enable the pupils to have the good moral character and behavior of loving the motherland, the people, labor, science, and socialism; (2) to equip the pupils with the abilities to read, express, and calculate and with the knowledge of natural and social sciences, and to enable the pupils to observe, think, and operate; (3) to ensure healthy development of the pupils in body and mind and to train them to have a good living and labor habit as well as self-reliant ability; and (4) to equip the pupils with the interest of aesthetics.[51]

The academic year is forty weeks, with twelve weeks off for winter and summer vacations. During each school week, there are twenty-four or twenty-five hours of instruction for lower, twenty-six for middle, and twenty-seven for higher grades.

Minimal graduation requirements from primary school are that students should be able to read 2,500 commonly used Mandarin characters and be proficient in reading, writing, and basic arithmetic. Those failing to attain this minimal level are retained. Each province, autonomous region, and municipality determines its own examination procedures.[52]

Secondary Schools

Access to secondary schooling, the schools' organization, and the graduates' destinies are often based on political and economic policies and needs. The PRC's secondary schooling has reflected official ideological shifts. Prior to the Cultural Revolution, secondary schools were organized according to a variety of patterns. Academic secondary schools prepared students for university entrance, paving the way for higher socioeconomic status. Entry into upper secondary schools was determined by students' academic achievement, social class origins, and Communist Party affiliation. Despite government proclamations about classlessness, upper secondary schools admitted children of the educated classes in much greater numbers than working-class children.[53] In 1965, only 9 percent of the age-specific group was enrolled in upper secondary schools. In addition to highly selective academic secondary schools, there were specialist technical schools, workers training schools, vocational schools, and agricultural secondary schools.

Chairman Mao saw upper secondary schools as bastions of what he despised in China's educational tradition—intellectualism disconnected from work—and as perpetuating the class structure that he wanted destroyed. Therefore, the various secondary schools were collapsed into a unified ordinary secondary school. Homogeneous grouping was discontinued and entry examinations were abolished. The number of regular secondary schools grew from 8,102 in 1965 to 190,000 in 1976. Enrollments expanded from 14.4 million students in 1965 to 68.5 million in 1976.[54] As a result of this expansion, academic standards declined. Instruction emphasized vocational training and political indoctrination.[55]

When the Four Modernizations replaced the Cultural Revolution, secondary schools returned to offering either an academic curriculum or specialized training. Academic quality replaced egalitarian leveling. Key schools were reopened with an even greater emphasis on academic competency and competition. The examination system, too, was reestablished. The use of key schools to prepare the PRC's modernizing elites marks an important policy decision in secondary education.[56]

Chinese secondary education is divided into the junior middle school, or *chuzhong,* and senior middle school, or *gaozhong.* The junior middle school, with grades one, two, and three, enrolls students ages twelve through fourteen. The junior middle school together with primary school constitutes the nine years of compulsory education, which the 1990 educational reform mandates. This reform increased access to junior middle schools in these selected urban regions. Senior middle schools, grades four, five, and six, enroll students ages fifteen through eighteen. Along with technical schools, normal schools for primary teacher preparation, and agricultural schools, senior middle schools constitute higher secondary education.[57] Less than half of the age cohort in the PRC attends middle school; only 10 percent of the age cohort attends senior middle school. Students, however, may enroll in alternative secondary institutions such as agricultural, vocational, and technical schools.[58]

Secondary education is structured in various ways. After the six-year primary school, students may enter the lower middle school, a lower secondary three-year institution, or the complete secondary school that offers the three-year lower and three-year upper secondary programs in one institution. Those who have completed the three-year lower secondary program at an incomplete secondary institution enter the comprehensive upper-secondary school, a three-year institution, offering both regular academic and vocational tracks. Also, a few seven-year secondary schools, on an experimental basis, offer four years of junior and three years of senior secondary education.

Dynamics of Chinese Secondary Education

A fascinating account of the dynamics of Chinese secondary education was provided by Martin Schoenhals, an American anthropologist, who did ethnographic research in a Chinese urban key middle school. His research focused on the interplay of "face," criticism, and evaluation.

The school week in Third Affiliated School, Schoenhals's pseudonym for the real school he observed, followed a six-day schedule, Monday through Saturday, 7:40 AM to 5:00 PM, with a lunch break from noon until 2:00 PM. Instruction was organized into forty-minute periods. Unlike U.S. students, Chinese students remained in the same classroom while their teachers moved from class to class. The average class size was sixty students, much larger than in the U.S. Students, seated at individual desks, faced the front of the room.[59] Although a few innovative teachers experimented with discussion groups, the pervasive method was lecturing. As they lectured, teachers asked questions to which students responded either in unison or individually.

Pursuing a prescribed curriculum, students used standardized textbooks in such required subjects as Chinese, English, mathematics, politics, physical education, physics, chemistry biology, history, geography, drawing, and music. There were no electives. While students were examined and graded in their courses, teacher-determined grades were not considered important since they were not relevant to university admission—students' primary goal at academic secondary schools.

Students were organized into units of sixty, called a *ban,* analogous to a U.S. homeroom group. As a unit, ban members took classes and participated in extracurricular activities. The ban was useful for: (1) scheduling; (2) discipline and social control; and (3) providing identification for its members. A *banzhuren,* a faculty member, was accountable for a particular ban's academic performance, social development, political correctness, and discipline. Students in a ban elected a cadre of student leaders such as the *xuexi weiyuan,* the study monitor; the *xuanchuan weiyan,* the propaganda representative; the *wenyi weiyuan,* the arts and entertainment leader; the *shenghuo weiyuan,* the supervisor for cleaning; the *tiyu weiyuan,* the extracurricular athletic organizer; and the *banzhang,* the overall student leader.[60]

Schoenhals's findings on evaluation, criticism, and "face" in Third Affiliated Middle School are representative of the larger Chinese society.[61] He noted the importance of rankings, a strong Confucianist hierarchical residue, and the use of continuous formative evaluation to establish student rankings. The emphasis on evaluative rankings, in turn, reflected the teacher's strategy for cultivating students' talents. For example, a high ranking in a particular skill or subject meant the student had a special talent in that area. Related to evaluative rankings is the teacher's use of criticism, usually private but occasionally public, to motivate and discipline students. While private criticism is more often used since it causes a lesser loss of face, severe misbehavior may invoke public criticism. For example, students may be required to write self-criticisms and to read them to the class or to post them on bulletin boards.[62]

While using rankings to designate merit is a Confucianist legacy, criticism comes from the Maoist era when it was used extensively for self- and group criticism. Teachers use both private and public criticism to motivate, discipline, and rank students. Highly powerful socially and emotionally, criticism relates to one's public persona or "face," the merit by which one is held by others.[63] Because ranking is emphasized, Chinese classrooms are covertly competitive. Though competing for rank, students are to appear humble and not be "show-offs." Winning an honor reflects positively on a student's entire family, including his or her ancestors, but losing face publicly has pervasive negative consequences.[64]

The emphasis on "face" and rankings often turns the classroom into a stage in which teachers and students perform before a potentially critical audience. Like actors in a play, lectures and recitations become a script that the teacher and students act out, trying to avoid missing lines or cues. This "performative" aspect of classroom behavior often creates an anticipatory anxiety in which the performer awaits the audience's judgment. These secondary school dynamics are a rehearsal for the national university entrance examinations, a highly competitive national performance.

Curriculum

The ordinary secondary school curriculum includes political science, Chinese language and literature, mathematics, foreign language, physics, chemistry, history, geography, biology, health and physical education, music, and art. Elective courses are also available. The curriculum of key schools varies from the ordinary secondary curriculum. In key schools, a student's program reflects enrollment in either liberal arts or science tracks. The academic year for secondary schools is forty weeks. There are six classes a day with thirty or thirty-one classes for junior and twenty-six to twenty-nine for senior students.[65]

Secondary school graduates seeking university admission face the hurdle of passing complex and highly selective nationally administered examinations, or *gaokao*. All applicants sustain a common core of examinations in Chinese, a foreign language, and mathematics. In addition, those planning to specialize in arts and sciences take examinations in history and geography while those seeking admission to engineering, agricultural, and medical schools must pass examinations in chemistry, physics, and biology. Passing or failing the examination has serious lifelong consequences. Those earning high scores have a better chance to enter prestigious universities. Those who fail are unlikely to find appropriate employment and may even be unemployed.

Many issues in Chinese secondary education relate to establishing and implementing priorities in a climate of economic change and rising expectations. Where and for whom should limited resources be expended? Since modernization and preparing scientific and technological elites is the government's highest priority, many Chinese youths are undeserved at the secondary level because of limited educational alternatives.

Vocational and Technical Schools

The government is emphasizing vocational and technical secondary education to complement modernization and economic restructuring. Vocational and technical education also absorbs many of the students who fail to qualify for admission to general academic secondary schools. The government also claims these schools are increasing women's employment opportunities. There are three types of secondary vocational and technical schools: specialized, technical, and vocational.

Sponsored and operated by ministries and commissions under the state council or local professional departments, specialized secondary schools prepare midlevel technical and managerial personnel in such programs as engineering, agriculture, forestry, medicine, law, finance, and economics. These semiprofessional programs generally require four to five years of study. Technical schools are operated by large and medium-sized enterprises or local professional departments to train technicians. Their programs are generally three years of training in technical skills, some of which is in-service. Upon completing their training programs, graduates often work in the enterprises that provided their training. Vocational schools include vocational middle schools in urban areas and agricultural middle schools in rural areas. They are operated by local authorities to train people for local needs. Occupational training programs, usually lasting two years, include agriculture, forestry, health, secretarial and clerical, hotel and restaurant service, cooking, tailoring, and similar fields. Currently, there is a great emphasis on training tourist guides and restaurant and hotel employees, as China seeks to attract foreign visitors and investors. The 33,464 vocational and polytechnic schools enroll approximately 18,700,000 students.[66]

Higher Education

Higher education in the PRC, too, has been shaped by ideological shifts. As indicated, when the Communists came to power in 1949, they reorganized higher education on Soviet models. Seeking to build a collectivist industrial economy, Chinese higher education sought to prepare needed scientists and engineers.

Like the Soviet system, Chinese higher education included general universities and polytechnic and technical institutes. Admission to higher education was selective and determined by manpower projections. Despite its Marxist derivation, the selective system, with rigorous examinations, was compatible with the inherited Chinese Confucianist scholar tradition. The emphasis on science, engineering, and technology, however, was a new element.[67]

Mao attacked selectivity in higher education during the Great Leap Forward of 1957 when he sought to industrialize through mass popular efforts rather than using people with expertise in mathematics, science, and technology. Mao's Cultural Revolution unleashed his most severe attack on selectivity in higher education. From 1966 through the early 1970s, universities and other institutions of higher education either were closed or radically reconstructed. Workers attending part-time universities were trained to be technicians.[68]

The Four Modernizations commenced a concerted effort to restore higher education's academic quality as part of the national modernization policy. The Ministry of Education, now reconstituted, was in control of university supervision, curriculum, and faculty appointments. To repair the Cultural Revolution's deleterious effects, the government launched an ambitious program to improve science and technology curriculum and encourage international exchange and study.

The 1,020 colleges and universities enroll 3,170,000 students.[69] Along with comprehensive universities, the higher education system includes institutions for science and engineering, finance and economics, teacher education, and medical training. Many institutions are administered by regional bureaus of higher education, supervised by the reestablished central Ministry of Education. Thirty-five leading universities are directly controlled by the Ministry of Education. In addition, the Ministry of Agriculture, the Ministry of Commerce, and other government ministries control institutions in their specialties.

Each university is governed internally by its own university affairs committee. At the department level, a departmental affairs committee and chair are responsible for organizing and maintaining teaching and research. CP committees at each level act as ideological watchdogs. In the early stages of modernization, the party's role weakened but after the suppression of the prodemocracy movement it has recouped some of its influence.

Chinese leaders and people have great faith in education's power for economic development. Deng Xiaoping, architect of modernization, stated it would be "impossible to develop science and technology" without educational innovation.[70] Educational policy today seeks to relate planning and implementation to modernization. Market forces and incentives have been introduced into educational planning to reduce reliance on inherited Marxist collectivist manpower planning.

The government is admonishing institutions of higher education to become more cost effective by increasing professor–student ratios, by maximizing the use of facilities, and by developing new specialties needed in the economic sector.[71] Universities are advised to be guided by competition, reduce costs, improve services, generate more income, and enroll more students but maintain high academic standards.

While China has had some success in stimulating modernization through higher education, problems such as educated unemployables, underemployability, and "brain drain" are surfacing. These problems are also found in other LTDCs like India. Prior to the modernization policy, the PRC, like other Marxist countries, had a rigidly planned system for manpower production and utilization in which placement in higher education was related to projected employment needs. In the new economy, China has large numbers of graduates without jobs suited to their special training.

China shares the problem of brain drain with other LTDCs. Brain drain refers to university graduates who leave the country to work in more TDCs. Since Chinese university students enjoy government subsidies, the expenditures on students who leave the country to work elsewhere adds to the government's educational deficits. One survey reports that of five thousand university professors who went abroad for advanced study or research only two thousand returned to the PRC. More than 200,000 Chinese students are attending universities in more TDCs. Many of these students are unlikely to return to the PRC.[72]

Conclusion

China's history and culture, like that of India and Japan, is an ancient one of several thousand years' duration. While not a foreign colony like India, China was forced to grant concessions to the European powers and Japan. As with Japan, the ethical system of Confucianism is rooted in Chinese culture. Despite the momentous political changes that have taken place in the PRC, Confucianism remains a strong cultural legacy that often has a conservative impact on education. Rigorous university entrance examinations exert a powerful force in both China and Japan. A contrast between China and Japan has been the relative ease of Japan's modernization compared with China's historical reluctance to modernize.

China, the world's most populous country, shares with India the problem of setting and implementing educational priorities. While both countries have official policies that call for universal primary education, they have given priority to secondary and higher education. Democratic India and Marxist China have tended to rely on top-down rather than grassroots development. Both countries exhibit serious differences in the availability of educational resources in rural areas.

China, the remaining large Marxist nation, has made a pronounced use of ideology. Although still emphasizing ideology's role in shaping the nation's destiny, Chinese leaders today have difficulty in relating their Marxist past with the present semi-capitalist economic modernization program. Among the critical questions facing China are: What traditional cultural elements will be used in restructuring China? Will it be possible for China to become a modern nation relying on Western science, technology, and engineering while maintaining its Marxist ideological orientation? Will economic change bring about social, political, and educational consequences unanticipated by government planners and functionaries?[73]

Discussion Questions

1. Examine the influence of Confucianism on Chinese thought, culture, and education.
2. What has been the traditional impact of hierarchy and ranking on Chinese culture and education?
3. Describe the scholar gentry and its role in Chinese officialdom during the Imperial era.
4. How was the examination system used to identify and empower a leadership elite in Imperial China?
5. In comparison to and contrast with Japan, why did Imperial China fail to meet the challenge of modernization?
6. What educational policies were followed during the early stages of the PRC?
7. What has been the impact of ideology on educational policies in the PRC?
8. Compare and contrast the educational policies followed during the Cultural Revolution with those of the Four Modernizations.
9. Describe the differentials, areas of disparity, in the provision of education in the PRC.
10. What is the structure of secondary education in the PRC?
11. How is primary or elementary education defined? How are primary or elementary schools organized? What are the component skills and subjects of the curriculum? Who attends primary school? Are there differences between urban and rural schools?
12. How is secondary education defined? How is secondary education organized? Are there a variety of secondary school patterns of organization? Who has access to secondary education? Are there selective examinations? Does secondary education encourage or discourage socioeconomic mobility? What is the nature of the curriculum? Is there equal opportunity or ethnic, class, and gender discrimination?
13. How is higher education defined and organized? Who has access to higher education? Are examinations used to determine access? Is there equal access to higher education or is there ethnic, class, and gender discrimination?

RESEARCH TOPICS

1. Read and review a book on education in the contemporary PRC.

2. Organize a group to view and comment on a recent motion picture involving China.

3. Select one of the following areas for the basis of a paper that compares education in the PRC with education in the U.S.: early childhood education, primary schooling, secondary schooling, vocational education, higher education.

4. Invite an international student from the PRC to visit your class and discuss her or his educational experiences.

5. Begin a clippings file of articles on politics and education in the PRC.

6. Prepare a historical overview paper that describes in a general way how the past has had an impact on culture, politics, society, and education China. What major events of the past shaped the present situation in the country?

7. In a research paper, describe the philosophical and religious attitudes that have contributed to shaping contemporary Chinese culture.

8. In a country profile describe the contemporary government and political situation in the PRC and how that situation shapes educational policies.

9. After doing some research on the PRC's economy, determine if it is a technologically developed or technologically underdeveloped country.

10. In a profile paper on educational governance, policies, and financing, determine the government agencies responsible for providing and supervising educational services.

11. Prepare a paper that compares and contrasts preschool and early childhood arrangements in the PRC and another country of your choice.

SUGGESTIONS FOR FURTHER READING

Barnett, A. Doak, and Ralph N. Clough, eds. *Modernizing China: Post-Mao Reform and Development*. Boulder, CO: Westview Press, 1986.

Bettelheim, Ruth, and Ruby Takanishi. *Early Schooling in Asia*. New York: McGraw-Hill, 1976.

Borthwick, Sally. *Education and Social Change in China: The Beginnings of the Modern Era*. Stanford, CA.: Hoover Institution Press, 1983.

Calhoun, Craig. *Neither Gods nor Emperors: Students and the Struggle for Democracy in China*. Berkeley and Los Angeles: University of California Press, 1994.

Cherrington, Ruth. *Deng's Generation: Young Intellectuals in 1980s China*. New York: St. Martin's Press, 1997.

Gibney, Frank. *The Pacific Century: America and Asia in a Changing World*. New York: Charles Scribner's Sons, 1992.

Grasso, June, Jay Corrin, and Michael Kort. *Modernization and Revolution in China*. Armonk, NY: M. E. Sharpe, 1997.

Grunfeld, A. Tom. *The Making of Modern Tibet*. Armonk, NY: M. E. Sharpe, 1996.

Gutek, Gerald L. *Philosophical and Ideological Perspectives in Education*. Boston: Allyn and Bacon, 1997.

Hayhoe, Ruth. *Contemporary Chinese Education.* Armonk, NY: M. E. Sharpe, 1984.

Hayhoe, Ruth, and Marianne Bastid, eds. *China's Education and the Industrialized World: Studies in Cultural Transfer.* Armonk, NY: M. E. Sharpe, 1987.

Holmes, Brian. *Equality and Freedom in Education: A Comparative Study.* London: George Allen & Unwin, 1985.

Huang, Ray. *China, A Macro History.* Armonk, NY: M. E. Sharpe, 1997.

Jun, Li. *Chinese Civilization in the Making, 1766–221 B.C.* New York: St. Martin's Press, 1997.

Kessen, William, ed. *Childhood in China.* New Haven, CT: Yale University Press, 1975.

Kristol, Nicholas D., and Sheryl Wuduun. *China Wakes: The Struggle for the Soul of a Rising Power.* New York: Times Book/Random House, 1994.

Lin, Jing. *Education in Post-Mao China.* Westport CT: Praeger, 1993.

Lewin, Keith, Angela Little, Hui Xu, and Jiwei Zheng. *Educational Innovation in China: Tracing the Impact of the 1985 Reforms.* Essex, UK: Longman, 1994.

Link, Perry, Richard Madsen, and Paul G. Pickowicz. *Unofficial China: Popular Culture and Thought in the People's Republic.* Boulder, CO: Westview Press, 1989.

Meisner, Maurice. *The Deng Xiaoping Era: An Inquiry into the Fate of Chinese Socialism, 1978–1994.* New York: Hill and Wang, 1996.

Niu, Xiaodong. *Policy Education and Inequalities in Communist China since 1949.* Lanham, MD: University Press of America, 1992.

Ogden, Suzanne. *China's Unresolved Issues: Politics, Development, and Culture.* Englewood Cliffs, NJ: Prentice-Hall, Inc., 1989.

Pepper, Suzanne. *China's Educational Reform in the 1980s: Policies, Issues, and Historical Perspectives.* Berkeley, CA: Institute of East Asian Studies, 1990.

Pepper, Suzanne. *Radicalism and Educational Reform in Twentieth Century China: The Search or an Ideal Development Model.* New York: Cambridge University Press, 1996.

Rawski, Evelyn S. *The Last Emperors: A Social History of Qing Imperial Institutions.* Berkeley: University of California Press, 1998.

Schoenhals, Martin. *The Paradox of Power in a People's Republic of China Middle School.* Armonk, NY: M. E. Sharpe, 1993.

Schirokauer, Conrad. *A Brief History of Chinese Civilization.* New York: Harcourt Brace Jovanovich, 1991.

Spence, Jonathan D. *The Search For Modern China.* New York: W. W. Norton, 1990.

Thaxton, Ralph A., Jr., *Salt of the Earth: The Political Origins of Peasant Protest and Communist Revolution in China.* Berkeley: University of California Press, 1997.

Thomas, R. Murray, ed. *International Comparative Education: Practices, Issues, & Prospects.* New York: Pergamon Press, 1990.

Wasserstrom, Jeffrey N., and Elizabeth J. Perry, eds. *Popular Protest and Political Culture in Modern China: Learning from 1989.* Boulder, CO: Westview Press, 1991.

Welty, Paul Thomas. *The Asians: Their Evolving Heritage.* New York: Harper and Row, 1984.

Yang, Benjamin. *Deng: A Political Biography.* Armonk, NY: M. E. Sharpe, 1997.

NOTES

[1] CIA (Central Intelligence Agency), "World Factbook: China," January 18, 2004, http://www.cia/gov/cia/publications/factbook/geos/ch.html.

[2] "The 1990 Census," *Beijing Today* (48) (1990); and "China Population," *China Daily* (July 16, 1990).

[3] CIA.

[4] Michael G. Roskin, *Countries and Concepts: An Introduction to Comparative Politics* (Englewood Cliffs, NJ: Prentice-Hall, 1989), 282. Also, see CIA.

[5] Roskin, 284.

[6] Emily Hannum, "Political Change and the Urban-Rural Gap in Basic Education in China, 1949–1990," *Comparative Education Review* 43(2) (1999): 193.

[7] For a biography of Deng, see Benjamin Yang, *Deng: A Political Biography* (Armonk, NY: M. E. Sharpe, 1997).

[8] Julia Kwong, "Ideological Crisis among China's Youths: Values of Official Ideology," *British Journal of Sociology* 45(2) (1994): 249.

[9] CIA.

[10] Maurice Meisner, *The Deng Xiaoping Era: An Inquiry into the Fate of Chinese Socialism, 1978–1994* (New York: Hill and Wang, 1996), 466–467.

[11] Song Lijun and Shen Yefan, "Liaoning to Speed Up Reform," *China Daily* (5449) (February 26, 1998): 1.

[12] A highly readable general history is Ray Huang, *China, A Macro History* (Armonk, NY: M. E. Sharpe, 1997).

[13] Martin Schoenhals, *The Paradox of Power in a People's Republic of China Middle School* (Armonk, NY: M. E. Sharpe, 1993), 39–40.

[14] John K. Fairbanks, Edwin O. Reichsauer, and Albert M. Craig, *East Asia: The Modern Transformation*, II (London: Allen and Unwin, 1965), 80–85.

[15] Ibid., 39–40.

[16] Ibid., 40–42.

[17] Irwin T. Hyatt, Jr., "Protestant Mission in China, 1877–1890: The Institutionalization of Good Works," in *American Missionaries in China; Papers from Harvard Seminars,* ed. Kwang Ching Liu (Cambridge, MA: Harvard University, Eastern Research Center, 1966), 93–105.

[18] For an analysis of reform efforts, see Roger R. Thompson, *China's Local Councils in the Age of Constitutional Reform 1898–1911* (Cambridge, MA: Council on East Asian Studies, Harvard University Press, 1995).

[19] Fairbanks, Reichsauer, and Craig, 613–616.

[20] Ibid., 634.

[21] Ralph A. Thaxton, Jr., *Salt of the Earth: The Political Origins of Peasant Protest and Communist Revolution in China* (Berkeley: University of California Press, 1997).

[22] Keith Lewin, Angela Little, Hui Xu, and Jiwei Zheng, *Educational Innovation in China: Tracing the Impact of the 1985 Reforms* (Essex: Longman, 1994), 19.

[23] Hannum, 197.

[24] Ibid., 195.

[25] Ibid., 197–198.

[26] For an analysis of the Great Leap Forward, see Jean-Luc Domenach, *The Origins of the Great Leap Forward: The Case of One Chinese Province,* trans. A. M. Berrett (Boulder, CO: Westview Press, 1995).

[27] Schoenhals, 45–46.

[28] Lynn Paine, "In Search of a Metaphor to Understand China's Changes," *Social Education* 50 (February 1986): 107.

[29] Stanley Rosen, "New Directions in Secondary Education," in *Contemporary Chinese Education,* ed. Ruth Hayhoe (Armonk, NY: M. E. Sharpe, 1984), 66–69.

[30] Schoenhals, 46.

[31] Jurgen Henze, "Higher Education: Tension Between Quality and Equality," in *Contemporary Chinese Education,* ed. Ruth Hayhoe (Armonk, NY: M. E. Sharpe, 1984), 105–107.

[32] Schoenhals, 50–51.

[33] Paine, 108.

[34] Craig Calhoun, *Neither Gods nor Emperors: Students and the Struggle for Democracy in China* (Berkeley and Los Angeles: University of California Press, 1994), 244–249.

[35] Kwong, 250.

[36] Ibid.

[37] Kwong, 249.

[38] Gerald L. Gutek, *Philosophical and Ideological Perspectives in Education* (Boston: Allyn and Bacon, 1997), 139–155.

[39] Suzanne Ogden, *China's Unresolved Issues: Politics, Development, and Culture* (Englewood Cliffs, NJ: Prentice-Hall, 1989), 309–310.

[40] Pan Dianjun, Han Keshun, and Cai Zhonghua, "Reform the Structure of Secondary Education to Comply with the Needs of the Four Modernizations (1980)," *Chinese Education and Society*, 27(5) (1994): 51–52.

[41] "Education," www.chinatoday.com (accessed June 7, 2005), 1–2; State Education Commission, *Education in China, 1978–1988* (Beijing: State Education Commission, the People's Republic of China, 1989), 2–5.

[42] Hannum, 193–211.

[43] "Primary School Education (1985)," *Chinese Education and Society* 27(5) (1994): 90–94.

[44] State Education Commission, 5.

[45] Liu Heying, Jia Quanqing, and Liu Runzhi, "Structural Reform of Rural Middle and Primary School Education, Hebei (1985)," *Chinese Education and Society* 27(5) (1944): 81–89.

[46] Billie L. C. Lo, "Primary Education: A Two-Track System for Dual Tasks," in *Contemporary Chinese Education*, ed. Ruth Hayhoe (Armonk, NY: M. E. Sharpe, 1984), 57–58.

[47] State Education Commission, 71.

[48] Lo, 49.

[49] Chen Taolei, "On the Inevitability of the Two-Track Educational System (1979)," *Chinese Education and Society* 27(5) (1994): 26–27.

[50] Kam Wing Chan, "Post-Mao China: A Two-Class Urban Society in the Making," *International Journal of Urban and Regional Research* 20 (March 1996): 134–150.

[51] State Education Commission, 5.

[52] "Primary School Education (1985)," *Chinese Education and Society* 27(5) (994): 93.

[53] Rosen, 66–67.

[54] Ibid., 67–69.

[55] State Education Commission, 15–16.

[56] Rosen, 71.

[57] State Education Commission, 16.

[58] Schoenhals, 7.

[59] Ibid., 8–9.

[60] Ibid., 11.

[61] Ibid., 8.

[62] Ibid., 110.

[63] Ibid., 18–31.

[64] Ibid., 110–112.

[65] State Education Commission, 17.

[66] "Education in China," *Travel China Guide*, www.travelchinaguide.com (accessed June 8, 2005).

[67] Henze, 94.

[68] "Education in China."

[69] Ibid.

[70] Dalu Yin, "Reforming Chinese Education: Context, Structure and Attitudes in the 1980s," *Compare* 23(2) (1993): 116.

[71] Ibid., 119–121.

[72] Ibid., 118.

[73] Ogden, 306–307.

EDUCATION IN INDIA

India, an ancient culture, exhibits strong traditionalism along with trends to modernization. India is selected for discussion in the book because: (1) it is an ancient civilization that has endured into the present through processes of cultural assimilation and equilibrium; (2) it has the world's second largest population; and (3) it has immense cultural, ethnic, religious, and social diversity.

Geographic and Demographic Contexts

The Republic of India is located on the Indian subcontinent, a large triangular landmass jutting from Asia that also includes Pakistan, Nepal, Bhutan, and Bangladesh. A federal republic, India occupies 1,260,000 square miles of the subcontinent. Contemporary India is a nation of contrasts where urbanization and modernization coexist with ancient traditions. Traditional attitudes are especially strong in the more than 500,000 villages inhabited by three-fourths of the population. However, India is also the scene of huge, sprawling, teeming metropolises such as Calcutta, Bombay, and Madras.

Exceeded in population only by the PRC, India, with a population of over one billion people, is the world's second most populous nation. The population growth rate is 1.4 percent, reflecting a birthrate of 22.32 births and a death rate of 8.28 deaths per 1,000 people. Life expectancy is 63.6 years for men and 65.2 years for women.[1]

India's population growth, typical of less technologically developed countries (LTDCs) such as China, Nigeria, and Mexico, is a serious concern. While more technologically developed countries (TDCs) have stable or declining school-age populations, LTDCs have very high percentages of school-age children. Further, the growth of the school-age population is often unequally distributed in LTDCs, with the largest numbers in rural areas.

Hinduism → big – 35%
→ Influences how people view education
→ Reincarnation
→ Path towards unity with life

Sociocultural Context

Religion

Hinduism, India's largest religion, is observed by 82 percent of the population. Ethnically based, Hinduism has no founder, specific creed, or dogmas. It is a body of beliefs, myths, customs, and rituals. Resting on an idealist spiritual orientation, it postulates that the human purpose is to become one with the ultimate spiritual reality—an eternal and Universal Spirit.[3] Human beings experience a series of reincarnations (rebirths and deaths) until the soul reaches the highest spiritual plane of absorption in the Universal Spirit, Brahma or Atman, thus ending the process.

The Hindu belief in reincarnation generates powerful implications for life and education. Hinduism asserts that each person experiences a series of lives, each with a continuity of the self, either on earth or elsewhere. This implies that individuals are in differing stages on their journey to their ultimate unification with the ultimate reality. Hinduism's ethical system postulates that each person should follow the duties and responsibilities of his or her situation at each stage of the multilived journey. While some people have overcome earthliness and reached a transcendental state, most still are seeking it. Hinduism's sacred books form a strong literary tradition, based on Sanskrit, the ancient classical language, as well as an oral tradition of storytelling, poetry, and drama.[4]

India, with 75,000,000 Muslims (11.3 percent of the population), is the world's third largest Islamic nation after Pakistan and Indonesia. Muslims live throughout India, but many are urban dwellers. India's 16,000,000 Christians, 2.4 percent of the population, are divided into Protestant, Catholic, and Orthodox denominations. Christians tend to be urban in the north and rural in the south. About 75 percent of Christians are rural and were converts from lower castes. Educationally, Christians play a more significant role than their numbers indicate. Their educational importance dates from nineteenth and twentieth century missionary activities. Christian denominations operate a large number of private schools, especially at the secondary and higher levels, which attract significant enrollments, including many non-Christians, since they are often successful avenues to college and university entrance. Christian churches provide 20 percent of India's health-care and educational institutions.[5]

Sikhism, founded in 1469, rejecting caste, endeavored originally to integrate Hinduism's and Islam's most positive features into a common religion. India's 13,000,000 Sikhs, 1.97 percent of the population, while located primarily in the Punjab (a region in the northwest section of India), live throughout India.

Buddhism, originating as a reform movement within Hinduism, was at one time a major force in India; many Buddhists have been reabsorbed into Hinduism. Today, the Buddhist minority in India is a small 0.71% of the population. Significantly, Indian missionaries carried Buddhism to other parts of Asia such as Myanmar and Thailand. It remains a religio-cultural presence in China and Japan and is Thailand's predominant religion. The Parsis, or Zoroastrians, a very small minority of 91,226, constitute only 0.01 percent of the population. They are typically prosperous industrialists. Because of their wealth and high status, they enjoy a high representation in higher education and make substantial philanthropic contributions to educational and charitable institutions.

While living parallel communal lives, there is little integration between religious groups. Communalism has caused religious bloc voting, conflict, and often violence. The Indian religious situation is politically and educationally paradoxical. India's constitution, pledging religious freedom, recognizes the nation's responsibility to protect religious minorities. India is a secular nation with no formal involvement or affiliation between the government and organized religion. Paradoxically, some political parties have religiously based ideologies and constituencies and religious sectarianism strongly influences Indian politics.

Caste and Society

The caste system is a unique and often debated feature of Indian culture, society, politics, and education. Caste refers to the hierarchically arranged endogamous hereditary group into which one is born. As a pervasive socioreligious and cultural pattern, caste, which subdivides Indian society, exerts a powerful social hold on the large Hindu majority but deeply influences other groups as well.[6]

Although there are hundreds of castes and subcastes, or *jatis*, there is a marked distinction between the ritually clean, twice-born higher castes and the untouchables who are relegated to occupations regarded as unclean, such as scavenging, sweeping, and hide and leather work. The untouchables, called *harijans*, or "the people of God" by Gandhi, are 15 percent of India's population.[7] Like racism in the U.S., the caste system stereotypes individuals and creates a serious multicultural educational challenge.

Educational researchers and policy makers have examined the impact of caste on educational access, participation, retention, and mobility. While educators worldwide have analyzed the impact of socioeconomic class on educational access, participation, and success, issues related to caste are more complex than those involving class. Caste is totally ascribed in that a person cannot become disengaged from the caste into which he or she is born. An increase in personal income may result from educational and occupational access, but conditions of wealth and poverty cannot change one's caste membership. Socioeconomic mobility, often driven by income in the U.S., does not have the same effect in India.

In addition to the untouchables, another disadvantaged group is the "tribals," indigenous peoples whose origins predate the Aryan invasions.

Caste ? → Class that doesn't change
Untouchables ? → you HAVE to marry this
Person
cause group

Approximately 50,000,000 Indians belong to tribal communities, which are ethnically distinct from the mass of the Indian population. These aboriginal peoples, living in remote areas, have been and often remain aloof from the socioeconomic and political changes reshaping modern India. Following ancient folkways, they speak their own distinct tribal languages. The majority of tribals live primarily in the central states.

The educational issues of India's tribal population are comparable to that of indigenous minorities in other countries. In the U.S., with a large Native American minority, the official policy was once resettlement, confinement to reservations, and assimilation—all destructive of indigenous cultures. Mexico, with a large Native American population, has used both formal and non-formal education to improve the condition of is indigenous peoples. Mexico, however, still has a sizeable population of disadvantaged illiterates among its Native American population. China, too, has its ethnic minorities who live in seminomadic remote areas. India's tribals, living in remote regions, like indigenous minorities elsewhere, have endured centuries of discrimination. Today, India's government, like those of certain other countries, uses affirmative action and compensatory programs to improve their situation.

India's constitution guarantees protection and support to three identified disadvantaged groups: scheduled castes, because of untouchability; scheduled tribes, because of geographical isolation; and backward classes, because of educational deficits. Article 14 guarantees all citizens have legal equality. Article 15 prohibits discrimination because of religion, race, caste, sex, or place of birth and provides for the government to make special provisions for scheduled castes and scheduled tribes. Article 16 assures equality in public employment. Article 17 decrees abolition of untouchability. Article 29 prohibits discrimination in government-funded educational institutions. Article 46 provides for the educational and economic interest of scheduled castes and tribes. The union, or central, government has developed special compensatory education programs for scheduled castes and tribes. One program reserves 15 percent of the places or positions in federal and state educational institutions and agencies for scheduled castes and 7.5 percent for scheduled tribes.[8] As in the U.S., affirmative action programs generate controversy. While beneficiaries want them continued, opponents contend that jobs and educational places, especially in higher education, should be filled on merit rather than quotas.

Caste is a pervasive but slowly diminishing feature of Indian culture. Urbanization and modernization are eroding higher castes' socioeconomic power. Nevertheless, the caste system remains a significant social determinant, especially in traditional rural areas.

Gender Issues

Women throughout Indian history have been subordinate in a patriarchal male-dominated society. However, some women, such as Indira Gandhi

Art 30 15 major languages
Right to establish & administer based on beliefs

who was prime minister, have attained leadership roles. Although female subordination is not unique to India, women's status is further impacted by traditionalism, casteism, tribalism, classism, regionalism, religion, and underdevelopment. Women in India, as well as in other LTDCs, face conditions symptomatic of socioeconomic underdevelopment. Indian traditional folkways, as in the PRC, value the male child who guarantees continuity of family lineage. Further, India has a long tradition of arranged marriages in which the bride is to be subservient in her husband's parents' extended household. Brides are expected to bring large dowries to the marriage, which often results in their family's indebtedness. In rural agricultural settings, women are relegated to child rearing, cooking, gathering fuel, and doing farm chores. Girls, who in traditional LTDCS leave school earlier than boys, are generally underrepresented in educational institutions, especially secondary and higher ones.

Language Issues

Costly to develop ← Three-language approach → Testbooks

Language issues exist in many multiracial and multiethnic nations, including India, the RF, most of the successor states of the FSU, and Nigeria. Fifteen major languages and almost 700 minor languages and dialects are spoken in India. Derived from classical Sanskrit, Hindi is the vernacular of many northern Indians. In the south, several Dravidian-based languages are spoken. English, the official language during British rule, remains a link language used as an associate official language in government and law. The situation regarding English is similar in Nigeria where it serves as a link language. A minority of the population speaks both official national languages, Hindi and English. Fourteen regional languages are recognized as official state languages. Sanskrit, the ancient classical root language of Hindi, remains important for scholarship and performance of religious rituals. The constitution's Article 29 gives minorities the right to preserve their language, script, and culture and Article 30 guarantees the right to establish and administer educational institutions of their choice based on religion or language.

Politicians, primarily from India's northern states, seek to make Hindi India's official language. This, however, is resisted in the south. The politically charged language issue has educational consequences. A compromise, the three-language formula, was developed to resolve the educational issue. Students are to study their mother tongue, which, depending on the area may be Hindi or a non-Hindi Indian language. Then, they study a second language, which may be a non-Hindi Indian language for those whose first language is Hindi and Hindi for non-Hindi speakers. Then, they take a third language, which may be English or some other language. Because of the language issue and its compromise, much instructional time is devoted to language learning, which tends to dominate instruction to the detriment of other subjects. Furthermore, textbooks, syllabi, and other instructional materials also need to be prepared and published in several languages. So much time spent on language learning reinforces the traditional learning style that emphasizes memorization. Due to the high dropout rate, many children leave school speaking only one language.

Political Context

India became free of British rule on August 15, 1947. Its constitution, adopted in 1950, established India as a sovereign, secular, and democratic republic. Among the world's most detailed state documents, India's constitution contains 395 articles, eleven schedules, and numerous amendments. Providing for single and uniform citizenship throughout the nation, the constitution gives every citizen, age eighteen and older, the right to vote. It guarantees the fundamental rights of freedom of speech, expression, belief, assembly and association, migration, and choice of occupation or trade. The constitution also provides legal protection from discrimination because of race, religion, caste, or sex. While the constitution provides these antidiscriminatory protections, India has had to struggle against caste and gender discrimination, as noted earlier.

A Federal–State Government System

As in all countries, the government structure influences educational governance, organization, and financing. India is a union of twenty-five states and seven centrally administered union territories. India's government, like that of the U.S., Germany, and Nigeria, is a federal–state system, with the constitution specifically delimiting responsibilities to either the union or state governments. The constitution also specifies responsibilities shared jointly by union and state governments. The union government has exclusive authority over such national areas as foreign policy, defense, communications, currency, taxation on corporations and nonagricultural income, and railroads. The state governments have exclusive power over internal areas such as police, public health and sanitation, local government, and taxation on agricultural income. Some areas that are essentially a state matter but of national importance are concurrently shared by the union and state governments, including criminal law, marriage and divorce, economic and social planning, and education.

Education's presence on the concurrent list identifies it as a national priority and gives the union government some control over each state's activities. The union government is to "assume larger responsibility motivating" and "ensuring proper management" of educational programs for which it makes a large fiscal contribution.[9] The union government is responsible for reinforcing education's "national and integrative character," maintaining "quality standards," and promoting "excellence at all levels of the educational pyramid."[10] As a result, union and state prerogatives overlap in education. Since planning is also a concurrent power, India's five-year plans, continuous since 1950, include educational provisions, especially those relating to funding.[11]

The concurrent responsibilities of union and state governments produce some complicating factors that affect policy implementation. Under complex funding formulas, the union controls some funding to the states. While the states depend on the union for development funding, the union, in turn, relies on them to implement plans.[12]

Legislative, Executive, and Judicial Branches

India, the world's largest democracy, has a parliamentary government patterned on the British model but with some provisions borrowed from the U.S. Like the British parliament and the U.S. Congress, it is bicameral. The features of Indian government most similar to the U.S. pattern are the division of powers between federal and state governments and the presence of a supreme court with powers of judicial review.

India's parliament consists of an upper house, the *Rajya Sabha*, the Council of States, and a lower house, the *Lok Sabha*, the House of the People. With the exception of money bills, legislation may originate in either house. Passage by simple majority is needed for a bill to become law.

The Rajya Sabha, presided over by the republic's vice president, is composed of 250 members and resembles the British House of Lords more than the U.S. Senate. India's president appoints twelve members to represent literature, science, art, and social service. The other members are elected by state legislative assemblies. While the Rajya Sabha is not subject to dissolution, one-third of its members retire every two years.

The Lok Sabha, the House of the People, is composed of 543 members and, like the British House of Commons, is popularly elected for five-year terms. Additionally, two members are appointed to represent the Anglo-Indian community. Like the British House of Commons, each member is elected by the voters of a particular district in the states and union territories. The Lok Sabha elects its own presiding officer, the speaker, as in the UK. The popularly elected Lok Sabha, again like the House of Commons, is the more powerful of the two houses of parliament. All legislation of a financial nature—taxation, budgets, excises, and tariffs, for example—must originate in the Lok Sabha. The prime minister, the executive head of government, like the British prime minister, also must command a majority of seats in the lower house. If he or she loses a vote of confidence or a majority in the Lok Sabha, the prime minister must resign. Either he or she or his or her successor must gain a majority of the house to form a new government. If no one can muster a majority, the president of the republic dissolves the house and orders new elections.

The president of the republic is India's official head of state and commander in chief of the armed forces. The president is elected for a five-year renewable term by an electoral college, composed of members of parliament and state legislative assemblies. A ceremonial head of state, the president has nominal powers, except for in emergencies when presidential rule can be invoked where a state government cannot maintain law and order. Executive power, as in the UK, is vested in the prime minister, who governs with the support of a majority in the Lok Sabha. The prime minister appoints the Council of Ministers and the Cabinet, the key group in the council.

While electoral and political processes bring shifts in government leadership, the Indian Administrative Service (the civil service) staffs the ministries and departments on a continuing basis. Like civil services elsewhere, it is an instrument of stability, order, and continuity.[13]

India's judiciary, as in the U.S., is independent of the executive and legislative branches of government. As in the U.S., the Supreme Court is the country's highest judicial tribunal. Each state also has its own high court. There is a uniform code of civil and criminal laws for the entire nation.

State and Local Governments

The states' governing structure resembles the union. The executive branch is composed of a governor, a ceremonial post comparable to that of the president, and a chief minister and council of ministers, similar to the prime minister and cabinet. Each state has a popularly elected legislative assembly. A few states also have an upper house, the legislative council.

Grassroots citizen participation is encouraged through local councils, *Panchayati Raj*. While they bring some local involvement, most policy development and implementation, including that affecting education, remains hierarchical, from higher to lower units. Consequently, policy implementation slowly moves downward through administrative levels composed of political policy makers, civil servants, and practitioners.

Political Parties

India's political party system is highly complex and constantly shifting. Despite this complexity and high illiteracy rates, India has been a functioning democracy since independence in 1947. Symbols that represent the political parties are printed on ballots to assist illiterate voters.

Historically, the most successful national party has been the Indian National Congress Party (INC). Founded in 1885, it led the independence movement and enjoyed the support of Gandhi, Nehru, Patel, and other founders of the republic. The INC, with a national rather than regional base, is a middle-of-the-road centrist party that supports parliamentary government and secularism. Originally favoring a "mixed" public and private sector economy, it now favors economic liberalization. Throughout much of India's history, the INC has formed the government, and it does so currently.

The largest rival to the INC is the *Bharatiya Janata* Party (BJP), a right-wing nationalist, pro-Hindu and probusiness party. It usually garners the second largest bloc of votes in the Lok Sabha. Though supported by many Hindu religious and service organizations that give it a grassroots framework, it suffers from the infighting and splitting endemic to Indian politics. Economically, the BJP favors free market policies but is wary of globalization, which is not perceived to be in India's self-interest. The Left Front is a coalition of leftist parties such as the Communist Party of India (Marxist), the Revolutionary Socialist Party, and the All India Forward Bloc. Like many Indian political coalitions, the stability of such "marriages of convenience" is highly tenuous. Marxist in orientation, The Left Front is secularist and favors more public control over the economy.

The *Janata Dal*, or Peoples Party, a small left-of-center party, supports secularism, social democracy, and increased government reservations (affirmative action) for scheduled castes. It, too, suffers from factionalism and splitting. The *Samajwadi* Party, or Socialist Party, opposing the trend to privatization, supports maintaining and extending the public economic sector and increased social services.

Economic Context

India's economy includes, as does Nigeria's, both public (state) and private sectors. Independent India's early leaders, especially Nehru, were influenced by the British Labour Party model in which the state owned and operated some key sectors and engaged in long-range planning. This model of economic development included centrally designed five-year plans in which the union government was chief planner, investor, and regulator. Decision making featured political compromises to foster economic sharing among the states. Since the 1980s, India, like other nations, has moved toward less government involvement, more restructuring, and greater privatization. Some restrictions on foreign investment have been eased and import duties reduced.

India has a well-developed, government-regulated banking system. The Reserve Bank of India regulates circulation of bank notes, manages foreign exchange, and operates the currency and credit systems. Foreign aid, once a necessary and highly significant feature, has decreased in importance. In the past, considerable foreign aid, largely directed to agricultural development and irrigation projects, came from the U.S. and the USSR and from international organizations such as the World Bank and the International Monetary Fund.

Since independence, the union government has developed a series of plans to develop simultaneously the agricultural and industrial sectors. Agriculture, a historically prominent sector, occupies 65 percent of the population but accounts for 30 percent of India's GNP. India's major grain crops are wheat in the north and rice in the south. Other crops are tobacco, tea, cotton, jute, mangoes, and other fruits. In the 1960s and 1970s, the federal government undertook large-scale projects and dams for hydroelectric power and irrigation. The "Green Revolution," which encouraged the use of high-yield hybrid rice and wheat plants, fertilizers, and pesticides increased yields, brought more land under cultivation, and increased production.

India's manufacturing sector is diversified. A substantial majority of industrial workers work in small-scale handicraft industries, "cottage industries," such as weaving, pottery, metal and woodworking. State governments subsidize industrial parks, featuring cheap land and low taxes, to attract business and industry. While some factories remain government owned and operated, privatization is increasing. A similar trend toward privatization is also occurring in Mexico, the RF, and throughout Eastern Europe. Even in the Marxist PRC, the private sector is growing. Privatization produces important educational implications. While reducing central government manpower planning that once determined occupational assignment, it also carries economic risk in that jobs are no longer government subsidized and guaranteed. Consequently, secondary and higher education, especially vocational and technical training, are driven more by the marketplace than by government planning.

About 20 percent of India's vast labor force works in the "organized sector," which includes mining, industry, utilities, transportation, commercial, and service enterprises. Much of the organized sector is unionized. Strikes are frequent and protracted. Many unions are affiliated with one of the government's recognized and regulated all-India central trade union organizations, several with memberships in millions. Some trade unions identify with political parties.

Though making progress, India's economy faces significant problems. Obsolete equipment and outdated management strategies cause inefficiency. Working conditions in many factories are unsafe. Industrial production pollutes the environment, a condition found in other LTDCs such as Mexico and the PRC. As in other LTDCs, a large percentage of the population lives at or below the poverty line.

Historical Context

India's history reveals a general theme of intrusion by outside invaders, followed by a cultural clash with the indigenous people, and then a slow restoration of sociopolitical and cultural equilibrium. The reestablishment of cultural equilibrium involved assimilating the invaders into the cultural context and cultural borrowing from the invaders by the indigenous people.

Vedic Origins and Aryan Invasions

Like China, India is an ancient civilization whose origins can be traced to religious texts that date to 7000 BC. As in ancient Egypt's Nile Valley, river valley civilizations developed elaborate urban cultures in the Indus River Valley from 3000 BC to 1500 BC, with cities that boasted well-plotted brick houses, copper tools, and drainage and sanitation systems.

The Aryans were a significant formative force. Streaming into India from the northwest from 2500 to 1500 BC, the Aryan invaders, organized into tribes, were a central Asian nomadic people. Slowly, the Aryans conquered and imposed their rule over the indigenous Dravidians. They introduced their elaborately stratified social order that evolved into the caste system. The original four principal castes were (in order of importance): *Brahmins*, priest-scholars; *Kshatriyas*, rulers, judges, and warriors; *Vaishyas*, merchants; and *Shudras*, farmers. At very bottom of the caste hierarchy were outcastes, the untouchables who performed the most menial work.

Caste, historically, has a tight grip on education. The informal aspects of caste—rituals, duties, responsibilities, and roles—were learned by imitation. Formal schooling was for the upper castes, primarily the Brahmin scholar-priests.

The Aryans introduced their language, Sanskrit, the root language of modern Hindi, and their religious literature, the Vedas.[14] Without dogmatic creed, Hinduism, a syncretic religion, allowed multiple beliefs and rituals. Decidedly other-worldly, Hinduism emphasized reincarnation, a cycle of lives through which the soul must pass by undergoing a series births and deaths.

Following the historic pattern of invasion and assimilation, the Aryans imposed their social order on the conquered Dravidians, the indigenous people of south India, who began to follow Hinduism and caste. Resisting the imposition of Hindi, the Dravidians, however, preserved their own mother tongues.

269 BC–AD 1707

Rather than presenting a detailed history of India, we identify key formative periods. One such period was the Maurya dynasty, whose most famous ruler, the Emperor Ashoka, ruled almost the entire subcontinent from 269–232 BC.[15] In 262 BC, Ashoka became a convert to Buddhism, which originated as a reform movement in Hinduism. He devoted himself to diffusing Buddhism throughout Asia, where it became the paramount religion in countries such as Thailand and Sri Lanka. After enjoying an ascendancy in India, Buddhism declined as Hinduism regained its pre-eminence. After Ashoka's death in 232 BC, the Maurya empire disintegrated, collapsing in 184 BC.

After a period of political instability, the Gupta dynasty came to power, ruling India during the fourth and fifth centuries AD. Although their empire was not as extensive as the Mauryan, it included much of the subcontinent. During Gupta rule, certain enduring cultural patterns, especially caste, were firmly put in place as orthodox Hinduism reasserted itself against Buddhism and other sects. The Gupta era saw progress in scholarship and art, especially in literature, astronomy, and mathematics. The classical architectural tradition reached its definition and there were significant achievements in sculpture, dance, painting, and music.

In the thirteenth century, the process of invasion and assimilation continued. The new invaders, coming from central Asia, were Islamic tribes, the ancestors of India's Muslim population. In 1206, the Muslims established the Delhi Sultanate, named after its capital. By 1230, the Delhi Sultan controlled most of India. By the fourteenth century, the Sultanate, in decline, was replaced by another Islamic empire, the Mogul, founded by Zahiruddin Mohammad Babur in 1526. Akbar, ruling from 1556 to 1605, established the principal institutions of the Mogul dynasty. A skilled ruler, Akbar included Hindus in the imperial administration to ease tensions between Hindus and Muslims. The Mogul dynasty introduced a Persian and Arabic influence into India's art, music, literature, astronomy, mathematics, medicine, philosophy, religion, and architecture. When Aurangzeb, the last of the great Mogul emperors died in 1707, the empire fell to European incursions into the subcontinent.

Entry of Europeans

In the early eighteenth century, there was intense competition between Western colonial rivals such as the Portuguese, Dutch, Danes, French, and British for dominance in India. With the elimination of the minor contenders, France and Great Britain contested for control. After French military defeats, the Peace of Paris in 1763 marked the end of France's presence in India. From 1763 until 1857, the British East India Company, a trading company indirectly supervised by the British Parliament, governed India.

The East India Company exercised political as well as economic power in India. Initially, the Company did not interfere with the traditional Hindu and Muslim schools, many of which were typically one-room with a single teacher. Only a minority of high caste boys, about 10 percent, attended these schools where they engaged in religious reading, writing, and computation. School attendance was three or four years, with the hours of instruction irregular. Wealthier and higher caste families also employed tutors. Lower caste children informally learned their family's ascribed occupation.

Hindu higher schools, called *pathashalas* in western India and *tols* in Bengal, used ancient Sanskrit as the medium of instruction. Conducted by the priestly-scholarly Brahmins, they emphasized the Vedas (religious literature), mathematics, astronomy, and Sanskrit grammar. Muslim schools, called *madrassahs*, offered grammar, study of the Koran, and classes in the sciences. They used either Arabic or Persian as the language of instruction. Persian was India's official language until 1837.[16]

Under the first governor general, Warren Hastings, Company policy was to provide limited assistance to indigenous schools. In 1780, Hastings granted aid to support the Calcutta madrassah, an Arabic-language school that provided Islamic education. Not wishing to offend Calcutta's Hindu community, he provided similar support for a Hindu school, the Sanskrit College at Banaras, which provided instruction in the Hindu religion and literatures.[17]

Company policy makers were divided on their attitude to Indian culture and education. Some members, called Orientalists, were intrigued by India's cultures and founded the Royal Asiatic Society of Bengal to study India's history, antiquities, arts, and literature in 1784. Others, referred to as Anglicists, urged the Company to encourage Christianity, English language and literature, and Western sciences.[18]

In 1811, Lord Minto, the governor general, reported that indigenous education, literature, and science were decaying among natives of India. Recommending Company aid to improve education, Minto proposed assistance for the Calcutta madrassah and the Banaras Sanskrit College.[19] With the Charter Act of 1813, the Company began to introduce British education. The act directed the governor general to allocate 100,000 rupees annually for the "revival and improvement of literature" and "the introduction and promotion . . . of the sciences" in British India.[20]

From 1813 to 1823, the governor general continued to encourage indigenous education but encountered contentious factions. Christian missionaries, who had established a number of schools, were introducing English-language education and a Western curriculum. Upper-caste Hindus wanted control of their own schools. The Orientalist faction in the Company argued for noninterference in indigenous religion and education.[21]

In Calcutta, several English-medium language schools had been established by missionaries and as private ventures by Indians. While missionaries used English for religious conversion, enterprising Indians saw the English language and Western education as a means of securing positions in the British-controlled government and economy. In 1817, the Hindu College, the first college in India organized on Western lines, was established in Calcutta by Raja Ram Mohan Roy, David Hare, and Sir Edward Hyde East. Calcutta's educational situation signaled an alliance of British and Indians to develop the English educational model in India.

The Committee of Public Instruction, created in 1823, was to: (1) collect information on educational conditions and recommend policies to improve education; (2) devise a means to improve instruction and introduce useful knowledge; (3) oversee existing educational institutions; and (4) administer and allocate the annual education grant.[22] In the early years, Orientalists, following a policy of noninterference in Indian affairs, dominated the committee. While basically taking the Orientalist line, the committee made small concessions to English-language pressure groups. In 1834, it allowed English-language instruction in existing oriental colleges and authorized establishment of separate English schools at Delhi and Banaras.

Education in both England and India was influenced by the introduction and popularity of Joseph Lancaster's and Andrew Bell's methods of monitorial education. Bell's system was especially important. Bell, an Anglican clergyman in Madras, found he could teach the English language and the principles of the Church of England by having a few skilled master teachers train promising Indian students as teaching assistants. In turn, these students, acting as monitors, would instruct others in basic English-language skills and religious principles. Though limited to basic skills, Bell's method was an inexpensive way to teach large numbers of people.

Orientalist–Anglicist Controversies

From its establishment in 1823 until the issuance of Lord Macaulay's Minute in 1835, the Committee of Public Instruction faced controversies about the role of English-language instruction and introduction of a Western curriculum. Orientalists, preferring noninterference with indigenous Indian education, were continually challenged by Anglicist opponents who argued for English education. Finding Sanskrit and Persian inadequate in conveying modern knowledge, Anglicists claimed English, as a link language, would aid both the British governors and Indians.[23] By 1829, the Anglicists were on the ascendancy on the Committee of Public Instruction. Governor General Lord William Bentinck, arguing that India's economic progress needed "European knowledge, morals, and civilization," announced a policy to make English the "language of public business throughout the country." [24]

Macaulay's Minute, in 1835, ended Orientalist–Anglicist controversy and determined future educational policy in British India. Macaulay's Minute: (1) ended the Orientalist–Anglicists debates; (2) appeased the Christian missionary lobby; (3) imposed a solution to the issue of language conflicts by making English dominant; (4) satisfied the demands of India's middle classes for English-language and Western education; and (5) served British administrative and commercial needs. Macaulay's Minute significantly changed Company policy by ending support of indigenous education in Indian languages and restricted it solely to English-language schools. A highly important consequence was that many educated Indians would become isolated from their own country's cultural heritage. For promotion in the British-controlled system, Indians had to learn the language and imitate the style of British administrators. A wide chasm developed between India's urban elites and village masses. A practical consequence, however, was that English could serve as a link between the many native Indian languages and provide a means of communication, if even for an elite few.

English, rather than India's classical languages, became the language of instruction in higher education. For admission to institutions of higher education, applicants needed to attend English-language preparatory and secondary schools. With English as the language needed for official appointment, Indians, especially the middle classes and castes, increasingly demanded English education. Publishers began printing more books in English. Lord Harding's resolution in 1844 gave preference in government employment to Indians educated in English. The secondary and higher education system was reoriented to train Indians for lower administrative positions.

The implementation of the English-language policy in India, called the "filtration" or "trickle down" theory of education, was comparable to other colonial situations, including those in Nigeria. Once key Indians were educated in English, they would then transmit their knowledge to others in their own vernaculars. The upper and middle classes and castes would be educated first, then Western learning would be diffused throughout the population. In reality, the English language and Western education reached only a small urban elite. British educational policy actually created a new class, the Indian middle class, which used English education to their advantage. However, the imposition of English and the introduction of Western education also had a long-range unanticipated consequence in stimulating the independence movement, a situation that occurred in other colonial nations as well. Future leaders of the INC, such as Gandhi, Nehru, Patel, and others who read about English liberalism and socialism, applied the lessons learned to their own country.

In 1854, Sir Charles Wood's Educational Dispatch proposed the creation of a complete system of education in India. Wood believed that the Western system would rouse in Indians a desire "to emulate us" in developing their country's "vast resources" and provide them with "all the advantages" of commercial development. Such a system would also work to British advantage in securing "a larger and more certain supply of many articles necessary for our manufactures" as well as an "almost inexhaustible demand for the produce of British labour."[25]

The imposition of the British language and Western education had serious consequences. First, the education of the vast majority of the population, the millions of village children, was neglected. Second, the educated English-speaking elite tended to be separated from India's major problems. Although the British intended to Westernize this elite, their education, in the British tradition, was highly literary. In the British civil service tradition, the best preparation for administrative duties was the classics and English history and literature. This education lacked scientific, technological, engineering, and managerial subjects. The result was that the Indian-educated elite (about 2 percent of the total population) was prepared like English civil servants but, nonetheless, was regarded as inferior by their British supervisors.

As the nineteenth century ended, India—divided into British India ruled directly by Great Britain and the many princely states indirectly under English rule—was regarded as the crown jewel of the Britain's far-flung worldwide empire. British rule in India represented a classic illustration of European colonialism with an English touch. The British were primarily imperialistic colonists who exploited India but they, like other invaders who preceded them, contributed to Indian culture. While promoting imperial interests, they established a semblance of unified political and legal rule for India as they did in Nigeria. To rule such a vast territory and diverse population, the British brought civil servants and educators from the UK to staff upper positions in the colonial government. These English civil servant administrators, tending to live in protected enclaves, were socially isolated from the indigenous population. Their role was to protect and promote imperial interests, which meant establishing and maintaining a British version of law and order. To facilitate their rule, the British trained a small portion of the Indian population to fill subordinate civil service, administrative, and military posts. For example, a British administrator would generally have an

Indian deputy and staff working under his supervision. To control the country, the British developed an internal communications and transportation infrastructure—a network of roads, canals, railways, and telegraph lines.

Gandhi

In human history, certain individuals appear on the world stage, exerting an influence that transcends their life and times. Mohandas K. Gandhi (1869–1948) was such a person. In the PRC, the very different Mao Zedong was another such figure. Gandhi, the son of an upper-caste government official in Kathiawad, attended primary and secondary schools at Rajkot and the Sarmaldas College in Bhavnager and then studied law in the U.K. Completing legal studies, he returned to India in 1891 to practice law in Bombay.

With the exception of a year in India, Gandhi, from 1893 to 1914, was in South Africa as legal counsel for an Indian business firm. To deal with discriminatory practices in South Africa he developed strategies of nonviolent, passive resistance against the discriminatory laws. To prepare his followers for nonviolent protest, he established educational centers, or *ashrams*. Gandhi emphasized that Indians' mutual interests were stronger than the traditional barriers of religion, language, and caste.[26]

Between 1905 and 1914, Gandhi mobilized South Africa's Indian community using *satyagraha*, or "spiritual force," as a strategy of nonviolent civil disobedience, passive resistance, and noncooperation against unjust laws. The Indian Relief Act, passed in 1914, eased disabilities against the Indian population.

In 1915, Gandhi returned to India and commenced the independence movement that occupied the next thirty-three years of his life. Gandhi organized civil disobedience campaigns to persuade the British to voluntarily "quit" India. With their resources depleted by World War II and led by a Labour government, the British left India in 1947. With independence achieved, India began the process of nation building. Although Gandhi opposed India's division, two independent nations—India and Pakistan—were established rather than one united nation. The Hindu and Sikh minorities in Pakistan, a Muslim nation, began an exodus to India while many Muslims in India migrated to Pakistan. In the midst of this massive relocation, communal rioting and massacres erupted. Deeply saddened, Gandhi began a fast, which lasted until the rioting subsided. On January 30, 1948, he was assassinated by Vinayak Godse, a fanatical Hindu nationalist.

Gandhi's Educational Ideas

Gandhi's educational philosophy rested on the premise that human beings, for their own self-perfection and contribution to society should be developed intellectually, physically and spiritually.[27] He rejected the inherited British-imposed colonial education as causing dependency rather than independence. Independent India required an awakening of national cultural consciousness by the study of its indigenous history, languages, and literature. Gandhi wanted the study of one's own cultural heritage to lead to national and personal self-esteem but not to ethnonationalist chauvinism. His antidiscrimination philosophy opposed discrimination against lower castes and untouchables.

Gandhi believed that education could revitalize India's economy, especially in its many villages. For him, small industries, producing handicrafts, was the key to economic revitalization. However, government planners, paying lip service to Gandhi's theory, concentrated on large projects designed to stimulate industrial modernization.

Gandhi developed a plan for "Basic Education," which he believed would counteract the inherited Indian bias against manual labor and the modern tendency to antisocial individualism.[28] In *India of My Dreams*, he stated, "Unless the development of the mind and body goes hand in hand with a corresponding awakening of the soul, the former alone would prove to be a poor lop-sided affair."[29] He recommended that a child's education commence by learning a useful craft that enabled her or him "to produce from the moment" training begins.[30]

In 1937, an all-India educators' conference, endorsing Gandhi's "Basic Education," called for: (1) free and compulsory education for seven years throughout India; (2) the use of the pupil's mother tongue as the language of primary instruction; (3) the entire educational process to be craft centered, with instruction related to the central craft taught in the school.[31] After independence, the government took some limited efforts to implement Basic Education. Today, less than 20 percent of Indian school children of primary school age attend Basic Education schools. Instead of encouraging "bottom up" development education originating in the villages as Gandhi urged, the government strategy has generally been to modernize from the top downward by training scientific and technological elites.

Political Leaders 1949–2005

India's first prime minister, Jawaharlal Nehru, an associate of Gandhi in the National Congress, was a highly educated, cosmopolitan political leader. He was attracted to parliamentary government on the British model but in the context of a secular republic. Familiar with the works of British Fabian Socialists, Nehru believed that the new India should incorporate state-planned democratic socialism.

Facing highly complex challenges that appeared insurmountable, Nehru had to integrate the 500 princely states, which had their own nominal rulers under the British, into the new India. By 1950, the princely states had been brought into the republic, but the difficult challenge of demarcating state boundaries remained. As in the Balkans, India's various communal religious, language, and ethnic groups do not live in neatly contiguous land areas.

In 1966, Indira Gandhi, Nehru's daughter, became prime minister. A shrewd and determined politician, Mrs. Gandhi forcefully implemented her program of nationalizing banks and launching the Green Revolution in agriculture. In 1975, the High Court found Mrs. Gandhi guilty of corruption.

She responded by declaring a state of emergency from 1975 to 1977. A backlash against her split the INC into pro- and anti-Indira factions and she lost the 1977 elections. Winning the 1980 elections, she returned to office. India faced religious tensions between Hindus and Sikhs, some of whom demanded creation of a separate autonomous Sikh state. After a military action against the sacred Sikh Golden Temple, Mrs. Gandhi was assassinated by her own Sikh bodyguards.

Rajiv Gandhi, Indira's son, succeeded her as prime minister. He proposed to lead India to greater modernization with special efforts to develop industry and technology. In 1989, Rajiv Gandhi's party, Congress I, was defeated in the elections. The shaky coalition of parties that replaced him was forced to call new elections in 1991 and Gandhi launched a populist style campaign. While campaigning, Rajiv Gandhi was assassinated by a bomb detonated by a Sri Lankan Tamil nationalist.

Manmohan Singh, elected prime minister in 2004, heads a government that is a coalition of parties called the United Progressive Alliance (UPA). The UPA pledges to build "a prosperous, inclusive, equitable, humane, caring and just India."[32] Singh and the UPA are establishing a Knowledge Commission to educate India's large and growing young population so they are prepared for the challenges of the twenty-first century.[33]

Governance and Administration of Education

Governance and Finance

Unlike the U.S. where state and local governments have the primary responsibility for educational planning and policy making, in India this responsibility is shared by the union and state governments. Educational policy making is complicated by this concurrent relationship.[34] Policy implementation must filter from the top downward through four governmental layers—central, state, district, and local—and there is no guarantee that the states and local districts will actually implement the policies originating at the union level.[35] There is only limited opportunity for a reverse flow from the local level upward. Furthermore, an intricate network of planning agencies has been established to provide a coordinating mechanism to deal with India's complex socioeconomic and educational issues and future development. While the theory works to some extent, there is a tendency to sacrifice practical implementation to theoretical planning.

The administration of education in India is conducted by the Department of Education, a component of the Ministry of Human Resource Development (MHRD). The cabinet minister who heads the MHRD has overall responsibility, and subordinate to the cabinet minister is a minister of state for education. The Department of Education develops national educational policies and administers and finances certain national and regional educational institutions operated by the central government.[36] As in the U.S., India's Department of Education is a source of educational information and statistics. In particular, the union department is a key agency in the national literacy campaign. The states, however, exercise primary but concurrent control for primary and secondary education.

Like the central government in France, the union government in India has encouraged more local authority over schools. For example, a new and ambitious project, *Lok Jumbish*, seeks to stimulate grassroots popular involvement in education in Rajasthan. The project creates Village Education Committees, elected by the community, to survey local elementary education needs, prepare an improvement plan, and implement change. Supported by the state government, the project aims at decentralizing authority in what traditionally is a highly centralized area. The project is an initiative to encourage local participation.[37]

Each state and union territory has its own ministry of education, headed by a secretary who generates policies in conjunction with the state legislature. The states are subdivided into districts, each of which has an educational administration headed by a district education officer in charge of elementary and secondary education. Assisted by deputies and subdeputies, the district education officer inspects and supervises schools. The districts are further subdivided into smaller units called blocks. Each block has a block educational officer in charge of elementary and nonformal education. Most schools have a headmaster or headmistress, who establishes the schedule, implements curriculum, and supervises teachers. In very small one-room or two-room schools, teachers perform these functions. In rural areas, primary education is organized through legislatively empowered village councils, or *panchyats*.

A persistent theme in India's educational planning is prioritization. Which educational levels should be allocated scarce economic resources? Though theoretically committed to universal education, India's planners tend to give greater priority to higher education, particularly in professional and technical fields. They believe that advances in higher education will seep downward and eventually benefit elementary and secondary schools. Other LTDCs employ this type of planning as well. Others argue for grassroots development that concentrates more resources on combating illiteracy and primary schooling. Generally, the top-down modernizers dominate policy making with 25 percent of total educational expenditures allocated to higher education. The scramble for a share of scarce economic resources generates continuing issues, not only in India, but also in other LTDCs.

The financing of education is rather complicated. Funds come from the union and state governments, local authorities, fees, endowments, and voluntary contributions. The union and state governments provide about 70 percent, fees about 16 percent, local bodies about 6 percent, and other sources about 8 percent. Although it varies from year to year, approximately 20 percent of total government spending is directed to education. Of these, approximately 65 percent comes from the states. The union contribution is channeled to states as part of their share of income and excise tax revenues.[38] Approximately 4 percent of the GNP is devoted to education.

Organization and Structure of Schools

In India's federal–state government system, as in the U.S., it is difficult to achieve educational standardization and articulation between state systems. The essential structure is the 10 + 2 + 3 pattern: that is, ten years of primary and lower secondary school, two years of higher secondary school, and three years of higher education for the bachelor's degree. Variations still exist, however, in that some states have ten and other states eleven years of primary–lower secondary schooling. The school year, which generally runs from July to April with short vacations in October and December, also varies from state to state.

Preprimary Education

Since compulsory education does not begin until age six, the union and state governments are not highly involved in preprimary education. Neither does the socioeconomic situation encourage preprimary education to the extent found in more technologically developed nations. Throughout rural and village India, the family pattern is the extended rather than the nuclear pattern. Grandparents, parents, aunts, cousins, and older siblings often care for children. Although the working mother phenomenon is beginning to occur in urban areas, it occurs much less in India than in more technologically developed nations. Due to the labor-intensive economy, wealthy families generally employ live-in "nannies" or servants to care for younger children.

India's recent history has shown that with the recent trend toward modernization, there is an increase in early childhood and preprimary education. Furthermore, kindergarten is well established in urban-area schools.

Another encouraging development is that some municipalities now operate nursery schools and integrated day care for infants and children in housing developments. The Central Social Welfare Board and the Community Development Administration also organize nursery schools, *balwadis*, in depressed rural areas. To improve low school attendance in tribal areas, the government sponsors residential programs.[39]

Elementary Education

Elementary education, a constitutional right of every Indian child, is a long-standing national priority. Despite this priority, India's elementary education has faced persistent problems involving: (1) improving curriculum; (2) providing facilities; (3) increasing participation; (4) reducing the dropout rate; (5) facilitating the education of working children; and (6) strengthening elementary teachers' professional training. In 1986, the National Policy on

Education addressed these problems through a strategy that: (1) promoted child-centered activity-based instruction; (2) ended retention at the primary level; (3) eliminated corporal punishment; and (4) created schedules suited to the needs of working children.[40]

Despite persistent problems and funding inadequacies, Indian elementary education has grown and developed. There has been a steady increase in the number and location of elementary schools so that 99 percent of the rural children can attend a school within two miles of their homes.[41] Lower primary schools exist in all villages with a population of three hundred or more.

Despite some state variations, primary schools generally follow a pattern that includes two levels: lower primary classes one through five and higher primary classes six through eight. In some states, primary education ends with class seven. The provision of higher primary schools, however, remains uneven, especially in remote rural and tribal areas.

India's educators have long struggled against the persistent problem of educational wastage, a high dropout rate that exceeds 40 percent. Children often drop out of school to work in local agriculture or craft industries. An estimated 49 percent of elementary pupils drop out before completing five years of primary schooling.[42] The lack of higher primary facilities is a major contributing factor to the high dropout rate, which approaches 80 percent in some states. Some states provide incentives such as scholarships, noon meals, and free uniforms and textbooks to encourage students to stay in school.

Primary schools are generally coeducational and follow a calendar of two hundred days of instruction. The responsibility for developing the primary curriculum resides primarily with the state education departments. With some variations from state to state, the primary curriculum includes reading, writing and spelling in the regional language, Indian culture and history, geography, arithmetic, science, and hygiene. Some states begin instruction in English as a second language in class three; other states, however, delay such instruction until class five or six. Both lower and higher primary examinations, set largely by municipal boards of education, are held at the end of each term. The examinations tend to be flexible, and students are usually not retained in the early classes. By class five, however, the examinations take on a rigidity similar to those in secondary and higher schools. Certificates of completion, needed for admission to secondary schools, are awarded to those completing primary school.

Operation Blackboard
Indian educational researchers identify inadequate primary school facilities as a significant factor in of the high dropout rate. For example, some primary schools lack such basic amenities as blackboards, drinking water, and sanitary facilities. Nearly two-thirds of the primary schools were one- or two-room facilities, with classes taught by one or two teachers.[43] "Operation Blackboard," a national program designed to upgrade elementary education by bringing schools up to national minimum norms, established the following

standards: (1) schools, of all-weather construction, are to have two large rooms; (2) classrooms are to be provided with essential furniture and supplies such as necessary toys, blackboards, maps, charts, and other learning materials; and (3) schools are to be staffed by at least two teachers, one of whom is a woman.[44]

While Operation Blackboard succeeded in bringing two-thirds of India's elementary schools into conformity with minimum standards, the school improvement strategy also revealed discrepancies between top-down planning and grassroots implementation. While the union government sought uniformity in facilities and instructional materials, state and district variations made standardization very difficult. Also, teachers were not always adequately inserviced in using new materials. Comfortable with the conventional textbook-based recitation, some teachers were reluctant to try new methods.[45]

Navodaya Vidyalayas

Navodaya Vidyalayas are coeducational residential "pace setting schools," usually one per district, in which talented pupils pursue an accelerated curriculum. These accelerated schools are operated by the *Navodaya Vidyalaya Samiti*, an autonomous society, under the Ministry of Human Resource Development and in affiliation with the Central Board of Secondary Education. The major objectives of Navodaya Vidyalayas are: (1) providing modern education for talented pupils without regard to socioeconomic background; (2) developing competence in three languages; and (3) serving as model schools for developing and sharing innovative instructional strategies. These schools are similar to magnet schools in the U.S. or key schools in the PRC.

Secondary Schools

The secondary education tradition in India has been highly academic rather than technical or vocational. Indigenous secondary schooling before British rule was literary and religious for both Hindus and Muslims. With the decision to impose a British model, secondary schools, designed for the elite rather than the masses, prepared students for university entry, which, in turn, prepared educated generalists rather than specialists. The academic pattern of secondary schooling continues to exercise a strong hold in India.

After achieving independence in 1947, India emphasized development and modernization as a national policy. However, India's modernization encountered a formidable obstacle in the inherited pattern of the educating nonspecialist generalists. At the policy-making level, there was debate over which type of secondary schooling should prevail: general academic or technical-vocational secondary education. Also, there were those who argued that Indian secondary education should be comprehensive.

The predilection for humanistic, general, academic education remains very strong among policy makers and the public. This tendency is accentuated by the power of higher institutions, universities, to set the curriculum of the secondary schools. University entry examinations virtually dictate the secondary school curriculum and teaching style. Further, the more affluent castes and classes, seeking the most effective route of entry to prestigious universities, patronize private preparatory secondary schools as do the elites in the UK. Despite the persistence of the academic preparatory function of secondary school, some inroads have been made for technical-vocational education. The Indian education system, like the country's political system, gravitates toward consensus in which contending factions achieve partial rather than complete satisfaction of their demands.

At the time of independence, the organization and structure of elementary and secondary schooling varied considerably in the states and territories. In the late 1960s, the Korthari Education Commission achieved a degree of standardization between the states. Secondary education consists of lower secondary classes nine and ten, and higher secondary classes eleven and twelve. Higher secondary education continues the traditional emphasis of preparing students for university entry. Approximately 40 percent of males and 22 percent of females in the age cohort fifteen to seventeen attend secondary schools.

The secondary curriculum, set by union and state boards of secondary education, includes mathematics, science, history, geography, languages, arts, health, and physical education. English is often studied as a second language. Since the lower secondary classes are often terminal for the majority of students, its curriculum also emphasizes community and civic competencies and service. For example, an objective of mathematics and science education is the application of knowledge to issues such as conservation of natural resources; reduction of environmental pollution; and proper hygiene, diet, and health. Some vocational courses are included in the curriculum.

Secondary schools are in session for 220 days each year. The school day is five hours in lower secondary and six to seven hours in higher secondary schools. Indian secondary teachers typically follow very closely the official curriculum and syllabus. Unlike American teachers, those in India have only a slight influence on curriculum development, which tends to be examination-driven. In school systems closely tied to external examinations such as in India, Japan, and the PRC, secondary teachers are constrained to adhere closely to approved syllabi and to follow textbooks. Deviations from the syllabi for discussion purposes is discouraged and often resisted by students. Based on examination results, the boards of education award certificates needed for admission to higher education or vocational training.

Vocational and Technical Education

In line with modernization efforts, Indian policy makers have sought to develop more industrial training institutes and polytechnic institutions to provide vocational education. Diploma courses in engineering and technology are offered at four hundred government-approved polytechnics, which enroll approximately 70,000 students. An approved polytechnic institution is one accredited by the All India Council for Technical Education and affiliated with the respective state board of technical education. While most are coeducational, forty-two approved polytechnics are women's institutions. Programs typically require three years to complete. In addition to approved institutions, there are many nonapproved institutions. Industrial training institutes offer vocational training and crafts courses. While entry requirements and programs vary, training programs typically require two years and an apprenticeship.

Teacher Preparation

Most primary teachers complete eight years of primary school and two years of lower secondary school. About half of India's lower and upper primary teachers have completed lower secondary school and completed additional education in upper secondary and teacher preparation institutions. Teachers at the lower and upper secondary levels have completed secondary school and earned an undergraduate bachelor's degree, with at least a year of study for the diploma or certificate of education. The central government sponsors pre-service and in-service teacher education programs.

Higher Education

India's university system was modeled after the University of London. The Universities of Calcutta, Bombay, and Madras were established in 1857 and made responsible for coordinating affiliated colleges by setting standards for courses and examinations, prescribing texts, and conferring degrees. By 1902, 191 colleges had been established and enrollments increased rapidly.

India's government has placed priority on higher education as the key to national development. India's emphasis on higher education is similar to other LTDCs such as Nigeria and Mexico. Earning advanced degrees is seen by many, especially the middle classes and castes, as the avenue to socioeconomic status and security.

Expansion of higher education has led to the currently existing 144 universities and twenty-five autonomous institutions with university status. Of these, five universities are exclusively for women's higher education. There are 6,912 colleges, of which 825 are exclusively for women.[46]

The union government created the University Grants Commission (UGC) as a national coordinating agency for higher education. The UGC, modeled after a similar agency in the UK, is a statutory, autonomous body that coordinates higher education, maintains standards, assesses institutions' financial needs, and allocates and disburses funds.

The major sources of income for state-sector higher education is funding from the union government for central institutions and from state governments for state ones. Federal and state funds constitute about 80 percent of the total income of institutions of higher education. Other government-provided income are UGC grants given to universities for special purposes, allotments from municipal boards, and endowments. These federal and state funds are supplemented by student tuition and fees.

From 1950 through the 1980s, expenditures for higher education grew at the rate of 14.8 percent annually, an impressive rate for an LTDC.[47] The real effect of these increased expenditures have been seriously eroded, as in other developing nations, by the general increase in population, economic inflation, and accelerating demand, especially by the middle classes, for increased student enrollment. Changes in higher education, such as fiscal retrenchment and privatization, can be anticipated as the Indian government follows the worldwide economic patterns of structural adjustment and economic stabilization at work in LTDCs.[48]

Governance

External guidelines for India's universities are determined by such higher education coordinating agencies as the UGC, the Medical Council, the Bar Council, and the All India Council for Technical Education. These external agencies provide some overall coordination and strategic planning for the largely autonomous institutions.

The internal governance and administration of universities tends to be uniform. The state's governor, as the chancellor of all universities in the state, acts as the formal head of the university and president of its senate. Actual administrative authority is exercised by the vice chancellor. Each university has a senate, a syndicate, and academic council that are its principal governing bodies. The senate, the highest internal governing body, establishes policies, controls the budget, reviews reports and accounts from lower units, establishes teaching and administrative positions, and confers degrees. The syndicate, monitoring operations, appoints, promotes, and determines the salaries of the teaching staff and manages the university's colleges, libraries, laboratories, dormitories, and hostels. The academic council, responsible for academic policy and affairs, establishes admission requirements and regulations, coordinates the faculty, and approves curricula and courses.

Programs, Degrees, and Participation

The minimum admission requirements are that the applicant have completed twelve years of schooling and earned a pass in a higher secondary and/or preuniversity examination. Additionally, some universities require students to pass their own entrance examinations. There is vigorous debate over making these requirements more academically rigorous or relaxed.

Most universities offer undergraduate degree programs in such major fields as humanities, social and natural sciences, and business. Some offer undergraduate professional degree programs in agriculture, engineering, medicine, and veterinary science. The program for the first degree, the bachelor's, is three years and the professional bachelor's is five years. The time required for postgraduate degrees varies with the particular field and requires the standard written and oral examinations and theses or dissertations.

Although possession of university degrees has been a well-established mark of status in Indian society among higher castes and social strata, there is an accelerating demand among the general population for greater and easier access to higher education. Rising expectations and possession of higher education degrees causes professionals in science, engineering, and medicine to abandon rural areas for urban amenities. (The phenomenon of rising higher education expectation is also a general trend among developing nations such as Mexico and Nigeria.) As a result, there is a steadily escalating pressure to create new institutions and to enlarge existing ones to accommodate more students. Critics of expansion counter that the rapid growth of higher education has not been matched by adding adequately prepared faculty, libraries, and laboratories. The result, they say, is an erosion of standards. Critics also contend that relaxed standards produce overcrowded campuses and admission of many students who lack needed academic background and skills.

Despite its expansion, wide disparities in access and representation in higher education exist between and within states, between urban and rural areas, between men and women, and between scheduled and non-scheduled castes. Significant differences exist in the ability of the different states and regions to support higher education. India has an inherited residue of discrimination against lower castes, untouchables, and tribals. As indicated, the constitution outlaws disabilities because of caste, and the union and state governments seek to ensure equitable access and treatment of members of scheduled castes and tribes. Government "affirmative action" provides access for members of scheduled castes and tribes to colleges and universities through more relaxed entrance requirements, a quota of reserved places, and financial aid. Since Indian higher education operates in an environment of scarce resources, these affirmative action provisions are controversial. Opponents argue that aid should be based on merit rather than on reserved quotas.

India has a historical residue of gender discrimination that union and state governments are seeking to reverse by implementing strategies to equalize women's educational opportunities.[49] Although their access to higher education is increasing at undergraduate and graduate levels, women constitute only one-third of total enrollment. Attitudes favoring traditional gender roles persist. For women, the rewards of continuing their education still appear to be less than for men, who see continuing and higher education as opening new career possibilities. For some young women of certain castes and classes, higher education is regarded as a necessary qualification for securing a desirable husband. Family expectations often cluster around this traditional goal.[50] This initial reinforcement of traditional gender views are changing, however, as women enjoy more opportunities and become open to wider career possibilities.

India, like the PRC, faces the problem of "educated unemployability," as universities produce more graduates than the economy can employ. The consequence is either unemployment or the employment in positions for which graduates are overqualified. Educated unemployability leads to the migration of university-educated persons from their own country, as is the case of the PRC and Nigeria, to technologically developed Western countries. This "brain drain" is problematic for a country that has spent scarce resources on educating individuals who then decide to leave and no longer contribute to the nation that educated them.

Nonformal Education

In India, Mexico, Nigeria, and other LTDCs, nonformal education—educational and training efforts largely outside of schools and universities—is highly important. Formal institutions may lend personnel, facilities, and other resources to nonformal programs, but these programs do not have entrance, curricular, and other requirements found in formal settings. For example, a nonformal education experience might be a literacy class for illiterate adults in a village. The goal would be to develop basic reading and writing skills for adults who have not attended school. Or, it could be a demonstration of how to dig a tube well to irrigate fields or a project to inform village women about family planning. Nonformal education becomes an important substitute or complement in countries with large numbers of illiterate or undereducated persons who live in remote areas underserved by formal institutions. As part of its continuing literacy program, the union government sponsors a comprehensive program, the National Literacy Mission, in adult education.

In India as well as other LTDCs, nongovernmental private, voluntary, and philanthropic organizations (NGOs) sponsor and conduct nonformal education. Nonformal education, also emphasized in Mexico and Nigeria, is intended to substitute for or complement schooling. In India, for example, where large numbers of people have difficulty in participating or have dropped out of the formal school system.

To be effective nonformal education must be taken to the people and places where it is most needed—to rural areas, remote villages, and tribal regions. It must be flexible so that scheduling and content fit local needs rather than institutionally set standards. Despite its strengths, nonformal education is limited by its specificity and short duration. It often depends on voluntarism, which may be sporadic and short-lived. It is estimated that approximately 250,000 nonformal education centers in India serve more than five million persons.

Conclusion

The study of education in India is an opportunity to examine the processes of both tradition and change. One of the world's oldest civilizations, India is a highly traditional society that is making concerted efforts at modernization and development. The context of Indian education, a rich and often confusing mosaic, involves ancient religious heritages, residues of caste and colonialism, and language issues along with efforts to use education as an instrument of national modernization. India's movement to modernization can be contrasted with that of the PRC; while the process in India involves federal–state negotiations and compromises, the Chinese situation is organized and controlled by the national government.

India, as a former colony of Great Britain, has neo-colonial residues. Its language situation can be compared with Nigeria where there are many distinct languages and dialects. In both countries, the former colonial language, English, acts as a link language. Both Nigeria and India, as well as many other countries, have language controversies based on ethnic tensions. As a former colonial nation, there is an emphasis in India on humanistic and literary rather than applied and technological training.

India, Nigeria, and LTDCs share major educational issues. They have very high dropout rates, with many students leaving prior to completion of elementary schooling. They also have high illiteracy rates among adults and a tendency for young people, who drop out, to slip back into illiteracy. These countries, with very limited financial resources, must make difficult strategic decisions. The pronounced trend is to give higher education the highest priority, under the assumption that the development of the higher education sector will eventually trickle down to and benefit elementary and secondary schooling. Further, in India and Mexico a growing middle class, with rising economic and social expectations, has pressured politicians to expand higher education.

Indian culture reveals processes of assimilation of new trends and movements into the ancient social and cultural fabric. India's movement to the future is a story of slow and sometimes halting progress. Its governance of education shows policies and plans developed at the top, slowly filtering downward, through layers of bureaucracy. Its school system, struggling to modernize, also reveals strong traditionalism.

DISCUSSION QUESTIONS

1. Analyze the impact of Hinduism on Indian culture and education.
2. How has Indian culture tended to assimilate invading peoples?
3. Describe the educational effects of imperialism on Indian culture and education.
4. What was the context of British India and how did it affect education?
5. Identify the key events in Gandhi's life. Indicate how these events contributed to shaping his character.
6. Identify aspects of Indian culture and education that might be relevant to the study of multiculturalism in American schools.
7. Examine India's government and politics. How is the country governed? Is it a republic, a dictatorship, a constitutional monarchy? Is there a par-

liament or legislature? Is it a one- or multiparty nation-state? Is the provision of education centralized, regional, local, or decentralized?

8. Examine India's economy. Is it a capitalist or socialist country? Does it have a state planned or a free market economy? What is the GNP? Is it a technologically developed or technologically underdeveloped country? What are the economic problems?

9. Examine educational governance, policy, and financing in India. Which government agencies are responsible for providing and supervising educational services? How are educational policies developed and implemented?

10. Examine preschool and early childhood arrangements in India. Are preschools available? Who attends? What are the purposes and programs in early childhood education?

11. Discuss elementary or primary schools. How is primary or elementary education defined and organized? How are primary or elementary schools organized? What are the component skills and subjects of the elementary curriculum? Who attends primary school? Are there differences between urban and rural schools?

12. Discuss secondary education. How is secondary education defined? How is secondary education organized? Are there a variety of secondary school patterns of organization? Who has access to secondary education? Are there selective examinations? Does secondary education encourage or discourage socioeconomic mobility? What is the nature of the curriculum? Is there equal opportunity or racial, class, and gender discrimination?

13. Examine higher education. How is higher education defined and organized? Who has access to higher education? Are examinations used to determine access? Is there equal access to higher education or is there racial, class, and gender discrimination?

RESEARCH TOPICS

1. In a research paper, examine an aspect of the imposition of British educational structures on India during the colonial era.

2. Review a biography of Gandhi.

3. Prepare a research paper that compares Gandhi and Martin Luther King, Jr., on the use of nonviolent passive resistance.

4. In a paper, compare the impact of untouchability on India's society and education with racism's effects in the U.S.

5. In a short paper, examine the geography and demographics of India.

6. Prepare a historical overview that describes in a general way how the past has had an impact on culture, politics, society, and education in India. What major events of the past shaped the present situation in the country? Was it a former colonial possession? Did invasions introduce new ideas? How did the country face its future?

7. In an overview paper, describe the cultural and religious context of India. Is there an official state church or a dominant religion, or is there separation of church and state? Are there pervasive cultural elements that have had an impact on educational philosophy? Are there religious tensions that have had an impact on educational philosophy, policy, and schooling?

SUGGESTIONS FOR FURTHER READING

Andrews, C. F. *Mahatma Gandhi at Work*. New York: Macmillan, 1931.

Ashe, Geoffrey. *Gandhi*. New York: Stein and Day, 1968.

Duncan, Ronald. *Gandhi: Selected Writings*. New York: Harper and Row, 1972.

Erikson, Erik. *Gandhi Truth*. New York: Norton, 1972.

Fischer, Louis. *The Essential Gandhi: His Life, Work, and Ideas, An Anthology*. New York: Vintage Books, 1962.

Fischer, Louis. *The Life of Mahatma Gandhi*. New York: Harper and Row, 1952.

Gandhi, Mohandas K. *An Autobiography or the Story of My Experiments with Truth*. Boston: Beacon Press, 1957.

Gibney, Frank. *The Pacific Century: America and Asia in a Changing World*. New York: Charles Scribner's Sons, 1992.

Holmes, Brian. *Equality and Freedom in Education: A Comparative Study*. London: George Allen & Unwin, 1985.

Ignas, Edward, and Raymond J. Corsini. *Comparative Educational Systems*. Itasca, IL: F. E. Peacock Publishers, 1981.

Iver, Raghavan. *The Moral and Political Writings of Mahatma Gandhi*. Oxford: Clarendon Press, 1986.

Kabir, Humayun. *Education in New India*. London: George Allen & Unwin, 1956.

Kabir, Humayun. *Indian Philosophy of Education*. New York: Asia Publishing House, 1961.

Mukerji, S. N. *History of Education in India*. Anand, India: Anand Press, 1957.

Ramanathan, G. *Education from Dewey to Gandhi*. London: Asia Publishing House, 1965.

Saiyidain, K. G. *The Humanist Tradition in Modern Indian Educational Thought*. Madison, WI: Dembar Educational Research Services, Inc., 1967.

Shirer, William. *Gandhi: A Memoir*. New York: Simon and Schuster, 1979.

Thomas, R. Murray, ed. *International Comparative Education: Practices, Issues, & Prospects*. New York: Pergamon Press, 1990.

Welty, Paul Thomas. *The Asians: Their Evolving Heritage*. New York: Harper and Row, Publishers, 1984.

NOTES

[1] CIA (Central Intelligence Agency), "The World Factbook: India," http://www.cia.gov/cia/publications/factbook/geos/in.html (accessed May 12, 2005), 3–4. Also see D. S. Muley, "The Indian Experience," *International Review of Education* 39(1–2) (1993): 118–124.

[2] Muley, 121–123.

[3] D. S. Sharma, "The Nature of Hinduism," in *The Religion of the Hindus*, ed. Kenneth W. Morgan (New York: Ronald Press, 1953), 3–27.

[4] Ibid.

[5] Karuna Chanana, "Accessing Higher Education: The Dilemma of Schooling Women, Minorities, Scheduled Castes and Scheduled Tribes in Contemporary India," *Higher Education* 26 (1993): 71–72.

[6] Ibid., 70.

[7] Ibid., 70–71.

[8] Ibid., 74–75.

[9] *Program of Action* (New Delhi: Government of India, 1986), 198–199.

[10] *National Policy on Education* (New Delhi: Government of India, 1986), 5.

[11] Caroline Dyer, "Education and the State: Policy Implementation in India's Federal Polity," *International Journal of Educational Development* 14(3) (1994): 243.

[12] Ibid.

[13] Ibid.

[14] Percival Spear, *A History of India* (London: Penguin Books, 1990), 156.

[15] Ibid., 259.

[16] Michael Edwards, *Raj: The Story of British India* (London: Pan Books, 1967), 133.

[17] Ibid., 134.

[18] S. N. Mukerji, *History of Education in India* (Anand, India: Anand Press, 1957), 97.

[19] Edwards, 134–135.

[20] Ibid., 135.

[21] Ibid.

[22] Ibid., 136.

[23] Ibid., 133.

[24] Ibid., 137.

[25] Ibid., 144–145.

[26] Shriman Narayan, ed., *The Selected Works of Mahatma Gandhi*, vol. 2 (Ahmedabad: Navajivan Publishing House, 1968), 496.

[27] Shriman Narayan, ed., *The Selected Works of Mahatma Gandhi*, vol. 6 (Ahmedabad: Navajivan Publishing House, 1968), 104.

[28] K. G. Saiyidain, *The Humanist Tradition in Modern Indian Educational Thought* (Madison, WI: Dembar Educational Research Services, 1967), 89.

[29] M. K. Gandhi, *India of My Dreams* (Ahmedabad: Navajivan Publishing House, 1947), 185.

[30] Ibid., 186.

[31] G. Ramanathan, *Education from Dewey to Gandhi* (London: Asia Publishing House, 1965), 4–5.

[32] "Release of Report: 'A Caring Government—One Year of UPA'" (May 22, 2005), 1. http://pmindia.nic.in/lspeech.asp?id=131 (accessed May 26, 2005).

[33] Ibid., 3. Since the political situation in India is subject to frequent changes, consult newspapers, journals, and the Web for the current state of affairs.

[34] Dyer, 241–253.

[35] Ibid., 249.

[36] J. C. Aggarwal and Sarita Aggarwal, *Education in India (Comparative Study of States and Union Territories)* (New Delhi: Concept Publishing, 1990), 15.

[37] David Archer, "The Changing Roles of Non-Governmental Organizations in the Field of Education (in the Context of Changing Relationships with the State)," *International Journal of Educational Development* 14(3) (1994): 226.

[38] Aggarwal and Aggarwal, 16–17.

[39] Robert Cowan, *International Handbook of Education Systems* (New York: John Wiley & Sons, 1985), 198.

[40] *National Policy on Education* (New Delhi: Government of India), 1986), 11.

[41] Dyer, 241.

[42] Ibid.

[43] Ibid., 241–242.

[44] *National Policy on Education*, 11.

[45] Dyer, 251.

[46] University Grants Commission, *Annual Report for the Year 1988–1989* (New Delhi: University Grants Commission, 1989), 59.

[47] Jandhyala B. G. Tilak, "Financing Higher Education in India: Principles, Practice, and Policy Issues," *Higher Education* 26 (1993): 49.

[48] Ibid., 43.

[49] For more information on women's issues and their access to higher education see: Government of India, *Report of the Committee on the Status of Women* (New Delhi: Ministry of Human Resource Development, 1959); Government of India, *Towards Equality: Report of the Committee on the Status of Women* (New Delhi: Ministry of Human Resource Development, 1975); Government of India, *National Policy of Education* (New Delhi: Ministry of Human Resource Development, 1986); Government of India, *National Perspective Plan for Women 1988–2000 A.D.* (New Delhi: Department of Women & Child Development, Ministry of Human Resource Development, 1988).

[50] Carol Vlassoff, "Hope or Despair? Rising Education and the Status of Adolescent Females in Rural India," *International Journal of Educational Development* 14(1) (1994): 3–12.

EDUCATION IN NIGERIA

The newly independent nations of Africa that emerged as sovereign nation-states when the European colonial empires dissolved in the late 1950s and the 1960s faced problems of constructing national political and economic infrastructures. Each of these nations represents a developing area, a region of world importance, and forms an important link in making multicultural connections. Nigeria, like other newly independent African nations, has faced serious challenges of nation building. Social, political, economic, and educational conditions in Nigeria, including remnants of former colonial patterns; the need to create national institutions; and the special situation created by language, tribal, and ethnic divisions are illustrative of less technologically developed countries (LTDCs) in Africa as well as in other parts of the world.

Geographic and Demographic Contexts

The Federal Republic of Nigeria occupies 360,269 square miles and is located in west Africa. Bordering the Gulf of Guinea, it lies between the two smaller countries of Benin and Cameroon; it is bordered by Niger to the north and Chad to the northeast. Nigeria's climate ranges from equatorial in the southern lowland region, tropical in the central plateau and hill region, and arid to semi-arid in the northern plains. Recent estimates place its population at 133,881,703, making it Africa's most populous nation. A high 43.6 percent of its population is young, with the age cohort from 0–14 years. The age cohort from 15–64 years is 53.6 percent and that over 65 is 2.8 percent of the population.[1] The median age is 18 years. These statistics indicate that well over 50 percent of Nigeria's population is at primary and secondary school age. The need to provide schools and educational resources to such a large sector of the population presents an immense challenge for a country struggling for political stability and economic development.

Illiteracy is a very serious problem, also faced by India and other LTDCs. About 32 percent of Nigerians are illiterate. The rate is higher among women, estimated at 60.6 percent.[2] Typical of LTDCs, illiteracy rates are highest in rural areas.

Like other countries in sub-Saharan Africa, Nigeria has a serious AIDS problem. The adult HIV/AIDS prevalence rate is 5.8 percent, and an estimated 3,500,000 people have HIV/AIDS. These factors have lowered the life expectancy to 51.89 years and raised the infant mortality rate to 71.35 deaths per 1000 live births.[3]

Sociocultural Context

When Nigeria became independent in 1960, a new nation-state had to be built from what was really a collection of regions administered by British colonial rulers. Some observers contended that Nigeria was not a nation but rather an administrative convenience created by the British colonialists. Nigeria's road to nation building has been marked by a bloody civil war, tribal and religious antagonisms and rivalries, political turmoil, and successive coups.

Nigeria is composed of more than 250 ethnic groups. The largest of these groups are the predominately Islamic Hausa and Fulani, 29 percent of the population, who dominate the northern region; the Yoruba at 21 percent of the population are concentrated in the southwest; and the Igbo (Ibo), with a sizable Christian population, at 18 percent, live in the southeast. Among the other larger ethnic groups are the Annang, Ibibio, Kanuri, Tiv, Edo, Nupe, Ijaw, and Efik.[4] In addition to its major ethnic tribes, each region also has smaller tribes that tend to ally themselves with the larger and more dominant group.

In Nigeria as well as many other Africa nations, a person's primary identity is based on tribal membership. Shared beliefs, customs, and values are important elements in the cultural repository of tribal membership. Similar to ethnonationalism in Eastern Europe, tribalism, while providing identity, can also be a highly divisive force, especially because the first basis of loyalty, commitment, and identification is tribal rather than national.[5] Many of the internal political issues that have weakened the sense of national unity stem from the efforts of one tribe to secure status, jobs, and power over other tribes.[6] Tribalism has also been a rallying cause for political parties in these countries that base their support on the members of particular tribes.

The Nigerian government identifies education as a key agency in nation building, especially in achieving the goals of national integration and economic development. Many nation-states historically have relied on organized education, or schooling, as a form of civic education to create a sense of national identity among peoples of different ethnic, tribal, cultural, and language backgrounds. In the case of Nigeria, education is seen as an important agency for creating a political culture conducive to economic improvement.

Language Issues

Historically, nation-states such as France and the UK used a common culture and language to construct a sense of national identity. In these countries, schools, by teaching a common language, conveyed a national history and literature to create a national identity and ethos. The use of a common language in the language arts area in the school curriculum has been most effectively implemented in homogenous nations such as Denmark or Iceland. However, language policy, reinforced in national school systems, has provoked serious conflicts in multiethnic and multilanguage nation-states. In these nation-states, dominant language groups have often attempted to impose their language as the official one. The imposition of a particular language as the official one is often related to gaining and maintaining power. Key government, economic, and military positions are often held by those who use the official language.

As in other newly independent LTDCs, Nigeria's government planners emphasized education's role in nation building, especially with regard to the study of Nigerian history and culture as an ideological foundation for national unity. The problem, however, has been to create a shared national history where none existed. Educational planners who emphasized the need to use English as the official national language throughout the country faced resistance in that English, spoken by the elite groups, represented the colonial past of British rule. Nevertheless, English, which is used throughout the regions, has become the official language. In terms of Nigeria's native languages, students are to study the three major Nigerian languages—Igbo, Yoruba, and Hausa.[7]

Language teaching, which occupies so much instructional time, is a persistent concern for educators in any country. A common language, particularly one with a long history of use, conveys a certain worldview, or *Weltanschauung*, and values. For any people, the use of their language and its transmission to the young is a way of guaranteeing survival and perpetuation of the cultural heritage. A multiplicity of languages in countries such as Nigeria where historically there is no common link language makes it difficult to shape a unified national identity. For educational policy makers, language issues are often complex, controversial, and difficult to resolve, making it difficult to develop national plans and a common curriculum for nation building. Educational situations where there is a multiplicity of languages require large outlays of resources for language learning. In terms of instructional time, language learning, especially of languages other than one's vernacular, requires time-consuming drill and memorization. The more time spent on languages means that less time will be devoted to science, technical subjects, and other areas needed by LTDCs. Further, designing curricula and preparing textbooks, syllabi, and other educational materials in several languages means that they need to be prepared and duplicated in multiple-language editions. For LTDCs where trained educational specialists are few and financial resources are scarce, the cost is indeed heavy.

Nigeria, like other LTDCs in sub-Saharan Africa, exhibits a pattern of linguistic and tribal factionalism. Like India, Nigeria has resorted to compromises on the language issue. When Nigeria gained independence from Britain in 1960, it was decided that the languages of the major tribes should be adopted as national languages. Hausa and Fulani were to be used in the North, Yoruba in the West, and Igbo is the East. While Hausa, Fulani, Yoruba, and Igbo are the major languages, Nigeria has 250 different languages and dialects,[8] and the compromise did not work. After all, language is closely related to tribal membership, which in turn influences identification with regional rather than national political parties. People with particular tribal and language identification naturally fear domination by other tribes and language groups.

In addition to the problems caused by language and tribal factionalism, Nigeria, as well as other LTDCs, especially former colonial nations, face the issue created by the presence of a superimposed colonial language, which often serves as the link language. In Nigeria, as in India, the superimposed colonial language is English, which during British rule was the official language of government and education. The ability to speak English gave the speaker status and prepared the way for entry into the colonial civil service, military, and business communities. Ambitious parents who could afford to pay their children's tuition selected schools that enjoyed a reputation for their success in educating students in the English language and style of behavior. English remains an important link language within Nigeria as well as for its international contacts outside of the country.[9]

Countries with multiplicity of languages frequently have difficulties in establishing a language policy for education. Often such countries have a highly divisive political situation that can be aggravated by regionalism. In addition to Nigeria, India has had persistent language issues. Linguistic politics are not confined to LTDCs. Technologically developed nations such as Canada and Belgium have also experienced political conflicts over language divisions that may threaten the country's unity.

Since each group's language is intimately related to its cultural heritage, efforts to determine a single national language to unite all groups have been very difficult for the political and educational leaders of newly independent nations such as Nigeria. In their national plans for education, Nigerian leaders have frequently identified the need to create a cohesive sense of national identity shared by the nation's constituent ethnic, tribal, and language groups. However, which language should it be? To determine that one language is the official one could generate fear, resentment, and even insurrection among groups who do not use it.[10]

There is considerable rivalry between tribal and language groups who fear domination by rival groups. To maintain an ethnic and linguistic identity, it is important for these groups that schools do what the oral tradition did in the past, namely transmit and thus perpetuate the particular group's language and values. At times, the degree to which the various groups have either tried to maintain autonomy or to dominate the nation politically and economically has impeded national integration. Since the ethnic and language groups are regionally located, as in the countries that once comprised the former Soviet Union, social interaction and assimilation is limited. Nigeria and the nations of west Africa represent case studies of the need for multicultural education to foster interethnic and intertribal understanding.

Religion

Nigeria has considerable religious diversity. Religious affiliation is often concurrent with ethnic and regional identification. Fifty percent of the population are Muslims, 40 percent are Christians, and 10 percent follow indigenous naturalist religions. Embedded in language, ethnic, tribal, and regional differences, religious affiliations have generated serious tensions, especially between Muslims, notably the Hausa and Fulani, who follow Islam in the North and Christians, especially Igbo (both Catholic and Protestant), in the South. As noted, religious identification tends to follow tribal lines. Politically and educationally, one religious group fears domination by another. For example, Christians oppose the adoption of Islamic law as has occurred in several northern states. Voting also follows these religious, ethnic, tribal, and language divisions.

Political Context

As indicated, the British united the various regions constituting present-day Nigeria as an administrative convenience and as a counterforce to German colonial ambitions in Africa prior to World War I. By the end of World War II, movements for independence had surfaced in Nigeria as in the other African and Asian colonies of the European powers. The National Council of Nigerian Citizens (NCNC), founded by the Igbo leader Nnamdi Azikiwe, was organized as a national political party in 1944. In the early 1950s, the Action Group, largely a Yoruba party, and the Northern People's Congress (NPC) were organized. These parties were regionally and tribally rather than nationally based.

From 1960 to 1963, the central government was a coalition formed by the NPC and the NCNC. The early optimism of independence faded and weakened; tribally dominated politics disintegrated the governing coalition. Two political alliances were formed prior to the elections that were to be held in December 1964: The Nigerian National Alliance (NNA) and the United Progressive Grand Alliance (UPGA). The NNA consisted of the NPC and several other parties representing ethnic minorities. The NPC hoped to gain control of the government through an alliance with the Western Region. The UPGA consisted mainly of the NCNC, which wanted full control of the government, and other minor groups. The UPGA planned to divide the country into states so that the existing power structure would dissolve. The election was postponed due to voting irregularities and boycotting. In the end, the NNA prevailed, and the UPGA became the official opposition. The election results caused protests, violence, and disagreements within the government.[11] The contending regions challenged the validity of the 1964 elections.

Although officially a federal republic with a parliamentary government, Nigeria's fragile political reality erupted on January 15, 1966, in a coups d'état conducted by a clique of military officers who assassinated a number of leading politicians. The pretext for the coup was that the army was purging the country of corrupt politicians who were unable to effectively govern the nation.[12]

The 1966 coup inflamed tribal rivalries. The coup leader, Major Chukwuma Nzeogwu was an Igbo, from the southern region. Many killed in the coup were from the Hausa and Fulani tribes of the North. When political control was taken by Major-General Johnson Aguyi-Ironsi, also an Igbo, Hausa army officers staged a countercoup. Ironsi was assassinated and widespread tribal violence erupted.[13]

After the coup of January 15, 1966, which forced President Nnamdi Azikiwe to flee the county, army officers took control of Nigeria. Once in power, the ruling officer clique entrenched itself in the government structure, subverting the constitutionally established representative political processes.[14]

Nigeria has experienced ethnic tensions similar to those of the Balkans. On May 30, 1967, the Igbo area of eastern Nigeria, led by Lt. Colonel Chuknumeka Ojuku, proclaiming its independence as Biafra, seceded from Nigeria. The Nigerian government was determined to crush the secessionist movement, and a bloody civil war took place that did not end until 1970. The civil war has left deep scars and divisive memories.[15]

After nearly sixteen years of military rule, a new constitution was adopted in 1999. This was followed in the same year by the military's relinquishing of power and a peaceful transition to an elected civilian government headed by President Olusegun Obasanjo, a member of the People's Democratic Party. G. O. Enukora is secretary of the Federal Ministry of Education and Youth Development.

Today, Nigeria, officially the Federal Republic of Nigeria, consists of 36 states and the Federal Capital Territory. The president is both the chief of state and the head of the government as in the U.S. and Mexico. The president is elected by popular vote for a four-year term and, as in the U.S., is limited to two terms.

Nigeria's federal legislative branch, the bicameral National Assembly, consists of the Senate, the upper house, and the House of Representatives, the lower house, whose members are elected by popular vote for four-year terms. The Senate is composed of 109 members, three of whom are elected from each of the 36 states and one from the Federal Territory. The House of Representatives is composed of 346 members.

Nigeria has a multiparty system. Among the major political parties are the Alliance for Democracy (AD), the All Nigeria Peoples Party (ANPP), the All Progressive Grand Alliance (APGA), the National Democratic Party (NDP), the Peoples Democratic Party (PDP), the Peoples Redemption Party

(PRP), the People's Salvation Party (PSP), and the United Nigeria Peoples Party (UNPP).[16]

Nigeria's legal system is based on the English common law, traditional law, and in some northern states on Islamic Shariah law. Based on the Koran, the Shariah law is a common law to govern the lives of Muslims. There have been serious controversies regarding the imposition of Shariah in northern areas, especially in relation to women's rights. The highest court is the Supreme Court, whose members are appointed by the president. The federal court of appeals is appointed by the federal government on the advice of the Advisory Judicial Committee.

Economic Context

Nigeria is a potentially rich nation in terms of resources, including natural gas, tin, columbite, iron ore, coal, limestone, lead, zinc, and most importantly, large petroleum reserves, but these have been often misused. Nigeria's economic history tells how the nation attempted to develop and often failed in its economic planning and implementation.

As early as the 1960s, government leaders recognized the relationship between investment in education and the development of the economy. Nigerian economic planners followed an essentially linear development strategy in which infrastructure modernization was centrally planned and implemented. *Investment in Education*, the Ashby Commission's report on Post-School Certificate and Higher Education in Nigeria, stated education's economic role: Secondary and higher education were to prepare technically skilled people needed for modernization. To implement the plan, Nigeria made a significant initial investment in education. As the comparative educator John Hanson then stated, the "quality of human resources . . . largely accounts for the change in economic output." The quality of human resources, or trained personnel, in turn, depended upon the quality of the nation's "educational system." To Hanson, "one of the greatest investments Nigeria" could "make in its economic future" was to invest in "the appropriate education of its people."[17] This goal has also been paramount in India.

By the late 1980s, however, many international development experts had abandoned top-down linear modernization models because they often required economic resources that exceeded LTDCs' realistic possibilities. Further, the modernization strategies, developed some twenty years earlier, were now criticized for neglecting local options and generating inequalities that exacerbated urban–rural differentials. Pointing to Nigeria and other LTDCs that had used top-down centralized development strategies, critics contended that their emphasis on higher education had not only neglected primary schooling but had created discontented classes of degree-holding unemployables.

Despite its wealth of natural resources, including petroleum, Nigeria's economy shows serious weaknesses. Some commentators on economic development contend that LTDCs like Nigeria have excessively intervened in their economics, creating "parasitical" states with "bloated" bureaucracies that stifle private-sector growth.[18] The World Bank and other international agencies have encouraged greater privatization and structural adjustment policies to reduce the government's involvement in running industries. It is assumed that privatization of industries will induce greater competition, efficiency, and growth. By eliminating government ownership and adding private businesses to the tax rolls, revenues for education and infrastructure development will increase.[19] Nevertheless, the actual consequences of privatization have been a reduction in government spending on social services, pensions, and often education.

Despite an announced commitment for infrastructure building, Nigeria shows serious weaknesses in its economic development. Mexico is also an LTDC that is striving for infrastructure development. Comparisons between Mexico and Nigeria illustrate Nigeria's staggering problems. For example, infant mortality in Nigeria is twice as high as it is in Mexico; only 64 percent of Nigeria's children under age five are free from malnutrition as compared to 86 percent in Mexico. Nigeria's primary school enrollment is only 40 percent that of Mexico. Basic infrastructure developments lag in availability of potable drinking water, electrical power generation, and roadway construction and maintenance. A report of the World Bank, noting that Nigeria's potential for development remains unfulfilled, found microeconomic and fiscal policies to be the chief impediments to economic growth. Among the serious economic issues facing Nigeria are a high rate of inflation, mounting government budget deficits, and inadequate mechanisms of revenue collection. Public service delivery is also poor with little accountability in managing resources.[20] The World Bank and the International Monetary Fund and other international agencies have urged Nigeria, like other LTDCs, to liberalize trade, embark on structural adjustment of the economy with greater privatization and accountability, and begin serious agricultural reform. A major requirement of restructuring lies in reducing government expenditures by streamlining government.

Still another related issue in many LTDCs such as Nigeria is the environment. Nigeria has serious problems of soil degradation, deforestation, and urban air and water pollution. China, India, and Mexico, as well as Nigeria, are becoming more industrial but often without the necessary safeguards for environmental protection. Russia, too, inherited environmentally damaging industries from the Soviet period. Critics contend that the government-owned steel industry in Nigeria generates large amounts of hazardous wastes. Its petroleum refining industries are regarded as highly inefficient and a major source of pollutants.

In addition to its ethnic, religious, tribal, and language tensions, Nigeria shows urban–rural differentials found in many LTDCs. Nigeria is 77 percent rural and agricultural and 23 percent urban.

Like other LTDCs such as Mexico and India, Nigeria has experienced a migration from rural to urban centers. This migration is generally stimulated by greater employment opportunities and social services in the cities. The average per capita income in Nigeria's urban areas is about 30 percent higher than in rural areas.[21] The urban population in cities such as Lagos, Enugu, Onitsha, and Port Harcourt enjoys extensive school systems, especially at the secondary level. As a result, compared to rural areas, urban school attendance is higher and urban children have more opportunities to attend primary and secondary schools. Despite the attractive pull of cities, Nigeria, like other LTDCs, faces serious urban infrastructure problems. The large cities are ringed by urban slums that lack many basic amenities such as pure drinking water, sanitation, and other services. Additionally, the rapid movement of rural people to large cities creates problems of social adaptation as the new urbanites, familiar with only rural skills, have a difficult adjustment to a more complex lifestyle.

Agriculture, both for domestic consumption and export, remains one of Nigeria's leading economic sectors. Nigeria is the leading producer of coca, palm kernel, peanuts, cotton, sorghum, and millet. About 77 percent of Nigeria's population is rural and engaged in either subsistence farming or agribusiness export production. As in other LTDCs such as India, the Nigerian government has developed programs to improve agricultural production such as Operation Feed the Nation, the Accelerated Industrial Crop Production Program, and other efforts to bring about a "Green Revolution," such as that which occurred in India. The Nigerian Agricultural Research Institute seeks to develop and disseminate agricultural improvement information. There is a need for irrigation projects and efforts to counter soil depletion. Agricultural education in Nigeria, as in other LTDCs, needs expansion, particularly in diffusing practical sustainable development farming practices.

A serious issue is that Nigeria's population growth is outdistancing domestic food production, and the country must now import some foodstuffs. While there is an annual population increase of 3 percent, agricultural production has increased at 1.3 percent. The recent slight increases in agricultural output have come from expanding tillable land usage rather than increasing the productivity of existing acreage. A consequence of this expansion has been reduced soil fertility, erosion, and deforestation. Although there was some discussion in planning circles of encouraging a four-child per family policy, no action was taken. Large extended families are customary features of Nigerian society as they are in India. Muslims and many Christians resist a government role in family planning.

The Nigerian economy, long plagued by political instability, corrupt practices, and inefficient management, is currently undergoing serious efforts at reform. Nigeria's former military rulers relied so much on oil production for revenues that they failed to diversify the economy. Petroleum production, however, remains highly important to the Nigerian economy in that it provides 20 percent of the country's GNP and 65 percent of its government's revenues. Like many other LTDCs, Nigeria is in the process of controversial economic restructuring.

Fueled by globalization, the World Bank, the International Monetary Fund (IMF), and other world financial organizations have pushed an agenda of economic restructuring, especially for those countries with large debts. In the case of Nigeria, this economic restructuring involved initiating free market reforms, modernizing the banking system, curbing inflation by controlling demands for higher wages, and resolving regional disputes for the distribution of oil-generated earnings.[22] Although the government has taken some steps in the direction of economic restructuring, the process has been slow and uneven. The proposals for greater privatization and reduction of social services has caused controversy, especially by those who contend that the restructuring demands are an interference with Nigeria's internal political and economic processes.

Historical Context

Three important periods can be identified in Nigeria's educational history: that of indigenous African education, that of British colonial rule, and that after independence. Before the European entry into west Africa, the social foundations of indigenous education rested on kinship, tribal, and regional patterns. The northern region of present-day Nigeria was populated by Yorubas, a tribal group who followed Islam. The southern region was home to the Igbos, who practiced animism prior to the European Christian missionaries' arrival.

Before its administrative organization as a colony by the British, Nigeria did not exist as a clearly defined nation. The various regions were ruled by kings, pre-eminent chieftains, who with their courts exercised political control in a given territory. The economy centered on farming and herding, supplemented by hunting and fishing. Social relationships were organized around the family and the kinship group with clearly specified rights and responsibilities resting on duties to parents and kindred.

Precolonial education was primarily a process of informal and nonformal education. Relying on an oral tradition, group identity was formed through stories told by tribal elders and religious rituals conducted by priests. This extensive oral tradition was the means by which knowledge and values were transmitted from one generation to the next. Social and political life based on the responsibilities of tribal and kinship membership were impressed on the young. Many practical life skills, such as farming, food gathering, and hunting, were taught to the young by parents or elders in the kinship group.

Colonial Education

In the case of Africa, European slavers raided coastal settlements and sent their captured inhabitants as slaves to other colonies, especially to North and South America. In addition to the Europeans dealing in the slave trade, they also developed the pattern of colonization in the late eighteenth and early nineteenth centuries. First, explorers, traders, and missionaries entered a region to establish trading posts and to convert the indigenous peoples to Christianity. After a period of time, the various European nations—in the case of Africa, the Portuguese, Spanish, British, French, Belgians, Germans, and Italians—would often establish a protectorate, a region in which they had special trading prerogatives, and then transform the protectorate into a colony. European control of a region of Africa would come as the particular European country imposed its administration, soldiers and police, customs officials, and educators on the region.

When the regions that compose modern Nigeria came under British control in 1852, the British colonial style of administration and education were introduced. Although the British made some attempts to establish primary schools, the actual number and enrollment in them were small. Over time, a small cadre of Nigerians, usually enlisted as soldiers in military units commanded by British officers or as lesser officials in the civil service, were prepared in schools to assist the British administrators in ruling the large colony. These Nigerians, who received a Western-style education, slowly developed into an elite body in their own country.

European-influenced education made its initial entry into Nigeria in the mid-nineteenth century through the activities of Christian missionaries. Among the earliest missionaries was Reverend Thomas Birch Freeman of the Wesleyan Methodist Missionary Society. Freeman established a mission in Badagry, near the major city of Lagos. Missionaries from such denominations as the Church of England, Methodists, Baptists, and Roman Catholics established churches, clinics, and schools. The various Christian churches engaged in intense denominational competition to win converts among the indigenous peoples. By 1860, about fifty mission schools were operating in what is now Nigeria.[23]

Christian evangelization and educational activities were more successful among the Igbos in the south and other tribes (primarily along the coast) who were following animist religions than among the Muslims in the northern areas. Christian mission schools were conducted by the minister or priest, assisted by a small staff that included African converts to the particular Christian religion. Their curriculum consisted of religious instruction in the creed and practices of the church that supported the mission, Bible reading and the learning of religious hymns, and reading, writing, and arithmetic. The schools' curriculum and milieu reflected British conceptions of knowledge and values, which were preferred over African culture. The Islamic Hausa and Fulani already had a system of religious Koranic schools attached to mosques. In the early twentieth century, approximately 20,000 Koranic schools with 150,000 students were operating in the predominately Muslim areas. The Koranic schools, conducted by mullahs, emphasized an Islamic religious education that involved reading and memorizing the Koran and learning prayers, ritual, and religious principles.

Twenty years after the British colonized Nigeria, the British colonial government began its first state-supported educational efforts. (It should be mentioned that a state system of local primary schools was not established in the UK itself until 1870.) The British colonial government's role in education began through a system of grants that were given to the Wesleyan Methodists, the Anglican Missionary Society, and Roman Catholics. In 1886, the colonial administration promulgated an education ordinance that gave the government limited control over the schools. In 1899, the colonial government established a primary school in Lagos for Muslims who refused to attend Christian missionary schools. In 1903, the colonial government established a department of education, with a small staff to minimally superintend schools in Nigeria.[24]

By the early twentieth century, Nigeria's educational system consisted of newly established government-sponsored schools, Islamic Koranic schools, and Christian missionary schools. Coexisting simultaneously with these formal schools that rested largely on European antecedents, African indigenous education through an oral tradition and nonformal learning processes persisted.

Education in Nigeria followed the typical colonial pattern, which would continue after independence. There were sharply contrasting rural–urban differentials. Schools were more available in urban areas and educational participation in the cities was much higher than in rural areas.

In 1906, the British established the Colony and Protectorate of Southern Nigeria as a unit of administrative and military governance. The northern region was separately administered as the Protectorate of Northern Nigeria. In 1908, an educational ordinance was enacted for Southern Nigeria. In 1909, the first government-sponsored secondary school was established at Lagos. As of 1912, there were fifty-nine government primary schools and one secondary school in Southern Nigeria. Along with the government schools, ninety-one missionary primary schools and four missionary secondary schools, which received government grants, also were operating. (Again, it should be mentioned that the central government in the UK also provided grants to voluntary schools, most of which were religious ones.) These government-assisted missionary schools enrolled some 16,000 students. In addition to the schools recognized by the government, there were also nonassisted missionary and private schools.[25]

Because of the variety of educational arrangements in British-ruled Nigeria, there was little uniformity or standardization in the colonial era. In 1923, the Advisory Committee on Native Education in the British Tropical African Dependencies was established. The Advisory Committee's recommendations led to the enactment of the Nigerian Educational Code in 1926 that sought to bring about standardization and uniformity. A Board of Education, composed of a director and representatives of the religious missions and other voluntary agencies, was established to administer the code. The code sought to designate levels of schools. For example, classes one and two were designated as infant classes, standards first through six as primary, and forms one through six as secondary levels. These classifications standardized Nigerian education into eight years of primary and six years of secondary schooling. In 1927, all school agencies were required to appoint supervisors whose salaries were paid by the government. In 1929, the colonial administration determined to create still greater educational uniformity in the northern and southern regions. In 1930, the departments of education in Southern and Northern Nigeria were merged under the directorship of E. R. J. Hussey. The first director of education in Nigeria, Hussey proposed a 6–6 system that was comprised of six years of primary schools, two years of middle school, and four years of secondary school. While the government schools followed Hussey's recommendation, mission schools tended to follow the older classifications.[26]

During the 1920s, the British colonial government entered into post-secondary and higher education. Queen's College was established in Lagos in 1927. Training colleges were also established at Ibadan and Umuahia in 1929.[27]

After World War II, the British colonial government continued its efforts to standardize the Nigerian educational system. It devised a Ten Year Development Plan in 1946 to coordinate and expand educational efforts. Eager for more educational opportunities, the population saw schooling as the key to economic security and mobility. Primary school enrollments increased from 670,000 in 1947 to 1,002,599 in 1951. Secondary enrollments, however, remained limited, with only a modest attendance of 31,425. During this period of educational expansion, Nigeria faced the serious problem of trying to staff the schools with qualified teachers. Of the 39,573 teachers, only 11,032 held degrees or teaching certificates.[28]

Standardization, a goal of the Ten Year Development Plan, was elusive. In 1947, the Memorandum of Education attempted to standardize the system by dividing primary schooling to two years of junior primary, two years of elementary, and two years of senior primary. These efforts at standardization were implemented in the southern but not the northern region.[29]

In 1951, four educational regions were organized: the Western Region where schooling was divided into six years of primary and six years of secondary; the Eastern Region where the schooling was divided into seven years of primary and five years of secondary; the Northern Region where there were seven years of primary education and six years of secondary; and Lagos where there were eight years of primary and six years of secondary schooling. Currently, Nigerian schools have been reorganized on a six-year primary cycle and a six-year secondary cycle (three years of junior secondary and three years of senior secondary).[30]

Despite the organizational differences between the government and the mission schools and the regions of Nigeria, the formal school system functioned, in the colonial era, according to the British style or idiom with its strong bias toward traditional schooling and emphasis on the classics, history, literature, and languages. The British influence with its legacy of a model of the educated person who was liberally educated but not a specialist coincided with and reinforced the African view that the educated person should not enter vocational occupations. Although Nigeria was economically an under-developed region, European-imposed schooling discouraged needed voca-tional and technical education. (Again, it needs to be pointed out that a similar situation was taking place in the UK as well as in India regarding vocational and technical schooling.) Especially at the secondary level, the schools operated according to the ideal of the educated gentleman rather than producing technically-trained people needed for economic development.

Education after Independence

When Nigeria became an independent and sovereign nation in 1960, early educational efforts in the newly independent nation were directed to eradicating neocolonialism, especially the concept that schooling had to be conducted in the Western frame of reference.[31] It proved difficult politically to weld the various tribal, linguistic, and religious groups into a unified nation-state, however.

The devastation caused by the civil war conflict in the 1960s disrupted education, especially in the Igbo areas. In the post–civil war era, the govern-ment sought to restore the educational system and to use schools for "rehabil-itation, reconstruction, and reconciliation." Despite these efforts, the war left a residue of bitterness that was slow to heal.

As indicated, Nigeria has a strong tradition of Christian missionary schools, both Roman Catholic and Protestant. In addition to tribal differ-ences, church–state issues have also surfaced in Nigeria. Even prior to inde-pendence, the government, in 1957, attempted to limit the expansion of voluntary schools and assume more authority over private education. These actions sparked resistance from Roman Catholics who sought to maintain control of their schools with only limited government supervision.

After independence, Nigerian national planners emphasized the power of formal education to contribute to economic growth and development. In many respects, formal schooling did contribute but educational expansion and economic development did not proceed at a balanced pace. More stu-dents completed secondary and higher education than the economy could absorb. This led to the problem of the "educated unemployed," individuals who had completed secondary or even higher education but could not find jobs, especially in the field in which they had been trained. A closely related phenomenon was to find a job for which one was overqualified. For example, clerical positions might have required some secondary education in the past. Now, these positions might be filled by university graduates. The response of many Nigerians was to seek more advanced education in order to compete for existing jobs. The result was greater pressure on political and educational leaders to create more places for applicants in secondary schools and univer-sities. When the pressure was yielded to, the ensuing consequence was trying to maintain quality in terms of overused facilities and an expanded but unevenly trained faculty.

Organization and Structure of Schools

Under Nigeria's federal system of government, authority and responsibility is shared between the federal and the state governments' ministries of education.[32] The Nigerian federal government has consistently emphasized education's crucial role in the nation's development and in creating a unified nation. A federal government policy statement proclaimed education as an instrument for "effecting national development." The federal government has worked to create greater standardization in educational institutions and practices in the various parts of the republic.[33]

Although Nigerian educators were determined to redesign the educational system from the British style so that it corresponded to the needs of development and nation building, Nigerian education continued to reflect the structures of the colonial past. Fufunwa, a leading Nigerian educator, commented that even after independence, Nigerian education continued to follow "the British pattern very closely in structure, organization, administration, and content." British education was undergoing significant changes; thus Nigerian education followed an older model that itself was being changed in the country of its origin.[34]

Preprimary and Primary Schools

The education of preschool-age children in Nigeria has traditionally been the responsibility of families. Nevertheless, preschool education has expanded with the help of the Nigerian federal government and UNICEF, who jointly established the Early Child Care Development and Education (ECCDE) Program and the Early Child Care (ECC) Project. ECC takes a holistic approach to child development, focusing on parenting, training, and retraining of caregivers.[35] Early childhood programs are designed for children age three to six. In many areas, day-care centers and nursery schools are located close to or on the same premises as primary schools. Still, the percentage of primary grade-one students who attended a preprimary program is very low, especially in rural areas. Although the government is not directly involved in the establishment and day-to-day running of day-care centers and nursery schools, it has established guidelines and objectives, including ensuring that the medium of instruction is principally the mother tongue, or the language of the immediate community, and that the main method of teaching is activity- or play-centered. Although these and other national guidelines have been established, preprimary programs are implemented in varying ways. Furthermore, the official curriculum has not circulated widely and teacher training is inadequate.[36]

There are approximately 36,000 primary schools in Nigeria. Under the provisions of the national Universal Primary Education Scheme, primary schooling is compulsory and free for children ages six through twelve. It is organized into six grades. While official statistics indicate a national enrollment of 98 percent of the primary-age cohort, there are significant regional, urban–rural, and gender differentials that make actual attendance much lower; for example, males are more likely to attend school than females. Another serious problem for primary education is created by the large numbers of unqualified and uncertificated teachers. Many teachers are untrained, especially in rural areas, having only a primary education themselves.

The primary school curriculum, developed and controlled by the state ministries of education, stresses basic literacy and numeracy—reading, writing, and arithmetic. Furthermore, primary education includes instruction in citizenship, provides tools for educational advancement, and helps the child learn how to adapt to a changing environment.[37] Like primary and elementary schools throughout the world, the early years of Nigerian primary schooling accentuates teaching language skills such as listening, reading, and writing. However, language learning on a national basis is complicated by the presence of important regional languages and the multiplicity of minor languages and dialects.

For the first three years of primary school, the mother tongue or vernacular of the area in which the school is located is the medium of instruction. Children are expected to learn one of the three major national languages—Hausa, Igbo, or Yoruba. English, the language that links the regions of Nigeria linguistically, is then taught for the remaining three years of primary school. Since the dropout rate is high in the rural areas, many of the students know only their vernacular. In the urban areas, many private schools use English throughout the curriculum. When there are multiple languages, instructional effort and time is taken up with language learning. This effort tends to detract from other subjects.

In addition to basic language and numeracy, the primary curriculum also includes social studies, stressing geography and history, elements of natural science, health education, domestic skills such as cooking and needlecraft, drawing and crafts, moral education, and physical education.

As is the case in many former British colonies, instruction is driven by preparation for examinations. Curriculum and instruction is organized to conform to the examination structure. At the end of primary schooling, students take the examinations for the first school-leaving certificate. Those who seek admission to secondary school also take the common entrance examination, prepared by the West African Examinations Council.[38]

In addition to government-operated and the religious missions' primary schools, a large number of Muslim Koranic schools operate in the northern region. For example, in Kano, the most heavily Muslim state, some 200,000 children attend the 10,000 Koranic schools. Koranic schools are often very small and the malams, the teachers, who hold their positions because of their knowledge of the Koran and religious rituals, may not be professionally prepared and credentialed as teachers. Students enter the Koranic schools, which may combine primary and secondary schooling, at age five, six, or seven, and a few students may continue until age seventeen. The curriculum is not highly structured. Primary studies include the memorization of the first ten chapters of the Koran and reading and writing Arabic. Secondary studies emphasize Islamic studies, Arabic grammar and literature, and arithmetic.[39]

Secondary Education

Secondary schooling is currently a six-year program that begins at age twelve. Only about one-third of the appropriate age group is enrolled in Nigeria's 6,000 secondary schools. This low enrollment is caused by several factors. First, Nigeria, like many other former colonial nations, continues to be influenced by the inherited British model in which secondary school admission was highly selective and reserved for an elite. Second, secondary schools are more available in urban rather than rural areas where the majority of the population lives. Third, secondary schooling is still expensive in that many secondary schools are residential, charge tuition fees, and require school uniforms. Despite these factors, the Nigerian federal government has endeavored to develop a more extensive secondary school system and to gradually increase participation.

Again following the inherited British pattern, secondary school admission is based upon passing the entrance examinations that are prepared, administered, and graded by the West African Examination Council. Until the end of the 1970s, Nigerian secondary schools, following the British pattern, consisted of grammar, modern, and comprehensive schools. The trend has been to eliminate the modern and comprehensive schools and to make grammar schools dominant institutions. (Note that this trend is counter to that in the UK where comprehensive secondary schools are increasing.) Subjects taught in junior secondary schools include English, math, integrated science, social studies, French, Nigerian languages, Christian religious knowledge, and Islamic religious knowledge.

The senior secondary school curriculum includes English language and literature, higher mathematics, social studies with an emphasis on history and geography, physics, chemistry, biology, economics, physical education, French, Nigerian languages, Christian religious knowledge, and Islamic religious knowledge. Some critics contend that secondary school contains too many subjects. It is possible for a junior and senior secondary student to study more than twelve subjects in an academic year. Such extensive coverage leans more to information-dispensing than to in-depth knowledge.

Higher Education

Higher education in Nigeria is primarily the responsibility of the federal government. The overall coordination and supervision of higher education is exercised by the federal government's Ministry of Education and the National Universities Commission. The Commission has the important responsibility of allocating funds, approving programs, and approving faculty appointments. Each university is headed by a vice chancellor who is appointed by the president of Nigeria. Each university has considerable autonomy and is governed internally by its own university council. Although tuition pays part of the operating costs of universities, they are largely funded by the federal government.

Until independence in 1960, the sole university in Nigeria was the University of Ibadan. Since independence, the expansion of higher education in

Nigeria has been phenomenal. In 1962, the country's four universities enrolled 3,646 students. Ten years later in 1972, enrollments had reached 20,889. By 1982, enrollments were 104,774. By 1987, enrollment figures in state and federal universities had reached 160,767. As of 1990, Nigeria had twenty-nine universities in operation.[40]

Admission to universities is highly competitive and selective. On average, slightly more than 10 percent of the applicants are admitted. For example, 11.65 percent of the applications every year from 1978 to 1983 were admitted to universities. Students who hold a West African High School Certificate or an Advanced General Certificate of Education are admitted directly into degree programs. Students holding a West African School Certificate or an Ordinary General Certificate of Education must first complete preliminary courses, which may take from one to two years of study. The usual degree courses are of three years duration. Among the leading areas of study are programs in education, with 18.25 percent of the total enrollment; programs in the arts, with 13.92 percent; social and behavioral science programs, with 12.25 percent; law, with 6.41 percent; medicine and health care, with 6.24 percent; agriculture, with 5.96 percent; engineering, with 8.69 percent; natural sciences, with 15.84 percent; and administration, with 6.20 percent.[41] Programs in medicine, dentistry, and veterinary medicine require five years of study. The universities also offer advanced graduate degrees at the master's and doctoral levels.

The federal government faces a persistent problem in Nigerian higher education of trying to respond to the demand for more accessibility to universities by a growing number of applicants. Higher education is regarded as a means of economic mobility—a way to gain employment and improved social status. At the same time that efforts have been made to increase participation in higher education, there is also the problem of maintaining quality standards regarding facilities and faculty. This dilemma of increasing enrollments and maintaining quality standards is faced by systems of higher education throughout the world. However, it is a critical issue in LTDCs like Nigeria where expectations for higher education are escalating but funds are limited.

The condition of Nigeria's economy has been weakened by fluctuations in the price of oil, chronic political instability, and demands for economic restructuring. The nation's economic problems have adversely affected the federal government's ability to fund higher education. Despite the dramatic increase in the number of institutions and accelerating enrollments, it has been difficult to maintain the quality of instruction as well as library and laboratory facilities and support services. The problem has been further aggravated by the "brain drain," in which Nigerian professors, particularly those in medicine, have relocated to more technologically developed nations.

In addition to the universities, colleges of technology offer programs in practical and technical fields that lead to the Nigerian National Diploma. Since Nigeria is an important petroleum exporting nation, petroleum technology is an important area of study. There are also specialized training institutes for such technical-vocational areas as agriculture, metallurgy, meteorology, and oceanography. Recognizing the role that technology education and training plays in infrastructure and industrial building, the government had stipulated that both domestic and foreign construction companies should provide training opportunities to Nigerian engineers and managers.[42]

Nigeria, like other LTDCs, especially those in Africa, faces a twofold problem in higher education. Due to rising expectations and the belief that higher education is the avenue to employment and status, there is intense pressure to expand the system to accommodate a larger student enrollment. Simultaneously, the country lacks the means of financially supporting such a large higher education system. The quality of education has declined because of weaknesses in funding, administration, and management of resources. Teachers' salaries are less than those of civil servants and are often not paid in a timely fashion. In addition to the problems of expansion and funding, there are serious questions if the nation's commerce and industry can absorb larger numbers of degree holders.

Conclusion

Nigeria is an LTDC that desperately needs a stable government and political order that functions democratically. The government needs to rebuild its most important economic asset, the petroleum industry, which has been plagued by mismanagement and corruption causing much needed revenues to be wasted. Nigeria has used national planning to improve its educational infrastructure to meet the needs of a growing population that is eager for more educational opportunities. The population growth and increased educational demands, however, have limited Nigeria's educational response and success.

Tribalism in sub-Saharan Africa represents a culturally evolved source of ethnic, religious, and language identification. Nigerian tribalism presents a different factor than the issues faced by Mexico and the U.S. Nigeria's tribalism more resembles the ethnic and language identification found in Russia and many Eastern European nations—identifications so deeply embedded that losing them for the sake of national identity causes tension and conflict. Like other formal colonial countries, Nigeria must figure out a way to unify different groups to create a national identity and address other issues involved with nation building. Mexico and the U.S. have also struggled with nation building, working their way to national integration through often tortuous conflicts. For example, Mexico had a series of revolutions that pitted class against class. The American Civil War was a five-year bloody struggle of North against South. In both Mexico and the U.S. reconciliation and reconstruction was a difficult but successful process. Although Nigeria has had its share of internal conflicts, its history since independence is much shorter than that of the U.S. or Mexico. An instructive comparison regarding the principle of "unity in diversity" comes from India. While India has had serious religious and communal conflicts, it has managed to maintain highly diverse ethnic, religious, and language groups in a common and democratic political framework.

Realistically, tribalism will remain a primary source of identification for Nigerians. Thus a major challenge for education is enlarging tribal identification to include the nation itself. Nigerian education needs to borrow and apply some of the principles of multiculturalism to its social and educational climate. A goal of Nigerian education might be to transfer attachments "from a smaller to a larger community through integration."[43]

DISCUSSION QUESTIONS

1. Examine the historical context of Nigerian education and identify the factors that have had an impact in shaping its educational structures.
2. Describe the general patterns of colonial education during British rule in Nigeria and compare them with India.
3. What is nation building? What problems does Nigeria face in the process of nation building?
4. How does Nigeria illustrate the educational ambitions and needs of an LTDC?
5. Identify and analyze the factors that have had an impact on the development of education in Nigeria.
6. Analyze the language issue in Nigerian education.
7. Analyze the problems of access and selectivity in Nigerian higher education.
8. Consider tribalism as a feature of Nigerian culture, politics, and society. Does the U.S. have a comparable situation?

RESEARCH TOPICS

1. Develop a "clippings file" of articles from newspapers and magazines that examines events in sub-Saharan Africa.
2. Develop a "map exercise" that illustrates changes of a political nature in Africa. Identify the nations of Africa and how their official designations have changed over time.
3. If there are international students from Nigeria or other African nations on your campus, invite them to speak to your class about their educational experiences.
4. Prepare a demographic profile on Nigeria and the countries of sub-Saharan Africa.
5. Prepare a research paper that examines a selected aspect of Nigerian education.
6. Prepare a research paper that examines nation building and development in an Africa nation such as Nigeria.
7. Prepare a comparative study of education in Nigeria and another African country.

SUGGESTIONS FOR FURTHER READING

Achebe, Chinua. *The Trouble with Nigeria*. London: Heinemann, 1983.

Altbach, Philip G., and Gail P. Kelly. *Education and Colonialism*. New York: Longman, 1978.

Arnold, G. *Modern Nigeria*. London: Longman, 1977.

Bendix, John. *Nation-Building and Citizenship*. New Brunswick: Transaction, 1996.

Brock-Utne, Birgit. *Whose Education for All? The Recolonization of the African Mind*. New York: Falmer Press, 2000.

Buchanan, K. M. *Land and People in Nigeria: The Human Geography of Nigeria and its Environmental Background*. London: University of London Press, 1987.

Coombs, Philip H. *The World Crisis in Education: The View from the Eighties*. New York: Oxford University Press, 1985.

Diamond, Larry. *Class, Ethnicity and Democracy in Nigeria*. Syracuse, NY: Syracuse University Press, 1988.

Ekwe-Ekwe, Herbert. *Conflict and Intervention in Africa*. New York: St. Martin Press, 1990.

Hanson, John W., and Cole S. Brembeck. *Education and the Development of Nations*. New York: Holt, Rinehart and Winston, 1966.

Harbeson, John W., and Donald Rothchild. *Africa in World Politics*. Boulder, CO: Westview Press, 1991.

Harbeson, John W. *The Military in African Politics*. New York: Praeger, 1987.

Ikejiani, Okechukwu. *Nigerian Education*. Bristol: Longmans of Nigeria, 1964.

Laitin, David D. *Hegemony and Culture: Politics and Religious Change Among the Yoruba*. Chicago: University of Chicago Press, 1986.

Lewis, L. J. *Society, Schools and Progress in Nigeria*. New York: Pergamon Press, 1965.

Mazrui, Ali A. *The African Condition*. London: Cambridge University Press, 1980.

Nzeribe, Francis A. *Nigeria: Another Hope Betrayed*. London: Kilimanjaro, 1985.

Ogbu, Osita dn Mihyo, Paschal. *African Youth on the Information Highway: Participation and Leadership in Community Development*. Ottawa, Canada: International Development Research Centre, 2000.

Okafor, Nduka. *The Development of Universities in Nigeria*. London: Longman, 1971.

Sigmund, Paul E. *The Ideologies of the Developing Nations*. New York: Praeger, 1972.

NOTES

[1] CIA (Central Intelligence Agency), "World Factbook: Nigeria," January 21, 2004, http://www.cia.gov/cia/publications/factbook/geos/ni.html.

[2] Ibid.

[3] Ibid.

[4] Ibid. For Nigeria's ethnic tribal groupings, see K. M. Buchanan, *Land and People in Nigeria: The Human Geography of Nigeria and Its Environmental Background* (London: University of London Press, 1987) and Frederick A. Schwarz, *Nigeria: The Tribe, the Nation, or the Race—the Politics of Independence* (Cambridge: M.I.T. Press, 1965).

[5] Walker Connor, *Ethnonationalism: The Quest for Understanding* (Princeton: Princeton University Press, 1994), 43.

[6] O. Ikejiani, "Education and Tribalism," in *Nigerian Education*, ed. Okechukwu Ikejiani (Bristol: Longman of Nigeria, 1964), 116–123.

[7] Ibid., 125.

[8] Philip H. Coombs, *The World Crisis in Education: The View from the Eighties* (New York: Oxford University Press, 1985), 257–258.

[9] Ibid., 258.

[10] Ibid., 259–260.

[11] "1964–1965 Elections," http://www.globalsecurity.org/military/world/war/nigeria1.htm (accessed May 16, 2005).

[12] W. F. Gutteridge, *The Military in African Politics* (London: Metheun, 1975), 69.

[13] Accounts of the tribal hostilities are F. R. Metrowich, *Nigeria: The Biafran War* (Pretoria: Africa Institute, 1969) and Arthur Nwankwo, *Nigeria: The Challenge of Biafra* (Enugu: Fourth Dimension, 1972).

[14] John W. Harbeson, *The Military in African Politics* (New York: Praeger, 1987), 12.

[15] Herbert Ekwe-Ekwe, *The Biafra War* (Lewiston, PA: Edwin Mellon, 1990).

[16] Because of frequent changes in Party affiliation, the major parties are identified so that readers have some reference to the political situation. For up-to-date changes in the political situation, readers should consult media and Internet reports.

[17] John W. Hanson, "Educational Tasks for a Nation," in *Education and the Development of Nations*, ed. John W. Hanson and Cole S. Brembeck (New York: Holt, Rinehart, and Winston, 1966), 16.

[18] James H. Weaver et al., "Competing Paradigms of Development," *Social Education* 53 (April–May 1989): 209.

[19] Claire Liuksila, ed., *External Assistance and Policies for Growth in Africa* (Washington, DC: IMF Publication Services, 1995), 9–10.

[20] *Nigeria: Federal Public Expenditure Review* (Washington, DC: World Bank Publications, 1995), 1.

[21] Alan Carroll and Oluwole Komolafe, eds., *A Strategy for Restoring Urban Infrastructure and Services to Nigeria* (Washington, DC: World Bank Publications, 1995), 9.

[22] CIA.

[23] George Kurian, "Nigeria," in *World Education Encyclopedia*, ed. George T. Kurian (New York: Facts on File, 1988), 945.

[24] Ibid.

[25] Ibid.

[26] Ibid., 945–946.

[27] Ibid., 946.

[28] Ibid.

[29] Ibid.

[30] http://www.nigeriaembassyusa.org/students/shmtl (accessed May 17, 2005).

[31] Abdulhamide Saleemi et al., "Primary Education in Nigeria," *Journal of Research in Childhood Education* 4(1) (1989): 30.

[32] Kurian, 947.

[33] Federal Republic of Nigeria, *National Policy on Education* (Lagos, Nigeria: Government Publications, 1991), 5.

[34] A. Babs Fufunwa, *History of Education in Nigeria* (Ibadan, Nigeria: NPS Educational Publishers, 1991), 205.

[35] "Nigeria," http://www.ibe.unesco.org/International/Databanks/Dossiers/inigeria.htm (accessed May 16, 2005).

[36] "Nigeria: Report: Part II: Analytic Section," http://www2.unesco.org/wef/countryreports/nigeria/rapport_2.html (accessed May 16, 2005).

[37] Ibid.

[38] Kurian, 948.

[39] Ibid., 947–948.

[40] Akin O. Adesola, "The Nigerian University System: Meeting the Challenges of Growth in a Depressed Economy," *Higher Education* 21 (1991): 121–133.

[41] Ibid.

[42] Federal Republic of Nigeria, 25.

[43] Albert Breton, ed., *Nationalism and Rationality* (New York: Cambridge University Press, 1995), xv.

INDEX